The Interaction between Enforcers of Competition Law, the DMA, and the GDPR

Information Law Series (INFO)

VOLUME 49

Editor

Prof. Martin R.F. Senftleben, Institute for Information Law, University of Amsterdam.

Objective & Readership

Publications in the Information Law Series focus on current legal issues of information law and are aimed at scholars, practitioners, and policy makers who are active in the rapidly expanding area of information law and policy.

Introduction & Contents

The advent of the information society has put the field of information law squarely on the map. Information law is the law relating to the production, marketing, distribution, and use of information goods and services. The field of information law therefore cuts across traditional legal boundaries, and encompasses a wide set of legal issues at the crossroads of intellectual property, media law, telecommunications law, freedom of expression, and right to privacy. Recent volumes in the Information Law Series deal with copyright enforcement on the Internet, interoperability among computer programs, harmonization of copyright at the European level, intellectual property and human rights, public broadcasting in Europe, the future of the public domain, conditional access in digital broadcasting, and the "three-step test" in copyright.

The titles published in this series are listed at the back of this volume.

The Interaction between Enforcers of Competition Law, the DMA, and the GDPR

An Inquiry into the Coherence of Enforcement across Legal Domains

Belle Beems

Wolters Kluwer

Published by:
Kluwer Law International B.V.
PO Box 316
2400 AH Alphen aan den Rijn
The Netherlands
E-mail: lrs-sales@wolterskluwer.com
Website: www.wolterskluwer.com/en/solutions/kluwerlawinternational

Sold and distributed by:
Wolters Kluwer Legal & Regulatory U.S.
920 Links Avenue
Landisville, PA 17538
United States of America
E-mail: customer.service@wolterskluwer.com

ISBN 978-94-035-4259-1

e-Book: ISBN 978-94-035-4269-0
web-PDF: ISBN 978-94-035-4279-9

About the Author

Belle Beems (1994) completed her PhD at Radboud University. She obtained her Bachelor's degree (*cum laude*) at Utrecht University and holds a (*cum laude*) Master's degree in European Law from the same university. During her Bachelor's, she studied for one semester at University College Dublin.

Before joining Radboud University, Belle worked as a lecturer and junior researcher at KU Leuven and Utrecht University. During her PhD, she undertook research stays at Pompeu Fabra University in Barcelona, Heinrich Heine University in Düsseldorf and the Vienna University of Economics and Business.

In addition to her research responsibilities at Radboud University, Belle was actively involved in teaching. She contributed to several courses at Radboud's Department of International and European law. Her teaching focused in particular on internal market and competition law. Furthermore, Belle supervised multiple Bachelor's and Master's theses.

Belle published on various topics related to EU law, competition law and data protection law in several national and international peer-reviewed journals, including the European Competition Journal, SEW, the Competition Law Review and the European Data Protection Law Review. She presented her work at various academic events, among others, organised by ASCOLA, CLASF, NVER, iHub and the Sectorplan Digital Legal Studies. Furthermore, she served as a board member of the Dutch Association for European Law (*NVER*).

As of October 2025, Belle is affiliated with Leiden University as an assistant professor.

Table of Contents

List of Abbreviations

ACM	*Autoriteit Consument en Markt*
Advisory Committee	Advisory Committee on Restrictive Practices and Dominant Positions
AEC	As Efficient Competitor
Annual Report DMA 2023	Annual Report on Regulation (EU) 2022/1925 of the European Parliament and of the Council of 6 March 2024 on contestable and fair markets in the digital sector and amending Directives (EU) 2019/1937 and (EU) 2020/1828 (Digital Markets Act)
ATT	App Tracking Transparency
Charter	Charter of Fundamental Rights of the European Union
CJEU	Court of Justice of the European Union
CMA	Competition and Markets Authority
Commission	European Commission
Cooperation Protocol	Samenwerkingsprotocol tussen Autoriteit Consument en Markt en Autoriteit Persoonsgegevens, 18 June 2020, Staatscourant 2020, 36741
DCA	Dutch Competition Act

Decision on the High-Level Group	Commission Decision of 23 March 2023 on setting up the High-Level Group for the Digital Markets Act, C(2023)1833 final
DG	Directorate-General
DMA	Digital Markets Act
DMAC	Digital Markets Advisory Committee
DPA	Data Protection Authority
DPC	Data Protection Commissioner
DPO	Data Protection Officer
Draft Guidelines on the Application of Article 102	Draft Guidelines on the Application of Article 102 of the Functioning of the European Union to abusive exclusionary conduct by dominant undertakings
DSA	Digital Services Act
ECN	European Competition Network
EDPB	European Data Protection Board
EDPS	European Data Protection Supervisor
EU	European Union
Federal Commissioner	Federal Commissioner for Data Protection and Freedom and Information
GAFA	Google, Amazon, Facebook, Apple and Microsoft
GALA	General Administrative Law Act
GC	General Court
GDPR	General Data Protection Regulation
GWB	Gesetz gegen Wettbewerbsbeschränkungen
High-Level Group	High-Level Group of Regulators
ICN	International Competition Network
MFN	Most Favoured Nation
MTB	Markttoezichthoudersberaad
NCA	National Competition Authority
Network Notice	Commission Notice on Cooperation Within the Network of Competition Authorities
Relevant Markets Notice	Commission Notice on the definition of the relevant market for the purposes of Union competition law

SDT	Samenwerkingsplatform Digitale Toezichthouders (*Digital Regulation Cooperation Platform)*
SMEs	Small and Medium-Sized Enterprises
SSNDQ	Small but Significant Non-transitory Decrease in Quality
SSNIP	Small but Significant Non-transitory Increase in Price
TEU	Treaty on the European Union
TFEU	Treaty on the Functioning of the European Union
The Committee	Advisory Committee on Restrictive Practices and Dominant Positions

The thesis takes into account developments up until **1 January 2025**. Some developments after this point in time are mentioned but not discussed in detail.

CHAPTER 1

Introduction

1.1 INTRODUCTION

The fact that digitalisation has changed society and the economy over the past few decades is undeniable. The Internet and digital technologies have transformed the way we work, live and interact.[1] The rise of the digital economy has even been coined as 'the Fourth Industrial Revolution'.[2] In the wake of this revolution, digital markets have emerged. In such markets, business models increasingly rely on digital technologies and use 'bits instead of atoms'.[3]

Despite the fact that digital markets come in various shapes, sizes and guises, such markets have certain idiosyncrasies. These include the omnipresence of platforms, strong (in)direct network effects, zero-price business models and data-driven transactions.[4] Within the broader category of digital markets, undertakings active on *personal data markets* create revenue by the collection, exchange and monetisation of personal data.[5]

1. Zingales et al. 2019, p. 6.
2. Drexl 2017, p. 259.
3. OECD 2013, p. 5; Schmidt 2019, p. 31; Rusu, Looijestijn-Clearie and Veenbrink 2018, p. 2.
4. *See* Chapter 2.
5. Personal data is defined in accordance with the GDPR. According to Article 4(1) GDPR, 'personal data' means 'any information relating to an identified or identifiable natural person ("data subject"); an identifiable natural person is one who can be identified, directly or indirectly, in particular by reference to an identifier such as a name, an identification number, location data, an online identifier or to one or more factors specific

Although the benefits and opportunities associated with digital markets have been broadly acknowledged, the rise of such markets also presents significant risks and challenges. Due to the characteristics of digital markets, a high level of concentration may occur, and tech giants – collectively referred to as GAFA, GAFAM or FAANG – rule over various markets.[6] This raises several concerns, including the existence of barriers to entry, customer lock-ins, unequal bargaining power and a lack of privacy-friendly options for consumers.[7] On personal data markets, several market failures, including concentration of power, information asymmetries, externalities and rationality problems, may occur.[8] Practical and technical barriers can limit switching possibilities, thereby making consumers hesitant to alternate between platforms.[9]

The legal frameworks of the EU and of the Member States provide various legal tools to address the range of concerns related to personal data markets. The areas of competition law, the Digital Markets Act (henceforth: DMA) and the General Data Protection Regulation (henceforth: GDPR) are particularly relevant in this regard. Various provisions of both national and EU competition law tackle issues of market power by prohibiting abusive behaviour by dominant undertakings.[10] Furthermore, the GDPR provides a framework for the protection of natural persons with regard to the processing of personal data and rules relating to the free movement of personal data.[11] Lastly, a myriad of novel initiatives, including the DMA and Section 19a of the German Competition Act, i.e., the *Gesetz gegen Wettbewerbsbeschränkungen* (henceforth: GWB), target Big Tech platforms by imposing rules on, for example, gatekeepers or undertakings with paramount significance for competition across markets.[12]

This increasing overlap between fields of the law triggers complex questions, particularly in the context of competition law, the DMA and the GDPR. These questions are both substantive and institutional in nature. From a substantive perspective, it remains, for example, uncertain to what extent one legal domain could be impacted by considerations related to another branch of law. In this light, the question of to what extent data protection considerations can and should be taken into account in a competition law

---

to the physical, physiological, genetic, mental, economic, cultural or social identity of that natural person'. *See also*: Schneider et al. 2023.

6. GAFA: Google, Facebook, Amazon and Apple; GAFAM; Google, Facebook, Amazon, Apple and Microsoft; FAANG: Facebook, Amazon, Apple, Netflix and Google; *See, e.g.*, Fox 2019, p. 101.
7. Botta and Wiedemann 2019, p. 432; Haucap and Heimeshoff 2013.
8. Economides and Lianos 2021.
9. Furman et al. 2019, p. 36.
10. *See* Article 102 TFEU; Article 24 Dutch Competition Act and Section 19 GWB.
11. Article 1(1) GDPR.
12. Opinion AG Bobek in CJEU 22 March 2022 Case C-117/20, *bpost*, para. 2.

assessment is a hot topic.[13] Apart from substantive challenges, *institutional challenges* arise because the overlap in substantive legal fields also results in overlapping competences of different enforcers at the national and EU level. Such overlapping competences manifest themselves in different ways. *First,* more than one authority may have the competence to initiate an enforcement action. These overlapping competences can either be complementary or conflicting and potentially result in parallel or consecutive proceedings. *Second,* an authority may 'borrow' concepts from one area of law to interpret concepts of another legal branch. In this situation, an authority internalises rules of concepts associated with a different field of law.[14]

Example I: the prohibition of self-preferencing behaviour – i.e., the provision of preferential treatment of a platform's own products and services over goods and services provided on the platform by third parties – constitutes an example of the first manifestation of norm overlaps. The DMA prohibits gatekeepers from treating their own services more favourably in ranking than services offered by third parties and hence prohibits self-preferencing behaviour by gatekeepers.[15] At the same time, this conduct can also amount to abuse of dominance within the meaning of Article 102 TFEU. Google was – for example – fined by the Commission for abusing its dominant position as a search engine by treating its own comparison shopping services more favourably than the services of third parties.[16] Consequently, the conduct of self-preferencing may be sanctioned both under the DMA and Article 102 TFEU.

Example II: the *Meta Bundeskartellamt* case illustrates the second manifestation of norm overlaps. In this case, the German *Bundeskartellamt* concluded that Meta's use of plug-ins and third-party cookies violated the GDPR and, therefore, also constituted an abuse of a dominant position.[17] The CJEU ruled that it may be necessary for a national competition authority (henceforth: NCA) to examine whether an undertaking's conduct complies with the GDPR in the context of assessing an abuse of dominance.[18] In this context, an NCA can thus internalise data protection considerations.

In the multi-level legal order of the EU, this competence overlap has an additional dimension. The overlap is not limited to competences of authorities of different legal branches, but potentially also entails an overlap between competences of authorities at *different levels* or in *different jurisdictions*. This dimension is particularly relevant in the case of digital markets, because physical borders are less relevant for the online world.

13. *See,* for example, CJEU 4 July 2023 Case C-252/21, *Meta Bundeskartellamt*; Robertson and Majcher 2022; Costa-Cabral and Lynskey 2018; Economides and Lianos 2021; Gorecka 2024.
14. Yakovleva, Geursen and Arnbak 2020, p. 1465.
15. Article 6(5) DMA.
16. European Commission 27 June 2017 Case AT.3970, *Google Shopping.*
17. Bundeskartellamt 6 February 2019 B6-22/16, *Facebook.*
18. CJEU 4 July 2023 Case C-252/21, *Meta Bundeskartellamt*, para. 48.

Therefore, digital transactions often entail a cross-border element.[19] This can simultaneously trigger the competence of enforcers of multiple jurisdictions.

As a result of the trends described above, a complex 'regulatory puzzle' has emerged in the digital arena and the competences of enforcers of: (i) various legal branches; and (ii) different legal orders or jurisdictions, increasingly overlap.[20] The involvement of multiple authorities has the potential to reinforce oversight over personal data markets. The objectives of the different legal branches are – despite their commonalities – not identical, and different authorities can thus take a broad range of considerations into account.[21] On top of this, many hands may make light work and the resources of individual authorities are limited. Yet, at the same time, overlapping competences result in a risk of divergent approaches in enforcement and of undue consumption of an enforcer's resources.[22] In this light, isolated approaches potentially bring a risk of incoherent enforcement actions.[23] This risk can be mitigated by well-functioning mechanisms of cooperation.[24]

1.2 STATE OF THE ART AND RESEARCH QUESTIONS

In academic (legal) literature, the regulation of Big Tech is a topical and much-debated issue. Platform regulation is discussed from multiple angles and perspectives. Various contributions study the key characteristics of digital markets, as well as their implications for competition on such markets.[25] Studies are not only conducted within the boundaries of a single legal branch, but also provide cross-disciplinary analyses on, for example, the relationship between competition law and the GDPR, as well as the interaction between competition law and the DMA.[26] The question of to what extent competition law should leave room for data protection considerations

19. Wiggers, Struijlaart and Dibbits 2019, p. 120; Communication from the Commission to the European Parliament, The Council, The European Economic and Social Committee and The Committee of Regions of 6 May 2015 on 'A Digital Single Market Strategy', COM(2015) 192 final, p. 2.
20. Podszun 2024, p. 10.
21. *See* sections 5.3 and 6.3.
22. Graef 2024, p. 174; Robertson 2024, p. 328.
23. De Streel and Monti 2022, p. 50; Reyna 2024.
24. Yakovleva, Geursen and Arnbak 2020, pp. 1467 and 1479.
25. Zingales et al. 2019; Furman et al. 2019.
26. *See,* for example, Beems, Van de Gronden and Rusu 2023; Wagner-von Papp 2024; Hornung 2023.

is, for example, discussed extensively in literature.[27] Moreover, the relationship between competition law and the DMA received ample academic attention.[28]

Since cross-disciplinary research takes into account multiple fields of the law, such studies are particularly well-placed to analyse the interrelationships between different areas of the law.[29] Yet, in this (cross-disciplinary) debate, the substantive rules are often in the spotlight. Institutional frameworks, laying down rules concerning rules on the enforcement of laws and policies by formal and informal bodies, receive far less attention.[30] Against this background, the topic of the interaction between different authorities is also overlooked in academic writing.[31] Despite the fact that the need for cooperation is generally recognised, the means to do so and the implications of such cooperation are under-explored.[32]

This study aims to fill this gap by providing an analysis of the institutional frameworks of the areas of competition law, the DMA and the GDPR at the EU level and in The Netherlands and Germany, with a particular focus on cooperation between authorities. The assessment focuses on the way in which: (i) competences of enforcers of these frameworks interrelate; and on (ii) the mechanisms that facilitate the interaction between different enforcers. In order to analyse these topics, this study addresses the question of to what extent the institutional frameworks and cooperation mechanisms of national and EU competition law, the DMA and the GDPR can guarantee the coherent application of these instruments to personal data markets.

In order to answer this question, the analysis is structured according to the following sub-research questions. The research questions aim to guide and structure the analysis and are answered in the different chapters, as well as in Synthesis I and II:

- What are the characteristics of personal data markets?
- How are institutions designed in the multi-level legal order of the EU, and which (general) principles govern the (complementary) enforcement of the selected legal branches?

27. Robertson 2020; Botta and Wiedemann 2019; Costa-Cabral and Lynskey 2018; Graef, Clifford and Valcke 2018; Kalimo and Majcher 2017; Majcher 2023; Robertson and Majcher 2022.
28. Van den Boom 2022; Schroeter and Hoyng 2021, p. 165; Schweitzer 2021, p. 4; Ibáñez Colomo 2021, p. 568; Cioffi 2021.
29. The term *cross-disciplinary* is also used by other authors to describe legal research that transcends the boundaries of legal branches, *see*: Majcher 2023, p. 274; Yakovleva, Geursen and Arnbak 2020, p. 1482.
30. Marsden and Podszun 2020, p. 48; Crane 2011, p. xi; M. Trebilcock and Iacobucci 2010, p. 455.
31. There are some important exceptions. *See, e.g.,* Yakovleva, Geursen and Arnbak 2020; De Streel and Monti 2022; Crémer et al. 2023a.
32. Abate, Bianco and Casalini 2024, p. 26.

- How do competition authorities of the selected legal orders address (potential) abuses of a dominant position on personal data markets?
- To what extent do competition law and the DMA overlap, and what is (or should be) the relationship between these two instruments?
- To what extent do the competition law and the GDPR overlap and what is (or should be) the relationship between these two instruments?
- Which mechanisms are in place to resolve conflicts between EU and national competition law, and to what extent do these mechanisms guarantee the coherent application of EU and national competition law to personal data markets?
- Which mechanisms are in place to resolve conflicts between competition law, the DMA and the GDPR, and to what extent do these mechanisms guarantee the coherent application of competition law, the DMA and the GDPR to personal data markets?
- Which mechanisms are in place to facilitate cooperation between (i) competition authorities and (ii) enforcers of the DMA and the GDRP respectively, and to what extent do these mechanisms guarantee the coherent application of competition law, the DMA and the GDPR to personal data markets?

1.3 METHODS, DEFINITIONS AND SCOPE

The overarching objective of this project is to provide a coherence analysis of the institutional frameworks of competition law, the DMA and the GDPR in the context of personal data markets. As explained in section 1.1, due to the economic reality of personal data markets and regulatory developments, competition law overlaps to an increasing extent with other legal branches and instruments. This overlap is the impetus for this cross-disciplinary research on the intersection between different fields of law.

1.3.1 Methodology

The assessment relies on a *legal doctrinal methodology* and 'black letter law' or the law on paper takes centre stage in the analysis.[33] I combine different supplementary methods of legal research, i.e., descriptive, theory-building, evaluative and normative research.[34] *First,* the research provides a description and analysis of the most important concepts and

33. Doctrinal legal research focuses on 'doctrine'. The word doctrine 'means instruction knowledge or learning' and includes legal concepts and principles of all types – cases, statutes, and rules. *See*: Hutchinson 2012, p. 84; Van Gestel, Micklitz and Maduro 2012, p. 7.
34. For an elaborate overview of legal research methods, *see*: Kestemont 2018.

frameworks, particularly including personal data markets, the legal frameworks of competition law, DMA and the GDPR. *Second,* the research has a theory-building objective. In order to map the mechanisms that are in place to streamline the interaction between authorities and to be able to analyse these mechanisms in a structured way, Chapter 8 provides a typology of different forms and types of cooperation. *Third* – and most prominently – I use evaluative and normative techniques. The ultimate objective is to analyse existing frameworks in light of the coherence principle. On the basis of this evaluation, and insofar as necessary, recommendations to reinforce the coherence of the frameworks are provided. Section 1.4 of this Introduction further elaborates on the principle of coherence, i.e., the main evaluative criterion.

In this project, the main research question is answered by applying a legal doctrinal methodology. This means that I study legislation, case law, policy documents and (legal) literature to answer the main research question. The analysis takes a *cross-disciplinary* approach by transcending the boundaries of a single legal branch and by focusing on the interaction between different (or *across*) areas of the law.[35] By considering and comparing different areas of the law, the book engages in *internal comparative law*.[36] The cross-disciplinary focus of the analysis allows for conclusions on the interactions between competition law, the DMA and the GDPR.

The research does not rely on multi-disciplinary methods. Despite the fact that it would be interesting to use empirical methods, and in particular qualitative methods such as interviews, to test the main findings, such analysis does not fall within the scope of this work. This limitation in terms of methodology aims to safeguard the focus of the project. Given this methodological limitation, the implications of *informal* cooperation between authorities can – despite their relevance – only be taken into account to a limited extent. Empirical research into informal cooperation mechanisms could be an interesting avenue for further research.[37]

1.3.2 Scope of the Research

Competition law is the 'traditional' field to address the issue of market power. Therefore, and despite the cross-disciplinary focus, the analysis takes *competition law* as a starting point. The focus on competition law is reflected in the way in which the relationship between EU and national competition

35. The interpretation of the terms inter-, multi- and cross-disciplinary research are subject to debate. In the context of this work, cross-disciplinary research refers to research that transcends the borders of a single legal branch, but takes a holistic approach by focusing on the interplay between different legal branches. The term cross-disciplinary is also used to refer to research that integrates different scientific disciplines. This interpretation of the concept cross-disciplinary is more encompassing than my definition. *See*: Guerra 2018, p. 590-591.
36. Vranken 2006, p. 88; Herweijer 2003, para. 5.
37. *See,* for example, Freeman and Rossi 2012. *See* section 10.4.

law, the DMA and the GDPR is approached. The analysis starts with an assessment of the relationship between the EU and national competition law. Next, I study the relationship between (i) competition law on the one hand and (ii) the DMA and the GDPR on the other hand. This analysis takes a *unidirectional* approach: the analysis considers the impact of the DMA and the GDPR on the competition law framework. The effect of competition law on the frameworks of the DMA and the GDPR does not fall within the scope of this work. Similarly – albeit very interesting – the interplay between the DMA and the GDPR is not part of this book. The limitation of a unidirectional approach ensures the focus of the project.

The DMA and the GDPR are selected given their close link with and undeniable relevance for the application of competition law to personal data markets. This close link is reflected in developments at the EU and national level. The *Meta Bundeskartellamt* judgment, which was handed down on 4 July 2023, unequivocally makes the connection between competition law and the GDPR.[38] On top of this, in the Notice on the Relevant Market, the Commission lists privacy protection as a relevant parameter of competition.[39] Hence, the relevance of data protection considerations cannot be overlooked, and the intersection between the GDPR and competition law deserves further academic attention. The DMA entered into force on 2 May 2023 and was adopted against the backdrop of the shortcomings of the competition law framework, as outlined by the Commission.[40] Yet, the DMA is not a competition law instrument according to the EU legislator, but aims to be complementary to competition law.[41] This makes the relationship between the DMA and competition law complicated, interesting and a topical subject for research.

Furthermore, the interplay between competition law, the DMA and the GDPR is studied in the context of the multi-levelled legal order of the EU. This means that developments at both the national and the EU level are relevant. However, an analysis of the national frameworks of 27 Member States is not feasible within this project. Therefore, this study is limited to the frameworks of: (i) the EU; (ii) Germany; and (iii) The Netherlands. The *EU framework* is selected for obvious reasons: both the DMA and the GDPR were adopted at the EU level. Moreover, the EU competition law framework has had a significant impact on the development of national competition laws.[42] An analysis of the EU framework is therefore inevitable. In order not

38. CJEU 4 July 2023 Case C-252/2, *Meta Bundeskartellamt*.
39. Commission Notice of 22 February 2024 on the definition of the relevant market for the purpose of Union competition law, C/2024/1645, para. 15.
40. Commission Staff Working Document Impact Assessment Report Accompanying the document Proposal for a Regulation of the European Parliament and of the Council on contestable and fair markets in the digital sector (Digital Markets Act), SWD(2020) 363 final, para. 10.
41. Preamble DMA, recital 10.
42. *See* section 8.3.1.

to overlook the relevance of national laws, the analysis is not limited to EU law, but also takes into consideration national frameworks. The analysis of national laws is limited to the legal orders of Germany and The Netherlands. *Germany* is selected for its pioneering role in the supervision of personal data markets. The proactive attitude of the German legislator, as well as that of the *Bundeskartellamt,* provides relevant insights into the interplay between the selected fields of law. The *Bundeskartellamt*'s *Facebook* (or *Meta*) decision is groundbreaking and has played a pivotal role in shaping the relationship between competition law and the GDPR.[43] At the same time, Sections 19a and 32f GWB – which lay down rules for undertakings which are of paramount significance for competition across markets and redraft the *Bundeskartellamt*'s competence to perform sector inquiries respectively – are considered to be revolutionary in the supervision of Big Tech. The legal order of *The Netherlands* is particularly interesting for reasons relating to the institutional design of its competition authority. The Dutch NCA, the *Autoriteit Consument en Markt* (henceforth: ACM), is shaped according to an integrated agency model.[44] The authority combines the enforcement of competition law, consumer law and certain sector-specific regulations. Additionally, in The Netherlands, *cross-disciplinary cooperation* between different authorities is well-developed.[45] The Dutch framework provides several fora for cooperation between enforcers of different legal branches, including a particular forum for cooperation in the field of supervision of digital markets.[46] For this reason, the institutional framework of The Netherlands provides interesting insights into the embedding of cooperation mechanisms in the institutional framework. Apart from those substantive reasons, the selection of Germany and The Netherlands is prompted by practical reasons, relating to language, expertise and access to sources.

1.3.3 Limitations

It makes sense to point out what this book does and does not cover. The analysis spans multiple legal branches, and the scope of cross-disciplinary research is inherently broad. It is nonetheless necessary to introduce certain constraints.

First, the analysis focuses on *unilateral behaviour.* This means that the project merely focuses on the behaviour of a single undertaking. Given their

43. *Bundeskartellamt* 6 February 2019, Case B6-22/16, *Facebook.*
44. *See* section 8.3.2.
45. Van den Boom, Bostoen and Monti 2024.
46. The *Digital Regulation Cooperation Platform* (*Samenwerkingsplatform Digitale Toezichthouders*) (henceforth: SDT). *See* section 9.8.1.4.

considerable economic power, unilateral behaviour by large platforms can have detrimental effects on competition and consumers. In this light, provisions targeting unilateral behaviour are particularly relevant, and the analysis of competition law is limited to national and EU provisions on abuse of dominance or other unilateral conduct. The topic of collective dominance does not fall within the scope of the analysis. Similarly, merger control – which focuses on a change of control and therefore amounts to a transaction between at least two undertakings – is out of scope. Lastly, rules governing agreements between undertakings, such as Article 101 TFEU, are – for similar reasons – not included in the assessment.

Second, as also explained above, the cross-disciplinary analysis is limited to the intersection between competition law, the DMA and the GDPR. Yet, these areas of the law are not the only fields intersecting with competition law. The intersection between, for example, competition law and consumer law, competition law and unfair commercial practices law, competition law and 'traditional' sector-specific regulation and/or competition law and the AI Act may be interesting too. Yet, and in order to safeguard the focus of this project, these areas of law are excluded from its scope.[47] Additionally, within the EU framework, the GDPR is not the only instrument that regulates the use and processing of data. More recent initiatives, including the Data Act and Data Governance Act, expand the field of 'data law'.[48] On top of this, the principles of data protection and privacy are also enshrined in the Charter of Fundamental Rights of the European Union (henceforth: Charter). In the *Meta Bundeskartellamt* case, the CJEU clearly established a link between competition law and the GDPR.[49] In contrast, the relationship between competition law and other fields of data law is still more ambiguous.[50] Therefore, at this point, an institutional analysis of the intersection between competition law and the GDPR is most relevant.

Third, and in line with the emphasis on cooperation between enforcement agencies, the research focuses on cooperation in the context of public enforcement. This means that considerations relating to private enforcement, notwithstanding their relevance, do not fall within the scope of the book. Given the focus on the interaction between administrative authorities, the preliminary reference procedure, and the issue of cooperation with (national) courts does not take centre stage in the analysis.

Lastly, in line with the cross-disciplinary focus of the research, the inquiry emphasises conduct by businesses that qualify as: (i) dominant undertaking; (ii) gatekeeper; *and* (iii) data controller or processor. I focus in particular on unilateral conduct by undertakings that fall within the scope of

---

47. For further reading *see,* for example: Bostoen 2025; Helberger, Zuiderveen Borgesius and Reyna 2017; Graef, Clifford and Valcke 2018.
48. Streinz 2021.
49. CJEU 4 July 2023 Case C-252/21, *Meta Bundeskartellamt.*
50. Schweitzer and Metzger 2023.

competition law, the DMA and the GDPR. In line with this delineation, the analysis takes into consideration particularly the behaviour of large platforms.

1.3.4 Definitions

This book relies on certain important notions and concepts. Most of these definitions are discussed in more detail elsewhere. However, for the sake of comprehensiveness and readability, I define some key notions here:

- *Personal data markets:* markets on which undertakings operate a business model that relies on the collection, exchange and/or monetisation of personal data.49[51]
- *Institutions:* 'formal and informal bodies that are charged by society with making, administrating, enforcing or adjudicating its laws or policies'.[52]
- *Institutional design:* an agency's mandate and organisational design, which includes the structures and processes that have a bearing on enforcement and the application of the law.[53]
- *Unidirectional:* only in one direction, meaning that the impact of: (i) the DMA on competition law; and (ii) the GDPR on competition law are analysed. The effect of competition law on both these instruments does not fall within the unidirectional scope of the research.
- *Cross-disciplinary:* transcending the boundaries of one legal branch.
- *Intra-disciplinary:* within one legal branch.
- *Mono-jurisdictional:* within a single legal order or jurisdiction.
- *Multi-jurisdictional:* across multiple jurisdictions or legal orders.
- *Polycentric cooperation:* cooperation between enforcers of more than two legal branches.

1.4 COHERENCE

As explained in sections 1.2 and 1.3, the main research question of this project pursues evaluative and normative research objectives. These objec

51. Personal data is defined in accordance with the GDPR. According to Article 4(1) GDPR, 'personal data' means 'any information relating to an identified or identifiable natural person ("data subject"); an identifiable natural person is one who can be identified, directly or indirectly, in particular by reference to an identifier such as a name, an identification number, location data, an online identifier or to one or more factors specific to the physical, physiological, genetic, mental, economic, cultural or social identity of that natural person'. *See also*: Schneider et al. 2023.
52. Balogh and Cseres 2013, p. 345.
53. Balogh and Cseres 2013, p. 345.

tives are also reflected in the main research question, and particularly in the requirement of *coherence*. The evaluative standard of coherence has been selected for multiple reasons.

First, and in line with my normative conception of coherence (*see* cf. section 1.4.2), the coherence between different branches of the law is important for the overall functioning of a legal system.[54] The importance and relevance of the principle of coherence are reflected in the fact that the Treaties contain a provision on consistency. According to Article 7 TFEU, '[t]he Union shall ensure consistency between its policies and activities, taking all of its objectives into account and in accordance with the principle of conferral of powers'. Despite the fact that consistency and coherence are not identical concepts, Article 7 TFEU is relevant from a coherence perspective. As will be explained below, consistency constitutes a component of coherence. Moreover, the EU law framework employs confusing terminology regarding coherence and consistency. Where the English version of Article 7 TFEU refers to consistency, other language versions of the same provision refer use terms equivalent to the English notion of coherence.[55] This indicates the relevance of the requirement of coherence for the EU law context.

Second, the requirements of coherence and consistency are relevant in light of the cross-disciplinary focus of the research. As explained above, the overlapping competences between different enforcers pose risks of divergence. The CJEU highlights that authorities must cooperate to ensure consistency.[56] Moreover, policymakers and academics emphasise the relevance of the coherent enforcement of competition law, the DMA and the GDPR more specifically.[57] Consequently, the requirement of coherence provides a useful normative tool to assess the interrelationship between these areas of the law.

Third, the multi-layered nature of the enforcement frameworks of various legal branches imposes a need for a certain degree of coherence between the EU and different national frameworks.[58] This is clearly reflected in the history and development of the institutional frameworks of both

54. Majcher 2023, p. 150.
55. Other language versions, for example, refer to *Kohärenz, cohérance, coerenza* and *samenhang*. A similar divergence is present in para. 52 of the *Meta Bundeskartellamt* case. The English version refers to the *consistency of application*. Conversely, the Dutch text alludes to *een coherente toepassing*. *See also*: Mathisen 2010, p. 1024;*See also* Ruiz Feases 2020a, p. 44; Langer and Sauter 2017, p. 42.
56. CJEU 4 July 2023 Case C-252/21, *Meta Bundeskartellamt*, para. 52. The relationship between coherence and consistency is discussed below.
57. *See* section 1.5.
58. Rodrigo, Allio and Andres-Amo 2009, p. 15.

competition law and the GDPR. As a result of the process of decentralisation of EU competition law, enforcement became the responsibility of both the Commission and the NCAs of the Member States. This development triggered widespread concern about the coherent application.[59] Different cooperation mechanisms laid down in Regulation 1/2003 and the ECN+ Directive aim to address these concerns.[60] The introduction of the GDPR was also fostered by a desire for a strong and more *coherent* data protection framework in the EU.[61] On top of this, the GDPR explicitly provides a consistency mechanism to streamline enforcement related to cross-border processing.[62] The division of overlapping competence in the application of competition law, the DMA and the GDPR also materialises at both the national and EU level. This begs the question of to what extent the approach taken by authorities at: (i) the EU; and (ii) the national level is coherent.

Lastly, the criterion of coherence aligns well with the legal doctrinal methodology. The methodological approach of doctrinal legal research is less suitable for assessing other evaluation criteria, such as effectiveness or efficiency. The de facto effectiveness of the cooperation mechanisms cannot be assessed by an analysis of the law on paper. Consequently, an assessment of the effectiveness of the framework would require a different methodology.

1.4.1 Defining Coherence

The notion of coherence is broad and multi-interpretable. According to the Oxford Dictionary, coherence means 'the situation in which all parts of something fit together well'.[63] In the context of legal systems, the principle of coherence requires the system to 'make sense as a whole'.[64] To this end, the objectives, substantive norms, procedures and institutions need to align. In order to further define the principle of coherence, I build on Sauter's definition. Coherence is understood as the extent to which a framework is:

> (i) logically consistent, and (ii) part of, or in itself constituting a unified systemic (or in other words functional) whole […] and (iii) the former two factors should serve a clearly identifiable objective and/or set of principles.[65]

---

59. Kjolbe 2020, p. 456. Chiriţoiu 2017, p. 4; Communication from the Commission to the European Parliament and the Council, 9 July 2014, Ten Years of Antitrust Enforcement under Regulation 1/2003: Achievements and Future Perspectives, COM(2014)453 final, p. 4.
60. *See* sections 8.3 and 8.4.
61. Preamble GDPR, recitals 5-7.
62. *See* section 9.6.1.
63. *See*: https://www.oxfordlearnersdictionaries.com/definition/english/coherence accessed 29 August 2025.
64. MacCormick 1978, p. 152.
65. Sauter 2016, p. 9.

This definition has a broad perception of coherence. Coherence is not limited to *consistency*, i.e., the absence of contradictions, but comprises a broader cluster of properties.[66] This broader interpretation is reflected under (ii) and (iii) in the abovementioned definition. The criteria of 'a unified systemic whole' and a clearly identifiable objective and/or set of principles are collectively referred to as *cohesion*. Since the principle of coherence is interpreted broader than mere consistency, it cannot be considered a binary concept. Rather, coherence is a matter of degree.[67]

The coherence analysis takes a two-step approach. First, the consistency of the legal frameworks of competition law, the DMA and the GDPR is taken into account by identifying potential contradictions, as well as mechanisms to avoid such contradictions.[68] Second, the frameworks are analysed in light of the principle of cohesion by identifying to what extent they constitute a unified, systemic whole serving overarching objectives and/or principles. In order to analyse to what extent the framework constitutes a 'unified and systemic whole', it will be assessed to what extent the different elements of the framework 'harmonically' link with each other.[69] In other words, a framework is cohesive if the different building blocks align well.

To further operationalise this analysis, I rely on the theoretical framework of Kress, who lists different criteria to assess the degree of coherence of a theory.[70] In an adjusted form, these criteria can also be used to analyse the degree of coherence of a legal framework.[71] For this study, the criteria of *comprehensiveness, completeness,* and *articulateness* are particularly relevant. The criteria of comprehensiveness and completeness entail the degree to which answers to all legal questions within the scope of a framework can be provided. If a framework is comprehensive and complete, there are no gaps or irresolvable issues in the system. The principle of articulateness requires that methods for deciding issues and for resolving conflicts are expressed and not merely intuitive. Such mechanisms can include various types of rules. These rules can either determine whether a conflict arises or how a conflict can be resolved. Mechanisms of scope and pre-emption determine to what extent rules can co-exist, and whether a conflict between frameworks arises. Potential conflicts can either be resolved by a lexical ordering, i.e., a hierarchy of norms. Alternatively, mechanisms of weighing and balancing can provide a solution in the case of a conflict between norms.

66. Wintgens 1993, p. 484 and 503; Schiavello 2001, p. 236; Guest 1992.
67. Alexy and Peczenik 1990, p. 145.
68. Consistency can entail 'static consistency', i.e., consistency at a specific moment in time and 'dynamic consistency' or the consistency over the year. *See, e.g.*, Ruiz Feases 2020a, p. 33; Ibáñez Colomo 2018, pp. 25-27.
69. Schiavello 2001, p. 237.
70. Kress 2010.
71. Kress also lists the criteria of monism, unity and justification. These criteria are well-suited to analyse the coherence of a theory, but are less suitable to analyse the degree of coherence of the institutional framework of competition law, the DMA and the GDPR.

1.4.2 A Normative Conception of Coherence

This project relies on a normative conception of coherence. The assumption is that a certain degree of coherence between the different building blocks of a legal system is an important value for the functioning of that legal system. This normative conception is grounded in legal theory. Dworkin, for example, highlighted the normative value of coherence by stating that coherent legal systems are more capable of legitimising the law.[72] In a legitimate framework, different interests should be balanced in a coherent fashion.[73] A coherent approach results in a degree of predictability, which reinforces the legitimacy of a legal framework. A normative conception of coherence can also be derived from its material effects: in a coherent legal system, the realisation of the objectives of the respective legal branches is more likely.[74] A sufficient degree of coherence between different policies is essential to provide legal certainty. Legal certainty – in turn – contributes to compliance, thereby enhancing the effectiveness of the legal framework.

1.5 RELEVANCE

The previous sections of this Introduction already touched upon the *academic* relevance of this project. By combining a cross-disciplinary approach and institutional focus, this book aims to fill gaps in academic literature.[75]

Apart from academic relevance, this project also has practical relevance. *First,* the project is relevant from a *governmental perspective.* Various public authorities and bodies have to position themselves in the ever-complex regulatory landscape. For instance, Martijn Snoep – chairman of the Dutch NCA – highlights that there are a lot of different national and EU regulators involved in the oversight over digital platforms. In his view, this exacerbates the need for cooperation between different enforcers.[76] The issue of cross-disciplinary cooperation is also on the agenda of the European Data Protection Board (henceforth: EDPB). The EDPB has highlighted the importance of cooperation between different legal branches on multiple occasions and has established a 'Taskforce on the Interplay between Data Protection, Competition and Consumer Protection Law'.[77] This shows that

72. Canto 2014, p. 38; Dworkin 1986.
73. Van Cleynenbreugel 2012, p. 312.
74. Sauter 2016, p. 10.
75. *See* sections 1.2 and 1.3.
76. Snoep 2023a; Snoep 2024.
77. Letter EDPB of 7 October 2024, EDPB on the interplay between EU data protection and competition law, COM A4/MK. *See also*: https://www.edpb.europa.eu/about-edpb/who-we-are/edpb-plenaries-subgroups-and-taskforces_en accessed 30 March 2025.

the issue of the institutional implications of cross-disciplinary norm overlaps is relevant for different (supervisory) bodies and authorities.

Second, the topic is relevant for *businesses*. Overlapping norms and parallel or consecutive procedures can increase compliance costs of undertakings. Moreover, navigating in a complex regulatory landscape further increases these costs.[78] Henceforth, it is unsurprising that the business community generally comments critically on divergent standards and regulatory complexities.[79] Since cross-disciplinary research on the coherence between legal branches helps to understand the interplay between the different fields of the law, such research can be interesting for businesses.

Lastly, the research can be relevant from a *customer* or *citizen* perspective. Individuals can benefit from the effective enforcement of competition law, the DMA and the GDPR, because this can, *inter alia*, reinforce consumer welfare and fairness.[80] The effective enforcement of competition law, the DMA and the GDPR requires a certain degree of coherence. Against this backdrop, well-developed cooperation mechanisms can be helpful to realise the objectives of the different legal branches. This can ultimately reinforce the position of customers or citizens.

1.6 STRUCTURE AND OUTLOOK

In order to answer the main research question, this study addresses the different sub-questions in three main parts. *Part I* sets the scene by providing the necessary background on personal data markets and institutional design in the multi-level legal order of the EU. *Part II* zooms in on the application of competition law, the DMA and the GDPR to personal data markets. The analysis focuses in particular on the interplay between these different instruments. *Part III* examines existing mechanisms of pre-emption, hierarchy of norms and cooperation and provides an overview of the mechanisms that are in place to facilitate the coherent application of the different frameworks.

Parts I, II and III are further subdivided into chapters according to the following structure.

78. Yakovleva, Geursen and Arnbak 2020, p. 1482.
79. The inconsistencies regarding unilateral conduct in competition law are, for example, subject to criticism from the business community. *See*: Commission Staff Working Paper of 29 April 2009 accompanying the Communication from the Commission to the European Parliament and Council, Report on the functioning of Regulation 1/2003, SEC(2009)574 final, p. 6. In the EU Fitness Check of Consumer Law stakeholders stress the fact that the proliferation of EU legislation in the digital area has increased regulatory complexity. *See*: Commission Staff Working Document 3 October 2024, Fitness Check of EU consumer law on digital fairness, SWD(2024)230 final, p. 58.
80. The objectives of the different legal branches are discussed in more detail in Part II.

In *Part I*, *Chapter 2* provides an analysis of the concept of personal data markets. The main aim of this chapter is to give an overview of the characteristics that distinguish personal data markets from traditional markets. To this end, the chapter elaborates on multiple concepts, including multi-sided platforms, network effects, 'free' services and data-driven transactions. *Chapter 3* zooms in on institutional design in the multi-level legal order of the EU in order to understand the broader context in which the enforcement of competition law, the DMA and the GDPR takes place. The chapter elaborates on the terms institution and institutional design, zooms in on the division of tasks between national and EU authorities and introduces important principles of EU law governing the complementary application of EU and national rules.

Part II addresses the application of competition law, the DMA and the GDPR to personal data markets. *Chapter 4* covers the application of EU and national competition law to personal data markets. This chapter aims to assess how the Commission and the Dutch and German NCAs rely on the competition law framework to respond to potential abuses of dominance in personal data markets. *Chapter 5* considers the interplay between competition law and the DMA. The goal of this chapter is to provide an understanding of the relationship between those instruments. *Chapter 6* takes a similar approach, but addresses the relationship between the competition law and the GDPR. The findings of Part II are wrapped up in *Synthesis I.*

Part III concerns mechanisms of pre-emption, hierarchy of norms and cooperation. Within Part III, *Chapter 7* addresses the issues of hierarchy of norms and pre-emption. Principles of pre-emption and hierarchy of norms determine to what extent legal frameworks can co-exist and which set of norms prevails in the case of a conflict. This analysis not only addresses the issue of conflicting norms but also takes into consideration the overlap between complementary norms. The principles of pre-emption and hierarchy of norms are less suitable to streamline the application and interaction of complementary norms. Against this backdrop, Chapters 8 and 9 address the issue of cooperation. *Chapter 8* starts with a theoretical analysis in order to provide a typology of different mechanisms for cooperation. This typology serves as the foundation for further analysis. After providing the theoretical analysis, Chapter 8 proceeds with an assessment of the mechanisms that facilitate cooperation between competition authorities at the national and the EU level. *Chapter 9* takes a cross-disciplinary approach and focuses on the mechanisms that are in place to facilitate cooperation between competition authorities and enforcers of the DMA and GDPR. *Synthesis II* builds on the findings of Part III and provides a coherence analysis of the different institutional frameworks.

Chapter 10 draws upon Synthesis I and II by providing the final conclusion by addressing the question of to what extent the institutional frameworks and cooperation mechanisms of competition law, the DMA and the GDPR can guarantee the coherent application of these instruments to personal data markets. Moreover, the Conclusion provides suggestions for improving the overall coherence of the framework and proposes suggestions for further research.

Part I
Setting the Scene

This part sets the scene and provides the necessary background and context for the research. To this end, *Chapter 2* studies the concept of personal data markets. Next, *Chapter 3* discusses the concepts of institutions and institutional design and studies the multi-level order of the EU.

Chapter 2
Personal Data Markets

2.1 INTRODUCTION

Over the past few decades, many aspects of our lives and the economy have become digitalised. In the wake of this process of digitalisation, various (new) digital markets have emerged. This process undeniably yields certain advantages. By facilitating speedy and efficient transactions, digitalisation leads to significant efficiency and financial gains.[81] Nowadays, we can, for example, communicate with virtually everyone around the world – mostly for free. Furthermore, various sectors, including healthcare, mobility and education, have been revolutionised.[82]

The positive impact of digital technologies is visible throughout (almost) all sectors of our economy and society.[83] Despite these opportunities, digitalisation also presents multiple challenges. Large platforms, and GAFAM in particular, have been labelled as *BAADD*, i.e., big, anti-competitive, addictive and destructive to our democracy.[84] The challenges associated with large platforms are broad in scope, and range – *inter alia* – from democratic concerns, to worries about the spread of disinformation and

81. Zingales et al. 2019, p. 6; Wiggers, Struijlaart and Dibbits 2019, p. 1.
82. Crémer, De Montjoye and Schweitzer 2019, p. 6.
83. Crémer, De Montjoye and Schweitzer 2019, p. 12.
84. Fox 2019, p. 102.

to issues of cybersecurity.[85] Moreover, the strong *economic* position of large platforms raises concerns.

Within this broader category of digital markets, *personal data markets* have emerged. On such markets, undertakings operate a business model that relies on the collection, exchange and/or monetisation of personal data.[86] This inquiry focuses particularly on personal data markets. However, since personal data markets are a subset of digital markets, their respective characteristics overlap significantly. Therefore, in order to provide an understanding of the functioning of personal data markets, this chapter addresses certain relevant particularities of digital markets as well.

Several characteristics distinguish digital and personal data markets from traditional or 'brick-and-mortar' markets. To provide further understanding of the concept of personal data markets, this chapter sets out the main characteristics or idiosyncrasies of such markets. To this end, I take stock of the concepts of online platforms (section 2.2), network effects (section 2.3), economies of scale and scope (section 2.4), zero-price markets and the monetisation of personal data (section 2.5), tipping markets, platform ecosystems and gatekeepers (section 2.6), information asymmetries and rational behaviour (section 2.7) and dynamic competition and innovation (section 2.8). Section 2.9 provides the chapter's conclusion.

2.2 ONLINE PLATFORMS

The omnipresence of online platforms is a first important characteristic of digital markets. Yet, despite the important role platforms play in the contemporary economy, there is no uniform definition of this concept. Some authors rely on a broad notion and define platforms, for example, as 'a service whose role it is to allow end users to access other providers upstream in the value chain'.[87] This definition does not explicitly refer to the potential two- or multi-sided nature of a platform, nor to the use of the Internet. In contrast, according to other, narrower definitions, the multi-sided nature is a, if not *the,* key characteristic of a platform.[88] The European Commission (henceforth: Commission), for example, defined a platform as 'an undertaking operating in a two or multi-sided market, which uses the Internet to enable interactions between two or more distinct but interdependent groups of users so as to generate value for at least one of the two groups'.[89]

---

85. It goes beyond the scope of the analysis to provide an extensive overview of all challenges relating to digitalisation and Big Tech. For further reading, *see, e.g.,* Rathenau Instituut 2021.
86. For a more extensive taxonomy of personal data markets *see*: Schneider et al. 2023.
87. Allen and Flores 2013, p. 11.
88. Lynskey 2017, p. 5.
89. EU Survey European Commission, Regulatory environment for platforms, online intermediaries, data and cloud computing and the collaborative economy (2015) https://

This book uses the narrower definition of online platforms. This narrow definition aligns particularly well with business models of platforms operating in personal data markets. The multi-sided nature of platforms is a key element for the monetisation of personal data, which – in turn – results in an overlap between the GDPR and competition law.[90] Hence, a narrow understanding of the concept of platform fits better within the analysis.

Online platforms can be categorised in different ways. In literature, transaction and non-transaction platforms are distinguished.[91] *Transaction platforms*, such as eBay, Mastercard and Amazon Marketplace, facilitate transactions between both sides of the platform.[92] Conversely, the absence of a transaction between different sides of the market characterises *non-transaction platforms*, such as social networking or general search platforms.[93] The distinction between transaction and non-transaction platforms is further addressed in the context of defining the relevant market in section 4.2.2.1.

2.3 NETWORK EFFECTS

Digital markets are characterised by the presence of (strong) direct and indirect network effects.[94] Network effects occur when the net value of a good or service for one user is affected by the use of *other* users.[95] On markets where network effects are present, the value of the offered services consists of two components. The *autarky value* of the service, i.e., the value of the service itself even if there were no other users, comprises the first component. The second component consists of the *synchronisation value*. In the case of a *positive* network effect, this entails the additional value derived

ec.europa.eu/newsroom/dae/document.cfm?doc_id=10932 accessed 3 March 2025, pp. 3-4. Several authors take a similar approach. Bostoen, for example, defines a platforms as 'intermediaries operating in two-sided markets in which they seek to facilitate interactions between different sides of the platform'. *See*: Bostoen 2019, p. 263.

90. *See* section 6.4.2.
91. The US Supreme Court also relies on the notion of transaction platforms in the case US Supreme Court 25 June 2018, 138 S. Ct. 2274, *Ohio v. American Express Co.*
92. Petit 2021, pp. 1433-1434; Zingales et al. 2019, p. 91; Baker 2021, p. 498; Bostoen 2019, p. 274.
93. Filistrucchi et al. 2014, p. 298.
94. European Data Protection Supervisor March 2014, 'Privacy and competitive in the age of big data: The interplay between data protection, competition law and consumer protection in the Digital Economy' https://www.edps.europa.eu/sites/default/files/publication/14-03-26_competitition_law_big_data_en.pdf accessed 24 March 2025, p. 8.
95. Autorité de la Concurrence and Bundeskartellamt 2016; Yun 2020, p. 11. This inquiry focusses largely on services rather than on goods. Therefore, I will discuss network effects in the context of services.

from the potential to interact with other users.[96] This synchronisation value amounts to the essence of network effects: the utility of a service increases when more people use it.[97] In other words, a service can become more attractive if more people use it.[98]

Network effects can take several forms. It is important to distinguish between direct and indirect network effects. *Direct network effects* occur on *one and the same* side of the market and directly relate to the size of the network or to the number of users on this one side.[99] Direct network effects materialise, for example, in the context of two-way telecommunication systems. The utility of the telephone is directly linked to the size of the network. If more households own a telephone and are connected to the network, it becomes more attractive to purchase a telephone.[100]

Indirect or *virtual network effects* manifest themselves *across* market populations. This means that the value a consumer derives from a good can increase with an increase in the use of complementary goods or services.[101] Such an indirect network effect can be apparent in two- or multi-sided markets. In this case, the network effects are present on *different* sides of the platform.[102] A particular Appstore will, for example, become more attractive for app developers if it has a large customer base. *Vice versa*, the app store will be more useful for customers if it offers a broad range of apps.[103]

The presence of network effects can be relevant for the application of competition law. The presence of such network effects can, for example, bear an effect on defining the relevant market or establishing a position of dominance. This issue is further studied in Chapter 4.

---

96. Network effects can also be negative. If a telephone or computer network, for example, becomes overloaded, the value for the individual consumer will decrease. *See*: Liebowitz and Margolis 1994, pp. 132-133.
97. Katz and Sharpio 1985, p. 424; Newman 2002, p. 671; European Data Protection Supervisor March 2014, 'Privacy and competitive in the age of big data: The interplay between data protection, competition law and consumer protection in the Digital Economy' https://www.edps.europa.eu/sites/default/files/publication/14-03-26_competiti tion_law_big_data_en.pdf accessed 24 March 2025, p. 35.
98. Ministry of Economic Affairs and Climate Policy, Letter to The Speaker of the House of Representatives, 17 May 2019, Future-proofing of competition policy in regard to online platforms, CE-MC/19129028, p. 3.
99. Haucap 2019a, p. 202.
100. Veljanovski, 2007, para. 07-013; Liebowitz and Margolis 1994, p. 135.
101. Parker and Van Alstyne 2005, p. 1496; Newman 2002.
102. Haucap 2019a, p. 202.
103. Zingales et al. 2019, p. 38.

2.4 ECONOMIES OF SCALE AND SCOPE

Strong economies of scale and scope are the next relevant characteristics of digital platforms. These scale and scope economies occur due to low marginal costs and certain characteristics of data.

First, on digital markets, *economies of scale* are present because marginal costs are often low, particularly in comparison to investment and/or fixed costs. Buying a rack of servers or developing a new and innovative service often requires a substantial investment.[104] Conversely, the marginal costs for adding an extra user are quite low, often even near-zero.[105] Therefore, as a platform becomes larger, the average total costs decrease as the output expands.[106]

Economies of scale are further reinforced by data benefits associated with the size of a platform. Bigger companies have access to larger data sets and are therefore more capable of exploiting the benefits of personal data. The more data a company can harvest, the greater the value that can be extracted from these data sets becomes. Large undertakings can thus 'leverage' their data.[107] Various business models on personal data markets rely on the use of (self-learning) algorithms. In such circumstances, larger data sets yield better outcomes.[108] Search engines, for example, work with a system of 'trial and error' and 'learning-by-doing' to increase the likelihood of providing the most relevant search results. If users tend to click on links with a lower ranking, the search engine identifies this and moves the search result to a more prominent place. Naturally, this process becomes more efficient if more users enter search queries and click on certain results. Increased traffic improves the service, which attracts more users. This – in turn – results in even more possibilities to reinforce the quality of the service. Henceforth, economies of scale result in a positive feedback loop.[109]

Besides economies of scale, in many digital markets, *economies of scope* can be identified. This means that the average total costs of production are often lower if two or more products are produced jointly.[110] As explained above, access to large data sets allows platforms to leverage data. This dynamic not only results in the possibility to improve existing services, but also provides the opportunity to develop high-quality products to enter

104. Schmidt 2019, p. 51.
105. Zingales et al. 2019, p. 32; Bostoen 2019, p. 265; European Commission, Proposal of 15 December 2020 for a Regulation of the European Parliament and of the Council on contestable and fair markets in the digital sector (Digital Markets Act), COM(2020)842 final, para. 2.
106. Yun 2020, p. 7.
107. Zingales et al. 2019, p. 37.
108. Gambaro 2018, p. 111.
109. Stucke and Grunes 2016, p. 171.
110. Yun 2020, p. 7.

adjacent markets.[111] By entering different markets, platforms can create a platform ecosystem, encompassing multiple adjacent services. If a large platform like Google could combine data aggregated from (*inter alia*) e-mail, search queries and videos watched on YouTube, the algorithm can provide an ever more detailed personalised profile.[112] This dynamic further reinforces the positive feedback loop described above.

2.5 ZERO-PRICE MARKETS AND THE MONETISATION OF PERSONAL DATA

As explained above, undertakings active on personal data markets thrive by the collection, exchange and/or monetisation of personal data.[113] Given the data-driven nature of transactions on such markets, personal data becomes an asset with an economic value.[114] Collecting (customer) data to improve profits is not a novelty of the online world. However, digital technologies enable online platforms to collect, store and process an unprecedented amount of data. Moreover, on digital markets, data has evolved to a crucial input for many online services which has significantly reinforced its importance over the past few decades.[115]

On digital markets, multiple undertakings offer their services free of charge. This means that many platforms do not aim to set prices as high as possible in order to maximise profits. Yet, the absence of a monetary price does not mean that platforms offer their services for philanthropic reasons.[116] Indeed, platforms rely on various strategies to effectively cross-subsidise between user groups on different sides of the platform. There are different strategies to facilitate this process of cross-subsidisation *across* groups.[117] These strategies are not mutually exclusive, but are often combined.[118]

Direct cross-subsidy occurs when a single undertaking subsidises across different product or service groups. The services offered can be tied or non-tied, and the strategy can be commercial or technological. For example, Microsoft tied its operating system to the web browser, and Amazon offered free shipping for certain orders because it makes sufficient profit on the order

111. Zingales et al. 2019, p. 37.
112. Stucke and Grunes 2016, p. 188.
113. For a more extensive taxonomy of personal data markets *see*: Schneider et al. 2023.
114. Roosendaal, Van Lieshout and Van Veenstra 2014, p. 4.
115. Crémer, De Montjoye and Schweitzer 2019, p. 2; Shelanski 2013, p. 1679.
116. Newman 2015, p. 154.
117. These strategies are not mutually exclusive and can be combined. For a more elaborate overview of different zero-price business models, *see*: Bostoen 2019, p. 263.
118. YouTube, for example, combines a freemium model with indirect cross-subsidy. *See*: https://www.youtube.com/static?gl=CA&template=terms accessed 20 March 2025.

itself.[119] Alternatively, business models can be based on a *freemium model.* A freemium model allows customers to use a basic service free of charge. In order to get access to a more advanced service, consumers can pay a monetary fee. LinkedIn and Skype, for example, offer a zero-price basic version, as well as a more advanced paid version. Furthermore, multi-sided platforms can rely on *indirect cross-subsidy.* In this case, platforms offer and distribute their services at zero prices for one side of the platform, while the other side pays for it.[120] This business model thus relies on the fact that user groups positively value each other's presence and exploits the indirect network effects. The fact that one side of the platform does not pay a monetary fee does not mean that the use of the service is entirely free. Instead of a monetary fee, users transfer something else to the platform, in particular their personal information and their attention.[121] Subsequently, business models on digital markets thrive by indirect cross-subsidisation through the monetisation of personal data.[122] Personalised advertisements constitute a clear example of indirect cross-subsidy by platforms. Platforms monitor the behaviour of users on one side of the platform to use the collected information to provide individually targeted advertisements.[123] The monitoring allows platforms to create precise user profiles, containing personal features, such as gender, age, location, education level, online shopping behaviour, etc.[124] Advertisers and data-seekers are willing to pay for access to target groups that share specific characteristics.[125] A bike manufacturer would, for example, be particularly keen on reaching an audience with an interest in cycling.

The previous sections explained that people exchange their personal data and/or attention in order to use online services without paying a monetary fee.124F This begs the question as to whether attention and/or personal data can be equated with money or currency. It is hard to deny that the value of personal data has increased significantly with the rise of personal data markets. In this light, some authors refer to data as 'the new oil', a new currency or revolutionary method of payment.[126] These analogies are not undisputed.[127] There are significant differences in place between data and 'regular' currencies. Data is, for example, not scarce and does not have a

119. Tying by dominant undertakings or gatekeepers can amount to a violation of competition law or the DMA. This is further discussed in sections 4.2.2, 4.3.2 and 5.2.3.
120. Newman 2015, p. 149.
121. In this light, I prefer the terminology 'free of charge' over 'free'. *See also*: Bostoen 2019, p. 266.
122. Douglas 2021, p. 18.
123. Boerman, Kruikemeier and Zuiderveen Borgesius 2017, p. 364.
124. Boerman, Kruikemeier and Zuiderveen Borgesius 2017, pp. 363 and 367.
125. Newman 2015, p. 157; Furman et al. 2019, p. 29.
126. Ezrachi and Stucke 2016, pp. 28-29; Varnali 2021, p. 98; Colaps 2017, p. 34; Schmidt 2019, p. 52.
127. For further reading, *see*: Haucap 2019a.

uniform value recognised by all participants in the market.[128] Despite the fact that there is debate on the qualification of data as currency, it is now acknowledged that personal data constitutes a competitive parameter.[129] This issue is further explored in Chapter 6.

2.6 TIPPING MARKETS, PLATFORM ECOSYSTEMS AND GATEKEEPERS

The characteristics of digital markets – as set out above – can result in a shift from competition *in* the market to competition *for* the market. In this context, a 'winner-takes-it-all' dynamic may emerge.[130] This makes digital markets prone to *tipping*. If a market tips, it reaches a point where a single player achieves a critical mass. This undertaking 'wins' the market and gets to extract the benefits associated with the characteristics of digital markets. This means the winning undertaking can exploit the network effects, economies of scale and scope and the benefits of the self-reinforcing positive feedback loop.[131] This further strengthens its position in the tipped market and may even create a position of 'ultra-dominance'.[132] At this point, potential new entrants will face significant difficulties. New entrants do not have access to similar customer bases, data sets and scale and scope benefits, making it unlikely for them to overcome these barriers.[133] Innovation by new entrants is the only possibility to overcome the incumbency advantage. However, even if a new entrant were able to develop an innovative service, the strong network effects, data advantages and economies of scale and scope can still make it difficult to gather the critical mass that is required to challenge the incumbent's position.[134] In other words, once a market has tipped, the 'winner' is 'unlikely to be pushed off its pedestal anytime soon'.[135]

Admittedly, not *all* digital markets show tendencies towards tipping.[136] Although digital markets are characterised by features that make such markets prone to tipping, certain countervailing factors may be in place. Customers can, for example, 'multi-home' by using different services

128. Gambaro 2018, p. 107.
129. Commission Notice of 22 February 2024 on the definition of the relevant market for the purpose of Union competition law, C/2024/1645, para. 15; CJEU 4 July 2023 Case C-252/21, *Meta Bundeskartellamt*, para. 51.
130. Rusu, Looijestijn-Clearie and Veenbrink 2018, p. 2; Beems, Van de Gronden and Rusu 2021, p. 260.
131. Lancieri and Morita Sokwski 2021, p. 75; Gal and Petit 2021, p. 6.
132. Lancieri and Morita Sokwski 2021, p. 75.
133. Zingales et al. 2019, pp. 8 and 29.
134. Van Gorp and Batura 2015, p. 64.
135. Robertson 2020, p. 171.
136. Motta and Peitz 2020, p. 12.

simultaneously or by switching between services.[137] Additionally, customers may have different tastes and/or preferences. Under these circumstances, multiple platforms can share a significant part of the customer base, which allows different platforms to co-exist.[138] In this case, the platform diversification is sufficiently strong and no tipping occurs.

Due to this tendency towards tipping, certain platforms have the opportunity to create a *platform ecosystem* and become a so-called *gatekeeper. First,* platforms can develop an ecosystem by offering multiple complementary goods and services, and by expanding to adjacent markets. By offering various services across different levels of the value chain, large players further cement their position.[139] Various large platforms are embedded in such an ecosystem and offer an integrated 'coral reef' of products and services.[140] Amazon, for example, controls an ecosystem by operating as a retailer, a marketing platform, a delivery and logistics network, a payment service, a credit lender, an auction house, a book publisher, a producer of television and films, a fashion designer, a hardware manufacturer and a host of cloud space.[141] *Second,* as a result of the tipping of the market and/or the expansion of the portfolio, a platform can become a so-called gatekeeper. In this scenario, there are no longer 'real' alternatives available for businesses and customers. Gatekeepers act as competitive bottlenecks or main gates by controlling: (i) access to necessary information; and/or (ii) by acting as a critical intermediary.[142] In both scenarios, (business) users can no longer avoid the platform and new entrants are prevented from entering certain markets.[143] The presence of gatekeepers results in significant risks, e.g., relating to dependencies of (business) users on the platform, limited contestability of the market or the imposition of unfair prices or conditions.[144] The topic of gatekeepers and the corresponding risks is addressed in Chapter 5.

---

137. Furman et al. 2019, p. 35.
138. Motta and Peitz 2020, p. 12.
139. According to the European Commission 'gatekeepers frequently provide the portfolio of their services as part of an integrated ecosystem [...]'. *See*: European Commission Proposal of 15 December 2020 for a Regulation of the European Parliament and of the Council on contestable and fair markets in the digital sector (Digital Markets Act), COM(2020)842 final, para. 14. *See also*: Furman et al. 2019, p. 40; Lancieri and Pereira Neto 2020, p. 6.
140. Ezrachi and Stucke 2016, p. 30.
141. Khan 2017, pp. 710 and 755.
142. Helberger, Kleinen-von Königslöw and Van der Noll 2015, p. 52.
143. Ministry of Economic Affairs and Climate Policy, Letter to The Speaker of the House of Representatives, 17 May 2019, Future-proofing of competition policy in regard to online platforms, CE-MC/19129028, p. 2.
144. European Commission Proposal of 15 December 2020 for a Regulation of the European Parliament and of the Council on contestable and fair markets in the digital sector (Digital Markets Act), COM(2020)842 final, p. 1.

2.7 INFORMATION ASYMMETRIES AND RATIONAL BEHAVIOUR

The previous sections of this chapter identified certain dynamics associated with the strong economic position of large online platforms. Concerns about personal data markets are not limited to the issue of market power. There are also various other challenges and market failures associated with personal data markets. This section examines information asymmetries and the privacy paradox.

On personal data markets, *information asymmetries* can occur. This means that consumers can lack sufficient information to make an informed decision about their market behaviour. Alternatively, information asymmetries can arise if there are substantial differences in place between the information available for customers and providers.[145] On personal data markets, information asymmetries relate in particular to the volume and means of data collection and processing.[146] Many users of the internet lack essential knowledge about privacy policies and the technical nature of data processing.[147] Relevant information is often concealed in hefty, vague and complex terms and conditions.[148] This makes it hard for consumers to understand to what extent and by what means their data is collected. Also, beyond the data collection stage, consumers are often unaware of what happens to their data. Platforms could, for example, distribute and exchange data with third parties or across services.[149] Moreover, many individuals are unaware of the far-reaching potential and scope of data analysis. Data analysis allows platforms to combine data and create detailed and extensive user profiles on the basis of the data collected. Research, for example, shows that the likelihood of a person suffering from depression can – quite accurately – be predicted by data analysis on the basis of Instagram posts. Apparently, depressive people are, for example, more likely to post photos in black and white and share fewer group pictures.[150] Given the lack of knowledge about data collection, processing and analysis, consumers often lack the necessary information to make privacy-sensitive decisions. This results in information asymmetries between consumers and platforms.[151]

Apart from the fact that consumers can lack information about how their data is collected and processed, individuals are often unaware of the value of their personal data.[152] In this light, consumers may be unwilling to

---

145. Van de Waerdt 2020, p. 2; Ogus 1994, p. 38.
146. Zuiderveen Borgesius 2015, p. 189.
147. Schwartz 2000, p. 822; Weinstock Netanel 2000, p. 476.
148. Lynskey 2017, p. 23; Roosendaal, Van Lieshout and Van Veenstra 2014, p. 13.
149. The DMA and GDPR impose certain limitations in this regard. This topic is further addressed in sections 5.3.2.1 and 6.2.3.
150. Reece and Danforth 2017.
151. Zingales et al. 2019, p. 60; Rhoen, 2019, p. 11; Acquisti and Grossklags 2005, p. 26.
152. Roosendaal, Van Lieshout and Van Veenstra 2014, p. 13.

pay for a privacy-friendly alternative, even if one were available.[153] Although individuals state that they are concerned about the protection of their personal data and privacy, this concern is often not reflected in their actual behaviour. In other words, a discrepancy exists between people's attitudes towards privacy and their actual behaviour. Despite seemingly valuing their personal data, in practice, people often disclose it imprudently or in exchange for minimal benefits. This discrepancy between attitude and action has been coined as the *privacy paradox*.[154] As explained above, the privacy paradox can partially be explained by information asymmetries in personal data markets.

Additionally, concerning their data protection and privacy, people do not always act fully rationally.[155] Individuals, for example, tend to value benefits more strongly than future risks. Against this background, the current benefits of disclosing information can be prioritised over future privacy losses. On top of this, due to 'optimism bias', individuals consider themselves to be less at risk of a privacy intrusion than others.[156] The interplay of these different biases can – at least partially – explain the privacy paradox.[157]

People's limited or bounded rationality is not only relevant in the context of the privacy paradox. The fact that humans are unable to process unlimited amounts of information and draw accurate conclusions from it can affect their degree of rationality.[158] Consumers, for example, tend to be very sensitive to nudges.[159] Differences in the presentation of options can have a strong impact on an individual's choice and platforms can easily steer consumer behaviour by different nudging strategies.[160] These strategies have evolved with the rise of Big Data and the use of algorithms. Novel technologies enable platforms to nudge in a highly sophisticated way by creating highly personalised environments or 'hyper-nudges'.[161]

Pre-installation and the use of default settings constitute examples of nudges. For example, the use of a default browser greatly increases the

153. Bamberger et al. 2020, p. 339.
154. Economides and Lianos 2021, p. 803; Zuiderveen Borgesius 2015, p. 197; W. Kerber 2016, p. 859; Haucap 2019b, p. 3; Acquisti and Grossklags 2005, p. 26.
155. Acquisti 2004. According to Sunstein, the fact that individuals act not always fully rational in an economic sense does not mean that 'people's behaviour is unpredictable, systematically irrational, random, rulefree, or elusive to social scientists'. *See*: Sunstein 2000, p. 1.
156. Acquisti and Grossklags 2005, p. 27; Kokolakis 2017, pp. 124 and 129.
157. Holland 2010, p. 906.
158. Baldwin, Cave and Lodge 2012, p. 74; Acquisti 2004, p. 24.
159. A nudge entails 'any aspect of choice architecture that alters people's behaviour in a predictable way without forbidding any options or significantly changing their economic incentives' and is intentionally designed to respond to cognitive limitations. *See*: Thaler and Sunstein 2009, p. 6; Yeung 2017a, p. 120; Furman et al. 2019, p. 4.
160. Crémer, De Montjoye and Schweitzer 2019, p. 47.
161. Yeung 2017a, pp. 120-122; Morozovaite 2022.

likelihood that a user will continue using this particular browser.[162] Similarly, people often accept standardised and pre-set privacy terms by simply agreeing to what is offered to them.[163] Subsequently, the use of defaults and pre-installation affects consumer behaviour, making it less likely for consumers to switch to alternatives. Hence, pre-installation can further reinforce and expand the strong position of a large platform or gatekeeper. Competition law and the DMA impose limitations on the use of defaults by gatekeepers and dominant undertakings. This issue is further addressed in sections 4.2.2 and 5.2.3.

2.8 DYNAMIC COMPETITION AND INNOVATION

The sections above discussed the main characteristics of digital markets, as well as some of the problems and market failures associated with these markets. This analysis highlighted the existence of entry barriers and the strong competitive position of large platforms. However, there is another side to the coin as well. Dynamic effects of competition are highly relevant for digital markets. The data-driven economy is dynamic, and new markets can be created through innovation. In light of this dynamic competition, new players can challenge the incumbent's position with innovative services.[164] If a new entrant does so successfully, a paradigm shift may occur. This can indicate that competition in digital markets is more sequential than simultaneous.[165] In the past, Google, for example, replaced AltaVista in the market for general search.[166] The effects of dynamic competition have implications for competition in the market. The successful entry of innovative, new challengers arguably indicates low entry barriers.[167]

The Commission has recognised the relevance of dynamic competition and innovation in previous decisions. In the *Facebook/Whatsapp* merger decision, for example, the Commission acknowledged that the communication sector is 'a recent and fast-growing sector which is characterised by short innovation cycles in which market shares may turn out to be ephemeral'.[168] In *Cisco,* the GC concurs with this approach.[169] The Commission and the General Court (henceforth: GC) thus seem to acknowledge

162. Zingales et al. 2019, p. 42.
163. Schwartz 2000, p. 822.
164. Costa-Cabral and Lynskey 2018, p. 11; Schmidt 2019, p. 60.
165. Shelanski 2013, p. 1669; OECD 2013, p. 6.
166. Autorité de la Concurrence and Bundeskartellamt 2016, p. 29.
167. Tucker and Wellford 2014, p. 7; Lilico and Sinclair 2017, p. 64.
168. European Commission 3 October 2014 COMP/M7216 *Facebook/WhatsApp*, para. 99; Commission, DRAFT Guidelines on the application of Article 102 of the Treaty on the Functioning of the European Union to abusive exclusionary conduct by dominant undertakings, [...](2024)xxx draft, para. 28.
169. GC 11 December 2013 Case T-79/12, *Cisco*, para. 69.

that, on such markets, market shares for a brief period of time may overstate the actual market power of a dominant player, since it is under threat of dynamic entry.[170] Hence, digital markets can be cyclical in nature, and successful firms with a large market share can be vulnerable to displacement by the next innovative cycle.[171]

Although dynamic competition can positively impact the competitiveness of digital markets, it does not always provide a sufficient counterweight to compensate for the effects of strong network effects, economies of scale and scope, information asymmetries and data advantages. Where innovation has indeed transformed certain digital markets, other markets appear more mature and less dynamic.[172] This nuance is also accepted by the Commission and the CJEU. In the *Google Shopping* case, Google argued that its dominant position was fragile and that dynamic competition threatened this position. The Commission rejected these arguments, stressing that the market did not show 'signs of market instability' and that 'on the contrary, a rather stable hierarchy is established'.[173] Notwithstanding the relevance of innovation, dynamic competition is more relevant for some digital markets than for others.[174] Consequently, it cannot be concluded that dynamic competition is always sufficient to safeguard the competitiveness of all digital markets.

2.9 CONCLUSION

Despite the fact that the term *digital market* is very broad and encompasses an umbrella concept, such markets have certain idiosyncrasies. Since personal data markets are a subset of digital markets, most of these characteristics are also relevant for personal data markets. The omnipresence of digital platforms, the existence of network effects, economies of scale and scope and the monetisation of personal data are, for example, important features that impact the functioning of personal data markets. Due to these characteristics, such markets are prone to tipping and 'winner takes it all' dynamics. Ultimately, large platforms may establish a platform ecosystem and gain a gatekeeping position.

The characteristics of personal data markets trigger multiple concerns. On personal data markets, various market failures may be present. Large platforms can, for example, gain a position of market power, and there are often strong information asymmetries in place between platforms and users.

170. Whish and Bailey 2018, p. 7.
171. OECD 2013, p. 6.
172. Schmidt 2019, p. 68.
173. European Commission 27 June 2017, Case AT3970, *Google Shopping*, para. 267.
174. Schmidt 2019, p. 62.

Furthermore, the use of nudging techniques, such as defaults and pre-installation, can exploit consumer irrationalities, further consolidating the powerful position of large platforms on personal data markets.

Several frameworks of EU and national law can potentially curb the strong economic position of Big Tech. Within this broader framework, this inquiry focuses on the application of competition law, the DMA and the GDPR to personal data platforms. Part II builds on this descriptive chapter and further assesses the application and interrelation of these fields in the context of personal data markets.

Chapter 3
Institutional Design in the Multi-Level Legal Order of the EU

3.1 INTRODUCTION

This inquiry assesses the institutional frameworks of national and EU competition law, the DMA and the GDPR in light of the principle of coherence.[175] Institutions are thus at the core of the analysis. The institutions responsible for the enforcement of these legal branches operate within the multi-level legal order of the EU. Against this backdrop, and in order to establish the relevant context, this chapter elaborates on the concepts of institutions and institutional design and on the dynamics of enforcement in the multi-level legal order of the EU. Moreover, EU law contains several legal principles that are relevant for the enforcement of competition law, the DMA and the GDPR. Given their general and overarching relevance, these principles are also addressed in this chapter. Part II builds on the general analysis by addressing the individual legal branches in more detail.

This chapter starts by defining the concepts of institutions and institutional design in section 3.2. Next, section 3.3 zooms in on the multi-level legal order of the EU. Within the broader framework of EU law, important (institutional) principles govern the complementary application of EU and national law. The principles of institutional and procedural autonomy and the principle of sincere cooperation are particularly relevant in this regard. Furthermore, the principle of *ne bis in idem* provides important limitations on the parallel or consecutive application of frameworks. Given their relevance

175. *See* sections 1.2 and 1.3.

to the research, section 3.4 analyses these principles in more detail. Section 3.5 provides the chapter's conclusion.

3.2 INSTITUTIONS AND INSTITUTIONAL DESIGN

The concept *institution* is rather broad and has multiple context-dependent meanings. Definitions range from very broad to rather narrow and stretch from 'rule of the game in a society' to an agency formally established by the law.[176] For the purpose of this inquiry, institutions are defined as 'formal and informal bodies that are charged by society with making, administrating, enforcing or adjudicating its laws or policies'.[177] In line with this inquiry's focus on public enforcement, the *enforcement* function of institutions will be in the spotlight.

The institutional dimension is important for the effective application of substantive frameworks and should therefore not be overlooked.[178] Institutions and institutional design are inherently linked to the effectiveness of the law: institutional and procedural differences likely result in different substantive outcomes.[179] Hence, institutions are 'a critical and underappreciated driver' of policy.[180]

Institutional design refers to an agency's *mandate* and *organisational design*, which includes the structures and processes that have a bearing on enforcement and the application of the law.[181] Despite the fact that the word *design* implies that these elements are always shaped by deliberate choices, reality is often much more complex.[182] The mandate and organisational design of an authority are not merely the result of deliberate, conscious choices, but are impacted by multiple factors, including historical developments, the political climate, interaction with other institutions, and social and economic forces.[183] Certain elements of an institution's mandate and/or structure will be shaped by deliberate choices. Yet, other features will be strongly impacted by different factors, including economic reality and political willingness. For example, originally, NCAs were not mandated to take data protection considerations into account. However, in light of the economic reality, such considerations can no longer be overlooked by competition authorities.[184] Considering the relevance of such developments,

176. Fox 2010, p. 473; North 2012; Menard and Shirley 2005; Crane 2011, p. xxi.
177. Balogh and Cseres 2013, p. 345.
178. Hyman and Kovacic 2014; Van Cleynenbreugel 2012, p. 308.
179. Trebilcock and Iacobucci 2010, p. 455.
180. Crane 2011; Kovacic 2012, p. 1020.
181. Balogh and Cseres 2013, p. 345.
182. Crane 2011, p. xiii.
183. Crane 2011, p. xiii.
184. CJEU 4 July 2023 Case C-252/21, *Meta Bundeskartellamt*, para. 51; *See* section 4.4.2.3.

my research is not merely focused on deliberate choices, but adopts a broader interpretation of institutional design.

3.3 THE MULTI-LEVEL LEGAL ORDER OF THE EU

The frameworks of competition law, the DMA and the GDPR are enforced within the multi-level legal order of the EU. National rules are – naturally – enforced at the national level. Conversely, the public enforcement of EU law is more complex and takes place at both the national and the EU level. The enforcement of the competition law framework is, for example, the shared competence of the Commission and NCAs.[185]

Initially, the EU was largely shaped as a model of *executive federalism,* meaning that, despite the fact that substantive EU laws were established at the EU level, executive action was largely taken at the national level by Member States' authorities.[186] The institutional and procedural frameworks were laid down at the national level, in line with the principles of institutional and procedural autonomy.[187] These principles, which are subject to the principles of equivalence, effectiveness and effective judicial protection, are further discussed in section 3.4.1.

With the development and expansion of the EU, it became apparent that these national approaches triggered a risk of inconsistencies in the application of EU law. To mitigate the negative consequences of these inconsistencies, in the context of the enforcement of EU laws, national institutional and procedural frameworks were increasingly Europeanised.[188] Hence, despite the institutional and procedural autonomy of the Member States, the EU framework does not leave national institutional and procedural frameworks entirely untouched. Rather, the impact of EU law on national procedures has gradually increased over time.[189] The EU has harmonised national procedural frameworks in a myriad of legal fields. For example, the ECN+ Directive introduces a set of investigative, decision-making and fining powers in the area of competition law.[190]

Apart from the Europeanisation of national procedural frameworks, EU bodies, agencies and networks have progressively reinforced their role in the enforcement of the EU substantive law framework. Since the 1980s, such institutions have been established in the context of various legal branches. The Commission, for example, is the 'sole enforcer' of the DMA, and the European Competition Network (henceforth: ECN) plays an important role

185. *See* section 4.2.3.
186. Hijmans 2019, p. 365.
187. De Moor-van Vught 2010, p. 67.
188. Scholten and Ottow 2014, p. 80.
189. Cseres 2013, p. 15.
190. Widdershoven 2019, p. 12.

in the enforcement of competition law. The actual degree of Europeanisation of procedural frameworks, as well as the level of *centralisation,* varies per legal branch. The (de)centralised enforcement of competition law, the DMA and the GDPR are discussed in more detail in sections 8.3.1, 9.2.1 and 9.5.1, respectively.

3.4 IMPORTANT (INSTITUTIONAL) PRINCIPLES

Despite the fact that the institutional frameworks of competition law, the DMA and the GDPR diverge, some important overarching (institutional) principles are relevant. The objective of this section is not to provide an exhaustive overview or catalogue of general principles of EU law. However, certain principles will be addressed since they are directly related to the core of the analysis. The principles of institutional and procedural autonomy are of key importance for understanding enforcement in the multi-layered legal order of the EU. Furthermore, the principle of sincere cooperation is the backbone of cooperation between different enforcers. For example, this became apparent in the *Meta Bundeskartellamt* case.[191] Moreover, the principle of *ne bis in idem* is particularly relevant for the parallel and/or consecutive application of different frameworks. Since overlapping norms between different enforcers are at the heart of the inquiry, this principle cannot be overlooked.

3.4.1 Institutional and Procedural Autonomy

As mentioned earlier, the implementation and enforcement of EU law partially takes place at the Member State level.[192] This means that EU law depends on national institutional and procedural frameworks for the achievement of its objectives.

According to the principle of *procedural autonomy,* the procedural frameworks that are relevant for the application and enforcement of EU substantive rules are – in the absence of EU law dealing with procedural matters – governed by national laws. In principle, Member States can enforce EU law through their own national systems and have the freedom to shape their own procedures.[193] However, this freedom is not unlimited: the procedural autonomy of Member States is subject to two conditions, i.e., the principles of equivalence and effectiveness.[194] These principles are grounded

191. CJEU 4 July 2023 Case C-252/22, *Meta Bundeskartellamt.*
192. *See, e.g.,* Article 291 TFEU.
193. Biondi and Gentile 2019, para. 1.
194. In the *Rewe* case, the CJEU established that 'in the absence of [Union] rules on this subject, it is for the domestic legal system of each Member State to designate the courts having jurisdiction and to determine the procedural conditions governing actions at law

in the principle of sincere cooperation.[195] According to the principle of equivalence, Member States cannot treat claims arising out of EU law less favourably than claims based on national law. The principle of effectiveness means that national procedural rules cannot make the enforcement of EU law rights impossible or excessively difficult.[196] Beyond the constraints imposed by the so-called *Rewe* principles of equivalence and effectiveness, national procedural autonomy can be limited by the principle of effective judicial protection, which is enshrined in Article 47 CFR.[197]

The principle of *institutional autonomy* means that the institutional structure of the Member States is, in the absence of EU law provisions, a matter of national law.[198] National governments have the freedom to establish the national institutional infrastructure. This institutional freedom does not merely relate to the organisation of courts, but also to that of administrative authorities.[199] In this light, Member States have discretion to determine which administrative authority is competent to apply and enforce EU law.[200]

The principle of institutional autonomy is not absolute. While there is (academic) debate as to the extent to which the principles of equivalence and effectiveness are relevant in the context of the principle of institutional autonomy, it is evident that the principle does not have an unlimited reach.[201] When the exercise of national institutional autonomy poses a threat to the uniform application of EU law, a Member State's autonomy may be curbed.[202] In this context, the principle of effectiveness is used as a limitation

---

intended to ensure the protection of the rights which citizens have from the direct effect of [Union] law, it being understood that such conditions cannot be less favourable than those relating to similar actions of a domestic nature'. *See*: CJEU 25 May 1976 Case 33/76, *Rewe*, para. 5; CJEU 16 December 1976 Case 45/76, *Comet*, para. 13.

195. *See* section 3.4.2; In *Rewe,* the CJEU stresses that '[a]pplying the principle of cooperation […] it is the national courts which are entrusted with ensuring the legal protection which citizens derive from the direct effect of the provisions of [EU] law'. *See*: CJEU 25 May 1976 Case 33/76, *Rewe*, para. 5. *See also*: De Baere and Roes 2015, p. 836.
196. Bobek 2011, p. 1. *See also*: CJEU 5 March 1996 Joined Cases C-46/93 and C-48/93, *Brasserie du Pêcheur*, para. 83.
197. Prechal and Widdershoven 2011; Widdershoven 2019.
198. Verhoeven 2010, p. 27.
199. Bois and Van Cleynenbreugel 2021, p. 11.
200. Verhoeven 2010, p. 27; Jans et al. 2007, pp. 54-56.
201. Bois and Van Cleynenbreugel 2021, p. 11. However, according to AG Bobek, the principle of institutional autonomy is also limited by those principles. He stresses that '[…] the institutional and procedural autonomy enjoyed by Member States […] are limited not only by the EU's dual requirements of equivalences and effectiveness, but also by the Charter'. *See*: Opinion of AG Bobek of 25 July 2018 in Case C-310/16, *Dzivev*, p. 119.
202. *See,* for example: CJEU 21 September 1983 Joined Cases 205 to 215/82 *Deutsche Milchkontor*, para. 17; CJEU 7 December 2010 Case C-439/08, *VEBIC*. In para. 64 of

to the principle of institutional autonomy.[203] Additionally, the protection of fundamental rights as enshrined in the CFR imposes a further limitation on the principle of institutional autonomy.[204]

When the exercise of national procedural and/or institutional autonomy threatens the uniform application of EU law, action can be taken at the EU level. In such circumstances, the EU legislator can harmonise national administrative procedures.[205] Against this background, the EU has increasingly established 'minimum standards' for national authorities, for example, relating to independence, funding, investigation and sanctioning powers, due process and fundamental rights.[206] The ECN+ Directive serves as a clear example in this regard.

3.4.2 Sincere Cooperation

The principles of institutional and procedural autonomy, as well as multiple duties to cooperate, are grounded in *the principle of sincere* or *loyal cooperation.*[207] According to the principle of sincere cooperation, which is enshrined in Article 4(3) TEU, the EU and the Member States shall 'in full mutual respect, assist each other in carrying out tasks which flow from the Treaties'. Article 4(3) TEU further establishes that Member States shall 'take any appropriate measure, general or particular, to ensure fulfilment of the obligations arising out of the Treaties or resulting from the acts of the institutions of the Union', and that 'Member States shall facilitate the achievement of the Union's tasks and refrain from any measure which could jeopardise the Union's objectives.' Consequently, the duty of sincere cooperation imposes both positive and negative obligations upon Member States and on the EU.[208] Article 13(2) TEU takes into consideration loyalty

---

the *VEBIC* case, the CJEU stresses that if an NCA consistently fails to enter an appearance in judicial proceedings 'the effectiveness of Articles 101 and 102 TFEU is jeopardised'.

203. AG Jacobs, for example, stresses that '[t]he principle of institutional autonomy […] governs the relationship between the [EU] and its Member States. According to the system of division of powers established by the EC Treaty, in absence of applicable [EU] rules, the responsibility for the implementation, application and enforcement of Community rules falls upon the Member States in accordance with their national legal systems, subject, of course, to the constraints of the principle of effectiveness as developed by the Court'. *See*: Opinion of AG Jacobs of 24 February 2005 in Case C-394/02, *Commission of the European Communities v. Hellenic Republic*, p. 27.
204. Opinion of AG Bobek of 25 July 2018 in Case C-310/16, *Dzivev*, p. 119.
205. Bois and Van Cleynenbreugel 2021, p. 12; Schütze 2010, p. 1407.
206. De Streel and Monti 2022, p. 16.
207. Despite the importance of this principle, the terminology of *sincere* and *loyal* cooperation is not used consistently in the literature and by the CJEU. Therefore, the terms sincere and loyal cooperation are used interchangeably. *See*: Jorens et al. 2017, p. 28.
208. Whish and Bailey 2021, p. 225; Guastaferro 2018, p. 351.

between EU institutions and states that '[e]ach institution shall act within the limits of the powers conferred on it' and that '[t]he institutions shall practice in mutual cooperation'.

Historically, the principle of sincere cooperation played a pivotal role in shaping the decentralised and shared enforcement framework of the EU. Given the important role of national authorities in the enforcement of EU law, a certain degree of loyalty is essential for maintaining the 'federal' balance in the EU.[209] In this context, the principle of sincere cooperation finds a broad application in EU law. For instance, the principle is discussed extensively in the context of EU external relations.[210] Moreover, there is a clear link between the principle of sincere cooperation and the notion of trust in EU law. This issue of trust can have implications for cooperation between national authorities, particularly in times of democratic backsliding.[211] Despite their relevance, the topics of external relations and democratic backsliding fall outside the scope of the analysis. Yet, the duty of sincere cooperation also establishes various obligations for authorities to cooperate. In its case law, the CJEU has derived more specific obligations from the general principle of sincere cooperation. In the *Meta Bundeskartellamt* case, the CJEU, for example, established a duty for national competition authorities to cooperate with national data protection authorities, potentially across jurisdictions.[212] Consequently, the duty of sincere cooperation can require cooperation between different actors within the multi-level legal order of the EU.[213] These duties to cooperate are highly relevant and, hence, constitute a crucial element of the analysis.

The principle of sincere cooperation has multiple dimensions. The *horizontal* dimension requires cooperation between authorities established at the same level, i.e., between different EU institutions *or* between different national authorities.[214] In the context of national authorities, the principle of sincere cooperation finds a broad application by addressing different national branches of government, including the legislator, administrative and judicial authorities.[215] Similarly, at the EU level, all Union institutions are bound by the principle.[216] The *Meta Bundeskartellamt* case – which is discussed in

209. Guastaferro 2015, pp. 3-4.
210. For further reading, *see*: Cremona 2008; Neframi 2010.
211. Kozak 2020a.
212. CJEU 4 July 2023 Case C-252/21, *Meta Bundeskartellamt*, paras 52-53.
213. Whish and Bailey 2021, p. 225; Guastaferro 2018, p. 351. According to Klamert, the duties of cooperation can be considered a subcategory of the more general principle of loyalty. *See*: Klamert 2014, p. 12.
214. The obligations based on loyalty that apply between different Union institutions are also referred to as *institutional loyalty. See*: Klamert 2014, pp. 22 and 28.
215. Guastaferro 2018, p. 355.
216. Klamert 2019, p. 56; Order of the CJEU of 13 July 1990 Case C-2/88, *Zwartveld*, para. 17.

more detail in section 4.4.2.3 – clearly reflects the national horizontal dimension of the principle of sincere cooperation.[217]

The principle of sincere cooperation not only applies horizontally but also governs the relationship between national and EU institutions. Therefore, the principle of sincere cooperation has a *vertical* dimension as well. Consequently, the principle addresses the position of Member States in relation to EU institutions.[218] Considering the position of Member States, it should be mentioned that Article 4 TEU does not only impose obligations upon Member States but also enshrines the principle of respect for Member States' national identities. In conjunction with the principle of subsidiarity, the principle protects national values and interests within the EU legal order. [219]

The principle of Union loyalty does not only apply to national institutions, but can also impose obligations on EU institutions vis-à-vis national authorities.[220] By referring to a duty of *mutual* respect, the Lisbon Treaty acknowledges a certain degree of reciprocity and thereby endorses the *reverse vertical* dimension of loyalty in Article 4(3) TEU. Although it is clear that loyalty is a two-way principle, the scope and reach of reverse vertical loyalty remain subject to debate.[221]

In legal literature, it is widely accepted that the duty of sincere cooperation may impose obligations upon EU institutions, including the Commission.[222] However, most cases on reverse vertical sincere cooperation, which predate the Lisbon Treaty, have focused on the Commission's cooperation with the national judiciary. In the *Zwartveld* case, the CJEU, for example, highlighted that the duty of sincere cooperation imposed on EU institutions is particularly important in relation to the *judicial* authorities of

217. CJEU 4 July 2023 Case C-252/22, *Meta Bundeskartellamt.*
218. The vertical dimension of loyalty 'finds its limits with purely political matters'. Member States are, for example, not required to cooperate in the Council. *See*: Klamert 2014, p. 24.
219. Guastaferro 2015, p. 4.
220. Klamert 2019, p. 54.
221. Molinari 2021, p. 270; Klamert 2014, p. 28. In the provision on the principle of sincere cooperation, the Lisbon Treaty included a reference to obligations of 'the Union'. By including this reference to the Union, the EU legislator incorporated case law of the CJEU establishing that the obligations derived from the principle of sincere cooperation do not fall merely upon Member States but 'are reciprocal and include all elements and institutions of the Union'. *See*: Jorens et al. 2017, p. 28.
222. De Baere and Roes stress that '[c]rucially, the duty of loyal cooperation not only imposes obligations on the Member States but also on the Union institutions'. Klamert puts forward that '[the CJEU] emphasized what is now explicitly stated in Article 4(3) TEU, namely that loyalty rests on mutual duties, which bind not only the Member States but also the Union institutions'. Lenaerts, Van Uffel and Corhaut put forward that '[t]he principle of sincere cooperation also holds good for the Union institutions, which must cooperate in good faith with the Member States'. *See*: De Baere and Roes 2015, p. 835; Klamert 2014, p. 25; Lenaerts, Van Nuffel and Corhaut 2021, para. 16.0003.

the Member States.[223] In other cases, the CJEU has also imposed a duty of sincere cooperation upon the Commission in relation to national actors beyond the judiciary. In the *IMO* case, the CJEU imposed a duty of best effort on the Commission vis-à-vis the Hellenic Republic.[224] The hypothetical application of the *Meta Bundeskartellamt* theories of harm by the Commission could – if this approach were to be adopted – be a good occasion for the CJEU to provide further guidance on the reverse vertical application of the duty of sincere cooperation in the executive sphere.[225] This issue is further addressed in section 7.6.2.

3.4.3 *Ne bis in Idem*

The principle of *ne bis in idem*, or the prohibition of double jeopardy, constitutes a fundamental principle of EU law. The principle prevents someone from being punished twice for the same offence and is enshrined in Article 50 CFR and Article 4 of Protocol No. 7 of the European Convention on Human Rights. According to Article 50 CFR '[n]o one shall be liable to be tried or punished again in criminal proceedings for an offence for which he or she has already been finally acquitted or convicted within the Union in accordance with the law'. The principle of *ne bis in idem* prohibits the duplication of procedures and penalties for the same act and against the same person.[226] If multiple authorities engage in different proceedings against one and the same person, the principle of *ne bis in idem* imposes limitations. It is important to stress that the principle of *ne bis in idem* does not constitute a mechanism for resolving conflicts, but rather remedies the 'side effects' of the parallel application of different sets of norms.[227] Since the norms of competition law, the DMA and the GDPR increasingly overlap, parallel or consecutive cases may arise.

As mentioned before, the principle of *ne bis in idem* prevents the duplication of proceedings: (i) against the same person; (ii) for the same, identical facts. In the past, in the context of competition law, a third relevant factor was applied. The principle of *ne bis in idem* could only be successfully invoked if the sanction concerned the same person, the same facts and *the*

223. In the *Delimitis* case, the CJEU also focused on cooperation with judicial authorities by stating that the Commission 'is bound by a duty of sincere cooperation with the judicial authorities of the Member State, who are responsible for ensuring that [EU] law is applied in the legal order'. *See*: CJEU 28 February 1991 Case C-234/89, *Delimitis*, para. 53; Order of the CJEU of 13 July 1990 Case C-2/88, *Zwartveld*, para. 18.
224. CJEU 12 February 2009 Case C-45/07, *Commission v. Hellenic Republic (IMO)*, para. 25; Klamert 2014, p. 240.
225. *See* sections 4.4.2.3 and 7.6.2.
226. CJEU 15 October 2002 Joint Cases C-238/99P, C-244/99P, C-245/99P, C-247/99P, C-250/99P and C-251/99P, *Limburgse Vinyl Maatschappij*, para. 59; CJEU 22 March 2022 Case C-117/20, *bpost*, para. 22.
227. Cappai and Colangelo 2021; Majcher 2023, p. 253.

same protected legal interest.[228] This third criterion – relating to the protected legal interest – was absent in other areas of EU law.[229] The CJEU abolished the identity of the legal interest as a separate criterion for the application of the *ne bis in idem* principle in a competition law context in the *Nordzucker and Bpost* cases and moved towards a more uniform interpretation of the *ne bis in idem* principle in EU law.[230] Consequently, the CJEU follows a two-prong test: the principle is violated if the duplication of procedure concerns: (i) the same person; and (ii) the same facts. Considering the criterion of *the same person,* in a competition law context, this criterion can be understood as an act by one and the same undertaking.[231] The criterion of the same material facts is discussed in the context of competition law, the DMA and the GDPR in sections 3.4.3.1, 3.4.3.2 and 3.4.3.4.

The principle of *ne bis in idem* is not absolute, and violations may be justified in accordance with Article 52(1) CFR. According to this provision, 'any limitation on the exercise of the rights and freedoms recognised by the Charter must be provided for by law and respect the essence of those rights and freedoms'. Limitations should be necessary and should genuinely meet the objectives of general interest recognised by the EU or the need to protect the rights and freedoms of others.[232] To justify a *ne bis in idem* violation specifically, the objectives of the respective procedures or penalties should serve 'complementary aims relating [...] to different aspects of the same unlawful conduct'.[233] Lastly, justification is subject to the principle of proportionality. The next Sections further elaborate on the (technical) details of the justifications of *ne bis in idem* violations in relation to the parallel or consecutive application of EU and national competition law (section 3.4.3.1),

228. Tavares 2018, p. 183.
229. In those areas the so-called *Menci* test was applied. According to the *Menci* test, the principle of *ne bis in idem* can be invoked if the duplicated procedures concern: (i) the same person; and (ii) the same facts. *See*: CJEU 20 March 2018 Case C-524/15, *Menci*, para. 25.
230. CJEU 22 March 2022 Case C-151/20, *Nordzucker*, paras 39-40; CJEU 22 March 2022 Case C-117/20, *bpost*, para. 35. The AG stresses that the scope of the ne bis in idem principle 'cannot, unless otherwise provided by EU law, vary from one field to another'. This is reiterated by the CJEU. *See*: Opinion of AG Bobek 2 September 2021 in Case C-117/20 *bpost*, paras 95 and 122. In the past, the different test that was used in a competition law context has been criticised by various authors. *See,* for example: Tavares 2018, p. 245; Devroe 2009, p. 145; Veenbrink 2019. In 2011, AG Kokkot invoked similar arguments, stressing that that '[t]here is no objective reason why the conditions to which the *ne bis in idem* principle is subject in competition matters should be any different from those applicable to it elsewhere'. *See*: Opinion of AG Kokkot 8 September 2011 in Case C-17/10, *Toshiba*, para. 118.
231. CJEU 22 March 2022 Case C-151/20, *Nordzucker*, para. 37; Cappai and Colangelo 2021, p. 16.
232. CJEU 22 March 2022 Case C-151/20, *Nordzucker*, paras 49-51; CJEU 22 March 2022 Case C-117/20, *bpost*, para. 41.
233. CJEU 22 March 2022 Case C-151/20, *Nordzucker*, para. 52.

competition law and the DMA (section 3.4.3.2) and competition law and the GDPR (section 3.4.3.3).

3.4.3.1 *Ne bis in Idem*: EU and National Competition Law

In order to identify whether cases concern the *same material facts* within a competition law context, it is necessary to examine whether the parallel or consecutive proceedings cover the same geographic and product market. Consequently, if the material facts concern similar conduct, but address the effects on different territories, no *ne bis in idem* violation can be established.[234] The fact that an authority refers to a factual element relating to the territory of another Member State is insufficient to meet the criterion of the same material facts. Only if an authority 'has actually ruled on that factual element in order to make out the infringement', can the *ne bis in idem* principle be invoked successfully.[235] On top of the geographic dimension, the time frame in which the infringement occurred is relevant in order to assess the identity of the material facts. This condition presupposes that the fact occurred within a similar timeframe.[236]

If a duplication of competition law proceedings amounts to a violation of the *ne bis in idem* principle, the violation can potentially be justified. To justify a *ne bis in idem* violation, the consecutive procedures must pursue complementary aims. In *Nordzucker,* the CJEU held that two NCAs engaging in proceedings and penalising the same facts to ensure compliance with Article 101 TFEU and its national equivalents would 'pursue the same objective of general interest of ensuring that competition in the market is not distorted'.[237] Consequently, the duplicated proceedings did not pursue complementary aims and the violation of the *ne bis in idem* principle could not be justified. To support this conclusion, the CJEU heavily relies on *the first sentence of* Article 3 Regulation 1/2003 and highlights the 'close link' between Article 101 TFEU and its national counterparts. Furthermore, it highlights the full convergence of Article 101 TFEU and national rules on cartels under the first sentence of Article 3(2) Regulation 1/2003. It remains unclear how this line of reasoning would translate to the Article 102 TFEU context. Article 3 Regulation 1/2003 leaves more room for NCAs to apply national rules on unilateral conduct.[238] In this line, the boundaries of a justification of a *ne bis in idem* principle in an Article 102 TFEU context remain unclear. This issue requires further clarification by the CJEU.[239]

---

234. Van Cleynenbreugel 2022, pp. 363 and 365.
235. CJEU 22 March 2022 Case C-151/20, *Nordzucker*, para. 44.
236. CJEU 22 March 2022 Case C-151/20, *Nordzucker*, para. 15; CJEU 22 March 2022 Case C-117/20, *bpost*, para. 51; Van Cleynenbreugel 2022, p. 365.
237. CJEU 22 March 2022 Case C-151/20, *Nordzucker*, para. 56.
238. *See* section 7.4.1.
239. Mayr 2022.

3.4.3.2 *Ne bis in Idem*: The DMA and Competition Law

Where the *Nordzucker* case provides useful insights into the application of the *ne bis in idem* principle in a competition law context, the *bpost* judgment concerns the duplication of competition law and postal regulation and is relevant in light of the consecutive application of competition law and sectoral regulation. The DMA is formally not part of the competition law framework, despite the similarities between these fields.[240] This means that the DMA – arguably – qualifies as an instrument of sectoral regulation.[241] In this light, the *bpost* case is relevant in the context of the parallel or consecutive application of competition law and the DMA.[242]

Considering the criterion of the same *material facts,* in the context of sectoral regulation and competition law, it must be assessed whether the facts of consecutive procedures are *identical.*[243] To make this assessment: (i) the facts taken into account; and (ii) the infringement period should be considered.[244] As explained above, in a competition law context, the definition of the relevant geographical market can provide useful insights. For the application of the DMA, it is not necessary to define the relevant market to designate gatekeepers.[245] Hence, in the context of competition law and the DMA, the geographical market is a less suitable tool to determine whether consecutive procedures cover the same material facts.[246]

In *bpost,* the CJEU also considers the *justification* of double jeopardy for a violation of competition law and sector-specific regulation. In order to justify such a violation, the duplication of proceedings must be provided for by law.[247] The DMA provides for this possibility in Article 1(6). Furthermore, it should be assessed whether the respective frameworks pursue distinct legitimate objectives.[248] The EU legislator expressly sets the objectives of competition law and the DMA apart.[249] However – as explained in section 5.3.1 – the respective objectives are arguably more closely related than portrayed by the EU legislator.[250] This begs the question of whether the

240. *See* sections 5.3 and 5.4.
241. *See* section 7.5.
242. *See also*: Beems 2023.
243. The *ne bis in idem* principle only applies if the facts are identical, not if they are merely similar. *See*: Van Cleynenbreugel 2022, p. 362.
244. CJEU 22 March 2022 Case C-117/20, *bpost*, para. 38.
245. *See* section 5.2.2.
246. *See also*: Ribera Martínez 2023a.
247. CJEU 22 March 2022 Case C-117/20, Bpost, paras 41-42.
248. In the *bpost* case, the CJEU ruled that postal regulation and Article 102 TFEU pursue distinct legitimate objectives. Postal regulations aim to facilitate the 'liberalisation of the internal market for postal services' and rules on abuse of a dominant position pursues the objective of ensuring that competition is not distorted in the market, which is indispensable for the functioning of the internal market. *See*: CJEU 22 March 2022 Case C-117/20, *bpost*, paras 45-46.
249. Preamble DMA, recital 10.
250. Beems 2023.

objectives are sufficiently distinct indeed. Ultimately, it is up to the CJEU to decide and provide further guidance in this regard.[251] *Ne bis in idem* issues could also arise in the context of the consecutive application of the DMA and *national* competition law. In this regard, the German Section 19a GWB is particularly relevant. This Section of the German Competition Act is, to a certain extent, similar to the DMA. The framework shares certain traits with the DMA, but qualifies as an instrument of competition law under German law.[252] In this context, similar questions arise regarding the criterion of sufficiently distinct objectives. In my view – as argued in section 7.5.2.3 – the objectives of the DMA and Section 19a GWB are, indeed, sufficiently distinct and the *ne bis in idem principle* does not necessarily prevent the parallel application of the DMA and Section 19a GWB.[253]

Lastly, in order to successfully justify an infringement of the *ne bis in idem principle*, the duplication of proceedings must be proportionate. In the context of the proportionality requirement, the CJEU stresses that the complementary legal responses must form 'a coherent whole so as to address the different aspects of the societal problem involved, provided that the accumulated legal responses do not represent an excessive burden for the individual concerned'.[254] To assess this criterion of strict necessity, it should be considered: (i) whether there are clear and precise rules to predict which acts may lead to duplication of proceedings; (ii) there must be coordination between different authorities; and (iii) the two sets of proceedings must have been conducted in a sufficiently coordinated manner and within a proximate timeframe.[255] During the legislative procedure of the DMA, the EU legislator seems to have taken notice of the *bpost* criteria. While the initial proposal of the Commission did not touch upon cooperation between NCAs and the Commission, the final version establishes various mechanisms for cooperation – primarily within the European Competition Network (henceforth: ECN).[256] Moreover, recital 86 DMA explicitly refers to the principle, stressing that 'appropriate levels of fines and periodic penalties should be laid down for non-compliance' in accordance with the principle of *ne bis in idem*. Similarly, this recital provides that the Commission and relevant NCAs should coordinate their enforcement actions. Therefore, previous fines under a parallel regime should be taken into consideration.[257] If this cooperative approach is implemented in practice, potential *ne bis in idem* violations can be successfully justified.[258] Furthermore, solid cooperation mechanisms may

---

251. Monti 2021a, p. 15.
252. *See* section 7.5.2.3.
253. Podszun 2022a, p. 9.
254. CJEU 22 March 2022 Case C-117/20, *bpost*, para. 49.
255. CJEU 22 March 2022 Case C-117/20, *bpost*, para. 51.
256. *See* section 9.3.1.
257. Schweitzer 2021, p. 13.
258. Beems 2023, p. 19; Ribera Martínez stresses that 'a limitation of Article 50 of the Charter will rarely be spotted from the duplication of proceedings when competition law

prevent *ne bis in idem* issues from arising in the first place, because parallel proceedings can be identified in an early stage.[259]

In sum, the CJEU's interpretation of the *ne bis in idem* principle in *bpost* leaves room for the parallel application of the DMA and national and EU competition law. However, *bpost* was about the consecutive application of competition law and sectoral regulation, rather than the consecutive application of the DMA and competition law. Given the fact that the application of the *ne bis in idem* principle is complex and intricate, it is likely that – if parallel proceedings were to be adopted – litigation will follow. Such cases may provide an opportunity for the CJEU to further crystallise the application of the *ne bis in idem* principle.[260]

3.4.3.3 *Ne bis in Idem*: The GDPR and Competition Law

So far, the CJEU has not yet analysed the *ne bis in idem* principle in the context of consecutive procedures under competition law and the GDPR. In the past, the principle was not very relevant in this context. As outlined above, the CJEU previously applied the criterion of the same legal interest to assess the scope of the *ne bis in idem principle.* Since the GDPR and competition law – despite their overlapping objectives – protect different legal interests, the *ne bis in idem* principle would not limit the imposition of consecutive sanctions under competition and data protection law.[261] In *bpost* and *Nordzucker*, the CJEU changed its approach by abolishing the criterion of 'the same legal interest'. This means that consecutive competition and data protection law sanctions concerning the same facts and the same persons can amount to a *ne bis in idem* violation.

Since the *ne bis in idem* principle is not absolute, double jeopardy under competition law and the GDPR is potentially justifiable. The CJEU has not yet interpreted the *ne bis in idem* principle in this particular context. Despite the absence of a case directly assessing the consecutive application of competition law and the GDPR, the *bpost* case provides relevant guidance and can (partially) be transposed to this scenario. The fact that there are no mechanisms for cooperation between competition authorities and DPAs in a trans-jurisdictional context may, for example, be problematic in light of the justification of a *ne bis in idem* violation. This issue is further considered in section 9.6.2.

The fact that competences of data protection and competition authorities apply in parallel is not the only manifestation of norm overlaps in the context of competition law and the GDPR. Competition authorities can take

---

and the DMA are involved'. *See*: A. Ribera Martínez 2023b, p. 25.

259. Van den Boom 2022, p. 29.

260. Harrison, Zdzieborska and Wise 2022, p. 58; Petterson 2022, p. 11.

261. OECD 2020, para. 102; De Waerdt 2023, p. 1094.

data protection considerations into account in their competition law assessment. Section 6.4.2 delves into this dynamic in greater detail. If the competition authority and data protection authority impose a fine for the same conduct, this potentially amounts to a *ne bis in idem* violation. In his opinion on the *Meta Bundeskartellamt* case, AG Rantos briefly touches upon this issue. He emphasises that the NCA's assessment is carried out in an incidental manner and is without prejudice to the application of the GDPR by DPAs.[262] Moreover, he concludes – in a footnote – that the *Meta Bundeskartellamt* scenario is not covered by the principle of *ne bis in idem*. The use of the phrase *not covered* is ambiguous: is AG Rantos implying that the principle is not applicable in this case, or alternatively, that a violation could be justified? The wording 'not covered' implies that the principle would not be applicable at all. However, in the footnote, Rantos refers to the paragraphs of *bpost* concerning *justification*. This suggests that the *ne bis in idem* is applicable indeed, but that a violation can be justified. In my view, given the CJEU's interpretation in *bpost,* the argument that the principle would not be applicable is unconvincing after the abolishment of the 'legal interest criterion': if a competition authority and a DPA both impose sanctions on the same undertaking and for the same facts, the principle applies. As explained above, a violation can potentially be justified, provided that the criteria for justification are met.

3.5 CONCLUSION

This chapter provided the necessary background and context for the research. To this end, it defined institutions and institutional design, addressed the intricacies of the multi-level legal order of the EU and discussed important overarching principles. The principles of procedural and institutional autonomy, sincere cooperation and *ne bis in idem* are particularly relevant in this regard. The chapter serves as a stepping stone for further analysis in Parts II and III.

262. Opinion of AG Rantos 20 September 2022 in Case-252/21, *Meta Bundeskartellamt*, para. 21.

Part II
Intervention on Personal Data Markets

Part II studies the regulatory responses of enforcers of competition law, the DMA and the GDPR to personal data markets. In line with the methodology of this work, the approach of the analysis is *unidirectional* and positions competition law as the central element.[263] *Chapter 4* discusses the application of national and EU competition law to personal data markets. The objectives of this analysis are to assess the extent to which the field of competition law can address market failures in personal data markets and to identify which institutions play a role of importance in this regard.

This project is not limited to the boundaries of the competition law framework, but instead adopts a *cross-disciplinary* approach. Consequently, the interaction between competition law, the DMA and the GDPR are at the core of the research. The cross-disciplinary focus of this project is reflected in Chapters 5 and 6, which build on Chapter 4 and aim to map the interplay between competition law, the DMA and the GDPR. *Chapter 5* studies the relationship between competition law and the DMA, while *Chapter 6* focuses on the relationship between competition law and the GDPR.

After studying the individual frameworks of competition law, the DMA and the GDPR and in order to analyse the relationship between (i) competition law and the DMA and (ii) competition law and the GDPR in a structured manner, both intersections are analysed using a similar structure. The analysis takes a three-step approach.

First, the *common features and denominators* of the respective fields are identified in order to understand whether, and if so, to what extent, the fields overlap. To this end, the main similarities and differences between the

263. *See* section 1.3.1.

areas of the law are considered. In order to provide a systematic overview, the analysis considers various perspectives by focusing on: (i) objectives; (ii) substantive provisions; and (iii) institutional and enforcement frameworks.

Second, the interaction between the legal branches is further *analysed.* To this end, the GDPR and the DMA are positioned in the broader regulatory framework of the EU. Next, I assess the extent to which the legal frameworks: (i) can reinforce each other by relying on synergies between the legal branches; and (ii) identify whether and to what extent frictions and clashes between the legal branches may occur.

Third, the sub-conclusions of Chapters 5 and 6 provide preliminary conclusions on the interplay between competition law and, respectively, the DMA and the GDPR. The sub-conclusions reflect on the relationship between the instruments and establish the degree to which interaction between the legal branches is desirable. The last step of the analysis has a stronger normative component, especially in the field of data protection law.

Chapter 4
Competition Law

4.1 INTRODUCTION

As explained in Chapter 2, due to the characteristics of personal data markets, such markets tend to be concentrated, and large platforms can obtain a position of market power. The field of competition law can address this issue of market power by prohibiting abusive behaviour by dominant undertakings. The application of EU and national provisions on abusive unilateral conduct by dominant players constitutes the focus of this chapter. In this chapter, I analyse how competition law is or can be used to address alleged abuses of dominance in personal data markets. Section 4.2 focuses on EU competition law, section 4.3 zooms in on Dutch competition law, and section 4.4 examines the German framework. Section 4.5 provides a conclusion.

The different frameworks of EU and national competition law are discussed in the context of their application to personal data markets and according to a similar structure. *First,* I study the objectives of the respective frameworks. *Second*, the substantive rules of competition law are explored. *Third,* the institutional and procedural frameworks are examined.

Over the last few decades, the frameworks of EU and national competition law have converged. This means that the substantive frameworks overlap to a significant extent. Moreover, similarities can be identified in the procedural rules.[264] Given these similarities and in order to avoid repetition, the national competition law frameworks are not discussed

264. Gerbrandy 2009.

exhaustively. Rather, the Sections on national competition law emphasise the main differences between EU and national competition law. To this end, I aim to identify to what extent the Dutch and German frameworks: (i) deviate from EU competition law; and/or (ii) complement EU competition law.

4.2 EU COMPETITION LAW

The powerful position of large platforms in digital markets is high on the political agenda of the EU. This is, for example, reflected in the adoption of the EU's Digital Strategy, which aims to ensure that the digital transformation works for people and businesses.[265] EU competition law has an important role to play in the achievement of these objectives and the pillar 'a fair and competitive digital economy' constitutes one of the main focal points. Former Commissioner Vestager has shown a clear ambition to contribute to these goals. She is even described as 'Big Tech's Tormenter in Chief' and 'Europe's top tech cop'.[266] Ever since her appointment in 2010, she has gained a reputation for taking on high-profile cases against major tech companies.[267] The question is now whether Vestager's successor, Teresa Ribera, can live up to the legacy of her predecessor. During her confirmation hearing, Ribera appeared ambitious, highlighting the importance of 'vigorous enforcement' of both competition law and the DMA.[268] Although Ribera received criticism for allegedly delaying the imposition of DMA to avoid escalation, the Commission issued the first DMA fines against Meta and Apple under her leadership.[269] While the amounts of the fine were not record-breaking (yet?), this suggests that Ribera takes DMA enforcement seriously. Still, only time will tell whether the new Commissioner can truly fill Vestager's big shoes.[270]

This section assesses how EU competition law addresses the issue of market power in personal data markets. As explained in section 3.3, the enforcement of EU competition law takes place in the multi-level legal order of the EU. This means that national procedural and institutional frameworks are relevant for the enforcement of EU competition law. Accordingly,

265. European Commission, Press Release 15 December 2020, Europe fit for the Digital Age: Commission proposes new rules for digital platforms, IP/20/2347, 1.
266. Scott 2019; Heath and Reingold 2021.
267. Subiotto, Lepetska and Nobbs 2022, p. 52.
268. Questionnaire to the Commissioner-Designate Teresa Ribera, Executive Vice-President for the Clean, Just and Competitive Transition, available at: https://hearings.elections.europa.eu/documents/ribera/ribera_writtenquestionsandanswers_en.pdf accessed 29 August 2025, p. 4.
269. Micheletti and Parry 2025.
270. European Commission, Press Release 23 April 2025 'Commission finds Apple and Meta in breach of the Digital Markets Act', IP/25/1085.

sections 4.3 and 4.4. address the national context of Germany and The Netherlands.

4.2.1 Objectives of EU Competition Law

Historically, the objectives of competition law have been subject to debate. Competition law has a range of different goals, and there is no consensus on the exact scope and reach of these objectives. This section addresses the different (potential) objectives of EU competition law in turn.

4.2.1.1 Consumer Welfare

Nowadays, the notion of *consumer welfare* constitutes one of the key objectives of EU competition law.[271] Despite the importance of this goal, the standard of consumer welfare is not clearly defined in the competition law framework.[272] Yet, and notwithstanding the discussion on the exact meaning of the concept, in a competition law context consumer welfare is usually defined through a 'lens of economic efficiency calculations'.[273] Ultimately, the focus lies on the calculation of the losses and gains to consumers: if certain conduct increases prices, reduces quality or limits output and/or innovation, this conduct is deemed to be detrimental to consumer welfare.[274]

The notion of consumer welfare can be interpreted broadly or narrowly. A *narrow* interpretation focuses on increases in price and on limitations in output and innovation. Hence, this narrow interpretation emphasises economic interests and leaves limited room for non-economic objectives. A *broader* interpretation is more open to *non-economic* interests, such as privacy, social justice or sustainability.[275] This discussion is also relevant in light of the 'twin transition' towards a digital and green economy.[276] By

---

271. The CJEU refers to the consumer welfare standards on multiple occasions. *See,* for example, CJEU 9 October 2015, Case C-23/14 *Post Danmark II*, para. 49; CJEU 27 March 2012, Case C-209/10, *Post Danmark I*, para. 42; CJEU 21 December 2023 Case C-333/21, *Super League*, para. 204; AG Pitruzzella even refers to consumer welfare as *the main (and some say the only) objective of competition law. See*: Opinion of AG Pitruzzella 16 July 2020 in Case C-372/19, *SABAM*, para. 22.
272. Arguably, the consumer welfare standard is even defined differently by lawyers and economists. *See*: Cseres 2006, p. 123.
273. These efficiencies can take several forms and relate to allocative, productive and dynamic efficiencies. Claassen and Gerbrandy 2016, p. 2; Van de Gronden and Rusu 2021, p. 11.
274. Claassen and Gerbrandy coin this standard as *an inclusive welfare standard. See*: Claassen and Gerbrandy 2016, p. 2.
275. Gerbrandy 2019, p. 131.
276. Communication from the Commission to the European Parliament, the European Council, the European Economic and Social Committee and the Committee of the Regions of 2 March 2022, Towards a green, digital and resilient economy: our European Growth Model, COM(2022)83 final, p. 1; Majcher and Robertson 2024.

broadening the notion of consumer welfare, competition law could take into consideration a wider range of objectives. This approach is particularly relevant for objectives which – to a certain extent – can be quantified, for example, by asking about consumers' preferences or using a 'willingness-to-pay' test.[277] In the context of digital markets, the debate impacts the interplay between the GDPR and competition law, because data protection can constitute part of the quality of a service.[278] Against this background, data protection considerations can enter the realm of competition law via the standard of consumer welfare.[279] This dynamic is further addressed in Chapter 6.

4.2.1.2 Internal Market

Consumer welfare is not the only goal of EU competition law. EU competition law also aims to contribute to the integration of the *internal market* of the EU. Article 3(3) TEU highlights that the EU shall establish an internal market. According to the Protocol on the internal market, a system of undistorted competition is part of the integration of a market.[280] Moreover, Article 3(1) sub b TFEU sets out that establishing a competition law framework is 'necessary for the functioning of the internal market'. In the *TeliaSonera* case, the CJEU confirmed the relevance of this market integration objective for Article 102 TFEU by highlighting that this provision is 'one of the competition rules referred to in Article 3(1) sub b TFEU'.[281] Moreover, paragraph 3 of the Relevant Markets Notice mentions 'the resilience of the single market'.[282] Consequently, EU competition law, including Article 102 TFEU, pursues a market integration objective.[283]

277. Claassen and Gerbrandy 2016, p. 3.
278. Majcher 2023, p. 31.
279. This approach is supported by data protection advocates. *See,* for example: Graef 2016, p. 5; Svantesson 2018, p. 28; European Data Protection Supervisor March 2014, 'Privacy and competitive in the age of big data: The interplay between data protection, competition law and consumer protection in the Digital Economy' https://www.edps.europa.eu/sites/default/files/publication/14-03-26_competitition_law_big_data_en.pdf accessed 24 March 2025.
280. Van de Gronden and Rusu 2021, p. 10. The area of competition law is not the only field of EU law that aims to safeguard the establishment and integration of the internal market. The provisions on free movement (i.e., Articles 34-36 and 45-66 TFEU, as well as relevant secondary regulation) aim at facilitating an internal market as well. These legal instruments are targeted at Member States, and can be seen as a 'different side of the same coin' in relation to Articles 101 and 102 TFEU, which address the behaviour of undertakings. *See also*: Consolidated version of the Treaty on the European Union, Protocol No. 27 of 9 May 2005 on the internal market and competition, O.J. 115, p. 0309.
281. CJEU 17 February 2011 Case C-52/09 *TeliaSonera*, para. 21.
282. Commission Notice of 22 February 2024 on the definition of the relevant market for the purpose of Union competition law, C/2024/1645.
283. Whish and Bailey 2018, p. 52.

4.2.1.3 The Structure of the Market and Competition as such

The structure of the market and the protection of competition as such constitute the next objective of EU competition law.[284] The CJEU has referred to these objectives on multiple occasions. In *GlaxoSmithKline,* the CJEU, for example, stressed that competition law 'aims to protect not only the interests of competitors or of consumers, but also the structure of the market and, in doing so, competition as such'.[285] Furthermore, the ECN+ Directive highlights that effective enforcement of Article 102 TFEU is necessary to ensure fairer and *more open competitive* markets in the EU.[286]

In order to protect the competitive process, it may be necessary to – either directly or indirectly – protect competitors to ensure that rivals remain in the market to compete with a dominant undertaking.[287] This issue of the protection of competitors is controversial: in reality, it is difficult to determine whether short-term protection of competitors is necessary in order to safeguard the long-term protection of competition (and ultimately of consumer welfare).[288] In this light, the CJEU and Commission have stipulated that the use of competition law in order to protect competitors is subject to limitations. For various pricing practices, the Commission and CJEU have endorsed the 'as efficient competitor' test as a method for assessing whether a practice is capable of producing exclusionary effects.[289] The rationale behind the test is that it is unlawful to exclude equally efficient competitors and that less efficient competitors may be forced to leave the market because they are unable to compete on the merits.[290]

4.2.1.4 Non-economic Objectives and Fairness

The objectives of competition law, and particularly the role of *non-economic values,* have been subject to a heated (academic) debate. This topic is sensitive and centres around the question of whether competition law should merely promote economic efficiency or should also serve broader goals by

---

284. Whish and Bailey 2021, p. 21.
285. CJEU 6 October 2009 Case C-501/06P, *GlaxoSmithKline*, para. 6.
286. ECN+ Directive, preamble para. 1.
287. Dunne 2015, p. 29.
288. Jones, Sufrin and Dunne 2019, p. 56.
289. *See* section 4.2.2.3; Communication from the Commission – Guidance on the Commission's enforcement priorities in applying Article 82 of the EC Treaty to abusive exclusionary conduct by dominant undertakings, 2009/C 45/02, paras 23-24. In the Draft Guidelines on the Application of Article 102 TFEU, the Commission also refers to the 'as efficient competitor' test. *See, e.g.,* DRAFT Guidelines on the application of Article 102 of the Treaty on the Functioning of the European Union to abusive exclusionary conduct by dominant undertakings, [...](2024)xxx draft, paras 73, 124 and 134. *See also*: CJEU 9 October 2015 Case C-23/14 *Post Danmark II*, para. 57; CJEU 19 January 2023 Case C-680/20, *Unilever*, para. 57; GC 19 September 2024 Case T-334/19, *Google Adsense*, para. 664.
290. Whish and Bailey 2021, p. 374.

guaranteeing welfare and liberty for the powerless. This debate is fundamental in nature and, ultimately, boils down to the 'soul of antitrust'. [291] By triggering a broad range of concerns, including the protection of privacy, the reliability of media and the functioning of democracy, the rise of Big Tech has intensified the debate. This development has provided a new impetus for the discussion.[292] The relevance of the debate is further reinforced by discussions relating to the relevance of sustainability-related objectives for EU competition law.[293]

In legal literature, it has been suggested that certain non-economic goals should be endorsed as self-standing objectives of competition law. This would broaden the goals of EU competition law by adding new objectives.[294] Moving to a more polycentric model would allow to take into consideration the complexity of the economic reality (of the digital economy) by acknowledging that dominance and power in the economic sphere can more easily be leveraged to other spheres, such as academia, politics, media or culture.[295] In my view, a shift towards more polycentric or broader objectives would be desirable, especially in relation to Big Tech. However, at this point in time, extending the goals of competition law is still a very controversial topic, and there is limited experience with this approach.

Non-economic objectives can be relevant for competition law, even if they are not recognised as self-standing goals. As explained above, certain considerations enter the realm of competition law through the lens of consumer welfare. On top of this, the concept of *fairness* may offer another possibility to embrace and incorporate certain non-economic values. The Preamble to the TFEU recognises *fair* competition as an important value of EU law. Moreover, both Articles 101 and 102 TFEU contain explicit references to the notion of fairness. In order for an Article 101 TFEU violation to be successfully justified, consumers must receive a *fair* share of the benefits, and Article 102(a) TFEU prohibits *unfair* selling prices or trading conditions. The notion of fairness is also present in secondary legislation. The Preamble to the ECN+ Directive, for example, stresses that the effective enforcement of Articles 101 and 102 TFEU is necessary to ensure *fairer* and more open competitive markets in the Union.[296]

The notion of fairness is undeniably present in EU competition law, as shown by the examples above. Yet, the interpretation of the principle is not unequivocally clear. A first problem relates to the question of *to whom* an outcome should be fair. What may be fair for one party can have detrimental

291. Ezrachi and Stucke 2018, pp. 1-2.
292. Van Dijck, Nieborg and Poell 2019, p. 6.
293. Relevant Market Notice, para. 15; For further reading on competition law and sustainability, *see,* for example: Monti and Mulder 2017; Gerbrandy 2017; Malinauskaite 2022; Nowag 2024.
294. Cseres 2006, p. 170; Ezrachi 2018; Lianos 2013a.
295. Lianos 2018, p. 165; Gerbrandy and Phoa 2022.
296. Preamble ECN+ Directive, recital 1.

effects on other market players. In a market context, it is very rare that every party will consider itself a winner, and certain trade-offs are inevitable.[297] It might, for example, be regarded as fair to protect smaller firms against larger undertakings. However, if this approach results in higher prices for end-consumers, the measure can be considered unfair from the consumers' perspective.

The second and arguably the main issue relates to the lack of a proper definition. Despite the fact that fairness is not defined in an EU competition law context, the implications of the principle are closely connected to its interpretation. Article 101(3) TFEU, for instance, aligns fairness with the maximisation of the overall consumer surplus. In the interpretation of fairness in the context of Article 102a TFEU, the CJEU focuses on the relationship between the price, cost and revenue.[298] This interpretation corresponds to the narrow standard of consumer welfare and is rather uncontroversial.[299] However, a broader interpretation of the principle of fairness is necessary in order to embrace a wider range of societal concerns.[300] Vestager seemed to endorse this approach in some of her speeches, for example, by highlighting that competition law is about fairness and that start-ups 'deserve the same chance to compete as the bigger, more established players in the market'.[301] In my view, these statements and references in EU primary and secondary legislation show that fairness is indeed one of the objectives of competition law. Yet, and despite Vestager's ambitious statements, the broad interpretation of fairness in a competition law context is still highly controversial. Hence, the reach and scope of the principle need to be clarified by the CJEU in order to understand what the implications of the principle are.

4.2.1.5 The Goals of Competition Law: Final Remarks

In sum, competition law has multiple goals, and there is no consensus on the exact reach and scope of these objectives. The debate on the goals of EU competition law is not yet settled, and probably never will. Yet, the discussion on the (development) of the objectives is relevant for the intersection between competition law, the DMA and the GDPR. The concept of fairness, for instance, establishes a potential parallel between these different legal branches. The parallels, overlapping and diverging objectives of competition law, the DMA and the GDPR are further studied in Chapters 5 and 6.

---

297. Dunne 2021, p. 247.
298. Dunne 2020, pp. 246-247.
299. Kalimo and Majcher 2017, p. 6.
300. Graef, Clifford and Valcke 2018, p. 205.
301. Berkley Law Borderlines 2022.

4.2.2 Scope and Substantive Framework

This section addresses the scope and substantive framework of EU competition law and focuses on unilateral behaviour.[302] This means that the analysis focuses on Article 102 TFEU, according to which:

> 'Any abuse by one or more undertakings of a dominant position within the internal market or in a substantial part of it shall be prohibited as incompatible with the internal market in so far as it may affect trade between Member States'.
>
> Such abuse may, in particular, consist in:
>
> (a) directly or indirectly imposing unfair purchase or selling prices or other unfair trading conditions;
> (b) limiting production, markets or technical development to the prejudice of consumers;
> (c) applying dissimilar conditions to equivalent transactions with other trading parties, thereby placing them at a competitive disadvantage;
> (d) making the conclusion of contracts subject to acceptance by the other parties of supplementary obligations which, by their nature or according to commercial usage, have no connection with the subject of such contracts.

Article 102 TFEU prohibits: (i) abusive behaviour by (ii) dominant undertakings.[303] The next sections further elaborate on both conditions.

The application of Article 102 TFEU is limited to *dominant* undertakings.[304] The CJEU defined the concept of dominance in the case *United Brands* and has established that a dominant position entails a position of 'economic strength enjoyed by an undertaking which enables it to prevent effective competition being maintained on the relevant market by giving it the power to behave to an appreciable extent independently of its competitors, customers and ultimately of its consumers'.[305] A dominant undertaking is not subject to competitive constraints and can act insensitively to the actions and reactions of competitors, customers and consumers.[306]

302. *See* section 1.3.3.
303. Article 102 TFEU also refers to 'multiple undertakings' and therefore covers more than unilateral behaviour. However, since this work is focused on unilateral behaviour, only matters relating to abuse of dominance by a single firm will be addressed.
304. An undertaking encompasses 'every entity engaged in an economic activity'. The fact no monetary fee is paid, does not mean that an activity is not considered economic. In *Google Android,* the Commission, for example, stresses that 'even though users do not pay a monetary consideration for the use of general search services, they contribute to the monetisation of the service by providing data with each query'. *See*: European Commission 18 July 2018, Case AT40099, *Google Android*, para. 326; CJEU 29 April 1991; Case C-41/90, *Höfner and Elser*, para. 20.
305. CJEU 14 February 1978 Case 27/76, *United Brands*.
306. Communication from the Commission – Guidance on the Commission's enforcement priorities in applying Article 82 of the EC Treaty to abusive exclusionary conduct by

In some cases, for example, when an undertaking enjoys a statutory monopoly, dominance is easy to establish.[307] Yet, in most cases, the assessment of a dominant position is less straightforward. A position of dominance can be derived from 'a combination of several factors', even when such factors independently would not amount to a dominant position.[308] In this case, the assessment takes into consideration multiple factors, including market shares. The next Sections address the issues of the relevant market, market shares and dominance in turn. The analysis is focused on defining relevant markets in the context of personal data markets.

4.2.2.1 The Relevant Market

Market shares are used by the Commission and the CJEU as a first indication for assessing the market structure. In order to calculate market shares, it is necessary to define the *relevant market*. The concept of market definition is a tool to identify and define the boundaries of competition between undertakings and to assess the relative competitive strength of undertakings.[309] The relevant market comprises the relevant product and the relevant geographical market.

The relevant *product market* covers all products that consumers regard as interchangeable or substitutable based on the product's characteristics, prices and intended use, taking into consideration the conditions of competition and the structure of supply and demand on the market.[310] Traditionally, the SSNIP test – which entails a speculative experiment to evaluate the reaction of consumers to a small, lasting change in price – was the main tool for assessing interchangeability.[311] However, the SSNIP test is price-centred and therefore difficult to apply to multi-sided platforms and zero-price markets, in which undertakings compete on parameters *other* than price.[312] Under these circumstances, price is not a relevant parameter and the Commission focuses on *other* relevant factors.[313] Moreover, in the Relevant

dominant undertakings, 2009/C 45/02, paras 10 and 11; DRAFT Guidelines on the application of Article 102 of the Treaty on the Functioning of the European Union to abusive exclusionary conduct by dominant undertakings, [...](2024)xxx draft, para. 25.

307. Jones, Sufrin and Dunne 2019, p. 332.
308. CJEU 14 February 1978 Case 27/76 United Brands, para. 66.
309. The concept of market definition is a tool and not an end in itself. Its main purpose is 'to identify in a systemic way the effective and immediate competitive constraints faced by the undertaking(s) involved [...]'. Market definition is not a mandatory step in all EU competition law assessments. *See*: Relevant Markets Notice, paras 6 and 8.
310. Relevant Markets Notice, para. 12.
311. SSNIP stands for Small Significant Non-transitory Increase in Price. *See also*: CJEU 14 February 1978 Case 27/76 *United Brands*, paras 12-35.
312. Relevant Markets Notice, para. 30. *See also*: European Commission 18 July 2018, Case AT40099, *Google Android*, paras 266-267.
313. According to para. 98 of the Relevant Markets Notice, the Commission can focus on factors such as product functionalities, intended use, evidence of past or hypothetical

Markets Notice, the Commission endorses the SSNDQ test, which entails an assessment of the switching behaviour of customers of the zero-price product in response to a small but significant non-transitory decrease in quality.[314] The main problem with the SSDQ test is that quality is more difficult to quantify than price.[315] The Commission and GC have acknowledged the limitations of the SSNDQ test and stressed that this test should be considered a framework for *qualitative* assessment. Therefore, according to the GC, defining a 'precise quantitative standard of degradation of quality' cannot be a prerequisite for the application of the SSNDQ test.[316] In applying the SSNDQ test to personal data markets, the data protection framework cannot be overlooked. The GDPR, and in particular the provisions on data minimisation and purpose limitation, limit undertakings in their data collection possibilities. This impacts the degree to which the level of data protection can be decreased. These limitations should be taken into consideration in the application of the SSNDQ test.[317] This SSNDQ test will probably gain importance, particularly in the context of personal data markets. However, at this point, there is limited experience with the application of the SSDNQ test. The test is thus still in its infancy and will likely develop further in the future.[318]

The mismatch between the SSNIP test and zero-price markets is not the only challenging aspect for defining personal data markets. Other characteristics of such markets, in particular the presence of multi-sided markets and ecosystems, have challenged traditional tools for defining markets.[319] *First*, the *multi-sided* nature of platforms triggers the question of whether both sides of the platform amount to two (or more) relevant markets, or conversely, whether one and the same market should encompass both sides of the platform.[320] Neither the case law of the CJEU, nor the decision-making practice of the Commission provides an unequivocal answer to this question.[321]

In academic literature, various authors have proposed solving the matter by distinguishing between transaction and non-transaction (or matching)

---

substitution, barriers or costs of switching, such as interoperability with other products, data portability and licensing features.

314. SSNDQ stands for small but significant non-transitory decrease in quality; Relevant Markets Notice, para. 98.
315. Mândrescu 2018, p. 253.
316. GC 14 September 2022 Case T-604/18, *Google Android*, paras 177 and 180; European Commission 18 July 2018, Case AT40099 (*Google Android*), pp. 284-305.
317. Mândrescu 2018, pp. 250-253.
318. Beems and Rusu 2024, p. 409.
319. The previous Notice on the relevant market dated from 1997 and, henceforth, did not take the specificities of digital markets into consideration. *See* Chapter 2.
320. Filistrucchi et al. 2014, p. 293.
321. The GC touches upon this issue in *Google Shopping,* but does not provide a definitive answer to this question. *See*: GC 14 September 2022 Case T-604/18, *Google Android*, p. 273. *See also*: Beems and Rusu 2024, p. 406.

platforms.[322] Where the absence of a transaction between both sides of the platform characterises non-transaction platforms, transaction platforms facilitate interactions between the different sides of the platform.[323] For transaction platforms, both sides of the platform would be included in one and the same relevant product market.[324] Non-transaction platforms would cover multiple markets, because the interests of the different sides are too far removed from each other to include them within one relevant product market.[325] In the Notice on the Relevant Markets, the Commission addresses the topic of multi-sided markets explicitly in paragraph 4.4 on 'Market definition in the presence of multi-sided platforms'. The Commission leaves open the possibility to define either: (i) separate product markets for each side of the platform; or (ii) one relevant market encompassing all user groups.[326] Thus, the Commission endorses both the *single-* and *multi-market* approach.[327] The multi-market approach is particularly suitable if there are significant differences in the substitution possibilities across the different sides of the platform. In order to assess this, the Commission takes multiple factors into account, including whether the products for each user group differ, the degree of product differentiation, behavioural factors such as homing decisions and the nature of the platform (i.e., a transaction or non-transaction platform). Moreover, the Commission takes stock of the indirect network effects between user groups when defining the relevant market or in the competitive assessment.[328] The Commission does not opt for a hard distinction between transaction and non-transaction platforms, but relies on a more flexible approach. Given that the binary approach distinguishing transaction from non-transaction platforms has not yet been established in case law or decision-making, this is a reasonable approach. The Relevant Markets Notice is an instrument of soft law and should therefore consolidate existing practices, rather than introducing novel theories.[329]

Second, the presence of *ecosystems* has posed challenges for defining relevant markets in a competition law context.[330] The integrated and

322. Van Gorp and Batura 2015.
323. *See* section 2.2.
324. Transaction platforms allow users on both sides of the platform to enter into a transaction through the platform. eBay, for instance, facilitates a transaction between buyers and sellers.
325. On non-transaction platforms, the different sides of the platform do not engage in a transaction. For example, on a social media platform, there is no direct transaction between platform users and advertisers. *See* for a more elaborate analysis: Knapstad 2024, pp. 293-339.
326. Relevant Markets Notice, para. 95.
327. Mândrescu 2024a.
328. Relevant Markets Notice, para. 95.
329. Beems and Rusu 2024, p. 407; Eben 2024; For a more theoretical analysis of soft law instruments, *see*: Chalmers 2024, pp. 108-110.
330. *See* section 2.6.

multi-layered nature of an ecosystem makes defining the relevant market a complicated exercise and requires a tool that acknowledges the complexities of the system.[331] In the Notice, the Commission extends existing concepts and builds on experience with *after-markets*.[332] In an after-market, the consumption of the primary product leads to the consumption of a secondary or connected product.[333] The Commission stresses that the criteria for defining after-markets can be useful for analysing competitive dynamics in relation to digital ecosystems.[334] Discussing the after-market approach in detail is beyond the scope of the analysis.[335] What is relevant is that the Commission uses the flexibility of the competition law framework by relying on existing concepts and by tweaking them to capture the reality of personal data markets.

The process of defining the relevant market is not limited to the product market but also encompasses the *geographic market* which covers the area in which 'the conditions of competition are sufficiently homogeneous, and which can be distinguished from neighbouring areas because the conditions of competition are appreciably different in those areas'.[336] As explained in the Introduction, digital transactions are often cross-border in nature, because physical boundaries are less relevant in the digital world. Against this background, in relation to digital markets, the relevant geographic market can exceed national or EU boundaries. For instance, in the *Microsoft* case, the relevant geographic market was defined as worldwide.[337] Yet, also in personal data markets, the geographic market can also be more narrowly defined, e.g., when customers in different countries have diverging (language) preferences. In *Google Shopping,* the Commission, for example, defined multiple national markets for general search.[338]

331. Jacobides and Lianos 2021; Robertson 2021, pp. 4-5.
332. The Commission establishes that '[d]igital ecosystems can, in certain circumstances, be thought of as consisting of a primary core product and several secondary (digital) products whose consumption is connected to the core product, for instance by technological links or interoperability. When considering digital ecosystems, the Commission may thus apply similar principles to those applied to after-markets to define the relevant product market'. *See*: Relevant Markets Notice, para. 104.
333. In the General Electric/Alstom the Commission, for example, established one product market for the sale of gas turbines and subsequent servicing. *See*: European Commission 9 September 2015, Case M.7278, *Generic Electric/Alstom*, para. 7.2.3.3.
334. However, the Commission does acknowledge that the analogy is not always suitable. Relevant Markets Notice, para. 104.
335. For further reading, *see*: Eben and Robertson 2021; Robertson 2021; Lancieri and Morita Sokwski 2021; Jacobides and Lianos 2021; Beems and Rusu 2024.
336. Commission Notice of 9 December 1997 on the definition of relevant market for the purposes of Community competition law, C 372/8, paras 8 and 20.
337. GC 17 September 2017, T-201/04, *Microsoft*, para. 29.
338. European Commission 27 June 2017, Case AT3970, *Google Shopping*, para. 256.

4.2.2.2 Market Shares and Dominance

After the relevant market has been defined, market shares can be calculated. These market shares constitute a first indication for assessing the market structure and potentially for establishing dominance. A market share of over 50% is considered to provide 'evidence of the existence of a dominant position' and results in a rebuttable presumption of dominance.[339] Undertakings with a market share below 40% are not likely to be considered dominant.[340] Consequently, market shares between 40% and 50% amount to the 'crucial range'. In this range, other factors – which will be discussed below – are particularly relevant. In the context of zero-price markets, the calculation of market shares is not as straightforward as it is in 'traditional' markets. Against this background, the tools for calculating market shares have required updating, particularly because the value of sales cannot always be quantified. In the Relevant Markets Notice, the Commission updates the framework by taking into consideration certain specificities of digital markets. Market shares can, for instance, be determined on the basis of the volume of sales, which can be calculated by considering multiple metrics, including the number of active users, the number of visited websites or streams, time spent on the platform or audience numbers, the number of downloads and updates and the number of interactions.[341] This approach is also endorsed in the Draft Guidelines on the application of Article 102 TFEU. The Commission highlights that, despite the fact that market shares based on sales value are typically the most appropriate indicator, sales volumes and other indicators may better reflect the competitive strength of undertakings in some instances.[342]

Despite the fact that market shares are one important factor in assessing dominance, they are not considered in isolation. The Commission interprets market shares in light of relevant market conditions and market dynamics. If market shares remain stable over time, they can be a reliable indicator of

339. CJEU 13 February 1979, Case C-85/76, *Hoffmann-La Roche*, paras 39-41; CJEU 3 July 1991, Case C-62/86, *AKZO*, para. 60.

340. Draft Guidelines on the Application of Article 102, para. 26. Communication from the Commission – Guidance on the Commission's enforcement priorities in applying Article 82 of the EC Treaty to abusive exclusionary conduct by dominant undertakings, 2009/C 45/02, paras 14-15 (henceforth: Draft Guidelines on the Application of Article 102). This does not mean that undertakings with a market share below 40% can never be found to be dominant, since 'there may be specific cases below that threshold where competitors are not in the position to constrain effectively the conduct of a dominant undertaking'. In European Commission 14 July 1999, IV/D-2/34780 Virgin/British Airways the Commission exceptionally established dominance at a market share below 40%, namely at 39.7%.

341. Relevant Market Notice, para. 108; This approach consolidate previous cases, such as: European Commission 18 July 2018, Case AT40099, *Google Android*, paras 591-594; European Commission 3 October 2014 COMP/M7216, *Facebook/WhatsApp*, para. 99; CJEU 11 December 2013 Case T-79/12 *Cisco Systems*, para. 69.

342. Draft Guidelines on the Application of Article 102, para. 26.

dominance. However, in rapidly changing markets, those market shares may be less useful.[343] Furthermore, market shares are not the only indicator of dominance. The Commission also takes stock of other factors, such as barriers to expansion and entry and countervailing buyer power. In personal data markets, market power and access to data are inherently linked because data amounts to a competitive parameter. The degree to which an undertaking and its competitors have access to a certain volume and variety of data can be relevant when assessing dominance.[344] This dynamic is acknowledged by the Commission in the Draft Guidelines which explicitly stress that *data-driven* advantages may amount to entry barriers, such as access to unique data, economies of scale and scope relating to data, or data-driven network effects.[345] Furthermore, in the Draft Guidelines, the Commission also takes stock of other characteristics of digital markets. As explained in section 2.3, digital markets are often characterised by strong network effects. The Commission highlights that such network effects can create entry barriers.[346]

The *degree of dominance* is another relevant issue concerning the dominance of large platforms. Given the vast power of certain Big Tech platforms, the question arises whether the concept of 'regular' dominance accurately reflects their position of strength. Article 102 TFEU allows for a certain range or degree of dominance: in *IMS Health*, the Commission referred to a 'quasi-monopoly situation'; in *Microsoft,* the Commission highlighted the 'overwhelmingly dominant position' of Microsoft; and in *Google Shopping,* Google's position was considered to be 'superdominant'.[347] Furthermore, the CJEU highlights that the degree of dominance is relevant for the assessment of the effects of an abuse, rather than for the question of whether an abuse exists.[348]

In conclusion, the characteristics of digital markets play an important role in defining relevant markets and in establishing dominance. In the past, the framework was challenged by these particular features, and it appeared

343. Draft Guidelines on the Application of Article 102, para. 28; *See* section 2.8.
344. Robertson 2021, p. 11; Drexl 2017, pp. 280-281.
345. Draft Guidelines on the application of Article 102 TFEU, para. 30. *See also*: GC 10 November 2021 Case T-612/17, *Google Shopping*, para. 287; GC 14 September 2022 Case T-604/18, *Google Android*, para. 115.
346. Draft Guidelines on the application of Article 102 TFEU, para. 31.
347. GC 10 November 2021 Case T-612/17, *Google Shopping*, para. 182; European Commission 3 July 2001 Case COMP D3/38044, *IMS Health*, para. 58; European Commission 24 March 2004 Case COMP/C-3/37792, *Microsoft*, para. 435; Whish and Bailey 2021, p. 193.
348. In *TeliaSonera,* the CJEU establishes that the degree of dominance in the market is not relevant regarding the assessment of dominance, but that the degree of market strength may, nonetheless, be '[...] significant in relation to the effects of the conduct of the undertaking concerned rather than in relation to the question of whether the abuse exists'. CJEU 17 February 2011 Case C-52/09 TeliaSonera, paras 80-81.

difficult to apply existing tools to the new economic reality.[349] However, case law and soft law measures illustrate competition law's flexibility. Although certain challenges remain, the tools of competition law have evolved with the rise of personal data markets. Important concepts and metrics have been updated. These inevitable changes ensure that the competition law framework remains relevant in the context of the digital economy.

4.2.2.3 Abuse

Dominant undertakings are under a special responsibility not to abuse their dominance. Obtaining a dominant position is not prohibited per se, but dominance may not be abused. Abuses can be *exclusionary* or *exploitative* in nature. Exploitative abuses amount to an exploitation of market power by directly harming consumers, e.g., through excessive prices.[350] Exclusionary abuses aim to exclude (remaining) competitors in order to further cement a position of dominance. In the *Hoffmann-La Roche* case, the CJEU stated that undertakings with a dominant position should refrain from 'methods different from those which condition normal competition' and that such undertakings cannot reinforce their position by 'using methods other than those within the scope of competition on the merits'.[351] If a dominant undertaking forces a less efficient competitor to leave the market as a result of a process of competition on the merits, this is not necessarily abusive, but rather a result of market dynamics.[352] Thus, dominant undertakings can compete on the basis of price, choice, quality and innovation.[353] Even if the constitutive criteria of Article 102 TFEU are fulfilled, dominant undertakings can escape the prohibition of Article 102 TFEU if the conduct is *objectively justified*. Abusive behaviour can be justified if it is objectively necessary or counterbalances or outweighs the negative effects of the conduct on competition. In other words, undertakings can invoke an *objective necessity defence* or an *efficiency defence*.[354]

The concept of *exclusionary* abuse encompasses multiple types of abuse. Historically, exclusionary abuses took centre stage in the enforcement

349. *See,* for example: Lancieri and Morita Sokwski 2021.
350. Whish and Bailey 2024, p. 218; Akman 2024, para. 408.
351. CJEU 13 February 1979 Case C-85/76, *Hoffmann-La Roche*, para. 91; CJEU 14 October 2010 Case C-280/08P, *Deutsche Telekom*, para. 174.
352. CJEU 9 October 2015 Case C-23/14, *Post Danmark II*, para. 21.
353. Communication from the Commission – Guidance on the Commission's enforcement priorities in applying Article 82 of the EC Treaty to abusive exclusionary conduct by dominant undertakings, 2009/C 45/02, para. 6; DRAFT Guidelines on the application of Article 102 of the Treaty on the Functioning of the European Union to abusive exclusionary conduct by dominant undertakings, [...](2024)xxx draft, para. 51.
354. Draft Guidelines, para. 67 and case law cited.

of competition law.[355] The interpretation of the concept of competition on the merits has been subject to debate over the past few decades.[356] While EU competition law initially was criticised for adopting an overly formalistic approach, with excessive emphasis on the protection of competitors, the Commission gradually shifted to a more economic and effects-based approach. In such an effects-based approach, the actual or potential *effects* of the conduct play a determinative role in the analysis.[357] In its case law, the CJEU allows for an effect-based approach, without always requiring the application of an 'as efficient competitor' test.[358] At this point, it is expected that the CJEU will mix a traditional and more economic approach. Yet, it remains uncertain 'how far the tide will go'.[359]

In contrast to the CJEU, the Commission appears to shy away from the more economic approach.[360] The Draft Guidelines on the Application of Article 102 illustrate this dynamic, for example, by introducing the category of 'naked restrictions'.[361] Admittedly, the *Draft* Guidelines are not yet definitive and may still be subject to change. Nevertheless, the document provides valuable insights into the Commission's vision. Given that the Guidelines are not yet final, this section also refers to the current *enforcement* priorities.[362]

The Commission aims to adopt new Guidelines in order to consolidate the case law of the EU Courts and to provide legal certainty and transparency of the principles underpinning its enforcement actions.[363] In the Draft Guidelines, the Commission establishes a two-prong test to determine

355. This is reflected in the Communication from the Commission – Guidance on the Commission's enforcement priorities in applying Article 82 of the EC Treaty to abusive exclusionary conduct by dominant undertakings, 2009/C 45/02.
356. Geradin 2002.
357. Witt 2019; Ibáñez Colomo 2023.
358. In *Post-Danmark* the CJEU stressed that there is no obligation to apply the AEC test to assess whether a rebate scheme is abusive. In the *Unilever* case, the CJEU establishes that the AEC test is 'only one of a number of methods for assessing whether a practice is capable of producing exclusionary effects; moreover, that method takes into consideration only price competition'. The GC repeats these considerations in the *Google AdSense* case. *See*: CJEU 9 October 2015 Case C-23/14 *Post Danmark II*, para. 57; CJEU 19 January 2023 Case C-680/20, *Unilever*, para. 57; GC 19 September 2024 Case T-334/19, *Google Adsense*, para. 664; CJEU 6 September 2017 Case C-413/14P, *Intel*.
359. Akman 2024.
360. Akman, Fumagalli and Motta 2024, pp. 12-13.
361. Draft Guidelines on the Application of Article 102 TFEU.
362. Communication from the Commission – Guidance on the Commission's enforcement priorities in applying Article 82 of the EC Treaty to abusive exclusionary conduct by dominant undertakings, 2009/C 45/02, p. 22.
363. European Commission, Call for Evidence for An Initiative – Guidelines on Exclusionary Abuse by Dominant Undertakings, Ref. Ares (2023)2189183, 27 March 2023.

whether conduct is abusive.[364] Conduct can amount to exclusionary abuse if: (i) it departs from competition on the merits; and (ii) it is capable of producing exclusionary effects. Next, the Draft Guidelines identify three categories of conduct, i.e.: (a) practices for which the EU Courts have not specified a test; (b) conduct for which the EU Courts have developed a specific framework; and (c) 'naked' restrictions, i.e., certain types of conduct that 'have no other interest […] than that of restricting competition'. If conduct falls within the third category, or within the second category and meets the conditions of the 'specific legal test', the conduct is presumed to depart from competition on the merits.[365] For conduct falling within the first category, the specific circumstances of the case must be taken into account.[366] Interestingly, the factor of 'whether dominant undertakings violate rules of other areas of the law (for instance, data protection law) and thereby affect a relevant parameter of competition, such as price, choice, quality or innovation' is listed explicitly.[367] By recognising compliance with the GDPR as relevant parameter of competition, the Commission explicitly endorses the link between competition law and the GDPR as established in the *Meta Bundeskartellamt* case. This intersection is further analysed in Chapter 6.

In assessing the second limb of the test, i.e., the exclusionary effects, the Commission lists several presumptions, depending on the category of conduct. For the first category, the burden of proof largely rests on the Commission, which must demonstrate that the practice is 'at least capable of having exclusionary effects'.[368] For the second category, it is presumed that the conduct has an exclusionary effect, though the dominant undertaking can rebut this presumption.[369] Practices falling within the third category are 'by their nature capable of restricting competition'.[370] In such cases, rebuttal of the presumption will be exceptional.[371]

The categorisation of certain practices and linked presumptions is among the main novelties of the Draft Guidelines.[372] Presumptions can be helpful in speeding up proceedings. Given the fact that antitrust proceedings tend to be very long, this is a noble objective. Yet, the current use of presumptions has not been received unequivocally positively: Akman, Fugmalli and Motta highlight, for example, that some of the presumptions are not grounded in economics and that not all presumptions can be linked

364. This Section provides a general overview of this two-prong test. For further reading and analysis, *see*: Akman, Fumagalli and Motta 2024.
365. Draft Guidelines on the Application of Article 102, paras 53 and 54.
366. For an overview of the circumstances, *see*: Draft Guidelines on the Application of Article 102, para. 55.
367. Draft Guidelines on the Application of Article 102, para. 55(c).
368. Draft Guidelines on the Application of Article 102, paras 60(a) and 61.
369. Draft Guidelines on the Application of Article 102, para. 60(b).
370. Draft Guidelines on the Application of Article 102, para. 60(c).
371. Draft Guidelines on the Application of Article 102, para. 60(c).
372. Akman, Fumagalli and Motta 2024, p. 12.

to existing case law. Moreover, they criticise the fact that it remains unclear whether the presumptions will be genuinely rebuttable in practice.[373] In my view, the use of presumptions can be a useful methodology to expedite competition law procedures, provided that the presumptions are linked to existing case law and that the option of rebuttal is genuinely feasible. It is important to firmly embed these guarantees in the final version of the new Guidelines on the Application of Article 102 TFEU.

4.2.2.4 Exclusionary Abuse of Dominance on Personal Data Markets

Over the past few years, the enforcement of competition law in personal data markets has undoubtedly been a hot topic. The Commission has imposed multiple sky-rocketing and record-breaking fines on Big Tech platforms.[374] This Section zooms in on the application of Article 102 TFEU to personal data markets. Since competition law in the national context will be discussed in the subsequent section, this section focuses on the decision-making practice of the Commission. This chapter does not provide an overarching overview of the different types of abuse and the relevant legal tests.[375] Rather, I aim to illustrate how Article 102 TFEU is used, and could be used, to address anticompetitive behaviour by dominant firms on personal data markets. To this end, I will discuss some important competition law cases addressing such behaviour. Since anti-competitive practices on personal data markets cover a broad range of conduct, the section touches upon multiple types of abuse.

In *Google Android,* the Commission imposed a record-breaking fine of EUR 4.3 billion on Google for anti-competitive conduct.[376] Google, *inter alia,* required manufacturers to pre-install the Google Search and browser apps in order to be able to license Google's app store (the Play Store). According to the Commission, this conduct amounted to illegal *tying* because pre-installation created a *status quo* bias, meaning that users were likely to stick with the pre-installed apps.[377] This tying practice constitutes an abuse of dominance.[378] The Commission's approach, particularly its scrutiny of

373. Akman, Fumagalli and Motta 2024, p. 12.
374. *See, e.g.,* European Commission 18 July 2018, Case AT40099, *Google Android*; European Commission 27 June 2017, Case AT3970, *Google Shopping*.
375. For such overview and analysis, *see,* for example: Bostoen 2023a; Akman 2024.
376. European Commission 18 July 2018, Case AT40099, *Google Android*, para. 1480; The GC adjusted the fine but considered a, still record-breaking fine, of EUR 4.1 billion appropriate. GC 14 September 2022 Case T-604/18, *Google Android*, para. 1101.
377. European Commission 18 July 2018, Case AT40099, *Google Android*, pp. 778 and 781.
378. Tying practices are assessed by the application of a four-tier test. In order to prove anti-competitive tying, the following elements need to be established: (i) a dominant position in the tying market; (ii) the tying and tied product are separate products; (iii) customers are coerced to buy the products together; and (iv) the tying leads to anti-competitive foreclosure. In its current Guidance, the Commission highlights two

pre-installation practices, has been subject to criticism. Default settings do not prevent users from installing another competing app, and competition would, therefore, merely be 'one click away'.[379] Yet, behavioural evidence shows that default settings indeed significantly impact consumer choice, because consumers are highly unlikely to use any other service than the pre-installed application.[380] The *Google Android* case was (largely) upheld by the GC, but an appeal is still pending before the CJEU.[381] The fact that pre-installation can amount to illegal tying is highly relevant for personal data markets, because the use of default and pre-installations is common practice in such markets.[382] Consequently, in *Google Android,* the Commission (so far) successfully tweaked a legal test in order to apply it to the economic reality of personal data markets, but it remains to be seen how the CJEU will evaluate this approach.[383] The *Google Android* case is not the only relevant case on tying practices in personal data markets. In *Facebook Marketplace*, the Commission fined Meta – Facebook's parent company – for (*inter alia*) tying Facebook Marketplace to the personal social network of Facebook.[384] At this point, the full decision is not yet available, but Meta has already announced its intention to appeal the decision. This litigation will potentially provide further insight into tying on personal data markets.[385] Furthermore, the Commission has sent a statement of objections to Microsoft for tying *Microsoft Teams* with Microsoft's productivity apps.[386]

In several cases, the Commission has established *exclusivity*-related abuses in personal data markets. Exclusivity clauses require customers to purchase (to a significant extent) exclusively from the dominant undertaking.[387] Article 102 TFEU not only prohibits abusive contractual exclusivity

---

elements of the four-tier test, i.e.: (i) the tying and tied product are distinct products; and (ii) the tying is likely to lead to anti-competitive foreclosure. Section 4.2.2 of the Draft Guidelines on the Application of Article 102 lists tying as 'conduct subject to a specific legal test'. *See also*: CJEU 9 October 2015 Case C-23/14 *Post Danmark II*, para. 44; Communication from the Commission – Guidance on the Commission's enforcement priorities in applying Article 82 of the EC Treaty to abusive exclusionary conduct by dominant undertakings, 2009/C 45/02, paras 47-74.

379. Gerbrandy and Phoa 2022, p. 177.
380. European Commission 18 July 2018, Case AT40099, *Google Android*, p. 781.
381. GC 14 September 2022 Case T-604/18, *Google Android*; Case C-738/22P, *Google Android* (Case in Progress).
382. Bergqvist 2020, p. 22.
383. Musielak 2021, p. 137.
384. European Commission 11 November 2024, 'Commission fines Meta €797.72 million over abusive practices benefitting Facebook Marketplace', IP/24/5801.
385. Meta 2024.
386. European Commission 25 June 2024, Commission sends Statement of Objections to Microsoft over possibly abusive tying practices regarding Teams, IP/24/3446.
387. The legal test for rebates is complicated and subject to debate and litigations. The *Intel* saga is particularly relevant in this regard. Where the GC initially established that exclusivity rebates are presumed to be unlawful, the CJEU ruled that the Commission is obliged to conduct an economic analysis if an undertaking submits evidence that its

but also covers de facto exclusivity, as well as certain discounts and rebates.[388] In *Google AdSense,* the Commission fined Google EUR 1.49 billion for abusing its dominant position by engaging in exclusivity contracts with several major third-party publisher websites.[389] These publisher websites, including newspapers, blogs and travel sites, offer advertisement space and often rely on an advertisement broker to interact with advertisers. Google's Adsense service is likely 'the biggest of those brokers'.[390] By engaging in exclusivity purchasing agreements and in 'relaxed exclusivity' clauses,[391] Google abused its dominant position.[392] The *Google AdSense* case has multiple interesting dimensions but the legal standard for addressing exclusivity is particularly important. The standard for assessing rebates and exclusivities is subject to an intense debate, and the *Intel* saga reflects the complexity of the matter.[393] Discussing this line of case law in further detail goes beyond the scope of this work.[394] However, what is relevant is that the *Google AdSense* case reveals that the degree to which the Commission has to show the anti-competitive effects of exclusivities and rebates is still a topic of debate. In *Google Adsense*, the Commission argued that: (i) it was not required to show that the conduct was capable of restricting competition; and that (ii) although it was not required to do so, it did show the anti-competitive effects of Google's allegedly abusive conduct.[395] Yet on appeal, the GC

conduct was not capable of restricting competition and producing foreclosure effects. The CJEU thus seems to endorse an effects-based approach for rebates in general. The CJEU referred the case back to the GC, and it became apparent that the Commission failed to assess the rebates' capability to foreclose competition. *See*: GC 12 June 2014, Case T-286/09, *Intel v. Commission*, pp. 74-78; CJEU 6 September 2017 Case C-413/14P, *Intel*, p. 138; *See,* for further reading: Whish and Bailey 2021, p. 773.

388. CJEU 28 September 2006 Case C-552/03P, *Unilever*; Communication from the Commission – Guidance on the Commission's enforcement priorities in applying Article 82 of the EC Treaty to abusive exclusionary conduct by dominant undertakings, 2009/C 45/02, paras 33-34; Whish and Bailey 2021, p. 720; Petit 2015.
389. European Commission 20 March 2019, Case AT40411, *Google AdSense.*
390. Vestager 2019b.
391. The 'relaxed exclusivity' entailed, among others, a Premium Placement and a Minimum Google Add Clause. On top of this, partners could not display other adds above or next to Google's adds, and Google required a minimum of AdSense adds from their partners. *See*: European Commission 20 March 2019, Case AT40411, *Google AdSense*, para. 355.
392. Monti 2022, p. 18.
393. CJEU 6 September 2017 Case C-413/14 P, *Intel* GC 12 June 2014, Case T-286/09, *Intel v. Commission* GC 26 January 2022, Case T-286/09, *RENV, Intel Corporation v. Commission.*
394. *See* for a more elaborate analysis: Whish 2015; Petit 2015; Geradin 2015; Monti 2021b.
395. The legal standard and degree of economic analysis is interesting. Google claims – with reference to the *Intel* saga – that the Commission has to show that its conduct was capable of restricting competition. However, the Commission argues that: (i) the Intel-precedent should be interpreted restrictively and only applies to rebate schemes; and (ii) that – although it was not required to do so – it did show the anti-competitive effects of Google's alleged abusive behaviour. The European Commission seems to play safely. It will be interesting to see which approach will be followed by the GC (and, in

annulled the *Google Adsense* decision and found that the Commission had erred in determining the duration of contract clauses, as well as in supporting the conclusion that the clauses had foreclosure effects.[396] It will be interesting to see whether the case will be appealed and how the CJEU will deal with the matter.[397] Further clarity on this matter will be highly relevant for digital markets. Exclusivities and rebate schemes negatively affect the possibility of multi-homing, i.e., relying on multiple platforms at the same time.[398] Discouraging multi-homing, for example, by providing monetary benefits or by offering a better ranking in the case of the exclusive use of a particular service, enables large platforms to make it less attractive to use multiple platforms simultaneously. This incentive to single-home further cements the position of the dominant platform.[399] By prohibiting exclusivity clauses and rebates, Article 102 TFEU may cover such behaviour. Consequently, it is important for the CJEU to clarify these types of conduct.

The Commission's cases on *self-preferencing* reflect the open-ended nature and flexibility of Article 102 TFEU. The Commission has addressed self-preferencing behaviour in personal data markets in multiple instances, including cases and investigations such as *Google Shopping, Google Adtech* and *Amazon BuyBox.*[400] In the *Google Shopping* case, the Commission fined Google for displaying its own comparison shopping services more favourably than its competitors' comparison shopping services.[401] This practice diverts traffic from Google's general search result pages to competing comparison shopping services, thereby leveraging its position in the market for general search to the market for comparison shopping.[402] The Commission's approach in the *Google Shopping* case triggered intense (academic)

---

case of a further appeal, the ECJ). If the courts side with the former approach, the Commission would not have to conduct an effect-based approach in future cases on exclusivity. This would be an interesting shift, and is highly relevant for future case law and decision-making. *See:* European Commission 20 March 2019, Case AT40411, *Google AdSense*, paras 344-345; Monti 2022, p. 18.

396. GC 19 September 2024 Case T-334/19, *Google Adsense*, para. 717.
397. In the Draft Guidelines the Commission makes a distinction between exclusive supply or purchasing agreements, rebates conditional upon exclusivity, a threat of withdrawing discounts benefiting the distributor to agree with the distributer that they will swap a competing product with the dominant undertaking's product, conditional rebates that are not subject to exclusive purchase or supply requirements and multi-product rebates. The different exclusivities and rebates fall within different categories of conduct. *See:* Draft Guidelines on the Application of Article 102, para. 60, sections 4.3.1 and 4.3.2.
398. Lancieri and Morita Sokwski 2021, p. 150.
399. Crémer, De Montjoye and Schweitzer 2019, para. 57.
400. European Commission 12 December 2022 Commitment Decision in Cases AT40462 and AT40704, *Amazon Marketplace* and *Amazon Buybox*; European Commission Initiation of Proceedings of 14 June 2023, Case AT40670, *Google Adtech*; European Commission 27 June 2017, Case AT3970, *Google Shopping*. For an analysis of the *Amazon* case, *see:* Bougette, Budzinski and Marty 2022.
401. European Commission 27 June 2017, Case AT3970, *Google Shopping*.
402. European Commission 27 June 2017, Case AT3970, *Google Shopping*, para. 7.2.

debate, in which the qualification of the abuse became one of the most salient topics. This issue is not merely theoretical in nature, but has significant consequences for the applicable legal test and the corresponding burden of proof.[403]

In *Google Shopping,* the Commission does not opt for qualifying this behaviour as a previously existing form of abuse (e.g., refusal to supply or margin squeeze), but construes a concept of *leveraging*.[404] The GC upheld the Commission's decision but took a slightly different approach by focusing on the 'favouring' and the 'abnormality'.[405] Yet, the GC did not refer to the *MEO* case on discriminatory behaviour. This is remarkable because *MEO* also seems applicable to discriminatory practices by dominant firms.[406] By treating self-preferencing as a self-standing type of abuse, the standard of infringement is arguably lower. The *MEO* case establishes a rather high legal standard, including an as-efficient-as competitor test.[407] In its long-awaited judgment, the CJEU confirmed that the as-efficient-competitor test is just one way to establish abuse. Moreover, the CJEU clarified that it is not necessary to apply the *Bronner* criteria in every case concerning access.[408] In the Draft Guidelines, the Commission lists self-preferencing behaviour as a self-standing type of abuse with no specific legal test, but for which the Union Courts have provided guidance as to how to apply the general legal principles to determine if conduct is liable to be abusive.[409] Currently, the fact that self-preferencing qualifies as a self-standing form of abuse is thus well established. Yet, the development of the applicable legal test requires more case law and further clarification by the CJEU.

Apart from the abovementioned case, the Commission has accepted commitments in multiple proceedings.[410] In *Amazon Buy Box* and *Amazon Marketplace,* the Commission, for example, closed the case by accepting binding commitments.[411] Despite the fact that commitments are rather efficient and can speed up proceedings, these cases result in more questions than answers. It would be interesting to see how the EU Courts will scrutinise Amazon's use of non-publicly available third-party seller's data. The case

403. Bostoen 2022a, p. 75.
404. The Commission highlights that 'conduct consisting in the use of a dominant position on one market to extent that dominant position to one or more adjacent markets […] constitutes a well-established, independent, form of abuse […]', European Commission 27 June 2017, Case AT3970, *Google Shopping*; According to some authors, leveraging is a *category* of different types of abuses, rather a type in itself. *See:* Deutscher 2021, p. 1355.
405. GC 10 November 2021 Case T-612/17, *Google Shopping*, para. 179.
406. Deutscher 2021, p. 1355; CJEU 19 April 2018 Case C-525/16, *MEO*.
407. Lindeboom 2022, p. 69.
408. CJEU 10 September 2024 Case C-48/22P, *Google Shopping*, pp. 118 and 265.
409. Draft Guidelines on the Application of Article 102, para. 137.
410. *See* section 4.2.3.2.
411. European Commission 12 December 2022 Commitment Decision in Cases AT40462 and AT40704, *Amazon Marketplace* and *Amazon Buybox.*

does not neatly fit into one of the established categories of abuse. Both the legal tests for margin squeezes and self-preferencing could provide useful guidance but there are many unclarities as to the applicable legal standards.[412]

The application of Article 102 TFEU to MFN clauses is currently subject to similar uncertainties. In the *Amazon E-Books* case, the Commission addressed Amazon's parity, or MFN clauses.[413] An MFN clause is a clause in which a party agrees to treat the goods or services of a certain party as favourable as, or more favourably than, those of other parties.[414] Amazon required its e-book suppliers to notify and offer Amazon 'the same or equivalent terms for the distribution of e-books' as any other e-book retailer.[415] According to the Commission, the clauses reduce the suppliers' incentive to support and invest in alternatives to Amazon's e-book service. Therefore, the clause reduces the capability of Amazon's competitors to develop and differentiate their products. This deters the entry and expansion possibilities of (potential) competitors.[416] In this case, the Commission also adopted a commitment decision. The EU Courts have, therefore, not yet ruled on this issue.

The above-mentioned examples illustrate how the Commission and EU Courts use Article 102 TFEU to assess anti-competitive conduct by large platforms active on personal data markets. Apart from these concrete, real-life examples of the application of Article 102 TFEU in this context, various suggestions to extend the application of Article 102 TFEU to address anti-competitive behaviour by dominant platforms have been made in legal literature. Some authors, for example, propose that the concept of *margin squeeze* could encompass self-preferencing behaviour by dominant firms.[417] Furthermore, the conduct of *price discrimination* – which is listed in Article 102(2)(c) TFEU – could be relevant for personal data markets.[418]

Price discrimination is not inherently bad from an economic perspective, but can: (i) be detrimental for the competitive process; and/or (ii) exploit

412. Reverdin 2021.
413. MFN means Most Favoured Nation. MFNs clauses are also be subject to scrutiny under Article 101 TFEU. *See:* Bostoen 2017.
414. Whish and Bailey 2021, p. 682.
415. European Commission 4 May 2017 Commitment Decision in AT40153, *Amazon E-Books*, para. 74.
416. European Commission 4 May 2017 Commitment Decision in AT40153, *Amazon E-Books*, para. 76.
417. Bostoen 2018, p. 373; Reverdin 2021. A margin squeeze occurs when a vertically integrated undertaking with a dominant position on the upstream market, leaves insufficient margins between the price of the up- and downstream products. This forecloses competitors on the downstream market. *See:* CJEU 17 February 2011 Case C-52/09 *TeliaSonera*; CJEU 14 October 2010 Case C-280/08P, *Deutsche Telekom*; CJEU 25 February 2021 Case C-857/19, *Slovak Telekom*.
418. CJEU 9 October 2015 Case C-23/14, *Post Danmark II*; CJEU 19 April 2018 Case C-525/16, *MEO*.

consumers. In other words, price discrimination can be both exploitative and exclusionary in nature.[419] Price discrimination existed long before the rise of digital markets. Yet, the rise of Big Data and modern technology makes a far-reaching degree of price discrimination more realistic.[420] The collection of vast amounts of data allow platforms to provide personalised and targeted advertisements or even individualised prices.[421] Therefore, the application of the doctrine of price-discrimination could be a future avenue for addressing anti-competitive behaviour on personal data markets.

Furthermore, the doctrines of *essential facilities* and *refusal to supply* have been put forward as tools to facilitate access to data. Despite the fact that the freedom of contract is the point of departure in competition law, refusal to supply a good or service can amount to an abuse of a dominant position – albeit in very specific circumstances.[422] The doctrine of essential facilities may be relevant for personal data markets, particularly insofar as dominant platforms control crucial technologies or essential data sets.[423] The magnitude of data available to Big Tech platforms, such as Google, could make it impossible for new entrants without access to similar data sets to enter the market.[424] If the data amounted to an essential facility, Google's refusal to provide access to such data sets could be considered an abusive refusal to supply. At this point, this analogy is merely made in academic writings. The Commission has not gone down this avenue. The high threshold for refusal to supply, and in particular the indispensability criterion, will likely impose significant obstacles. To meet the indispensability requirement, it is necessary that: (i) the facility cannot be replicated; and (ii) that there are no alternative distribution systems available. The impossibility of

419. Graef 2018, p. 543.
420. Steppe 2017, p. 770.
421. Townley, Morrison and Yeung 2017, p. 685; Poort and Zuiderveen Borgesius 2019, p. 3; Townley, Morrison and Yeung 2017, p. 687.
422. The legal test on refusal to supply flows from the *Bronner* judgment. In line with these *Bronner* criteria, refusal to supply can be considered abusive if: (i) the input at hand is indispensable; (ii) the refusal to supply eliminates competition; and (iii) is not objectively justified. In the cases, *IMS Health* and *Magill,* the CJEU establishes a fourth criterion, i.e., the emergence of a new product for which there is customer demand. In *Microsoft,* the CJEU broadened this category by including the further development of an existing product. *See:* CJEU 26 November 1998 Case C-7/97, *Oscar Bronner*, para. 41; CJEU 6 April 1995 Joined Cases C-241/91P and C-242/91P, *Magill*; CJEU 29 April 2004 Case C-418/01, *IMS Health*, para. 38; GC 17 September 2017, T-201/04, *Microsoft*. In the Guidance on Enforcement Priorities, the Commission uses similar criteria, but refers to 'objectively necessary' instead of 'indispensable'. In the Draft Guidelines on the Application of Article 102, the Commission invokes the indispensability criterion in para. 99. The CJEU's judgment in CJEU 25 February 2025 Case C-233/23, *Android Auto* is also highly relevant in this regard. For an analysis of this case, *see:* Colangelo 2025a.
423. Vanberg and Ünver 2017, p. 8.
424. Kuschewsky and Geradin 2014, p. 16.

replication can have various reasons, for example, physical, legal or economic impossibilities.[425]

Considering access to data sets, it may be difficult to argue that different data sets cannot serve as replication.[426] Moreover, dominant platforms could argue that competitors could create their own databases, for example, by acquiring the relevant data.[427] These issues are probably difficult to overcome, and this may explain why the Commission – so far – has not invoked the essential facilities doctrine to force access to data. Yet, in *Google Shopping,* the GC stressed that Google has 'characteristics akin to an essential facility'.[428] Therefore, it cannot be ruled out that the essential facilities doctrine may be relied on in the future. If this approach were to be taken, the GDPR cannot be overlooked. If data sets concern personal data, sharing may be problematic from the perspective of the GDPR. In this light, hypothetical conflicts between data protection and competition law could arise if this approach were to be adopted.

4.2.2.5 Exploitative Abuse on Personal Data Markets

Historically, exclusionary abuses took centre stage in the enforcement of Article 102 TFEU. Although exclusionary abuses remain undeniably relevant, exploitative abuses are receiving an increasing amount of attention – particularly in the context of digital markets. The data-driven and zero-price business models of large platforms can allow for the exploitation of consumers, for instance, through excessive data collection. Against this backdrop, the threat of exploitative behaviour has significantly expanded in digital markets.[429]

So far, the Commission has already addressed exploitative, abusive behaviour by large platforms in multiple cases.[430] Yet, the Commission does not refer to exploitative abuses in its Draft Guidelines. The reluctance to focus on exploitative abuses has multiple potential explanations. One of the main reasons probably relates to the challenges associated with exploitative abuses. It is conceptually difficult to establish what exploitative abuses precisely entail, and in practical terms, it is not always straightforward to determine the borderline for unfair prices or conditions.[431] From an enforcement perspective, it is hard to establish which cases of exploitation should be

---

425. CJEU 26 November 1998 Case C-7/97, *Oscar Bronner.*
426. Kuschewsky and Geradin 2014, p. 14.
427. Vanberg and Ünver 2017, p. 11.
428. GC 10 November 2021 Case T-612/17, *Google Shopping*, p. 224.
429. Buiten 2021, p. 275.
430. *See, e.g.,* European Commission 4 March 2024, Case AT40437, *Apple Appstore Practices – music streaming*; European Commission 11 November 2024, 'Commission fines Meta €797.72 million over abusive practices benefitting Facebook Marketplace', IP/24/5801.
431. Balasingham and D'Amico 2024, p. 4; Robertson 2020, p. 173; Graef 2016.

subject to competition law scrutiny. According to some authors, exploitative abuses should not be enforced under EU competition law.[432] Conversely, Balasingham and D'Amico convincingly argue that addressing exploitative abuses has merit.[433] Exploitative conduct covers different types of abuse. Article 102 TFEU explicitly refers to unfair prices and unfair conditions. Moreover, the conduct of price discrimination can have an exploitative dimension. The different types of behaviour are addressed in turn.

Excessive pricing by dominant firms amounts to abusive behaviour. As explained above, determining at which point a price becomes excessive is a difficult exercise.[434] The main question is whether the dominant undertaking has made use of the opportunities of its dominant position 'in such a way as to reap trading benefits which it would not have obtained if there had been normal and sufficiently effective competition'.[435] The CJEU has developed a two-prong test to assess (excessive) prices: *first*, it has to be determined whether the price is *excessive* by comparing the price and production costs to determine profit margins. *Second*, it is to be assessed whether the price is *unfair*, either in itself or in comparison to competing products.[436] Although there are several tests available,[437] it remains difficult to apply such tests in practice, since – regardless of the methodology – further economic analysis is required to determine whether a price is excessive.[438] Presuming that some large platforms collect an excessive amount of data and consumers 'pay' with their data, the question arises whether this excessive data collection amounts to an excessive 'price'.[439] Applying the doctrine of excessive prices to data collection by analogy sparks various complexities. First, it is uncertain whether the level of data protection can be equated with the price of a product. Second, even if it were to be accepted that the personal data collected constitutes the price, several practical difficulties remain. Quantifying the actual value of personal data is far from straightforward, and the

---

432. Werden 2021.
433. Balasingham and D'Amico 2024.
434. There is no consensus on the interpretation of the concept excessive price. *See:* Ayata 2021, p. 181.
435. CJEU 14 February 1978 Case 27/76, *United Brands*, para. 249.
436. CJEU 14 February 1978 Case 27/76, *United Brands*, paras 249-252; CJEU 14 September 2017 Case C-177/16, *AKKA/LAA*.
437. In *AKKA/LA* the CJJEU highlights that competition authorities have 'margin of manoeuvre and [that] there is no single method', *see* CJEU: 14 September 2017 Case C-177/16, *AKKA/LAA*, para. 48.
438. If an authority, for example, makes an assessment on the basis of a comparison with other Member States it should make the assessment based on 'objective, appropriate and verifiable criteria', for example, by taking into account 'economic and social factors'. In *AKKA/LA* the Latvian authority, for example, made a comparison between the rates applied in Latvia, Lithuania and Estonia, supported by rates charged in other Member States adjusted in accordance with the PPP index (*see* CJEU 14 September 2017 Case C-177/16, *AKKA/LAA*, paras 39-42). *See* for a more elaborate overview of this matter: Ayata 2021.
439. Buiten 2021, p. 275.

value of data is context-dependent. The actual value of personal data may, for instance, be different for the data subject than for the data controller.[440] Moreover, by quantifying the monetary value of personal data, the fundamental rights dimension is disregarded. In legal literature, it has been suggested that other legal branches could provide useful guidance to overcome the challenges mentioned.[441] Other regulatory frameworks could give insight into the degree to which the amount of collected data is excessive. The fact that a data collection practice violates another regulation, for example, the GDPR or the Unfair Commercial Practices Directive, is arguably an indication that the data collection is unfair.[442] If this approach were to be adopted, it would no longer be necessary to determine the monetary value of personal data in order to conclude that data collection is excessive. At this point, neither the Commission nor the EU Courts have adopted this approach and have generally refrained from qualifying a certain level of data collection as an unfair price.

Article 102(a) TFEU not only refers to unfair prices but also addresses *unfair trading conditions*. Exploitative conduct is not limited to price-related behaviour but also covers other ways of exploiting economic power.[443] Again, it is difficult to determine when a trading condition is unfair. In the *SABAM* case, the CJEU concluded that a collective management organisation abused its dominance by imposing trading conditions that exceeded what was necessary to protect the organisation's rights and interests.[444] In *SABAM,* the CJEU established the key factors for assessing the fairness of a trading condition.[445] A practice is unfair when the trading conditions are: (i) disproportionate; (ii) not necessary for the objectives that the undertaking is meant to pursue; and (iii) misleading in terms of the information supplied to the contracting parties.[446]

In the context of personal data markets, the Commission has established, on several occasions, that certain conduct amounted to unfair conditions. In the *Apple App Store* case, the Commission ruled that Apple abused its dominant position by imposing unfair conditions, notably anti-steering provisions.[447] These provisions prohibited music streaming services from notifying iOS users about available alternatives and therefore prevented these users from effectively choosing between options. As a result, consumers were not adequately informed about alternative subscription and payment

440. Robertson 2020, p. 173.
441. Robertson 2020, p. 177.
442. The intersection between the GDPR and competition law will further be assessed in Chapter 6.
443. Gebicka and Heinemann 2014, p. 162.
444. CJEU 16 February 2012 Case C-360/10, *SABAM*; Schneider 2018, p. 221.
445. Graef 2021, p. 488.
446. Schneider 2018, p. 221.
447. European Commission 4 March 2024, Case AT40437, *Apple Appstore Practices – music streaming*, p. 567.

mechanisms, nor about the costs associated with these subscription and payment mechanisms.[448] Since Apple imposed high commission fees on in-app purchases, and because consumers were not informed about cheaper alternative subscription services, users paid significantly higher prices for their music subscriptions. Moreover, consumers faced non-monetary harms, including less choice, a degraded user experience and frustration at being unable to subscribe to certain music streaming apps.[449]

The *Apple Appstore* case is not the only investigation into exploitative abuse on personal data markets. The *Facebook Marketplace* decision also has a clear exploitative component. The case not only focused on tying but also addressed the unilateral imposition of unfair trading conditions on ad service providers who advertise on Meta's platforms (and in particular on Facebook and Instagram).[450] The case is very interesting and indicates the relevance of exploitative abuses for personal data markets. At this point, the full decision has not yet been published. Moreover, Meta has already announced that it will appeal the decision.[451] The appeal procedure will provide a good opportunity for the CJEU to provide insight into the applicable legal tests for such exploitative abuse.

Apart from using Article 102(a) TFEU to address certain unfair conditions imposed by platforms, the doctrine could – by analogy – be applied to data collection. Against this backdrop, excessive data collection could potentially amount to unfair trading conditions.[452] Where the application of the doctrine on excessive pricing mostly relates to the *amount* of the collected data, the application of the test for unfair conditions concerns *the way* in which data is collected and processed. This, for example, includes the way in which data is used, as well as the transparency of the processing.[453] This approach would clearly integrate data protection considerations into the realm of competition law.[454] So far, the Commission has not adopted this approach. However, the German *Bundeskartellamt* has already incorporated data protection considerations into its assessment of abuse of dominance in the Meta or Facebook case.[455] Moreover, the CJEU clarified that data protection considerations can indeed be relevant for competition law

448. European Commission 4 March 2024, Case AT40437, *Apple Appstore Practices – music streaming*, section 9.3.
449. European Commission 4 March 2024, Case AT40437, *Apple Appstore Practices – music streaming*, paras 599 and 681. For a further analysis of the *Apple Appstore* case, *see:* Bostoen and Mândrescu 2020; Geradin and Katsifis 2021.
450. European Commission 11 November 2024, 'Commission fines Meta €797.72 million over abusive practices benefitting Facebook Marketplace', IP/24/5801.
451. Meta 2024.
452. Robertson 2020; Botta 2019, p. 466.
453. Botta 2019, p. 469.
454. Zingales 2017, p. 557.
455. Schneider 2018, p. 214.

assessments.[456] This issue is further discussed in sections 4.4.2.3 and 6.4.2.[457]

4.2.3 The Institutional and Enforcement Framework

This Section examines the institutional and enforcement framework of EU competition law. This area of law is enforced in the EU's multi-level legal order, and both the Commission and national enforcers are involved. *First*, I consider the institutional framework by briefly elaborating on the system of parallel enforcement of EU competition law. *Second*, the mechanisms for enforcement, including fact-finding and decision-making powers, are discussed. This section focuses on enforcement by the Commission. Enforcement by the Dutch and German NCAs is discussed in sections 4.3.3 and 4.4.3, respectively.

4.2.3.1 The Institutional Framework

The institutional framework of EU competition law has significantly developed over the past few decades.[458] For several years, the enforcement of EU competition law was the sole responsibility of the Commission.[459] Regulation 1/2003 dismantled this system of centralised enforcement.[460] While the Commission still plays an important role in the enforcement of EU competition law, the regulation introduced a system of 'multi-level governance' or 'multi-level administration'. This marked a substantial shift in the institutional framework by decentralising the enforcement of competition law – at least to a certain extent.[461] With the entry into force of Regulation 1/2003, national authorities were granted the competence to apply EU competition law in individual cases.[462] In cases with a cross-border effect, Article 3(1) Regulation 1/2003 even requires NCAs to apply EU competition law in parallel to national competition law.[463]

Although Regulation 1/2003 granted NCAs the competence (and in some cases even the obligation) to apply EU competition law, the enforcement and procedural frameworks largely remained governed by national law,

456. CJEU 4 July 2023 Case C-252/21, *Meta Bundeskartellamt*.
457. *Bundeskartellamt* 6 February 2019 B6-22/16, *Facebook*.
458. *See* for the history and development of the procedural framework of competition law, e.g., Wils 2013.
459. Article 89 EC Treaty (Treaty of Rome); Monti 2014, p. 1.
460. Ibáñez Colomo 2013, p. 364.
461. Article 4 Regulation 1/2003; Cseres 2017, p. 184.
462. Article 5 Regulation 1/2003.
463. *See* section 8.4.2.1.

reflecting the procedural autonomy of the Member States.[464] The enforcement of EU competition law by NCAs, therefore, primarily relied on the national domestic procedures.[465] However, some NCAs lacked the necessary means and instruments to enforce competition law effectively, leading to divergences between Member States.[466] In this light, the ECN+ Directive was introduced in 2019 in order to harmonise parts of the national enforcement frameworks by laying down 'necessary guarantees of independence, resources, and enforcement and fining powers to be able to effectively apply Article 101 and 102 TFEU'.[467] To this end, the ECN+ Directive provides, for example, investigation and fact-finding powers, sanctioning tools and requirements of independence. Importantly, the ECN+ Directive also addresses the cooperation between authorities.[468] This topic is further discussed in section 8.4.

4.2.3.2 The Enforcement Framework

The Commission has several tools at its disposal to enforce EU competition law, including investigative and sanctioning powers. Considering the tools of investigation, the Commission can, for instance, engage in a sector inquiry, file a request for information, take statements and inspect premises.[469]

Once the Commission finds an infringement of competition law, it can adopt various types of decisions. If competition law is infringed, the Commission may impose *an infringement decision* ordering the termination of the violation.[470] Before adopting such a final decision, the Commission has the possibility of taking *interim measures*.[471] Such measures can be imposed in cases of 'urgency due to the risk of serious and irreparable harm to competition'.[472] The instrument allows the Commission to speedily intervene in cases with a pressing need to prevent further damage to competition.

464. Although procedural and institutional frameworks largely remained the responsibility of the Member States, Regulation 1/2003, and Articles 5 and 35 in particular, had an impact on the way in which these national frameworks developed. For an elaboration on procedural autonomy. *See* section 3.4.1.
465. Dzino and Rusu 2019, p. 132.
466. Sinclair 2017, p. 625; Dzino and Rusu 2019, p. 132.
467. Article 1 ECN+ Directive.
468. *See* Chapter VII ECN+ Directive.
469. Articles 17-23 Regulation 1/2003.
470. Article 7 Regulation 1/2003.
471. In IMS Health, the Commission, for example, imposed such measures. The GC upheld IMS Health's appeal and suspended the interim measures. *See:* European Commission 3 July 2001 Case COMP D3/38044, *IMS Health.*
472. Article 8 Regulation 1/2003.

However, it should be stressed that the threshold for 'serious and irreparable damage' is astronomically high.[473] Consequently, the Commission is reluctant to impose interim measures and has rarely made use of the instrument in the past decades. Interestingly, the Commission adopted interim measures in the *Broadcom* case, after a nearly 20-year period of 'dormancy'.[474] So far, the *Broadcom* case is a rather unique example.[475] Although the practical relevance of the instrument has been very limited over the past decades, the use of the instrument of interim measures could help to expedite competition law procedures.

In legal literature, it is suggested that the fact that a market is susceptible to tipping could make it easier to meet the threshold of irreparable damage.[476] The instrument of interim measures could provide an instrument to swiftly respond to anti-competitive behaviour, thereby potentially preventing the market from tipping.[477] The approach is reasonable since the risk of tipping constitutes a serious risk of irreparable harm to competition. By endorsing this approach in case law, the EU courts could contribute to the revival of the instrument of interim measures.

Additionally, scholars have suggested redesigning the test for interim measures by lowering the threshold of 'irreparable damage' and replacing it with a less stringent test, such as 'preventing significant damage'.[478] This lower bar would make it easier for the Commission to impose interim measures. In my view, although providing concrete suggestions for changing the instrument of interim measures does not fall within the scope of the research, in order for the instrument to be genuinely effective, it is necessary to explore avenues for reform.[479] The review and potential upcoming revision of Regulation 1/2003 offer a good opportunity to reconsider the instrument of interim measures, e.g., by relaxing the threshold to impose interim measures.

Apart from infringement decisions and interim measures, the Commission has the competence to adopt *commitment decisions*. Undertakings can offer commitments to address certain anti-competitive concerns, and the Commission can make these commitments binding, *without* issuing an infringement decision. When commitments are binding and complied with

473. In its most recent review of Regulation 1/2003, the Commission acknowledges that 'a more efficient use of this tool may to some extent be prevented by time-intensive procedural requirements and the widespread perception of an overly demanding test'. *See:* European Commission, Commission Staff Working Document, Evaluation of Regulation 1/2003 and 773/2004, SWD(2024)216 final.
474. European Commission 10 October 2019 Case AT40608, *Broadcom; Caminade, Chapsal and Penglase* 2021, p. 437.
475. Steppe, Devroe and Deblander 2024, p. 201.
476. Alexiadis and De Streel 2020, p. 48.
477. *See* section 2.6.
478. Masquelier 2021.
479. Ruiz Feases 2020b, pp. 427-428; Farinhas 2025.

by the undertaking concerned, the Commission can no longer take action. However, a commitment does not constitute a final ruling on a case. Therefore, NCAs and national courts are not bound by these decisions.[480] Moreover, it should be stressed that the Commission is under no obligation to accept commitments. In the *Google Shopping* case, the Commission, for instance, rejected Google's commitments and continued its investigation.[481] In general, if the Commission intends to impose a fine, commitment decisions are not an appropriate instrument.[482]

In practice, commitment decisions are a useful tool because they are relatively inexpensive and easy to adopt. Since the Commission does not take an infringement decision, it is not bound to provide certain complex economic and legal analyses.[483] Moreover, the CJEU established in the *Alrosa* case that the obligations of a commitment decision can exceed those that could have been imposed in an infringement decision, provided that the proportionality principle is observed by the Commission.[484] Lastly, commitment decisions can facilitate swift procedures, in particular when coupled with interim measures. In the *Broadcom* case, the Commission combined interim measures and a commitment decision.[485] Particularly in complex cases, this approach can offer a quick resolution.[486] This combination could be valuable for addressing the position of large platforms in innovative and rapidly evolving markets.

An infringement decision can order the termination of the infringement. In addition, the Commission can take *positive steps* to end an infringement by imposing *behavioural* or *structural remedies*.[487] Where structural remedies affect the structure of the undertaking by creating legally and operationally independent entities to maintain competition, behavioural remedies impose obligations relating to the undertaking's behaviour or operation to prevent anti-competitive conduct.[488] Structural remedies are a matter of last resort: they can only be adopted if behavioural remedies would not be equally effective of if such remedies are more burdensome.[489] Structural remedies are often proposed as a solution to address problems

480. CJEU 23 November 2017 Case C-547/16, *Gasorba*.
481. Jones, Sufrin and Dunne 2019, p. 940; European Commission 27 June 2017, Case AT3970, *Google Shopping*.
482. Preamble Regulation 1/2003, recital 13.
483. Van de Gronden and Rusu 2021, p. 204.
484. CJEU 29 June 2010 Case C-441/07P, *Alrosa*, para. 41; Van de Gronden and Rusu 2021, p. 206.
485. European Commission 10 October 2019 Case AT40608, *Broadcom*.
486. Mantzari 2020, p. 1.
487. Article 7 Regulation 1/2003.
488. In practice, the distinction is not always evident. *See:* Lianos 2013b, p. 50.
489. According to the text of Article 7 Regulation 1/2003, '[s]tructural remedies can only be imposed either where there is no equally effective behavioural remedy or where any equally effective behavioural remedy would be more burdensome for the undertaking concerned than the structural remedy'. *See also*: Jones, Sufrin and Dunne 2019, p. 934.

associated with large platforms. Breaking up Big Tech is frequently put forward as the ultimate solution to curb platform power.[490] However, it is not evident that structural remedies within the meaning of Regulation 1/2003 can facilitate this ambition. Article 7 Regulation 1/2003, read in conjunction with recital 12, seems to leave room to change the structure of an undertaking, provided that the principles of necessity and proportionality are met.[491] Arguably, this could facilitate the divestiture of one or more units of a large platform. Yet, in practice, the Commission has never imposed such structural remedies. Therefore, the practical relevance of this instrument can be questioned.[492] At present, there are no clear indications that the Commission will invoke structural remedies to break up large platforms.

Apart from structural or behavioural remedies, the Commission can impose fines and periodic penalty payments. Article 23 Regulation 1/2003 stipulates that the Commission can impose fines up to 1% of the total annual turnover of an undertaking for procedural violations, such as providing misleading or incorrect information or breaking seals during on-site inspections. Moreover, the Commission can impose fines of a maximum of 10% of the undertaking's annual turnover for an infringement of Article 102 TFEU, for contravening an interim measure or for a failure to comply with binding commitments. The Commission determines the amount of the fine within the limits of this 10% cap. To this end, the Commission has formulated its *Guidelines on the method of setting fines.*[493] Apart from fines, the Commission can adopt periodic penalty payments, not exceeding 5% of the daily turnover of the undertaking concerned.[494] Such payments can compel an undertaking to terminate its infringement of Article 102 TFEU, its non-compliance with an interim decision or its violation of binding commitments.

4.2.4 EU Competition Law: Final Remarks

The Commission has invoked Article 102 TFEU to address anti-competitive conduct of large platforms on multiple occasions. This demonstrates that the competition law framework can play an important role in addressing the behaviour of large platforms. However, in the past years, the rise of personal data markets has challenged the EU competition law framework. Well-established concepts, such as the notion of the relevant market and the SSNIP

490. Akman 2019, p. 589.
491. Recital 12 of Regulation 1/2003 provides that '[c]hanges to the structure of an undertaking as it existed before the infringement was committed would only be proportionate where there is a substantial risk of a lasting or repeated infringement that derives from the very structure of the undertaking'.
492. Van de Gronden and Rusu 2021, p. 201.
493. Guidelines of 1 September 2006 on the method of setting fines imposed pursuant to Article 23(2)(a) of Regulation No. 1/2003, C 210/8.
494. Article 24 Regulation 1/2003.

test, have proven to be difficult to apply to this new economic reality. Furthermore, some of the existing types of abuses have been tweaked to accommodate their application to personal data markets. For example, the doctrine of tying was adjusted and currently also covers certain practices of default settings and pre-installation. Moreover, anti-competitive conduct of large platforms does not always fit neatly into the established categories or types of existing abuses. Experience with personal data markets illustrates the flexibility of the competition law framework. Various tools, including those for defining the relevant market, have been adjusted and updated. Moreover, the open-ended nature of Article 102 TFEU allows for new categories of abuse. The abuse of self-preferencing, which is now also adopted in the Draft Guidelines, constitutes a clear example in this regard. By virtue of its flexible nature, competition law can adjust in light of changes to markets and remains relevant for the new economic reality. Furthermore, the broad nature of Article 102 TFEU enables it to be used to address exploitative abuses in personal data markets. The characteristics of personal data markets pose a risk of consumer exploitation by Big Tech. In this light, Article 102 TFEU may prove useful again in the future, despite the Commission historically not emphasising exploitative abuses.

Notwithstanding these adjustments and the flexibility, the application of the competition law framework to personal data markets still faces challenges. *First,* while the framework is flexible, the reach and scope of Article 102 TFEU is not unlimited. At some point, the framework may be overstretched. In this light, the development and adjustment of theories of harms should be done in a prudent manner and require diligence.[495] Moreover, to get clarity on the lawfulness of new approaches, consolidation by the CJEU is necessary. Hence, diligently developing and adjusting theories takes time. This is particularly problematic in the context of digital markets where dynamics are changing rapidly and markets are prone to tipping.[496] *Second,* competition law procedures tend to be notoriously lengthy (and, consequently, costly). For instance, in *Google Shopping,* the Commission launched its investigation in 2010. The CJEU published its final ruling in the appeal procedure in 2024.[497] Similarly, the Google Android investigation started in 2015. At this point in time, the appeal procedure before the CJEU is still in progress.[498] The lengthy duration of competition law proceedings is particularly detrimental in the context of personal data markets. By the time a ruling is final, the market can have changed, and the technology underlying the investigated practice may have become outdated

495. Mândrescu 2024b, p. 116.
496. *See* section 2.6.
497. European Commission 27 June 2017, Case AT3970, *Google Shopping*, p. 6; CJEU 10 September 2024 Case C-48/22P, *Google Shopping*.
498. European Commission 18 July 2018, Case AT40099, *Google Android*, p. 10; Case C-738/22P, *Google Android* (Case in Progress).

and obsolete.[499] One proposed solution for speeding up and simplifying procedures is to rely on more per se rules. Per se rules do not rely on an in-depth assessment of individual cases, but rather establish legal presumptions of illegality for certain types of conduct that are particularly likely to have a detrimental effect.[500] By introducing the category of 'naked restrictions', the Commission seems to shift in this direction.[501] However, this approach is still very controversial and appears to contradict the effects-based approach that is central to competition law. Moreover, per se rules are more rigid and could undermine the flexible nature of EU competition law – which has proven to be highly valuable.[502] *Lastly,* EU competition law targets anti-competitive *behaviour* by dominant undertakings. Given the focus on firm conduct, EU competition law cannot address market failures related to the structure of the market. Consequently, competition law is not suitable for tackling issues relating to market tipping associated with the market structure rather than with specific conduct.[503]

The EU competition law framework provides several procedural tools for accelerating proceedings. The instruments of interim measures and commitments are highly relevant in this regard. Despite their potential, there are currently procedural obstacles. This explains why the Commission has been reluctant to adopt interim measures. It will be interesting to see how these tools evolve in the ongoing review and potential revision of Regulation 1/2003. Similarly, structural remedies could be an asset for addressing concerns relating to Big Tech. However, at this point in time, this instrument has not yet been used in practice. Therefore, the practical relevance of structural is currently limited.

4.3 COMPETITION LAW IN THE NETHERLANDS

Competition law is not only enforced at the EU level. On the contrary, national competition authorities play an important role in the enforcement of competition law. These national authorities enforce both (i) EU and (ii) national competition laws. This section focuses on the enforcement of competition law in The Netherlands. The objectives, scope and substantive provisions and institutional and enforcement framework are addressed in turn. Since the frameworks of EU and national competition law partially overlap and clear similarities are apparent, the national frameworks will not

499. Witt 2022, p. 676.
500. Witt 2022, p. 683.
501. Draft Guidelines on the Application of Article 102, para. 60 sub c ; *See* section 4.2.2.3.
502. Witt 2022, pp. 682-683.
503. Impact Assessment DMA, para. 120.

be addressed exhaustively. Rather, the main differences between the respective national frameworks and EU competition law are highlighted. Ultimately, I aim to provide an overview of the relevance of these national frameworks in addressing the issue of market power on personal data markets.

In the enforcement of Dutch competition law, personal data markets receive a lot of attention. Over the past few years, digital markets have been high on the political agenda of the ACM. In 2018, the ACM, for instance, highlighted that rapid developments in the digital sphere call for alertness of supervisors, and that the existing competition law instruments were potentially not suitable for resolving all difficulties relating to digital markets.[504] In fact, the ACM was one of the first authorities to signal the need for *ex-ante* regulation.[505] The ACM's current chairman is particularly ambitious and aims for the ACM to act as a leading actor in platform supervision by running at the forefront.[506]

4.3.1 Objectives of Dutch Competition Law

The objectives of Dutch competition law largely align with those of European competition law. The goals of the Dutch framework are not explicitly mentioned in the 'Dutch Competition Act' (*de Mededingingswet*)(henceforth: DCA). However, the Explanatory Memorandum to the initial DCA states that competition law has the objective of promoting competition (*het bevorderen van de mededinging*) in order to contribute to consumer welfare. Moreover, the Establishment Act of the ACM provides some guidance on the objectives of Dutch competition law. Admittedly, the tasks of the ACM are broader than only the enforcement of competition law.[507] Therefore, these statements do not merely relate to competition law. Yet, by stressing that the ACM must 'ensure that markets function well, that market processes are orderly and transparent, and that consumers are treated with due care', the Establishment Act gives a hint as to the objectives of

504. ACM 11 April 2028, 'ACM Signal 2018' https://www.acm.nl/nl/publicaties/acm-signaal-2018 accessed 31 March 2025.
505. Snoep 2024; Ministry of Economic Affairs and Climate Policy, Letter to The Speaker of the House of Representatives, 17 May 2019, Future-proofing of competition policy in regard to online platforms, CE-MC/19129028; Benelux Memorandum of the Belgian, Dutch and Luxembourg competition authorities on challenges faced by competition authorities in a digital world, 2 October 2019, https://www.acm.nl/sites/default/files/documents/2019-10/benelux-memorandum-over-toezicht-mededinging-in-digitale-economie.pdf accessed 20 March 2025.
506. Dekker, Gerbrandy and Niels 2019, p. 87.
507. *See* sections 4.3.3.1 and 8.3.2.

Dutch competition law.[508] Moreover, in its Annual Report, the ACM stresses that it aims to 'make markets work well for people and businesses, now and in the future'.[509] The ACM thus emphasises a standard or *well-functioning market.*

Moreover, the goal of *consumer welfare* is reflected in the Dutch competition law framework. In the Explanatory Memorandum to the DCA, the Dutch legislator, for instance, highlighted that competition can stimulate the growth of the economy, thereby contributing to *welfare.* The objective of consumer welfare can be derived from these statements.[510] The relevance of *consumer welfare* is also illustrated by the fact that the District Court of Rotterdam has referred to consumer welfare (*consumentenwelvaart*) expressly.[511] The ACM appears to adhere to a rather broad interpretation of the consumer welfare standard by paying attention to a wide range of interests, including innovation, sustainability and product diversity.[512] Debates on the role of non-economic objectives and societal harm in competition law have been prominently present in The Netherlands.[513] The Dutch discussion on the endorsement of non-economic objectives of competition law, for example, predates the EU discussion, and the ACM is particularly open to sustainability considerations.[514] Moreover, Martijn Snoep, the ACM's chairman, stressed that '[…] fairness is perhaps even more important than efficiency'.[515]

In sum, the objectives of Dutch competition law to a significant extent mirror those of EU competition law. Naturally, the objective of market integration is not relevant in the Dutch context, since the national framework focuses on merely one market.[516]

---

508. Tweede Kamer der Staten Generaal, 9 May 1996, Memorie van Toelichting Nieuwe regels omtrent de economische mededinging (Mededingingswet), 1995-1996, 24707, nr. 3 (Explanatory Memorandum DCA).
509. ACM, 'ACM Annual Report' (2021) https://www.acm.nl/sites/default/files/documents/2021-acm-annual-report_0.pdf accessed 11 March 2025, p. 5.
510. Van de Gronden 2022, p. 25.
511. District Court Rotterdam 25 August 2011 ECLI:NL:RBROT:2011:BT8903, Nederlandse Melkveehouders Vakbond en Nederlandse Bond voor Handelaren in vee/de NMA, paras 2.8.2.1 and 2.8.2.2.
512. Gerbrandy et al. 2020, p. 7.
513. Gerbrandy et al. 2020, p. 7; ACM 11 April 2028, 'ACM Signaal 2018' https://www.acm.nl/nl/publicaties/acm-signaal-2018 accessed 31 March 2025, p. 2.
514. Dekker, Gerbrandy and Niels 2019, p. 90.
515. Snoep 2023b.
516. Although it is generally assumed that market integration does not encompass the objective of national, and therefore of Dutch, competition laws, the *Nordzucker* case causes some confusion. In this case, the CJEU states that 'if two national competition authorities were to take proceedings against and penalise the same facts in order to ensure compliance with the prohibition on cartels under Article 101 TFEU and the corresponding provisions of their respective national law, those authorities would pursue the same objective of general interest of ensuring that competition in the internal market is not distorted […]'. This seems to imply that by enforcing national competition laws,

4.3.2 Scope and Substantive Provisions

In The Netherlands, the substantive rules of national competition law are set out in the DCA. The DCA builds on EU competition law concepts and establishes clear links between the national and EU level. The interpretation of important concepts, such as *agreement* and *undertaking*, is aligned with EU competition law interpretations.[517]

Like EU competition law, the Dutch framework prohibits abuse of a dominant position. In terms of substance, the Dutch framework closely aligns with EU competition law.[518] Article 24 DCA codifies the Dutch equivalent of Article 102 TFEU. Despite the similarities, there are some differences between the two provisions. Where Article 102 TFEU contains a list of potential abuses, Article 24 DCA does not refer to particular practices, but merely stresses that it is prohibited for undertakings to abuse their dominant position.[519] Furthermore, the territorial scope of Article 24 DCA is narrower than the scope of Article 102 TFEU and only covers conduct with an effect on the Dutch market.[520] Another major difference between Dutch and EU competition law relates to the fact that Article 24(2) DCA establishes that a concentration cannot amount to an abuse of dominance. Article 102 TFEU does not contain a similar reference. In the past, this divergence was largely theoretical in nature, because mergers were generally not reviewed in light Article 102 TFEU. This changed with the *Towercast* case, in which the CJEU established that NCAs are not precluded from applying Article 102 TFEU to concentrations not subject to EU or national merger control.[521] This raises the question of whether Article 24(2) DCA is at odds with the *Towercast* judgment. The answer to this question is not unequivocal and depends on the scope of Article 24(2) DCA. If Article 24(2) DCA only precludes the application of Article 24 DCA, the provision is not problematic in light of the *Towercast* judgment. However, if Article 24(2) DCA would also preclude the application of Article 102 TFEU to concentrations, it

NCAs pursue a market integration objective as well. It remains to be seen how this statement will be developed in the future. CJEU 22 March 2022 Case C-151/20, *Nordzucker*, para. 56; *See also*: Wirtz, 2006, p. 99; E. Zippro 2008, para. 2.2.3.3.

517. Article 1(1) DCA; Van de Gronden 2022, p. 176.
518. Appeldoorn and Vedder 2010, p. 298.
519. Despite the fact that Article 24 DCA does provide a list of potentially abusive behaviour, the Explanatory Memorandum lists various types of abusive behaviour, such as excessive pricing, fidelity rebates, refusal to supply and tying. *See:* Tweede Kamer der Staten Generaal, 9 May 1996, Memorie van Toelichting Nieuwe regels omtrent de economische mededinging (Mededingingswet), 1995-1996, 24707, nr. 3 (Explanatory Memorandum DCA).
520. Dutch competition law can – similar to EU competition law – be applied extraterritorially. Undertakings without an establishment in The Netherlands can still be subject to Dutch competition law, insofar their behaviour affects the Dutch market. *See:* Zippro 2008, p. 17; Van de Gronden 2022, p. 177.
521. CJEU 16 March 2023 Case C-449/21, *Towercast.*

cannot be reconciled with *Towercast*. Rusu and Van de Gronden convincingly argue that the provision should be interpreted narrowly, confining itself to excluding the application of Dutch competition law to concentrations.[522] Yet, given the current uncertainties in the aftermath of the *Towercast* case, it should be explicitly clarified whether Article 24(2) DCA also covers Article 102 TFEU. If this is the case after all, I would recommend abolishing this provision.[523]

The Dutch ACM has shown its willingness to address anti-competitive behaviour in personal data markets. The *Apple App Store* case is the clearest example in this regard. The ACM established that Apple abused its dominance by imposing unreasonable conditions on dating app providers for access to the App Store. The unreasonable conditions are, according to the ACM, two-fold. *First,* Apple prevents dating app providers from using alternative payment systems to facilitate payment for digital content and prohibits app providers from referring to payment options outside the app. *Second,* Apple refuses to give dating app providers access to its customer data, including customer services, invoices, cancellations and refunds.[524] To terminate the infringement, the ACM imposed an order sanctioned by the forfeiture of penalty payments.[525]

In the *Apple App Store* case, the ACM took into consideration the specificities of digital markets by acknowledging the importance of single and multi-homing and by considering the importance of network effects.[526] In the assessment of Apple's dominant position, the fact that most Dutch consumers only use a single operating system (and thus *single-home*) constituted a relevant factor. Dating app providers strongly depend on network effects and desire to reach and connect users of different operating systems. Hence, dating app providers envision offering their service in both the Apple App Store and Google Playstore. In order to reach Apple users, dating app providers are bound by the App Store, since no alternatives are allowed by Apple. Due to this dependence, Apple can act independently from the dating app providers – at least to a significant extent. This allows Apple to dictate its terms and conditions.[527] The *Apple App Store* case shows that the ACM has an eye for the specific characteristics of personal data markets and is willing to address exploitative abuses in such markets.[528] However, since the full decision has not (yet) been published, this analysis is merely based on the summary decision. It remains to be seen when the full decision

522. Rusu and Van de Gronden 2024, p. 30.
523. Sauter and Mulder 2023, p. 142.
524. ACM 24 August 2021 ACM/19/035630, *Apple* (Case Summary), paras 15-19.
525. ACM 24 August 2021 ACM/19/035630, *Apple* (Case Summary), paras 8-13.
526. *See* section 2.3.
527. ACM 24 August 2021 ACM/19/035630, *Apple* (Case Summary), paras 8-13.
528. The District Court Rotterdam acknowledges that the ACM focusses on exploitative abuses, *see:* Court of First Instance Rotterdam 24 December 2024 Case ROT 21/4781 and 21/4782, *Apple v. ACM*, para. 4.5.

will be published, whether the case will be appealed and which further insights can be derived from it.

The *Apple App Store* case is interesting from multiple perspectives. *First,* it reflects the ACM's ambition to address the challenges associated with digital markets.[529] In *Apple App Store*, the ACM is pioneering by being one of the first authorities to address anti-competitive behaviour in the context of App Stores.[530] Moreover, the ACM shows boldness by experimenting with the application of the doctrine of unfair conditions in this context. *Second,* the case is interesting in light of the relationship between the Commission and NCAs. As explained in section 4.2.2.5, the Commission engaged in a rather similar case, but did not relieve the ACM of its competence to apply Article 102 TFEU. This issue is further discussed in section 7.4.2. *Third,* the case is relevant from a remedy perspective and illustrates the deep pockets of Big Tech. Initially, Apple did not comply with the ACM's decision and ultimately received the maximum amount of periodic penalties.[531] This approach could be considered a strategy of refusal to comply.[532] Former Commissioner Vestager even stressed that 'Apple essentially prefers to pay periodic fines rather than comply with the decision of the ACM' and that some gatekeepers may be 'tempted to pay for time'. [533] In the Dutch case, Apple ultimately changed its behaviour and complied with the ACM's decision.[534] In this light, the enforcement action was effective. However, the fact that Apple initially chose to pay rather than comply demonstrates that large platforms may opt for paying large sums of money in order to be able to postpone their behavioural changes as long as possible. Admittedly, the *Apple App Store* case merely constitutes an individual example, but if such strategies were to be or become more widespread, this may jeopardise the effectiveness of competition law remedies.

4.3.3 The Dutch Institutional and Enforcement Framework

This section addresses the Dutch institutional and enforcement framework. Section 4.3.3.1 zooms in on the position of the Dutch NCA, i.e., the ACM and section 4.3.3.1 studies the Dutch enforcement framework.

529. ACM, 'Focus Werkzaamheden ACM 2022' (2022) https://www.acm.nl/sites/default/files/documents/focus-2022.pdf accessed 11 March 2025.
530. Bostoen 2022b, p. 584.
531. ACM, 'Focus Werkzaamheden ACM 2022' (2022) https://www.acm.nl/sites/default/files/documents/focus-2022.pdf accessed 11 March 2025.
532. Geradin 2022.
533. Vestager 2022.
534. ACM, 'Focus Werkzaamheden ACM 2022' (2022) https://www.acm.nl/sites/default/files/documents/focus-2022.pdf accessed 11 March 2025.

4.3.3.1 The Dutch Institutional Framework

In The Netherlands, the ACM is responsible for the enforcement of EU and Dutch competition law.[535] The enforcement of competition law is not the only responsibility of the ACM. Rather, the authority has multiple tasks and is also responsible for the enforcement of consumer law, as well as postal, telecom, energy and healthcare regulation.[536] The broad mandate of the ACM is further discussed in section 8.3.2.

The Dutch ACM has several tools at its disposal to enforce Dutch and EU competition law. The Dutch General Administrative Law Act (henceforth: GALA) and the Establishment Act ACM contain several investigative and fact-finding powers, including the power to inspect houses or require information.[537] Even before the adoption of the ECN+ Directive, the ACM had a rather strong position and had the competence to invoke a range of investigative and sanctioning powers.[538] Subsequently, the Dutch legislator did not have to realise significant changes in order to implement the sanctioning and fact-finding competences of the ECN+ Directive. Yet, the Dutch legislator made certain other adjustments, e.g., relating to independence, to interim measures and to the ACM's cooperation with other authorities.[539]

4.3.3.2 The Dutch Enforcement Framework

The ACM has an internal decision-making tool to determine which investigative and sanctioning powers it uses in a particular case. Since this tool is not publicly available, it is not possible to discuss its content in detail.[540] The ACM can take multiple types of decisions. It has the possibility to take an *infringement decision* in order to establish a violation of the law.[541] Moreover, it may impose a *binding instruction*. This instrument is rarely used in practice.[542] To realise swift intervention, the ACM has the competence to

535. Articles 2, 88 and 89 DCA.
536. *See:* https://www.acm.nl/nl/organisatie/onze-organisatie/de-autoriteit-consument-en-markt accessed 20 March 2025; Bok-Wicherts et al. 2020.
537. Section 5 GALA; the competence to inspect private premises (including homes) is established in Article 50 DCA.
538. Kamerstukken Tweede Kamer der Staten Generaal, Wijziging van de Mededingingswet en de Instellingswet Autoriteit Consument en Markt in verband met de implementatie van richtlijn (EU) 2019/1, 2019/2020 35 467, Memorie van Toelichting; Letter of the Minister of Economic Affairs of 18 December 2015, Kamer Stukken Tweede Kamer der Staten Generaal, 2015/2016, 25 268, nr. 132; *See also*: De Groes and Raats 2021, p. 294.
539. The mechanisms governing the cooperation with other authorities are further analysed in Chapters 8 and 9.
540. Bok-Wicherts et al. 2020, p. 39.
541. Article 56 DCA.
542. *See* for an elaboration on binding instructions Jansen 2013; Bredenoord-Spoek and De Jong 2020.

impose *interim measures*.[543] After a few years of absence, this competence was reintroduced in the DCA in the implementation process of the ECN+ Directive.[544] Interim measures may be imposed in the case of a threat of serious and irreparable harm to competition.[545] As explained in section 4.2.3.2, this threshold is very high. The fact that the Dutch legislator copies the standard from Regulation 1/2003 makes it likewise difficult to use the instrument in the Dutch context. Besides interim measures, the ACM may accept *binding commitments* according to Article 12h Establishment Act ACM. However, where Article 12 ECN+ Directives stresses that commitments can be accepted if they meet the concerns expressed by the NCA, the Establishment Act ACM highlights that commitments can be accepted insofar as they are more efficient than imposing a fine or periodic penalty payment. Since the Dutch provision requires an efficiency test, it appears more stringent than the ECN+ Directive. The Dutch provision thus arguably does not implement the Directive properly. However, this divergence will probably not lead to a different outcome in practice.[546]

Furthermore, the ACM has several remedial powers. The ACM may impose a fine of maximum EUR 900,000 or up to 10% of the annual turnover of the undertaking concerned.[547] Furthermore, the ACM also has the competence to impose a fine of maximum EUR 900,000 or 1% of the annual turnover for procedural infringements.[548] Moreover, the DCA give the ACM the possibility to impose an order sanctioned by forfeiture of penalty

543. Article 58b DCA.
544. In the past, Article 83 DCA provided the ACM with the competence to adopt interim measures in competition law cases. The ACM's predecessor imposed several interim measures under Article 83 DCA, for example, in NMA 11 August 1998 Case 803, Edipress/Audax. However, in 2014 this DCA competence was removed, because the ACM has – according to the general Article 5:7 GALA – the possibility to impose an order subject to a periodic penalty payment. This GALA competence would have made Article 83 DCA obsolete. *See:* Kamerstukken Tweede Kamer der Staten Generaal, Wijziging van de Instellingswet Autoriteit Consument en Markt en enige andere wetten in verband met de stroomlijning van het door de Autoriteit Consument te houden markttoezicht, 2012/2013 33622, 3; Van de Gronden 2022, p. 200.
545. Kamerstukken Tweede Kamer der Staten Generaal, Wijziging van de Mededingingswet en de Instellingswet Autoriteit Consument en Markt in verband met de implementatie van richtlijn (EU) 2019/1, 2019/2020 35 467, Memorie van Toelichting; Van de Gronden 2022, p. 301.
546. Dzino, Van de Gronden and Rusu 2019, p. 542.
547. Article 56-57 DCA and Article 5:40 GALA. The ACM uses the *Fining Guidelines ACM 2014* to determine the amount of the fine. This document largely reflects the fining policy of the European Commission. Contrary to the European Commission, the ACM did not develop this policy itself. Rather, the Fining Guidelines are developed by the Minister of Economic Affairs. The ACM has the possibility to deviate from the Guidelines. *See:* Beleidsregel van de Minister van Economische Zaken van 4 juli 2014, nr. WJZ/14112617, Stcrt. 19776 (Boetebeleidsregel ACM 2014)(Fining Guidelines 2014); *See also* Van de Gronden 2022, p. 411; Veenbrink, Van de Gronden and Aronstein 2022, p. 552.
548. *See, e.g.,* Article 70a DCA.

payments (*last onder dwangsom*).[549] Such measures can be imposed for a period of maximum two years and the competence to impose penalty payments expires five years after the infringement.[550]

Apart from fines and periodic penalty payments, the ACM can impose structural and behavioural remedies.[551] Structural remedies may only be imposed if the remedy is proportionate to the infringement, and necessary to bring the infringement effectively to an end. In the case of various structural and behavioural remedies which are equally effective, the least burdensome remedy should be imposed.[552] The Dutch legislator highlights the importance of the corporate structure of the undertaking concerned and stresses that structural remedies are therefore stringent measures. Therefore, structural remedies should be considered an *ultimum remedium*. Such measures are only proportionate in the case of a 'reasonable likelihood of a continuous or repeated infringement' (*een gerede kans op een voortdurende of herhaalde inbreuk*). So far, the ACM has not imposed structural remedies to address abusive behaviour.[553]

Apart from the ACM's existing enforcement and decision-making powers, in The Netherlands, discussions about the establishment of a 'New Competition Tool' at the national level are ongoing. This tool would grant the ACM the power to impose remedies on undertakings to promote effective competition after conducting a market investigation. The ACM has advocated for the introduction of this tool on various occasions. Chairman Martijn Snoep is a strong proponent of the tool. In multiple blogs and speeches, he has addressed the need for and benefits of introducing a New Competition Tool in The Netherlands.[554]

4.3.4 Dutch Competition Law: Final Remarks

The Dutch competition law framework is rather similar to the EU competition law framework. Despite some differences, Article 24 DCA to a

549. Article 56 DCA.
550. Article 12r Establishment Act ACM.
551. Article 58a DCA. The ACM, for example, imposed a remedy sanctioned by forfeiture of penalty payments on Apple. The ACM required Apple to change their conditions regarding the payment system in the App Store. *See* section 4.3.2.
552. Article 58a(2) DCA.
553. Heideman 2025.
554. Snoep 2024; Ministry of Economic Affairs and Climate Policy, Letter to The Speaker of the House of Representatives, 17 May 2019, Future-proofing of competition policy in regard to online platforms, CE-MC/19129028; Benelux Memorandum of the Belgian, Dutch and Luxembourg competition authorities on challenges faced by competition authorities in a digital world, 2 October 2019, https://www.acm.nl/sites/default/files/documents/2019-10/benelux-memorandum-over-toezicht-mededinging-in-digitale-economie.pdf accessed 20 March 2025.

significant extent mirrors Article 102 TFEU. Moreover, the Dutch enforcement tools resemble the tools available in EU competition law. The fact that the Dutch and EU competition law frameworks share important traits does not imply that Dutch competition law is obsolete, nor that the ACM does not play an important role in addressing anti-competitive conduct on personal data markets. The challenges associated with personal data markets are high on the agenda of the Dutch competition authority. Over the last few years, the ACM has not only launched multiple studies and inquiries into the digital sector but has also – proactively – launched investigations and imposed fines on large platforms.[555] The *Apple App Store* case is the clearest and most important example of this.[556] In this case, the ACM was 'ahead of the curve' in addressing exploitative behaviour relating to App Stores.[557] This reflects the potential pioneering role of NCAs and shows a willingness to apply competition law to personal data markets.

4.4 COMPETITION LAW IN GERMANY

This section analyses the application of competition law to personal data markets in Germany. The German legislator is particularly ambitious when it comes to addressing the challenges associated with digital markets and has introduced several tools for addressing platform power – even before the introduction of the DMA. Moreover, the *Bundeskartellamt* has a very proactive attitude in addressing abuses in digital markets. This section zooms in on the application of EU and German competition law in the German context. I study: (i) the objectives of German competition law; (ii) its scope and substantive provisions; and (iii) the institutional and enforcement framework in turn.

4.4.1 Objectives of German Competition Law

The objectives of German competition law are, like the goals of EU and Dutch competition law, subject to an ongoing debate. The German Competition Act, the GWB, provides a first useful indication of the objectives of German competition law. The legislator stresses that the GWB constitutes 'one of the most important foundations for promoting and maintaining a market economy', and that it intends to 'ensure the freedom to compete' and that it eliminates 'economic power where it impairs the effectiveness of

555. ACM 6 October 2017, 'A Closer Look at Online Video Platforms' (2017) https://www.acm.nl/en/publications/closer-look-online-video-platforms accessed 31 March 2025.
556. ACM 24 August 2021 ACM/19/035630, *Apple* (Case Summary).
557. Bostoen 2022b, p. 584.

competition [...] where it jeopardises the optimal supply to the consumer'.[558] The Explanatory Memorandum to the GWB emphasises the *Freiheit des Wettbewerbs.* This concept is closely related to the protection of the competitive process and the freedom to compete and is of pivotal importance for German competition law.[559] Market power may impede this freedom to compete, thereby undermining other undertakings' ability to participate freely in the market. According to Ordo-liberal theory, such circumstances necessitate competition law intervention, since a *laissez faire* approach would result in an undesirable outcome and should be prevented from 'destroying its own prerequisites'.[560]

The Freiburg School of Ordo-liberalism has significantly influenced the development of German competition law. Leading academics associated with this school, including Eucken, Böhm and Großmann-Doerth, have pursued the ideal of a well-functioning market economy, in which individual freedom is protected against state intervention, as well as against undue interference by other market players.[561] The aversion to concentration of power has to be understood in the context of Germany's history and the Second World War, and in particular against the backdrop of the significant degree of public and private power wielded by the Nazi regime, influential interest groups and cartelised industries.[562]

Despite its (historical) relevance, the *Freiheit des Wettbewerbs* is not the only objective of German competition law. The initial memorandum to the GWB also refers to other goals, including efficiency-related concerns. Yet, there is no consensus on the role of efficiency considerations in German scholarship. Maier-Rigaud endorses efficiency and argues that the Ordo-liberal references in the legislative history of the GWB are scarce.[563] Other prominent German scholars, such as Mestmäcker and Hellwig, stress the

---

558. The original text of the Explanatory Memorandum reads: 'Das GWB stellt eine der wichtigsten Grundlagen zur Förderung und Erhaltung der Marktwirtschaft dar. Es soll die Freiheit des Wettbewerbs sicherstellen und wirtschaftliche Macht da beseitigen, wo sie die Wirksamkeit des Wettbewerbs und die ihm innewohnenden Tendenzen zur Leistungssteigerung beeinträchtigt und die bestmögliche Versorgung der Verbraucher in Frage stellt'. *See:* Entwurf eines Gesetzes gegen Wettbewerbsbeschränkungen of 22 January 1955, BT-Drs. 1158.
559. Maier-Rigaud 2012, p. 135. The importance of the *Freiheit des Wettbewerbs* is also reflected by statements of the Federal Ministry of Economic Affairs and Energy in which it stresses that the goal of the GWB is to protect the freedom to compete, the preservation of a market based economic system, to protect individual freedom of all market participants and to limit economic power. *See:* Bundesministerium für Wirtschaft und Energie, 'Informationen zum Nationalen Kartell- und Wettbewerbsrecht' https://www.bmwk.de/Redaktion/DE/Downloads/I/informationen-zum-nationalen-kartell-und-wettbewerbsrecht.pdf?__blob=publicationFile&v=1 accessed 30 March 2025.
560. Deutscher and Makris 2016, p. 186; Kerber 2007, p. 9.
561. Böhm, Eucken and Großmann-Dörth 1936/2008; Riesenkampff 2011, p. 789. *See,* for a more elaborate work on Ordoliberalism: Gerber 1994.
562. Behrens 2014, p. 11.
563. Maier-Rigaud 2012, p. 152.

importance of economic liberty and argue against too much emphasis on efficiencies.[564] Hence, the Ordo-liberal standard finds ample support in German legal literature.

Following up on debates about efficiency and the freedom to compete, the relevance of the *consumer welfare* standard for German competition law has triggered a lot of debate in the German competition law community.[565] According to critics, the objective of consumer welfare would be difficult to reconcile with the original Ordo-liberal roots of German competition law.[566] Where the German school focuses on a 'consumer choice' paradigm, the consumer welfare standard is more rooted in the Chicago School-oriented economic welfare approach.[567] The question arises of whether competition policy should aim to protect consumer welfare or, instead, ought to aim at advancing '*Wettbewerbsfreiheit*' or the freedom to compete.[568] Against this background, the consumer welfare standard is particularly controversial in Germany.

The discussion on the inclusion of non-economic objectives in the goals of competition law has also been present in the context of German competition law.[569] This discussion flared up in the aftermath of the *Meta Bundeskartellamt* case, in which the German NCA incorporated data protection considerations into an antitrust assessment.[570] According to critics, this approach unduly complicates competition law by mingling the goals of competition law and privacy protection.[571] Yet, in my view, the *Meta Bundeskartellamt* case does not recognise considerations of privacy as self-standing goals of competition law. Rather, the German NCA extends traditional goals by including data protection considerations in existing notions of competition law. In fact, the *Bundeskartellamt* puts a lot of emphasis on the notion of consumer choice in relation to data accumulation.[572] The *Bundeskartellamt*'s chairman, e.g., stressed that, due to Facebook's market power, users only have the *choice* either to accept Facebook's conditions or to refrain from using the social media network. In this scenario,

564. Mestmäcker 2005, p. 35; Hellwig 2006, p. 7.
565. *See, e.g.,* Immenga 2006; Budzinski 2007; Körber 2020.
566. Maier-Rigaud 2012, p. 136; Vanberg 2009.
567. Behrens 2014, p. 32.
568. Vanberg 2009, p. 4.
569. Bueren and Crowder 2024.
570. *See* section 4.4.2.3.
571. Van den Bergh and Weber 2021, p. 43.
572. Colangelo and Maggiolino 2019, p. 355.

the *choice* cannot be considered voluntary consent.[573] This approach seems to reflect the Ordo-liberal roots of German competition law.[574]

In sum, German competition law has – like its EU and Dutch counterparts – multiple objectives. Yet, the objectives of German and EU competition law are not identical. In the German context, the consumer welfare and efficiency standards are more controversial, and the relevance of Ordo-liberal ideas can hardly be overlooked. In this light, the protection of consumer choice and the protection of competition play a more prominent role. Apart from these discussions, given the national focus of German competition law, the objective of market integration cannot be considered to be a goal of German competition law. Like the Dutch framework, the German competition rules are adopted within the context of one Member State. Therefore, the internal market rationale of EU competition law is not present within German competition law.

4.4.2 Scope and Substantive Provisions

This section addresses the scope and substantive provisions of German competition law. To this end, the scope and the concept of abuse are discussed in turn. Given the importance of the *Meta Bundeskartellamt* case for the inquiry, a separate Section is devoted to this case.

4.4.2.1 The Scope of German Competition Law

The German framework on rules for unilateral behaviour is broader than its EU law equivalent. The German framework is – like the EU and Dutch frameworks – addressed to *undertakings*.[575] Subsequently, Section 18 GWB elaborates on the concept of market dominance by stressing that an undertaking is dominant, when: (i) it has no competitors (e.g., a legal monopoly); (ii) it is not exposed to any substantial competition; or (iii) it has a paramount position in relation to its competitors. The category of undertakings with a paramount position in relation to its competitors amounts to an independent and self-standing form of dominance and focuses on undertakings with a paramount position *in relation* to their competitors.

573. Bundeskartellamt 7 February 2019, Bundeskartellamt prohibits Facebook from combining user data from different sources Background information on the Bundeskartellamt's Facebook proceeding (2019) https://www.bundeskartellamt.de/SharedDocs/Publikation/EN/Downloads/FAQ_Facebook.pdf?__blob=publicationFile&v=2 accessed 11 March 2025.

574. Van den Bergh and Weber 2021, p. 43.

575. The GWB refers to *Unternehmen. See also*: Koenig and Bremenkamp 2022, p. 4.

Hence, the personal scope is broader and the threshold for dominance is lower than that of Article 102 TFEU.[576]

To assess an alleged dominant position, market shares play a pivotal role in the German context. According to Section 18(4) GWB, an undertaking is considered to have a position of 'single dominance' if its market share exceeds 40%.[577] The use of a market share-based presumption mirrors the AKZO approach.[578] However, while the German framework codifies an explicit threshold of 40%, the AKZO presumption is only triggered where an undertaking has a market share of over 50%. Hence, the German framework establishes a lower threshold.[579] Similar to the EU framework, the GWB does not merely rely on market shares to assess dominance, but also takes other factors into consideration. The GWB refers to several 'traditional' factors, such as market shares, access to supply or sale markets and the ability to shift supply and demand to other goods and services. Interestingly, Section 18(2a) and (3a) GWB also set out certain criteria relating to the specificities of digital markets – already before the adoption of the Commission's Notice on the Relevant Market.[580] Section 18(2a) GWB establishes that the assumption of a market shall not be invalidated by the fact that a service is provided free of charge. Furthermore, Section 18(3a) GWB lists certain criteria that are particularly relevant for personal data markets. The provision, for example, mentions 'access to data relevant for competition' as a relevant criterion. Additionally, Section 18(3a) and (3b) addresses the particularities of multi-sided markets by clarifying that direct and indirect network effects, multi-homing, economies of scale and scope, access to data and the competitive pressure of innovation cannot be overlooked.

The GWB does not limit the concept of dominance to undertakings with a 'traditional dominant position', but extends the application of the rules on the prohibition of abuse of dominance to undertakings with *relative* or *superior market power* (*relative oder überlegene Marktmacht).* Relative market power does not flow from a position of dominance vis-à-vis all market players, but from a position of strength in the bilateral relationship with certain suppliers or customers.[581] According to Section 20 GWB, the German prohibition for abuse of dominance also applies to undertakings on which *other undertakings* are dependent in such a way that possibilities of switching do not exist, resulting in a significant imbalance in power. Furthermore, the concept of relative dominance includes intermediary

576. Section 18(1) sub 3 GWB refers to an undertaking that possesses 'eine im Verhältnis zu seinen Wettbewerbern überragende Marktstellung'. *See also*: Fuchs 2019, para. 1-207.
577. The GWB also contains criteria to establish collective dominance. However, since the scope of the analysis is limited to unilateral behaviour (*see* section 1.3), collective dominance is not taken into account.
578. CJEU 3 July 1991, Case C-62/86, *AKZO*, para. 60; *See* section 4.2.2.2.
579. Oppermann and Chmeis 2017, p. 204.
580. *See also*: Budzinski, Gaenssle and Stöhr 2016.
581. Markert 2019, paras 5-9.

services for accessing supply and sales markets for which no reasonable alternatives are available. According to Section 20(1a) GWB, relative market power can also arise if an undertaking is dependent on accessing data controlled by another undertaking. Section 20(1a) GWB stresses explicitly that, in this scenario, refusing to grant access to data in return for adequate compensation may constitute an abuse of a dominant position.

Besides relative market power, Section 20(3) GWB refers to *superior market power*. Undertakings with a superior market position *vis-à-vis* SMEs cannot abuse their market power by impeding such competitors directly or indirectly in an unfair manner.[582] Initially, the concept of superior market power mostly referred to the relationship between SMEs and larger firms. This changed with the 10th Amendment to the GWB.[583] Currently, according to Section 20(3a) GWB, a superior market position can also arise in multi-sided markets with network effects. The scope of the concept of superior market powers is thus extended and now also potentially includes large online intermediaries and gatekeepers.

Apart from undertakings with 'single dominance' or 'relative or superior market power', the German GWB also targets *undertakings of paramount significance for competition across markets* in Section 19a GWB. Section 19a GWB addresses behaviour by undertakings that are: (i) active on a market in the meaning of Section 18(3a) GWB; and (ii) are of paramount significance for competition across markets. The first criterion establishes that Section 19a GWB applies to multi-sided markets and networks.[584] The scope of Section 19a GWB is thus not limited to certain specific 'core platform services', but covers potentially all multi-sided markets and networks.[585] To assess the second criterion – i.e., the paramount significance – the *Bundeskartellamt* takes several factors into consideration, including dominance on one or several markets, financial strength, vertical integration, access to data relevant for competition and the relevance of the undertaking's

582. An unfair impediment exists in particular when an undertaking: (i) offers food within the meaning of Article 2 Regulation 178/2002 below cost price; (ii) offers other goods or commercial services not occasionally below cost price, or (iii) demands from SMEs with which it competes on the downstream market a price which is higher than the price it itself offers on such markets.

583. Gesetz zur Änderung des Gesetzes gegen Wettbewerbsbeschränkungen für ein fokussiertes, proaktives und digitales Wettbewerbsrecht 4.0 und anderer Bestimmungen (GWB-Digitalisierungsgesetz), 18 January 2021, Bundesgesetzblatt Jahrgang 2021, 1.

584. Section 18(3a) GWB refers to *the case of multi-sided markets and networks*. *See also*: Bauermeister 2022, p. 78.

585. It is controversial whether Section 19a GWB merely applies to digital markets, or also to other multi-sided markets such as credit card systems. Since the scope of the analysis is limited to personal data markets, which are inherently digital, this discussion goes beyond scope of this work.

activities for third-party access to supply and sales markets. Unlike the DMA, Section 19a GWB does not contain any quantitative thresholds for assessing the market position of an undertaking. Defining the relevant market is not strictly required for the application of Section 19a GWB. Yet, some of the sub-criteria for establishing a position of paramount importance for competition across markets are related to the concept of definable markets.[586] This means that disputes relating to market definition could arise in a Section 19a GWB case.

Although the criterion of 'paramount significance' seems relatively hard to meet, this is not necessarily the case. The criterion was introduced as a concept below the threshold of dominance in the meaning of Article 102 TFEU or Section 19 GWB.[587] So far, the *Bundeskartellamt* has designated Google (Alphabet),[588] Facebook (Meta),[589] Apple,[590] Amazon[591] and Microsoft[592] as undertakings of paramount significance for competition across markets.

In sum, the scope of dominance in German competition law is broader than the scope of a dominant position within the meaning of Article 102 TFEU. Apart from 'single' dominance – which in itself already seems broader than the EU concept – it also covers undertakings with a relative or superior market position, as well as undertakings of paramount significance for competition across markets. Consequently, the GWB uses the leeway of Article 3(2) Regulation 1/2003.[593] The relationship between German and EU competition law, as well as Article 3(2), is further discussed in section 7.4.1. The different types of dominance in German competition law are summarised in the table below.

586. Franck and Peitz 2021, p. 517.
587. The text of the provision and the parliamentary memorandum make it clear that Section 19a GWB can also apply to undertakings that do not (yet) meet the standard of dominance in a relevant market. *See also*: Franck and Peitz 2021, p. 517.
588. *Bundeskartellamt* 5 January 2022 B7-61/21, *Google* – Feststellung der überragenden marktübergreifenden Bedeutung für den Wettbewerb.
589. *Bundeskartellamt* 2 May 2022 B6-27/21, *Meta* – Feststellung der überragenden marktübergreifenden Bedeutung für den Wettbewerb.
590. *Bundeskartellamt* 3 April 2023 B9-67/21, *Apple* – Feststellung der überragenden marktübergreifenden Bedeutung für den Wettbewerb.
591. *Bundeskartellamt* 5 July 2022 B2-55/21, *Amazon* – Feststellung einer überragenden marktübergreifenden Bedeutung für den Wettbewerb.
592. *Bundeskartellamt* 27 September 2024 B6-26/23, *Microsoft* – Feststellung der überragenden marktübergreifenden Bedeutung für den Wettbewerb.
593. Koenig and Bremenkamp 2022, p. 1.

Table 4.1 Dominance in German Competition Law

Type of Dominance	*Sub-categories*	*Provision*
Single dominance	(1) No competitors. (2) No substantial competition. (3) Paramount market position in relation to competitors.	Section 18 GWB
Relative dominance	(1) No sufficient and reasonable possibilities for switching and a significant imbalance in power. (2) Multi-sided intermediaries on which undertakings are dependent for accessing supply and sales markets. (3) Undertakings controlling data to which other undertakings require access in order to conduct their activities.	Section 20 GWB
Superior market position	(1) Undertakings with superior market position vis-à-vis SMEs. (2) Undertakings with superior market position in multi-sided markets characterised by network effects.	Section 20 GWB
Paramount importance of competition across markets	(1) Undertakings with paramount significance for competition across markets.	Section 19a GWB

4.4.2.2 Abuse in German Competition Law

Considering the concept of abuse, Section 19 GWB largely reiterates the structure of Article 102 TFEU. Section 19 GWB contains a widely phrased prohibition norm, stressing that 'any abuse of a dominant position by one or several undertakings is prohibited'. The open norm is combined with a non-exhaustive list of different types of abuse, largely mirroring the examples of Article 102 TFEU. Despite the similarities between Article 102 TFEU and Section 19 GWB, there are some differences in place. The main difference relates to the GWB's first listed example. The GWB stresses that a dominant undertaking abuses its position if it 'directly or indirectly impedes another undertaking in an unfair manner or indirectly treats an undertaking differently from another undertaking without any objective justification'. Section 19 GWB thus contains a rather generally framed ban on discrimination and abusive behaviour. Article 102(c) TFEU also applies to discriminatory behaviour, but this prohibition on discrimination is phrased more narrowly and only applies if the undertaking concerned is placed at a competitive disadvantage.[594]

Furthermore, the *Bundeskartellamt* and German courts have interpreted the prohibition of the abuse of dominance quite broadly.[595] In the context of personal data markets, the *Meta Bundeskartellamt* case is particularly ground-breaking. Given the importance of the judgment, section 4.4.2.3 analyses the case in detail.

Although the *Meta Bundeskartellamt* sparked the most debate, it is not the only German case relating to personal data markets. In 2019, the *Bundeskartellamt*, for example, closed its proceedings against Amazon. This case concerned Amazon's general terms of business, in particular vis-à-vis sellers. The *Bundeskartellamt* stressed that 'inappropriate business terms imposed by a dominant company can constitute exploitative abuse [...] if the business terms no longer reflect a balance of interests [...]'.[596] In this case, the *Bundeskartellamt* merely focused on Section 19 GWB, without applying Article 102 TFEU in parallel. In the *Amazon* case, the *Bundeskartellamt* terminated proceedings without adopting a formal decision.[597] Amazon changed its general terms of business and thereby addressed the concerns of the *Bundeskartellamt*. According to the *Bundeskartellamt*, the proposed amendments, 'will achieve considerable improvements for marketplace sellers without adversely affecting the interests of consumers in the marketplace'.[598] In light of these amendments, the *Bundeskartellamt* closed its investigation. Although it did not adopt any formal commitments, it published a case summary on its website.[599]

Apart from Section 19 GWB, the German competition law framework imposes additional obligations on undertakings with relative or superior dominance and on undertakings with a position of paramount significance for competition across markets. Section 20 GWB lists the prohibited conduct for undertakings with *relative* or *superior* market power. As explained above, a refusal to grant access to data can amount to abusive behaviour. In Section 20(1) sub a, the German legislator thus explicitly extends the application of

594. Oppermann and Chmeis 2017, p. 203.
595. *See:* Bundesgerichtshof 7 June 2016 Az KZR 6/15, Pechstein; Bundesgerichtshof 24 January 2017 KZR 47/14, Az VBL Gegenwert.
596. *Bundeskartellamt* 17 July 2019 B2-88/18, *Amazon* (Case Summary), p. 7.
597. As the press release does not have binding effect, Article 3(1) Regulation 1/2003 cannot be applied.
598. *Bundeskartellamt* 17 July 2019 B2-88/18, *Amazon* (Case Summary), p. 1.
599. Heinz 2019.

the essential facilities doctrine to access to data.[600] This approach can make the market more competitive, but can also be problematic in light of data protection law.[601] The exact reach of Section 20(1a) GWB's right to access to data is disputed. Despite the fact that Section 20(1a) GWB addresses the issue of data sharing by dominant undertakings, some uncertainty remains about the analytical framework for determining the potential anti-competitiveness of refusals of access to data. The scope of the obligation needs to be determined on a case-by-case basis, and Section 20(1a) GWB provides little guidance in this regard. According to some authors, the denial of access to data in the context of Section 20(1a) GWB should be interpreted in line with existing case law on Article 102 TFEU.[602] If this approach is taken, the added value of Section 20(1a) GWB would be limited. Others suggest a different approach. Schweitzer et al. point out that Section 20(1a) GWB, in the case of bilateral dependency, seems to impose an 'increased responsibility to grant access to data'.[603] In the same report, it is suggested that further clarification is needed as to when a refusal to share data should be analysed in light of the essential facilities doctrine, or under which circumstances German law imposes a stricter requirement in the case of bilateral dependency.[604] On top of this, Section 20 GWB lists prohibited behaviour for undertakings with superior market power. According to Section 20(3a), undertakings with superior market power on a multi-sided market with network effects cannot impede the independent attainment of network effects by competitors in a way that creates serious risks of significantly restricting competition on the merits.

Since the 10th Amendment of the GWB, German competition law imposes additional obligations on *undertakings of paramount significance for competition across markets*. The framework aims to reinforce the enforcement of competition law on markets where digital ecosystems are controlled by undertakings with a gatekeeper position (*Gatekeeper-Funktion*).[605] To this end, Section 19a GWB provides a basis for controlling

---

600. Körber 2019; Budzinski and Polk 2021.
601. Picht 2022, p. 323.
602. Hoppner 2020.
603. Schweitzer et al. 2022, p. 244.
604. Schweitzer et al. 2022, p. 244.
605. The explanatory memorandum stresses: 'Gleichwohl besteht gesetzgeberischer Bedarf, noch besser mögliche wettbewerbsschädliche Wirkungen und Gefährdungen des Wettbewerbs im Bereich digitaler Ökosysteme, in denen einzelne Unternehmen eine sog. Gatekeeper-Funktion einnehmen, zu erfassen. Mit § 19a wird daher eine Grundlage geschaffen, die dem Bundeskartellamt eine effektivere Kontrolle derjenigen großen Digitalkonzerne ermöglichen soll, denen eine überragende marktübergreifende Bedeutung für den Wettbewerb zukommt.' *See:* Entwurf eines Gesetzes zur Änderung des Gesetzes gegen Wettbewerbsbeschränkungen für ein fokussiertes, proaktives und digitales Wettbewerbsrecht 4.0 und anderer wettbewerbsrechtlicher Bestimmungen (GWB-Digitalisierungsgesetz) 19 October 2020, 19/23492, p. 73.

large digital undertakings with a paramount position across markets effectively.[606] The instrument lowers the burden of proof for the *Bundeskartellamt* and can speed up procedures.[607]

The German Section 19a GWB is – unlike the DMA (*see* cf. section 5.4) – part of the competition law framework. The qualification of this instrument in the broader regulatory landscape is an interesting exercise. Under German law, Section 19a is part of the GWB and qualifies as competition law. There are clear similarities between Section 19a GWB and 'traditional' competition law. Both areas of law, for instance, prohibit self-preferencing, as well as certain practices of pre-installation.[608] Yet, the approach of Section 19a GWB also includes some characteristics of a more regulatory approach, since it determines its addressee in an *ex ante* manner by a decision of the *Bundeskartellamt*.[609] Furthermore, certain Section 19a GWB obligations overlap with Articles 5 and 6 DMA. However, the German obligations are phrased in a shorter and less detailed manner and place less emphasis on per se obligations.[610] This overlap complicates the relationship between Section 19a GWB and the DMA.[611] The nature of Section 19a GWB, as well as its relationship with EU competition law and the DMA, is further discussed in the context of its relationship with the DMA in section 7.5.2.3.

Section 19a GWB provides the *Bundeskartellamt* with the possibility to designate an undertaking as 'undertaking of paramount significance for competition across markets'. Once the *Bundeskartellamt* has issued a decision declaring an undertaking of paramount significance for competition across markets for a period of five years, the authority has the competence to take a decision establishing that the undertaking violates one of the pre-defined prohibitions of Section 19a GWB. Despite the fact that the obligations of Section 19a GWB are predefined, the German instrument cannot be fully considered a per se tool. Although Section 19a GWB shifts the burden of proof, undertakings have the possibility to objectively justify their behaviour.[612] On top of this, Section 19a GWB does not encompass a prohibition in itself and does not contain self-executory obligations.[613] Rather, it provides the *Bundeskartellamt* with the possibility to declare

606. Franck and Peitz 2021, p. 515.
607. Bauermeister 2022, p. 88.
608. *See, e.g.,* European Commission 27 June 2017, Case AT3970, *Google Shopping*; European Commission 18 July 2018, Case AT40099, *Google Android.*
609. According to Section 19a GWB, the *Bundeskartellamt* may 'issue a decision declaring that an undertaking which is active to a significant extent on markets [… .] is of paramount significance for competition across markets'. *See also*: Mohr 2023, p. 70.
610. Botta 2021, p. 507.
611. Bechtold and Busch stress that the co-existence of the DMA and Section 19a GWB can lead to 'komplexe Kollisionsfragen'. *See:* Bechtold and Bosch 2021, para. 3.
612. Witt 2023, pp. 661-662.
613. Podszun 2022a, p. 9.

certain activities prohibited.[614] The *Bundeskartellamt* thus needs to take action in two instances in order to apply the provisions of Section 19a GWB. First, it needs to designate an undertaking as being an undertaking of paramount significance for competition across markets, and second, it has to take a decision prohibiting certain conduct. Only after these two steps have been taken can an undertaking be fined for infringing the prohibition decision. This approach, in combination with the possibility for objective justification, thus seems to leave some room for a degree of case-by-case assessment.[615]

As mentioned previously, Section 19a GWB provides a catalogue of conduct that can be prohibited by the *Bundeskartellamt.* The catalogue encompasses various types of behaviour, including:

(i) favouring its own offers over the offers of its competitors when mediating access to supply and sales markets and in particular presenting its own offers in a more favourable manner or exclusively pre-installing its own offers or integrating them in any other way in offers;

(ii) taking measures that impede other undertakings from carrying out their business activities on supply or sales markets where the undertaking's activities are of relevance for accessing such markets, in particular taking measures that result in exclusive pre-installation of offers provided by the undertaking or preventing other undertakings from advertising their own offers or reaching their purchasers through other channels or making it more difficult for undertakings to do so;

(iii) directly or indirectly impeding competitors on a market on which the undertaking can rapidly expand its position even without being dominant, in particular by linking the use of an offer provided by the undertaking to the automatic use of another offer provided by the undertaking or making the use of an offer provided conditional on the use of another offer provided by the undertaking;

(iv) creating or appreciably raising barriers to market entry or otherwise impeding other undertakings by processing data relevant for competition, in particular by making use of services conditional to users agreeing on the processing of data from other services of the undertaking or a third-party provider without giving the user sufficient choice or processing data relevant for competition received from other undertakings for purposes other than those necessary for the provision of its own services;

---

614. Section 19a(2) GWB stresses that '[i]n the case of a declaratory decision issued pursuant to subsection (1), the Bundeskartellamt may prohibit such undertaking from […]'.
615. Bauermeister 2022, p. 82.

(v) refusing interoperability of products and services or data portability, or making it more difficult and in this way impeding competition;
(vi) providing other undertakings with insufficient information about the scope, quality or success of the service rendered or commissioned or making it otherwise difficult for such undertakings to assess the value of this service;
(vii) demanding disproportionate benefits, in particular demanding the transfer of data or rights that are not absolutely necessary for the purpose of presenting these offers or making the quality in which these offers are presented conditional on the transfer of data or rights which are not reasonably required for this purpose.

So far, the *Bundeskartellamt* has concluded various cases and is currently engaged in multiple ongoing procedures.[616] The cases concern different Big Tech platforms and address a wide range of behaviour. In *Google News Showcase,* the *Bundeskartellamt* assessed the adequate balance between the rights and obligations of content providers and Google, as well as possible discrimination between individual publishers and an examination of whether competing services are being squeezed out or the market or whether Google is preferencing its own services. In the course of the proceedings, Google changed or stopped several of the examined practices and declared its willingness to address the remaining issues.[617] The measures taken by Google addressed the concerns of the *Bundeskartellamt*, which discontinued the examination.[618] In the *Google/Data Processing Conditions* case, the *Bundeskartellamt* adopted a commitment decision. The case concerns Google's data processing terms for end-users, providing for the possibility to process user data across services without effective consent.[619] The *Bundeskartellamt* accepted Google's commitments and closed proceedings. Interestingly, the commitments do not cover services that are subject to the DMA.[620] This is relevant for the relationship between the DMA and Section 19a GWB. This issue will be further addressed in section 7.5.2.3. In *Facebook/VR Headsets* (or *Facebook Oculus*), the *Bundeskartellamt* addressed the linkage between VR Headsets (formerly Oculus) and Facebook's social network. These concerns have been addressed, and the headsets can now also be used without a Facebook or Instagram account. However, and

616. Witt 2023, p. 661.
617. *Bundeskartellamt* 1 August 2023 V-43/20, *Google News Showcase* (Case Summary), p. 6.
618. *Bundeskartellamt* 1 August 2023 V-43/20, *Google News Showcase* (Case Summary), p. 1.
619. *Bundeskartellamt* 5 October 2023 B7-70/21, *Google/Data processing conditions*, pp. 10-11.
620. *Bundeskartellamt* 5 October 2023 B7-70/21, *Google/Data processing conditions*, para. 40.

despite these developments, the proceedings have not been closed. The *Bundeskartellamt* is still assessing the specific choice of architecture regarding the usable accounts and whether and how data is processed and combined.[621] Apart from the concluded cases, the *Bundeskartellamt* is engaged in various ongoing proceedings. These procedures entail investigations into Google Maps Platforms and Google Automotive Services,[622] Amazon's Price Control and Brandgating (i.e., an examination of possible disadvantages for marketplace sellers)[623] and Apple's App Tracking Transparency Framework.[624]

4.4.2.3 The Meta Bundeskartellamt Case

In 2019, the German NCA adopted a revolutionary and groundbreaking decision by concluding that the data-protection policy of Meta (then still Facebook) amounted to abusive behaviour. The *Bundeskartellamt* prohibited Meta from combining data sets from different sources.[625] This section addresses the facts of the decision, zooms in on the case and subsequent procedures and highlights the main takeaways from the case. The decision is relevant for the relationship between EU and national competition law, as well as for the interplay between competition law and the GDPR. These topics are discussed in more detail in sections 8.4.2.1 and 9.6.2.2.

The *facts* of the *Meta Bundeskartellamt* case concern the combining of different data sets by Meta. Meta is a platform that operates and offers a range of (online) services and products. Meta's flagship product, Facebook, is a social network service with an integrated service for real-time communication, i.e., Facebook Messenger. Apart from the core service, Meta provides a service called 'Meta Business Tools', which allows third parties to integrate Facebook features into their own websites and/or apps. The tools include various social plugins, such as 'Like' and 'Share' buttons, Facebook

621. *Bundeskartellamt* 23 November 2022, 'Meta (Facebook) responds to the Bundeskartellamt's concerns – VR headsets can now be used without a Facebook account' (2022) https://www.bundeskartellamt.de/SharedDocs/Meldung/EN/Pressemitteilungen/2022/23_11_2022_Facebook_VR_Brillen.html accessed 12 March 2025.
622. *Bundeskartellamt* 21 June 2023, 'Statement of objections issued against various of Google's practices in connection with Google Automotive Services and Google Maps Platform' (2023) https://www.bundeskartellamt.de/SharedDocs/Meldung/EN/Pressemitteilungen/2023/21_06_2023_Google.html accessed 12 March 2025.
623. *Bundeskartellamt* 14 November 2022, 'Extension of ongoing proceedings against Amazon to also include an examination pursuant to Section 19a of the German Competition Act (GWB)' (2022) https://www.bundeskartellamt.de/SharedDocs/Meldung/EN/Pressemitteilungen/2022/14_11_2022_Amazon_19a.html accessed 12 March 2025.
624. *Bundeskartellamt* 14 June 2022, 'Bundeskartellamt reviews Apple's tracking rules for third-party apps' (2022) https://www.bundeskartellamt.de/SharedDocs/Meldung/EN/Pressemitteilungen/2022/14_06_2022_Apple.html accessed 12 March 2025.
625. *Bundeskartellamt* 15 February 2019 B6-22/16, *Facebook* (Case Summary), p. 1.

logins or analytical services. Besides Facebook and the Business Tools, Meta offers other online services, including Instagram, Whatsapp, Masquerade and Oculus.[626] The use of Facebook's social media service is conditional upon agreement with Meta's terms and conditions which, *inter alia,* stipulate that Facebook processes personal data, including data collected *outside* the platform via the Business Tools. In doing so, Facebook combines the data from various sources. According to Meta, this practice is required to provide Meta's services and to fulfil Facebook's legitimate interest.[627]

In its *Meta Bundeskartellamt* decision, the German NCA concluded that this behaviour amounts to an abuse of a dominant position in violation of Section 19 GWB. In assessing the dominant position, the *Bundeskartellamt* pays attention to the particularities of digital markets and takes stock of Facebook's position as a multi-sided network providing 'free' services.[628] The *Bundeskartellamt* defines the geographic market as national, i.e., Germany-wide. According to the *Bundeskartellamt*, Facebook holds a dominant position in the German market for social networks for private users. The dominant position is derived from Facebook's market shares in the relevant market, especially among daily active users.[629] A further 'key element of market dominance' is the presence of strong direct and indirect network effects, as well as Facebook's access to competitively relevant data. Lastly, the *Bundeskartellamt* addresses Facebook's arguments relating to innovation and dynamic competition by stating that there is no trend of users withdrawing from Facebook or Facebook losing market shares despite the Internet's high rate of innovation.[630]

The *Bundeskartellamt* concludes that Facebook's data policy, which allows the undertaking to 'collect user and device-related data from sources outside Facebook and to merge it with data collected on Facebook' constitutes an abuse of dominance in the form of exploitative terms according to the 'general clause' of Section 19(1) GWB.[631] According to the *Bundeskartellamt*, Facebook's terms violate the GDPR, as well as Section 19(1) GWB. The *Bundeskartellamt* builds on German case law regarding the agreement of contract terms, in order to assess the appropriateness of

626. Instagram is a social media service for the sharing of photos and short videos; WhatsApp entails a communication service and allows users to send and receive, among others, text and voice messages, photos, videos and locations; Masquarade is a service for editing and sharing pictures with masks and filters; Oculus provides virtual reality headsets and software.
627. *Bundeskartellamt* 15 February 2019 B6-22/16, *Facebook* (Case Summary).
628. *Bundeskartellamt* 6 February 2019 B6-22/16, *Facebook*, paras 213 and further.
629. The *Bundeskartellamt* considers the 'daily active users as the key indicator and relevant measure for assessing the network's competitive significance and market success'. *See:* Bundeskartellamt 15 February 2019 B6-22/16, *Facebook* (Case Summary), p. 6.
630. *Bundeskartellamt* 15 February 2019 B6-22/16, *Facebook* (Case Summary), p. 6.
631. *Bundeskartellamt* 6 February 2019 B6-22/16, *Facebook*, para. 305.

conditions 'agreed in unbalanced negotiation'.[632] According to the *Bundeskartellamt*, the GDPR is relevant in this regard, since it aims to 'counter asymmetries of power between organisations and individuals and ensure an appropriate balance of interests'. Against this backdrop, data protection safeguards the fundamental right to self-determination and the right to decide freely and without coercion on the processing of personal data.[633] The *Bundeskartellamt* continues by stressing that it is 'indispensable to examine conduct of dominant undertakings also in terms of their data processing procedures' and that the responsibility and consistency mechanism of the GDPR (*see* section 9.6.1) does not prevent the *Bundeskartellamt* from assessing compliance with the GDPR, since data protection regulations do not suspend abuse control.[634]

In the assessment of Facebook's conduct, the *Bundeskartellamt* first concludes that Facebook's comprehensive processing of personal data violates the requirements of the GDPR since effective consent pursuant to Article 6(1) sub a GDPR is lacking. Since Facebook does not need to process the data to fulfil its contractual requirements and no other justification grounds for processing are provided, there is no sufficient legal basis to justify data processing. This amounts to a violation of the GDPR, which in turn, is a manifestation (*Ausfluss*) of Facebook's market power and constitutes a restriction of the user's right to self-determination.[635] Moreover, Facebook's conduct would impede the position of competitors, because it provides Facebook with access to a large number of data sources, resulting in an unlawful competitive advantage and increased entry barriers.[636] In other words, Facebook's behaviour would provide it with a competitive advantage over undertakings that *do* comply with the GDPR. As a result, the *Bundeskartellamt* prohibited the data processing policy and ordered the termination of the conduct.[637] The *Bundeskartellamt* based this decision primarily on *exploitative abuse* vis-à-vis the user, but also addressed exclusionary abuse vis-à-vis competitors.[638]

The *Meta Bundeskartellamt* case was highly controversial and resulted in a lengthy legal battle. Initially, Meta successfully challenged the decision before the Higher Regional Court in Düsseldorf (*Oberlandesgericht Düsseldorf*) in an interim procedure. This court suspended the decision due to weaknesses in the motivation concerning the required proof of damage to

---

632. *Bundeskartellamt* 6 February 2019 B6-22/16, *Facebook*, para. 527; *Bundeskartellamt* 15 February 2019 B6-22/16, *Facebook* (Case Summary), p. 8; Bundeserichtshof 7 June 2016 AzKZR 6/15, Pechstein; Bundesgerichtshof 24 January 2017 Az KZR 47/14, VBL Gegenwert.
633. *Bundeskartellamt* 15 February 2019 B6-22/16 *Facebook* (Case Summary), p. 8.
634. *Bundeskartellamt* 15 February 2019 B6-22/16 *Facebook* (Case Summary), p. 9.
635. *Bundeskartellamt* 6 February 2019, B6-22/16, *Facebook*, para. 524.
636. *Bundeskartellamt* 15 February 2019 B6-22/16 *Facebook* (Case Summary), p. 11.
637. Sections 19(1) and 32 GWB.
638. Van den Bergh and Weber 2021, p. 34.

competition and causality.[639] In addition, the Higher Regional Court, *inter alia*, stressed that the criteria of Section 19(2) sub 2 GWB were not fulfilled since no but-for market scenario was put forward and criticised the lowering of the standard for causality.[640] The *Bundeskartellamt* appealed the decision in the interim procedure before the German Federal Supreme Court (*Bundesgerichthof*). This highest German court annulled the suspensive effect of the Higher Regional Court's decision. In its decision, the German Supreme Court emphasised the importance of users' personal autonomy and right to self-determination by arguing that there is a lack of choice for users who wish to use the platform, but have objections against sharing an excessive amount of data.[641] The interim decision was not the end of the story, and the proceedings on the merits continued before the Higher Regional Court which referred preliminary questions to the CJEU.

The CJEU ruled that it may be necessary for NCAs to examine whether an undertaking's conduct complies with rules other than those relating to competition, such as the GDPR.[642] After the CJEU's judgment, the proceedings before the Düsseldorf Higher Regional Court were no longer continued and ultimately terminated after Meta withdrew its appeal. In October 2024, the *Bundeskartellamt* issued a publication stressing that Meta had significantly improved the options regarding the combination of data and announced that it had closed the proceedings.[643]

4.4.3 The German Institutional and Enforcement Framework

This section further addresses, in turn, the German institutional and enforcement frameworks.

4.4.3.1 The German Institutional Framework

Within the German context, competition law is enforced at various levels. According to Section 48 GWB, competition law enforcement is the joint responsibility of the federal *Bundeskartellamt*, the Federal Ministry for Economic Affairs and Energy and the regional *Land* authorities. The

639. Oberlandesgericht Düsseldorf 28 August 2019 openJur 2019, 30575, Facebook Bundeskartellamt; *See also*: Van den Bergh and Weber 2021, p. 34; Podszun 2020, pp. 1271-1272.

640. Oberlandesgericht Düsseldorf 28 August 2019 openJur 2019, 30575, *Facebook Bundeskartellamt*, paras 7-19.

641. Bundesgerichtshof 23 June 2020 Decision Az KVR 69/19, *Facebook Bundeskartellamt*, para. 86.

642. CJEU 4 July 2023 Case C-252/21, *Meta Bundeskartellamt*, para. 48. The *Meta Bundeskartellamt* case and its implications for the relationship between competition law and the GDPR are further discussed in Chapter 6.

643. *Bundeskartellamt* 10 October 2024 B6-22/16, *Facebook* – Implementation of the Bundeskartellamt's decision of 6 February 2019.

Bundeskartellamt exercises its competence when anti-competitive conduct has an effect beyond the territory of a *Land.*[644] Furthermore, the *Bundeskartellamt* is the German authority responsible for applying Articles 101 and 102 TFEU.[645] The conduct of large platforms, i.e., the focus of the analysis, will most likely fall within the competence of the *Bundeskartellamt.* Therefore, the position of the *Land* authorities will not be taken into further consideration.[646]

The competences of the *Bundeskartellamt* are not limited to competition law, but also encompass certain elements of consumer law.[647] Yet, the range of competence of the German NCA is not as wide as the mandate of the Dutch ACM.[648] Electricity, gas and telecom regulation, for example, do not fall within the mandate of the *Bundeskartellamt*, but are instead enforced by the Federal Network Agency for Electricity, Gas, Telecommunication, Post and Railway.[649]

The independence of the *Bundeskartellamt* is set out in the GWB. According to Section 51(1) GWB, the authority acts as an independent higher federal authority (*selbständige Bundesoberbehörde*). Although the *Bundeskartellamt* is organisationally subordinate to the Ministry for Economic Affairs and Energy and can receive general instructions from the Ministry of Foreign Affairs, the authority enjoys independence in substantive terms.[650] Despite their organisational links, the Ministry cannot impose instructions regarding substantive issues.[651] The internal structure of the *Bundeskartellamt* is arguably more similar to the organisation of German courts than to the hierarchical organisation of other executive agencies. According to Podszun and Overhoff, this means that the *Bundeskartellamt* 'seems to be pretty immune from political influence'.[652]

4.4.3.2 The German Enforcement Framework

The *Bundeskartellamt* has several investigative and decision-making powers at its disposal. The German authority can take an *infringement decision* and

644. Section 48(2) GWB.
645. Section 50(1) GWB.
646. *See* in this regard Section 49 GWB.
647. The 9th amendment of the GWB granted the *Bundeskartellamt* with competencies in the field of consumer protection. The *Bundeskartellamt* can, for example, launch a sector-inquiry if there is a suspicion that consumer law has been violated and can act as an amicus curiae in a consumer law procedure. *See:* Neuntes Gesetz zur Änderung des Gesetzes gegen Wettbewerbsbeschränkungen 1 June 2017, Bundesgesetzblatt Jahrgang 2017, nr. 33.
648. *See* sections 4.3.3.1 and 8.3.2.
649. Section 47a GWB.
650. Section 52 GWB.
651. *See also* Article 87(3) Grundgesetz für die Bundesrepublik Deutschland (Basic Law for the Federal Republic of Germany).
652. Podszun and Overhoff 2024, p. 8.

may order the termination of a violation in accordance with Section 32(1) GWB. Moreover, the authority may adopt *commitments*. The *Bundeskartellamt* can declare such commitments binding according to Section 32b GWB. The German provision on commitments is clearly modelled on Article 9 Regulation 1/2003.[653] This reflects an endeavour on the German legislator's behalf to align the procedural instruments of EU and German competition law.[654] Furthermore, the *Bundeskartellamt* may impose interim measures pursuant to Section 32a GWB. Interim measures may be imposed if (i) an infringement is more likely than not to exist and if provisional measures are (ii) necessary to protect competition or due to an imminent threat of serious harm to another undertaking. On paper, the German standard for interim measures is not identical to the high European threshold. It appears easier to adopt interim measures under the GWB, since the legal standard is formulated less stringently than its EU equivalent. Yet, in practice, the interpretation of the German threshold seems to be rather high as well. In this light, the relevance of interim measures is – also in the German context – questioned.[655]

The German NCA has the competence to impose a range of remedies. According to Section 81 GWB, the authority may impose *fines* for violations of EU or German competition law. The amount of the fine will be determined in line with Section 81c GWB, in conjunction with the Fining Guidelines of the *Bundeskartellamt*.[656] The GWB sets a 10% fine cap for intentionally committed offences.[657] Moreover, the *Bundeskartellamt* can impose *behavioural* remedies, or *structural* remedies if there is no equally effective behavioural remedy available.[658] Furthermore, according to Section 32(3), the *Bundeskartellamt* has the competence to reimburse benefits generated through the infringement.[659] If the *Bundeskartellamt* concludes that there is no ground for taking any action, it can issue a decision stating that it will not exercise its power to render an infringement decision or adopt interim measures.[660]

Apart from addressing the conduct of individual firms, the *Bundeskartellamt* can start an investigation into a specific sector or across sectors.[661] With the 11th Amendment to the GWB, the German legislator significantly

---

653. Otto 2020, paras 1 and 2.
654. Bach 2020, para. 2.
655. Otto 2020, paras 1-2.
656. Bundeskartellamt, Guidelines for the Setting of Fines in Cartel Administrative Offence Proceedings 7 October 2021.
657. Section 81(4)(2) GWB; *See also*: Koenig and Bremenkamp 2022, p. 11.
658. Section 32(1)(2) GWB.
659. Section 32(2a) GWB.
660. Section 32c GWB.
661. Such investigation can also be started if the *Bundeskartellamt* has reasonable ground to suspect substantial, permanent or repeated infringements of consumer law. *See* Section 32e(5) GWB.

strengthened the instrument of the sector inquiry (*Sektoruntersuchung*). The instrument of the sector inquiry was already part of the GWB before the 11th Amendment. However, such sector inquiries usually ended with a report of the *Bundeskartellamt*, with no further remedies available. With the 11th Amendment to the GWB, the German instrument of the sector inquiry has obtained significantly stronger teeth.

In the Explanatory Memorandum to the 11th Amendment, the German legislator acknowledges that competition law has so far emphasised the behaviour of firms. As a result, existing anti-competitive or dysfunctional structures, as well as oligopolistic markets, could not be addressed adequately.[662] To address these shortcomings, the German legislator has reinforced the instrument of the sector inquiry. According to Section 32f(3) GWB, following a sector inquiry, the *Bundeskartellamt* is granted the power to determine, within 18 months from the start of the sector inquiry and by means of an order, that there is a 'significant and continuous malfunctioning of competition' on at least one market which is at least nation-wide, on several individual markets or across markets.[663] Section 32f(5) GWB further specifies the concept of malfunctioning of competition. Such *malfunctioning* exists, in particular, in the case of: (i) unilateral supply or demand power; (ii) restriction on market entry, exit or switching possibilities; (iii) uniform or coordinated behaviour; or (iv) input or customer foreclosure. Additionally, Section 32f(5) GWB lists factors to examine whether there is an interference with *competition*. These factors include, *inter alia*, the number, size, financial strength and turnover of the undertakings active in the market, the interrelationships of undertakings affected and prices, quantity, choice and quality of the products offered in the market. A restraint of competition is considered to be *continuous* if it has 'existed permanently over a period of three years or has occurred repeatedly and there is no indication […] that the restraint is more likely than not to cease within two years'.[664]

In the case of a *significant and continuing malfunctioning of competition*, the *Bundeskartellamt* can counteract the identified malfunctioning by imposing structural or behavioural remedies. Such remedies are a matter of last resort and should only be adopted when the application of the other powers under the GWB[665] is unlikely to be sufficiently effective.[666] The

662. Referentenentwurf des Bundesministeriums für Wirtschaft und Klimaschutz 15 September 2022, Entwurf eines Gesetzes zur Verbesserung der Wettbewerbsstrukturen und zur Abschöpfung von Vorteilen aus Wettbewerbsverstößen (Wettbewerbsdurchsetzungsgesetz), p. 1.
663. This quote is taken from an unofficial translation (*see:* https://www.d-kart.de/wp-content/uploads/2023/05/GWB11-engl.pdf accessed 29 August 2025). The original Section 32f(3) GWB refers to 'eine erhebliche und fortwährende Störung des Wettbewerbs'.
664. Section 32f(7) GWB.
665. That is, the termination of anticompetitive conduct (Section 32 GWB), interim measures (Section 32a GWB), commitments (Section 32b GWB) (or a decision not to intervene (Section 32c GWB)).

remedies should be addressed to one or more undertakings, and it is not necessary to establish an abuse of a dominant position.[667] These undertakings *may* have contributed significantly to the distortion of competition by their behaviour, and in selecting the addressees of the remedies, the market position of the undertakings concerned should be taken into account.[668] Section 32f(3) GWB provides a non-exhaustive list of behavioural and structural remedies that may be imposed. These include measures to grant access to data, interfaces, networks or other facilities; requirements for business relationships between companies; obligations to establish transparent, open and non-discriminatory norms and standards; requirements for certain forms of contracts; the prohibition on unilateral disclosure of information and the organisational separation of company or business divisions. Moreover, the *Bundeskartellamt* may require undertakings with market dominance or undertakings with paramount significance for competition across markets to dispose shares or assets if it is expected that 'this measure will eliminate or substantially reduce the significant and continuing malfunctioning of competition'.[669] Such measures can only be taken if the other previously mentioned 'new' remedies are not possible, not equally effective or more burdensome for the undertaking concerned.[670]

Amendment 11 of the GWB allows for structural intervention, even in the absence of anticompetitive conduct. This approach arguably amounts to a paradigm shift in German competition law, since it entails a far-reaching competition law instrument encompassing intervention powers to address market structures.[671] Such an approach either amounts to a revolution of competition law or further blurs the boundaries between competition law and market design by regulation by adopting an instrument with regulatory features in the competition law framework of the GWB.[672] According to Körber, Section 19a GWB and Section 32f reflect a broader trend towards a more *ex-ante* regulation.[673]

Given the significance of the Amendment, it is unsurprising that the development has fostered a great deal of (academic) debate. Critics of the

666. Pauer 2023, p. 355.
667. The application of Section 32f GWB is 'misbrauchsunabhängig'. *See:* Bundesministerium für Wirtschaft und Klimaschutz 2023.
668. Section 32(f) GWB.
669. Section 32(f)4 GWB.
670. Section 32f(4) GWB.
671. According to Mundt, this is not necessarily the case, since the current paradigm entails 'das Vertrouwen in die Kräfte eines functionerenden Wettbewerb', which does not necessarily exclude the approach taken in Amendment 11 GWB. In contrast, Körber argues that 'Das wäre ein grundlegender Paradigmenwechsel' *See:* Mundt 2023; Körber 2023. *See also*: Pauer 2023, p. 356; Wagner-von Papp 2023a.
672. Wagner-von Papp 2022, p. 607.
673. The President of the ACM, for example, pleas in favour of the adoption of a similar instrument in the Dutch context. *See:* Snoep 2024; Körber 2023, p. 6.

approach emphasise the risk of over-enforcement and consider the competence to be a *carte blanche* for the *Bundeskartellamt*.[674] The instrument arguably does not allow for a distinction between 'good' and 'bad' monopolies.[675] Moreover, the *Bundeskartellamt's* freedom to determine which sectors or industries should be subject to *ex-ante* regulation is considered unconstitutional: such regulatory choices would belong in the realm of the legislator.[676] This criticism relates to the broad scope of the instrument. Proponents of the instrument highlight the exceptional nature of the novel remedies, as well as the procedural safeguards. Given the controversies surrounding the tool, it is expected that future enforcement actions will lead to litigation. At this point, the Amendment was only adopted quite recently, and there is no experience with its application yet. Therefore, it is too early to draw any conclusions regarding the practical relevance of the remedy.[677]

4.4.4 German Competition Law: Final Remarks

Generally speaking, the German competition law framework is broader in scope than its EU law counterpart. The prohibition of abuse of dominance has a wider application and also includes relative or superior market power as well as the concept of undertakings with a paramount position in relation to competitors. Furthermore, and importantly, Germany takes a central position in the regulation of Big Tech platforms. The German legislator is very proactive, adopting multiple instruments without an EU counterpart. Section 19a GWB constitutes a clear example in this regard, particularly because the tool was adopted prior to the DMA. The ambitious attitude of the German legislator has not diminished following the adoption of Section 19a GWB. The newly adopted Section 32f GWB provides another example of the introduction of a revolutionary instrument of competition law in the national context. Admittedly, the instrument to a certain extent resembles the New Competition Tool, which was proposed by the Commission in 2020, but which was never adopted.[678] The New Competition Tool aimed to provide a market-based tool to address structural competition problems relating to market characteristics such as network effects, scale and scope economies and lock-in effects, as well as structural market failures such as high

674. Körber 2023, p. 6.
675. Wagner-von Papp 2022, p. 606.
676. Grünwald et al. 2023.
677. *See also*: Budzinski 2023.
678. The fact that the German legislator adopted the instrument, despite the fact that the Commission did not, results in criticism. Körber, for example, stresses that the German legislator did not explain explicitly why a tool would not be necessary in the EU context, but would have merit in the German context. This line of reasoning questions the necessity of the instrument. *See:* Körber 2023, p. 7.

concentration and barriers to entry.[679] Since the New Competition Tool never made it to the finish line, Section 32f enters uncharted territory, and its practical implications remain unpredictable.[680]

In the German context, the legislator is not the only proactive actor in the context of competition law. The German *Bundeskartellamt* also acts as a forerunner. The authority demonstrates a willingness to engage in controversial theories of harm. The *Meta Bundeskartellamt* case is particularly groundbreaking in the context of personal data markets. In this case, the *Bundeskartellamt* incorporated elements of data protection law in the context of the assessment of an abuse of dominance, thereby 'internalising' GDPR considerations into competition law.

4.5 CONCLUSION

This chapter analysed whether and how the competition law framework can address problems related to abuse of dominance by large platforms in personal data markets with a focus on the EU, Dutch and German frameworks. Over the years, competition law authorities have gained experience with the application of EU and national competition law to personal data markets. Initially, it appeared challenging to apply the 'traditional' competition law framework to personal data markets as some existing tools did not align with the new economic reality.[681] Yet, by virtue of the competition law's flexibility, tools and instruments have been updated and adjusted.

At the *EU* level, the Commission, for example, adopted an updated Notice on the Relevant Market, taking stock of the characteristics of digital markets.[682] Moreover, in several cases, theories of harm were tweaked or even introduced. The *Google Shopping* case and subsequent litigation in which the conduct of self-preferencing is recognised as a novel type of abuse, constitutes a clear example in this regard.[683]

The Commission is not the only authority playing an active role in addressing anti-competitive conduct by large platforms. Digital markets are high on the agenda of the authorities of various Member States, and both the Dutch and German NCA have adopted decisions resulting in behavioural changes of Big Tech. The *Dutch* authority is ambitious and aims to play a key

679. European Commission, Inception Impact Assessment New Competition Tool (NCT), 4 June 2020, (2020)2877634, p. 2.
680. Schwintowski 2023, p. 172.
681. Zingales et al. 2019; Furman et al. 2019.
682. Commission Notice of 22 February 2024 on the definition of the relevant market for the purpose of Union competition law, C/2024/1645.
683. European Commission 27 June 2017, Case AT397, *Google Shopping*; GC 10 November 2021 Case T-612/17, *Google Shopping* CJEU 10 September 2024 Case C-48/22P, *Google Shopping*.

role in curbing platform power. So far, this authority has played in particular a pioneering role by addressing exploitative behaviour on markets for app stores.[684] Furthermore, *Germany* acts as a forerunner. Traditionally, German competition law casts a wider net and is broader in scope than its EU counterpart. Legislative developments have broadened the scope of German competition law even further. The German framework, for example, explicitly qualifies the refusal to supply data as a potential abuse in Section 20(1a) GWB. Section 19a GWB provides a swift procedure and lowers the burden of proof for the *Bundeskartellamt*. Moreover, the newly adopted Section 32f GWB allows structural competition problems to be addressed. Apart from the proactive and innovative attitude of the German legislator, the *Bundeskartellamt* acts as a forerunner. It not only actively applies the Section 19a GWB to large platforms but also adopted the pioneering *Meta Bundeskartellamt* decision.[685]

Experience with personal data markets shows that competition law remains a suitable instrument for addressing issues associated with platform power. Yet, certain challenges remain, particularly concerning the length of procedures. This is problematic in light of digital markets which require swift intervention due to the fact that such markets are prone to tipping.[686] The development of the framework and new theories of harm is a time-consuming process. Competition law cases tend to extend over years or even decades. In this light, it will take a substantial amount of time before the CJEU can confirm new theories and approaches. Admittedly, within the competition law framework, several procedural tools can expedite proceedings. Instruments such as commitment decisions and interim measures can facilitate a swifter approach. However, in the EU, The Netherlands and Germany, interim measures are rarely used. At this point, the practical relevance of interim measures is limited.

In sum, the competition law framework is developing, albeit not always at a sufficiently rapid pace. Developments are fostered not only by action at the EU level but also Member States (and particularly Germany) contribute to the development of the competition law framework by experimentation and the introduction of novel (procedural) tools and instruments. In my view, this is a necessary and positive development. Yet, divergent enforcement actions result in a risk of incoherencies.[687] Against this background, it is inevitable that these approaches should be coordinated and that different authorities cooperate. This need for cooperation does not only relate to the intra-disciplinary competition law context but also has a cross-disciplinary dimension. Shortcomings of the competition law framework are not merely addressed by changes to the framework itself, but also by the introduction of

---

684. ACM 24 August 2021 ACM/19/035630, *Apple* (Case Summary).
685. *Bundeskartellamt* 15 February 2019 B6-22/16, *Facebook* (Case Summary).
686. *See* section 2.6.
687. Mândrescu 2024b, p. 116.

novel instruments, such as the DMA. On top of this, due to the monetisation of personal data, competition law overlaps to an increasing extent with the GDPR. The overlap between competition law on the one hand, and the DMA and the GDPR, on the other hand, is further discussed in Chapters 5 and 6.

Chapter 5

Competition Law and the DMA

5.1 INTRODUCTION

This chapter studies the relationship between the DMA and competition law. The DMA, which became applicable in May 2023 after a relatively swift legislative procedure, was adopted as part of the Commission's *Digital Service Act Package.*[688] The DMA aims to ensure *contestable* and *fair* markets by imposing prohibitions and obligations upon so-called *gatekeepers*. The DMA and the competition law framework share important traits, and the DMA aims to resolve certain shortcomings of competition law.[689] To this end, the DMA not only addresses issues resulting from the behaviour of dominant firms but also problems associated with the structure of the market. On top of this, the DMA aims to remedy competition law's lack of speed by establishing competences to address certain procedural pitfalls of competition law.[690] Yet, the EU legislator does not qualify the DMA as competition law.[691] This begs the question of how the domains of competition law and the

688. The Digital Service Act Package consists of the DMA and the DSA and has the objective to facilitate an ambitious reform of the digital space by creating a safer digital environment and by establishing a level playing field on digital markets. *See:* European Commission, Press Release 15 December 2020, Europe fit for the Digital Age: Commission proposes new rules for digital platforms, IP/20/2347, 1, p. 8.
689. Commission Staff Working Document Impact Assessment Report Accompanying the document Proposal for a Regulation of the European Parliament and of the Council on contestable and fair markets in the digital sector (Digital Markets Act), SWD(2020) 363 final.
690. Andriychuk 2022, p. 124; Bostoen 2023b, pp. 264-265.
691. Preamble DMA, recital 11; Vestager 2021.

DMA relate to each other. This chapter zooms in on the relationship between competition law and the DMA by analysing to what extent the fields overlap and by assessing what the relationship between the instruments is (or should be).

To this end, section 5.2 provides an overview of the legal framework of the DMA. The relationship is further analysed in accordance with the analytical structure provided in the Introduction of Part II. I study the interaction between the DMA and competition law by mapping the common features and main differences in section 5.3. Subsequently, section 5.4 further analyses the interaction and aims to position the DMA in the broader regulatory context. Section 5.5 provides the conclusion to the chapter.

5.2 THE LEGAL FRAMEWORK OF THE DMA

This Section sets out the legal framework of the DMA by discussing the instrument's: (i) objectives, (ii) scope, (iii) substantive provisions, and (iv) the enforcement and institutional framework.

5.2.1 Objectives

The DMA aims 'to contribute to the proper functioning of the internal market by laying down harmonised rules ensuring for all businesses, contestable and fair markets in the digital sector across the Union where gatekeepers are present for all businesses users and end users'.[692] Consequently, the instrument serves a dual objective of *contestability* and *fairness* for the benefit of business users and end users.[693] Both objectives are intertwined: weak contestability on particular markets potentially allows undertakings to engage in unfair practices.[694] At the same time, unfair practices can reduce the ability of competitors to contest the gatekeeper's position.[695] On top of this, the DMA has a *market integration* goal, since it aims to contribute to the functioning of the internal market.[696]

The DMA aims to guarantee *contestability* on markets where gatekeepers are present. In the context of the DMA, contestability relates 'to the ability of undertakings to effectively overcome barriers to entry and

692. Article 1(1) DMA.
693. Article 1(1) DMA.
694. In the Preamble of the DMA, the EU legislator establishes a clear connection between the principles of fairness and contestability. The concepts are intertwined and a lack of or weak contestability can enable a gatekeeper to engage in unfair practices. Similarly, unfair practices can reduce competitor's possibility to contest the gatekeepers position. *See:* Preamble DMA, recitals 16 and 34; *See also*: Crémer et al. 2023b, p. 107.
695. DMA, Preamble para. 34.
696. Podszun 2024, p. 12.

expansion and challenge the gatekeeper on the merits of their products and services'.[697] The DMA endorses a rather broad interpretation of contestability, since it not only focuses on competition *on* the market and short-term entry but also includes obligations relating to competition *for* the market and competition on *other* markets.[698] This is, for example, reflected in the prohibition of self-preferencing of Article 6(5) DMA, which focuses on competition on other markets.[699] Despite this broad interpretation, in the DMA, contestability is understood in a very particular context since it is clearly linked to entry barriers resulting from the gatekeeper position of large platforms.[700]

Next, the DMA aims to safeguard *fairness*. Despite the fact that fairness is a broad and elusive concept, the DMA attempts to provide a definition by stressing that unfairness should relate to 'an imbalance between the rights and obligations of business users where the gatekeeper obtains a disproportionate advantage'.[701] Although the Preamble to the DMA provides a clue as to the interpretation of the fairness principle in the context of the DMA, the exact meaning of the principle remains unclear. An important interpretative element for defining the fairness principle relates to the question of *to whom* an outcome should be fair. In the context of the DMA, there is no unequivocal answer to this question. In interpreting the principle of fairness, recital 10 of the DMA's preamble emphasises the position of *business* users. Yet, Article 1(1) DMA stresses that the instrument must be applied for the benefit of *both* business and *end users*. This indicates that the DMA has a *vertical* dimension.

Finally, the DMA aims to safeguard the *functioning of the internal market*. According to the Preamble to the DMA, a number of initiatives at the national level aim to address the issues of unfairness and a lack of contestability on gatekeeper markets. Divergent national regulations can amount to a risk of fragmentation of the internal market.[702] Against this backdrop, the DMA aims to provide a framework of harmonised rules.[703]

---

697. DMA, Preamble para. 32.
698. Schweitzer 2021, p. 8.
699. Beems 2023, p. 5.
700. Budzinski and Mendelsohn 2021, p. 17.
701. Preamble DMA, recital 33.
702. Preamble DMA, recitals 6 and 7; The existence of these divergent national solutions have been subject to debate. Some authors stress that the sources of regulatory fragmentation are not properly identified and specified in the DMA Proposal, nor in the Impact Assessment. *See* for a more elaborate analysis: Lamadrid de Pablo and Bayón Fernández 2021.
703. Witt 2023, p. 660.

5.2.2 Scope

According to Article 1(1) DMA, the instrument applies to 'core platform services provided or offered by gatekeepers'. The DMA provides a list of *core platform services*, including online intermediaries, online search engines, online social networking services, video-sharing platforms and online advertisement services.[704] Consequently, the DMA applies to a wide range of services and a broad variety of business models. The DMA is not limited to a specific service or economic sector, but covers multiple services relevant to most sectors of the economy.[705] Despite the broadness of the DMA's scope, the different core platform services share a number of characteristics, such as extreme economies of scale, very strong network effects, an ability to connect many businesses and end users through the multi-sidedness of the service, lock-in effects and vertical integration.[706] As a result, such markets tend to be highly concentrated, and a small number of large platforms enjoy considerable economic power.[707] The Commission can conduct a market investigation for the purpose of investigating whether other services within the digital economy should be added to the list of core platform services providers.[708]

The DMA obligations do not apply to all providers of core platform services. Rather, only undertakings with a particular position can be designated as a *gatekeeper.* Article 3(1) DMA sets out what a gatekeeper exactly entails, i.e., an undertaking: (i) with a significant impact on the internal market, (ii) providing a core platform service which is an important gateway for business users to reach end users, and (iii) enjoying an entrenched and durable position in its operations or foreseeably will enjoy such position in the near future. If an undertaking meets the quantitative thresholds of Article 3(2) DMA, it is presumed to meet the mentioned criteria.[709] If an undertaking has: (i) an annual turnover equal to or above EUR 7.5 billion in each of the last three financial years;[710] (ii) its core platform service has at least 45 million monthly active end users established or located in the Union and at least 10,000 yearly active business users established in the Union; and (iii) has met the aforementioned criteria in each of at least three financial years, it is presumed to have a gatekeeper position. If an undertaking meets the above-mentioned quantitative criteria, it is

704. Article 2(2) DMA.
705. Larouche and De Streel 2021, p. 545.
706. *See* Chapter 2.
707. Preamble DMA, paras 2-3.
708. Article 19(1) DMA.
709. The quantitative criteria of Article 3(2) DMA are subject to criticism. Geradin, for example, questions to what extent absolute numbers provide a useful parameter to assess whether an undertaking serves as an important gateway. *See:* Geradin 2021, pp. 14-15.
710. Or where its average market capitalisation or its equivalent fair market value amounted to at least EUR 75 billion in the last financial year, and it provides the same core platform service in at least three Member States.

obliged to notify the Commission thereof without delay, or in any case, two months after those thresholds are met.[711] Importantly, the turnover requirement applies to the undertaking of which the core platform provider is part and not merely to the revenue of the core platform service.[712] The last criterion, according to which the turnover and amount of user requirements have to be met for at least three financial years, provides new market entrants with leeway. New market players have a three-year immunity from designation. During this 'gratis vacation time', the entrants can scale up, mature and institutionalise their market presence.[713]

Despite the importance of the presumptions of Article 3(2), the DMA incorporates mechanisms to prevent over-inclusiveness or under-inclusiveness stemming from the application of a quantitative standard.[714] To prevent *over-inclusiveness*, an undertaking can rebut the presumption of a gatekeeping position by providing arguments demonstrating that it does not meet the qualitative criteria of Article 3(1) DMA, despite the fact that it does meet the quantitative thresholds of Article 3(2) DMA. According to the DMA's text, such rebuttals are exceptional.[715] The Commission can reject the rebuttal if the arguments submitted by the undertaking are 'not sufficiently substantiated because they do not manifestly call into question the presumption'.[716] If the arguments *are* sufficiently substantiated, the Commission can conduct a market investigation to assess whether the undertaking demonstrated that the relevant core platform service does not satisfy the requirements of Article 3(1) DMA. Apple, for example, successfully rebutted the gatekeeper presumption for iMessage, and Microsoft filed successful rebuttal for its Bing and Edge services.[717] Similarly, X successfully rebutted its

711. Article 3(3) DMA. If an undertaking fails to meet this notification requirement, the Commission can request information. If the undertaking concerned fails to provide access to the requested information, the Commission may impose a fine of maximum 1% of the undertaking's total worldwide turnover in the preceding year. *See also*: Article 21 DMA; Article 30(3)(e) DMA.
712. Geradin 2021, p. 12.
713. Andriychuk 2022, p. 127.
714. Chirico 2021, p. 494.
715. Article 3(5) DMA.
716. Article 3(5) DMA.
717. Summary of Commission Decision of 12 February 2024 relating to a decision pursuant to Article 17(3) of Regulation (EU) 2022/1925, Cases DMA100015 – *Microsoft* – Online Search Engines, DMA100028 – *Microsoft* – Web Browsers, DMA100034 – *Microsoft* – Online Advertising Services; Summary of Commission Decision of 5 September 2023 relating to a decision pursuant to Article 3 of Regulation (EU) 2022/1925, Cases DMA100020 – *Meta* – online social networking services; DMA100024 – *Meta* – Number-independent interpersonal communications services; DMA100035 – *Meta* – Online advertising services; DMA100044 – *Meta* – Online intermediation services – Marketplace.

qualification as a gatekeeper in relation to its online social networking service.[718]

In the *ByteDance* judgment, the GC addressed the topic of rebuttal for the first time. According to ByteDance, the Commission erred in concluding that the arguments presented to rebut the presumption of Article 3(2) DMA were not sufficiently substantiated so as to manifestly call into question the presumption. ByteDance criticised: (i) the rejection of certain 'qualitative' arguments and evidence; as well as (ii) the high standard of proof consisting in requiring 'convincing' evidence.[719]

In its judgment, the GC highlights that it may be difficult, if not impossible, to distinguish between quantitative and qualitative evidence and that qualitative arguments are not to be excluded from the assessment. Both quantitative and qualitative arguments may be invoked, insofar as they relate to the quantitative criteria.[720] Moreover, the list of elements that may be taken into account according to recital 23 of the DMA's preamble is not exhaustive.[721]

The only category of arguments or evidence explicitly excluded as irrelevant by the EU legislator is 'those deriving from a justification on economic grounds seeking to enter into market definition or to demonstrate efficiencies'.[722] Other arguments would be admissible, provided that they are sufficiently substantiated to manifestly call into question the presumptions. Rather than focusing on *what* may be argued, the GC highlights the relevance of *how* arguments should be substantiated.[723] With regard to the standard of proof, the CJEU clarifies that the standard of proof to rebut the presumption of a gatekeeper position is high and that it is not sufficient to prove the existence of mere doubts or prima facie evidence.[724]

Consequently, the *ByteDance* case shows that the bar for rebutting the quantitative presumption of the gatekeeper is rather high.[725] Moreover, although the GC allows for the consideration of a non-exhaustive list of arguments, it avoids competition law-like analysis by confirming that arguments relating to market definition or efficiencies cannot be taken into account. This can safeguard the speedy designation of gatekeepers, which is necessary to keep up with rapidly changing market developments in the digital realm.[726] Furthermore, despite the fact that the Commission had made

718. European Commission 13 May 2024, Case DMA100232, *X – Online advertising services*.
719. GC 17 July 2024, Case T-1077/23, *Bytedance*, paras 34 and 36.
720. GC 17 July 2024, Case T-1077/23, *Bytedance*, paras 59 and 60.
721. GC 17 July 2024, Case T-1077/23, *Bytedance*, paras 39-45; Butorac Malnar and Kunda 2024, p. 245.
722. GC 17 July 2024, Case T-1077/23, *Bytedance*, para. 46.
723. Butorac Malnar and Kunda 2024, p. 245.
724. GC 17 July 2024, Case T-1077/23, *Bytedance*, para. 71.
725. Van den Boom and Hinck 2024.
726. Butorac Malnar and Kunda 2024, p. 246.

some small procedural errors, the GC did not annul the designation. This implies that the GC is largely limiting itself to ensuring that all the evidence and arguments have been given due consideration.[727] The *ByteDance* case is currently under review at the CJEU, and the outcome of this case will reveal whether the CJEU is aligned with the Commission and the GC.[728]

To prevent *under-inclusiveness*, a gatekeeper can also be designated if the quantitative criteria are not met. The Commission can conduct a market investigation taking into account various considerations, including the size of the undertaking, the number of businesses and end users, the network effects and data-driven advantages, any scale and scope effects from which the undertaking benefits, user lock-ins, the vertical integration of an undertaking and other structural business or service characteristics.[729] The Commission, for example, designated Apple for its operating system for iPad, despite the fact that the quantitative thresholds were not met. The Commission reflected on Apple's ability to act as a gatekeeper in relation to iPad operating systems, and considered, *inter alia*, Apple's user numbers and the lock-in of consumers and businesses.[730] The market investigation-based designation is more burdensome for the Commission, but arguably generates more accurate and future-proof results than the more 'crude' quantitative metrics of Article 3(2) DMA.[731]

If an undertaking meets the criteria of Article 3 DMA, the Commission can designate the provider of the core platform services as a gatekeeper. The Commission has designated multiple platforms providing different core platform services.[732] To date, the Commission has designated seven gatekeepers, offering a range of core platform services, including social networks, a number of independent communication services, intermediation platforms, a video sharing platform, a search engine, web browsers, providers of advertisement services and operating systems. So far, the Commission has designated several Big Tech platforms as gatekeepers, namely Alphabet,[733] Amazon,[734] Apple,[735] ByteDance,[736] Meta,[737] Microsoft[738] and Booking.com.[739]

727. Humpe et al. 2024, p. 112.
728. CJEU Case C-627/24P, *ByteDance v. Commission* (Case in Progress).
729. Article 3(8) DMA; Article 17(1) DMA.
730. Commission Decision of 29 April 2024, Case DMA100047, *Apple – iPadOS.*
731. Akman 2022, p. 92.
732. For an overview of the designated gatekeepers, *see:* https://digital-markets-act.ec.europa.eu/gatekeepers_en accessed 29 August 2025.
733. For the provision of Google Maps, Google Play, Google Shopping, YouTube, Google Ads, Chrome, Google Search and Google Android.
734. For Amazon Marketplace and Amazon Ads.
735. For App Store, Safari, iOs and iPadiOS.
736. For Tiktok.
737. For Facebook, Instagram, Whatsapp, Messenger, Meta Marketplace and Meta Ads.
738. For LinkedIn and Windows PC OS.
739. For Booking.com.

5.2.3 Substantive Obligations and Prohibitions

According to Article 3(10) DMA, a gatekeeper shall comply with the DMA obligations within six months after being designated by the Commission. The DMA's substantive obligations are enshrined in Articles 5, 6 and 7 DMA. Despite the fact that all obligations apply automatically, the obligations of Article 5 are 'self-executing', whereas the obligations of Article 6 are 'susceptible of being further specified'.[740] This means that Article 6 DMA allows for a regulatory dialogue between the gatekeeper and the Commission. However, the regulatory dialogue is not a *condition sine qua non* in order for Article 6 DMA to be enforceable.[741] Lastly, Article 7 contains specific rules regarding horizontal interoperability for communication applications. The complexity of such services renders a specific provision necessary.[742]

The obligations listed in the DMA are per se rules, which means that the Commission does not have to establish the anticompetitive effects or the effect on consumer welfare in order to establish a violation of the DMA. As such, the listed behaviour is illegal.[743] Although per se obligations yield certain advantages, particularly relating to cost and time efficiencies, such obligations are by their nature blunt and error-prone.[744] Furthermore, there is very limited room for justifying a violation. Generally, the DMA does not allow for efficiency defences. Yet, two lines of defence can be invoked by an undertaking. In 'exceptional circumstances', the Commission can suspend the application of certain DMA provisions insofar as these obligations would endanger gatekeeper's 'economic viability' of operations in the EU.[745] Furthermore, the Commission may grant exemptions on grounds of public health and public security.[746] In order to suspend the application of DMA obligations for a certain gatekeeper, the Commission must adopt an implementing act. Hence, the application of an exemption ground requires the Commission's prior approval. Moreover, the grounds of public health and public security must arguably be interpreted narrowly.[747]

Apart from the general exemption grounds, some of the specific obligations provide leeway to balance different interests. For instance,

740. Some academics express their critique on the distinction between the obligations in Articles 5 and 6 DMA. It is, for example, argued that – from an economic perspective and in light of the underlying theories of harm – the conduct listed in Article 6 is not necessarily less relevant or more ambivalent that the behaviour listed in Article 5. *See, e.g.*, Budzinski and Mendelsohn 2021, p. 13.
741. Akman 2022, p. 96.
742. De Streel et al. 2020, p. 32.
743. Witt 2023, p. 641.
744. Witt 2023, p. 665.
745. Article 9 DMA.
746. Article 10 DMA.
747. These exception grounds are not a novelty of the DMA, but can be found in multiple instruments in internal market law. In the past, the grounds have been interpreted very

Article 5(6) DMA clarifies that the prohibition to prevent or restrict business or end users from raising any issue of non-compliance with the EU or national authorities does not prejudice the possibility of agreeing on the use of lawful complaint mechanisms. Moreover, several obligations leave room to consider data protection law. Article 5(9) and 5(10) DMA, for example, allow consideration of the publisher's and advertiser's consent concerning the provision of information relating to advertisements. Furthermore, despite the obligation of Article 6(4) DMA to enable the installation of third-party software, gatekeepers are not prevented from taking necessary and proportionate measures to ensure that third-party software does not endanger the integrity of the hardware or operating system.

Despite the fact that the DMA relies on a closed-shop list with pre-defined obligations and prohibitions, the instrument does provide some flexibility. Articles 12 and 19 DMA empower the Commission to adopt delegated acts to update the obligations of Articles 5 and 6 DMA based on a market investigation.[748] Given the rapidly changing and innovative nature of digital markets, a degree of flexibility is a prerequisite for guaranteeing the effective application of the DMA in the future.[749] Yet, the Commission's freedom to update is not unlimited. After conducting a market investigation, the Commission can add obligations that address the contestability of core platform service or services that are unfair *in the same way* as the practices of Articles 5 and 6 DMA. Furthermore, the delegated act can only: (i) extend obligations that only apply to certain core platform services to other core platform services; (ii) extend obligations that benefit certain business or end users to benefit other business or end users; (iii) specify the way in which the existing obligations are to be performed; (iv) extend obligations to other services that are provided with, or in support of core platform services; (v) extend obligations that apply to certain types of data to other types of data; (vi) add further conditions where an obligation imposes certain conditions on the behaviour of a gatekeeper; and (vii) apply these obligations that govern a certain relation to another relation.

Consequently, the Commission does not have *carte blanche* to come up with entirely novel obligations. For such adjustments, a delegated act does not suffice. Rather, the Commission would have to rely on the legislative procedure by submitting a legislative proposal to update the DMA. Such legislative action cannot be taken without the involvement of the Council and the European Parliament.[750]

---

narrowly. Since the DMA is also adopted on the basis of Article 114 TFEU, it is likely that the exemptions of Article 10 DMA will be applied in a narrow way. *See:* Kessedjian 2007.

748. *See also* Article 49 DMA.
749. Preamble DMA, recital 77; Beems, Van de Gronden and Rusu 2023, p. 69.
750. Witt 2023, p. 652.

The closed-shop list of the DMA contains several substantive obligations ranging, for example, from a prohibition to combine data sets to an obligation to provide access to information to advertisers. In line with the unidirectional focus, the substantive obligations of the DMA are discussed in relation to (potentially) overlapping abuses of a dominant position. A more detailed analysis of the different prohibitions and obligations of the DMA is provided in section 5.3.2.

5.2.4 The Institutional and Enforcement Framework

The DMA not only establishes a substantive framework but also lays down a detailed enforcement and institutional framework. The institutional and enforcement framework is discussed respectively in this section.

5.2.4.1 The Institutional Framework

The DMA is enforced in a (largely) centralised fashion at the EU level. The Commission is the 'sole enforcer' of the DMA and the only authority competent to apply the regulation.[751] The centralised nature of the institutional framework aims to ensure the uniform application of EU law.[752]

Throughout the DMA's legislative procedure, the internal division of work within the Commission was subject to debate.[753] Given the complex position of the DMA in the regulatory landscape – which is discussed in section 5.4.1 – it was not apparent which Directorate-General (henceforth: DG) would be best suited to take the lead in DMA enforcement. Given the legal basis of the DMA, i.e., Article 114 TFEU, DG GROW – responsible for the Internal Market, Industry and Entrepreneurship and SMEs – appeared to be a logical candidate. However, due to the DMA's close relationship with competition law, DG COMP could also be a strong contender. Lastly, in line with the emphasis on the *digital* world, enforcement by DG CONNECT could be a valid option. Ultimately, the Commission opted for a joint team, and the DMA is enforced collectively by DG COMP and DG CONNECT.[754]

---

751. Preamble DMA, para. 91.
752. Witt 2023, p. 646.
753. *See also*, section 9.2.2.
754. Both DG COMP and DG CONNECT have a unit dedicated to digital platforms. Within DG COMP this is unit COMP.J.3. Within DG CONNECT, this is unit COMP.J. *See:* https://competition-policy.ec.europa.eu/document/download/82bca9b5-7a94-45bc-9d51-ae24c09cf71c_en and https://op.europa.eu/en/web/who-is-who/organization/-/organization/COMP/COM_CRF_246548 accessed 4 March 2025. The joint efforts are also reflected in the Commission's Decision on the establishment of a High-level group of regulators, which establishes that this High-Level Group shall be chaired by the Commission's DG CNCT and DG COMP. *See:* Commission Decision of 23 March 2023 on setting up a High-Level Group for the Digital Markets Act, C(2023) 1833 final.

In the speech, Breton indicated that the team will have 100 FTEs for the enforcement of both the DSA and the DMA.[755]

Despite the central DMA enforcement, national authorities are involved in the enforcement of the DMA.[756] In the initial DMA Proposal, the position of NCAs was not addressed, leading to dissatisfaction among NCAs and the ECN regarding the institutional choice.[757] In the final version of the DMA, the role of national authorities is strengthened, albeit limited to the investigative stage of DMA enforcement. According to Article 37(7) DMA, Member States may empower national authorities to conduct an investigation into non-compliance with the DMA.[758] The involvement of NCAs in the investigative stage reinforces their position, even though the Commission remains the DMA's sole enforcer. NCA investigations may incentivise the Commission to take action against certain practices. In this way, Article 37(7) offers NCAs a useful tool to influence the Commission's DMA enforcement agenda.[759] However, so far, NCAs have not yet engaged in such investigations.[760] It remains to be seen whether national authorities will use this competence in practice.[761] Investigations are cost-intensive, and no fines can be imposed at the national level. Hence, engaging in DMA investigations may not be appealing from a financial perspective. This may discourage national authorities from prioritising DMA enforcement actions over the application of EU or national competition law.

In The Netherlands, the legislator proposed the adoption of an implementing act for the DMA. In the Draft Act, the Dutch NCA – the ACM – is appointed as the authority responsible for enforcing the DMA in The Netherlands.[762] The act empowers the ACM to execute the tasks conferred upon it by the DMA.[763] The Dutch legislator explicitly establishes that the authority's competence is limited to supervision and monitoring compliance and does not entail the competence to enforce the DMA.[764] The ACM reacted positively to the proposed act and considers the approach workable. In order to take up its new responsibilities, the ACM expects to need seven additional FTEs on a structural basis.[765]

---

755. Breton 2022.
756. *See also* section 9.2.1.
757. European Competition Network 2021.
758. Preamble DMA, recital 91.
759. Beems, Van de Gronden and Rusu 2023, p. 70.
760. Annual report on Regulation (EU) 2022/1925 of the European Parliament and of the Council on contestable and fair markets in the digital sector and amending Directives (EU) 2019/1937 and (EU) 2020/1828 (Digital Markets Act), COM/2024/106, p. 42.
761. Beems, Van de Gronden and Rusu 2023, p. 70.
762. Article 2 Dutch Draft Implementing Act DMA.
763. Article 2(3) Dutch Implementing Act DMA.
764. Explanatory Memorandum Dutch Draft Implementing Act DMA, para. 4.2.4.
765. ACM, Uitvoerings- en handhavingstoets Digital Markets Act (DMA), 29 maart 2023, ACM/INT/468084.

In Germany, the *Bundeskartellamt* is the authority responsible for the enforcement of the DMA. The 11th Amendment to the GWB appoints the *Bundeskartellamt* as the responsible actor.[766] Section 32g GWB emphasises that the investigative powers of the competition law framework apply *mutatis mutandis* to DMA investigations. Moreover, Section 32g(3) GWB establishes an obligation for the *Bundeskartellamt* to report to the Commission on the results of DMA investigations. The German *Bundeskartellamt* has been granted broader competences than the Dutch ACM. According to the novel Section 32g GWB, the *Bundeskartellamt* has the competence to publish a report on the results of the investigation.[767] Apart from the competence to monitor compliance with the DMA, the 11th Amendment of the GWB thus confers two additional competences upon the *Bundeskartellamt*, i.e.: (i) the competence to draw its own conclusions on the findings of a DMA investigation; and (ii) the competence to publish these findings. These competences seem to grant the *Bundeskartellamt* the ability to make a public pre-decision.[768] It should be stressed that the *Bundeskartellamt's* competence to publish its conclusions cannot undermine the Commission's position as the 'sole enforcer' of the DMA.[769] Consequently, the *Bundeskartellamt* should limit its 'pre-decision' to a summary of its findings in the investigative stage. By engaging in decision-making, the German authority would overstep its competences. This approach would stand at odds with the DMA's objective of avoiding fragmentation of the internal market.[770]

5.2.4.2 The Enforcement and Compliance Framework

According to recital 80 of the DMA's Preamble, the Commission needs 'strong investigative and enforcement powers, to allow it to investigate, enforce and monitor' the DMA. To this end, the Commission has several fact-finding powers.[771] Furthermore, the Commission has multiple decision-making powers at its disposal. According to Article 29 DMA, the Commission can adopt a *non-compliance decision*. Moreover, Article 24 DMA establishes the competence to adopt an interim decision in the case of 'urgency due to the risk of serious and irreparable damage for business users or end users'.[772] In this scenario, the Commission may take the interim decision on the basis of prima facie evidence of an infringement.

766. Section 32g GWB. *See also*: Entwurf eines Gesetzes zur Änderung des Gesetzes gegen Wettbewerbsbeschränkungen under anderer Gesetze, 16 May 2023, 20/6824.
767. The original German text of Section 32g(3) states that the *Bundeskartellamt* 'kann einen Bericht über die Ergebnisse der Untersuchung veröffentlichen'.
768. Ribera Martínez 2023a.
769. Article 38(7) DMA; Preamble DMA, recital 91.
770. Ribera Martínez 2023a.
771. Articles 16-19 DMA.
772. *See also*: Preamble DMA, recital 84.

Experience with competition law shows that the interpretation of the legal threshold has a significant impact on the effectiveness of the instrument of interim measures: if the standard is too high, the instrument will rarely be used in practice. In the competition law context, it has become apparent that the standard of 'serious and irreparable damage' is very high indeed. In this light, the criterion of serious and irreparable damage can also present a hurdle for imposing interim measures in the context of the DMA.[773] However, the DMA does not fully replicate the standard of Regulation 1/2003. It refers to damage to *business users* and *end users* rather than damage to competition. This standard is less abstract and, therefore, easier to prove in practice.[774]

Furthermore, the DMA provides the Commission with the competence to adopt binding commitments in Articles 18(6) and 25 DMA. The instrument of commitments is much more limited than its competition law equivalent. Commitments can only be adopted in the context of market investigations into systemic non-compliance.[775] The 'regular' non-compliance procedure does not allow for the adoption of binding commitments. The rationale behind this limitation is that the regulatory dialogue serves a somewhat similar function and pattern as commitments.[776] As argued elsewhere, the absence of the instrument of commitments in the DMA is a missed opportunity. In my view, the regulatory dialogue serves a purpose different from that of the tool of commitments, i.e., it addresses issues relating to non-compliance rather than facilitating compliance.[777] Given the fact that experience with competition law shows that the instrument of commitments is a useful and effective tool, it is a missed opportunity that the DMA only reintroduces the tool to a very limited extent.

Apart from the range of decision-making powers, the Commission can impose several remedies. The Commission can impose fines of up to 10% of the gatekeeper's annual total worldwide turnover.[778] In the case of repeated infringements, the fine cap is raised to 20% of the total worldwide turnover.[779] Furthermore, the Commission can impose a fine of up to 1% of the annual turnover for procedural infringements, such as a failure to provide information or refraining from notifying that the quantitative thresholds of Article 3(2) DMA are met.[780] Apart from fines, the Commission can impose

773. Witt 2023, p. 652.
774. Beems, Van de Gronden and Rusu 2023, pp. 63-64.
775. Preamble DMA, recital 76.
776. Beems, Van de Gronden and Rusu 2023, pp. 63-64.
777. Beems, Van de Gronden and Rusu 2023, p. 64.
778. Article 30 DMA.
779. A repeated infringement occurs if the gatekeeper committed 'the same or a similar infringement' in relation to the same core platform services in a timeframe of eight years. *See:* Article 20(2) DMA.
780. Article 10(3) DMA.

periodic penalty payments not exceeding 1% of the daily worldwide turnover.[781]

The Commission can impose behavioural and structural remedies in the case of systemic non-compliance. Systemic non-compliance occurs if the gatekeeper receives at least three non-compliance decisions within a period of eight years, and has maintained, strengthened or extended its gatekeeper position. According to Article 18(1) DMA, the Commission may conduct a market investigation in order to assess whether a gatekeeper has engaged in systemic non-compliance.[782] Interestingly, unlike Regulation 1/2003, the DMA does not establish a preference for behavioural remedies. Rather, structural and behavioural remedies are viewed on (almost) equal footing.[783] This could be an indication that structural remedies are more likely to be imposed in the context of the DMA than in the context of competition law.[784]

Within the framework of competition law, the Commission cannot only assess the behaviour of individual firms but also has the competence to engage in a sector inquiry. This competence is not copied in the DMA. However, the DMA does include the competence to conduct a market investigation to designate gatekeepers, assess non-compliance with DMA obligations or identify novel harmful conduct.[785] This competence can be considered a rebranded sector inquiry.[786]

781. Article 31 DMA.

782. For this threshold, infringements by the gatekeeper are taken into account. The threshold is therefore not limited to a single core platform service or a particular obligation. The test is thus slightly different than the test that is used for a repeated infringement as used in Article 20(2) DMA. *See:* Preamble DMA, recital 75.

783. Admittedly, the language used in recital 75 of the DMA suggests that the threshold for structural remedies is still slightly higher than that for behavioural remedies: 'The Commission should investigate and assess whether additional behavioural or, *where appropriate,* structural remedies are justified … '. Nevertheless, the threshold for structural remedies is definitely more relaxed than under Article 7(1) Regulation 1/2003: 'Structural remedies can only be imposed either where there is no equally effective behavioural remedy or where any equally effective behavioural remedy would be more burdensome for the undertaking concerned than the structural remedy.'

784. Ibáñez Colomo 2021, p. 561; Beems, Van de Gronden and Rusu 2023, p. 66.

785. In the past, the Commission investigated the possibility to introduce a New Competition Tool. In one of the proposed scenarios, this tool would entail an instrument to identify competition problems in certain markets and intervene on such markets without having to proof violations of competition law. Such tool – which is ultimately not adopted – would add significant remedies to the instrument of the sector inquiry. Although this instrument is ultimately not introduced in EU competition law, in German national competition law a similar instrument is introduced (*see* section 4.4). *See also*: European Commission, Inception Impact Assessment New Competition Tool (NCT), 4 June 2020, (2020)2877634, p. 2.

786. Beems, Van de Gronden and Rusu 2023, p. 63.

The enforcement framework of the DMA not only lists competences for the Commission but also establishes compliance requirements for gatekeepers. According to Article 28 DMA, gatekeepers 'shall introduce a compliance function, which is independent from the operational functions of the gatekeeper'. Such compliance function shall be composed of one or more compliance officers with sufficient authority, stature and resources.[787] The compliance function should have a head in the function of an independent senior manager with distinct responsibility for the compliance function.[788] The compliance function should have access to the management body of the gatekeeper.[789] Gatekeepers are not only under the obligation to set up a compliance function but also have to report to the Commission. According to Article 11 DMA, gatekeepers shall submit an annual compliance report. This report shall provide a detailed and transparent description of the measures that are implemented to ensure compliance.[790] These reports will be an important source of information for the Commission. However, the compliance reports, and in particular the quality standard in this regard, may lead to a 'game' played by the Commission and gatekeepers as gatekeepers may make a strategy out of the level of information supply.[791] Arguably, precise and detailed compliance reports will make the monitoring task of the Commission easier. Unclear reports however will make it more difficult to get insight into the gatekeeper's activities. Without proper information, it can be difficult for the Commission to assess whether a given gatekeeper complies with the obligations of the DMA. This could provide an incentive to focus on gatekeepers that provide informative reports. However, such an approach would provide a significant incentive to provide unclear reports, which is not desirable.[792]

5.3 THE DMA AND COMPETITION LAW: COMMON FEATURES AND MAIN DIFFERENCES

The previous section set out the legislative framework of the DMA and drew some parallels with competition law. This Section builds on this analysis by mapping the common features of the DMA and competition law, as well as the main differences. The (i) objectives, (ii) scope and substantive provisions, and (iii) institutional and enforcement frameworks are addressed in turn.

---

787. The compliance officers shall have 'the professional qualifications, knowledge, experience and ability necessary to fulfil [their tasks]'. *See* Article 28(3) DMA.
788. Article 28(1)(3) DMA.
789. Article 28(2) DMA.
790. For an overview of the submitted compliance reports, *see:* https://digital-markets-act-cases.ec.europa.eu/reports/compliance-reports accessed 15 March 2025.
791. Crémer et al. 2023a, p. 326.
792. Crémer et al. 2023a, p. 326.

5.3.1 Objectives of the DMA and Competition Law

As explained in section 5.2.1, the DMA pursues various objectives. The EU legislator explicitly distinguishes those objectives from the goals of competition law.[793] However, a closer look at the goals of the respective legal branches arguably reveals a closer relatedness than that portrayed by the legislator.[794]

First, the objective of *contestability* partially overlaps with the goals of EU competition law. As explained in section 4.2.1, EU competition law aims not only to contribute to consumer welfare but also has the objective of keeping markets open and competitive. In the *GlaxoSmithKline* case, the CJEU endorsed the protection of the structure of the market and of competition as such as objectives of competition law.[795] Moreover, in the ECN+ Directive, the EU legislator refers to a contestability-related goal of competition law by stressing that enforcement of competition law is necessary to ensure *more open competitive markets in the Union* in which undertakings compete on the merits and without company-erected barriers to entry.[796] The objective of the structure of the market is even more clearly reflected in German competition law.[797] Both the DMA and competition law thus aim to address the issue of entry barriers. Against this backdrop, the goal of contestability clearly interacts with the objectives of competition law. Admittedly, the interpretation of contestability is not identical for both legal fields. Competition law primarily focuses on entry barriers created by anticompetitive behaviour of dominant firms, such as exclusivity or tying agreements. While the DMA also addresses barriers related to undertakings' behaviour, its framework additionally covers entry barriers arising from the inherent characteristics of gatekeeper markets.[798]

Second, the principle of *fairness* bridges the fields of competition law and the DMA and is part of the broader objectives of both areas of the law. Despite its appearance in both legal branches, the extent to which the concept of fairness connects the goals of the DMA and the competition law framework remains hard to determine. As explained earlier, fairness is a broad and elusive concept, and its meaning is context-dependent. This begs the question of whether the principle can be interpreted uniformly in both fields of law. In both areas, the concept of fairness seems linked to the *exploitation* of customers or consumers. The DMA links fairness to an imbalance between the rights and obligations of *business* users, where the gatekeeper obtains a *disproportionate* advantage.[799] In this context, fairness

793. Preamble DMA, recital 11.
794. Beems 2023, p. 4.
795. CJEU 6 October 2009 Case C-501/06P, *GlaxoSmithKline*.
796. Preamble ECN+ Directive, recital 1.
797. *See* section 4.4.1.
798. Preamble DMA, recital 16.
799. Preamble DMA, recital 33.

seems to be understood in an *intraplatform* setting, focusing on the relationship between the platform and its users. This shows clear parallels with the notion of fairness as established in Article 102 TFEU, prohibiting unfair prices and trading conditions. The question of *to whom* an outcome should be fair leads to some confusion in the context of the DMA. As explained in section 5.2.1, it is not entirely clear whether the principle merely governs the relationship between the platform and *business* users or also covers the platform's relationship with *end* users. Recital 33 of the DMA focuses on the position of business users vis-à-vis the platform. However, by stressing that DMA pursues its objectives for the 'benefit of business and end-users' Article 1(1) DMA takes a different approach and includes concerns relating to the position of the end consumer. In an earlier version of the DMA, the European Parliament put even more emphasis on the end consumer by endorsing consumer welfare as a goal of the DMA.[800] However, the final version of the DMA does not include the notion of consumer welfare, and the exact interpretation of the fairness principle remains ambiguous.

Furthermore, the DMA has, in alignment with the legal basis of Article 114 TFEU, an EU market integration objective. It is well-established that market integration constitutes one of the objectives of EU competition law.[801] Against this background, market integration can be considered another common objective shared by the competition law framework and the DMA.

5.3.2 Scope and Substantive Provisions of the DMA and Competition Law

Apart from the objectives, the DMA's substantive provisions partially overlap with those of competition law. While the scope of the instruments is clearly not identical and is determined by relying on different tools and methodologies, the material scope of the DMA to a certain extent mirrors that of the competition law framework. Several DMA obligations overlap with past and ongoing antitrust investigations relating to personal data markets.

Before addressing the main parallels between specific DMA obligations and their competition law counterparts, it is important to acknowledge the fact that the scope and methodologies of the respective fields are significantly different. Notwithstanding the similarities of the instruments, the following fundamental differences cannot be overlooked.

First, the personal scopes of Article 102 TFEU and the DMA are not identical. Article 102 TFEU applies to a dominant undertaking, whereas the

800. Amendments adopted by the European Parliament on 15 December 2021 on the proposal for a regulation of the European Parliament and of the Council on contestable and fair markets in the digital sector (Digital Markets Act) (COM(2020)0842 – C9-0419/2020.
801. *See* section 4.2.1.2.

DMA targets gatekeepers. These concepts are fundamentally different. While the application of Article 102 TFEU requires an assessment of dominance (including the delineation of the relevant market), the DMA takes a more formal approach by establishing quantitative thresholds. [802]

Second, DMA obligations are shaped as per se rules, meaning that conduct is not inconsistent with competition on the merits, nor that anti-competitive effects must be proven to establish a violation of the DMA. While competition law provides an open clause in Article 102 TFEU, the DMA is based on a closed-shop list of per se rules with no room for efficiencies or objective justifications. The Preamble of the DMA highlights this difference by stressing that competition law enforcement 'occurs *ex post* and requires an extensive investigation of often very complex facts on a case by case basis'.[803] Conversely, the DMA provides self-executing, directly applicable rules that gatekeepers have to adhere to.[804] In this light, the DMA shifts from a 'system of control of abuse' to a 'system of prohibition'.[805]

Despite these differences, important substantive parallels between the DMA and competition law are in place. The DMA was clearly designed with competition law in mind. This is unsurprising given the background of the DMA; the instrument was adopted in order to address certain shortcomings of the competition law framework, in particular its lack of speed and the impossibility of addressing problems relating to the structure of the market.[806]

Mapping and classifying the parallels between the DMA and existing categories of abusive behaviour is not a straightforward exercise. As explained in the previous chapter, competition law prohibits different types of abusive behaviour. In the past, there has been a lot of debate on the classification and categorisation of abuses, particularly in the context of personal data markets.[807] Since the boundaries between the different types of abuse are not always clearly defined within the competition law context, it is not evident how the different DMA provisions relate to the existing types of abuse. The different prohibitions and obligations are further explored below. The analysis addresses the DMA's relationship with 'traditional' competition law and Section 19a GWB in turn.

5.3.2.1 'Traditional' Competition Law and the DMA

Notwithstanding the important differences in scope and methodologies, the DMA and competition law partially address similar conduct.[808] While some

802. Käseberg and Gappa 2024b, p. 69.
803. Preamble DMA, recital 5.
804. Podszun 2023, p. 7.
805. Komninos 2022, p. 1.
806. Gal and Petit 2021, p. 8.
807. *See* section 4.2.2.
808. *See also* section 5.4.3.

DMA obligations have a clear competition law counterpart, others cannot easily be linked to an existing type of abuse. Hence, the DMA's obligations and prohibitions can be subdivided into three categories:

(i) conduct that is also prohibited under EU or national competition law and has a precedent;
(ii) conduct that could potentially be qualified as abusive under Article 102 TFEU, but has not (yet) a precedent in EU or national competition law;
(iii) conduct without an EU competition law counterpart.

The existence of the third category confirms that the fields are not identical: the DMA does not cover all existing types of abusive behaviour, and some of the DMA's substantive provisions transcend the traditional competition law framework. For instance, Article 5(6) DMA states that gatekeepers shall not prevent or restrict business users from raising any issues of non-compliance with EU or national law with the relevant public authorities. This prohibition cannot be derived from EU competition law. DMA conduct without a competition law counterpart is unlikely to cause coherence problems between competition law and the DMA as there is no risk of a divergent interpretation.

Many DMA obligations fall within the first or second category and have a (potential) competition law counterpart.[809]

First, the DMA contains several provisions addressing the issue of *tying*. In a competition law context, anti-competitive tying can constitute an abuse of dominance.[810] The DMA addresses tying in multiple provisions, including Articles 5(7), 5(8), 6(3), 6(4) and 6(6) DMA. In this context, both instruments address the issue of defaults and pre-installations.[811] For instance, the Commission investigated Apple's user choice obligations, including its pre-installation and change default setting, under the DMA and closed its investigation following a constructive dialogue.[812]

Second, a dominant undertaking's *refusal to supply* certain goods and services may amount to an abuse of dominance. Arguably, this doctrine could be extended to the refusal to supply data or interoperability information. German competition law also recognises the refusal to provide access to data as a potential abuse.[813] Several provisions of the DMA include obligations to supply certain services or information. Article 5(9) DMA, for example,

---

809. For a more elaborate overview of the concept of abuse in the context of EU competition law, *see* section 4.2.2.
810. *See* section 4.2.2.4.
811. European Commission 18 July 2018 Case AT40099, *Google Android*; GC 14 September 2022 Case T-604/18, *Google Android.*
812. European Commission 23 April 2025, 'Commission closes investigation into Apple's user choice obligations and issues preliminary findings on rules for alternative apps under the Digital Markets Act', IP25/1086.
813. *See* section 4.4.2.2.

establishes that gatekeepers shall provide advertisers and publishers with information, fees, remuneration and metrics on which these indicators are calculated. Furthermore, Article 6(8), 6(9), 6(10), 6(11) and 6(12) DMA provide business and end users with the right to data access and data portability.

Third, the DMA's provisions on interoperability, i.e., Articles 6(7) and 7 DMA, arguably overlap with competition law.[814] In the past, the Commission and the EU Courts have considered the refusal to provide interoperability information as a refusal to supply.[815] Furthermore, the Commission addressed the issue of interoperability in its statement of objections concerning Microsoft's alleged tying practices regarding Teams.[816] In the context of the DMA, the Commission started a procedure to specify Apple's interoperability obligations in the context of several iOS connectivity features and functionalities for connected devices and for interoperability requests by developers and third parties of iOS and IPadOS.[817]

Fourth, Article 6(5) DMA prohibits *self-preferencing* behaviour. According to this provision, gatekeepers shall not treat their own services more favourably in ranking and related indexing and crawling than services offered by third parties. Similarly, competition law prohibits self-preferencing behaviour by dominant firms.[818] The DMA's prohibition on self-preferencing illustrates a clear parallel with competition law; it is clearly inspired by the *Google Shopping* saga.[819]

Fifth, the DMA contains several other obligations relating *to unfair prices and conditions*. Accordingly, there are also certain parallels between the DMA and the exploitative dimension of Article 102 TFEU. Article 5(2) DMA limits the gatekeeper's possibility to use data, e.g., by prohibiting the merging and combining of certain data sets. The Commission imposed a DMA fine on Meta for its 'Pay or Consent' model. The Commission considers Meta's policy which offers undertakings a binary choice forcing them to consent to the combination of their personal data as a violation of Article 5(2) DMA.[820] Article 5(2) DMA and the Commission's investigation

814. Graef 2014, p. 9.
815. *See* section 4.2.2.4.
816. European Commission 25 June 2024, Commission sends Statement of Objections to Microsoft over possibly abusive tying practices regarding Teams, IP/24/3446.
817. European Commission 19 September 2024, Commission starts first proceedings to specify Apple's interoperability obligations under the Digital Markets Act, IP/24/4761.
818. European Commission 27 June 2017, Case AT3970 (*Google Shopping*); Draft Guidelines on the Application of Article 102, section 4.3.3.
819. *See* section 4.2.2.4.
820. European Commission 1 July 2024, Commission sends preliminary findings to Meta over its 'Pay or Consent' model for breach of the Digital Markets Act, IP/24/3582; European Commission 23 April 2025, 'Commission finds Apple and Meta in breach of the Digital Markets Act', IP/25/1085. The Commission's decision was issued subsequent to the cutoff date for this research and is therefore not analysed in more detail. *See also*: Frank and Emma 2024.

mirror the German *Meta Bundeskartellamt* case.[821] Furthermore, Article 6(13) DMA prevents gatekeepers from imposing disproportionate conditions for terminating the provision of core platform services. Arguably, such conditions could also be qualified as unfair trading conditions within the meaning of Article 102(a) TFEU.

Sixth, the overlap between competition law and the DMA is also clearly represented in relation to the prohibition on *anti-steering obligations*, i.e., clauses prohibiting or limiting the use of secondary services outside the core platform. The ACM imposed a competition law fine on Apple for prohibiting the use of secondary services outside the core platform service.[822] Similarly, the Commission fined Apple for abusing its dominant position by preventing app developers from informing iOS users about alternative and cheaper music subscriptions outside the app.[823] Yet, anti-steering clauses are not only subject to antitrust scrutiny but are also prohibited by Article 5(4) DMA. In fact, the Commission assessed Apple's anti-steering practices under the DMA and imposed one of the first-ever DMA fines for this conduct.[824]

Seventh, the DMA prohibits the use of *MFNs* by stating that gatekeepers shall not prevent business users from offering the same products and services through third-party intermediation services or through their own direct sales channels. Despite some uncertainties as to the application of Article 102 TFEU to MFNs, such clauses are prohibited under competition law too.[825]\\

Lastly, the DMA contains provisions that are clearly linked to competition law, but for which it remains unclear which specific type of abuse the corresponding obligations align with. Article 6(2) DMA, for example, contains a prohibition for gatekeepers on the use of non-publicly available data to compete with business users. Gatekeepers cannot use data collected in the context of their relevant CPS to compete with business users. This prohibition mirrors the *Amazon Marketplace* and *Facebook Marketplace* cases.[826] As noted in section 4.2.2.4, it is not unequivocally clear which type of abuse constitutes the core of these cases.

---

821. *See* section 4.4.2.3.
822. ACM 24 August 2021 ACM/19/035630, *Apple* (Case Summary); Graef 2022, p. 580.
823. European Commission 4 March 2024, Case AT40437, *Apple Appstore Practices – music streaming*; *See* section 4.2.2.5.
824. European Commission 23 April 2025, 'Commission finds Apple and Meta in breach of the Digital Markets Act', IP/25/1085. The Commission's decision was issued subsequent to the cutoff date for this research and is therefore not analysed in more detail.
825. *See* section 4.2.2.4.
826. European Commission 12 December 2022 Commitment Decision in Cases AT40462 and AT40704, *Amazon Marketplace* and *Amazon Buybox*; European Commission 11 November 2024, 'Commission fines Meta €797.72 million over abusive practices benefitting Facebook Marketplace', IP/24/5801.

5.3.2.2 Section 19a GWB and the DMA

The DMA not only overlaps with 'traditional' competition law but also with novel national instruments. Section 19a GWB is particularly relevant in this regard. Section 19a GWB targets undertakings with a position of paramount significance for competition across markets by imposing certain pre-defined obligations on such undertakings.[827] Unlike the DMA, Section 19a GWB is enshrined in the German *competition* act and, thus, amounts to part of the national competition law framework. Yet, Section 19a GWB is (to a certain extent) 'comparable' with the DMA.[828] By introducing certain *ex ante* features into antitrust law, the instrument has fostered a 'paradigm shift' in German competition law. Section 19a GWB sits somewhere between competition law and economic regulation and is referred to as a competition and regulatory law *chimera*.[829]

The qualification of Section 19a GWB as either competition law or sector-specific regulation is highly relevant for its relationship with the DMA. The pre-emptive effect of the DMA is different for competition law than it is for economic regulation. This issue is further discussed in section 7.5.

5.3.3 The Enforcement and Institutional Framework

The similarities between the DMA and Article 102 TFEU are not limited to the substantive framework but also relate to the institutional and enforcement frameworks. Considering the *institutional framework,* the enforcement of the DMA is largely in the hands of the same actors as the enforcement of competition law, namely the Commission and – to a limited extent – NCAs. Yet, and despite these similarities, the division of tasks between the respective authorities is rather different. Where competition law has, since the entry into force of Regulation 1/2003, become to a significant extent decentralised, the Commission is in the driver's seat for DMA enforcement. NCAs only play a role of importance in the investigative stage.[830] Henceforth, the role of NCAs is much more limited in this context. This institutional model mirrors the competition law's institutional framework before the entry into force of Regulation 1/2003. In the past, EU competition law was enforced centrally by the Commission for about 40 years.[831]

827. *See* section 4.4.2.2.
828. Bechtold and Bosch 2021, para. 3.
829. Zilsdorf 2023; A Chimera is a creature with a lion's head, a goat's body, and a snake's tail (*see:* Oxford Dictionary, Chimera, https://www.oxfordlearnersdictionaries.com/definition/american_english/chimera#:~:text=chimera-,noun,that%20can%20breathe%20out%20fire accessed 29 August 2025).
830. Article 37(8) DMA.
831. *See* Regulation 17/62/EEC.

Moreover, within the Commission, the internal division of tasks is also different. Where the enforcement of competition law is the responsibility of DG COMP, the DMA is enforced by a joint team, and involves DG CONNECT too.[832]

Considering the institutional dimension, there are clear parallels between the DMA's and competition law's network for cooperation. In the context of the DMA, authorities will cooperate through the ECN. It is remarkable that the European legislator selected a network for cooperation in the field of *competition law* to streamline the application of the DMA and competition law, since it explicitly stresses that the DMA should not be considered part of the competition law framework.[833]

The DMA's enforcement toolbox is undoubtedly modelled on Regulation 1/2003.[834] A large part of the DMA's enforcement framework clearly resembles the enforcement framework of competition law. Various enforcement powers, including the competence to take non-compliance decisions, impose fines and periodic penalty payments, adopt interim measures and impose structural and behavioural remedies, draw inspiration from existing competition law tools. Despite the clear similarities in investigative and decision-making powers, the DMA does not copy and paste competition law frameworks. For some competences, the thresholds are formulated slightly differently, and other competition law enforcement tools are absent in the DMA or formulated much narrower. Furthermore, in comparison to Regulation 1/2003, the DMA puts more emphasis on the reality of digital markets. Articles 21 and 23 DMA, for example, allow the Commission to access data, algorithms and information about IT systems.

5.4 THE DMA AND COMPETITION LAW: ANALYSIS

The previous sections aimed to map the main differences and similarities between the DMA and competition law. This section deepens the analysis by further assessing the interplay between the DMA and competition law. To this end, first, I aim to position the DMA in the broader regulatory context of EU law. Next, this Section highlights to what extent the DMA and competition law can: (i) reinforce each other; or (ii) potentially conflict. In line with the unidirectional focus of the research, the discussion emphasises the impact of the DMA on competition law.[835]

---

832. *See* section 9.2.2.
833. Vestager 2021.
834. Beems, Van de Gronden and Rusu 2023, p. 53.
835. *See* section 1.3.2.

5.4.1 The DMA in the Broader Regulatory Context

As explained in the previous Sections, the EU legislator does not consider the DMA to be part of the competition law framework. Yet, the instrument aims to address competition law shortcomings and clearly draws inspiration from the 'traditional' competition law.[836] Thus, these fields of law are inevitably intertwined.

Within the regulatory landscape of the EU, various *types of market intervention* can be distinguished. Traditionally, the arsenal of market regulatory tools is subdivided into multiple categories, in particular: (i) competition law; (ii) economic regulation; and (iii) social, human rights and solidarity regulation. The relationship between these instruments is context-dependent and not always straightforward: the instruments are neither identical, nor wholly distinct and neither fully co-extensive, nor mutually exclusive.[837] Generally speaking, economic regulation amounts to a more far-reaching intervention in the market by proscribing particular market conduct in an *ex-ante* manner.[838] Conversely, competition law prohibits certain behaviour, such as abuse of a dominant position, *ex post.*[839] Apart from competition law and economic regulation, social, human rights and solidarity regulations aim to protect non-market values.[840] This illustrates that economic inefficiencies are not the only imperative for market intervention.[841]

The EU has a longstanding tradition of the parallel or consecutive application of competition law and regulation.[842] In *Deutsche Telekom* and *Telefónica,* the competition law framework is applied to the regulated telecommunications sector.[843] In *Telekomunicacja Polska,* the Commission takes this a step further by endorsing a conglomerate approach: the failure to comply with regulatory obligations amounts to the abuse of a dominant

---

836. Akman 2022, pp. 94-95.
837. Dunne 2015, p. 40.
838. Economic regulation is 'State-directed, positive, coercive alteration or derogation from the operation of the free market […], typically undertaken to address market failure, and to be distinguished from regulation that pursues a predominantly "social" aim'. *See:* Dunne 2015, pp. 3 and 40.
839. Dunne 2015, p. 36.
840. Prosser 2006.
841. Baldwin, Cave and Lodge 2012, pp. 15, 21-22; Feintuck 2010, p. 39.
842. Where the EU framework considers sectoral regulation as complements, in the US framework the two forms of markets intervention are considered substitutes. *See,* for example, Supreme Court of the United States 13 October 2004 540 US 398, *Verizon v. Trinko*. In this case, the US Supreme Court limits the scope for antitrust intervention to regulated sectors, such as network industries.
843. CJEU 14 October 2010 Case C-280/08P, *Deutsche Telekom*; European Commission 21 May 2003 COMP/C-1/37451, 37578, 37579 *Deutsche Telekom*, para. 54. In the Deutsche Telekom decision, the Commission stresses that: 'the competition rules may apply where the sector-specific legislation does not preclude the undertakings it governs from engaging in autonomous conduct that prevents, restricts or distorts competition'.

position within the context of Article 102 TFEU.[844] The two regimes are considered to pursue divergent objectives by imposing different obligations upon undertakings. Where competition law has a generic application and imposes economy-wide prohibitions, regulation addresses specific and identified market failures in certain sectors.[845] Moreover, where economic regulation often oversteps the market mechanism, competition law can contribute to this process by fostering competition within the market.[846] Furthermore, the consecutive application of competition law and economic regulation can be explained by the constitutional setup of the EU: neither national regulatory law nor EU secondary legislation can limit the application of Treaty provisions, including Article 102 TFEU.[847]

Historically, the dichotomy between competition law and economic regulation was rather clear. Economic regulation imposed *ex-ante* rules to meet specific regulatory objectives, mostly relating to specific (liberalised) sectors. Competition law applied *ex post* and pursued broader and more generic objectives, particularly consumer welfare. Over the last years, the distinction between the frameworks has become blurred. Regulatory authorities are increasingly applying *ex-post* interventions to conduct that is already present in the market.[848] At the same time, competition authorities increasingly rely on *ex-ante* instruments.[849] This process has been accelerated by the adoption of multiple novel instruments in the context of digital markets. Several tools, including the DMA, Section 19a GWB, and Section 32f GWB, have simultaneously competition law and economic regulation traits. This means that novel instruments do not neatly fit into previously established categories of market intervention. The next sections examine the DMA's position in the regulatory landscape in more detail.

5.4.1.1 The DMA as Competition Law

The Preamble to the DMA explicitly states that the regulation pursues 'an objective that is complementary to, but different from that of protecting undistorted competition on any given market'.[850] Similarly, former Commissioner Vestager has stressed that the DMA is 'not a competition law instrument'.[851] This approach is also reflected in the legal basis for the instrument, i.e., Article 114 TFEU. The EU legislator relies merely on the 'general' legal basis for the internal market, rather than on a combination

844. Dunne 2015, p. 213.
845. Dunne 2015, p. 42.
846. Intven, Oliver and Sepúlveda 2000, p. 12.
847. De Streel et al. 2020, p. 87. *See* section 7.2.1.
848. De Streel 2008, p. 56.
849. Actis Perinetto and Marquis 2017, p. 144.
850. Preamble DMA, para. 11.
851. Vestager 2021.

with the more specific Article 103 TFEU, which constitutes the legal basis for competition law instruments.

Despite the fact that the EU legislator clearly distinguishes between the DMA and traditional competition law, the relationship between these fields of law is, in my view, more complicated. As explained in the previous sections, the DMA cannot be considered in isolation from the competition law framework. It was adopted in order to address certain competition law shortcomings and shares objectives, procedures, and enforcement and institutional tools with the competition law framework.[852] It is unsurprising that the DMA's nature and qualification have been subject to academic debate in the wake of its entry into force. In academic debates, some scholars have considered the DMA as a self-standing regulatory instrument, whereas others have made a clear connection with competition law. Cioffi, for example, considers the DMA as a 'distinct and ancillary body of regulation' and Ibáñez Colomo refers to the instrument as 'more than a simple tweak of competition law'.[853] Conversely, Schweitzer qualifies the DMA as a 'highly simplified version of competition law' and Schroeter and Hyong consider the DMA as an *ex-ante* instrument of competition law.[854] In previous work, I agreed with the latter perspective. In my view, it would have been reasonable to have adopted the DMA as part of the EU competition law framework by considering it as a special sub-branch containing rules for gatekeepers.[855] The similarities of the fields would have justified this approach. Furthermore, another main benefit would be that the DMA could rely on past experience from competition law, for example, in the area of private enforcement. This would have allowed the fields to develop alongside each other. In this way, it would have been easier to guarantee the coherent application of common notions, thereby fostering cross-fertilisation between both areas of the law. Despite the fact that the Commission did not opt for this approach, and the DMA cannot be considered a new branch of EU competition law, the clear parallels between the fields cannot be neglected. Therefore, despite the fact that the DMA is not competition law, it could be considered part of the 'competition law family'.[856]

5.4.1.2 The DMA as (Sector-Specific) Regulation

Although the DMA and the competition law framework overlap to a certain extent, it is clear that the EU legislator considers the DMA as an instrument beyond competition law. Therefore, the question arises whether the DMA can be qualified as sector-specific regulation. Provided that the DMA does not

852. Larouche and De Streel 2021, p. 545.
853. Ibáñez Colomo 2021, p. 568; Cioffi 2021.
854. Schroeter and Hoyng 2021, p. 165; Schweitzer 2021, p. 4.
855. Beems 2023, pp. 10-11; Beems, Van de Gronden and Rusu 2023, p. 80.
856. Van de Gronden and Rusu 2024, p. 337.

amount to competition law, this could be a logical avenue. Yet, the DMA does not share some of the typical traits of sector-specific or economic regulation.[857]

First, the DMA applies to 'providers of core platform services' with a gatekeeper position and, thus, targets a very limited number of undertakings in comparison with competition law.[858] Yet, and as explained in section 5.2.2, the concept of 'core platform service' is rather broad and encompasses a wide range of online services. Against this background, the DMA focuses on a spectrum of digital services throughout the economy, rather than on pre-determined and specific sectors.[859]

Second, the nature of DMA obligations is not merely *proscriptive,* but is also *prescriptive.* In general, competition law obligations are framed negatively and reactively, whereas regulation tends to impose positive or proactive obligations.[860] The DMA lays down both positive and negative obligations. Article 5(2) and 5(3) DMA, for instance, contain negative obligations stressing that gatekeepers should refrain from certain conduct. Conversely, Article 5(4) and 5(5) DMA stress what a gatekeeper should do, thereby establishing a positive obligation. In other words, the DMA contains both *dos* and *don'ts.*[861]

Consequently, the DMA does not neatly fit into the traditional dichotomy between competition law and economic regulation. The instrument is not considered to be competition law, but also differs from other instruments of economic regulation. In this context, the DMA is arguably a novelty with a 'difficult epistemological' position.[862] This unique position has consequences for the consecutive application of the DMA and competition law. This issue is further discussed in the following Sections, which elaborate on the potential interactions between the DMA and competition law.

5.4.2 The DMA and Competition Law Can Reinforce Each Other

The Preamble to the DMA explicitly emphasises that the DMA is 'complementary' to the application of competition law.[863] This implies that the frameworks can reinforce each other. The DMA aims to address some of competition law's shortcomings by providing a swift instrument for market intervention with the capacity to tackle issues associated with the structure of the market. The DMA can, for example, be well-placed to address issues

857. Akman 2022, p. 106; Beems 2023, p. 15.
858. Podszun 2023, p. 7.
859. Larouche and De Streel 2021, p. 545.
860. Dunne 2015, p. 45.
861. Akman 2022, p. 105.
862. Larouche and De Streel 2021, p. 542.
863. Preamble DMA, recital 11.

relating to tipping markets.[864] In this context, the proactive *ex-ante* enforcement framework of the DMA complements the 'traditional' *ex-post* competition law framework.[865] In the context of the competition law and DMA intersection, the complementary relation can unfold in multiple ways.

First, by introducing quantitative criteria, the DMA offers a useful method to complement market definition in the digital context. Defining digital markets can be a cumbersome and complex process, and by providing an alternative tool for scoping, the DMA can help to resolve issues relating to market definition.[866] The concept of gatekeeper is new and distinct from that of a dominant position. Accordingly, gatekeepers do not necessarily hold a dominant position within the meaning of competition law.[867] The quantitative threshold-based presumptions in the DMA are significantly different from the process of defining the relevant market in a competition law context.[868] By explicitly confirming that arguments relating to market definition are not admissible for rebutting a presumption of a gatekeeper position, the GC confirms that the tools to determine the scope of competition law and the DMA respectively are indeed divergent.[869]

Second, the tools and methodologies of competition law and the DMA are not identical. While the application of Article 102 TFEU relies on an individualised assessment, the DMA imposes *ex-ante* pre-defined obligations. Although this divergence may give rise to potential frictions, as discussed in section 5.4.3, it also allows for a certain complementarity. The DMA requires gatekeepers to submit compliance reports to 'ensure and demonstrate' effective compliance with the DMA.[870] The obligation placed on the regulated entities to proactively explain their adherence to the law and prove effective implementation is a 'remarkable turn in comparison to traditional enforcement'.[871] The enforcement framework of the DMA relies on compliance and regulatory dialogue along with the possibility of imposing non-compliance decisions and remedies in case of non-compliance. The relevance of dialogue in DMA enforcement is clearly reflected in the Commission's first DMA cases. In the Press Release, the Commission emphasises the 'extensive dialogue' and 'multiple exchanges' that took place

864. Commission Staff Working Document Impact Assessment Report Accompanying the document Proposal for a Regulation of the European Parliament and of the Council on contestable and fair markets in the digital sector (Digital Markets Act), SWD(2020) 363 final, para. 5.1.
865. Andriychuk 2022, p. 124.
866. *See also* section 4.2.2.1.
867. GC 17 July 2024, Case T-1077/23, *Bytedance*, para. 298.
868. Thépot 2025, p. 67.
869. GC 17 July 2024, Case T-1077/23, *Bytedance*, para. 46; *see also* section 5.2.2.
870. Article 8(1) DMA.
871. Van den Boom and Podszun 2025, p. 3.

between the Commission and the gatekeepers.[872] The combination of: (i) compliance by the gatekeeper; (ii) ongoing supervision by the Commission; and (iii) ad hoc enforcement can complement the more *ex-post* oriented enforcement mechanisms of traditional competition law.[873]

Third, and in my view most importantly, the DMA offers a speedy alternative to the notoriously lengthy procedures under EU competition law. The tools and methodologies of the DMA allow for quicker intervention, which is particularly desirable in innovative and fast-changing markets that are prone to tipping. When it comes to the speed of procedures, the (limited) enforcement experience with the DMA is rather promising. So far, the Commission has designated multiple gatekeepers, engaged in compliance workshops and sent statements of objections. In April 2025, the Commission imposed its first DMA fines for Apple's steering terms and Meta's consent-or-pay model.[874] Given that the DMA entered into force in 2023 and that designated gatekeepers had to comply with the DMA's obligations in 2024, the Commission has acted at a remarkably fast pace. This is promising and reflects the DMA's potential to address certain gaps in the competition law framework, especially the concerns relating to speed.

At the same time, considering the DMA's objective to provide a swift regulatory response to conduct in gatekeeper markets, there are potential risks. These may undermine the complementary relationship between the DMA and competition law. Given the emphasis on speed, certain procedural aspects of the DMA could have been more robust. The threshold for interim measures is, for example, rather high, and the DMA does not contain a general tool for commitments. Since commitments can allow for speedy intervention, this is a missed opportunity.[875]

Furthermore, and notwithstanding the DMA's potential to complement competition law enforcement, it should be stressed that competition law by no means becomes obsolete. As explained in section 5.2.3, the DMA works with a closed-shop list of obligations and prohibitions. This means that the framework is inherently less flexible than competition law, although the Commission has the possibility to update the list according to Article 12 DMA.[876] Given the more rigid nature of the DMA and its focus on a closed-shop list of conduct, competition law will remain relevant. The open-ended and flexible nature of Article 102 TFEU allows for continuous scrutiny of new practices that are not (yet) included in Articles 5, 6 and 7 DMA. These novel competition law cases can, in turn, provide inspiration for future updates of the DMA.

---

872. European Commission, Press Release 23 April 202 'Commission finds Apple and Meta in breach of the Digital Markets Act', IP/25/1085.
873. Tzanaki and Nowag 2023, p. 19.
874. European Commission, Press Release 23 April 202 'Commission finds Apple and Meta in breach of the Digital Markets Act', IP/25/1085.
875. Beems, Van de Gronden and Rusu 2023, p. 64.
876. Monti 2022, p. 62.

In sum, the DMA clearly has the potential to complement the application of competition law. Against this background, the instrument can play an important role in guaranteeing contestability and fairness in gatekeeper markets by filling some of the current gaps in the competition law framework. At the same time, antitrust law remains relevant and may continue to serve as a continuous source of inspiration for future updates of the DMA.

5.4.3 Competition Law and the DMA: Potential Conflicts

The previous section addressed the reinforcing relationship between the DMA and competition law. However, in order to map the relationship between the instruments properly, it does not suffice to merely consider how the instruments strengthen each other or contribute to the realisation of (shared) objectives. Rather, in order to paint a nuanced picture, potential conflicts and clashes between the branches must also be identified. In other words, are there potential conflicts between the DMA and competition law, or can the application of the DMA be detrimental to the application of competition law?

Regarding potential clashes between competition law and the DMA, it should be stressed that the DMA applies 'without prejudice' to EU competition law.[877] Although the relationship with national law is more complicated, the DMA also leaves room for national competition rules. At first glance, this thus seems to indicate that the DMA will not limit the application of competition law. The specificities relating to hierarchies of norms and mechanisms of pre-emption are further discussed in Chapter 7. This section aims to identify (potential) friction between the instruments.

As explained in sections 5.3.2 and 5.4.2, the DMA was designed with competition law in mind. Therefore, it is unlikely that the parallel or consecutive application of the DMA and competition law will result in direct conflicts in individual cases.[878] Yet, and despite the unlikelihood of direct clashes between the DMA and competition law, the entry into force of the DMA may have a practical effect on the application of competition law. The obligations of the DMA overlap with different types of abuse of a dominant position, both with and without precedent.[879] The close link between the two fields can have implications for the parallel or consecutive application of the respective areas of the law. The main question in this regard is whether the application of the DMA will lead to fewer antitrust cases on personal data markets. If the application of the DMA indeed results in a decrease in the

877. Article 1(6) DMA.
878. Such a situation could arise if one decision would authorise, or even require, a specific course of action, whereas another decision would prohibit the same behaviour. Larouche and De Streel 2021, p. 2.
879. *See* section 5.3.2.

application of competition law to such markets, the relevance of competition law in this context may decrease as a result of the DMA's entry into force. The fact that regulators do not have unlimited resources could constitute an incentive to focus on the application of one framework, rather than engaging in parallel proceedings addressing similar conduct. Such parallel investigations could be considered a waste of regulatory resources.[880] In this light, the application of DMA obligations with a competition law counterpart may decrease the relevance of corresponding competition law provisions in practice.

Considering the position of the Commission, which enforces both the DMA and EU competition law, it is likely that the Commission will rely on the stronger DMA tool to maximise the speed and strength of its intervention. Multiple separate and uncoordinated enforcement actions by the Commission addressing one and the same conduct are thus not to be expected. This situation is particularly complex if a DMA obligation overlaps with an ongoing antitrust investigation. In this scenario, the Commission has multiple options. It could decide to: (i) continue the competition law case and apply the DMA at a later stage; (ii) close the competition law case with a commitment decision, taking into account the DMA obligations; (iii) abandon the antitrust case and apply the DMA; or (iv) abandon the 'duplicate' part of the antitrust case for the concerns addressed by the DMA.[881]

The effects of the DMA on the application of EU and national competition law by NCAs are less straightforward. While these authorities are competent to apply EU and national competition laws, their involvement in DMA enforcement is limited to the investigative stage.[882] Since the DMA does not fully limit the competence of NCAs to apply EU and competition laws, parallel cases may arise. The overlap between the DMA, EU and national competition law is governed by multiple clauses of pre-emption and hierarchy of norms. These mechanisms are further studied in section 7.5.

The different methodologies used in the context of competition law and the DMA may lead to further tension. As explained in section 4.2.2.4, the assessment of the *effects* of alleged anti-competitive behaviour constitutes an important step in an Article 102 TFEU analysis. In contrast, the DMA contains per se rules and does not require such an assessment of anti-competitive effects. The fundamental differences in methodology may amount to tension. Given the fact that violation of DMA does not require an analysis of the anti-competitive effects, the threshold for establishing a violation of a DMA prohibition is lower than the threshold for its competition law counterpart. Against this background, similar competition law and DMA obligations can be interpreted differently depending on the applicable legal

880. Freeman and Rossi 2012, p. 1145; Robertson 2024, pp. 327-328.
881. Crémer et al. 2023a, pp. 333-338.
882. *See* sections 4.2.3 and 5.3.3.

instrument. Although this potentially raises concerns relating to legal certainty and equality of treatment, certain divergences are unavoidable in light of the different methodologies and approaches enshrined in the DMA and competition law.[883]

5.5 CONCLUSION

This chapter aimed to map and analyse the relationship between the DMA and competition law. Despite the fact that the DMA is formally not included in the competition law framework, there are significant parallels in place between the two areas of law. The DMA was adopted in order to address the gaps in the application of competition law to personal data markets. Moreover, the framework undeniably draws inspiration from 'traditional' competition law. The objectives of both fields are partially overlapping, the majority of the DMA obligations are derived from competition law, and even the procedural and institutional frameworks share important similarities. Despite the fundamental differences in approach and methodology, both frameworks seek to control the use of market power by gatekeepers.[884] This begs the question of how the frameworks relate to each other.

As a starting position, the different frameworks apply in parallel, in line with the regulatory tradition of the EU. The DMA builds on the EU's longstanding tradition of the parallel or consecutive application of competition law and regulation to certain markets. Yet, there are significant differences in place between the DMA and other instruments of regulation. Accordingly, the DMA is a 'strange animal' which neither constitutes part of the competition law framework nor perfectly fits into the category of sector-specific regulation.[885] Henceforth, the DMA does not fit within the existing dichotomy between competition law and sector-specific regulation. In this light, past experience with the parallel application of competition law and sectoral regulation is not directly applicable to the DMA's relationship with competition law. The fact that the goals of the DMA are related to the objectives of competition law can, for example, have consequences for the application of the *ne bis in idem* principle.[886] The difficult epistemological position of the DMA begs the question of how the complementary relationship between the DMA and competition law should be shaped in practice.[887] In this context, the principles of hierarchy of norms, pre-emption and cooperation between authorities are highly relevant. These mechanisms are further explored in Part III.

883. Akman 2024, p. 432.
884. Akman 2024, pp. 431-432.
885. Podszun 2022c, p. 197; Vezzoso 2021.
886. *See* section 3.4.3.
887. Larouche and De Streel 2021, p. 542.

CHAPTER 6
Competition Law and the GDPR

6.1 INTRODUCTION

This chapter addresses the relationship between competition law and the GDPR. The debate on the relationship between the GDPR and competition law has been ongoing for years, but after the issuing of the *Meta Bundeskartellamt* judgment, the overlap between the two branches has become undeniable.[888] This chapter studies this interplay in more detail and aims to map the relationship between competition law and the GDPR by assessing how the relationship between the respective instruments is (or should be) shaped. To this end, the analysis is conducted in accordance with the structure put forward in Part II – Intervention on Personal Data Markets.

In line with this structure, section 6.2 sets out the legal framework of the GDRP by taking into account the objectives, scope, substantive provisions and institutional and enforcement framework of the instrument. Subsequently, section 6.3 identifies the GDPR's and competition law's common features, as well as the main differences between the respective instruments. Next, section 6.4 analyses the interaction between both frameworks in more detail and aims to place the GDPR in the broader regulatory context of EU law. Lastly, section 6.5 provides the chapter's conclusion.

888. CJEU 4 July 2023 Case C-252/21, *Meta Bundeskartellamt*; Graef 2016.

6.2 THE LEGAL FRAMEWORK OF THE GDPR

This section studies the legal framework of the GDPR which constitutes the backbone of EU data protection law. Data protection law is a relatively new field within EU law. In the 1970s, Germany – and subsequently some other Member States – started to adopt data protection legislation to control the processing of personal data by public authorities and large undertakings.[889] Although the EU initially refrained from adopting data protection rules, it began initiating such legislation in the 1990s. Over the decades, EU data protection law has become to a significant extent Europeanised and the field has grown into an important and independent branch of EU law.[890] The EU data protection framework is laid down in multiple instruments. The fundamental right to data protection and privacy is, for instance, enshrined in Articles 8 and 16 CFR. The right to data protection is further specified in the GDPR which is at the heart of EU data protection law.[891] This section further analyses the framework of the GDPR.[892]

6.2.1 Objectives of the GDPR

The objectives of the GDPR are manifold and ambitious. According to the Preamble to the GDPR, the processing of data should be designed to serve mankind.[893] In this context, the principles and rules on data protection should respect fundamental rights and freedoms, in particular the right to data protection and any processing of personal data should be lawful and fair.[894] Moreover, the GDPR aims to provide an equivalent level of data protection throughout the EU to ensure a consistent and high level of protection and to remove the obstacles to the free flow of personal data within the Union.[895] This section addresses the objectives of: (i) promoting the free flow of personal data in the EU; (ii) the safeguarding of fundamental rights and in particular the right to data protection; and (iii) fairness and lawfulness of processing, in turn.[896]

First, the GDPR has a *market integration* objective. This is unsurprising given that the GDPR originates from internal market law.[897] The GDPR's

889. European Union Agency for Fundamental Rights 2018, p. 18.
890. Streinz 2021.
891. Communication from the Commission to the European Parliament and the Council of 24 June 2020, Data Protection as a pillar of citizens' empowerment and the EU's approach to the digital transition – two years of application of the General Data Protection Directive, COM(2020)264 final, p. 2.
892. The analysis is limited to the GDPR. *See* section 1.3.3.
893. Preamble GDPR, recital 4.
894. Preamble GDPR, recitals 2 and 39.
895. Preamble GDPR, recital 10.
896. Bygrave 2002, p. 2.
897. Granger and Irion 2018.

internal market goal is reflected in the instrument's ambition to establish a level playing field for the flow of data in the EU. In this capacity, the GDPR has the potential to strengthen the functioning of the internal market.[898]

Second, the GDPR intends to contribute to the *protection of fundamental rights* and in particular the right to data protection. Given that the fundamental rights dimension is strongly reflected in the GDPR, this objective has gained importance with the development of EU personal data law.[899] In order to protect the right to personal data protection, the GDPR framework aims to provide a tool for ensuring that individuals have control over their personal data, and that data processing serves a legitimate purpose and is conducted in a lawful and transparent way.[900] In the context of EU law, the right to data protection is not subsumed to the right to private life or the right to privacy. Instead, the right to data protection is a self-standing and independent right.[901] Although the right to data protection, the right to private life and the right to privacy are closely related, their scope is not identical. Not every privacy issue will be relevant from a data protection perspective, and vice versa.[902] Privacy primarily focuses on independence and control, and covers a broad range of facets, including intimacy, seclusion and personhood.[903] Although the right to data protection is related to privacy, it places emphasis on the way information about an individual is used. Data protection serves as a 'catch-all' term for a series of ideas regarding the processing of data. Against this background, the ideal of informational autonomy is central to data protection law.[904]

Third, the principle of *fairness* constitutes an important overarching objective of data protection law. Arguably, fairness even amounts to the 'ultimate goal' of data protection law.[905] The notion takes centre stage in the GDPR. Article 5(1)(a) GDPR, for example, provides that 'personal data shall be processed lawfully, fairly, and in a transparent manner'. Despite the

---

898. Communication from the Commission to the European Parliament and the Council of 24 June 2020, Data Protection as a pillar of citizens' empowerment and the EU's approach to the digital transition – two years of application of the General Data Protection Directive, COM(2020)264 final, p. 2.
899. Hoofnagle, Van der Sloot and Zuiderveen Borgesius 2019, p. 72.
900. Communication from the Commission to the European Parliament and the Council of 24 June 2020, Data Protection as a pillar of citizens' empowerment and the EU's approach to the digital transition – two years of application of the General Data Protection Directive, COM(2020)264 final, p. 1.
901. European Union Agency for Fundamental Rights 2018, p. 18; Vogiatzoglou and Valcke 2022, p. 18.
902. In this light, the GC, for example, stressed that 'the fact that the concept of "private life" is a broad one [...] does not mean that all personal data necessarily fall within the concept of private life'. *See:* GC 8 November 2007 Case T-194/04, *Bavarian Lager*, para. 118.
903. Blume 2010, p. 153.
904. Tzanou 2013, p. 89.
905. Tzanou 2013, pp. 89-91.

prominent position of fairness, the GDPR does not define the principle. Therefore, the exact scope and meaning of the principle remain elusive and subject to debate. The GDPR links the fairness of data processing to other key principles, namely lawfulness and transparency.[906] Although these other principles can provide guidance for understanding the meaning of fairness in the context of data protection law, fairness cannot be reduced to lawfulness and transparency. Another important issue relates to the question of *to whom* an outcome should be fair.[907] The GDPR imposes obligations upon data controllers and grants rights to the data subject.[908] Against this background, fairness within the context of the GDPR focuses on the relationship between the data subject and the data controller.[909] In this relationship, the GDPR can be used to address market failures in personal data markets by rebalancing asymmetries in information and data access. By offering tools to the data subject, the GDPR reinforces its position vis-à-vis the data controller. This interpretation of the fairness principle is relevant to the GDPR's relationship with competition law. This issue is further addressed in section 6.3.

6.2.2 Scope

The scope of the GDPR is limited to the 'processing of personal data'.[910] According to Article 4(1) GDPR, *personal data* entails 'any information relating to an identified or identifiable person'. The GDPR does not apply to anonymous data that cannot be linked to an identifiable natural person. A person can be identifiable by various means, such as name, an identification number, location data, an online identifier, or by one or more factors related to the physical, psychological, genetic, mental, economic, cultural or social identity of that natural person. In order to determine whether an individual is identifiable, 'all means reasonably likely to be used' should be taken into account:[911]

> Example: a name is the most straightforward means of identifying someone. However, other identifiers, such as fingerprints, IP addresses or cookie identifiers, could also make someone identifiable, since such

906. Articles 13(2) and 14(2) GDPR and Article 6 GDPR.
907. This question also arises in the context of competition law and the DMA. *See* section 5.3.1.
908. European Union Agency for Fundamental Rights 2018, p. 118.
909. For an elaborate analysis in this regard *see:* Clifford and Ausloos 2018.
910. Articles 1(1) and 2(1) GDPR.
911. In order to conclude whether means are reasonably likely to be used, 'account should be taken of all objective factors, such as the costs of and the amount of time required for identification, taking into consideration the available technology at the time of the processing and technological development', *see:* Preamble GDPR, recital 26.

identifiers may leave traces that can be used to create profiles of natural persons in order to identify them.[912]

Next, *processing* refers to 'any operation or set of operations which is performed on personal data or sets of personal data, whether or not by automated means'.[913] The GDPR provides a non-exhaustive list of operations that may qualify as processing, including the collection, recording, organisation, structuring, storage and adaptation of personal data. Under the GDPR, two entities may be responsible for the processing of personal data. The 'controller' is the 'natural or legal person, public authority, agency or other body which, alone or jointly with others, determines the purposes and means of the processing of personal data'.[914] The processor is the entity which 'processes personal data on behalf of the controller'. The distinction between processors and controllers is relevant as the responsibilities of the respective actors differ:[915]

> Example: a brewery signs a contract with a payroll company to pay wages to its employees. The brewery decides when the wages should be paid and provides all details regarding the salary slip and payment. The payroll company relies on this information and uses its own IT system to store the employees' data. In this scenario, the brewery qualifies as the data controller and the payroll company constitutes the processor.[916]

6.2.3 Substantive Obligations and Prohibitions

The GDPR is based on a number of key principles and only allows data processing on the basis of an applicable legal basis.[917] This Section addresses the GDPR's main principles and legal bases, as well as the most important substantive obligations and prohibitions.

First, personal data should be processed *fairly, lawfully* and *transparently*.[918] The concept of fairness has been discussed in section 6.2.1. According to the principle of lawfulness, data can only be processed based on one of the six lawful grounds, i.e.: (i) consent; (ii) necessity for contractual performance; (iii) necessity for a task carried out in the exercise of public authority; (iv) compliance with a legal obligation; (v) a legitimate

---

912. Preamble GDPR, recital 30.
913. Article 4 (2) GDPR.
914. Article 4(7) GDPR.
915. Carey 2020, p. 19; For the sake of the readability, I will only refer to the data controller.
916. *See:* https://commission.europa.eu/law/law-topic/data-protection/rules-business-and-organisations/obligations/controllerprocessor/what-data-controller-or-data-processor_en accessed 29 August 2025.
917. Communication from the Commission to the European Parliament and the Council of 24 June 2020, Data Protection as a pillar of citizens' empowerment and the EU's approach to the digital transition – two years of application of the General Data Protection Directive, COM(2020)264 final, p. 2.
918. Article 5(1)(a) GDPR.

interest of the controller or a third party; and (vi) the protection of the vital interest of the data subject. In the private sector, the grounds of necessity for contract performance, legitimate interest and consent are the most relevant.[919] The central role of the notion of consent in the GDPR framework has been heavily criticised. This criticism mostly relates to the ability of the average user to make an informed choice about privacy policies, which are often hefty and complex. The rationality of individual users can be affected by several behavioural biases.[920] This raises the question of whether consent adequately reflects a real choice on the part of the individual or data subject.[921] Considering the principle of transparency, data processors are under an obligation to take appropriate measures to ensure that the data subject is informed about the use of its data. The information should be available before the processing starts, but must also be provided upon request. The means and terms of processing should be explained in an easily accessible way, and processors are obliged to use clear and plain language.[922]

Second, the principle of *purpose limitation* requires that personal data is merely collected for specified, explicit and legitimate purposes.[923] The data can only be processed for a well-defined purpose and for additional purposes that are compatible with the initial purpose. In short, data collected for objective X cannot be used or processed to pursue goal Y.[924]

Third, according to the principle of *data minimisation*, data should be 'adequate, relevant and limited to what is necessary in relation to the purposes for which they are processed'.[925] This means that only the data that are necessary to achieve the declared purpose of the processing can be collected.[926] Disproportionate data processing is, therefore, prohibited.

Fourth, the principle of *accuracy* establishes that stored data must be accurate and up-to-date. Controllers must take reasonable steps to guarantee that inaccurate data is erased or rectified.[927]

Fifth, the GDPR establishes a principle of *storage limitation*, prohibiting data from being stored for unreasonably long periods. This means that data cannot be stored in a form that allows the identification of the data subject for longer than is necessary for the purpose of data processing.[928]

919. Helberger, Zuiderveen Borgesius and Reyna 2017, p. 1432.
920. *See* section 2.7.
921. Gil González and De Hert 2019, p. 601.
922. Articles 12, 13 and 14 GDPR; Preamble GDPR, para. 39; *See also*: European Union Agency for Fundamental Rights 2018, p. 120.
923. Article 5(1)(b) GDPR For a more elaborate analysis of the principle of purpose limitation, *see:* Von Grafenstein 2018.
924. Helberger, Zuiderveen Borgesius and Reyna 2017, p. 1432.
925. Article 5(1) sub c GDPR.
926. European Union Agency for Fundamental Rights 2018, p. 125.
927. Article 5(1)(d) GDPR.
928. Article 5(1)(e) GDPR.

Once it is no longer necessary to store personalised data, such data should therefore be anonymised or erased.[929]

Sixth, the principles of *data security* and *confidentiality* establish that data controllers are responsible for safeguarding data protection rights. Data shall be processed in a manner that ensures security by using appropriate technical and organisational measures, including protection against unlawful processing, as well as accidental loss, destruction and damage.[930]

Seventh, the principle of *accountability* establishes that data controllers are responsible for safeguarding data protection rights.[931] Data controllers are obliged to actively and continuously implement measures to safeguard these rights. To this end, the GDPR sets out various mechanisms of compliance. Article 24 GDPR, for instance, stresses that controllers have to implement appropriate technical and organisational measures to ensure compliance. Moreover, other specific obligations, such as requirements relating to privacy by default, keeping appropriate records of processing and the obligations to notify personal data breaches, further substantiate the accountability principle.[932] Lastly, data processors should be capable of demonstrating compliance.

Apart from the seven key principles, the GDPR lays down various additional rights and obligations for users, processors and controllers. Individuals have the *right to be informed* and may require controllers (or processors) to provide processing information, including the controller's identity and contact details as well as the legal basis for processing.[933] Furthermore, data subjects have the right to *access their own personal data.*[934] This right to access is considered a key element of data protection law. In line with the principle of accuracy, data subjects have a *right to rectification* without undue delay.[935] To guarantee the effective application of the data protection principles and the principle of data minimisation in particular, data subjects have the *right to erasure* or the *right to be forgotten*:9[936]

> Example: In the *Google Spain* case, the CJEU stressed that individuals have the right to request erasure of their personal data if this data is inaccurate, inadequate, irrelevant or excessive.[937] Article 18 GDPR provides data subjects with the *right to restriction of processing.* This means that an individual can file a request to restrict processing if, for

929. European Union Agency for Fundamental Rights 2018, p. 129.
930. Article 5(1)(f) GDPR.
931. Article 5(2) GDPR.
932. Articles 25, 30, 33 and 34 GDPR. *See also*: Van Alsenoy 2019, pp. 44-45.
933. Articles 13 and 14 GDPR.
934. Article 15 GDPR.
935. Article 16 and 19 GDPR; *See also*: European Union Agency for Fundamental Rights 2018, p. 217.
936. Article 17 GDPR.
937. CJEU 13 May 2014 Case C-131/12, *Google Spain*, para. 93.

example, the accuracy of the data is contested or if the processing is unlawful.

If data is processed on the basis of consent or a contract, data subjects have the right to *data portability*.[938] This means that they have the right to have their data transferred from one controller to another, insofar as this is technically feasible.[939] The right to data portability is also relevant from the perspective of competition law. This issue is further addressed in section 6.4.2. Furthermore, data subjects have the *right to object* to processing where processing is based on the controller's performance of tasks in the public interest or on a legitimate interest. Lastly, the GDPR provides data subjects with a remedy. They have the *right to lodge a complaint* with a supervisory authority and/or a national court.[940]

The GDPR not only establishes rights for individuals but also imposes specific obligations on controllers and processors. Certain processors and controllers are obligated to designate a data protection officer (henceforth: DPO).[941] Generally speaking, this DPO is responsible for monitoring the controller's compliance with the GDPR.[942] Furthermore, the GDPR requires the implementation of data protection by design and data protection by default.[943] Data protection by design lays down the obligation to take data protection into account from the earliest stages in the development of new means of processing. Data controllers must take the necessary technical and organisational steps to implement the data protection principles. The obligation to provide data protection by default requires that the most data protection-friendly setting constitutes the default setting.[944]

6.2.4 Institutional and Enforcement Framework

This section addresses the GDPR's enforcement and institutional frameworks. The institutional and enforcement frameworks are addressed in turn.

6.2.4.1 The Institutional Framework

The enforcement of the GDPR is decentralised and largely takes place at the Member State level.[945] According to Article 55 GDPR, each supervisory

938. Article 20 GDPR.
939. European Union Agency for Fundamental Rights 2018, p. 228.
940. Articles 21(1), 13(2)(d) and 14(2)(e) GDPR.
941. The obligation to designate a DPO applies, among others, to controllers and processors whose core activity consist of processing operations which require systematic monitoring of data subjects on a large scale (Article 37(1)(b) GDPR).
942. Article 37 GDPR.
943. Article 25 GDPR.
944. Preamble GDPR, recital 78.
945. The decentralisation of the GDPR is further studied in section 9.5.1.

authority is competent to enforce the GDPR within the territory of its own Member State. Member States are not obligated to establish only one competent authority, but can opt for a plethora of DPAs.[946] Furthermore, the tasks of DPAs are not necessarily limited to GDPR enforcement. In contrast, these authorities may engage in other functions as well.[947]

In *The Netherlands*, the *Autoriteit Persoonsgegevens* (henceforth: AP) is responsible for the enforcement of the GDPR.[948] To this end, this authority can rely on the competences established in the GDPR.[949] While the enforcement of data protection law is the responsibility of a single authority in The Netherlands, in *Germany*, multiple authorities are involved. The Federal Commissioner for Data Protection and Freedom of Information (*Bundesbeauftragte für den Datenschutz und die Informationsfreiheit*) (henceforth: Federal Commissioner) is the supreme and federal authority.[950] The Federal Commissioner is responsible for the supervision of federal public bodies as well as for the oversight of certain telecom providers.[951] Moreover, the Federal Commissioner serves as the single point of contact for the GDPR's consistency mechanism. The Federal Commissioner shares the competence to enforce the GDPR with several decentralised authorities. The 16 federal states (*Bundesländer*) each have their own decentralised data protection authority.[952]

Although the GDPR relies on a system of decentralised enforcement, the regulation establishes a one-stop-shop mechanism for cross-border processing. According to this mechanism, the supervisory authority of the main or single establishment of a controller acts as the competent supervisor.[953] The GDPR establishes various mechanisms to facilitate cooperation between the lead supervisor and other DPAs.[954] These mechanisms are further addressed in section 9.5.1.

Although the enforcement of the GDPR is to a significant extent decentralised, certain bodies have been established at the EU level. The European Data Protection Supervisor (henceforth: EDPS) and the European Data Protection Board (henceforth: EDPB) are the most relevant in this regard. The EDPS is an independent body responsible for the monitoring of

946. Recital 117 of the GDPR's preamble stresses that 'Member States should be able to establish more than one supervisory authority, to reflect their constitutional, organisational and administrative structure'.
947. In The Netherlands, the Dutch DPA is, for example, responsible for the supervision on algorithms and AI. *See:* Letter Ministerie van Binnenlandse Zaken en Koninkrijksrelaties aan de Voorzitter van de Tweede Kamer der Staten-Generaal 22 December 2022, 2022-0000689652.
948. Article 6(2) Dutch Implementation Act GDPR.
949. Article 14 Dutch Implementation Act GDPR.
950. Section 8 German Federal Data Protection Act.
951. Section 9 Bundesdatenschutzgesetz.
952. *See,* for example, Hamburgisches Datenschutzgesetz 18 May 2018, HmbGVBI. S. 67.
953. Article 56 GDPR.
954. Articles 60-67 GDPR.

the application of data protection laws to all processing operations carried out by EU institutions and bodies.[955] The EDPB is an independent body comprised of the heads of the DPAs of the Member States and the EDPS.[956] The Commission has the right to participate in the activities and meetings of the EDPB without a voting right.[957] This body has the responsibility to 'ensure the consistent application' of the GDPR.[958]

6.2.4.2 The Enforcement Framework

Prior to the adoption of the GDPR, data protection law was enforced at the Member State level.[959] This resulted in significant divergences in national enforcement frameworks.[960] The GDPR addresses these issues by partially harmonising the enforcement of EU data protection law. Yet, the regulation still allows Member States to adopt additional powers at the national level, provided that the GDPR's mechanisms for cooperation and consistency are not affected.[961] National procedural rules must comply with national and EU safeguards, including the right to an effective judicial remedy and due process.[962] The opening clause of the GDPR leaves room for divergence in national enforcement frameworks.[963]

Although Member States may adopt additional procedural frameworks, the GDPR grants several competences to national DPAs. In this regard, Article 58 GDPR makes a distinction between investigative and corrective powers. DPAs shall have various corrective powers at their disposal, including the power to issue a warning or reprimand, order the controller to comply with certain GDPR obligations, impose a temporary ban on processing, impose an administrative fine or order the suspension of data flows to recipients in third countries. Thus, DPAs can impose a broad range of behavioural remedies and sanctions. DPAs can impose relatively mild

955. Article 1(3) Regulation (EU) 2018/1725 of the European Parliament and of the Council of 23 October 2018 on the protection of natural persons with regard to the processing of personal data by the Union institutions, bodies, offices and agencies and on the free movement of such data, and repealing Regulation (EC) No. 45/2001 and Decision No. 1247/2002/EC.
956. Articles 68, 69 and 70(1) GDPR.
957. Article 68(5) GDPR.
958. Article 70 GDPR.
959. Directive 95/46/EC (Data Protection Directive).
960. These divergencies, among others, are related to the resources and powers of the DPAs and can be explained by differences in history, case law, culture and internal organisation of the Member States. *See:* Article 29 Data Protection Working Party and Working Party on Policy and Justice 1 December 2009, Joint contribution to the Consultation of the European Commission on the legal framework for the fundamental right to protection of personal data, 02356/09/EN.
961. Article 58(6) GDPR; Voigt and Von dem Bussche 2017, pp. 201-202.
962. Article 58(4) GDPR.
963. Georgieva and Schmidl 2020, p. 946.

sanctions, such as warnings and reprimands. However, some other listed remedies are more far-reaching. The DPAs possibility to impose a ban on processing constitutes a stringent behavioural remedy. In theory, this remedy could even have more impact than a fine, since data processing is at the core of business models on personal data markets.[964]

The GDPR grants DPAs the competence to impose fines. The GDPR allows DPAs to impose fines of up to EUR 20,000,000 or 4% of the annual turnover of the undertaking concerned.[965] This remedy is considered the strongest and most coercive competence of DPAs.[966] The GDPR lists certain factors which shall be taken into account in establishing the amount of the fine. These factors, which partially mirror the relevant competences in a competition law context and encompass, *inter alia,* the nature, gravity and duration of the infringement, the intentional or negligent character of the infringement and the action taken to mitigate damage and relevant previous infringements.[967] Despite the general factors that shall be taken into account, the GDPR leaves the imposition and calculation of fines largely at the discretion of the respective DPAs. Given this broad discretion, the level of fines can differ between Member States since national practices relating to the use of financial sanctions diverge and DPAs have different priorities and resources.[968] Against this backdrop, it is to be applauded that the EDPB has issued guidelines on the calculation of administrative fines.[969] However, and despite the guidelines, the imposition of fines remains subject to controversy. This is clearly reflected in a case considering Meta's data transfers to the US. In this case, the Irish DPA, the Data Protection Commission (henceforth: DPC) ordered Meta to bring its data processing operations in compliance with the GDPR by suspending any future transfers of personal data to the US. In its initial decision, the DPC did not impose a fine upon Meta which was criticised by various other DPAs who raised objections and triggered the consistency mechanisms of the GDPR which is discussed in section 9.5.1.[970] In its binding decision the EDPB concluded that the DPC's decision to refrain from the imposition of a fine did not comply with the GDPR.[971] This case shows the disagreement among the various DPAs when it comes to the imposition of fines.

964. Lintvedt 2022, p. 11.
965. Articles 58(2)(i) and 83 GDPR.
966. Giurgiu and Larsen 2016, p. 348.
967. Articles 58(2) and 83 GDPR.
968. Lintvedt 2022, pp. 1-2.
969. European Data Protection Board, Guidelines of 12 May 2022 on the calculation of administrative fines under the GDPR, 04/2022.
970. Article 63 GDPR; The consistency mechanisms will be further discussed in section 9.5.1.
971. EDPB Binding decision 1/2021 of 28 July 2021 on the dispute arisen on the draft decision of the Irish Supervisory Authority regarding WhatsApp Ireland under Article 65(1)(a) GDPR.

6.2.4.3 Institutional and Enforcement Framework: Final Remarks

The institutional and enforcement frameworks of the GDPR are subject to criticism, especially concerning divergences between Member States and GDPR enforcement in the context of cross-border cases. The weaknesses in the enforcement and institutional framework arguably result in a dichotomy between the law in the books and its practical application.[972] The Commission acknowledges the shortcomings in the enforcement and institutional framework and has highlighted that 'further progress is needed to make the handling of cross-border cases more efficient and harmonised across the EU'.[973] The issues associated with the weaknesses in the GDPR's enforcement framework have various dimensions.

First, various data protection authorities suffer from a lack of resources.[974] The overall combined budget of the 45 data protection authorities in the EU is a mere EUR 325 million a year, and half of the authorities have a budget not exceeding EUR 10 million a year.[975] Against this background, it is unsurprising that the Dutch DPA has requested an increase in resources.[976] This lack of resources is not merely an issue at the national level, but also the EDPS and EDPB have expressed concerns about their financial situation and requested an increase in human resources.[977] This issue of limited financial and human resources is particularly problematic in the context of large platforms, which have significant resources at their disposal.

Second, the one-stop-shop mechanism for cross-border cases – which is further addressed in section 9.5.1 – can hamper the effective application of the GDPR.[978] As a result of this mechanism, the authority in which a data controller has its main establishment acts as the leading supervisory authority in cross-border cases. In practice, this means that many investigations into Big Tech platforms are led by very few authorities. The Irish DPA is mainly responsible for the supervision of Tech giants, including Google, Meta,

972. Gentile and Lynskey 2022.
973. Communication from the Commission to the European Parliament and the Council of 24 June 2020, Data Protection as a pillar of citizens' empowerment and the EU's approach to the digital transition – two years of application of the General Data Protection Directive, COM(2020)264 final ; Proposal for a Regulation of the European Parliament and Council on a Regulation laying down additional procedural rules relating to the enforcement of Regulation 2016/679, COM(2023) 348 final.
974. EPDB and EDPS 13 September 2021, Lack of resources puts enforcement of individuals' data protection rights at risk https://www.edps.europa.eu/press-publications/press-news/press-releases/2022/edpb-edps-lack-resources-puts-enforcement-individuals-data-protection-rights-risk_en accessed 14 March 2025.
975. Tombal 2021, p. 18.
976. Barkhuysen 2021, p. 585.
977. EDPB and EPDS 12 September 2022, OUT2022 – 0068 https://www.edpb.europa.eu/system/files/2022-09/letteronbudget_out2022-0068.pdf accessed 14 March 2025.
978. Kerber and Specht-Riemenschneider 2021, p. 13.

Microsoft and Twitter.[979] This concentration of cases creates bottlenecks due to a lack of capacity of the Irish authorities.[980] Furthermore, the Irish authority has received criticism as its alleged reluctance to intervene can result in a large platform escaping the application of the GDPR.[981]

In July 2023, the Commission adopted a proposal for further harmonisation of the procedural framework of the GDPR. The Proposal, *inter alia*, streamlines the filing and handling of complaints. Moreover, the proposed procedural regulation aims to address cooperation within the context of GDPR enforcement.[982] This topic of cooperation is further discussed in section 9.6.

6.3 COMPETITION LAW AND THE GDPR: COMMON FEATURES AND MAIN DIFFERENCES

The frameworks of competition law and the GDPR are separate areas of the law with distinct objectives, substantive provisions, enforcement and institutional frameworks. However, in personal data markets, these areas of the law increasingly interact and intertwine.[983] Although these areas of law are clearly not identical, they share some common features or 'family' ties.[984] This section further examines the interaction between competition law and the GDPR by mapping the main commonalities and differences between the respective frameworks. The objectives, scope and substantive provisions and enforcement and institutional frameworks are addressed in turn.

6.3.1 Objectives

The primary goals of competition law and data protection law are not identical. Nevertheless, these legal fields share some common objectives.[985] While EU competition law (*inter alia*) aims to contribute to consumer welfare by safeguarding undistorted competition on the market, data protection law focuses on protecting the rights and freedoms of the data subject so as to ensure fair data processing without restricting the free movement of

979. Nicolas Vinocur 2019.
980. Tombal 2021, p. 18.
981. Geradin, Karanikioti and Katsifis 2021, p. 68.
982. Proposal for a Regulation of the European Parliament and Council on a Regulation laying down additional procedural rules relating to the enforcement of Regulation 2016/679, COM(2023) 348 final.
983. Svantesson 2018, p. 25; Graef 2016.
984. Graef 2016.
985. Wiedemann 2021, p. 923.

data.[986] Arguably, the areas of law serve an overarching aim of the protection of 'welfare of individuals in the modern economy'.[987] More specifically, both fields: (i) contribute to the integration of the EU's internal market; (ii) share a concern for the consumer; and (iii) pursue a fairness objective.[988]

First, the objective of integration of the EU's internal market amounts to a shared objective of EU competition law and the GDPR. Although both fields of law rely on different means to achieve this objective, market integration constitutes a common goal. While the GDPR fosters *positive* integration via secondary legislation, the main substantive provisions of EU competition law facilitate *negative* integration by ensuring that undertakings do not jeopardise the functioning of the internal market by engaging in anti-competitive behaviour.[989] It is important to stress that there are multiple instruments and areas of EU law with a market integration objective, particularly instruments adopted on the basis of Article 114 TFEU.[990] Therefore, the goal of market integration links multiple areas of EU law and does not establish a specific link between competition law and the GDPR. Against this backdrop, the market integration rationale can be considered a shared denominator, but not as a factor that inherently links the two areas of law or aligns their diverse underlying values.

Second, competition law and the GDPR share a *concern for the consumer*. In competition law, this concern is reflected in the consumer welfare standard. Data protection focuses on the position of the data subject, but in this capacity, it also touches upon the position of the online consumer. Thus, data protection can strengthen the online consumer's degree of data control as well as the individual's informational autonomy.[991] To this end, the GDPR addresses asymmetries between the data subject and data controllers or processors. This is relevant for the competitive process since information asymmetries may result in users accepting inferior privacy conditions even if better alternatives exist on the market.[992] In other words, well-informed consumers are a prerequisite for the existence of well-functioning markets and data protection laws can increase the online consumer's access to

986. Costa-Cabral and Lynskey 2018.
987. Botta and Wiedemann 2019, p. 435.
988. Lynskey 2015, p. 9.
989. Nevertheless, the EU competition law framework also encompasses some instrument of positive integration, especially in terms of the procedural framework. The Private Damages Directive and Regulation 1/2003, for example, constitute examples of positive integration. *See also*: Graef 2016, p. 9.
990. The Services Directive, for example, also aims at 'the establishment of a genuine internal market' and the DSA aims to 'safeguard and improve the functioning of the internal market'.
991. Wiedemann 2021, p. 926.
992. Buiten 2021, p. 282.

information. Therefore, the GDPR and competition law are complementary and protect 'different dimensions of consumer welfare'.[993]

The degree to which concern for the consumer in competition and data protection law overlaps depends on one's normative understanding of the goals of competition law and in particular of the consumer welfare standard. As explained in section 4.2.1, a narrow reading of the consumer welfare standard does not leave room for the incorporation of data protection considerations. However, by accepting that: (i) the available level of data protection constitutes part of the quality of an online service; or (ii) that the amount of data collected constitutes a part of the 'price', GDPR-related considerations enter the realm of competition law. Now, the relevance of privacy and data protection as relevant parameters has been endorsed by the Commission and the CJEU. In the Relevant Markets Notice, the Commission explicitly mentions the 'privacy protection afforded' as a parameter of competition.[994] Similarly, the CJEU established that data amounts to a 'significant parameter of competition' in the *Meta Bundeskartellamt* case.[995] Given the importance of data for the competitive process, the CJEU stressed that the legal framework for data protection may need to be taken into consideration in assessing potential abuses of dominance. Excluding the rules on data protection law, and the GDPR in particular would 'disregard the reality of this economic development [the increasing relevance of data] and undermine the effectiveness of competition law'.[996] The CJEU thus also explicitly acknowledged the link between data protection and competition law and made it clear that data considerations can constitute a relevant element of a competition law analysis since (the level of) data protection constitutes a relevant parameter of competition. In my view, the fact that the Commission and CJEU endorse the relevance of data and data protection in the context of a competition law assessment should be applauded. The flexibility of the competition law framework leaves room for this approach. As explained previously, undertakings active on such markets rely on business models in which personal data is monetised.[997] The monetisation of personal data makes such data relevant from a competitive perspective as well. As stated by the CJEU, neglecting this development by focusing merely on more 'traditional' parameters of competition would disregard economic reality. Subsequently, the consumer welfare standard in competition law and the consumer concern in the data protection law framework increasingly align. Therefore, the consumer welfare standard, and particularly a broader interpretation of this standard, can bridge the frameworks of data protection and competition law.

---

993. Graef, Clifford and Valcke 2018, p. 203.
994. Relevant Markets Notice, para. 15.
995. CJEU 4 July 2023 Case C-252/21, *Meta Bundeskartellamt*, para. 51.
996. CJEU 4 July 2023 Case C-252/21, *Meta Bundeskartellamt*, para. 51.
997. *See* section 2.5.

Third, the principle of *fairness* is a shared notion within the competition and data protection law frameworks. At first sight, the principle of fairness does seem a common feature of the frameworks of competition and data protection law. However, despite its presence in both frameworks, the relevance of the notion of fairness in connecting competition law and the GDPR depends on the way in which the principle is defined. If the interpretation of the principle is significantly divergent in the different contexts, it cannot amount to a common feature.

Although the principle of consistency of EU laws could indicate that the notion of fairness should have a similar meaning in the respective fields of EU law, reality is more complex.[998] The interpretation of the notion of fairness is context-dependent and diverges across legal fields. The fact that neither competition law nor the GDPR provide a definition of the concept of fairness further complicates the matter. Despite the absence of a definition, fairness in a GDPR context focuses on *fair processing* so as to rebalance the asymmetric data access in the relationship between the data subject and the data controller.[999] In a competition law context, the exact meaning and scope of the notion of fairness is subject to debate.[1000] It is uncertain whether the notion of fairness should be aligned with a narrow definition of consumer welfare or should be understood more broadly. Under the narrowest reading, consumer welfare arguably leaves little room for data protection considerations, while a broader understanding could incorporate the level of data protection as part of the quality of a service. Data protection and privacy can – under this approach – be considered indirect elements of the notion of fairness in a competition law context. If one agrees that competition law should pursue non-economic objectives as well, these commonalities would become even stronger.[1001] Despite the fact that the latter approach is not currently endorsed in EU competition law, the evolution of competition law may result in a closer alignment between the interpretation of the concept of fairness in the competition law and data protection law contexts. Despite the fact that data protection considerations 'are not, as such, a matter for competition law', the CJEU has acknowledged that it may be necessary to take such considerations into account.[1002] By allowing NCAs to incorporate GDPR considerations into a competition law assessment, the CJEU confirms that the GDPR can offer normative guidance for a competition law assessment.[1003] In other words, compliance with the data protection framework has become a relevant factor in assessing whether a condition is fair in a competition law context.

998. Kalimo and Majcher 2017, p. 4.
999. *See* section 6.2.1.
1000. *See* section 4.2.1.4.
1001. Kalimo and Majcher 2017, p. 7.
1002. CJEU 23 November 2006 Case C-238/05, *Asnef-Equifax*, para. 63; CJEU 4 July 2023 Case C-252/21 *Meta Bundeskartellamt*, para. 48.
1003. Majcher 2023, pp. 158-159.

In sum, data protection and competition law share some overlapping objectives and can complement each other in the regulation of personal data markets. These fields of law are undeniably intertwined. Yet, the desirable degree of overlap remains subject to debate and largely depends on one's understanding of the 'soul of antitrust'.[1004] At this point, the shared concern for consumers constitutes the clearest common goal of competition law and the GDPR. In case law, the CJEU seems to endorse a rather broad standard of consumer welfare by recognising data as a relevant parameter for competition. In this light, (the level of) data protection becomes relevant when assessing the level of consumer welfare and clearly enters the field of competition law. Data protection law is not endorsed as an objective in and of itself but becomes relevant for the objectives of competition law through the lens of consumer welfare. In my view, this is a desirable approach, given the new economic reality of digital markets and, in particular, the monetisation of personal data. Neglecting the relevance of personal data in a competition law assessment would overlook the new economic reality and thereby compromise the effectiveness of the competition law framework.[1005]

Apart from the principle of consumer welfare, the objective of fairness can serve as a bridge between the data protection and the competition law frameworks. This notion is present in both fields of law. However, the debate on the relevance of fairness in a competition law context, combined with the concept's elusive nature, makes it difficult to determine to what extent the notion of fairness may serve as a connecting objective in practice.

6.3.2 Scope and Substantive Provisions

The scope and nature of the substantive provisions of competition law and the GDPR are rather different. While the GDPR establishes a general framework with a broad scope applying to *all* processors and controllers, Article 102 TFEU applies exclusively to undertakings with a dominant position. Apart from the differences in scope, the nature of the substantive obligations of competition law and the GDPR are far from identical. Article 102 TFEU contains a broad and open-ended norm, whereas the GDPR establishes specific principles, rights and obligations. From a substantive perspective, the frameworks have – at first sight – little in common.[1006] Yet, the fact that the frameworks are designed differently does not mean that these areas of law do not have commonalities.

1004. Fox 1987.
1005. *See also* CJEU 4 July 2023 Case C-252/21 *Meta Bundeskartellamt*, para. 51.
1006. Lynskey 2015, p. 9.

Since undertakings operating on personal data markets 'monetise' personal data, such data becomes a parameter of competition.[1007] This dynamic establishes a clear substantive link between competition law and the GDPR. In the *Meta Bundeskartellamt* case, the German NCA concluded that Facebook had violated the GDPR and abused its dominant position by collecting data from third-party websites and by linking this data to the user's Facebook account.[1008] In this case, the *Bundeskartellamt* used the GDPR as a normative parameter in the competition law assessment.[1009] In the *Meta Bundeskartellamt* case, the CJEU established a clear connection between the substantive frameworks of data protection law and competition law, particularly in the context of exploitative abuses. The implications of this case are further analysed in section 6.4.2. By consolidating this approach in the Draft Guidelines on the application of Article 102 TFEU, the Commission takes a similar approach.[1010]

6.3.3 Institutional and Enforcement Frameworks

The enforcement frameworks of competition law and the GDPR share some similarities. In drafting the GDPR's enforcement framework, the EU legislator visibly drew inspiration from the competition law framework.[1011] The parallels between the enforcement frameworks are, for instance, clearly reflected in recital 151 of the GDPR's Preamble which stresses that where administrative fines are imposed on an undertaking, 'an undertaking should be understood to be an undertaking in accordance with Articles 101 and 102 TFEU […]'. Yet, and despite these parallels, the institutional and enforcement frameworks of competition law and the GDPR are notably distinct in their design. While the enforcement of EU competition law is the shared responsibility of the Commission and NCAs, the GDPR is enforced in a decentralised fashion by national DPAs. For cases relating to cross-border processing, the GDPR establishes a one-stop-shop mechanism.[1012]

Furthermore, there are significant divergences in the effectiveness of the enforcement frameworks. While the enforcement of competition law is considered relatively effective, the GDPR's enforcement and institutional

1007. In *Google Shopping,* the Commission, for instance, acknowledges that consumers contribute to the monetisation of personal data. *See:* European Commission 27 June 2017, Case AT3970, *Google Shopping*, para. 158.

1008. *Bundeskartellamt* 6 February 2019 Case B6-22/16, *Facebook*; *See* section 4.4.2.3.

1009. Van den Bergh and Weber 2021, p. 34.

1010. Draft Guidelines on the Application of Article 102, para. 55(c).

1011. Article 83(2) GDPR lists similar factors as the Guidelines of 1 September 2006 on the method of setting fines imposed pursuant to Article 23(2)(a) of Regulation No. 1/2003, C 210/8.

1012. *See* section 9.5.1.

frameworks have faced significant criticism.[1013] GDPR enforcement in a cross-border context appears particularly problematic.[1014] It has been suggested that the GDPR has 'much to learn from the elaborate procedural framework of competition law'.[1015] This statement does not only relate to the institutional set-up of the GDPR which may result in bottlenecks due to inactivity of the lead supervisory authority but also relates to the enforcement framework. Competition law fines tend to be much higher than GDPR fines. This can partially be explained by the fact that competition law establishes a 10% fine cap, whereas the GDPR caps fines at 4% of the annual turnover.[1016] Beyond differences in fining policies, the GDPR and competition law are not identical in terms of the available behavioural and structural remedies. On the one hand, unlike data protection law, competition law allows for the imposition of structural remedies, although these structural remedies are generally not imposed in practice.[1017] On the other hand, the GDPR contains some remedies that are absent in the EU competition law context. The GDPR, for example, includes remedies with an *ex-ante* character, such as the competence to issue a warning in the case of processing operations that are 'likely to infringe the provisions of the regulation'.[1018] This means that the GDPR provides for a remedy to issue warnings before an infringement has taken place or has been established. In this regard, the GDPR is more *ex ante*-focused than the procedural framework of competition law.[1019] Moreover, the GDPR provides competence to impose a ban on

1013. Wils, for example, stresses – with regard to the competition law framework and based on among others an analysis of the number of investigations and adopted fines or commitments – that '[t]en years after the adoption of Regulation 1/2003, there can be no doubt that [… .] the new enforcement system has been a major success'. *See:* Wils 2013, p. 7.

1014. In a Proposal for the new GDPR Procedural Regulation, the Commission, for example, stresses that 'further process was needed to make the handling of cross-border cases more efficient and harmonised across the EU'. *See:* Proposal for a Regulation of the European Parliament and Council on a Regulation laying down additional procedural rules relating to the enforcement of Regulation 2016/679, COM(2023) 348 final, p. 1; Various academics also express their concerns as to the effectiveness of the enforcement framework of the GDPR. *See,* for example: Geradin, Karanikioti and Katsifis 2021; Koops 2014.

1015. Lynskey 2015, p. 9.

1016. Article 23(2) Regulation 1/2003 and Article 83 GDPR.

1017. *See* sections 4.2.3, 4.3.3 and 4.4.3.

1018. Article 58(2)(a) GDPR.

1019. Georgieva and Schmidl 2020, p. 946. In a competition law context, the European Commission can adopt commitments. Since commitments can be adopted before a positive infringement decision is taken, there are some similarities between this commitment decision and the warnings in a GDPR context. However, commitments can only be adopted if the Commission intends to adopt a decision, where warnings can be issued where an infringement is likely. Furthermore, commitments are offered by the undertakings concerned. Against this background, the instrument of commitments and the warming mechanism in the GDPR are not identical.

processing activities.[1020] Such a ban could have large implications for a platform's ability to offer its services. Therefore, a ban on processing amounts to a stringent remedy. Yet, to my knowledge, such a ban has not yet been imposed, at least not to address violations by Big Tech platforms. In this light, there is a parallel in place with structural remedies in competition law: both instruments are strong on paper, but have not (yet) proven highly effective in practice.

In sum, the institutional and enforcement frameworks of competition law and the GDPR share some traits, but also display significant differences. Most importantly, competition law has stronger teeth. Against this backdrop, some authors suggest giving competition authorities more leeway to play a role in addressing data protection violations by dominant firms.[1021] If a relevant lead supervisory authority, for example, refuses to take action, the application of competition law by a competition authority could break the impasse. In my view, this is not a reasonable approach. Despite the fact that there are good reasons for incorporating data protection considerations into competition law, one field of law should not be applied to cover for the alleged shortcomings of another area. In other words, it is undesirable for EU competition law to be applied in order to compensate for the weaknesses of the GDPR's enforcement and institutional framework. Such shortcomings must be resolved by adjustments to the GDPR's enforcement framework, not by the application of competition law. Consequently, the initiative to update the GDPR's enforcement and institutional framework is a step in the right direction and to be applauded. Arguably, the coherence of the EU law framework could potentially benefit from more similar enforcement frameworks for competition law and the GDPR.[1022] It is recommended that this dimension be taken into consideration in the legislative procedure concerning the procedural regulation for GDPR enforcement.[1023]

6.4 COMPETITION LAW AND THE GDPR: ANALYSIS

The previous Section studied the main similarities and differences between the competition law and data protection frameworks. This section takes the analysis a step further and aims to analyse the interaction between the respective fields in more depth. To this end, the analysis starts by positioning the GDPR in the broader regulatory landscape of the EU. Next, I assess how the application of the GDPR can reinforce competition law. Lastly, this

1020. Article 51(2)(f) GDPR.
1021. Buiten 2021, p. 287.
1022. Lynskey 2015, p. 9; Buiten 2021, p. 287.
1023. Proposal for a Regulation of the European Parliament and Council on a Regulation laying down additional procedural rules relating to the enforcement of Regulation 2016/679, COM(2023) 348 final.

section examines whether and to what extent friction between competition law and the GDPR may occur.

6.4.1 The GDPR in the Broader Regulatory Landscape

As explained in section 5.4.1, in the EU regulatory framework, several instruments of market intervention can be distinguished, i.e.: (i) competition law, (ii) economic regulation, and (iii) social, human rights and solidarity regulation. The position of the GDPR within this framework is not self-evident. The GDPR serves a human rights objective. Against this background, the instrument undeniably serves a broader societal goal and could be qualified as social, human rights or solidarity regulation.[1024] Some authors refer to data protection authorities as enforcers of human rights regulation rather than as economic regulators.[1025]

Yet, and notwithstanding the relevance of the human rights-related tasks of data protection supervisors, it should be acknowledged that data protection regulation has an economic component as well. *First,* the market integration dimension of data protection law can be considered an aspect of economic regulation.[1026] *Second,* the GDPR addresses several market failures, such as information asymmetries and rationality problems.[1027] Regulatory intervention can be considered necessary to protect the 'weakest party' in online relationships, i.e., the data subject.[1028] Data protection law may, for example, resolve information asymmetries by imposing transparency requirements in order to reinforce the position of the individual.[1029] Similarly, several rights produce clear economic effects. For instance, the right to data portability can increase the likelihood of data sharing, thereby mitigating the market power of the data holder.[1030] *Third,* and as explained in section 2.5, data amounts to a competitive parameter on personal data markets. As a result, data protection laws directly impact one of the competitive parameters in personal data markets. Undertakings collect and process personal data to derive a positive monetary value from this data. This value can be affected by the right to be forgotten or the right to erasure since the data subject may request the erasure of this data at any time.[1031]

In sum, data protection law should not only be considered a human rights regulation but also amounts to economic regulation.[1032] Subsequently,

1024. Buiten 2021, p. 277.
1025. Lavrijssen and Ottow 2012, p. 423.
1026. Lynskey 2015, p. 76.
1027. Buiten 2018, p. 277.
1028. Monteleone 2015, p. 82.
1029. Kerber 2016, p. 857.
1030. Martens et al. 2020, p. 9 and footnote 63.
1031. Allen et al. 2020, p. 5.
1032. Lynskey 2015, pp. 76-77.

there can be a debate as to data protection law's leading objectives and conceptual foundations.[1033] This unclarity is exacerbated by the fact that it is difficult to frame data protection, and the GDPR in particular, in terms of *ex-ante* and *ex-post* regulation. In regulatory theory, *ex-ante* and *ex-post* regulation are traditionally distinguished. It is hard to fit the GDPR into this well-established dichotomy. The GDPR relies on a range of both *ex-ante* and *ex-post* approaches to fulfil its objectives. Although the system is not based on licensing and prior control, and therefore seems to focus on *ex-post* rather than *ex-ante* control, the instrument contains some mechanisms with an *ex-ante* dimension. Some mechanisms in the GDPR focus on accountability and responsibility of the data controller and could therefore arguably be qualified as *ex-ante* regulation.[1034] The rules relating to data protection by design and default (Article 25 GDPR), data protection impact assessments (Article 35 GDPR) and prior consultation in the case of high-risk operations (Article 36 GDPR) constitute the clearest examples in this regard.[1035] Furthermore, DPAs have some procedural powers that seem to imply a certain degree of *ex-ante* control (*see* cf. section 6.3.3).

Consequently, data protection law does not fit neatly into one of the traditionally distinguished categories of the arsenal of government intervention. This may explain why few attempts have been made to fit data protection into one of the existing categories.[1036] Yet, in my view, the partial economic nature of data protection cannot be neglected and is particularly relevant in the context of personal data markets.[1037] The economic dimension of data protection regulation constitutes the most important common denominator between the GDPR and competition law and, therefore, serves to bridge the two fields of law. Consequently, the economic dimension of data protection regulation is particularly relevant for the inquiry.

6.4.2 The GDPR Can Reinforce Competition Law

As explained in section 6.3, data protection law and competition law have – notwithstanding their significant differences – certain common features. Therefore, the application of these respective fields of law could have a positive effect on the achievement of each other's objectives. In other words, the frameworks can strengthen each other, and there is room for *synergies*

1033. Bygrave 2014, p. 117; Yeung 2017b, p. 41.
1034. Hoofnagle, Van der Sloot and Zuiderveen Borgesius 2019, p. 67.
1035. Yeung and Bygrave 2022, pp. 143 and 151.
1036. Lynskey 2015, p. 76.
1037. This dimension is also acknowledged by other authors. Hondius, for example, refers to data protection regulation as 'legal regulation of computers' and Miller draws a parallel between the regulation of computer transmissions (of which data protection forms an inherent part) and regulation for airlines, railroads, radio and television. *See:* Hondius 1980; Miller 1971, p. 8; Gellert 2020, p. 8.

between the two legal branches.[1038] This means that the application of the GDPR potentially reinforces the application of competition law.

First, the application of certain GDPR rights can have a *direct* beneficial effect on competition on the market. Certain GDPR rights stimulate or facilitate the competitive process and can, therefore, contribute to the achievement of certain competition law objectives. The instrument of data portability, as laid down in Article 20 GDPR, for example, provides data subjects with the possibility to switch between different providers by giving them access to their own data. Although this provision from a GDPR perspective mainly aims to reinforce self-determination and user control, it may also foster competition between services by facilitating switching possibilities.[1039]

Arguably, a right to data portability can also be derived from the competition law framework. If a data controller holds a dominant position on a certain market, a refusal to grant data portability could potentially amount to an abusive refusal to supply or to provide access to an essential facility.[1040] If a dominant undertaking refuses to grant access to data that is indispensable for potential new entrants to enter the market, such refusal could – in the absence of objective justifications – be qualified as abusive behaviour. Although the essential facilities doctrine has not yet been applied to data in the context of EU competition law, the German competition law framework is more explicit in this regard. According to Section 19 GWB, refusals to grant access to data may amount to an abuse of dominance. A right to data portability can have added value compared to the right to data protection as established in the GDPR. The right in Article 20 GDPR can only be invoked by data subjects, i.e., identifiable individuals (*see* cf. section 6.2.2). This means that businesses cannot rely on this right. Deriving a right to data portability from the prohibition of the abuse of dominance – and the doctrine on refusal to supply in particular – could fill this gap.[1041] Henceforth, in the context of data portability, certain synergies between the GDPR and competition law could emerge.[1042]

Second, data protection considerations can amount to a relevant factor for a competition law analysis. In this case, the synergetic effects of the GDPR are more *indirect*. Data protection law and competition law do not apply in parallel, serving an overlapping objective, but GDPR considerations are incorporated into the competition law assessment. In this scenario, competition authorities 'internalise' GDPR considerations. The need to take such considerations into account results from the monetisation of personal

1038. Graef, Clifford and Valcke 2018, p. 203.
1039. Article 29 Working Party 27 October 2017, Guidelines on the right to data portability, wp242rev.01.
1040. Lynskey 2017.
1041. Vanberg and Ünver 2017.
1042. Kerber and Specht-Riemenschneider 2021, p. 42.

data in data-driven markets.[1043] On personal data markets, the ability to process personal data determines an undertaking's competitive position and can thus be a relevant source of market power.[1044] Against this backdrop, data protection and privacy can be relevant in the context of a competition law assessment. The importance of data has, as stressed previously, also been acknowledged by the Commission. In the new Notice on the Relevant Market, it is stressed that, when defining the relevant market, the Commission takes into account 'the various parameters of competition'. Those parameters include 'quality in its various aspects'. The privacy protection afforded is explicitly mentioned as one of these aspects.[1045]

The CJEU takes a similar approach by bridging data protection and competition law in the *Meta Bundeskartellamt* case by stressing that personal data has become a 'significant parameter of competition' and that excluding data protection rules from the assessment of abuse of a dominant position would 'disregard the reality of this economic development' and 'undermine the effectiveness of competition law within the European Union'.[1046] The CJEU highlights that compliance or non-compliance with the GDPR can be 'a vital clue among the relevant circumstances' in order to assess whether certain conduct entails a method governing normal competition. The CJEU continues by stating that it may be necessary for an NCA to examine whether an undertaking's conduct complies with rules other than those relating to competition law, such as the GDPR.[1047] The CJEU thus explicitly acknowledges that (in)compliance with the GDPR can be a relevant element in the assessment of abuse of a dominant position. In such cases, the theory of harm centres around consumer exploitation, and the abusive imposition of unfair conditions in particular.[1048]

Where the CJEU clearly bridges data protection and competition law in the *Meta Bundeskartellamt* case, it has not always unequivocally endorsed the interaction between the respective fields of law. In the *Asnef-Equifax* case, the CJEU stressed that 'any possible issues relating to the sensitivity of personal data are not, as such, a matter for competition law, they may be resolved on the basis of the relevant provisions governing data protection'.[1049] Where some authors interpret this phrase as an indication that data protection cannot influence competition law, the CJEU is – in my view – more nuanced.[1050] The CJEU highlights that data protection considerations *as such* are not a matter for competition law. However, this does not mean that data protection considerations cannot be integrated in any way. Insofar

1043. *See* section 2.5.
1044. Graef 2015, p. 473.
1045. Relevant Markets Notice, para. 15; Beems and Rusu 2024.
1046. CJEU 4 July 2023 Case C-252/21, *Meta Bundeskartellamt*, para. 51.
1047. CJEU 4 July 2023 Case C-252/21, *Meta Bundeskartellamt*, paras 47 and 48.
1048. Jones, Sufrin and Dunne 2019, p. 570.
1049. CJEU 23 November 2006 Case C-238/05, *Asnef-Equifax*, para. 63.
1050. O'Callaghan 2018, p. 112; Botta and Wiedemann 2019, p. 436.

as data protection considerations entail a relevant element of competition, and in particular quality (of the services rendered), these considerations can still be relevant for a competition law analysis. In my view, the *Meta Bundeskartellamt* and *Asnef-Equifax* cases do not contradict each other.

Consequently, data protection considerations may be a relevant factor in the assessment of potentially abusive behaviour by dominant firms. Data-related considerations can thus be taken into account in a competition law assessment. At this point, it is not yet entirely clear how such considerations can or should be integrated.

On the one hand, data protection considerations can be considered 'internal constraints' of data protection law on competition law.[1051] This means that data protection considerations can be implemented in a competition law assessment by taking these values into account by acknowledging the GDPR's interaction with the normative values of competition law. As explained previously, the level of data protection is increasingly considered a competitive parameter since data protection can be conceptualised as part of the quality of online services.[1052] Accordingly, services with a more privacy-friendly processing policy could be considered to be of better quality than services with an inferior policy. Arguably, the level of data protection could be considered a 'normative yardstick for assessment of quality'.[1053] This yardstick could be relevant for the assessment of allegedly excessive prices or unfair conditions.

On the other hand, data protection could be considered *part of the relevant legal and economic context* of a competition law assessment. In assessing alleged abuse, a competition authority has to take into account the legal and economic context in which that conduct takes place.[1054] Against this background, the Commission lists the fact whether a dominant undertaking violates rules of other areas of the law, for instance, data protection law, as a relevant factor for establishing whether an undertaking has departed from competition on the merits.[1055] Although such an approach leaves room for data protection considerations, this approach would not be unique for data protection law. Under this approach, competition law authorities would consider data protection rules like any other form of regulation.[1056] In other words, data protection considerations could be taken into account in a competition law context, but do not have a 'special' position compared to other regulatory frameworks.

In my view, the approach of the CJEU in the *Meta Bundeskartellamt* case most closely aligns with the first conceptualisation of the interrelation

---

1051. Costa-Cabral and Lynskey 2015, p. 15.
1052. Robertson and Majcher 2022, p. 637.
1053. Costa-Cabral and Lynskey 2015, p. 15.
1054. CJEU 6 September 2017 Case C-413/14P, *Intel*, para. 136.
1055. Draft Guidelines on the application of Article 102 TFEU, para. 55.
1056. Costa-Cabral and Lynskey 2015, p. 3.

between data protection and competition law. The CJEU explicitly acknowledges that data constitutes a significant parameter of competition between undertakings in the digital economy and that excluding considerations relating to personal data protection when examining an abuse of a dominant position would disregard economic reality.[1057] Subsequently, the CJEU specifically addresses the relevance of data for the examination of the competitive process and seems to qualify the data protection framework as an 'internal constraint' of competition law. Admittedly, the CJEU also states that it may be necessary for NCAs to take into account whether an undertaking's conduct complies with rules 'other than those relating to competition law, *such as* the rules on the protection of personal data laid down by the GDPR'.[1058] By referring to rules *such as* data protection rules, the CJEU implies that the GDPR constitutes an example of the rules that can be taken into account in a competition law assessment. Yet, there may be room to take other frameworks into account as well.[1059] This statement could imply that the CJEU considers data protection rules as part of the 'relevant legal and economic framework'.[1060] However, in my view, given the extensive discussion on the relevance of personal data for the digital economy and the explicit reference to personal data as a 'significant parameter of competition', the CJEU does not merely take into account data protection considerations as part of the relevant legal context. Rather, the CJEU takes this a step further by qualifying data protection considerations as a part of the competitive context. Consequently, the principles of the GDPR become a benchmark for assessing the unfairness of trading conditions and the existence of an abuse.[1061]

6.4.3 Friction Between the GDPR and Competition Law

The previous Section addressed the potential synergies between the GDPR and competition law. While these areas of law can strengthen each other, a certain degree of friction, or even clashes, between the frameworks may also occur.

First, the GDPR may negatively affect competition in the market by imposing several obligations upon data processors and controllers, hence creating a regulatory burden. Generally speaking, larger undertakings are

1057. CJEU 4 July 2023 Case C-252/21, *Meta Bundeskartellamt*, para. 51.
1058. CJEU 4 July 2023 Case C-252/21, *Meta Bundeskartellamt*, para. 51.
1059. According to case law, a competition law assessment needs to take into account the legal context of a practice, and non-compliance with other branches of the law can be a relevant factor.
1060. *See, e.g.,* CJEU 14 March 2013 Case C-32/11, *Allianz Hungária*, para. 29.
1061. Wils 2019, p. 13.

better positioned to absorb the implementation costs associated with compliance.[1062] It is rather costly and labour-intensive to set up a system for the collection and processing of personal data in compliance with the requirements of the GDPR.[1063] The requirement to establish a system for obtaining opt-in consent is arguably more burdensome for smaller companies, as larger firms may more frequently rely on previously obtained consent, thereby benefiting from economies of scale and scope.[1064] Therefore, it may be easier for larger firms to obtain this consent. In other words, the GDPR compliance costs and the consent-based requirements for data protection in the GDPR may – in a way – even strengthen the economic position of large firms.[1065] As a result, the effects of the GDPR are not necessarily pro-competitive.

Second, the institutional and enforcement set-up of the GDPR may offer an unintended benefit to larger undertakings which can have a negative impact on the competitive landscape. The GDPR relies on a one-stop-shop system in cases of cross-border processing where the Member State of the single or main establishment is appointed as lead supervisor.[1066] As explained previously, this means that numerous Big Tech platforms will be supervised by the same few national data protection authorities. Lack of resources and/or reluctance of these authorities may thus result in serious enforcement bottlenecks. The resources and willingness of the Irish authority, the DPC, are considered to be particularly problematic. Since this authority is responsible for the oversight of, *inter alia*, Google and Meta, this lack of action is particularly problematic. At the same time, it appears that DPAs in other Member States, for example, in France, are much more active. As a result, smaller undertakings are – in a way – more likely to be punished for data protection violations.[1067]

Third, a tension between data protection and competition law can occur if privacy-enhancing policies adopted by dominant platforms pose exploitative or exclusionary risks. Certain strategies adopted by large tech firms can potentially *increase* rather than decrease privacy protection.[1068] While such policies may be laudable from a data protection standpoint, they can raise concerns from a competition law perspective. In this regard, Apple's App Tracking Transparency Framework (henceforth: ATT framework) and Google's Privacy Sandbox policies are particularly relevant. The ATT framework relates to Apple's introduction, in version 14.5 of its iOS and iPadOS

1062. Buiten 2021, p. 290; Tombal 2021, p. 5.
1063. Gal and Aviv 2020, p. 353.
1064. *See* section 2.4.
1065. According to Geradin, Karanikioti and Katisifis, the GDPR, for instance, strengthened Google's position vis-à-vis smaller rivals on the market for advertisement services. Geradin, Karanikioti and Katsifis 2021, pp. 3 and 15. *See also*: Kerber and Specht-Riemenschneider 2021, pp. 5, 15 and 35.
1066. *See* section 9.5.1.
1067. Geradin 2021, p. 22.
1068. Carugati 2023, p. 168.

operating systems, of a policy requiring user consent for data collection by third-party applications via a pop-up window in a partially standardised format.[1069] The French Autorité de la concurrence imposed a fine of EUR 150,000 on Apple for abusing its dominant position by implementing the ATT framework in the procedure on the merits, although it refused a request for interim measures in this case in 2021.[1070] While the French authority acknowledges that Apple's policy is not problematic in terms of the likely benefits for users as regards privacy protection, it finds implementation of the framework abusive, as the implementation method artificially complicates the use of third-party applications, distorts the neutrality of the framework and results in an asymmetry of treatment between Apple and its publishers. In Germany, the *Bundeskartellamt* addressed similar concerns on the basis of Section 19a GWB by issuing a statement of objections to Apple regarding the same ATT framework.[1071] In the UK, the Competition and Markets Authority (henceforth: CMA) scrutinised Google's phasing out of the support for third-party cookies and the introduction of the so-called Privacy Sandbox under competition law. In its commitment decision, the CMA highlighted the risks of the Privacy Sandbox, in particular in terms of third parties' unequal access to the functionality associated with user tracking, Google's self-preferencing of its own ad tech providers and owned and operated ad inventory and the imposition of unfair terms on Chrome's web browser.[1072]

The cases mentioned reveal a tension between competition law and data protection: while the policies in question can be data protection enhancing, they can have exploitative or exclusionary effects, in particular due to self-preferencing and/or leveraging dynamics.[1073] This raises the question of how competition and data protection should be reconciled in this scenario. Against this background, it is important to highlight that the analysis should

---

1069. Autorité de la concurrence, Press Release 31 March 2025, Targeted advertising: the Autorité de la concurrence imposes a fine of EUR 150,000,000 on Apple for the implementation of the App Tracking Transparency ('ATT') framework https://www.autoritedelaconcurrence.fr/en/press-release/targeted-advertising-autorite-de-la-concurrence-imposes-fine-eu150000000-apple accessed 29 August 2025.

1070. Although France and the UK do not fall within the scope of this research, the decision showcases a potential relevant friction between data protection and competition law and will therefore be discussed briefly.

1071. Bundeskartellamt 14 June 2022, 'Bundeskartellamt reviews Apple's tracking rules for third-party apps' (2022) https://www.bundeskartellamt.de/SharedDocs/Meldung/EN/Pressemitteilungen/2022/14_06_2022_Apple.html accessed 29 August 2025; Bundeskartellamt 13 February 2025, 'Bundeskartellamt has concerns about the current form of Apple's App Tracking Transparency Framework (ATTF)' (2025) https://www.bundeskartellamt.de/SharedDocs/Meldung/EN/Pressemitteilungen/2025/02_13_2025_ATTF.html?nn=49120 accessed 29 August 2025.

1072. CMA 11 February 2022 Case No. 50972, Decision to accept commitments offered by Google in relation to its Privacy Sandbox Proposals, para. 1.7. For a further analysis of this case, *see:* Geradin, Katsifis and Karanikioti 2021 and Gorecka 2024, pp. 136 and further.

1073. Colangelo 2025b, p. 134.

be context-dependent and can only be conducted on a case-by-case basis. Furthermore, it is essential to ascertain to what extent the proposed policies indeed genuinely enhance data protection. Geradin, Karanikioti and Katsifis, for example, convincingly argue that the proposed benefits in the Google Sandbox case are smaller than one would initially think because it does not curb surveillance by Google itself.[1074] Where the relevant policies genuinely improve data protection but also involve anti-competitive conduct, the policy's contribution to data protection could be considered in assessing whether the conduct is objectively justified, provided that there are no less restrictive alternatives which could have been pursued to promote privacy.[1075]

Lastly, further clashes could arise if dominant undertakings attempt to 'weaponise' data protection law in competition law proceedings. This scenario could be apparent in the case of an abusive refusal to supply by a dominant undertaking. As argued previously, the doctrines of essential facilities and refusal to supply could potentially be extended to the sharing of data.[1076] If the relevant data also concerns personal data, data protection law might limit the possibilities of data sharing, especially through the requirements relating to legitimate processing and consent. In this context, large firms may 'weaponise' data protection law by putting forward privacy considerations to justify potentially abusive behaviour.[1077] Data protection could be used as an objective justification for denying the grant of access to data. This could – if such approach were adopted – result in a conflict between data protection and competition law.[1078] However, to my knowledge, such conflicts have not yet arisen in practice.

Data protection can also be weaponised in a procedural setting. For instance, Meta argued that the 'virtual data room procedure'[1079] did not adequately protect the individual's right to privacy.[1080] In other words, Meta argued that submitting personal data in the virtual data room may violate the GDPR, since the data subjects concerned did not give their consent. The GC does not side with this line of reasoning and argues that consent is not required in this case, since the processing is lawful in that it is necessary for compliance with a legal obligation.[1081] In other words, data processing can be lawful on the basis of *one* legal basis. In this scenario, the processing of personal data is based on a legal obligation. Therefore, consent is not

1074. Geradin, Katsifis and Karanikioti 2021, p. 680.
1075. Geradin, Katsifis and Karanikioti 2021, p. 672.
1076. *See* sections 4.2.2.4 and 4.4.2.2.
1077. Geradin, Karanikioti and Katsifis 2021, p. 35.
1078. Graef, Clifford and Valcke 2018, p. 220; Kerber and Specht-Riemenschneider 2021, pp. 24 and 69.
1079. *See* for a more elaborate analysis of data protection and competition law enforcement, *see:* Kuschewsky and Geradin 2014.
1080. GC 24 May 2023 Case T-452/20, *Meta v. Commission*, para. 157.
1081. Article 6(1)(a) and 6(1)(c) GDPR.

required. If this approach is indeed adopted, data protection considerations cannot be 'weaponised' to refrain from compliance with procedural obligations in a competition law context. The case is currently under appeal before the CJEU.[1082]

In sum, there can be some friction between the frameworks of data protection and competition law. Although the frameworks potentially strengthen each other in certain cases, in other circumstances, the application of the respective frameworks can give rise to friction or even clashes.

6.5 CONCLUSION

This chapter studied the interplay between the GDPR and competition law and aimed to assess how the relationship between the respective frameworks is (or should be) shaped. Due to the new economic reality of personal data markets and business models that centre around the collection of personal data, the legal fields of competition law and the GDPR have become increasingly intertwined.[1083] Yet, the two instruments are different legal fields with separate objectives, substantive norms, enforcement and institutional frameworks. This begs the question of how the relationship between the legal areas should be shaped. The answer to this question is not straightforward, but multi-faceted and normatively coloured.

The desirable level of synergies between competition law and data protection law is a normative matter and largely depends on one's understanding of the objectives of competition law. This discussion is linked to the question of to what extent 'idiosyncratic' harms should be taken into account in competition law.[1084] Ultimately, the debate boils down to the conception of the 'soul of antitrust'.[1085] In the debate, two opposing views on the goals of antitrust are apparent. On the one hand, separatists or isolationists find that data protection and competition should be viewed separately. This means that a competition law analysis should leave no, or very little, room for data protection considerations. On the other hand, integrationists find that privacy arguments could and should be incorporated into antitrust.[1086]

In my view, the competition law framework leaves room for data protection considerations. Despite the fact that it may be relatively difficult to quantify data protection considerations, this is a reasonable approach. Data-driven business models are part of the new economic reality. Therefore, in order to develop the competition law framework in a way that is in line with this changing economic landscape, such considerations cannot be

1082. CJEU Case C-496/23P *Meta v. Commission* (Case in Progress).
1083. Kerber and Zolna 2022, p. 218.
1084. Petit 2020; Kalimo and Majcher 2017, p. 4.
1085. Fox 1987; Ezrachi and Stucke 2018.
1086. Gorecka 2020.

overlooked. Rather than neglecting the reality of data in modern markets, competition law needs tools to incorporate such considerations properly. The development of theories on the economics of data protection and privacy should help to achieve this integrated approach in a sound way.[1087]

In the *Asnef-Equifax* case, the CJEU initially showed reluctance to establish a bridge between the GDPR and competition law by stressing that data protection considerations as such are not a matter for competition law.[1088] Despite the fact that data protection considerations as such are not relevant for competition law, such considerations can enter the realm of competition law given that data constitutes a parameter of competition on personal data markets. Indeed, the CJEU acknowledged in *Meta Bundeskartellamt* that data protection considerations are relevant for competition law assessments concerning markets for personal data. In other words, the GDPR can offer valuable internal constraints for the competition law framework.[1089]

The fact that competition law internalises data protection considerations should be applauded. This approach is required in order to guarantee that the field of competition remains relevant for personal data markets and, thereby, future-proof. Yet, it should be stressed that there are also certain limitations that must be observed. The field of competition law should not be used to resolve the institutional and procedural shortcomings of the data protection law framework. In other words, competition law is not, nor should it be, a 'panacea' for all problems relating to Big Tech.

Furthermore, the increasing interaction between competition law and the GDPR comes with certain (institutional) challenges relating to the coherent application of both fields by the plethora of responsible authorities. If overlapping competences are not streamlined properly, a risk of incoherent application arises.[1090] On top of this, overlapping competences come with a risk of over- or underenforcement. Against this background, competition law and data protection authorities can no longer operate on their separate islands, but – at least to a certain extent – need to provide a more holistic or integrated approach.[1091] To this end, it is necessary that the authorities coordinate their enforcement actions and cooperate with each other. The mechanisms for cooperation are further studied in Part III.

1087. Acquisti, John and Loewenstein 2013; Acquisti, Taylor and Wagman 2016; Acquisti 2014; Kerber and Zolna 2022; Evans 2020.
1088. CJEU 23 November 2006 Case C-238/05, *Asnef-Equifax*, para. 63.
1089. Costa-Cabral and Lynskey 2015.
1090. Graef 2024, p. 158.
1091. Buiten 2021, p. 288.

Synthesis I: Part II

This part of the research assessed the application of competition law, the DMA and the GDPR to personal data markets, focusing particularly on the interplay between these legal branches.

Competition law applies to undertakings operating in digital markets. Its flexible nature enables the adaptation of the framework, allowing its application to the 'new' reality of personal data markets. Both the Commission and NCAs have adopted non-compliance decisions and imposed fines upon Big Tech companies. In several instances, these large platforms adjusted their behaviour following competition law intervention.[1092] Yet, despite the clear potential of the competition law framework to address the issue of market power within personal data markets, the field has faced several challenges.

Traditional competition law is not entirely apt to address the challenges associated with platform power. These shortcomings are partly procedural. Competition law proceedings are notoriously lengthy, which can render its application too slow to effectively address issues relating to rapidly changing and tipping markets. Moreover, competition law is not equipped to account for harms that stem from the characteristics of digital markets, rather than from the behaviour of dominant firms. To address these shortcomings, the EU legislator introduced a novel instrument: the DMA.[1093] Despite the similarities between competition law and the DMA, the instrument is not formally qualified as competition law. This creates complexities in the relationship between the two frameworks.

1092. *Bundeskartellamt* 10 October 2024 B6-22/16, Facebook – Implementation of the *Bundeskartellamt's* decision of 6 February 2019.

1093. Commission Staff Working Document Impact Assessment Report Accompanying the document Proposal for a Regulation of the European Parliament and of the Council on contestable and fair markets in the digital sector (Digital Markets Act), SWD(2020) 363 final, para. 5.1.

Furthermore, various tools in the competition law framework were not originally designed to be applied to data-driven markets. Against this background, it is unsurprising that the relevance of data protection considerations for competition law assessments has triggered a lot of (academic) debate. However, the flexibility of the competition law framework has enabled the field to adapt and adjust to the new economic reality. Data-related considerations have been incorporated into multiple tools, including instruments used to define the relevant market. Moreover, the CJEU has established that data protection considerations can be taken into account in the assessment of an alleged abuse of dominance.[1094]

In conclusion, the competition law framework has evolved, leveraging its inherent flexibility to remain relevant in the context of personal data markets. As a result of the developments outlined above, the area of competition law has become increasingly intertwined with other areas of the law. This increasing overlap stems from two main dynamics.

First, the regulatory environment is changing. Multiple initiatives to regulate the powerful position of platforms are emerging, both at the EU and the national level. These regulatory initiatives are partially rooted in the competition law framework, but also extend beyond it by taking a regulatory approach. For instance, Section 19a GWB qualifies as German competition law, whereas the DMA is considered an instrument of economic regulation. These novel instruments represent hybrids or 'chimeras' of competition law and regulation and are difficult to fit within the traditional dichotomy that distinguishes between these two types of market intervention.[1095] As a result, instruments of competition law and economic or sectoral regulation increasingly overlap. This dynamic is particularly relevant for the interaction between competition law and the *DMA*.

Second, competition law authorities may be required to go beyond their traditional field(s) of responsibility, as personal data increasingly serves as a competitive parameter. Consequently, it may be necessary for competition authorities to address data protection considerations in assessing abuses of dominance. For example, this approach was adopted by the *Bundeskartellamt* in its *Meta* case.[1096] This dynamic is relevant for the interplay between competition law and the *GDPR*.

As a result of these two dynamics, substantive legal fields increasingly overlap. This trend also has an institutional dimension, as it results in overlapping competences of different enforcers at the national and EU level. This institutional overlap manifests itself in two ways. On the one hand,

---

1094. CJEU 4 July 2023 Case C-252/21, *Meta Bundeskartellamt.*
1095. Zilsdorf 2023.
1096. Bundeskartellamt 6 February 2019 Case B6-22/16, *Facebook.*

multiple authorities may have the competence to initiate parallel or consecutive proceedings. In this scenario, specific conduct can be captured by more than one legal branch. As a result, more than one authority might regulate the same conduct.[1097] On the other hand, an authority may incorporate rules or concepts from areas of the law that do not fall within its original mandate. If a competition law authority addresses data protection concerns, it – for example – 'borrows' from the field of data protection law.[1098] In this scenario, a competition authority integrates or internalises data protection considerations.

In the multi-level legal order of the EU, institutional overlaps can have multiple dimensions. Overlaps may exist within a single legal order or jurisdiction. In such cases, the overlap is considered *mono-jurisdictional.* Furthermore, overlaps can relate to the competences of authorities across multiple jurisdictions or legal orders. In this case, the overlap is *multi-jurisdictional.*

However, overlaps can be *intra-* or *cross-disciplinary.* While an intra-disciplinary overlap entails an overlap between enforcers within one legal branch, a cross-disciplinary overlap concerns the interaction between enforcers of several legal branches.

Given the two variants, four distinct dimensions of overlapping competences can be identified.

Table 6.1 Dimensions of Institutional Overlap

Dimensions of Institutional Overlaps		
	Single legal branch	*Multiple legal branches*
Single legal order	*Mono-jurisdictional and intra-disciplinary*	*Mono-jurisdictional and cross-disciplinary*
Multiple legal orders	*Multi-jurisdictional and intra-disciplinary*	*Multi-jurisdictional and cross-disciplinary (transversal)*

Henceforth, overlaps in the context of competition law, the DMA and the GDPR can have multiple dimensions:

(i) Mono-jurisdictional and intra-disciplinary.
(ii) Multi-jurisdictional and intra-disciplinary.
(iii) Mono-jurisdictional and cross-disciplinary.
(iv) Multi-jurisdictional and cross-disciplinary, or transversal.

1097. De Streel and Larouche 2016, p. 46.
1098. Yakovleva, Geursen and Arnbak 2020, p. 1465.

A *mono-jurisdictional* and *intra-disciplinary* overlap can, for example, occur in the context of German data protection law. In Germany, the GDPR is enforced by multiple authorities, both at the federal and the local level.[1099] Overlapping competences between different German data protection authorities amount to mono-jurisdictional, intra-disciplinary overlaps.

A *multi-jurisdictional* and *intra-disciplinary* overlap can occur in the context of competition law. This dimension, for example, covers the relationship between the Commission and NCAs in a competition law context. Similarly, cooperation between DPAs of different Member States falls under this dimension.

A *mono-jurisdictional* and *cross-disciplinary* overlap arises if competences of enforcers of different legal branches within one and the same legal order overlap. This situation, for example, covers the interaction between the Dutch data protection authority and the ACM.

A *multi-jurisdictional* and *cross-disciplinary* overlap concerns overlapping competences of enforcers of different legal orders and different legal branches. I also refer to this dimension as a *transversal* overlap. The *Meta Bundeskartellamt* case clearly illustrates the relevance of the transversal dimension: The German NCA takes into account data protection considerations, while the Irish data protection authority is the lead supervisory authority in the context of the GDPR.

Apart from the different dimensions, overlapping norms and competences can manifest in various ways and may yield diverse consequences. *First,* norms may *conflict.* In this scenario, the application of one norm results in the violation of another norm. *Second,* norm overlaps can amount to *replication*, where norms confirm each other without adding or detracting from the relevant rights and obligations.[1100] *Third,* different norms can be *complementary.*[1101] In this scenario, the norm overlap neither amounts to a conflict nor a replication. Rather, the different norms can strengthen or reinforce each other. The latter category is most relevant for my research. As explained in this Part, certain conflicts or tensions between competition law, the GDPR and the DMA may occur. Moreover, in the context of competition law, the DMA and the GDPR, complementary norm overlaps are clearly visible. The application of national competition law complements the application of EU competition law; the DMA is 'complementary' to EU competition law, and the GDPR can strengthen the application of competition law in the context of personal data markets. Against this backdrop, the relevance of complementary norm overlaps cannot be overstated.

As explained in the Introduction, overlapping competences are not necessarily problematic. Yet, in order to guarantee the coherent application of the different legal branches, well-functioning cooperation mechanisms,

1099. *See* section 6.2.4.
1100. Hancox 2021, pp. 1061-1062.
1101. Burchardt 2019, p. 80.

covering the different dimensions of overlapping competences, are required. Without such cooperation mechanisms in place, the application of overlapping frameworks may result in the incoherent application of the rules, due to inconsistent interpretation of norms by different authorities, the disruption of existing cooperation mechanisms, over- or under-enforcement or conflicts between norms. The mechanisms of cooperation are at the heart of Part III.[1102]

1102. Yakovleva, Geursen and Arnbak 2020, p. 1479.

Part III

Pre-emption, Hierarchy of Norms and Cooperation

Part II explored the interaction between the areas of competition law, the GDPR and the DMA. On personal data markets, these fields of law, as well as the competences of enforcers of those branches, increasingly overlap. Overlapping competences are not problematic per se but call for effective cooperation between all relevant authorities in order to guarantee a consistent regulatory approach.[1103] The main question in this regard is: *who should do what?*[1104]

Overlapping norms and competences can be streamlined by substantive and institutional mechanisms. *First*, the substantive dimension centres around the degree to which the respective frameworks can be applied in parallel or consecutively. In this light, it should be assessed to what extent: (i) the frameworks can co-exist; and (ii) which framework takes precedence in the case of a potential conflict. Despite the institutional focus of the analysis, the substantive dimension of norm overlaps cannot be overlooked. If the competences of two enforcers overlap, but one instrument pre-empts the application of another set of rules, the norm overlap is not genuine. It is clear which framework takes precedence, and consequently, there can be no doubt as to the question of which entity should take action. In other words, there are mechanisms available to determine which framework prevails and thereby limits the application of the other field.

Second, the substantive dimension will not always resolve the norm or competence overlap. The different frameworks of EU law do not necessarily limit each other's application but often apply complementarily. In this

1103. De Streel and Larouche 2016, p. 11.
1104. Hyman and Kovacic 2014.

scenario, principles of hierarchy of norms or pre-emption do not provide a solution. Rather, this type of overlap calls for mechanisms that can strengthen the complementary relationship between different norms by providing mechanisms for cooperation between the frameworks. In this scenario, both frameworks apply in parallel or consecutively. In order to safeguard coherence under these circumstances, cooperation between different institutions is necessary. For the purpose of this inquiry, cooperation can also entail coordination between authorities. Since the notions of coordination and cooperation are very closely related and used interchangeably in literature, I do not rely on a strict dichotomy between these two notions.[1105]

Part III addresses both the substantive and the institutional dimension. *Chapter 7* focuses on the substantive dimension and studies relevant mechanisms of pre-emption and hierarchy of norms. This analysis is focused on the degree to which legal frameworks can limit each other's application. The institutional dimension of cooperation is reflected in Chapters 8 and 9. *Chapter 8* provides the theoretical background on the topic of cooperation between authorities and studies the mechanisms for intra-disciplinary cooperation in the field of competition law. *Chapter 9* analyses the frameworks for cross-disciplinary cooperation in the field of: (i) competition law and the DMA; and (ii) competition law and the GDPR. These chapters emphasise the complementary application of different frameworks.

1105. Sauter, for example, refers to mutual information sharing and discussion as a 'softer form of coordination'. Similarly, De Streel and Larouche consider the exchange of information as a mechanism of coordination at the agency level. However, Gerard refers to mechanisms for the exchange of information and mutual assistance as horizontal *cooperation* mechanisms and the Network Notice on *Cooperation* between authorities also addresses the exchange and use of information. A similar divergence is present in the case law of the CJEU. The English version of the *Meta Bundeskartellamt* case refers to the *consistency of application*. Conversely, the Dutch text alludes to *een coherente toepassing*. *See:* Sauter 2016, p. 143; De Streel and Larouche 2016, pp. 46-47; Gerard 2010, p. 3; Network Notice, para. 26; CJEU 4 July 2023 Case C-252/21, *Meta Bundeskartellamt*, para. 52.

CHAPTER 7

Pre-emption and Hierarchy of Norms

7.1 INTRODUCTION

The application of competition law, the DMA and the GDPR to personal data markets results in overlapping competences of different enforcers. Against this backdrop, the coherent application of these fields requires cooperation between authorities. The interaction between the competences of different enforcers has both a substantive and an institutional dimension. This chapter studies substantive mechanisms and aims to assess: (i) the extent to which the respective fields of the law can co-exist; as well as (ii) the means by which conflicts between the legal frameworks can be resolved. The principles of hierarchy of norms and pre-emption take centre stage.

In order to assess how the principles of pre-emption and hierarchy of norms can resolve overlapping competences between enforcers of competition law, the DMA and the GDPR, this chapter starts with a theoretical overview of the principles of hierarchy of norms and pre-emption in sections 7.2 and 7.3. Subsequently, section 7.4 applies these principles to EU and national competition law, section 7.5 studies the principles in the context of competition law and the DMA, and section 7.6 analyses the principles in the context of competition law and the GDPR. Section 7.7 provides the chapter's conclusion.

7.2 HIERARCHY OF NORMS

In most legal orders, the relationship between different norms is subject to a *hierarchy of norms* establishing a vertical order of legal acts in which lower level rules must comply with rules at a higher level.[1106] A hierarchy of norms clarifies the structure of a legal framework, thereby safeguarding its stability and predictability.[1107] Norm hierarchies are particularly relevant in complex legal systems, such as the multi-level legal order of the EU.

Norm hierarchies can be shaped in various ways and may be guided by different maxims.[1108] Legal frameworks can provide explicit norm hierarchies, such as 'takes precedence' clauses. In the absence of such clauses, various interpretative principles may establish a hierarchy of norms. The principles of *lex superior, lex specialis and lex posterior* are most common in this regard. Those principles establish 'interpretative maxims' to assist in the resolution of norm overlaps.[1109] The *lex superior* principle focuses on the author of or the procedure by which a norm is adopted and provides a hierarchy based on the formal source of each norm. If there is no explicit hierarchy between overlapping norms in place, the *lex specialis* principle, establishing that a more specialised rule takes precedence over a more general rule, can be applied. Furthermore, the *lex posterior* principle, which considers the moment of adoption, can be relied on.[1110]

7.2.1 Hierarchy Between Norms of EU Law

The Lisbon Treaty introduced a formal *lex superior* hierarchy of norms in EU law.[1111] Different EU laws and principles are subject to the following norm hierarchy:

(1) Primary law, i.e., the Treaties, their Protocols and the CFR.
(2) General principles of law.
(3) International agreements with third countries and international organisations.
(4) EU secondary law, i.e., legislative acts,[1112] including regulations, directives and decisions adopted in a special or ordinary procedure

1106. EURLEX, 'Hierarchy of Norms', *see:* https://eur-lex.europa.eu/EN/legal-content/glossary/eu-hierarchy-of-norms.html#:~:text=The%20hierarchy%20of%20norms%20refers,by%20the%20unratified%20Constitutional%20Treaty accessed 17 March 2025.
1107. Bieber and Solomé 1996, p. 908.
1108. Bieber and Solomé 1996, p. 910.
1109. Hancox 2021, p. 1062.
1110. Hancox 2021, p. 1063.
1111. Curtin and Manucharyan 2015, p. 103.
1112. Article 289 TFEU.

and non-legislative acts[1113] which can take the form of delegated and implementing acts.

The hierarchy of norms in EU law, as well as the distinction between the different instruments of EU law, is subject to debate. A detailed examination of this discussion is beyond the scope of this work.[1114] What is most important for this inquiry is the hierarchical relationship between primary and secondary law.

Primary EU law ranks higher than secondary EU law. Accordingly, secondary EU law can, in principle, not curtail the application of primary EU law.[1115] This norm hierarchy is clearly reflected in the *Towercast* case. In this case, AG Kokott stressed in her Opinion that 'it follows from the principle of hierarchy of norms and the principle *lex superior derogate legi inferiori* [...] that a provision of secondary law is not capable of restricting the scope or direct applicability of primary law'.[1116] Secondary EU law can, therefore, not modify or limit the scope of primary EU law.[1117] AG Kokott concluded, based on the *lex superior* principle, that the EU Merger Regulation cannot limit the application of Article 102 TFEU by NCAs. In its judgment, the CJEU largely follows AG's line of reasoning. It rejects the assertion that a provision of EU primary law, i.e., Article 102 TFEU, can be overruled by secondary legislation, in this case, the Merger Regulation. The CJEU acknowledges, in light of the objectives and general scheme of the Merger Regulation, that this regulation establishes a one-stop-shop mechanism for EU merger control.[1118] However, this system does not deprive national authorities of their competence to assess mergers on the basis of Articles 101 and 102 TFEU.[1119]

The sources of EU law are not limited to the (legislative) instruments mentioned above. Rather, the importance of case law of the CJEU and soft law instruments can hardly be overstated. From a hierarchy of norm perspective, soft law sits at the bottom of the EU's legal source hierarchy given its non-binding nature.[1120] Contrary to soft law, CJEU's case law

1113. Article 290 TFEU.
1114. *See* for a more elaborate analysis, for example, Curtin and Manucharyan 2015.
1115. Also, EU secondary law should, as far as possible, be interpreted 'in such way as not to affect its validity and conformity with EU primary law as a whole and, in particular, with the provisions of the Charter'. Nevertheless, in some cases the CJEU seems to interpret primary law in light of secondary legislation and an 'inversion of the hierarchy of norms' occur. This trend is particularly visible in the area of the free movement of persons and workers, and will not be discussed elaborately here. *See:* CJEU 2 February 2021 Case C-481/19, *Consob*, para. 50. For an elaborate analysis, *see:* Hancox 2021.
1116. Opinion of AG Kokott 13 October 2022 in Case C-449/21, *Towercast*, para. 30.
1117. Opinion of AG Kokott 13 October 2022 in Case C-449/21, *Towercast*, para. 35.
1118. CJEU 16 March 2023 Case C-449/21, *Towercast*, paras 40 and 53.
1119. Sauter and Mulder 2023, p. 141. This discussion is particularly relevant in the context of Article 24(2) DCA. *See* section 4.3.2.
1120. Stefan et al. 2019, pp. 9-10; Senden 2004, p. 45.

constitutes a binding source of law.[1121] Since Article 263(1) TFEU allows the CJEU to annul legislative acts, case law of the CJEU ranks above EU secondary legislation.[1122]

7.2.2 Hierarchy Between EU and National Laws

The multi-level nature of EU law requires rules or principles to resolve overlaps or conflicts between the national and EU spheres.[1123] In the context of EU law, this hierarchy is shaped by two important 'twin' principles: the principles of *primacy* and *pre-emption.*[1124] This section focuses on the principle of primacy, and section 7.3 addresses the principle of pre-emption.

The principle of *supremacy* or *primacy* constitutes one of the main principles of EU law. The principle of primacy was established in the seminal case *Costa v. ENEL* which builds on *Van Gend and Loos.* In *Van Gend and Loos,* the CJEU established the doctrine of direct effect by stressing the EU's status as a 'new legal order'.[1125] Subsequently, in *Costa v. ENEL,* the CJEU established the doctrine of primacy. Relying on a teleological interpretation and emphasising the aims and spirit of the EU and the Treaties, the CJEU stressed that EU law, as an independent source of law, 'could not, because of its special and original nature, be overridden by domestic legal provisions, however framed, without being deprived of its character as [EU] law and without the legal basis of the [EU] itself being called into question'.[1126] In the case of conflicts between national and EU law provisions with direct effect, the conflicting national provision should be disapplied.[1127] Even minor pieces of technical EU legislation rank higher than important national

1121. In case CJEU 15 January 2014 Case C-176/12, *Association de médiation sociale*, para. 50, the CJEU, for example, refers to its own *Francovich* judgment as source of law. Derlén and Lindholm 2015, p. 1074.
1122. Ziller 2014, pp. 344-345.
1123. Schütze 2006, p. 1023.
1124. Arena 2018.
1125. CJEU 5 February 1963 Case 26/62, *Van Gend & Loos*, p. 12.
1126. CJEU 15 July 1964 Case 6/64, *Costa v. ENEL*, p. 594; Despite the importance of the principle, there is still debate on the exact reach and scope of the principle of supremacy. This debate is beyond the scope of the analysis. For a more elaborate analysis, *see,* for example: Klamert 2022. Moreover, there is still debate on the relationship between the principle of primacy and German constitutional law. This issue goes beyond the scope of the analysis. *See* for a more elaborate analysis in this regard: Hilpold 2021; Tuominen 2020, p. 246.
1127. In the *Poplawski* case, the CJEU highlights that the principle of primacy does not require national courts to disapply incompatible national law provisions if the conflicting EU law provision does not have direct effect. *See:* CJEU 24 June 2019 Case C-573/17, *Poplawski*, para. 62. For a more extensive analysis of the *Poplawski* case, *see:* Haket 2020; Miasik and Szwarc 2021. For a more elaborate analysis of the remedy of disapplication, *see:* Dougan 2019.

constitutional norms.[1128] Consequently, the principle of primacy has important implications for the national legal order. In this context, it should be stressed that – despite the unconditional nature of the principle of primacy – certain other principles mitigate its effects. The principles of national identity, procedural and institutional autonomy, conferral and subsidiarity are particularly relevant in this regard.[1129] Moreover, EU secondary legislation only takes precedence over national laws if it has been validly adopted. *Ultra vires* legislation does not have primacy over national laws. Importantly, only the CJEU has the competence to rule on the validity of EU law acts.[1130]

The principle of primacy requires national courts to disapply national rules that conflict with EU law having direct effect.[1131] The disapplication of national laws by national courts does not fall within the scope of the analysis. However, in the *CIF* and *Fratelli Constanzo* judgments, the CJEU stressed that the duty to disapply national legislation contravening EU law applies not only to courts but also to all organs of the Member State, including administrative authorities.[1132] This means that the duty to disapply national measures which are contrary to EU law provisions with direct effect also applies to national competition authorities and national data protection authorities.[1133]

7.3 THE PRINCIPLE OF PRE-EMPTION

Apart from the principle of primacy, the principle of pre-emption co-determines the relationship between EU and national law. The principle of pre-emption originates from the US. Despite the fact that pre-emption does not amount to a fundamental principle of EU law, it can serve as a useful tool

---

1128. Weatherill 1995, p. 106. In the case, *Internationale Handelsgesellschaft* the Court stressed that 'the validity of a Community measure or its effect within a Member State cannot be affected by allegations that it runs counter to either fundamental rights as formulated by the construction of that State or the principles of a national constitutional structure'. *See:* CJEU 17 December 1970 Case 11/70, *Internationale Handelsgesellschaft*, para. 3.
1129. Claes 2015, p. 186; Von Bogdandy and Schill 2011.
1130. Claes 2015, p. 186.
1131. In the *Poplawski* case, the CJEU highlights that the principle of primacy does not require national courts to disapply incompatible national law provisions if the conflicting EU law provision does not have direct effect. *See:* CJEU 24 June 2019 Case C-573/17, *Poplawski*. For an more extensive analysis of the *Poplawski* case, *see:* Haket 2020.
1132. CJEU 9 September 2003 Case C-198/01, *CIF*, para. 49; CJEU 22 June 1989 Case 103/88, *Fratelli Costanzo*, para. 31.
1133. In the *CIF* judgment the CJEU establishes that competition law authorities should be able to declare a national measure contrary to EU law. A similar logic can be applied to data protection authorities. CJEU 9 September 2003 Case C-198/01, *CIF*, para. 50. *See also*: De Witte 2021, p. 196; Claes 2015, pp. 184-185; Dougan 2019, p. 1466.

in order to understand the relationship between EU and national laws. Various academics and Advocates-General have endorsed the principle. In the *Budějovický Budvar National Corporation* case, AG Colomer, for example, has acknowledged its importance stressing: '[w]hat we have here ultimately is the debate about [EU] "pre-emption" of a measure and the situation in which the consecutive competences of the Member States in a particular field may have been displaced by the activity of the [EU] legislator'.[1134]

While the principle of primacy focuses on *how* conflicts between EU and national law must be resolved, the principle of pre-emption concerns the question of *whether* such conflicts arise.[1135] In other words, the principle of pre-emption determines whether a conflict exists between national and EU law. [1136] In turn, the principle of primacy – as discussed above – concerns the way such conflict can be resolved.[1137] The principles of primacy and pre-emption should be separated, but cannot be considered in isolation, as their primacy grants EU law the capacity to pre-empt national law.[1138]

The doctrine of pre-emption thus concerns the question of whether a national law conflicts with EU law. This principle – which has received far less (academic) attention than the principle of primacy – is not covered by a uniform definition. Furthermore, pre-emption can take several forms. In the most far-reaching form of pre-emption, the mere existence of a national law can amount to a violation of EU law because EU law in a particular field prevents Member States from taking any action in this area at all.[1139] In this

---

1134. Opinion of AG Colomer 5 February 2009 in Case C-478/07, *Budějovický Budvar National Corporation*, para. 93; *See also*: Arena 2011.
1135. Arena 2018, p. 322. The principle of pre-emption is discussed by various AGs. AG Cápeta discusses pre-emption in the context of shared competences and mentions that 'because of the pre-emptive effect of the majority of shared competences under the Treaties: once the EU has regulated an issue, Member States cannot regulate it on their own force'. *See:* Opinion of AG Ćapeta 3 February 2022 in Case C-500/20, *ÖBB-Infrastruktur Aktiengesellschaft*, para. 73.
1136. Schütze 2006, p. 1023.
1137. Despite the fact that primacy and pre-emption constitute two separate principles, they represent 'two sides of the same coin': the principle of pre-emption will establish whether a conflict exists and triggers the coming into operation of the principle of primacy. At the same time, in order to understand *which* rule pre-empts the other, it is necessary to take into consideration the principle of primacy in order to know which rule is superior. *See:* Schütze 2006, p. 1023.
1138. The relationship can be clarified by making a distinction between primacy and supremacy. The principle of primacy would constitute a rule of conflict resolution on the basis of which national law can be set aside. However, this does not necessarily mean that the legal order as such is superior. Such superiority could be referred to as supremacy. If this line of reasoning is applied, EU law's capacity to pre-empt national laws would flow from the principle of supremacy. In turn, if a conflict arises, such conflict can be resolved on the basis of the principle of primacy. *See:* Tuominen 2020, p. 254; Avbelj 2011, p. 750.
1139. Schütze 2006, p. 1033; Avbelj 2011, p. 747.

scenario, the conflict between EU and national law stems from purely jurisdictional considerations.[1140] This type of pre-emption is referred to as *field pre-emption.*[1141]

In the case of *conflict pre-emption*, national laws are pre-empted by EU law due to the relationship between specific norms. In this scenario, national rules can only be pre-empted insofar as they amount to direct or indirect conflicts, either with particular EU rules or with EU objectives. Conflict pre-emption can take the form of rule or obstacle pre-emption. *Rule pre-emption* occurs if a national norm violates a provision of EU law. Moreover, in the case of *obstacle pre-emption,* a conflict can occur because a national provision endangers the objectives, obstructs the working of or interferes with the proper functioning of (secondary) EU law.[1142]

The pre-emptive effect of EU law can stem from EU secondary legislation but may also be triggered by executive action. A decision by an authority can limit the substantive discretion of other authorities. This scenario amounts to *executive pre-emption* and has multiple dimensions. *First,* in the context of EU law, authorities may be forced to respect an executive decision of another authority based on EU law. In this scenario, the EU law decision *directly* limits the discretion of the national authority.[1143] For example, Article 1(7) DMA, according to which national authorities shall not take decisions which run counter to a decision adopted by the Commission under the DMA, reflects this principle.[1144] The fact that NCAs cannot depart from prior decisions of a DPA if they incorporate data protection considerations in a competition law assessment constitutes another example.[1145] *Second*, national authorities may be required to take into account decisions and remedies imposed by another authority. In this situation, the pre-emptive effect is merely indirect and applies through the principle of mutual recognition.[1146] For instance, in the *Walt Wilhelm* case, the CJEU established that NCAs must 'take proper account of the effects of' a Commission decision.[1147] *Third,* certain executive actions can temporarily

1140. Schütze 2006, p. 1047.

1141. In the *Ratti* case, the CJEU discusses field pre-emption in the area of the classification, packaging and labelling of products. According to the CJEU, Directive 73/173 lays down provisions on classification, packaging and labelling of products and 'may not prohibit, restrict or impede on the grounds of classification, packaging or labelling the placing on the market of dangerous preparations which satisfy the requirements of the directive [...]'. In other words, the Directive prevents Member States from taking measures altogether and thereby amounts to field pre-emption. CJEU 5 April 1979 Case 148/78, *Ratti*, para. 12.

1142. Arena 2018, p. 330; *See,* for example: CJEU 29 March 2012 Case C-7/10 and C-9/10, *Kahveci* and *Inan*, paras 30-35.

1143. Schütze 2010, p. 1402.

1144. *See* section 7.5.3.

1145. CJEU 4 July 2023 Case C-252/21, *Meta Bundeskartellamt*, paras 56 and 63.

1146. Schütze 2010, p. 1402.

1147. CJEU 13 February 1969 Case C-14/68, *Walt Wilhelm*, paras 7-9.

pre-empt another authority's competence to apply certain rules. According to Article 11(6) Regulation 1/2003, the initiation of EU competition law proceedings by the Commission relieves NCAs of their competence to apply Articles 101 and 102 TFEU. In this scenario, NCAs are temporarily prohibited from exercising their competences in a particular case.[1148]

The multi-faceted principle of pre-emption is useful for assessing the range of tensions that may occur between national and EU laws. The tool is particularly helpful in evaluating to what extent EU law leaves room for national laws. Yet, the pre-emptive effect of EU law is context-dependent and can only be assessed on a case-by-case basis.[1149] In the analysis, the division of competences between the EU and the Member States and the degree of harmonisation of an EU instrument cannot be overlooked.

The *division of competences* between the EU and Member States is shaped by multiple principles. According to the principle of conferral, which is set out in Article 5(2) TEU, the EU can only act insofar as it has the competences conferred upon it by the Member States. The Treaty of Lisbon provides clarifications regarding the division of competences, by distinguishing three categories, i.e.: (i) exclusive, (ii) shared, and (iii) supporting competences. Generally speaking, in the field of exclusive competences, only the EU has the power to adopt legislation. Member States cannot adopt legislation in this field unless the EU legislator explicitly grants them the power to do so.[1150] In the field of shared competences, both the EU and Member States have the competence to adopt legislation. Member States can use their competences insofar as the EU has not exercised its competence in a particular field. In other words, when it comes to shared competences, national competences are pre-empted in areas where the EU has exercised its power.[1151] Consequently, in the context of shared competences, the different areas of EU law vary significantly in terms of division of competences.[1152] In the last category, i.e., the supporting competences, the ball is largely in the court of the Member States and the EU can merely take supporting, coordinating or complementary action.[1153]

For this inquiry, exclusive and shared competences are most relevant. The EU has exclusive competence in the area of competition law and shared competence in the field of internal market law.[1154] The field of data protection law is not mentioned in the competence catalogue. Yet, Article 16 TFEU grants wide powers to the EU legislator to take action in the fields of data protection and privacy.[1155] According to Hijmans, data protection can be

1148. Schütze 2010, p. 1404.
1149. Arena 2018, p. 332.
1150. Article 3 TFEU.
1151. Article 4 TFEU.
1152. Craig and De Búrca 2015, p. 114.
1153. Article 6 TFEU.
1154. Articles 3 and 4 TFEU.
1155. Hijmans 2016, p. 120.

considered a shared competence.[1156] The area is not listed in the competence catalogue of Articles 3 and 6 TFEU which lists exclusive and supporting competences in an exhaustive manner. The shared competences are listed in an 'open' fashion. Therefore, competences that are not listed as exclusive or supporting can be presumed to be shared. This line of reasoning can be applied to competences in the field of data protection.[1157]

Furthermore, the topic of *harmonisation* is inextricably linked with the pre-emptive effect of EU laws.[1158] In this context, various types of harmonisation should be distinguished. *First*, the scope of harmonisation is important. Harmonisation is *comprehensive* or *full* in scope if it comprehensively regulates a specific area. If an area is not regulated comprehensively, the harmonisation is *partial.*[1159] Second, and distinct from the differences in scope, harmonisation measures can vary in their intensity. *Exhaustive* or *maximum* harmonisation entails standards from which Member States cannot derogate.[1160] Such rules set both a floor and a ceiling.[1161] This means the national competence to take further action is pre-empted.[1162] By contrast, *minimum harmonisation* does not completely preclude complementary national laws. Rather, this form of harmonisation provides merely a floor, not a ceiling.[1163] Member States remain free to introduce stricter regulatory standards that are compatible with the Treaties.[1164] The pre-emptive effect of minimum harmonisation is thus less far-reaching: in the case of minimum harmonisation, national measures can fall within the scope of EU legislation without conflicting with EU law because the field is not pre-empted.[1165] According to Weatherill, the instrument of minimum harmonisation 'shielded Member States away from the brutal competences that apply under the orthodoxy of classical legislative pre-emption'.[1166] This type of harmonisation thus has an effect on the discretionary room that is left for the Member States. However, in practice, the dichotomy between exhaustive and minimum harmonisation is not always entirely clear. In fact, there are different

1156. Hijmans 2016, p. 120.
1157. Lenaerts, Van Nuffel and Corhaut 2021, p. 96.
1158. *See* for a more elaborate overview of the concept of harmonisation in EU law: Azoulai 2015.
1159. Klamert 2015, pp. 362-363.
1160. Klamert 2015, pp. 362-363.
1161. Weatherill 2012, p. 176.
1162. Dougan 2000, p. 854.
1163. Given the distinction of the scope and intensity of an harmonising measures, rules can be *exhaustive* and *minimum* at the same time. The CJEU, for example, refers to 'exhaustively common minimum standards'. *See:* CJEU 19 March 1998 Case C-1/96, *The Queen and Minister of Agriculture, Fisheries and Food v. Compassing in World Farming*, para. 56.
1164. Dougan 2000, p. 854; Weatherill 2012, p. 176.
1165. Arena 2018, p. 333.
1166. Weatherill 2012, p. 183.

shades of harmonisation, and it may be unclear whether a measure provides for minimum or exhaustive harmonisation.[1167]

7.4 EU AND NATIONAL COMPETITION LAW

As explained in Chapter 4, competition law frameworks are established at both the national and the EU level and EU competition law is enforced by both the Commission and NCAs. Given this multi-level nature and parallel enforcement framework, it is unsurprising that the relationship between EU and national competition law has been the subject of (academic) debate over the past decades.[1168] This section addresses part of this debate by considering the principles of the hierarchy of norms and pre-emption in the context of EU and national competition law. The hierarchy of norms is relatively straightforward in this context. Due to the primacy of EU law, EU competition law ranks higher than national competition law. The pre-emptive effect of EU competition law on national competition law is more complex.

Prior to the adoption of the Lisbon Treaty and Regulation 1/2003, the relationship between EU and national competition law was largely based on the doctrine established in the *Walt Wilhelm* case.[1169] In this case, concerning a cartel dispute, the CJEU built on the doctrine of primacy of EU law.[1170] The CJEU ruled that, in the absence of rules adopted pursuant to Article 103 TFEU, national authorities could apply national competition law to agreements, even if the Commission is examining similar conduct. The national procedure may not prejudice the full and uniform application of EU law nor the effects of measures taken or to be taken to implement EU law.[1171]

The situation changed with the adoption of the competence catalogue of the Lisbon Treaty. According to Article 3(1)(b) TFEU, 'the establishing of substantive competition rules necessary for the functioning of the internal market' amounts to an exclusive competence of the EU. Accordingly, Member States can only adopt additional regulations if the EU empowers them to do so. In the context of competition law, Article 103 TFEU allows the EU legislator to determine the degree to which national competition rules can be displaced by EU competition law. In other words, Article 103 TFEU allows the EU legislator to adopt rules that determine the pre-emptive effect of competition law.

1167. Klamert 2015, p. 363.
1168. *See, e.g.,* Deringer 1963, p. 30. In his Opinion in the *Walt Wilhelm* case, AG Roemer refers to this issue as a 'difficult question'. *See:* Opinion of AG Roemer in Case 14/68 19 December 1968, *Walt Wilhelm*, p. 20.
1169. CJEU 13 February 1969 Case C-14/68, *Walt Wilhelm*.
1170. Delgado and Petit refer to *Walt Wilhelm* as 'one of the earliest applications of the principle of primacy'. *See:* Mota Delgado and Petit 2023, p. 1.
1171. To this end, NCAs must 'take proper account of' Commission's decisions. *See:* CJEU 13 February 1969 Case C-14/68, *Walt Wilhelm*, paras 7-9.

There is some academic debate on the question of whether Article 103 TFEU allows for limitations on the primacy of EU law.[1172] In my view, this is not the case: Article 103(2)(e) TFEU permits determining the degree to which EU competition law leaves room for additional national rules, rather than establishing which framework takes precedence in the case of a conflict. Indeed, Article 3 Regulation 1/2003 does not establish that practices in violation of EU competition law can be considered lawful or permitted under national law.[1173] Therefore, the EU legislator can adjust the pre-emptive effects of EU competition law rather than the primacy of EU competition law and Article 103(2)(e) TFEU amounts to a tool of pre-emptive design.[1174] Article 103(2)(e) TFEU was used to adopt Regulation 1/2003. Considering the pre-emptive effect of EU competition law, Article 3 Regulation 1/2003 is the most relevant provision. The next sections discuss this provision in more detail.

7.4.1 Article 3(2) and 3(3) Regulation 1/2003

The pre-emptive effect of EU competition law is determined by Article 3(2) and 3(3) Regulation 1/2003. According to these provisions:

> 'Member States shall […] not be precluded from adopting and applying on their territory stricter national laws which prohibit or sanction unilateral conduct […]'
>
> 'Without prejudice to general principles and other provisions of Community law […] paragraphs 1 and 2 [of Article 3 Regulation 1/2003] do not apply when the competition authorities […] apply […] provisions of national law that predominantly pursue an objective different from that pursued by [Articles 101 and 102 TFEU]'

Consequently, Article 3(2) and 3(3) Regulation 1/2003 establish the pre-emptive effect of EU competition law by determining the extent to which

1172. Mota Delgado and Petit distinguish so-called *literalists* and *constructionists*. Literalists argue that Regulation 1/2003 leave the principle of primacy untouched. Conversely, constructionists argue that Article 3(2) Regulation 1/2003 amounts to a toleration of modulations of the principle of primacy. *See:* Mota Delgado and Petit 2023, pp. 9 and further.

1173. Feteira 2015, p. 58; Gerber and Cassinis 2006, p. 13.

1174. Tavares agrees with this approach and stresses that 'the exercise of powers under Article 103(2)(e) TFEU must respect the primacy of EU competition law' the Council could not 'establish a general rule according to which national laws prevail over EU competition laws, as that will go against the primacy principle'. Townley and Türk disagree with this approach, and question the use of Article 103(2)(e) TFEU 'if the principle of primacy is inviolable'. Szydlo also proposes a different view by stressing that 'the supremacy of EU competition law over national law has its clear and unequivocal limits that are set in Article 3 of Regulation 1/2003'. *See:* Townley and Türk 2019, p. 274; Tavares 2018; Szydlo 2010, p. 557; Mota Delgado and Petit 2023, p. 11.

EU law leaves room for additional national competition laws. The design of these provisions is rather complex, and Article 3 Regulation 1/2003 is not an 'easy read'.[1175] The competence catalogue and Article 103 TFEU would have allowed the EU legislator to establish a system of field pre-emption in the area of competition law rules necessary for the functioning of the internal market. Initially, the Commission pursued this avenue by proposing a full convergence rule.[1176] Such a rule would have amounted to maximum or exhaustive harmonisation of competition law rules applicable to conduct with an effect on interstate trade. In cases with an effect on the interstate trade, EU competition law would be applied exclusively. The Commission's Proposal received considerable criticism.[1177] Ultimately, the full convergence rule was not adopted, but Article 3(2) Regulation 1/2003 was introduced instead. Thus, Article 3 Regulation 1/2003 is the result of a compromise.[1178] Rather than a system of field pre-emption, Regulation 1/2003 introduces a complex model of conflict pre-emption.[1179]

Article 3(2) and 3(3) Regulation 1/2003 establish a classificatory system by dividing national rules and frameworks into different categories. Depending on the category, national governments are granted a certain amount of leeway or freedom to adopt national rules. To establish to what extent the EU framework leaves room for national laws, the classificatory system of Article 3 Regulation 1/2003 relies on various benchmarks, such as competition law, stricter rules and different objectives. The table below summarises the classificatory system.

1175. Mota Delgado and Petit 2023, p.1.

1176. Feteira 2015, p. 54; European Commission, Proposal of 19 December 2000 for a Council Regulation on the implementation of the rules on competition laid down in Articles 81 and 82 of the Treaty and amending Regulations (EEC) No. 1017/68, (EEC) No. 2988/74,(EEC) No. 4056/86 and (EEC) No. 3975/87 (Regulation implementing Articles 81 and 82 of the Treaty).

1177. Feteira 2015, p. 55.

1178. Against this backdrop, Wagner-von Papp stresses that provisions introduced 'at the last minute under political pressure are rarely a good vehicle for sound policy or careful drafting'. *See:* Wagner-von Papp 2023b, p. 12.

1179. *See* section 7.3.

Figure 7.1 Schematic overview of Articles 3(2) and 3(3) Regulation 1/2003

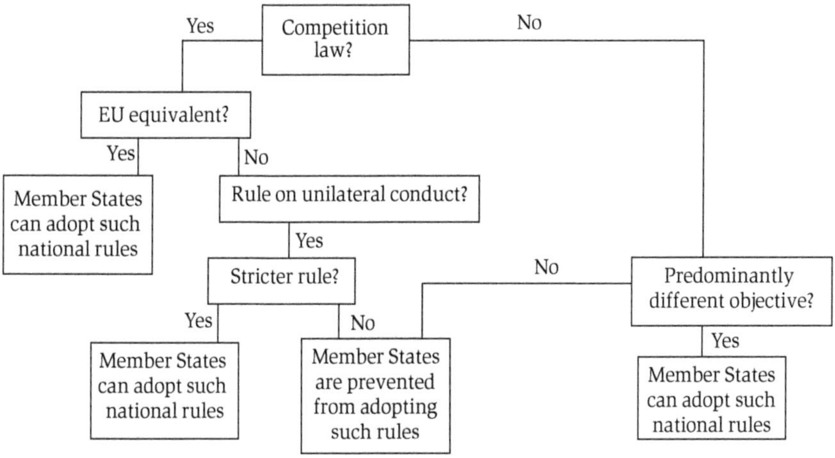

The main problem with the classificatory system of Article 3 Regulation 1/2003 is that several important benchmarks are unclear. The ambiguities relating to Article 3(2) Regulation 1/2003 and 3(3) Regulation 1/2003 are addressed in turn.

7.4.1.1 Article 3(2) Regulation 1/2003: Stricter National Competition Laws

Article 3(2) Regulation 1/2003 determines to what extent EU competition law leaves room for (complementary) national competition laws. According to this provision, Member States shall not be precluded from adopting stricter national laws prohibiting or sanctioning unilateral conduct.

The *first* issue concerning Article 3(2) Regulation 1/2003 relates to *scope*. It is generally presumed that Article 3(2) Regulation 1/2003 merely covers national *competition* laws.[1180] Yet, confusingly, the provisions refer to 'stricter national laws' rather than to stricter national competition laws. This begs the question of whether national rules on unilateral conduct that are not labelled as competition law can fall within the scope of Article 3(2) Regulation 1/2003. Unlike the text of Article 3(2) Regulation 1/2003, the Preamble to the Regulation does refer to national *competition* laws.[1181] Although the Preamble does not have binding force, this implies that Article

1180. Brook and Eben 2023a, pp. 57-58.
1181. Preamble 1/2003, recital 8.

3(2) Regulation 1/2003 is limited to national competition laws. Other interpretative principles support this approach.[1182]

Second, even if we presume that Article 3(2) Regulation 1/2003 only concerns national competition law, it remains unclear what the notion of competition law precisely entails. Regulation 1/2003 relies on a dichotomy between national competition laws and rules with a predominantly different objective. However, the regulation does not provide a definition of competition law. This raises the question under which circumstances national rules with similar objectives to those of EU competition law, but without a national competition law label, should be considered competition law. This issue is further discussed in section 7.4.1.2.

Third, Article 3(2) Regulation 1/2003 allows for *stricter* national competition laws. Yet, Regulation 1/2003 does not clarify the circumstances under which a national rule can be qualified as stricter. This raises the question of whether EU law provides an autonomous definition of the notion of stricter, or – alternatively – whether Member States have the freedom to determine if a national rule qualifies as stricter.[1183] According to some authors, the fact that Regulation 1/2003 does not make reference to Member States to determine the meaning of the concept of a 'stricter law' implies that the principle should be defined at the EU level.[1184] This discussion has important implications: if the CJEU adopts an autonomous definition, it could overrule Member States qualifying their national laws as being stricter.[1185]

Although a clear definition of the concept 'stricter' is absent, it is generally accepted that stricter rules can take various shapes. Stricter rules could be: (i) broader in personal scope; (ii) broader in material scope; or (iii) stricter in sanctions.[1186] Furthermore, it is questionable whether a stricter

1182. Mota Delgado and Petit stress, for example, that the title of Article 3 Regulation 1/2003 refers to 'national competition laws'. *See:* Mota Delgado and Petit 2023, p. 6.

1183. While some NCAs stressed that they have no doubts as to which laws are covered by the scope of Article 3(2) Regulation 1/2003, certain NCAs stressed that it is not clear to them which laws qualify as 'stricter' national laws. *See:* European Commission, Commission Staff Working Document, Evaluation of Regulation 1/2003 and 773/2004, SWD(2024)216 final, 238.

1184. Mota Delgado and Petit, for example, stress that the concept of 'stricter law' should be interpreted in an autonomous and uniform manner at the EU level. In order to support their approach, they refer to the 'well-established interpretative principle of EU law'. They refer to the case CJEU 29 October 2009, Case C-174/08, *Construction Danmark,* in which it is stressed that 'the term of a provision of [EU] law which makes no express reference to the law of the Member States for the purpose of determining its meaning and scope must normally given an autonomous and uniform interpretation throughout the EU'. Regulation 1/2003 refers to national laws, but does not give a meaning of the concept 'stricter national law'. Therefore, this concept should be determined at the EU level. *See:* Mota Delgado and Petit 2023, p. 5. *See also*: Podszun, p. 10 and CJEU 27 January 2005 Case C-188/03, *Junk*, para. 29.

1185. Brook and Eben 2023a, p. 58.

1186. Feteira 2015, p. 65.

interpretation of rules equivalent to Article 102 TFEU also qualifies as 'stricter rules' in the context of Article 3(2) Regulation 1/2003. The different categories of stricter rules are addressed in turn.

Stricter rules with a *broader personal scope* apply to the conduct of firms without a 'traditional' dominant position.[1187] In other words, such national laws allow NCAs to intervene below the standard of dominance. Recital 8 Regulation 1/2003 establishes that 'stricter laws may include provisions which prohibit or impose sanctions on abusive behaviour towards economically dependent undertakings'. Similarly, in its Report on the Functioning of Regulation 1/2003, the Commission qualifies national provisions regulating 'superior bargaining power' or 'significant influence' and national laws that 'foresee different standards for assessing dominance' as stricter national competition laws.[1188] In the German competition law framework, multiple examples of stricter rules are apparent, for example, rules for undertakings with relative dominance or a superior market position.[1189] These rules constitute 'stricter' national competition law rules on unilateral conduct for which EU competition law leaves room under Article 3(2) Regulation 1/2003. The German legislator adopted Section 19a GWB which establishes rules governing the position of undertakings of paramount significance for competition across markets. These rules arguably also constitute 'stricter' national competition law provisions on unilateral conduct. However, since Section 19a GWB also has regulatory features, this framework could potentially qualify as a rule with a predominantly different objective. Since the classification of Section 19a GWB is not straightforward, this topic is discussed in more detail in section 7.5.2.3.

Second, national rules can be stricter due to their broader material scope. Such rules allow NCAs to intervene below the threshold of abuse within the meaning of Article 102 TFEU. Against this backdrop, the Commission, for example, mentions 'legal provisions concerning resale at below cost or at loss' and 'stricter national provisions governing the conduct of dominant undertakings'.[1190]

Third, national prohibitions imposing stricter sanctions qualify as stricter competition law rules governing unilateral behaviour. Criminal sanctions for competition law violations constitute an example in this regard.[1191] Since criminal enforcement does not fall within the scope of the inquiry, this issue is not further addressed.

Lastly, it is questionable to what extent national equivalents of Article 102 TFEU can fall within the scope of Article 3(2) Regulation 1/2003.

1187. Brook and Eben 2023a, p. 58.
1188. European Commission, Report of 29 April 2009 on the functioning of Regulation 1/2003, COM(2009) 206 final, para. 21.
1189. *See* section 4.4.
1190. Mota Delgado and Petit 2023, p. 8.
1191. Feteira 2015, p. 66.

Against this backdrop, the *Meta Bundeskartellamt* case is highly relevant. In this case, as explained above, the *Bundeskartellamt* applied Section 19 GWB – the German counterpart of Article 102 TFEU – without applying Article 102 TFEU in parallel.[1192] The rationale behind this was that the German interpretation of Section 19 GWB – in which fundamental rights play a pivotal role – had not yet been endorsed in EU competition law. The *Bundeskartellamt* follows the line of reasoning that the German provision is stricter, because the concept developed in the *Meta Bundeskartellamt* case does not have an EU counterpart. The applied theory of harm would not have a counterpart in EU law.[1193] By taking this approach, the *Bundeskartellamt* relies on a rather broad interpretation of 'stricter' national laws by considering a national law stricter on the basis of a different interpretation of the standard of abuse.[1194] It is a missed opportunity that this issue was not taken into account in the preliminary ruling procedure in the *Meta Bundeskartellamt* case. Although no questions were posed relating to this issue, the CJEU could have taken this up ex officio.[1195] Doing so would have provided a (rare) opportunity to clarify the concept of 'stricter national rules' within the meaning of Regulation 1/2003.

7.4.1.2 Article 3(3) Regulation 1/2003: Rules with a Different Objective

Article 3(3) Regulation 1/2003 provides that Member States can adopt provisions of national law that predominantly pursue an objective different from the objectives pursued by Articles 101 and 102 TFEU. National frameworks that cannot be qualified as competition law are subject to Article 3(3) Regulation 1/2003.

In the context of Regulation 1/2003, the benchmark of 'predominantly different objective' from that of competition law gives rise to difficulties. For some national frameworks, it is rather evident that a different objective is pursued. Consumer laws, for example, serve objectives different from those of competition laws.[1196] Moreover, the Preamble to Regulation 1/2003 mentions rules on unfair trading practices as an example of rules with a predominantly different objective. It is explicitly stressed that 'such legislation pursues a specific objective, irrespective of the actual or presumed

1192. The duty of parallel application is discussed in section 8.4.2.1.
1193. The original German text stresses that: Die Prüfung hat jedoch gezeigt, dass das von der deutschen Rechtsprechung zur Generalklausel des § 19 Abs. 1 GWB entwickelte Schutzkonzept, das sich zur Feststellung der Missbräuchlichkeit maßgeblich auf grundrechtliche oder einfachgesetzliche Wertentscheidungen bezieht, in der europäischen Rechtsprechung und Anwendungspraxis bisher keine Entsprechung gefunden hat. *See:* Bundeskartellamt 6 February 2019 Case B6-22/16, *Facebook*, para. 914.
1194. Brook and Eben 2023b, p. 28.
1195. Brook and Eben 2023b, p. 28.
1196. Whish and Bailey 2018, p. 80.

effects of such acts on competition on the market'.[1197] In other instances, it is less evident whether a piece of legislation pursues a predominantly different objective. As explained in the previous Section, determining the objectives of a framework is not always a straightforward exercise. The application of Article 3(3) Regulation 1/2003 is further complicated by the fact that Regulation 1/2003 does not provide tools to determine the objectives of a national framework. It is, for example, unclear whether the national label of a framework is determinative or whether certain autonomous notions of EU law must be observed. In their extensive empirical study on Article 3 Regulation 1/2003, Brook and Eben assess various potential benchmarks in this regard, the application of which can lead to very different outcomes.[1198]

The *objective of the national statute* could be a first potential benchmark. This approach is formalistic and assigns great weight to the national label of a law. Subsequently, Member States could 'circumvent' the obligations of Regulation 1/2003 by adopting competition law-related rules in other statutes. An alternative benchmark could be the *objective of the specific provision*. This benchmark is also not unproblematic, since the objective of an individual legal provision is often not stipulated.[1199] A final benchmark relates to the *harm addressed in the enforcement of the national provision*. According to recital 9 Regulation 1/2003, unfair trading practices address *harms* that exist separately from the effects on competition in the market. In this case, the EU legislator seems to emphasise the harms addressed in enforcement.[1200] However, no uniform benchmark to determine whether a national rule pursues a 'predominantly different objective' from competition law can be identified in the application of Article 3 Regulation 1/2003 in the different jurisdictions in the EU.[1201]

The unclarities associated with Article 3(2) and 3(3) Regulation 1/2003 have practical implications. As explained in section 4.4, German competition law makes use of the freedom afforded by Article 3 Regulation 1/2003. While it is rather clear that the rules on relative and superior market power amount to stricter competition rules, the position of Section 19a GWB is less clear-cut. Section 19a GWB imposes certain pre-defined obligations upon undertakings with a position of paramount significance for competition across markets. Under German law, Section 19a GWB qualifies as competition law. It is questionable whether this automatically means that the framework also qualifies as such in the context of Article 3 Regulation

1197. Preamble Regulation 1/2003, recital 9.
1198. Brook and Eben 2023a, pp. 60 and further.
1199. Brook and Eben 2023a, p. 61.
1200. In the cases *VAG Händlebeirat* and *Metro* the CJEU takes the assumption that the German unfair competition rules are not competition laws. *See:* CJEU 5 June 1997 Case C-41/96, *VAG-Händlerbeirat*, para. 16; CJEU 25 October 1977 Case 26/76, *Metro*, para. 24. *See also*: Brook and Eben 2023a, pp. 51-52.
1201. For a very elaborate analysis in this regard, *see:* Brook and Eben 2023a.

1/2003. If the *objective of the national statute* were to constitute the relevant benchmark for determining whether national law pursues a predominantly different objective, Section 19a GWB indeed would be competition law. However, if (i) the objective of the specific provision or (ii) the harm addressed in enforcement would be leading, the qualification may be different. This issue is discussed in more detail in section 7.5.2.3.

In conclusion, this section assesses the described mechanisms of pre-emption and hierarchies of norms in the context of EU and national competition law. The pre-emptive effect of EU competition law is shaped by the classificatory system of Article 3(2) and 3(3) Regulation 1/2003. This provision determines to what extent EU competition law leaves room for certain additional national (competition) laws. In doing so, various categories of national regulation are set apart, i.e.:

- The national equivalents of Article 102 TFEU, e.g., Section 19 GWB or Article 24 Dutch Competition Act.
- National competition laws on unilateral conduct without an EU law counterpart which are stricter than Article 102 TFEU.
- National competition law rules which are not stricter than Article 102 TFEU without an EU law equivalent.
- Rules with a predominantly different objective.

The degree to which EU law leaves room for national rules depends on the category of which a national provision is considered to be part. The table below summarises under which conditions EU law allows for national provisions, provided that there is an effect on trade between Member States.

Table 7.1 The Pre-emptive Effect of EU Competition Law

Type of National Rule	*Application in a Case with an Effect on Trade Between Member States Possible?*	*Institutional and Procedural Obligations*
National equivalent of Article 102 TFEU	Yes	Institutional and procedural obligations Regulation 1/2003 Duty of parallel application of EU competition law applies

Stricter competition law rules without an EU equivalent	Yes	Duty of parallel application can apply Institutional and procedural obligations Regulation 1/2003 in the case of parallel application
National competition law rules which are not stricter than Article 102 TFEU without an EU law equivalent	No	
Rules with a predominantly different objective	Yes	

The classificatory system of Article 3 Regulation 1/2003 relies on various concepts. However, as explained above, many of these concepts are poorly defined. This blurs the line between the different categories which is detrimental for legal certainty. Article 3 Regulation 1/2003 relies on the following unclear concepts:

- national competition law;
- stricter;
- predominantly different objective.

In sum, the system established by Article 3 is highly complex, and the test of Article 3 Regulation 1/2003 is flawed in various ways. This is worrisome since the qualification of a national rule for the purposes of Article 3 Regulation 1/2003 has important consequences for the pre-emptive effect of EU competition law. The qualification of a national rule as competition law is not only important in order to determine whether only stricter rules can be imposed but also has procedural and institutional consequences relating to the parallel application of EU and national competition law and relating to the procedural and institutional obligations of Regulation 1/2003.[1202]

7.4.2 Executive Pre-emption in Competition Law

Apart from the legislative pre-emptive effect of EU competition law, the application of EU competition law by the Commission can amount to

1202. Brook and Eben 2023a, p. 54.

executive pre-emption. In this context, Articles 16 and 11(6) Regulation 1/2003 are particularly relevant. Both provisions are addressed in turn.

7.4.2.1 Article 16 Regulation 1/2003

Article 16 Regulation 1/2003, which codifies the *Masterfoods* doctrine, establishes that NCAs cannot take decisions that run counter to a decision adopted by the Commission.[1203] Consequently, by creating a mechanism to avoid conflicting decisions, Article 16 Regulation 1/2003 provides a mechanism of executive pre-emption.[1204] Article 16 Regulation 1/2003 reflects the Commission's general supervisory role and seeks to contribute to the uniform application of EU competition law in the parallel enforcement framework of EU competition law.[1205]

The scope of Article 16(2) is rather broad: in the *Toshiba* case, the CJEU established that 'the general wording of Article 16(2) of Regulation 1/2003 and its schematic position within the chapter on cooperation' shows that it is 'by no means limited to only one particular type of decision'.[1206] Despite its broad formulation, the reach of Article 16 Regulation 1/2003 depends on the nature of the decision at hand.[1207] The text of the article refers to a *decision of the Commission.* While it is generally recognised that this concept covers infringement decisions, interim decisions and decisions finding the inapplicability of EU competition law, the effect of commitment decisions is more complex.[1208] According to recital 22 of Regulation 1/2003, commitment decisions do not affect the power of national courts and NCAs. In the *Gasorba* case, the CJEU established – in the context of *national courts*

1203. In the initial Proposal for Regulation 1/2003, the text established that NCAs (and national courts) *shall use every effort* to avoid conflicting decisions. *See:* European Commission, Proposal of 19 December 2000 for a Council Regulation on the implementation of the rules on competition laid down in Articles 81 and 82 of the Treaty and amending Regulations (EEC) No. 1017/68, (EEC) No. 2988/74,(EEC) No. 4056/86 and (EEC) No. 3975/87 (Regulation implementing Articles 81 and 82 of the Treaty). Moreover, Article 16(1) Regulation 1/2003 establishes a similar obligation for national courts. For national courts, the obligation is extended to *decisions contemplated by the Commission in proceedings it has initiated.* Article 16(2) Regulation 1/2003 does not refer to ongoing competition law procedures. This is logical, because Article 11(6) Regulation 1/2003 reliefs NCAs from their competence to apply Articles 101 and 102 TFEU once the Commission initiated a decision.

1204. Explanatory Memorandum to European Commission, Proposal of 19 December 2000 for a Council Regulation on the implementation of the rules on competition laid down in Articles 81 and 82 of the Treaty and amending Regulations (EEC) No. 1017/68, (EEC) No. 2988/74,(EEC) No. 4056/86 and (EEC) No. 3975/87 (Regulation implementing Articles 81 and 82 of the Treaty), Article 16.

1205. Preamble Regulation 1/2003, recital 22; Article 105(1) TFEU; CJEU 14 December 2000 Case C-344/98, *Masterfoods*, para. 46; Wils 2019, p. 151; Riley 2003, p. 612.

1206. CJEU 14 February 2012 Case C-17/10, *Toshiba*, para. 87.

1207. Joncheray 2022, p. 399.

1208. Massa 2020, p. 132.

– that these decisions, despite the fact that they should be considered prima facie evidence, are a 'preliminary assessment' and do not establish whether there is or has been an infringement. Therefore, national courts may conclude that a practice that is subject to a commitment decision violates EU competition law. Yet, 'both the principle of sincere cooperation and the objective of applying EU competition law effectively and uniformly require the national court to take into account the preliminary assessment carried out by the Commission and regard it as an indication, if not prima facie evidence, of the anticompetitive nature of the agreement at issue'.[1209] National courts and competition authorities therefore cannot simply ignore a commitment decision taken by the Commission.[1210]

Article 16 Regulation 1/2003 thus shows that the EU legislator considered it necessary to establish a specific provision ensuring the uniform application of EU competition law, notwithstanding the general principles of EU law, as well as the other cooperation mechanisms introduced in Regulation 1/2003.[1211]

7.4.2.2 Article 11(6) Regulation 1/2003

According to Article 11(6) Regulation 1/2003, the Commission's initiation of proceedings in order to adopt an EU competition law decision relieves NCAs of their competence to apply EU competition law.[1212] Against this backdrop, Article 11(6) Regulation 1/2003 serves not only as a tool of executive pre-emption but also as a tool for the allocation of cases between the Commission and the NCAs. Article 11(6) Regulation 1/2003 in its capacity as an allocative tool is further discussed in section 8.4.2.2.

Article 11(6) Regulation 1/2003 reflects the Commission's managerial position in the ECN: if the Commission starts proceedings under EU competition law, NCAs can no longer do so. By initiating proceedings, the Commission temporarily prevents NCAs from using their competence to apply EU competition law.[1213] Hence, Article 11(6) Regulation 1/2003 provides a mechanism of *temporary executive pre-emption* and protects

1209. CJEU 23 November 2017 Case C-547/16, *Gasorba.*
1210. Joncheray 2022, p. 405.
1211. Joncheray 2022, p. 398.
1212. The concept of initiation of a procedure should be interpreted as 'an act of the Commission by which it announces to an undertaking its intention to bring proceedings in order to adopt [a decision]'. *See:* CJEU 25 February 2021 Case C-857/19, *Slovak Telekom*, paras 25-27; According De Smijter and Sinclair, Article 11(6) Regulation 1/2003 constitutes 'a rule of competence'. *See:* De Smijter and Sinclair 2014, para. 2.231.
1213. Sauter 2016, p. 170.

undertakings from parallel proceedings brought by NCAs and the Commission.[1214]

In the application of Article 11(6) Regulation 1/2003, two scenarios must be distinguished. The Commission can be the first to start an investigation into a particular conduct. In this case, Article 11(6) Regulation prevents NCAs from applying Article 102 TFEU to practices by the same undertaking on the same relevant market.[1215] The situation is more complicated if an NCA has already started a proceeding and has informed the Commission about this.[1216] In this scenario, the Commission can still start a procedure with a pre-emptive effect. Within the ECN, cases are normally re-allocated within a period of two months.[1217] During this initial allocation period, the Commission can initiate proceedings with a pre-emptive effect after having consulted the NCA concerned.[1218] After this two month period, the Commission only applies Article 11(6) Regulation 1/2003 in specific situations, for example, if NCAs envisions adopting a conflicting decision in the same case or if an NCA envisions adopting a decision which obviously conflicts with consolidated case law or previous decisions or if there is a need to adopt a Commission decision, in particular, if issues arise in multiple Member States or if the NCAs concerned do not object. In practice, the Commission has not yet relied on Article 11(6) Regulation 1/2003 in the situation where an NCA has already started proceedings.[1219]

Importantly, the pre-emptive effects of a Commission decision are limited to the facts that are subject to the proceedings initiated by the Commission.[1220] The CJEU established – in the *Slovak Telekom* and *Amazon* cases – that Member States are relieved of their competence to bring proceedings against 'the same undertaking for the same, allegedly anticompetitive, practices occurring on the same product market and geographical market or markets during the same period or periods'.[1221] Consequently, Article 11(6) Regulation 1/2003 ensures that undertakings are not subject to

1214. CJEU 25 February 2021 Case C-857/19, *Slovak Telekom*, para. 32; CJEU 29 January 2020 Case C-418/19P, *Silgan Closures*, para. 73; De Smijter and Sinclair 2014, p. 2.231.
1215. Commission Notice of 27 April 2004 on cooperation within the Network of Competition Authorities, C 101/43, Commission Notice of 27 April 2004 on cooperation within the Network of Competition Authorities, C 101/43 (henceforth: Network Notice).
1216. Article 11(3) Regulation 1/2003.
1217. Network Notice, para. 18.
1218. Network Notice, para. 54.
1219. Van Cleynenbreugel 2020, p. 419.
1220. CJEU 25 February 2021 Case C-857/19, *Slovak Telekom*, para. 28; CJEU 29 January 2020 Case C-418/19P, *Silgan Closures*, paras 73-75.
1221. CJEU 25 February 2021 Case C-857/19, *Slovak Telekom*, para. 30; CJEU 20 April 2023 Case C-815/21P, *Amazon v. Commission*, paras 27 and 31.

simultaneous parallel procedures under EU competition law.[1222] This limitation of the NCA's competence to apply EU competition law is limited to the product and geographical market of the Commission's proceedings. For instance, in the *Amazon* case, the CJEU ruled that Italy's competence to apply EU competition law was not limited because the territorial scope of the Commission's case did not include Italy. Hence, the protection against parallel proceedings did not apply.[1223]

Another important issue relating to Article 11(6) Regulation 1/2003 entails its effect on *national* competition laws. In the *Toshiba* case, the CJEU broadened the application of Article 11(6) Regulation 1/2003 by stressing that the provision does not only suspend the application of EU competition law but also of a 'part of [...] domestic competition law'.[1224] This pre-emptive effect, which only applies to cases with an effect on trade between Member States, stems from a joint reading of Articles 11(6) and 3(1) Regulation 1/2003. Article 3(1) Regulation 1/2003 establishes the duty of parallel application of EU competition law to conduct with an effect on trade between Member States. If NCAs are under the obligation to apply EU competition law in parallel to their national competition laws, but Article 11(6) prevents them from applying EU competition law, this means that national competition law cannot be applied either because the NCA cannot act in conformity with Article 3(1) Regulation 1/2003.[1225] The parts that remain applicable without limitations are the frameworks mentioned in Article 3(2) and 3(3) Regulation 1/2003, i.e., stricter national laws which prohibit or sanction unilateral conduct and national law that pursues a predominantly different objective.[1226]

7.5 COMPETITION LAW AND THE DMA

While the previous section focused on the intra-disciplinary context, this Section uses the concepts of pre-emption and norm hierarchies to analyse the cross-disciplinary interplay between competition law and the DMA. The DMA has a pre-emptive effect on certain national laws. Article 1(5), (6), and (7) DMA are particularly relevant in this regard. According to Article 1(5) DMA:

> In order to avoid the fragmentation of the internal market, Member States shall not impose further obligations on gatekeepers by way of laws, regulations or administrative measures for the purpose of ensuring

1222. Network Notice, para. 53; The Commission should be informed in accordance with Article 11(3) Regulation 1/2003. Article 11(3) Regulation 1/2003 is discussed in section 8.4.2.3.
1223. CJEU 20 April 2023 Case C-815/21P, *Amazon v. Commission*, para. 34.
1224. CJEU 14 February 2012 Case C-17/10, *Toshiba*, para. 75.
1225. Rayment and Grubeck 2018, pp. 1328-1330.
1226. CJEU 14 February 2012 Case C-17/10, *Toshiba*, paras 72-78.

contestable and fair markets. Nothing in [the DMA] precludes Member States from imposing obligations on undertakings, including undertakings providing core platform services, for matters falling outside the scope of this Regulation, provided that those obligations are compatible with Union law and do not result from the fact that the relevant undertaking has the status of a gatekeeper within the meaning of this Regulation.

Furthermore, Article 1(6) DMA establishes that:

[The DMA] *is without prejudice to the application of Articles 101 and 102 TFEU. It is also without prejudice to the application of:*

(a) National competition rules prohibiting anti-competitive agreements, decisions by associations of undertakings, concerted practices and abuses of dominant positions;
(b) National competition rules prohibiting other forms of unilateral conduct insofar as they are applied to undertakings other than gatekeepers or amount to the imposition of further obligations on gatekeepers; and
(c) Council Regulation No 139/2004 and national rules concerning merger control.

Lastly, Article 1(7) DMA stresses that 'national authorities shall not take decisions which run counter to a decision adopted by the Commission under this Regulation. The Commission and Member States shall work in close cooperation and coordinate their enforcement actions […]'.

Article 1(5), (6) and (7) DMA establish a classificatory system that, in part, mirrors Article 3 Regulation 1/2003. These provisions address the DMA's relationship with both national and EU competition law. Each of these dimensions is addressed in turn in the next Sections.

7.5.1 The DMA and EU Competition Law

The DMA is relatively straightforward as to its relationship with EU competition law: the instrument is 'without prejudice' to EU competition law. This 'without prejudice' clause means that the DMA and competition law can be applied in parallel. Consequently, the DMA does not pre-empt the application of Article 102 TFEU. This approach is sensible and inevitable: in light of the principle of the hierarchy of norms of EU law, the DMA – which constitutes an instrument of secondary EU law – cannot limit the application of primary EU law. Since Article 102 TFEU constitutes a norm of primary EU law, its application cannot be limited by the DMA.[1227]

Although the relationship between the DMA and EU competition law is relatively straightforward at first sight, Article 1(7) DMA introduces

1227. Beems 2023, p. 20.

complications regarding the application of Article 102 TFEU by NCAs. Confusingly, Article 1(7) DMA specifies that NCAs are prevented from taking decisions that run counter to DMA decisions of the Commission. This implies a certain degree of *executive pre-emption*: the Commission's application of the DMA limits NCA's room to manoeuvre.[1228] The text of the DMA does not provide clarity as to the scope and reach of the pre-emptive effects of Article 1(7) DMA. It remains unclear whether NCAs can, in the context of applying Article 102 TFEU, diverge from the Commission's DMA interpretation of a certain obligation. If a hypothetical conflict were to arise, it is not clear whether the NCA's interpretation of the primary law provision of Article 102 TFEU, or conversely, the Commission's interpretation of the DMA, should take precedence. Article 1(6) and 1(7) DMA do not provide clarity in this regard.[1229]

7.5.2 The DMA and National (Competition) Law

The DMA's relationship with national (competition) law is more complicated. In this context, Article 1(5) and 1(6) DMA establish a classificatory system resembling that of Regulation 1/2003. The system is, similarly to Article 3 Regulation 1/2003, not easy to read.[1230] The table below aims to summarise Article 1(5) and 1(6) DMA.

Figure 7.2 Schematic Overview of Article 1(5) and 1(6) DMA

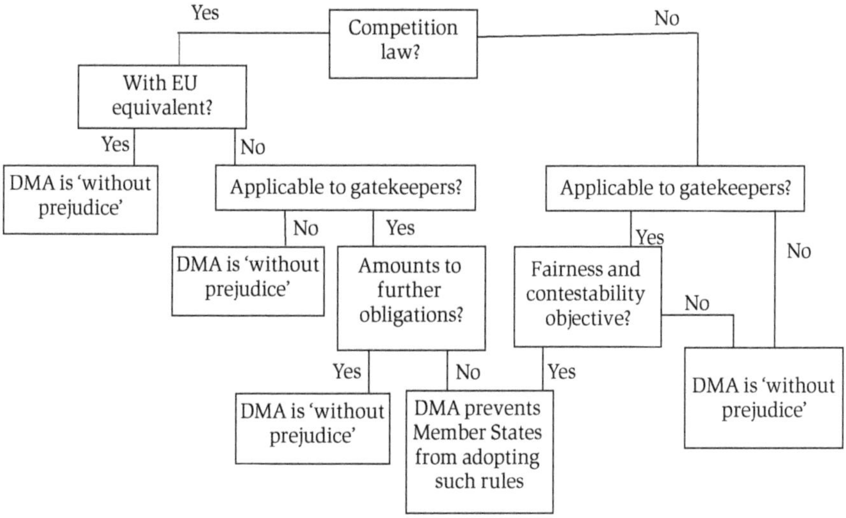

1228. *See* sections 7.3 and 7.4.2.
1229. Beems, Van de Gronden and Rusu 2023, p. 69.
1230. Mota Delgado and Petit 2023.

Before delving into the individual categories of national law as listed in the DMA, it is interesting to consider the relationship between Article 1(5) and 1(6) DMA and the principle of primacy of EU law. Generally, the DMA takes precedence over national laws according to the principle of primacy.[1231] There is (academic) debate regarding the question of whether Article 1(5) and (6) DMA bears an effect on the principle of primacy of EU law. This debate mirrors discussions on the implications of Article 3(2) and (3) Regulation 1/2003.[1232] The DMA provides an opening clause for certain national competition laws and regulatory instruments.[1233] According to some authors, this opening clause amounts to an exception to the principle of primacy.[1234] In my view, the provisions provide a tool of pre-emption, rather than an exception to the principle of primacy. The DMA leaves room for Member States to apply certain national frameworks in parallel to the DMA. This does not mean that these national frameworks may amount to a direct violation of the DMA, nor that national provisions would take precedence in the case of conflicting norms. According to the principle of primacy of EU law, the DMA's provisions are hierarchically superior to national laws and Article 1(5) and (6) DMA do not alter this hierarchy of norms. In other words, the DMA does not lay down that Member States can adopt rules that are in conflict with the DMA. Rather, it allows Member States to adopt certain additional national provisions that can be applied in parallel to the DMA's provisions. Similar to Article 3(2) and (3) Regulation 1/2003, Article 1(5) and (6) DMA relate to the pre-emptive effect of the DMA in relation to national law, rather than to the hierarchical relationship between the DMA and national law.

Furthermore, the DMA is based on Article 114 TFEU which constitutes the EU's legal basis for adopting rules with the objective of establishing and ensuring the functioning of the internal market.[1235] While the EU has exclusive competences in the area of competition rules necessary for the functioning of the internal market, the internal market is a shared competence according to Article 3 TFEU. This means that Member States have the competence to act insofar as the EU has not executed its power. With the establishment of the DMA, the EU has used its power to adopt rules to

---

1231. *See* section 7.2.1.

1232. *See* section 7.4.1.

1233. Podszun 2022a.

1234. Brook and Eben 2022, p. 2.

1235. It is questionable whether Article 114 TFEU allows for the adoption of measures of approximation of national competition laws. It could be argued that Article 114 TFEU allows the EU to adopt measures that harmonise national competition laws, insofar as that is deemed necessary for the functioning of the internal market. This approach seems to be taken by the EU legislator in the DMA. In my view, such an approach is reasonable. Tavares argues otherwise and stresses that the use of Article 114 TFEU for the approximation of national competition laws runs counter to the principle of conferral. *See:* Tavares 2018.

safeguard contestable and fair gatekeeper markets. However, the EU legislator did not fully pre-empt the application of national competition laws or other regulations. This means that the instrument does not establish a model of legislative field pre-emption. Rather, the system of the DMA focuses on conflict pre-emption: in the case of certain direct or indirect conflicts, the DMA does not leave room for additional national laws. This does not mean that these national frameworks may amount to an infringement of EU law. This is also confirmed by the text of Article 1(5) and (6) DMA: national competition laws without an EU equivalent can only amount to further obligations, and other national regulatory initiatives can only be imposed insofar as they are compatible with EU law.

7.5.2.1 Article 1(6) DMA: National Competition Laws

Article 1(6) DMA establishes that the DMA is 'without prejudice' to national competition laws. Similar to Regulation 1/2003, the classificatory system of the DMA relies on a distinction between competition laws and other regulatory instruments. This begs the question under which circumstances a national rule qualifies as competition law.[1236] As explained in section 7.4.1, Regulation 1/2003 provides very limited guidance on the concept of national competition laws and largely centres around the objective of a national law. Article 3(2) Regulation 1/2003 does not rely on a clear benchmark. Despite the fact that the DMA partially replicates the test of Article 3(2) Regulation 1/2003, the DMA's preamble provides some more guidance by establishing an autonomous EU law definition of competition law – at least in the context of the DMA.[1237] According to recital 10 of the DMA's preamble, national competition rules regarding unilateral conduct are 'based on an individualised assessment of market position and behaviour, including its actual or potential effects and the precise scope of the prohibited behaviour, and which provides for the possibility for undertakings to make efficiency and objective justification arguments for the behaviour in question […]'. In order to determine whether a national rule amounts to competition law, the degree to which a rule allows for an effect-based assessment is thus of key importance.

Consequently, laws that are formulated as rigid per se rules without a possibility for justification do not qualify as national competition laws within the meaning of the DMA, since such rules do not leave much room for an individualised assessment. If a national rule or framework does not qualify as competition law, the DMA's pre-emption rules on other regulatory instruments apply. In order to establish whether a national framework can be categorised as competition law within the meaning of the DMA, the formal qualification of the instrument is thus not determinative. Rather, the evaluative standard, and therefore the intensity of the market intervention,

1236. Hoffman, Herrmann and Kestler 2024, p. 130.
1237. Zilsdorf 2023, p. 305.

plays a role of key importance.[1238] The focus on an autonomous EU standard can be explained: if the DMA were merely to look at the formal status of a legal act, Member States could circumvent the DMA's limitations on certain regulatory instruments by labelling such rules as competition law.[1239]

In the broader category of national competition law, the DMA distinguishes between (i) national competition rules concerning abuse of a dominant position and (ii) national competition rules prohibiting other forms of unilateral conduct. Similar to Regulation 1/2003, the DMA thus separates between national competition laws with and without an EU equivalent. When it comes to competition law rules with an EU equivalent, the DMA does not seem to impose explicit limitations: the DMA applies *without prejudice* to such rules. This means that neither Section 19 GWB nor Article 24 DCA are affected by the introduction of the DMA.

The opening clause for rules on unilateral conduct without an EU equivalent is more complicated. Such rules can merely be adopted insofar as they are: (i) applied to undertakings other than gatekeepers; or (ii) amount to the imposition of further obligations on gatekeepers. For the purposes of the DMA, national competition rules without an EU equivalent are thus subdivided into two categories, namely rules that are applied to undertakings other than gatekeepers and rules that apply to gatekeepers. The DMA does not prevent Member States from adopting rules in the former category. However, the DMA does not provide further clarity on the meaning of 'rules applied to undertakings other than gatekeepers'. It remains unclear whether this category also encompasses rules that de facto (mainly) apply to gatekeepers, but are labelled differently. In this light, it is, for example, relevant whether the German Section 19a GWB on 'undertakings with a paramount position for competition across markets' can qualify as such. This issue is further discussed below.

The DMA does not fully prevent Member States from adopting rules that apply to gatekeepers. Under certain conditions, national rules without an EU equivalent can be applied to undertakings that have to be designated as gatekeeper. Such rules can be imposed if they amount to the imposition of *further obligations* on gatekeepers. The leeway to adopt further obligations indicates that the DMA – when it comes to national competition rules without an EU equivalent – provides minimum harmonisation: Member States are allowed to impose *further obligations* on gatekeepers.[1240] In my view, Article 1(6) DMA draws inspiration from Article 3 Regulation 1/2003 which allows for 'stricter' national competition laws on unilateral conduct. The DMA does not provide further indication as to the meaning of the concept 'further obligations'. Therefore, it remains uncertain to what extent 'further' obligations are similar to 'stricter' provisions. In legal literature,

1238. Zilsdorf 2023, p. 308.
1239. Brauneck 2023, p. 34.
1240. Van den Boom 2022, p. 10.

various examples of 'further obligations' are discussed. National rules on unilateral behaviour could, for example, address conduct related to services that do not qualify as 'core platform service' under the DMA.[1241] However, it remains questionable whether national frameworks containing stricter substantive provisions or stricter sanctions can also be considered 'further obligations'. The DMA is insufficiently clear in this regard.

7.5.2.2 Article 1(5) DMA: Other Regulatory Initiatives

As explained above, the text of the DMA not only addresses the relationship with national competition laws but also covers the relationship between the DMA and other national regulatory instruments. According to Article 1(5) DMA, such instruments can take the form of 'laws, regulations or administrative measures'. The Member States' discretion in this regard is not unlimited. According to recital 9 of the DMA, 'fragmentation of the internal market can only effectively be averted if Member States are prevented from applying national rules which are within the scope and pursue the same objective as [the DMA]'.[1242]

Article 1(5) DMA centres around the concepts of: (i) the same scope; and (ii) similar objectives. Both benchmarks are not sufficiently clarified in the DMA. *First,* regarding the personal scope, the DMA establishes that Member States shall not impose further obligations *on gatekeepers* for the purpose of ensuring contestable and fair markets. However, it remains uncertain whether this means that Member States cannot establish rules that are (also) applicable to undertakings that have been designated as gatekeeper or whether the DMA only limits the possibility of adopting rules which are specifically labelled as rules addressing gatekeepers. Section 19a GWB, for instance, addresses undertakings with a paramount position for competition across markets rather than gatekeepers. However, in practice, both instruments largely target the same online platforms. This raises the question of whether Section 19a GWB imposes rules applicable to gatekeepers. This issue is further discussed in the next Section. Furthermore, Article 1(5) DMA continues by stressing that the DMA does not prevent Member States from imposing obligations on undertakings, including core platform services providers, 'provided that those obligations […] do not result from the fact that the relevant undertaking has the status of a gatekeeper within the meaning of this Regulation'. However, as also pointed out by Brook and Eben, it is unclear under which circumstances an obligation results from a core platform provider's gatekeeper status.[1243] Given the importance of this criterion, further clarification is needed.

1241. Podszun 2022a, p. 6.
1242. Preamble DMA, recital 9.
1243. Brook and Eben 2022, p. 3.

Second, the DMA harmonises rules with the objective of 'ensuring contestable and fair markets'. Article 1(5) DMA allows Member States to introduce regulatory frameworks applicable to gatekeepers for other purposes. The objective of a national framework is, therefore, a determinative factor in assessing whether EU law leaves room for additional national regulatory frameworks. As explained in the context of Article 3 Regulation 1/2003, identifying the objective of a rule or framework is a difficult task. It remains, for example, unclear whether the objective of a provision should be considered in light of the provision itself, in light of the framework of which a provision is a part or in light of the harm addressed by a rule.[1244] By partially replicating the test of Article 3 Regulation 1/2003, Article 1(6) DMA may result in similar uncertainties.

7.5.2.3 Section 19a GWB

The discussion on the pre-emptive effect of the DMA is particularly relevant in the context of the German *Section 19a GWB* which imposes certain obligations on undertakings with a position of paramount importance for competition across markets.[1245] Interestingly, Section 19a GWB is not only labelled as an instrument of German competition law but is also referred to as an instrument 'comparable' to the DMA.[1246] This begs the question of how Section 19a GWB fits in the regulatory landscape after the adoption of the DMA. In order to assess whether the DMA leaves room for Section 19a GWB, it is necessary to establish whether the German instrument amounts to competition law or to (economic) regulation. This can be a difficult task since Section 19a GWB sits somewhere in between competition law and the DMA and is described as a competition and regulatory law 'chimera'.[1247] From a German perspective, Section 19a GWB constitutes a competition law instrument: the instrument is part of the German competition law act (the GWB) and mainly serves a competition law objective.[1248] Moreover, the *Bundesgerichtshof* confirmed that the instrument amounts to competition law.[1249] However, at the same time, the instrument has some regulatory

1244. Brook and Eben 2022, p. 6.
1245. *See* section 4.4.
1246. Bechtold and Bosch 2021, para. 3.
1247. Zilsdorf refers to Section 19a GWB as 'eine wettbewerbs- und regulierungsrecht Chimäre'. A Chimera is a creature with a lion's head, a goat's body, and a snake's tail. Zilsdorf 2023; *see also*: https://www.oxfordlearnersdictionaries.com/definition/americ an_english/chimera#:~:text=chimera-,noun,that%20can%20breathe%20out%20fire ac cessed 1 April 2025.
1248. Hornung 2023, p. 37.
1249. Bundesgerichtshof 23 April 2024, Case KVB 56/22, *Amazon*; Reetz and Iken 2025, p. 85.

characteristics and arguably amounts to a 'paradigm shift' in German competition law.[1250]

In order to determine the interrelation between the DMA and Section 19a GWB, the national qualification of the instrument as either regulation or competition law is of limited importance. Rather, it is relevant whether the instrument qualifies as competition law within the meaning of the DMA. According to recital 10 of the DMA's preamble, national competition rules are 'based on an individualised assessment of market positions and behaviour, including its actual or potential effects and the precise scope of the prohibited behaviour, and which provide for the possibility of undertakings to make efficiency and objective justification arguments'. The main question to be answered is whether the Section 19a GWB allows for an individualised assessment.[1251] In my view, Section 19a GWB allows for an individualised assessment. Various arguments support this conclusion.

Considering the scope of the instrument, the GWB does not establish quantitative criteria triggering a presumption of a position of paramount importance. Rather, designation can follow an investigation into the undertaking concerned.[1252] This approach leaves more room for an individualised assessment than quantitative parameters. Moreover, the prohibitions and obligations listed in Section 19a GWB are – unlike the DMA's obligations – not automatically applicable to all undertakings that have been designated as undertakings of paramount significance for competition across markets. Rather, the *Bundeskartellamt* needs to adopt a second decision in order to specify the application of the respective obligations to the undertaking concerned.[1253] Moreover, in an assessment under Section 19a GWB, the actual effects of a specific conduct on competition in the markets can be taken into consideration. Furthermore, Section 19a GWB allows undertakings to justify their alleged anti-competitive behaviour. This is an indication that there is room for an individualised assessment. Based on those arguments, various (German) authors contend that Section 19a GWB should indeed be qualified as competition law.[1254]

Yet, and despite these largely convincing arguments, it cannot be ignored that Section 19a GWB has close proximity to regulatory laws.[1255] Also, by rebutting the standard of proof of the anti-competitive effect, Section 19a GWB establishes that the *Bundeskartellamt* does not have to address the anti-competitive effects in each individual case. This could be an argument against qualifying the instrument as competition law and is referred

1250. Wagner-von Papp 2023a.
1251. Preamble DMA, recital 10.
1252. Van den Boom 2022, p. 75.
1253. Hornung 2023, p. 36.
1254. *See, e.g.,* Podszun 2022a, p. 9.
1255. Stöhr and Mendelsohn 2024, p. 24.

to as the 'proverbial Achilles' Heel' of Section 19a GWB.[1256] Because there is – given the novelty of the provisions – no existing case law on the interpretation of Article 1(5) and (6) DMA, it remains uncertain to what extent the above-mentioned arguments are valid. Further case law of the CJEU is necessary in order to provide insights into the exact scope and meaning of these proceedings.

Assuming that Section 19a GWB would indeed qualify as competition law, further questions arise. National competition laws can be applied insofar they: (i) are applied to other undertakings than gatekeepers; or (ii) amount to the imposition of further obligations.

As explained above, regarding national competition laws on unilateral behaviour, the DMA establishes two categories, namely rules that are applied to gatekeepers and rules that are applied to undertakings *other than gatekeepers*. On paper, the German rules have a scope different from that of the DMA, and the concept 'gatekeeper' is not used to determine the scope of Section 19a GWB. This begs the question of whether Section 19a GWB applies to gatekeepers. On the one hand, one could argue that Section 19a GWB is applied to undertakings with a position of paramount significance for competition across markets and therefore, does not apply to gatekeepers. On the other hand, despite the differences in scope, the DMA is used to address the behaviour of large platforms and will thus target largely the same undertakings as the DMA.

Against this backdrop, a distinction can be made between the application of the GWB to undertakings that have also been designated as gatekeepers and the application to undertakings that have not been designated as such. In the latter scenario, the DMA would not limit the possibility to apply Section 19a GWB: national competition rules can be applied to undertakings other than gatekeepers. The former scenario, however, can be more complicated. In practice, the latter scenario is more likely to occur: both the DMA and Section 19a GWB address the behaviour of 'Big Tech'. Also, the undertakings that so far have been designated under Section 19a GWB by the *Bundeskartellamt* overlap with the undertakings that provide one or more core platform services and are designated as gatekeeper in the context of the DMA.[1257]

If Section 19a GWB were to be qualified as a rule applicable to gatekeepers, the DMA still leaves room for the instrument if it would *amount to the imposition of further obligations*. However, as explained above, it is not clear under which circumstances a rule amounts to further obligations. The concept of core platform services and the question whether a Section 19a GWB case relates to a core platform service or to another service offered by a platform can be of key importance in this regard. Although the scope of the GWB is not limited to core platform services (*see* cf. section 4.4.2), it may

1256. Witt 2023, p. 663.
1257. *See* sections 4.4.2 and 5.2.2.

be determinative whether the obligations relate to core platform services in the meaning of the DMA. The application of Section 19a GWB to services that do *not* qualify as core platform services within the meaning of the DMA may amount to 'further obligations'. In a Section 19a GWB case on Google's data policy, the *Bundeskartellamt* probably follows this avenue. Without explicitly establishing how Section 19a GWB should be appraised under Article 1(5) and (6) DMA, the *Bundeskartellamt* limits its application of Section 19a GWB to 'those services which are not relevant core platform services'.[1258] The *Bundeskartellamt* – in this situation – thus seems to consider Section 19a GWB as an instrument of national competition law without an EU equivalent that is applied to gatekeepers. Although the *Bundeskartellamt*'s approach – which was coordinated with the Commission[1259] – provides interesting insights into the German NCA's perspective on the relationship between the DMA and Section 19a GWB, further clarification must be provided by the CJEU.

As explained above, there are various (convincing) arguments that support the qualification of Section 19a GWB as an instrument of competition law. In the alternative scenario, Section 19a GWB would *not* be qualified as competition law. In this case, the first relevant question would be whether the regulatory framework entails rules *imposed on gatekeepers.* As explained above, in the context of the DMA, it can be debated whether this amounts to obligations imposed on gatekeepers. The personal scope of Section 19a GWB is not directed at gatekeepers. However, the framework will impose obligations on undertakings that have also been designated as gatekeepers under the DMA. Consequently, it remains unclear whether Section 19a GWB would impose obligations on gatekeepers under Article 1(5) DMA.[1260]

The next relevant question would be whether Section 19a GWB pursues an objective similar to that of DMA. In other words, it should be established whether the Section 19a GWB pursues a fairness and contestability objective. Unlike the DMA, Section 19a GWB as such does not introduce novel objectives, but is rather embedded in the German competition law framework.[1261] This arguably indicates that the goals pursued by Section 19a GWB are different from the objectives of the DMA. However, at the same time and as explained section 6.3.1, the objectives of the DMA and competition law are closely related. In turn, this may indicate a rather close proximity of the objectives of the DMA and of Section 19a GWB. Furthermore, despite the fact that Section 19a GWB was adopted as part of the German competition law framework, the strong position of online platforms and their 'gatekeeper'

1258. *Bundeskartellamt* 5 October 2023 B7-70/21, *Google/Data processing conditions*, para. 40.

1259. The case stresses that the *Bundeskartellamt* and the Commission 'maintained close contact'. *See: Bundeskartellamt* 5 October 2023 B7-70/21, *Google/Data processing conditions*, para. 40.

1260. Witt 2023, p. 662.

1261. Podszun 2022a, p. 9.

role are part of Section 19a's *raison d'être*. The German legislator, for example, stresses that Section 19a GWB should reinforce the application of the German competition law framework to markets in which digital ecosystems are present and gatekeeper positions are controlled by a few undertakings.[1262] Although the term *gatekeeper* in this context does not have the exact same meaning as the term gatekeeper in the DMA, it indicates that Section 19a GWB addresses concerns similar to those of the DMA. This begs the question to what extent the objectives of the DMA and Section 19a can indeed be considered to be divergent.[1263]

In conclusion, the application of Article 1(5) and (6) DMA to Section 19a GWB show the unclarities, complexities and ambiguities of the pre-emptive effect of the DMA. In the context of Section 19a GWB, this results in uncertainties as to its position relationship and compatibility with EU law. Although there are various convincing arguments supporting the compatibility of the DMA and Section 19a GWB, uncertainties remain. This can lead to litigation challenging Section 19a's compatibility with EU law.[1264]

7.5.3 Executive Pre-emption

The DMA pre-empts parts of national competition law. Furthermore, the Commission's application of the DMA can have a pre-emptive effect on a national authority's competence to execute its investigative DMA powers. According to Article 38(7) DMA, the opening of DMA proceedings by the Commission relieves an NCA of its competence to conduct a DMA investigation. The Commission can also rely on its pre-emptive power if an NCA has already started a procedure. In this scenario, NCAs are under the obligation to report their findings to the Commission.

The executive pre-emptive effect of investigations launched by the Commission reflects the Commission's position as 'sole enforcer' of the DMA. The provision, to a significant extent, mirrors Article 11(6) Regulation 1/2003. However, there is an important difference between the provisions. Article 38(7) DMA explicitly obliges NCAs to report their findings in order to support the Commission. Against this backdrop, the pre-emptive effect in the context of the DMA does not necessarily have an adverse effect on the spending of regulatory resources. Ideally, the Commission can build on the

1262. The German legislator refers to 'digitaler Ökosysteme, in denen einzelne Unternehmen eine sog. Gatekeeper-Funktion einnehmen, zu erfassen'. *See:* Deutscher Bundestag 7 January 2022 'Die Anwendbarkeit von § 19a GWB im Lichte des europäischen Gesetzgebungsverfahrens zum Digital Markets Act' WD 7 – 3000 – 114/21; PE 6 – 3000 – 067/21, p. 75.
1263. Wagner-von Papp 2023a, p.
1264. Witt 2023, p. 662; Stöhr and Mendelsohn 2024, p. 24.

investigative actions of the NCA. This reflects the complementary relationship between both authorities. It is unsurprising that the DMA provides this obligation to share findings. Since the competences of NCAs are limited to the investigative stage, no decisions can be taken at the national level. This means that the case must eventually be transferred to the Commission.

7.5.4 Final Remark

In conclusion, the DMA pre-empts a national legislator's competence to adopt certain (competition) laws. While the DMA leaves national competition rules with an EU equivalent largely untouched, it affects national rules on unilateral conduct applicable to gatekeepers, as well as regulatory initiatives applicable to gatekeepers pursuing a fairness and contestability objective.[1265] The DMA relies on a highly complicated classificatory system, distinguishing between:

- EU competition law;
- national equivalents of Article 102 TFEU;
- national competition laws without an EU equivalent that are applicable to undertakings other than gatekeepers;
- national competition laws without an EU equivalent that are applicable to gatekeepers and impose further obligations;
- national competition laws without an EU equivalent that are applicable to gatekeepers and do not impose further obligations;
- other regulatory frameworks that are not applicable to gatekeepers;
- other regulatory frameworks that are applicable to gatekeepers and do not pursue a fairness and contestability objective;
- other regulatory frameworks that are applicable to gatekeepers and do pursue a fairness and contestability objective.

Again, as also seen in the context of Article 3 Regulation 1/2003, the category of which a national provision is considered to be part determines the degree to which EU law leaves room for such national frameworks. The following table summarises under which circumstances the DMA leaves room for national frameworks.

1265. *See* for an elaborate analysis: Van den Boom 2022.

Table 7.2 The Pre-emptive Effect of the DMA

Type of Rule	*DMA allows for the Application*	*Additional remarks*
Article 102 TFEU	Yes	However, NCAs can possibly be limited by the executive pre-emptive effect of Article 1(7) DMA
National equivalents of Article 102 TFEU	Yes	Duty of parallel application can apply under Article 3 Regulation 1/2003
National competition laws without an EU equivalent	*Scenario 1:* yes, if applicable to other undertakings than gatekeepers. *Scenario 2:* yes, if applicable to gatekeepers and amounts to the imposition of further obligations. *Scenario 3:* no, if imposed on gatekeepers and does not amount to the imposition of further obligations.	The DMA provides an *autonomous definition* of competition law.
Other regulatory frameworks	*Scenario 1:* yes, if not imposed on gatekeepers. *Scenario 2:* yes, if imposed on gatekeepers, but not for the objectives of fairness and contestability. *Scenario 3:* no, if imposed on gatekeepers for the objective of contestability and fairness.	

The classificatory system of Article 1(5) and (6) DMA centres around various concepts. However, as became apparent in the previous sections, several of these concepts are insufficiently clear which is detrimental to legal certainty. The DMA lists the following ill-defined concepts:

- competition law;
- applicable to undertakings other than gatekeepers;
- further obligations;
- objectives of contestability and fairness.

In the context of EU and national competition law, it became apparent that the unclarities regarding Article 3 Regulation 1/2003 result in uncertainties about the pre-emptive effect of EU competition law. The uncertainties relating to Article 1(5) and (6) DMA have a similar effect. This issue is further addressed in the Conclusion of this chapter (*see* cf. section 7.7).

7.6 COMPETITION LAW AND THE GDPR

Competition law and the GDPR increasingly overlap. Both frameworks not only apply in parallel but also intertwine since competition authorities can take data protection considerations into account in competition law assessments.[1266] This section addresses the extent to which the principles regarding norm hierarchies and pre-emption shape the relationship between competition law and the GDPR.

7.6.1 Norm Hierarchies

In the context of the GDPR and competition law, no explicit clauses on norm hierarchies or rules of pre-emption are established in EU primary or secondary law. Consequently, the relationship between both fields is governed by the general norm hierarchies of EU law.[1267] In principle, Article 102 TFEU takes precedence over the GDPR because primary EU law ranks higher than secondary EU law.[1268] However, the right to data protection is not merely enshrined in the GDPR, but also in Article 16 TFEU and in the CFR. Since Article 6 TEU determines that primary law and the CFR have 'the same legal value', they are on a comparable level in the hierarchy of EU laws, and the principle of norm hierarchy does not provide an unequivocal solution to clashes between both norms. In this scenario, the EU courts

1266. *See* section 6.4.2; *See also*: Costa-Cabral and Lynskey 2015.
1267. *See* section 7.2.1.
1268. The GC stresses, in the context of sectoral regulation and competition law, that 'in view of the principles governing the hierarchical relationship of legal rules, such secondary regulation could not, in the absence of any enabling provision in the Treaty, derogate from a provision of the Treaty, in this case [Article 102 TFEU]'. A similar line of reasoning can be applied to the GDPR and Article 102 TFEU. *See:* CJEU 13 May 2014, Case C-131/12, *Google Spain*, para. 55.

would have to carefully weigh and balance the respective frameworks on a case-by-case basis.[1269] Consequently, norm hierarchies do not always provide a clear-cut solution.[1270]

The relationship between *national* competition law and the GDPR is shaped by the principle of primacy of EU law which constitutes the rule of conflict that determines the relationship between national and EU law. In the case of a conflict, the GDPR which is an instrument of EU law would thus take precedence over national competition law. Moreover, it should be stressed that the GDPR – unlike the DMA – does not pre-empt the adoption of national competition law. This can be explained by the proximity and the development of the relationship between the different fields of law. While the DMA and competition law are closely related and the DMA was adopted in order to address certain shortcomings of the competition law framework, the GDPR and competition law constitute separate legal branches that – due to changing economic reality – have become increasingly overlapping.[1271]

7.6.2 Pre-emption

While the DMA imposes limitations on the Member State's ability to adopt (competition) laws to regulate personal data markets, the GDPR does not provide such limitations. Against this background, the GDPR does not have a legislative pre-emptive effect on national competition laws. However, the principle of pre-emption cannot be overlooked in the context of the interplay between competition law and the GDPR.

The application of the GDPR can have a (limited) *executive pre-emptive effect* on competition authorities' competences. This pre-emptive effect arises when a competition authority envisions addressing data protection considerations. In this scenario, the principle of sincere cooperation obliges NCAs to coordinate and cooperate with DPAs.[1272] This duty of cooperation has two dimensions. On the one hand, it can have an executive pre-emptive effect. On the other hand, it establishes certain concrete duties for institutional cooperation. This section addresses the pre-emptive effect. The issue of

---

1269. Such situation occurred in an intra-disciplinary data protection context. In the *Schrems* case, data protection authorities were confronted with conflicting legal obligations, namely the obligation to apply the Commission's Safe Harbour decision and the obligations to protect fundamental rights. The principle of primacy of EU law prevents Member States from setting aside the Safe Harbour Decision. The CJEU resolved this issue by applying the principle of due diligence. If a national authority has doubts as to the validity of the Safe Harbour decision, it should be able to put forward these concerns at a national court, which – in turn – should put forward preliminary questions as to the validity of this safe harbour decision. *See:* CJEU 6 October 2015 Case C-362/14, *Schrems*, paras 63-64. *See also*: Hijmans 2016, p. 154.
1270. ICN 2024, p. 22.
1271. *See* Synthesis I: Part II.
1272. CJEU 4 July 2023 Case C-252/21, *Meta Bundeskartellamt*, para. 53.

cooperation between competition and data protection authorities is studied in section 9.6.

Regarding the executive pre-emptive effect of the GDPR on competition law, two scenarios must be distinguished. *First,* NCAs can investigate behaviour that is the same or similar to conduct that has already been investigated by a DPA. In this case, NCAs cannot depart from the DPA's decision although NCAs remain free to draw their own conclusions from the point of view of the application of competition law.[1273] The fact that NCAs cannot depart from a DPA's decision reflects the 'interpretational primacy' of DPAs.[1274] The CJEU stresses that NCAs remain free to draw their own conclusions in the context of the application of competition law. In other words, the CJEU does allow for 'GDPR based competition law' and for a 'competition law assessment'.[1275] This confirms that, despite the overlap and interaction between the fields, the different areas have their own objectives as well as autonomous interpretations of various concepts.[1276] Hence, the NCA's competence to apply competition law is not curbed or limited by this obligation, and the pre-emptive effect remains very limited.

Second, the situation is different if a DPA has not (yet) adopted a (similar) decision. Where DPAs have not investigated a (similar) case, are simultaneously investigating a (similar) case, or when the DPA's assessment gives rise to doubts, NCAs must consult DPAs and seek cooperation in order to dispel these uncertainties. Importantly, the NCA has to determine whether 'it must wait for the supervisory authority concerned to take a decision before starting its own assessment'.[1277] Since the CJEU leaves open the possibility of NCAs having to wait for a DPA's decision, their procedures can temporarily be suspended due to a an ongoing investigation by a DPA. Consequently, the CJEU establishes a temporal executive effect for DPA investigations. This obligation can seriously delay competition law procedures. In this light, it is to be welcomed that DPAs concerned have the possibility to waive this obligation.[1278] According to Picht, the principle of sincere cooperation may even require such waiver if claiming the executive pre-emptive is not necessary from an enforcement perspective.[1279]

The temporarily pre-emptive effect of the GDPR introduces additional complexities in the hypothetical scenario in which the Commission would apply the *Meta Bundeskartellamt* theory of harm. Importantly, the CJEU only discusses the application of the GDPR by *national authorities.* However, since the CJEU addresses the relevance of the GDPR for Article 102 TFEU, i.e., *EU* competition law, the case can also be relevant for the

1273. CJEU 4 July 2023 Case C-252/21, *Meta Bundeskartellamt*, p. 56.
1274. Picht 2023, p. 2.
1275. Picht 2023, p. 2.
1276. Graef 2023, p. 333.
1277. CJEU 4 July 2023 Case C-252/21, *Meta Bundeskartellamt*, paras 57-59.
1278. CJEU 4 July 2023 Case C-252/21, *Meta Bundeskartellamt*, para. 59.
1279. Picht 2023, p. 2.

application of Article 102 TFEU by the Commission. In this context, an important initial question is whether the Commission is bound by: (i) the principle of sincere cooperation; and (ii) the CJEU's interpretation of this principle in the *Meta Bundeskartellamt case.* This situation is currently hypothetical: a strong need for cooperation would only arise if the Commission were to rely on the theories of harm as established in the *Meta Bundeskartellamt* case. At present, there have been no cases in which the Commission has established an Article 102 TFEU violation by taking into account a violation of the GDPR. However, after the preliminary ruling of the CJEU, the Commission could potentially take this avenue.

As explained in section 3.4.2, the principle of sincere cooperation not only imposes duties of cooperation upon Member States, but – due to its reciprocal nature – also applies to the Commission. If the Commission adopts an approach similar to the *Bundeskartellamt* in the *Meta* case, novel problems and additional open questions will arise. Although the duty of sincere cooperation can impose obligations on the Commission, it is unclear how this principle is to be interpreted in this context and which duties of cooperation can be derived from the principle. In the *Meta* case, the CJEU focused on the application of the principle of sincere cooperation to *national* competition authorities. Although the duty of sincere cooperation applies to the Commission too, it remains unclear whether the same concrete duties to cooperate can be derived from the principle. Assuming that the case *can* be transposed, issues relating to hierarchy of norms and executive pre-emption by national DPAs arise. In the scenario where the obligations *cannot* be transposed, there is no clarity as to the Commission's duties to cooperate.

If the obligations are, indeed, transposed, the Commission's application of Article 102 TFEU could be suspended by a GDPR procedure at the national level. This scenario poses challenges: the Commission, the guardian of the Treaty, would be limited in its application of primary EU law by the application of secondary EU law by a national DPA. Considering the hierarchy of norms within EU law, the Commission's power to start an infringement procedure against Member States under Article 258 TFEU, as well as (theories on) the principle of pre-emption, it would be very unusual for an action of a national actor to (temporarily) pre-empt the Commission from acting. Currently, the EU framework does not provide a solution or procedure for this situation, and it is desirable for further clarity to be provided.

Article 70(1) GDPR may provide a potential solution. Article 70(1) GDPR allows the Commission to seek advice from the EDPB. Rather than consulting with national DPAs, the Commission could approach the EDPB directly. The EDPB would be better placed to advise the Commission than national DPAs. Admittedly, this solution is not free of problems. In the current institutional framework, the GDPR is enforced by DPAs at the Member State level, rather than by the EDPB. Furthermore, the solution is arguably hard to reconcile with the position of the lead supervisory authority.

Moreover, the current institutional framework does not allow for the exchange of confidential information between the EDPB and the Commission, as became apparent in the context of the *Google Fitbit* case.[1280] This can be detrimental to the realisation of cooperation. If the Commission were to consult with the EDPB in the future, a legal basis for the exchange of information must be established.

On top of this, the fact remains that in light of the hierarchy of norms, Article 102 TFEU is hierarchically superior to the GDPR. This raises the question of whether the application of the GDPR can temporarily suspend the Commission's application of Article 102 TFEU. At this point, there are many uncertainties and no all-encompassing solution is available. Yet, and despite the obstacles mentioned in solving the matter within the context of the current institutional framework, a solution is needed to prevent further institutional problems relating to the integration of the GDPR in the assessment of Article 102 TFEU. It is recommended that this interaction be considered in the context of the adoption of the procedural GDPR regulation.[1281] Additionally, provided that a case reaches the CJEU, it is desirable that further clarity is given on the interpretation of the duty of sincere cooperation in this context. If the CJEU were given the opportunity, it should provide further clarity as to which duties of cooperation can be derived from this principle and can bind the Commission.

7.6.3 Final Remarks

The principles of hierarchy of norms and pre-emption are relevant for the relationship between competition law and the GDPR. In the case of conflicts, the general EU law principles on norm hierarchies are applicable. Moreover, the text of the GDPR does not pre-empt or limit the application of competition law. Yet, the principle of pre-emption is relevant in relation to the interaction between competition law and the GDPR. If a competition authority integrates GDPR considerations in a competition law assessment, its competence can be temporarily suspended by a parallel procedure of a DPA. This dynamic of temporary executive pre-emption is rather unproblematic if GDPR considerations are incorporated in the assessment of *national* competition laws. However, the situation is more complicated when it comes to the application of EU competition law. The pre-emptive effect of the GDPR sits at odds with the general principle of norm hierarchies of EU law since the GDPR, an instrument of secondary EU law, would limit the application of the primary law provision of Article 102 TFEU. This situation would be particularly challenging if the Commission were to adopt the theories of harm of the *Meta Bundeskartellamt* case.

1280. *See* section 9.6.1.3.
1281. *See* section 6.2.4.3.

7.7 CONCLUSION

This section addressed the mechanisms of pre-emption and hierarchy of norms that shape the interaction between competition law, the DMA and the GDPR. The section aimed to assess to what extent the fields of law can co-exist and how conflicts between them can be resolved.

The mechanisms available concerning hierarchy of norms are context-dependent and, therefore, vary across legal branches. Given the inherent differences between fields, their respective intersections are addressed in turn.

In the context of *EU and national competition law*, the principle of pre-emption plays an important role. The executive pre-emption of the application of EU competition law by the Commission reflects its managerial role within the ECN.[1282] Moreover, the principle of pre-emption helps to shape the relationship between national and EU competition law. Yet, the pre-emptive effect of EU competition law is subject to (academic) debate. Article 3 Regulation 1/2003 establishes a complex classificatory system and relies on various poorly defined concepts. This has a detrimental effect on the clarity of the pre-emptive effect of EU competition law: it remains uncertain how much room the framework leaves for additional national (competition) laws. Consequently, rather than streamlining the interaction between national and EU competition law, Article 3 Regulation 1/2003 creates confusion and uncertainty. The ambiguities are particularly problematic in the context of personal data markets where Member States adopt complementary (competition) laws to regulate the behaviour of large platforms.[1283] As a result, the relationship between EU and national competition law is not well articulated and, therefore, not shaped in a coherent manner. This issue is further addressed in Synthesis II.

The text of the *DMA* explicitly addresses its relationship with *competition law*. Considering EU competition law, the DMA is relatively straightforward: the instrument does not limit the application of Article 102 TFEU, in accordance with the principle of hierarchy of norms. However, by stressing that NCAs cannot take decisions that run counter to a Commission DMA decision, Article 1(7) DMA implies a certain degree of executive pre-emption of DMA decisions, causing confusion as to the relationship between the DMA and the application of EU competition law by NCAs. Furthermore, the DMA's interplay with national competition laws is more complicated. Like Article 3 Regulation 1/2003, the DMA establishes a classificatory system in Article 1(5) and 1(6) DMA. Unfortunately, these provisions contain various ill-defined concepts. Admittedly, by providing an autonomous definition of competition laws, the DMA offers more guidance

1282. Cengiz 2010, p. 663.
1283. *See*, in particular, section 4.4.2.

than Regulation 1/2003.[1284] Yet, the interpretation of certain important benchmarks remains unclear which has a detrimental effect on the pre-emptive effect of the DMA. The relationship between the DMA and competition law is, thus, not well-articulated. This issue is further addressed in Synthesis II.

While EU competition law and the DMA have a pre-emptive effect on national competition law by harmonising a part of this area, the GDPR does not have a similar effect. The GDPR does not have a legal pre-emptive effect on competition laws and, therefore, the fields of law can co-exist. Yet, the principle of pre-emption provides useful insights for mapping the relationship between competition law and the DMA. In the *Meta Bundeskartellamt* case, the CJEU recognised a certain executive pre-emptive effect of the GDPR on competition law: in certain circumstances, a DPA's application of the GDPR requires competition authorities to suspend their proceedings.[1285] If NCAs or the Commission were to integrate GDPR considerations into an Article 102 TFEU assessment, this pre-emptive effect would lead to a confusing situation. In this scenario, an instrument of secondary law temporarily pre-empts the application of an instrument of primary EU law. This amounts to friction within the hierarchy of norms in EU law and, therefore, affects the articulateness of competition law and the GDPR. This issue is further addressed in Synthesis II.

The principle of pre-emption determines whether frameworks can co-exist or whether this co-existence amounts to a conflict of laws. If a conflict arises, the principle of hierarchy of norms determines how such a conflict should be resolved. In the context of EU law, clear norm hierarchies are present. These will resolve conflicts between EU law and national law and between primary and secondary EU law. The situation would be more complicated in the case of a conflict between multiple frameworks established at the same level. For instance, it would not be straightforward to resolve a conflict between Article 102 TFEU, Article 16 TFEU and Articles 7 and 8 CFR. In such case, the CJEU should carefully balance the different interests involved.

Principles of hierarchy of norms and pre-emption are useful concepts for assessing whether frameworks can co-exist and how conflicts between overlapping norms can be resolved. They provide useful tools for analysing the relationship between competition law, the DMA and the GDPR. However, as explained in Chapters 5 and 6, it becomes apparent that these instruments can indeed co-exist and mainly apply in a *complementary* fashion. Since norm hierarchies focus on conflicting rules, such tools are not suitable for determining the complementary application of overlapping norms. In this context, (institutional) mechanisms of cooperation are highly relevant. These mechanisms are analysed in Chapters 8 and 9.

1284. Brook and Eben 2022, p. 8.
1285. CJEU 4 July 2023 Case C-252/21, *Meta Bundeskartellamt*, para. 59.

Chapter 8

Cooperation: Theory and Competition Law

8.1 INTRODUCTION

The previous chapter analysed the mechanisms of pre-emption and norm hierarchies shaping the interplay between competition law, the DMA and the GDPR. While these principles provide useful tools to examine to what extent the frameworks can co-exist and how conflicts between norms should be resolved, such principles are not sufficient to guarantee the coherent application of the mentioned legal branches. As explained in Part II, the overlaps between competition law, the DMA and the GDPR do not merely amount to potential conflicts, but also entail the complementary application of the legal fields. This complementary application calls for cooperation mechanisms facilitating the coherent application of the different frameworks in the case of overlapping competences. This chapter aims to evaluate which cooperation mechanisms are in place and assesses to what extent potential gaps exist in the institutional framework.

To this end, this chapter provides a theoretical framework on cooperation between authorities. The interaction between different authorities can be realised by a plethora of different cooperation mechanisms. To provide a structured analysis and to properly map the mechanisms available in the areas of competition law, the DMA and the GDPR, section 8.2 develops a theoretical framework that introduces a typology of different cooperation mechanisms. By mapping these mechanisms, the theoretical framework provides the necessary background for analysing the available mechanisms in competition law, the DMA and the GDPR. Following this, sections 8.3 and

8.4 apply the proposed structure to intra-disciplinary cooperation in the field of competition law in order to map the interaction between the Commission and NCAs. Section 8.3 studies the institutional design of competition law authorities. Subsequently, section 8.4 discusses intra-disciplinary cooperation mechanisms in the field of competition law. Lastly, section 8.5 provides concluding remarks on cooperation within the field of competition law.

8.2 THEORETICAL FRAMEWORK: INSTITUTIONAL DESIGN AND COOPERATION

This Section aims to provide a theoretical overview of cooperation between authorities. The theoretical framework serves as a blueprint for mapping, analysing and comparing the cooperation mechanisms within the areas of competition law, the DMA and the GDPR in a structured manner.

In order to understand the interaction between enforcers of overlapping legal branches, various institutional factors are relevant. *First,* the *institutional design* of the authorities concerned plays a significant role. As explained in section 3.2, institutional design denotes an agency's *mandate* and *organisational design* which includes the structures and processes that have a bearing on enforcement and the application of the law.[1286] The issue of cooperation cannot be decoupled from institutional design since this determines the extent to which the authorities have similar or overlapping competences. In this light, in order to understand the interaction between various authorities, it is necessary to map how the different mandates interrelate. *Second,* provided that two or more authorities do indeed have overlapping tasks, *cooperation mechanisms* can require, allow or stimulate these authorities to cooperate. Generally speaking, such mechanisms determine whether, when and how authorities may or should cooperate.[1287] Sections 8.2.1 and 8.2.2 address the topics of: (i) institutional design; and (ii) mechanisms for cooperation in turn.

8.2.1 Institutional Design

In the multi-level legal order of the EU, the topic of institutional design has two main dimensions. *First,* the issue is closely related to the division of tasks between the EU and the Member States' authorities. While national law is enforced by the Member States authorities, the enforcement of the EU framework is more complex. The enforcement of the EU substantive rules can be realised through a centralised or decentralised enforcement model. *Second,* from an institutional design perspective, the scope of an agency's

1286. Balogh and Cseres 2013, p. 345.
1287. Hyman and Kovacic 2014, pp. 1464-1465.

portfolio is relevant. While some authorities are responsible for the enforcement of a single legal branch, others have an integrated or more complex portfolio encompassing various fields of law.[1288] The Dutch ACM is, for example, responsible for the enforcement of competition law, consumer law and sector-specific regulation.[1289] Integrating the enforcement of various fields of law has implications for the interaction between these legal branches.

Before further addressing the topics of: (i) the level of centralisation; and (ii) agency mandates, it is important to stress that institutional design *can,* but need not necessarily, *have to* be a deliberate policy choice. In some circumstances, an authority acquires a competence by fortuity or by accident, rather than by a deliberate decision of the legislator.[1290]

8.2.1.1 The Level of (De)Centralisation

EU substantive laws can be enforced at a central or decentral level. In a *centralised enforcement model*, institutions at the EU level take the lead. In a *decentralised model*, enforcement is the responsibility of national authorities. Apart from a fully centralised or decentralised model, enforcement can be shared between the EU and national authorities. The allocation of competences between the EU and national level can, thus, be structured according to a whole range of hybrid forms and differing degrees of EU involvement.[1291] The institutional framework depends on the particular set of rules and varies from one policy area to another. It is not always straightforward why the EU legislator has chosen a certain model.[1292]

Centralised and decentralised models each have strengths and weaknesses. A decentralised model can be desirable for several reasons, including regulatory competition, the ability of national agencies to collect information from local companies and the opportunity to experiment through different authorities.[1293] At the same time, a centralised model also has its merits. Such a framework allows authorities to benefit from economies of scale and scope, could address fears of a race to the bottom and makes it easier to safeguard a coherent or uniform approach.[1294]

In a decentralised model, enforcement responsibilities are shared between multiple authorities. In the case of cross-border activities, there are various ways to divide competences between authorities. In a *country of*

1288. Kovacic and Hyman 2013.
1289. *See* sections 4.3.3.1 and 8.3.2.
1290. *See* section 3.2.
1291. Ottow 2012, p. 193.
1292. Scholten 2021, p. 8.
1293. Scholars disagree whether rivalry and competition between agencies is positive. An extensive debate on regulatory competition does not fall within the scope of the analysis. For further reading *see:* Ottow 2014.
1294. Geradin 2002, p. 3.

origin model, such as the one-stop-shop mechanism of the GDPR, the substantive rules are enforced by the authority where the company providing the regulated service is established. In a *country of destination model*, the Member States where the regulated service is offered have the competence to act.[1295] The competition law framework in the EU is modelled on a country of destination model. This model can give rise to serious obstacles to the internal market since undertakings can potentially be subject to enforcement by multiple authorities. In this light, a country of origin model – which allows for one-stop-shop mechanisms – is beneficial for market integration, particularly in industries where undertakings are engaged in cross-border activities and provide their services in multiple jurisdictions.[1296]

Despite the potential of the country of origin model, the system can only function properly if there are certain 'minimum common standards' and a certain degree of mutual trust that these standards will be enforced. Additionally, Monti and De Streel mention: (i) the ability for the country of origin's authority to apply EU law effectively; and (ii) the incentive to do so for the benefit of the EU as a whole as additional criteria for a successful realisation of the country of origin model.[1297]

8.2.1.2 Agency Mandates and Portfolios

The tasks assigned to a particular authority determine its mandate or portfolio. While some authorities have a single and clearly delineated task, other institutions have a broader mandate. Authorities can be structured as a separated agency, focusing on the enforcement of one field of law. Conversely, in an *integrated* model, an institution has a 'double mission', for example, because it enforces both competition and consumer law.[1298] In reality, many authorities apply multiple substantive frameworks, and an agency with a single function is the exception rather than the rule.[1299]

The creation of authorities with multiple functions presents certain opportunities. An integrated authority can be more *effective* and *efficient.* Information sharing may, for example, be easier within an integrated authority.[1300] Moreover, the expertise of the staff will be broader. Joint teams and integrated management teams may be better equipped to deal with complex issues effectively.[1301] Additionally, an integrated approach can facilitate a single point of contact for complainants.[1302] Furthermore, this

1295. De Streel and Monti 2022, p. 18.
1296. De Streel and Monti 2022, p. 18.
1297. De Streel and Monti 2022, p. 18.
1298. Cseres 2013, p. 19.
1299. Kovacic and Hyman 2013, p. 9.
1300. Schäfers and Houdijk 2012, p. 666.
1301. Cseres 2013, pp. 35-37.
1302. Henten, Smarajiva and Melody 2003, p. 34.

approach arguably allows for *synergies* between the legal branches.[1303] If multiple frameworks can address a particular market failure, it is not always obvious which field of law is best suited to be applied. In an integrated model, multiple frameworks are enforced by one and the same authority. This can make it easier to determine which framework proposes the best remedy or to provide a combined analysis of multiple legal branches.[1304]

Despite these benefits, integrating several tasks within one authority can be detrimental to the relatedness and coherence of the agency's function. Authorities with a single mandate are more specialised which can be desirable, especially when it comes to complicated legal frameworks and markets.[1305] In other words, if the different tasks lack a set of internally consistent goals or pursue inconsistent or unrelated objectives, an overly broad mandate is detrimental to an institution's *policy coherence*.[1306] Unrelated tasks can also result in practical difficulties. An expert in water technology, for example, does not necessarily have expertise in the technical aspects of telecommunication.[1307] Furthermore, in legal literature, it has been questioned whether one institution can simultaneously act as a regulator and a competition authority. The roles of the respective authorities are different, and a regulatory function, which usually focuses largely on *ex-ante* supervision, is not identical to an *ex-post* oriented competition law function. The different nature of regulatory and competition supervisors should be considered carefully and is, according to some authors, potentially problematic given the 'intrinsic' differences.[1308] Lastly, overly broad mandates could result in an 'organisational maze' due to bureaucracy and a lack of transparency.[1309]

Furthermore, the integration of different functions within one authority does not necessarily lead to coherence between tasks. Integrated authorities often create separate and specialised units for the different functions.[1310] Over time, these different units can become more autonomous and insular because they develop their own norms, goals, priorities and specialised skills.[1311] Coordination between the different functions will not be realised simply because separate organisations are combined. In this light, the integration of authorities may transform an issue of *inter-agency* cooperation into an *intra-agency* problem.[1312]

1303. Schäfers and Houdijk 2012, p. 661.
1304. Cseres 2013, pp. 35-37.
1305. Cseres 2013, pp. 35-37.
1306. Kovacic and Hyman 2013, p. 11.
1307. Garcia-Murillo and MacInnes 2003, p. 64.
1308. Schäfers and Houdijk 2012, p. 663.
1309. Henten, Smarajiva and Melody 2003, p. 34.
1310. Kovacic and Hyman 2013, p. 25.
1311. Hyman and Kovacic 2014, p. 1477.
1312. Freeman and Rossi 2012, p. 1156.

8.2.2 Cooperation

The analysis is focused on the interplay between enforcers of competition law, the DMA and the GDPR. Hence, it is not sufficient to focus on the institutional design of the individual enforcers of these legal branches. Rather, the available mechanisms for cooperation between authorities are at the heart of the research. This section provides the theoretical background on cooperation mechanisms. By providing a typology of different forms and types of cooperation, the theoretical framework serves as a tool to provide a structured analysis of existing cooperation mechanisms that are relevant for this project. In the literature, cooperation mechanisms are structured and classified in various ways.[1313] In order to provide a framework for the analysis, this Section relies on and builds on insights of other authors.

First, cooperation mechanisms can apply to the various *dimensions* of overlapping competences. As explained in Synthesis I: Part II, overlapping competences can be: (i) mono- or multi-jurisdictional; and (ii) intra- or cross-disciplinary. While mono-jurisdictional overlaps require cooperation between enforcers *within* a single legal order, multi-jurisdictional overlaps can only be streamlined by cooperation mechanisms that facilitate collaboration between enforcers of *different* legal orders. Moreover, intra-disciplinary overlaps call for cooperation between the enforcers of one and the same legal branch. Cross-disciplinary overlaps transcend legal branches and result in a need for cooperation between enforcers of different legal branches. Furthermore, cooperation mechanisms can be bilateral or multilateral. While *bilateral* cooperation relates to the interaction between two authorities, *multilateral* arrangements concern the interplay between more than two institutions. Multilateral cooperation can be *polycentric*. Polycentric cooperation entails the interaction between more than two legal branches.

Second, the *nature* of the cooperation mechanism is relevant. The nature of a cooperation mechanism may be formal or informal, depending on the legal basis for cooperation and on the applicable procedural rules of the network.[1314] Informal cooperation mechanisms can range from authorities simply observing each other to informal conversations and agreements between officials from different institutions. This form of cooperation largely takes place behind closed doors and is hard to track.[1315] It is thus challenging to analyse informal forms of cooperation in doctrinal legal research.[1316] Apart from informal agreements and understandings, cooperation can be arranged more formally. Such cooperation mechanisms are defined by clear

1313. *See,* for example, Majcher, who distinguishes between: (1) intra and inter-institutional cooperation; (2) formal and/or informal cooperation; (3) ad hoc and/or structured cooperation; and (4) open and/or closed cooperation. *See:* Majcher 2023, p. 261.

1314. Csatlós 2018, p. 58.

1315. Freeman and Rossi 2012, p. 1156.

1316. This is one of the limitations of this project, *see* section 1.3.3.

procedures and rules.[1317] In this case, the cooperation mechanisms are laid down explicitly in either: (i) inter-institutional agreements; or (ii) legislation and/or soft-law.[1318]

Third, cooperation can take place on a *structural* or ad hoc basis.[1319] Networks are a good avenue for structural cooperation. This form of cooperation occurs frequently in the EU context and provides a constant channel for systemic cooperation.[1320] This enhances performance, for example, by promoting, discussing and identifying best practices. Furthermore, networks can combat the risk of a divergent application of the substantive rules of EU law, while maintaining respect for differences between Member States. In this light, networks are useful tools for combining the advantages of centralised and decentralised enforcement.[1321] Importantly, fora are not the only way to facilitate structural cooperation. A more structural approach can also be realised through inter-institutional (bilateral) cooperation agreements.[1322]

Fourth, cooperation varies in its *intensity.* Authorities can *consult* each other while acting independently in their decision-making and remaining competent to apply their own regulatory frameworks. In a 'deeper' form of cooperation, authorities engage in joint work. In this case, authorities can, for example, exchange information or evidence related to specific cases, agree on joint remedies or collectively monitor certain markets. This can facilitate the exploitation of synergies and helps to avoid inconsistent decisions in the case of overlapping competences.[1323] Authorities can also cooperate beyond individual cases, such as by publishing common regulatory documents and guidelines. Such documents can serve as a basis for each authority in applying its framework to individual cases.[1324] Joint policymaking instruments or statements tend to be a rather visible form of cooperation and are therefore often transparent.[1325] As explained above, in the case of overlapping or complementary norms, authorities can also be integrated. In a way, an integrated authority can be considered the most far-reaching form of cooperation between the enforcers of different legal branches. In this situation, the legal branches will be enforced under one roof, albeit usually by different units.

Lastly, cooperation can pertain to various *stages* of the decision-making procedure. In an early stage of proceedings, authorities can, for example,

---

1317. Levi-Faur 2011, pp. 813-814.
1318. Reyna 2024, p. 14.
1319. Majcher 2023, p. 261.
1320. Levi-Faur 2011, p. 811; Csatlós 2018, p. 58.
1321. *See also* section 8.2; Potocnik-Manzouri 2021, p. 1005.
1322. In this light, there is a clear connection between the legal basis of the cooperation mechanisms and the structural or ad hoc basis.
1323. De Streel and Monti 2022, p. 25.
1324. De Streel and Monti 2022, p. 26.
1325. Freeman and Rossi 2012, p. 1165.

determine which authority is best placed to investigate or take the lead in a particular investigation. In a later stage, cooperation may focus on investigations and the collection of evidence. In the final stage of the decision-making process, cooperation efforts can centre around the imposition of sanctions and/or remedies.[1326]

8.3 COMPETITION LAW: INSTITUTIONAL DESIGN AND COOPERATION

This section applies the theoretical framework of section 8.2 to the field of competition law by mapping and analysing cooperation mechanisms in an *intra-disciplinary* context.[1327] While national competition law is, for obvious reasons, enforced by national competition authorities, the EU competition law framework is enforced by both the Commission and NCAs.[1328] This section focuses on the interplay between the Commission and NCAs. In order to map their interaction properly, this Section provides an overview of the institutional design of competition authorities by analysing the decentralisation of EU competition law, as well as the mandates of competition authorities. Afterwards, section 8.4 examines the mechanisms in place to facilitate cooperation between authorities.

8.3.1 (De)centralisation of Competition Law

In the field of EU competition law, a clear trend of *decentralisation* can be observed. Initially, the enforcement of EU competition law was dealt with by the Commission. The entry into force of Regulation 1/2003 dismantled this centralised enforcement framework by fostering a shift towards partially decentralised enforcement.[1329] Competition law evolved into a system of a multi-level governance or a multi-level administration model.[1330] After the decentralisation of competition law, this legal field relies on a *country of destination model* which means that multiple NCAs and the Commission share enforcement responsibilities.[1331]

The decentralised framework of EU competition law is praised for effectively reducing the Commission's workload by involving NCAs. This approach multiplied enforcement resources and enabled enforcement on a scale that far exceeds the capacity of the Commission.[1332] Despite the

1326. Reyna 2024, p. 2.
1327. *See* Synthesis I: Part II.
1328. *See* sections 4.2.3, 4.3.3. and 4.4.3.
1329. Article 89 EC Treaty (Treaty of Rome); Monti 2014, p. 1.
1330. Cengiz 2010.
1331. De Streel and Monti 2022, p. 20.
1332. Sinclair 2017, p. 625; Dzino and Rusu 2019; p. 132; Botta 2013, p. 108.

efficiency-enhancing potential of the decentralised framework, the application of EU competition law by multiple authorities introduces potential coherence-related challenges. Against this background, the process of decentralisation amplified the need for effective cooperation mechanisms to ensure the coherent application of EU competition law by multiple authorities.[1333]

Apart from prompting a need for cooperation, the decentralisation of competition law has impacted national institutional frameworks which have become increasingly Europeanised in the wake of the decentralisation of EU competition law. This trend was driven by various developments.

First, in the aftermath of the decentralisation of competition law, the CJEU has limited the institutional autonomy of Member States on multiple occasions. The CJEU has derived several institutional obligations from the broader EU competition law framework. For example, in the *VEBIC* case, the CJEU ruled that Article 35 Regulation 1/2003 precludes national rules that do not allow competition authorities to participate in judicial proceedings concerning their own decisions.[1334]

Second, harmonisation of national frameworks has fostered further 'Europeanisation' of procedural and institutional frameworks. Initially, frameworks aligned due to a dynamic of *spontaneous harmonisation*. Regulation 1/2003 establishes a duty of parallel application. This duty of parallel application – which will be discussed in more detail in section 8.4.2.1 – triggered a process of spontaneous harmonisation that impacted national substantive, procedural and institutional frameworks.[1335] In addition, the EU legislator played an important role in the harmonisation of national competition laws by harmonising certain aspects of procedural and institutional law. The ECN+ Directive, for instance, codifies various previously existing best practices and soft laws of the ECN, thereby harmonising national institutional frameworks.[1336]

Although the enforcement of EU competition law has been decentralised, the influence of the EU level has not merely diminished. On the

1333. Van de Gronden and De Vries 2006, p. 40.
1334. CJEU 7 December 2010 Case C-439/08, *VEBIC*, paras 57-59.
1335. Honnefelder and Kolassa 2016, p. 5.
1336. According to paras 5 and 6 of the Preamble of the ECN+ Directive: 'The lack of guarantees of independence, resources, and enforcement and fining powers for many NCAs […] effectively means that undertakings engaging in anti-competitive practices may face very different outcomes in proceedings, depending on the Member States in which they are active' and 'Uneven enforcement of Articles 101 and 102 TFEU, whether applied on a stand-alone basis or in parallel with national competition law, results in missed opportunities to remove barriers to market entry and to create fairer competitive markets throughout the Union where undertakings compete on the merits.' *See also*: Potocnik-Manzouri 2021, p. 1001. *See also*: Maher and Ştefan 2010, p. 190.

contrary, as the EU increasingly harmonised institutional frameworks, it reduced the Member States' freedom to establish such frameworks. This trend is coined as a process of recentralisation.[1337] In the context of institutional competition law frameworks, complex dynamics of decentralisation and Europeanisation are apparent. A trend of decentralisation shifts competences to the national level. However, in response to this shift, certain national laws may become Europeanised. In other words, the decentralisation of EU laws can result in the convergence and assimilation of national (institutional) frameworks.[1338]

This process of convergence can contribute to the uniform application of competition law. However, it is also criticised, particularly because its effect on national legal frameworks is not always acknowledged in the academic and policy debate.[1339]

8.3.2 Competition Law: Agency Mandates and Portfolios

Various enforcers of competition laws have mandates transcending the field of competition law. This means that authorities do not merely enforce competition law, but also perform broader tasks. The Commission has a broad range of tasks, extending far beyond competition law.[1340] Moreover, in Germany, the *Bundeskartellamt* has certain competences in the field of consumer law.[1341]

The discussion on agency mandates and portfolios has been prominently present in The Netherlands where the former Netherlands Competition Authority, the Dutch Consumer Authority and The Netherlands Independent Post and Telecommunication Authority were merged into a new authority, the ACM.[1342] Consequently, The Netherlands shifted from a *separated agency* model in which the enforcement of consumer and competition law was the responsibility of distinct administrative authorities, to an *integrated model*.[1343]

1337. McIntyre 2023, p. 268.
1338. Van Cleynenbreugel 2012, p. 290.
1339. According to Colomo, the effect on the national legal framework is not sufficiently acknowledged in the policy and academic debate. *See:* Ibáñez Colomo 2013, p. 383; Vedder 2004.
1340. *See:* https://commission.europa.eu/about/role_en#:~:text=Role%20of%20the%20European%20Commission,international%20development%20and%20delivering%20aid accessed 25 March 2025.
1341. *See* section 4.4.3.1.
1342. Instellingswet Autoriteit Consument en Markt van 28 februari 2013 houdende regels omtremt de instelling van de Autoriteit Consument en Markt, Stb. 2013, 102 (Instellingswet ACM)(henceforth: Establishment Act ACM); Similar institutional discussions took place in, for example, Denmark, Ireland, Finland and the United Kingdom. *See* for an overview in this regard: Cseres 2013, p. 6.
1343. Cseres 2013, p. 19.

The Dutch legislator invoked several arguments in favour of the integrated model which was intended to improve the *effectiveness and efficiency* of market supervision in The Netherlands. The new compact and decisive *(compacte en slagvaardige)* ACM would be better equipped to respond in a flexible and integral way to new developments in the market, such as internationalisation, technological developments and changing markets. It would be easier to capitalise on the available in-house expertise, knowledge and information. The improvement in effectiveness and efficiency was expected to improve the quality of supervision, while *reducing government spending* by eliminating concurrences of tasks, better use of staff and the sharing of expertise and knowledge.[1344]

Consequently, the Dutch legislator relied on reasons of cost-reduction, effectiveness and potential synergies. Despite this range of benefits, cost-reductions arguably played a guiding role. Indeed, the establishment of the ACM was part of a broader programme aimed at a 'compact government' with fewer civil servants, fewer rules and fewer directors.[1345] Moreover, the Dutch legislator elaborated on the potential synergies only to a limited extent and largely linked the synergy benefits to reasons of cost-reduction. Against this backdrop, the Dutch legislator has been criticised for disguising cost-saving objectives by referring to synergy benefits.[1346] Interestingly, the Dutch legislator acknowledges that synergy benefits cannot be realised if the tasks of an authority are too broad. For example, with regard to the media supervisor, a merger would not be desirable because a very large and broad range of tasks may have an adverse effect on the decisiveness of the authority.[1347] However, it remains unclear under which circumstances synergy benefits can be achieved and at which point a regulatory mandate becomes too divergent.

In sum, an agency's mandate is determined by various factors. Extending a portfolio may enhance the exploitation of synergies, but a merger of authorities can also be fostered by reasons of efficiency, effectiveness and cost-reduction. The Dutch example illustrates that multiple reasons can be invoked to justify a change in institutional design.

1344. Tweede Kamer Der Staten Generaal, Regels omtrent de instelling van de Autoriteit Consument en Markt (Instellingswet Autoriteit Consument en Markt), 2011-2012, 33 186, 3 (Explanatory Memorandum Establishment Act ACM), p. 1.

1345. This program is known as *het Uitvoeringsprogramma Compacte Rijksdienst.*

1346. De Bree 2012; Schinkel 2011.

1347. Tweede Kamer Der Staten Generaal, Regels omtrent de instelling van de Autoriteit Consument en Markt (Instellingswet Autoriteit Consument en Markt), 2011-2012, 33 186, 3 (Explanatory Memorandum Establishment Act ACM), p. 4.

8.4 COMPETITION LAW: MECHANISMS FOR COOPERATION

This section studies the mechanisms of intra-disciplinary cooperation that facilitate the interaction between competition authorities. Specifically, it explores the relevant fora, as well as the concrete mechanisms and provisions governing cooperation between authorities.

8.4.1 Fora for Cooperation

Cooperation between competition authorities takes place in two main fora, i.e., the ECN and the Advisory Committee on Restrictive Practices and Dominant Positions (henceforth: Advisory Committee). These fora are the cornerstones of cooperation among the Commission and NCAs and are addressed in turn.[1348]

8.4.1.1 The European Competition Network (ECN)

The ECN, comprising the Commission and NCAs, constitutes the main forum for intra-disciplinary cooperation in the field of competition law.[1349] According to recital 15 of Regulation 1/2003, the Commission and NCAs 'should form together a network of public authorities applying the [EU] competition rules in close cooperation'. To that end, it is necessary to 'set up arrangements for information and consultation'.

The ECN, which can be considered a 'manifestation of the duty of sincere cooperation', serves as a forum for the facilitation of the consistent application of EU competition law.[1350] The ECN aims to provide a forum for cooperation between competition authorities in order to create and maintain a 'common competition culture' in the EU.[1351] To this end, the network seeks to ensure an efficient division of work and the consistent application of EU competition law.[1352] The network contributes to cooperation concerning individual cases as well as to the development of policy.[1353]

The ECN is an 'atypical' network with a hierarchical and formal structure.[1354] While networks and management rules governing the network usually occur 'naturally', the design of the ECN was largely planned at the

1348. Brüggemann and Parmentier 2022, p. 354.
1349. Honnefelder and Kolassa 2016, p. 4.
1350. Whish and Bailey 2021, p. 303.
1351. Network Notice, para. 1.
1352. Network Notice, para. 3.
1353. Network Notice, para. 3.
1354. According to Cengiz, the network is 'different from other European regulatory policy networks' and 'it does not fully reflect the dynamics of policy networks as determined by political science literature'. *See:* Cengiz 2009, p. 4.

EU level.[1355] Although Member States played an important role in initiating the ECN and were consulted in the drafting process of the Network Notice, the ECN was largely formed according to the wishes of the Commission.[1356] The strong position of the Commission is reflected in the design of the ECN. As stressed above, the ECN consists of the Commission and NCAs. Within this structure, the Commission has a special or 'managerial' position in the network: it has certain powers that are not shared with the other members of the ECN.[1357] Consequently, the Commission acts as a *primus inter pares.*[1358]

The ECN plays an important role in mitigating the risks associated with the decentralised enforcement of EU competition law.[1359] Initially, the ECN was considered to be successful in this regard.[1360] In the five-year review, the Commission lauded the initiative.[1361] Ten years after the adoption of Regulation 1/2003, the Commission published another report on its functioning.[1362] Despite the fact that the Commission acknowledges the 'key role' of the ECN, this review was much more critical in tone.[1363] Although the new system has positively contributed to the stronger enforcement of competition rules and has allowed the competition rules to become the 'law of the land', it stressed that existing divergences between NCAs in

1355. There are indications that the different competition authorities also cooperated under Regulation 17/62 and that there was already a competition law network apparent, at least to a certain degree. Yet, this 'network' was not formalised and 'at best' comprised of 'irregular and ad hoc contacts' between Commission and NCA officials. *See:* Cengiz 2010, p. 663.
1356. This top down approach led to some scepticism towards the network in its early stages. *See:* Cengiz 2010, p. 663.
1357. Cengiz 2010, p. 661; Jones, Sufrin and Dunne 2019, p. 1018. *See, e.g.,* Article 10 Regulation 1/2003. *See also*: section 7.4.2.
1358. Maher and Ştefan 2010, p. 194; Sousa Ferro 2020, 414.
1359. Cengiz 2009, p. 10 European Commission, Commission Staff Working Document, Evaluation of Regulation 1/2003 and 773/2004, SWD(2024)216 final, p. 24.
1360. European Commission, Commission Staff Working Document, Evaluation of Regulation 1/2003 and 773/2004, SWD(2024)216 final, pp. 43 and 49.
1361. The Commission, for example, highlights 'the extensive efforts of the ECN in promoting the coherent application of the [EU] antitrust rules' established that 'cooperation mechanisms for fact-finding purposes within the ECN have worked well overall' and that the ECN has successfully contributed to ensuring consistency. *See:* Communication from the Commission to the European Parliament and the Council of 29 April 2009, Report on the functioning of Regulation 1/2003, COM(2009)206 final.
1362. Communication from the Commission to the European Parliament and the Council, 9 July 2014, Ten Years of Antitrust Enforcement under Regulation 1/2003: Achievements and Future Perspectives, COM(2014)453 final.
1363. Communication from the Commission to the European Parliament and the Council, 9 July 2014, Ten Years of Antitrust Enforcement under Regulation 1/2003: Achievements and Future Perspectives, COM(2014)453 final, para. 23; Honnefelder and Kolassa 2016, p. 17.

decision-making and fact-finding powers merited further evaluation.[1364] Ultimately, the procedural divergences led to the adoption of the ECN+ Directive. The latest review of Regulation 1/2003 again contains a more positive tone regarding the ECN. The Commission stresses that the network allows the Commission and NCAs to 'cooperate effectively and actively at multiple levels, with daily formal and informal exchanges on a confidential basis, far beyond the minimum legal requirements established by Regulation 1/2003'.[1365]

8.4.1.2 The Advisory Committee on Restrictive Practices and Dominant Positions

Article 14 Regulation 1/2003 establishes that the Commission shall consult the Advisory Committee prior to adopting certain decisions. The objective of the Advisory Committee is to 'help to safeguard the consistent application of [EU] competition rules'.[1366] The Advisory Committee is a specific instrument of EU antitrust law that does not fall within the scope of the comitology procedure.[1367] However, the DMA's Digital Markets Advisory Committee, which is an instrument of comitology, builds on experiences with the Advisory Committee in the context of competition law. This topic is further discussed in section 9.8.1.3.

The Advisory Committee is composed of representatives of NCAs and can discuss both Commission and NCA decisions. The Commission is obliged to consult the Committee prior to taking certain decisions in individual cases.[1368] Cases dealt with by national authorities can be put on the agenda of the Committee by the Commission or at the request of an NCA. Regulation 1/2003 stresses that NCAs may make such requests in particular where the Commission intends to invoke Article 11(6) Regulation 1/2003.[1369] When it comes to cases dealt with by national authorities, the Committee does not issue an opinion.[1370] Apart from individual cases, the Committee can discuss *general issues* of EU competition law.[1371] In the

1364. Communication from the Commission to the European Parliament and the Council, 9 July 2014, Ten Years of Antitrust Enforcement under Regulation 1/2003: Achievements and Future Perspectives, COM(2014)453 final, paras 3 and 42.
1365. Commission Staff Working Document, Evaluation of Regulation 1/2003 and 773/2004, SWD(2024)216 final, p. 245.
1366. Preamble Regulation 1/2003, recital 19.
1367. Regulation 182/2011.
1368. According to Article 14(1) Regulation 1/2003, '[t]he Commission shall consult an Advisory Committee on Restrictive Practices and Dominant Positions prior to the taking of any decision under Articles 7, 8, 9, 10, 23, Article 24(2) and Article 29(1)' Regulation 1/2003.
1369. Article 14(7) Regulation 1/2003. *See:* section: 7.4.2.
1370. Article 14(7) Regulation 1/2003.
1371. Article 14(7) Regulation 1/2003.

context of these general issues, Member States may appoint an additional representative, e.g., an official from the responsible ministry.[1372]

The Advisory Committee delivers a written (reasoned) opinion on the Commission's preliminary draft measure.[1373] According to Article 14(5) Regulation 1/2003, the Commission shall take *the utmost account* of the Advisory Committee's opinion. Moreover, the opinion should be appended to the draft decision if the Committee advises publication of the opinion. The Committee's opinion on the *Google Shopping* case was, for example, published.[1374] When publishing such an opinion, the Commission takes *into account the legitimate interest of undertakings in the protection of their business secrets.*[1375]

The Advisory Committee serves as an important forum for cooperation within the area of EU competition law as it provides a channel for NCAs to voice their opinions and influence decision-making by the Commission.[1376] In this light, it constitutes an important element of the institutionalised cooperation between the Commission and NCAs.[1377] Despite this relevance, certain remarks should be made regarding the functioning of this forum for cooperation. An important concern relates to timing: the Advisory Committee only comes into play at a relatively late stage of the procedure.[1378]

8.4.2 Mechanisms for Cooperation

Regulation 1/2003 and the ECN+ Directive establish multiple mechanisms for cooperation between competition authorities. Article 11 Regulation 1/2003 is the key provision in this regard.[1379] According to Article 11(1) Regulation 1/2003, the Commission and NCAs shall apply EU competition law in close cooperation. This cooperation is realised by various mechanisms, including a framework for notification and rules regarding the exchange of information. Before addressing these mechanisms in more detail, this section discusses the duty of parallel application of EU competition law, which is established in Article 3(1) Regulation 1/2003. The duty of parallel application of EU competition law is of the utmost importance for the functioning of the cooperation mechanisms, as the application of EU competition law triggers the duties to cooperate.

1372. Article 14(2) Regulation 1/2003.
1373. Article 14(4) Regulation 1/2003.
1374. Opinion of the Advisory Committee on restrictive practices and dominant positions given at its meeting of 20 June 2017 regarding a draft decision relating to Case AT39740 – *Google Search (Shopping).*
1375. Article 14(6) Regulation 1/2003; *see also* Network Notice, para. 68.
1376. Honnefelder and Kolassa 2016, p. 15.
1377. Van de Gronden and De Vries 2006, p. 40.
1378. Podszun 2022b, p. 988.
1379. Kjolbe 2020, p. 457.

8.4.2.1 The Duty of Parallel Application of EU Competition Law

According to Article 3(1) Regulation 1/2003, NCAs and national courts are under the obligation to apply EU competition law in parallel to national competition law in cases which may affect trade between Member States. According to recital 8 Regulation 1/2003, this obligation ensures the effective enforcement of EU competition law as well as the proper functioning of the cooperation mechanisms of Regulation 1/2003.

The duty of parallel application entails: (i) a duty to assess whether Article 102 TFEU applies; and subsequently, if so (ii) a duty to apply Article 102 TFEU in parallel.[1380] This obligation can also apply if an NCA relies on a 'stricter national rule on unilateral conduct'. If a rule with a broader scope is applied in a case where Article 102 TFEU would also be applicable, Article 102 TFEU must be applied.[1381] The German *Meta Bundeskartellamt* case, which is discussed below, is particularly noteworthy in this regard.

The duty of parallel application only applies in cases that may have an *effect on trade between Member States*. Consequently, the concept of trade between Member States is of key importance for the doctrine of parallel application.[1382] Yet, and despite the relevance of this criterion, NCAs and national courts do not always discuss explicitly whether an effect on trade between Member States is present or assume that there is no effect.[1383] This can undermine the functioning of Regulation 1/2003. This inquiry is focused on the behaviour of large platforms in personal data markets. Since such platforms usually act on a European or global scale, the criterion of an effect on trade between Member States will generally be met.[1384] Therefore, this notion is not discussed in further detail.

The duty of parallel application of EU competition law has contributed to an increase in the application of EU competition law, making 'a single legal standard a reality on a very large scale'.[1385] However, and despite the principle's contribution to the development of EU competition law as the 'law of the land', cases relating to anti-competitive conduct on digital markets, such as the *Meta Bundeskartellamt* case, raise questions about the scope and functioning of the duty of parallel application of EU and national competition law.[1386]

1380. Holzwarth and Woolfson 2022, p. 99.
1381. De Smijter and Sinclair 2014, para. 2.37.
1382. Whish and Bailey 2021, p. 78.
1383. Brook and Eben 2023a, pp. 48-49; Svetlicinii 2023.
1384. *See* Chapter 2.
1385. European Commission, Report of 29 April 2009 on the functioning of Regulation 1/2003, COM(2009) 206 final, p. 5.
1386. Wils 2019, p. 7.

In the *Meta Bundeskartellamt* case, the German NCA merely relied on national competition law. Accordingly, the *Bundeskartellamt* applied national law and refrained from analysing the conduct in question in light of Article 102 TFEU. Although the *Bundeskartellamt* does not apply EU competition law in parallel to Section 19 GWB, it touches upon the doctrine of parallel application. In paragraph 914 of its decision, the German NCA explicitly stated that Article 102(2) TFEU prohibits excessive prices and unfair trading conditions. However, the authority continued by stressing that the Meta case is based on Section 19 GWB which – in line with the *Pechstein* and *Gegenwert* cases – allows for the inclusion of fundamental rights and additional legislation in a competition law assessment. According to the *Bundeskartellamt*, this doctrine does not have a counterpart in EU law.[1387] The *Bundeskartellamt* reached these conclusions without providing an in-depth assessment of the applicability of Article 102 TFEU. Moreover, in an FAQ on the *Meta* case, the *Bundeskartellamt* emphasised that European competition law is also at issue since proceedings would generally be possible under Article 102 TFEU as well. Additionally, the German authority was in close contact with the Commission given the cross-border nature of the *Meta* case.[1388]

In my view, the approach of the *Bundeskartellamt* violated Article 3(1) Regulation 1/2003. Despite its brief references to Article 102 TFEU, the German authority does not fulfil its duty of parallel application. 'Applying' EU competition law requires an explicit reference to Article 102 TFEU in the operative part of the judgment.[1389] By disregarding the application of Article 102 TFEU through mentioning this EU provision in a single paragraph, the *Bundeskartellamt* did not meet this requirement. The German authority seems to presume that Article 102 TFEU only provides limited room for data protection considerations. However, despite the lack of precedents at the time, it was not evident that data protection considerations could *not* be taken into account in EU competition law assessments.[1390] Therefore, the *Bundeskartellamt* should have applied Article 102 TFEU in parallel to

---

1387. The original German text stresses that: Die Prüfung hat jedoch gezeigt, dass das von der deutschen Rechtsprechung zur Generalklausel des § 19 Abs. 1 GWB entwickelte Schutzkonzept, das sich zur Feststellung der Missbräuchlichkeit maßgeblich auf grundrechtliche oder einfachgesetzliche Wertentscheidungen bezieht, in der europäischen Rechtsprechung und Anwendungspraxis bisher keine Entsprechung gefunden hat. *See:* Bundeskartellamt 6 February 2019 Case B6-22/16, *Facebook*, para. 914; Bundesgerichtshof 7 June 2016 Az KZR 6/15, Pechstein; Bundesgerichtshof 24 January 2017 KZR 47/14, Az VBL Gegenwert.

1388. *Bundeskartellamt*, Hintergrundinformationen zum Facebook-Verfahren des *Bundeskartellamtes*, 19 December 2017 https://www.Bundeskartellamt.de/SharedDocs/Publikation/DE/Diskussions_Hintergrundpapier/Hintergrundpapier_Facebook.pdf;jsessionid=7DDD5AAC0E6B14B1A419869BDE65D948.1_cid362?__blob=publicationFile&v=5 accessed 31 March 2025, p. 1.

1389. Holzwarth and Woolfson 2022, p. 99.

1390. Wils 2019, p. 11; Article 16 TFEU; *See* sections 6.3 and 6.4.

Section 19 GWB. Admittedly, in applying Article 102 TFEU in parallel to national competition law NCAs walk a 'narrow path'.[1391] While Article 3(1) Regulation 1/2003 requires NCAs to 'apply' Article 102 TFEU in parallel in cases with an effect on trade between Member States, NCAs are not empowered to adopt a decision finding the inapplicability of EU competition law.[1392] Consequently, if NCAs find that national competition law applies to particular conduct, whereas Article 102 TFEU does not apply, they find themselves in a difficult position and may be incentivised to keep any reference to this provision short.[1393] A better alternative can be found in Article 10 Regulation 1/2003 and recital 14 of its Preamble. NCAs could consult with the Commission regarding the applicability of Article 102 TFEU. Recital 14 of Regulation 1/2003s Preamble allows the Commission to adopt a decision of a declaratory nature finding that Article 102 TFEU does not apply. According to the text of recital 14, this avenue is particularly relevant with regard to new types of practices that have not been settled in existing case law or decision-making. Consequently, this would have been a suitable avenue in the *Meta Bundeskartellamt* case.

The Düsseldorf court acknowledged that the *Bundeskartellamt* had not observed Article 3(1) Regulation 1/2003 and considered the limitation to the application of German competition law a 'procedural error'.[1394] Surprisingly, the duty of parallel application is not included in the preliminary reference procedure. The Düsseldorf court did not include this issue in its preliminary questions, and the CJEU did not address this issue ex officio.[1395] This is a missed opportunity since the *Meta Bundeskartellamt* case provided the CJEU a rare opportunity to clarify the consequences of an Article 3(1) Regulation 1/2003 violation.

Violations of Article 3(1) Regulation 1/2003 have serious procedural and institutional consequences as the application of EU competition law triggers institutional and procedural obligations.[1396] The application of Article 102 TFEU activates the cooperation mechanisms of Chapter IV Regulation 1/2003. The duty of parallel application thus safeguards the functioning of the cooperation mechanisms contained in Regulation 1/2003: without a duty of parallel application, Member States could refrain from applying EU competition law in cases with an effect on trade between Member States, thereby circumventing the cooperative obligations of Regulation 1/2003.[1397] The duty of sincere cooperation, thus, contributes to the effective functioning of the cooperation mechanisms, which in turn aim to

1391. Holzwarth and Woolfson 2022, p. 99.
1392. Article 10 Regulation 1/2003; CJEU 3 May 2011 Case C-375/09, *Tele2Polska*.
1393. Holzwarth and Woolfson 2022, p. 99.
1394. Brook and Eben 2023b, p. 27.
1395. Oberlandesgericht Düsseldorf 22 April 2021 VI-Kart 2/19 (V), Facebook gegen Bundeskartellamt.
1396. Brook and Eben 2023a, p. 54.
1397. De Smijter and Sinclair 2014, para. 2.40.

ensure the effective enforcement of EU competition and maintain its coherent application within the internal market.[1398] In a way, the duty of parallel application also 'gives a concrete shape to the general principle of sincere cooperation'.[1399] Given the relevance of parallel application for the functioning of competition law's cooperation mechanisms, an NCA's decision to refrain from complying with its duty of parallel application has an adverse effect on the ability of the Commission and other NCAs to influence the decision.[1400]

Despite the important institutional and procedural consequences of an Article 3(1) Regulation 1/2003 violation, the consequences of such an infringement are far from clear. It is highly unlikely that a violation would be addressed in front of a court. Undertakings have no incentive to raise the argument that their conduct should also be subject to Article 102 TFEU scrutiny. Arguably, national courts could bring up violations of Article 3(1) Regulation 1/2003 on their own motion, possibly in combination with a preliminary reference procedure.[1401] Even if national courts take this approach, the (legal) consequences of a violation remain unclear, and different approaches are put forward in the literature. While De Smijter and Sinclair stress that decisions adopted in violation of Article 3(1) Regulation 1/2003 are invalid and unenforceable given the provision's direct effect, Wils argues that such remedy is neither workable nor desirable.[1402] In my view, Article 102 TFEU decisions adopted in violation of Article 3(1) Regulation are not necessarily unenforceable.[1403] The consequences of such violation for the decision adopted under national law are *procedural*, and therefore, according to the principle of procedural autonomy, a matter of national law. Consequently, provided that the principles of equivalence, effectiveness and legal protection are respected, different remedies can be adopted.[1404] A national court could, for example, remedy the deficiency by applying Article

---

1398. Preamble Regulation 1/2003, recital 8.
1399. Holzwarth and Woolfson 2022, p. 100.
1400. Brook and Eben 2022, p. 3.
1401. Brook and Eben 2022, p. 4.
1402. De Smijter and Sinclair 2014, p. 107; Wils 2019, p. 17; Wils 2024, pp. 34-36.
1403. This situation is different in the scenario where national competition law is applied to an agreement which does not violate Article 101 TFEU. Since Article 3(1) Regulation 1/2003 provides that '[t]he application of national competition law may not lead to the prohibition of agreements, decisions by associations of undertakings or concerted practices which may affect trade between Member States but which do not restrict competition within the meaning of Article [101(1)] of the Treaty, or which fulfil the conditions of Article [101(3)] of the Treaty or which are covered by a Regulation for the application of Article 81(3) of the Treaty', this line of reasoning does not apply to Article 101 TFEU decisions adopted in violations of Article 3(1) Regulation 1/2003.
1404. *See* section 3.4.1; CJEU 25 May 1976 Case 33/76, *Rewe*; CJEU 16 December 1976 Case 45/76, *Comet*.

102 TFEU on its own motion.[1405] The duty of parallel application also applies to courts, and the courts of the Member States can ask the Commission to transmit its opinion on the application of EU competition law.[1406]

Furthermore, Article 258 TFEU can be helpful to address violations of Article 3(1) Regulation 1/2003. Theoretically, the Commission could start an infringement procedure against the Member State whose NCA violated Article 3(1) Regulation 1/2003. However, this procedure is rarely used for a single failure by an NCA.[1407] The infringement procedure, therefore, only seems useful in cases of systemic or repeated infringements of Article 3(1) Regulation 1/2003 by a particular national competition authority. In such circumstances, an infringement procedure could be helpful in order to deter future omissions in applying Article 102 TFEU. In its latest 'Evaluation of Regulation 1/2003 and 773/2004', the Commission stressed that, despite examples of NCAs potentially not fulfilling their duty of parallel application, there are no signs of systemic non-compliance with Article 3 Regulation 1/2003.[1408] Infringement procedures for non-compliance with the duty of parallel application are, at this point, thus unlikely. Yet, given the important procedural and institutional implications of Article 3(1) Regulation 1/2003, it would be advisable for the Commission to initiate an infringement procedure *if* certain NCAs systemically violate Article 3(1) Regulation 1/2003 in the future.

8.4.2.2 The Allocation of Cases

In a country of destination model, efficient tools for the allocation of cases can limit duplications of regulatory work. This can prevent an unnecessary regulatory burden on undertakings, as well as a waste of the limited resources by authorities.[1409] This section studies mechanisms for case allocation in the context of EU competition law.

Regulation 1/2003 does not contain clear criteria for the attribution of competence to a particular competition authority in the EU. Article 11(6) Regulation 1/2003 – which is discussed in more detail in section 7.4.2.2 –

1405. Holzwarth and Woolfson 2022, pp. 101-102. Article 101 and 102 TFEU are both 'fundamental provisions that are a matter of EU public policy' and can therefore be applied ex officio. *See:* CJEU 1 June 1990 Case C-126/97, *Eco Swiss*, para. 37; CJEU 21 December 2023 Case C-124/21P, *International Skating Union*, para. 193. *See also*: Geradin 2016.

1406. Article 15 Regulation 1/2003.

1407. Wils 2019, p. 16.

1408. European Commission, Commission Staff Working Document, Evaluation of Regulation 1/2003 and 773/2004, SWD(2024)216 final, p. 233.

1409. Brammer 2005, p. 1384; European Data Protection Supervisor 15 January 2025 'Towards a Digital Clearinghouse 2.0 – Concept Note' https://www.edps.europa.eu/system/files/2025-01/towards_a_digital_clearinghouse_2_0_january_2025_en_0.pdf accessed 20 March 2025, para. 17.

provides the main jurisdictional rule in Regulation 1/2003.[1410] According to this provision, NCAs can be relieved of their competence to apply EU competition law if the Commission initiates a procedure. Article 11(6) Regulation 1/2003 constitutes a tool of pre-emption, but can also serve as a tool for case allocation by allowing the Commission to deal exclusively with a case. In theory, this competence can also be used in scenarios where an NCA is already engaged in proceedings. Yet, in practice, the Commission has not relied on this 'draconian' or 'nuclear' option.[1411]

The Commission's reluctance to rely on Article 11(6) Regulation 1/2003 has been questioned. Despite the fact that different NCAs have adopted (inconsistent) decisions regarding Booking's practices relating to narrow and wide MFN clauses, the Commission has not intervened. This reveals the shortcomings of Article 11(6) Regulation 1/2003: the Commission can only take the drastic measure of withdrawing the case from the NCAs who most likely already have invested considerable resources in their ongoing investigation. Despite the fact that Article 11(6) Regulation 1/2003 is rarely used to take over ongoing cases from Member States, it can serve as leverage vis-à-vis NCAs. This leverage could be used to stimulate the consistent application of EU competition law.[1412]

Although EU competition law does not contain binding case allocation mechanisms apart from Article 11(6) Regulation 1/2003, certain more informal, non-binding mechanisms are in place. The *Network Notice* – which was adopted by the Commission in cooperation with the NCAs – provides allocation criteria.[1413] The Network Notice reiterates that cases can be dealt with by: (i) a single NCA, possibly with the assistance of other Member States; (ii) several NCAs acting in parallel; or (iii) the Commission. The case allocation mechanism is based on the idea that cases should be dealt with by a single authority wherever possible.[1414] Cases should be dealt with by 'a well-placed competition authority' and Member States should keep each other informed in order to detect parallel procedures. Under normal circumstances, the authority that has received a complaint or started an ex officio procedure and has notified the ECN remains in charge of the case.[1415] However, in some circumstances, re-allocation is 'found to be necessary for an effective protection of competition and for an [EU] interest'.[1416] If cases are reallocated, the process should be quick and efficient. Accordingly, the process should normally be resolved within two months after information has

1410. De Smijter and Sinclair 2014, para. 2.231.
1411. *See also* section 7.4.2.
1412. Sauter 2016, p. 154.
1413. Network Notice, para. 7; Brammer 2005, 1386.
1414. Brammer 2005, p. 1387.
1415. Network Notice, para. 6.
1416. Network Notice, para. 7.

been sent to the ECN.[1417] During this process, authorities should try to reach an agreement on the re-allocation and, where relevant, on the modalities for parallel action.[1418]

The Network Notice centres around the notion of 'well-placed' authority and takes a rather pragmatic approach to determine whether an authority qualifies as such, focusing on effects on a territory, the authority's capability to bring the infringement to an end and the possibilities for gathering evidence.[1419] Interestingly, the Network Notice relies on the notion of a 'well placed' authority, rather than the 'best placed' authority, thereby allowing a more flexible approach and not excluding the possibility of parallel enforcement actions.[1420] Paragraph 12 of the Network Notice provides that parallel enforcement actions may be appropriate insofar as a practice has a substantial effect on competition in the respective territories and action by a single NCA would not be sufficient to bring the entire infringement to an end. Yet, parallel control should be 'the exception rather than the rule'.[1421]

The Network Notice endorses the special position of the Commission.[1422] The Commission is particularly well-placed to deal with cases that have an effect on the territory of more than three Member States.[1423] The Commission is also well-placed 'for cases that are closely linked to other [EU] provisions which may be exclusively or more effectively [be] applied by the Commission' and 'if the [EU] interest requires the adoption of a Commission decision to develop [EU] competition policy when a new competition issue arises in order to ensure effective enforcement'.[1424] The fact that the Commission is particularly well placed to deal with cases that are closely linked to other EU provisions enforced by the Commission is relevant in the context of the DMA. Since the Commission is the 'sole enforcer' of the DMA, the provisions of the DMA could qualify as EU provisions applied by the Commission.[1425] This would mean that the Commission would be particularly well placed to deal with cases that overlap

1417. Despite the fact that cases are normally reallocated in a two month period, the Network Notice 'provides no precise assurance that the period for re-allocation would not exceed a period of two months'. Furthermore, the time allocated to the Commission to re-allocate the case only begins to run once it becomes aware of the infringement in question. *See:* CJEU 2 October 2024 Case T-587/22, *Crown v. Commission*, 47 and 100.

1418. Network Notice, paras 7 and 16-19.

1419. Network Notice, paras 8-15; Brammer 2005, pp. 1388-1389.

1420. Brammer 2005, p. 1388.

1421. Brammer 2005, p. 1390.

1422. The fact that the Commission is well-placed to deal with a certain case, does not mean that the Commission is forced to act. The Commission has the discretion to refrain from acting and leaving the case to NCAs. *See:* Dzino and Rusu 2019, p. 136.

1423. For example if a dominant firm abuses its position in four different national markets. *See:* Network Notice, para. 14.

1424. Network Notice, para. 15.

1425. *See* sections 5.2.4 and 9.2.1.

with the DMA. As explained in section 5.4.3, it is unlikely that the Commission will apply EU competition law and the DMA in parallel to address one and the same conduct. This means that the allocation mechanism of the Network Notice may result in fewer competition law cases involving conduct that is also subject to the DMA.

In 2017, the ECN demonstrated its commitment to ensuring consistency in future cases through the introduction of an 'early warning system'. This system aims to 'allow discussing ongoing cases that raise novel issues at the earliest possible stage' and to facilitate early case allocation and coordination in novel cases with a cross-border effect, handled by several authorities.[1426] The early warning mechanism allows for early coordination and case allocation, even at an earlier stage than that required by Article 11(2) and 11(3) Regulation 1/2003.[1427] According to the Commission's most recent review of Regulation 1/2003, the early warning mechanism is a 'concrete expression of 'lessons learned' within the ECN following the hotel booking cases'.[1428]

Apart from the criteria established in the Network Notice, Article 14(7) Regulation 1/2003 may play a role in the allocation of EU competition law cases. This provision allows the Commission to put cases dealt with by NCAs on the agenda of the Advisory Committee. In this context, the Advisory Committee can serve as a *forum for the discussion of case allocation*.[1429] Yet, the fact remains that the Advisory Committee cannot adopt a binding decision. Therefore, parallel proceedings will only be avoided if the different competition authorities agree to do so.[1430]

In sum, EU competition law has very limited instruments for binding case allocations. Yet, due to the well-functioning informal mechanisms, the current model 'overall works effectively and efficiently and there is an extensive practice of early coordination discussions'.[1431]

8.4.2.3 The Obligation to Notify

Regulation 1/2003 provides several mechanisms for notification and the exchange of information. These mechanisms not only facilitate the exchange of information but also allow the Commission to monitor decision-making

1426. Outcome of the Meeting of ECN DGs on 17 February 2017 https://www.konkurrensverket.se/contentassets/ad8356e1c8f148daa3287ffa3ab4bbdd/ecn_meeting_outcome_17022017.pdf accessed 20 March 2025.
1427. European Commission, Commission Staff Working Document, Evaluation of Regulation 1/2003 and 773/2004, SWD(2024)216 final, p. 240.
1428. European Commission, Commission Staff Working Document, Evaluation of Regulation 1/2003 and 773/2004, SWD(2024)216 final, p. 246.
1429. Network Notice, para. 62.
1430. Brammer 2005, p. 1403.
1431. European Commission, Commission Staff Working Document, Evaluation of Regulation 1/2003 and 773/2004, SWD(2024)216 final, p. 246.

and strategic choices at the national level. This enables the Commission to intervene, either through informal mechanisms or – as a matter of last resort – by relying on the pre-emptive effect of Article 11(6) Regulation 1/2003.[1432]

Article 11(3) Regulation 1/2003 obliges NCAs to inform the Commission in writing about formal EU competition law investigations.[1433] This enables the Commission – the 'guardian of the Treaty' – to confirm whether the NCA intends to apply EU competition law in conformity with the decisional practices of the Commission and the case law of the EU courts.[1434] The information can be made available to the NCAs of other Member States.[1435] Despite the fact that Regulation 1/2003 does not contain an identical obligation for the Commission, the Network Notice provides that the Commission 'has accepted an equivalent obligation to inform NCAs under Article 11(2) Regulation 1/2003'.[1436]

Apart from the obligation to inform the Commission about the start of an investigation, Article 11(4) Regulation 1/2003 requires NCAs to inform the Commission about a decision no later than 30 days before its adoption. Article 11(4) provides the obligation to share a summary of the case, the envisaged decision or other documents indicating the proposed course of action.

Given the good relationship between competition authorities, NCAs are generally willing to contribute to the coherent enforcement of EU competition law and usually comply with Article 11(3) and (4) Regulation 1/2003.[1437] However, in the 'rare case' where an NCA violates its duty to inform the Commission, the implications are not clear.[1438] The notification mechanisms should be considered an integral part of the cooperation mechanism, and refraining from informing the Commission *before* the conclusion of the proceedings could undermine the Commission's power to use Article 11(6) Regulation 1/2003.[1439] In this context, a violation of Article 11(4) Regulation 1/2003 is particularly problematic. Yet, it is not unequivocally clear what the consequences of an Article 11(4) violation are. Despite the fact that the article has a direct effect, national courts have given different

1432. Cengiz 2010, p. 667.
1433. The Commission must be notified before or without delay after commencing the first formal investigative measure. *See:* Network Notice, para. 17.
1434. Arsenidou et al. 2020, para. 19.33.
1435. The intention is 'to make any information exchanged pursuant to Article 11 available and easily accessible to all network members'. Network Notice, para. 17; Veenbrink suggests to explicitly include this obligation in Regulation 1/2003 to create more clarity. *See:* Veenbrink 2019, p. 85.
1436. Network Notice, para. 17.
1437. Communication from the Commission to the European Parliament and the Council, 9 July 2014, Ten Years of Antitrust Enforcement under Regulation 1/2003: Achievements and Future Perspectives, COM(2014)453 final, para. 28.
1438. Tountopoulos 2012, p. 475.
1439. Tountopoulos 2012, pp.483-484.

effects to a violation of the duty to inform the Commission.[1440] Where the Bulgarian Supreme Administrative Court stressed that a violation of Article 11(4) Regulation 1/2003 may result in a substantial procedural violation under national procedural law that leads to the annulment of the decision, Lithuanian, Greek and French courts have not taken this approach.[1441] The differences can be explained by the principle of procedural autonomy which gives Member States the freedom to establish the criteria for the annulment of an NCA's decision. According to De Smijter and Sinclair, 'there can be little doubt that decisions adopted in breach of Article 11(4) are invalid and unenforceable', because the obligation constitutes 'an essential procedural requirement that is closely linked to the substantive decision'.[1442] In my view, a violation of Article 11(4) Regulation 1/2003 does *not* necessarily lead to the inapplicability of the NCA's decision. The CJEU discussed the effects of a Member State's violation of a duty to inform the Commission in previous case law. If the duty to communicate a certain measure to the Commission does not infringe the rights of individuals, non-notification does not necessarily lead to enforceability.[1443] Since Article 11(4) Regulation 1/2003 does not confer rights upon individuals, the adoption of a competition law decision by an NCA in violation of Article 11(4) Regulation 1/2003 does not render the decision inapplicable.

Furthermore, the current reality does not require the procedural harmonisation of the consequences of a violation of Article 11(4) Regulation 1/2003 at the EU level. The Commission's evaluation of Regulation 1/2003 shows that violations of Article 11(4) Regulation 1/2003 are not commonplace. On the contrary, it concludes that compliance with this regulation is well respected overall.[1444] This means that it is, at this point, not necessary to harmonise the matter. If certain NCAs were to systematically violate Article 11(3) and (4) TFEU in the future, the Commission could exceptionally start an infringement procedure.

8.4.2.4 The Exchange of Information

In the pursuit of effective cooperation, the EU competition law framework includes a mechanism for the sharing of information.[1445] The exchange of information is considered 'a key element of the functioning of the [ECN]' and a 'precondition for efficient and effective allocation and handling of

1440. Tountopoulos 2012, p. 479.
1441. *See,* for a more elaborate analysis, Tountopoulos 2012.
1442. De Smijter and Sinclair 2014, para. 2.225.
1443. CJEU 30 April 1966 Case C-194/94, CIA Security International, paras 49-54; CJEU 13 July 1989 Case 380/87, *Enichem Base v. Comuni di Cinisello Balsamo*, paras 19-24.
1444. European Commission, Commission Staff Working Document, Evaluation of Regulation 1/2003 and 773/2004, SWD(2024)216 final, p. 227 and in particular footnote 270.
1445. Riley 2003, p. 610.

cases'.[1446] According to Article 12 Regulation 1/2003, the Commission and NCAs shall have the power 'to provide one another with and use in evidence in any matter of fact or of law, including confidential information'. The information exchanged can only be used for applying Articles 101 and 102 TFEU and in respect of the subject matter for which it was collected by the transmitting authority. However, the information may also be used for the parallel application of national competition law, provided that this does not lead to a different outcome.[1447] Section 2.2.3 of The Network Notice lays down further safeguards concerning the sharing of confidential information.

Despite the relevance of information sharing, neither Regulation 1/2003, nor the ECN+ Directive contain detailed procedural rules for the exchange of information.[1448] Recital 15 and Article 24(2) ECN+ Directive reiterates that the exchange of information between NCAs and the use of such information in evidence for the application of Articles 101 and 102 TFEU should be carried out pursuant to Article 12 Regulation 1/2003. Furthermore, the directive refers to more general principles of EU law and to the CFR.[1449] Yet, the ECN+ Directive does not include more specific safeguards. Kozak is critical in this regard and considers the absence of such guarantees as a missed opportunity for strengthening the procedural rights of parties.[1450]

8.4.2.5 Mutual Assistance and Joint Cases

Regulation 1/2003 not only provides a mechanism to exchange evidence but also establishes that an NCA may carry out an inspection or fact-finding measure under its national law *on behalf of another Member State.*[1451] Moreover, at the request of the Commission, NCAs *shall* undertake the inspections that the Commission considers necessary under Article 22(2) Regulation 1/2003. This provision stresses that NCA officials 'shall exercise their powers in accordance with national law' and can be accompanied or assisted by the Commission.

While the mutual assistance between the Commission and NCAs is subject to the provisions of Regulation 1/2003, the ECN+ Directive has further harmonised mutual assistance between NCAs.[1452] Given the focus on assistance among NCAs, the relationship between the Commission and

1446. Network Notice, para. 26.
1447. Article 12(2) Regulation 1/2003.
1448. Kozak 2020b, p. 60.
1449. Article 3(1) ECN+ Directive.
1450. Kozak 2020b, p. 77.
1451. Article 22(1) Regulation 1/2003; Under such circumstances, the exchange of evidence is subject to Article 12 Regulation 1/2003.
1452. Recital 7 of the Preamble of the ECN+ Directive establishes that a system of mutual assistance, 'does not work well when there are still NCAs that do not have adequate fact-finding tools'.

NCAs is not further harmonised by this instrument. Yet, since Regulation 1/2003 contains extensive provisions relating to mutual assistance between the Commission and NCAs, this is not problematic.[1453] In the implementation of the ECN+ Directive, both The Netherlands and Germany strengthened the framework for cooperation among NCAs. The Dutch legislator introduced specific rules governing the ACM's cooperation with other NCAs.[1454] The German framework also explicitly establishes competences for the *Bundeskartellamt* to cooperate (in the context of the ECN). Chapter 1 of Part 2 of the GWB addresses issues such as investigations within the European Competition Network, the exchange of documents and information and enforcement within the European Competition Network.[1455]

8.4.2.6 Informal Cooperation

While Regulation 1/2003 and the ECN+ Directive provide interesting insights into the functioning of the ECN, its meetings take place behind closed doors. A 'successful informal communication between officials' has emerged, resulting in the successful functioning of the network and a lack of conflict between network members.[1456] Yet, and despite these achievements, informal cooperation is opaque and cannot be fully comprehended from the outside.[1457]

Several cases concerning personal data markets imply a degree of informal cooperation. In various cases, the Commission and NCAs have engaged in parallel proceedings but focused on different relevant product markets. For instance, both the Commission and the Dutch NCA investigated Apple's conduct relating to the App Store. Where the Commission addressed music streaming platforms, the ACM targeted conduct concerning dating apps.[1458] Consequently, both authorities addressed behaviour in different product markets. While the focus on different product markets can be a way of avoiding overlapping decisions, this approach has been criticised in legal literature. It is questionable whether there are economically viable arguments for distinguishing between different types of App Store markets since all

1453. Dzino, Van de Gronden and Rusu 2019, p. 537.
1454. *See* Article 89ga, 89gb and 89gc of the Dutch Competition Act. *See also*: De Groes and Raats 2021, p. 297.
1455. Section 50a, 50b, 50c, 50d and 50f GWB.
1456. Honnefelder and Kolassa 2016, p. 18.
1457. This is also acknowledged in the methodology section. *See* section 1.3.3.
1458. The ACM focusses on the *market for Appstore services on mobile operating systems iOS for dating-app providers*; the Commission focusses on *the market for the provision to developers of platforms for the distribution of music streaming apps to iOS users. See:* ACM 24 August 2021 ACM/19/035630 *Apple* (Case Summary); European Commission 4 March 2024, Case AT40437, *Apple Appstore Practices – music streaming*.

kinds of (paid) apps 'appear to experience the same constraints when it comes to the distribution and capitalisation of iOS apps'.[1459]

The app store cases are not the only example of investigations in which different authorities focus on different parts of the relevant market. In the *Amazon Buy Box* case, the Commission carved out the territory of Italy from the geographic market by stating that its investigation will cover 'the European Economic Area, with the exception of Italy'. In the Press Release, the Commission highlights that 'the Italian Competition Authority started to investigate partially similar concerns last year, with a focus on the Italian market' and that the Commission will continue in close cooperation with the Italian authority.[1460] By not investigating the Italian territory, the Commission clearly shows self-restraint: under Article 11(6) Regulation 1/2003 including the entire territory of the EU would have relieved the Italian Competition Authority of its competence to apply EU competition law.[1461] By excluding the territory of Italy, the Italian authority's and the Commission's case do not focus on the same geographical market, meaning that Article 11(6) Regulation 1/2003 is not applicable.[1462]

Amazon challenged the Commission's decision to exclude the Italian market from the investigation. Both the GC and the CJEU declared the appeal inadmissible. The delimitation of the geographical scope of the investigation opened by the Commission amounts to a preparatory act since it paves the way for a final decision and may evolve during the administrative procedure.[1463] Such an act 'produced only the ordinary effects of any procedural step and, […] did not affect the legal position [of Amazon]'.[1464] Furthermore, the CJEU reiterates that Article 11(6) Regulation 1/2003 does not apply because the territorial scope of the Commission's proceedings does not include Italy and Article 11(6) does not 'imply any right for an undertaking to have a case dealt with in its entirety by the Commission'.[1465]

In the scenario where the Commission and an NCA engage in parallel procedures, but focus on different parts of the relevant markets, Article 11(6) Regulation 1/2003 does not apply. Consequently, NCAs are not relieved of their competence to apply EU competition law. Furthermore, under these circumstances, the *ne bis in idem* principle is not applicable since the parallel investigations do not concern the same material facts.[1466] In my view,

1459. Mândrescu 2024a.
1460. European Commission, Press Release 10 November 2020 'Antitrust: Commission sends Statement of Objections to Amazon for the use of non-public independent seller data and opens second investigation into its e-commerce business practices', IP/20/2077.
1461. Midri 2023, p. 3.
1462. CJEU 25 February 2021 Case C-857/19, *Slovak Telekom*, para. 30.
1463. Order of the GC 14 October 2021 Case T-19/21, *Amazon v. Commission*, para. 32.
1464. CJEU 20 April 2023 Case C-815/21P, *Amazon v. Commission*, para. 43.
1465. CJEU 20 April 2023 Case C-815/21P, *Amazon v. Commission*, para. 43.
1466. *See* section 3.4.3.

carving out specific parts of the relevant markets should not be used as a mechanism for allocating cases or circumventing the applicability of Article 11(6) Regulation 1/2003 and the *ne bis in idem* principle. Obviously, there may be valid economic reasons for excluding the territory of a particular Member State from the relevant market, for example, because consumer preferences are not sufficiently homogeneous.[1467] However, in the absence of such economic considerations, territories should not be excluded in order to grant leeway to Member States. Taking this approach jeopardises the functioning of the cooperation mechanisms of Regulation 1/2003 and also has a detrimental effect on the procedural rights of the parties concerned since the principle of *ne bis in idem* is circumvented.

8.5 CONCLUSION

This chapter studied which cooperation mechanisms are in place in the intra-disciplinary context of competition law and aimed to identify potential gaps in the institutional framework for cooperation. Before discussing the potential gaps, the table below offers a structured overview of the mechanisms that are in place. The table follows the typology outlined in section 8.2.

Table 8.1 Typology Institutional Design and Cooperation in Competition Law

Typology Institutional Design and Cooperation Competition Law		
(1) Institutional design	*1a level of centralisation*	Combination of central and decentral enforcement
	1b agency mandate or portfolio	Different competition authorities have different mandates, but the portfolio is often broader than 'traditional' competition law
(2) Cooperation	*2a dimension(s)*	Intra-disciplinary multi-jurisdictional; multi- and bilateral
	2b legal basis	Regulation 1/2003, the Network Notice and national law
	2c forum	European Competition Network Advisory Committee on Restrictive Practices and Dominant Positions
	2d intensity	Consultation; cooperation in individual cases; joint cases
	2e stage	Allocation of cases; investigative stage; decision-making stage.

1467. *See* section 4.2.2.1.

This chapter found that cooperation mechanisms in the field of competition law are widely available. Cooperation between the Commission and NCAs, as well as between different NCAs, takes place in multiple fora. The intra-disciplinary cooperation mechanisms in the context of competition law are, generally, well-developed. After the process of decentralisation, the coherent application of EU competition law has received significant attention. Moreover, in the wake of this process, the substantive, procedural and institutional frameworks have increasingly converged. This trend was fostered by the EU legislator, the ECN and the CJEU.[1468]

Despite the elaborate framework for cooperation and the institutional and procedural similarities between Member States, challenges remain. A *first* issue relates to the *allocation of cases*. EU competition law is enforced according to a country of destination model, without binding or absolute mechanisms for case allocation. Article 11(6) Regulation 1/2003 enables the Commission to pre-empt NCAs' competences to apply EU competition law. On paper, this offers an effective mechanism for the prevention of parallel proceedings. However, the mechanism appears to be rather drastic in practice, especially in scenarios where an NCA has already invested significant human and financial resources in a case. Consequently, in reality, Article 11(6) Regulation 1/2003 is not used to pre-empt an NCA's competence once it has already engaged in a procedure. The absence of binding rules for case allocation is partially resolved by the availability of non-binding and voluntary mechanisms. The Network Notice, for example, sets out criteria for establishing which authority is well-placed, (the risk of) parallel proceedings can be discussed in the context of the Advisory Committee under Article 14(7) Regulation 1/2003, and the 'early warning mechanism' allows for coordination at an early stage. Consequently, it is currently not necessary to provide set-in-stone mechanisms for the allocation of competition law cases. It is unlikely that there will be political willingness for the realisation of such a rigid system, and a certain degree of flexibility has merit to it. Consequently, it is neither realistic nor desirable to provide a bulletproof system.[1469]

A *second* potential gap relates to the *legal effect of violations* of important duties to cooperate. The duty of parallel application under Article 3(1) Regulation 1/2003 and the obligation to inform the Commission of proceedings and envisaged decisions as established in Article 11(3) and 11(4) Regulation 1/2003 are key provisions for the functioning of the cooperation framework in EU competition law. While the former is necessary to trigger the operation of existing cooperation mechanisms, the latter allows the Commission to fulfil its managerial role within the ECN. The exchange of information is the 'lifeblood of the network' and a precondition for a flexible

1468. *See also*: Gerbrandy 2009.
1469. Van Cleynenbreugel 2020, p. 420.

case-allocation mechanism.[1470] The level of trust and cooperative spirit between competition law authorities can partially compensate for these uncertainties since systemic violations of Articles 3(1), 11(3) and 11(4) Regulation 1/2003 have not systemically emerged in practice. Yet, the *Meta Bundeskartellamt* case shows that an infringement of the duty of parallel application can deprive other competition authorities of the opportunity to exercise their influence.[1471] This can adversely affect the coherent development of the competition law framework, particularly in the context of controversial or ground-breaking cases.

The *third* risk identified does not relate to the cooperative framework as such, but rather to its practical application. The practice of artificially dividing markets in order to circumvent the application of Article 11(6) Regulation 1/2003 and the *ne bis in idem* principle has a detrimental effect on the judicial protection afforded and poses a risk to the effective functioning of the cooperation framework in EU competition law. Therefore, the Commission should refrain from taking this approach.

Despite these gaps and risks, overall, the system of cooperation in the field of competition law functions well. The collaborative spirit of NCAs, combined with the voluntary mechanisms for case allocation and the extensive framework for cooperation, generally avoids positive norm overlaps and parallel procedures.[1472] The institutional and cooperation framework of competition law reflects the complexities of enforcement in the multi-level legal order of the EU. The decentralisation of EU competition law has shifted competences to the national level, but – at the same time – fostered a process of the Europeanisation of national procedural and institutional frameworks. The current framework combines the advantages of centralised and decentralised enforcement by building on strong networks and cooperation mechanisms.

1470. Communication from the Commission to the European Parliament and the Council, 9 July 2014, Ten Years of Antitrust Enforcement under Regulation 1/2003: Achievements and Future Perspectives, COM(2014)453 final, para. 26.
1471. *See* section 8.4.2.1.
1472. Brammer 2005, p. 1404.

CHAPTER 9

Cooperation: Competition Law, the DMA and the GDPR

9.1 INTRODUCTION

This chapter builds on the theoretical framework provided in Chapter 8 by studying *cross-disciplinary* cooperation mechanisms. The mechanisms for cooperation between enforcers of: (i) competition law and the DMA; and (ii) competition law and the GDPR are analysed in turn. The objective of this chapter is to map existing cooperation frameworks in these respective areas of the law in order to identify potential gaps in the frameworks.

To this end, section 9.2 introduces the institutional design of the DMA. Section 9.3 discusses cooperation between enforcers of competition law and the DMA, and section 9.4 provides a sub-conclusion in this regard. Section 9.5 analyses the institutional design of the GDPR, and section 9.6 studies the interaction between enforcers of competition law and the GDPR. Section 9.7 provides a sub-conclusion on cooperation between data protection and competition authorities. Next section 9.8 addresses the issue of polycentric cooperation, i.e., initiatives for cooperation between enforcers of more than two legal branches. In this analysis, broader fora for cooperation, such as the High-Level Group of Regulators (henceforth: High-Level Group), take centre stage. This Section also includes a discussion on the (un)desirability of establishing a 'super' regulator for digital markets. Lastly, section 9.9 provides the chapter's conclusion.

In accordance with the structure of the previous chapter (*see* cf. section 8.2), the relationship between competition law and the DMA, as well as the relationship between competition law and the GDPR, is analysed from multiple perspectives. I address: (i) the institutional design of the authorities concerned; and (ii) the existing mechanisms for cooperation in turn.

9.2 THE DMA: INSTITUTIONAL DESIGN

This Section examines the framework for cooperation between enforcers of competition law and the DMA. While competition law is enforced by the Commission *and* NCAs, DMA enforcement is notably more centralised. The Commission is the 'sole enforcer' and NCAs merely play a role during the investigative stage of DMA enforcement.[1473] This raises the question of how NCAs and the Commission should cooperate in the context of DMA and competition law enforcement. To address this question, this section addresses the level of centralisation of the DMA as well as the topic of agency mandates and portfolios.

9.2.1 Centralisation of the DMA

During the DMA's legislative procedure, the desirable level of enforcement generated significant debate. Initially, the Commission proposed a far-reaching form of centralisation with a very limited – or even nonexistent – role for NCAs. Ultimately, the role of NCAs was strengthened. Although the Commission remains the 'sole enforcer' of the DMA, Article 38(7) DMA permits NCAs to conduct investigations into non-compliance with the DMA.[1474]

Throughout the legislative procedure, various arguments were presented in favour of both a centralised and a decentralised approach. In the DMA Proposal and the Impact Assessment, the Commission advocated for a centralised model.[1475] This approach would be desirable since a decentralised system 'does not seem a convincible alternative', also in light of the 'risk of regulatory fragmentation' the DMA aims to address.[1476] Furthermore, decentralised enforcement would not be proportionate 'given the limited number of gatekeepers that would be in scope' of the DMA.[1477] These arguments are underscored by Monti who stresses that: (i) the global operation of gatekeepers; (ii) their similar operations across the EU and even the world; (iii) the high costs of ensuring compliance; (iv) the deep pockets of Big Tech;

1473. *See* sections 5.2.4 and 5.3.3.
1474. Preamble DMA, recital 91.
1475. Commission Staff Working Document Impact Assessment Report Accompanying the document Proposal of 15 December 2020 for a Regulation of the European Parliament and of the Council on contestable and fair markets in the digital sector (Digital Markets Act), SWD(2020)363 final.
1476. DMA Proposal, p. 9. *See also*: Chirico 2021, p. 498.
1477. DMA Proposal, p. 9.

and (v) the fact that the DMA is targeted at a relatively small number of firms justify a centralised approach.[1478]

Proponents of a more decentralised approach highlight the proven success of the decentralisation of competition law enforcement.[1479] Moreover, according to several Member States including The Netherlands and Germany, it would be desirable to involve NCAs in the enforcement of the DMA, particularly given the complementary relationship of competition law and the DMA.[1480] Over the years, NCAs have accumulated extensive experience with digital markets and leveraging this expertise could enhance synergies between competition law and the DMA.[1481] Beyond potential synergies, involving NCAs could improve the effectiveness of DMA enforcement. Neglecting their role may result in 'underutilization of existing resources causing an enforcement bottleneck and significant delays'.[1482] Although the DMA applies to a limited number of undertakings, NCAs argue that 'it will be difficult for the Commission alone to provide sufficient resources to enforce all obligations and prohibitions [...]'.[1483] Relying on NCA's could boost the capacity and lower costs for the Commission.[1484] Furthermore, NCAs could be valuable as their 'radar screen' is probably better.[1485] NCAs are arguably more accessible for complainants, since complicated procedures in Brussels constitute a hurdle for submitting a complaint or providing information.[1486] In comparison to the 'large, vertical and bureaucratic institution of the Commission', NCAs could be more approachable, especially given their proximity to the field.[1487] Lastly, involving NCAs in DMA enforcement could make cooperation between authorities easier.[1488]

In the final version of the DMA, the legislator adopted a *limited centralisation approach*:[1489] while the Commission retains its role as the sole enforcer of the DMA, NCAs can play a role in the investigative stage of

1478. Monti 2021a, p. 6.
1479. Schweitzer 2021, p. 32.
1480. Ministers of France, Germany and The Netherlands 27 May 2021, Friends of an effective Digital Markets Act – Strengthening the Digital Markets Act and Its Enforcement https://www.netherlandsandyou.nl/web/pr-eu-brussels/about-us/our-ideas-for-europe/digital-policy accessed 21 March 2025, p. 2.
1481. European Competition Network 2021; Schweitzer 2021, p. 32; Snoep 2021, p. 204.
1482. European Competition Network 2021, paras 20-21.
1483. European Competition Network 2021, para. 20; *See also*: Witt 2023, p. 657; Hoffman, Herrmann and Kestler 2024, p. 146.
1484. Crémer et al. 2023a, p. 323.
1485. European Competition Network 2021, paras 23-25.
1486. This is also highlighted by the President of the Dutch ACM: Snoep 2021. *See also*: Beems 2023, p. 22.
1487. McIntyre 2023, p. 274.
1488. European Competition Network 2021, paras 23-25.
1489. Hoffman, Herrmann and Kestler 2024.

enforcement.[1490] So far, various Member States, including Germany and The Netherlands, have already equipped their NCAs so that they can contribute to DMA enforcement.[1491]

The (academic) responses to this hybrid solution are mixed. According to McIntyre, this approach 'strikes an optimal institutional balance in its enforcement regime: maintaining centralised control whilst partially engaging the expertise and resources of national actors'.[1492] Other authors are more critical. Harrison, Zdzieborska and Wise, for instance, question whether the enforcement cooperation mechanisms under the DMA are sufficiently robust to provide adequate legal certainty.[1493] Furthermore, concerns have been raised about whether the DMA offers sufficient incentives to NCAs and Member States to engage in its enforcement.[1494] While NCAs can play a role in the investigative stage, they lack decision-making powers. The limited involvement reduces the recognition for their enforcement efforts which can be problematic in terms of political accountability at the national level.[1495]

Experiences with competition law, and Regulation 1/2003 in particular, demonstrate that the level of decentralisation within a particular legal field can adapt and change over time. The enforcement of competition law moved from a centralised to a decentralised mechanism after the establishment of a culture of competition law in the EU.[1496] Against this backdrop, the enforcement framework of the DMA may also evolve in the future. It is not unimaginable that the role of NCAs will expand over time, especially once the Commission gathers experience and provides further guidelines on the interpretation of the DMA.[1497] Keeping the evolution of competition law in mind, the EU legislator took a reasonable approach by opting for a limited centralisation approach. This approach does not disregard the position of NCAs but can facilitate the uniform application of the DMA. In due time, it should be examined whether there is room for strengthening the position of NCAs without jeopardising the coherent application of the instrument.

1490. Article 38(7) DMA.
1491. Voorstel Uitvoeringswet Verordening (EU) 2022/1925 van het Europees Parlement en de Raad van 14 september 2022 over betwistbare en eerlijke markten in de digitale sector, en tot wijziging van Richtlijnen (EU) 2019/1937 en (EU) 2020/1828, 2023-2024, 36 495, 2 (Uitvoeringswet digitalemarktenverordening) (Dutch Draft Implementing Act DMA); Section 32g GWB; *See also*: Reetz and Iken 2025.
1492. McIntyre 2023, p. 275.
1493. Harrison, Zdzieborska and Wise 2022, p. 59.
1494. Wagner-von Papp 2024, p. 343.
1495. De Streel et al. 2023, p. 185; Beems, Van de Gronden and Rusu 2023, p. 71.
1496. *See* sections 4.2.3 and 8.3.1.
1497. Witt 2023, p. 657.

9.2.2 Agency Mandates and Portfolios

The discussions on the institutional design of the DMA did not merely address its limited centralisation approach but also included the question of which DG would be best placed to enforce the instrument. This debate is linked to the Commission's internal division of tasks. The DMA is not a competition instrument but clearly shares common denominators with this area of the law.[1498] Consequently, it was not clear-cut which DG of the Commission would be best placed to take up the enforcement task. As explained in section 5.2.4.1, the DMA is enforced by a joint team in DG COMP and DG CONNECT. The fact that DMA enforcement has been shaped as a joint effort should be applauded. Since the DMA is a hybrid between competition law and 'traditional' regulation, the combined enforcement by DG COMP and DG CONNECT is a well-balanced institutional approach, reflecting the complex nature of the DMA. Moreover, combined efforts of different DGs have also 'worked well' in the past.[1499]

Despite the potential benefits of joint teams, in the context of the DMA, the Commission's internal division of tasks still raises some questions. *First,* neither the DMA nor the supporting documents provide adequate background on the rationale behind working in joint teams. Former Commissioner Breton shared some insights in a speech but overall the reasons behind the institutional design remain opaque.[1500] This is problematic, particularly because the current institutional set-up was not the only reasonable approach. The ECN proposed another solution by arguing in favour of enforcement by DG COMP.[1501] It would be valuable to understand how these institutional choices were made and which arguments played a decisive role in shaping the DMA's institutional framework. *Second,* information on the division of tasks or procedures governing the interplay between different units is rarely publicly available.[1502] The DMA Annual Report, for example, touches on the topic of cooperation between the Commission and national authorities, with a particular focus on the ECN and the High-Level Group. However, the interrelationship between different DGs within the Commission is not taken into consideration.[1503] Yet, and as stressed in the context of the integration of

---

1498. *See* sections 5.3 and 5.4.
1499. De Streel and Alexiadis refer to the revised regulatory framework for electronic communication of 2002, which was initially enforced by a Joint Task force constituted by members of the former DG COMP and the former DG CONNECT. Over time, the supervisory role was passed on to DG CONNECT. *See:* De Streel and Alexiadis 2023, p. 112.
1500. Breton 2022.
1501. European Competition Network 2021.
1502. *See also*: Beems 2023, p. 22.
1503. Annual report on Regulation (EU) 2022/1925 of the European Parliament and of the Council of 6 March 2024 on contestable and fair markets in the digital sector and amending Directives (EU) 2019/1937 and (EU) 2020/1828 (Digital Markets Act) (henceforth: Annual Report DMA 2023).

different authorities, the mere fact that different enforcers or units operate under one roof is not sufficient to ensure coherent enforcement or to leverage synergies effectively.[1504] Rather, internal mechanisms for cooperation should facilitate the interaction between the different units.[1505] Considering DMA enforcement by the Commission, these mechanisms are not publicly available. It remains, therefore, uncertain whether the different units interact effectively.

The relevance of agency mandates and portfolios is not limited to the EU level. Also, at the national level, the DMA interplays with multiple legal branches and, therefore, requires cooperation between different types of enforcers.[1506] This cooperation is particularly complicated in Member States where multiple authorities are involved in the enforcement of rules relating to unilateral conduct. In these circumstances, more than one authority can qualify as the authority referred to in Article 1(6) DMA. In the Dutch context, this issue does not arise due to the integrated model of the ACM.[1507] Chairman of the ACM, Martijn Snoep, mentions this as an additional benefit of an integrated model.[1508] In Germany, the telecommunication supervisor and NCA are not integrated.[1509] While the *Bundeskartellamt* is the authority competent to carry out investigations into non-compliance with the DMA, Section 32g(2) GWB also acknowledges the position of the German telecom supervisor, the *Bundesnetzagentur*. According to this provision, the *Bundeskartellamt* must provide the *Bundesnetzagentur* with the possibility to comment on inquiries in the context of Article 7 DMA, which establishes obligations for gatekeepers regarding the interoperability of number-independent interpersonal communication services.

9.3 THE DMA: COOPERATION

As explained in Chapter 5, the DMA overlaps (to some degree) with other EU and national legal frameworks, resulting in overlapping competences between enforcers. The DMA addresses this overlap by establishing various mechanisms for cooperation and distinguishes between: (i) authorities within

---

1504. *See* section 8.2.1.
1505. In this light, Podszun and Marsden argue for 'a much stronger interplay between, in particular, DG COMP and DG CNCT in enforcing the new rules effectively'. The enforcement of the DMA necessitates 'much stronger collaboration between COMP and CNCT, utilising their respective strengths on rulemaking and interpretation on the one hand and evidence-based attention to market developments on the other'. *See:* Marsden and Podszun 2020, pp. 50-51.
1506. *See* Synthesis I: Part II.
1507. *See* sections 4.3.3.1 and 8.3.2.
1508. Snoep 2021, p. 205.
1509. *See* sections 4.4.3.1 and 8.3.2.

the meaning of Article 1(6) DMA, such as NCAs; and (ii) other authorities.[1510] While the DMA establishes an extensive cooperation framework regarding cooperation between authorities within the meaning of Article 1(6) DMA, the cooperation with other authorities receives far less attention. Article 37 DMA establishes that 'the Commission and Member States shall work in close cooperation and coordinate their enforcement actions to ensure coherent, effective and complementary enforcement of available legal instruments applied to gatekeepers'. Although the DMA establishes several fora for the facilitation of this cooperation, in comparison to the rules governing the position of NCAs, it contains few elaborate procedural rules addressing the position of other national enforcers. Since the DMA's intersection with other regulatory instruments does not fall within the scope of the analysis, this Section focuses on mechanisms for cooperation in the context of DMA and competition law enforcement.

9.3.1 Fora for Cooperation

The DMA establishes and endorses multiple fora for cooperation between the Commission, national authorities and European bodies. This Section addresses the different fora in turn.

9.3.1.1 The European Competition Network

Article 38(1) DMA establishes that '[t]he Commission and national competent authorities of the Member States enforcing the rules referred to in Article 1(6) shall cooperate with each other and inform each other about their respective enforcement action through the European Competition Network'. The ECN allows the authorities concerned to make the necessary arrangements for cooperation and for the exchange of information. By relying on the ECN, the EU legislator has opted for extending the scope of an existing and well-functioning network.[1511] The reliance on an existing forum has efficiency benefits and may realise cooperation within a relatively short timeframe.[1512] Notwithstanding these benefits, the ECN was established as a *competition law* forum. Since it is formally not a part of the competition law framework, opting for the use of the ECN is a remarkable choice. According to the Network Notice, the ECN is *a forum for discussion and cooperation in the application and enforcement of [EU] competition policy.*[1513] If the DMA is indeed not a competition law instrument, why would cooperation

1510. De Streel et al. 2023, p. 184.
1511. *See* section 8.4.1.1.
1512. Graef 2024, p. 175.
1513. Network Notice, para. 1.

take place within a *competition* network?[1514] By adding cooperation in the field of the DMA to the responsibilities of the ECN, Article 38 DMA extends the scope of the ECN. Accordingly, it would be advisable to revise the Network Notice and specify that the ECN also serves as a forum for discussion and cooperation in the application of the DMA.

Despite the fact that the ECN is the main forum for cooperation in the context of competition law and the DMA, the DMA may require cooperation between the Commission and authorities that are not part of the ECN. In both Germany and The Netherlands, NCAs are appointed to monitor DMA compliance. These NCAs are already part of the ECN which makes cooperation relatively straightforward.[1515] However, the concept of 'national competent authorities enforcing the rules referred to in Article 1(6) DMA' does not merely cover NCAs. Member States are not obliged to appoint their competition authority as competent supervisor: they can also grant competences to another existing or new institution. In this regard, Article 38(1) DMA establishes that when an authority is not a member of the ECN 'the Commission shall make the necessary arrangements for cooperation and exchange of information on cases concerning the enforcement of [the DMA] and the enforcement of cases referred to in Article 1(6) of such authorities'. Consequently, if the monitoring of the DMA is the responsibility of authorities other than NCAs, cooperation must be arranged bilaterally or ad hoc. It is reasonable to refrain from discussions with non-members within the context of the ECN. Allowing different institutions and entities to participate in ECN meetings could be detrimental to the functioning of the network, and the Network Notice does not leave room for this approach.[1516] The Annual Review of the DMA does not elaborate on such ad hoc agreements but only states that 'cooperation between the Commission and national authorities, and in particular national competition authorities, has taken place mainly through the European Competition Network (ECN)'.[1517]

In sum, the ECN is the 'key venue' for cooperation and for the exchange of information between NCAs and the Commission.[1518] As noted in section 8.4.1.1, the ECN has functioned well in the past and has contributed to the good relationships between competition authorities in the EU. Therefore, the

---

1514. According to Witt, 'the role of DG COMP in enforcing the DMA, and the – more limited – involvement of the ECN and national competition authorities, could be seen as evidence that the DMA is an instrument of EU competition law'. *See:* Witt 2023, p. 649.

1515. The German framework establishes an obligation for the *Bundeskartellamt* to consult the *Bundesnetzagentur* in certain circumstances. *See* section 9.2.2.

1516. The Network Notice makes clear the ECN comprises of NCAs and the Commission (*see*, for example: Network Notice, para. 1). ACM Chairman Martijn Snoep highlights that it would not be desirable to involve different authorities and ministries with broad competences in ECN meetings with DMA subjects. *See:* Snoep 2021, p. 205.

1517. Annual Report DMA 2023, para. 42.

1518. Graef 2024, p. 175.

ECN will likely contribute to the achievement of constructive cooperation between NCAs and the Commission.[1519] However, despite this potential, certain open questions remain. The position of authorities within the meaning of Article 1(6) DMA that are not part of the ECN is, for example, less clear. Moreover, the Network Notice will need updating.

9.3.1.2 Other Fora

The ECN is not the only relevant forum for cooperation in the context of the DMA. The *High-Level Group of Regulators* and the *Digital Markets Advisory Committee* also play important roles. These fora do not merely govern the interaction between competition law and the DMA but have a broader application. Since these fora transcend the interaction between the DMA and competition law and are, consequently, polycentric in nature, these initiatives are discussed in section 9.8.1.

9.3.2 Mechanisms for Cooperation

This Section addresses the specific cooperation mechanisms governing the interaction between the Commission and authorities within the meaning of Article 1(6) DMA. Given the scope of the analysis and given the fact that NCAs are appointed as the national authority to monitor DMA compliance in both Germany and The Netherlands, this section assesses the aforementioned mechanisms in the context of national competition authorities.

Apart from the general obligation to cooperate as stressed in Article 38(1) DMA, the relationship between NCAs and the Commission is subject to more specific provisions on cooperation. These mechanisms establish, *inter alia*, rules on notification, on the exchange of information and on assistance. The mechanisms for cooperation established in the DMA clearly draw inspiration from Regulation 1/2003.

The DMA lays down obligations for NCAs to inform the Commission about enforcement actions relating to national laws referred to in Article 1(6) DMA. When an NCA intends to start an investigation into the conduct of a gatekeeper, it shall inform the Commission.[1520] Moreover, if an NCA intends to impose obligations on gatekeepers based on national laws referred to in Article 1(6) DMA, it is obliged to communicate the draft measure, including the reason for adopting the measure, to the Commission no later than 30 days before adoption of the decision.[1521] In the case of interim measures, the Commission should be informed as soon as possible and at the latest immediately after adopting such measures. Information on the launch of an investigation or the enforcement of the rules referred to in Article 1(6) DMA

1519. Graef 2024, p. 175.
1520. Article 38(2) DMA.
1521. Article 38(3) DMA.

may also be made available to other NCAs.[1522] In the competition law context, it became clear that there is a debate as to the effects of a violation of these obligations. This debate can be transposed to the obligation to notify the Commission in the context of Article 38(2) and (3) DMA. As explained in section 8.4.2.3, decisions adopted in violation of Article 11(4) Regulation 1/2003 are not necessarily unenforceable and invalid since the provision does not confer rights upon individuals. A similar line of reasoning can be applied to decisions adopted in violation of Article 38(2) and 38(3) DMA. Consequently, a decision adopted in violation of these provisions is not necessarily invalid and unenforceable.[1523]

Furthermore, the DMA allows NCAs and the Commission to exchange information. According to Article 38(5) DMA, information exchanged pursuant to Article 38(1), (2) and (3) DMA 'shall only be exchanged and used for the purposes of the coordination of the enforcement of this Regulation and the rules referred to in Article 1(6) DMA'. This means that the information exchanged can be used in the context of EU competition law, national competition rules with an EU equivalent and national rules prohibiting other forms of unilateral conduct. A strict reading of Article 38(5) DMA implies that the information exchanged cannot be used to coordinate the enforcement of the DMA and national regulatory instruments that do not qualify as competition law. The distinction between national competition rules and other regulatory instruments is not always clear-cut.[1524] In this light, it is not always evident whether a national instrument falls under Article 1(6) or 1(5) DMA. Yet, the qualification of a national framework has serious consequences for the extent to which information exchanged can be used. This constitutes yet another argument for clarifying the distinction between national competition laws and other regulatory instruments. Furthermore, Article 38(5) DMA puts forward that the information exchanged may only be used for coordination. The purpose limitation of this provision is thus narrower than that of Article 12(3) Regulation 1/2003.[1525]

As explained earlier, Member States can empower national authorities to play a role in the investigatory stage of DMA enforcement. If an NCA intends to conduct an investigation into non-compliance with the DMA, it shall inform the Commission in writing before taking the first investigative measure.[1526] If the Commission, at this stage or later on, decides to start an investigation, NCAs are relieved of the possibility of conducting a DMA investigation. As discussed in section 7.5.3, an investigation by the Commission has a pre-emptive effect. In this scenario, apart from the pre-emptive

1522. Article 38(3) DMA.
1523. CJEU 30 April 1966 Case C-194/94, CIA Security International, paras 49-54; CJEU 13 July 1989 Case 380/87, *Enichem Base v. Comuni di Cinisello Balsamo*, paras 19-24. *See* section 8.4.2.3.
1524. *See* sections 7.4.1 and 7.5.2.
1525. Gappa and Käseberg 2024, p. 460. *See* section 8.4.2.4.
1526. *See also*: Podszun 2022a.

dynamic, an obligation to cooperate arises. NCAs are required to report to the Commission on their findings in order to support the Commission in its role as sole enforcer of the DMA.[1527]

Apart from the obligation to inform the Commission, the DMA establishes several mechanisms which allow national authorities to assist the Commission in enforcing the DMA. In other words, NCAs may participate in certain enforcement tasks after being informed by or at the request of the Commission.[1528] Article 21(5) DMA establishes that the Commission can request NCAs to provide all relevant information in their possession to carry out its duties under the DMA. Article 22(2) DMA provides that, in the case of interviews, the Commission shall inform the NCA in whose territory the interview takes place. Upon request of the NCA, its officials may assist the Commission in conducting the interview. In order to carry out inspections, the Commission may request the assistance of NCAs according to Article 23(3) DMA. Moreover, Article 38(6) DMA states that the Commission can ask NCAs to provide support in any of its market investigations pursuant to the DMA.

The cooperation mechanisms establish certain obligations for NCAs but also grant Member States certain rights. For instance, Article 41 DMA sets out that three or more Member States may request the Commission to open a market investigation relating to the designation of a gatekeeper, to the addition of one or more services to the list of core platform services or to practices that are not effectively addressed by the DMA. Moreover, one or more Member States may request the Commission to launch a market investigation into systemic infringements. Member States must submit evidence in support of their request, and the Commission shall examine whether there are reasonable grounds for opening a market investigation.[1529]

9.4 SUB-CONCLUSION DMA

The DMA establishes various cooperating mechanisms governing its complementary application with competition law. In shaping cooperation between the Commission and national competition authorities, the DMA clearly draws inspiration from the cooperative frameworks established in a competition law context. The ECN serves as the most relevant forum for cooperation between the Commission and NCAs, also in the context of the DMA. According to the Annual Review of the DMA, the ECN was used to

1527. Article 38(7) DMA.
1528. Witt 2023, pp. 656-657.
1529. Article 41(4)(5) DMA.

exchange information between the Commission and NCAs.[1530] The system of notification, assistance and regulatory pre-emption clearly builds upon existing arrangements in the field of competition law. Despite the fact that Regulation 1/2003 has inspired the cooperative framework of the DMA, important changes have been implemented.

First, the DMA extends the cooperation within the ECN.[1531] Under Regulation 1/2003, the application of *EU* competition law triggered the cooperation mechanisms. An NCA's violation of the duty of parallel application can therefore jeopardise the functioning of the system (*see* cf. section 8.4.2.1). The notification system under the DMA is not limited to the application of EU law but also covers the application of certain national laws by NCAs. If an NCA applies the laws mentioned in Article 1(6) DMA, including national competition law and other national rules governing unilateral behaviour, the Commission should be notified. This means that the duty for national authorities to inform the Commission is clearly extended under the DMA.

Second, Regulation 1/2003 should be considered an intra-branch instrument: it covers cooperation between enforcers operating exclusively within the field of competition law. The cooperation mechanisms introduced in the context of the DMA are cross-disciplinary. Since the DMA is formally not an instrument of competition law, this concerns cooperation between enforcers of different legal branches.[1532] In this context, when enforcing the DMA, the Commission does not act in its capacity as a competition law enforcer.

In conclusion, the DMA establishes a rather elaborate framework in order to streamline cooperation between NCAs and the Commission as sole enforcer of the DMA. The DMA does not only provide a forum for cooperation but also sets out specific mechanisms for notification and the exchange of information. Despite the open questions and challenges identified in this Section, it is commendable that the DMA does explicitly address the issue of cooperation between authorities. The mechanisms set out can help to realise cooperation in DMA and competition law enforcement.

9.5 THE GDPR: INSTITUTIONAL DESIGN

This Section addresses the mechanisms for cooperation between competition and data protection law authorities. In the aftermath of the *Meta Bundeskartellamt* case – which is discussed in more detail in section 4.4.2.3 – it became

1530. According to the Annual Review of the DMA, '[t]o date, cooperation between the Commission and national authorities, and in particular national competition authorities, has taken place mainly through the ECN'. *See:* Annual Report DMA 2023, para. 42.
1531. Maher 2024, p. 278.
1532. *See* Chapter 5.

apparent that competition authorities can integrate GDPR-related concerns in their competition law assessments. This type of norm overlap underscores and amplifies the need for cross-disciplinary cooperation between these authorities.[1533] Following the structure outlined in section 8.2, this Section starts with an overview of the institutional design of data protection authorities. In order to properly understand the institutional dynamics at play, the institutional design of data protection authorities must be clearly conceptualised. Consequently, the analysis starts with an overview of: (i) the level of decentralisation of GDPR enforcement; and (ii) agency mandates in data protection law. Subsequently, the available mechanisms for cooperation are examined in the section 9.6.

9.5.1 Decentralisation and the GDPR

As explained in section 6.3.3, in the context of the GDPR, the EU legislator opted for a *decentralised enforcement model* meaning that the instrument is enforced at the Member State level. For cross-border cases, the GDPR introduced a system for allocating competences in order to streamline cooperation between DPAs.[1534] According to Article 56(1) GDPR, in the case of cross-border processing, the supervisory authority of the *main* or *single establishment* of the controller or processor shall be competent to act as the lead supervisory authority. This means that the GDPR – for cross-border cases – adopts a *country of origin model.*[1535] This mechanism aims to prevent parallel proceedings and provides a tool for case allocation among DPAs.[1536]

The one-stop shop mechanism and country of origin model are, contrary to the Commission's initial approach, not absolute.[1537] Rather, the GDPR establishes a 'complex cooperation and assistance framework between all

1533. CJEU 4 July 2023 Case C-252/22, *Meta Bundeskartellamt.*

1534. According to Article 4(23) GDRP, *cross-border processing* means either 'processing of personal data which takes place in the context of the activities of establishments in more than one Member State of a controller or processer in the Union where the controller or processor is established in more than one Member State' or 'processing of personal data which takes place in the context of the activities of a single establishment of a controller or processor in the Union but which substantially affects or is likely to affect data subjects in more than one Member State'.

1535. De Streel and Monti 2022, p. 18.

1536. Galetta and De Hert 2015.

1537. In the initial Proposal for the GDPR, the one-stop-shop mechanisms was more absolute. According to Article 51(2) of this Proposal, in case of cross-border processing 'the supervisory authority of the main establishment of the controller or processor shall be competent for the supervision of the processing activities of the controller or processor in all Member States'. *See:* Proposal of 25 January 2012 for a Regulation of the European Parliament and of the Council on the protection of individuals with regard to the processing of personal data and on the free movement of such data (General Data Protection Regulation), COM(2012)11 final.

DPAs involved in cross-border processing activities'.[1538] The GDPR, for example, allows DPAs apart from the lead supervisory authority to conduct independent supervisory activities in exceptional cases.[1539] On top of this, the lead supervisory authority is required to involve other DPAs according to the cooperation and consistency mechanisms established in the GDPR. Therefore, the lead supervisory authority does not act entirely on its own.[1540]

Article 60 GDPR states that the lead supervisory authority shall cooperate with the other supervisory authorities concerned and shall endeavour to seek consensus.[1541] To this end, the GDPR contains several provisions relating to mutual assistance and the exchange of information.[1542] Additionally, the GDPR establishes a *consistency mechanism.*[1543] The lead supervisory authority shall communicate a draft decision to the other supervisory authorities. These authorities can submit their relevant and reasoned objections to the draft decision within four weeks.[1544] The lead supervisory authority can decide to follow these reasoned objections and send a revised draft decision to the other supervisory authorities concerned.[1545] If the leading supervisory authority decides to refrain from following the objections, it shall submit the matter to the dispute resolution mechanism under Article 63 GDPR.[1546]

The consistency mechanism aims to contribute to the GDPR's consistent application throughout the EU.[1547] If the lead supervisory authority and other authorities concerned cannot reach consensus, the EDPB (*see* cf. section 6.2.4) may intervene by adopting a binding decision concerning all

---

1538. Matos Brandao 2023, p. 316. *See also*: CJEU 15 June 2021 Case C-645/19, *Facebook v. Belgian DPA*.
1539. Despite the fact that a data processor is established in multiple Member States, each supervisory authority not acting as lead supervisory authority remains competent to handle local cases concerning processing carried out in a single Member State and involving only data subjects in that single Member State. In such circumstances, the lead supervisory authority should be informed. The lead supervisory authority may decide to handle the case in accordance with the consistency mechanism of Article 60 GDPR. *See:* Article 56(2) GDPR and Preamble GDPR, recital 127.
1540. Gentile and Lynskey 2022, p. 704.
1541. According to Article 4(22) GDPR, 'supervisory authority concerned' means a supervisory authority which is concerned by the processing of data because, '(a) the controller or processor is established on the territory of the Member State that is the supervisory authority, (b) data subjects residing in the Member State of that supervisory authority are substantially affected or likely to be substantially affected by the processing or (c) a complaint has been lodged with that supervisory authority'.
1542. *See, e.g.,* Article 61 GDPR.
1543. The EPDB provides further Guidelines on the Application of Article 60 GDPR. *See:* European Data Protection Board, Guidelines of 14 March 2022 on the application of Article 60 GDPR, 02/2022.
1544. Article 60(3) GDPR.
1545. Article 60(5) GDPR.
1546. Article 60(4) GDPR.
1547. Article 63 GDPR.

matters which are the subject of the relevant and reasoned objections.[1548] According to Article 65(3) GDPR, this decision shall be adopted by a two-thirds majority of the members of the EDPB.[1549]

So far, the GDPR's allocation of competences and consistency mechanism has sparked debate, particularly in the context of large platforms. The unwillingness of lead supervisory authorities to act or impose sanctions can lead to a deadlock, thereby jeopardising the effective application of the GDPR. A case concerning a GDPR violation by Meta shows that the consistency mechanism can play an important role in practice. In this case, the Irish DPA – acting as the lead supervisory authority – ordered Meta to bring its processing operations in compliance with Chapter V GDPR by suspending the future transfers of personal data to the US.[1550] However, the Irish authority did not intend to impose a fine. This raised objections from various other DPAs who argued that imposing a fine would be appropriate in addition to the suspension of the violations.[1551]

Ultimately, the consistency mechanism was triggered, and the EDPB adopted a binding decision. In this binding decision, the EDPB stressed that the Irish DPA's decision to refrain from imposing a fine did not meet the relevant requirements of the GDPR. The EDPB ordered the Irish authority to impose a fine which was to be determined on the basis of the factors listed in Article 83(2) GDPR. The EDPB did not suggest a specific amount, but listed various relevant factors, such as the gravity of the infringement, the very large scope of the processing and the high numbers of data subjects affected. Furthermore, the fact that Meta committed the infringement with the 'highest degree of negligence' and bears a 'high level of responsibility' should be taken into consideration.[1552] Ultimately, and after the involvement of the EDPB, the Irish DPA imposed a fine of EUR 1.2 billion.[1553] Meta appealed the decision of the Irish DPA, as well as the EDPBs decision.[1554] In the latter procedure, Meta not only raised objections to the EDPB's decision

1548. Article 65 GDPR.
1549. The role of the EDPB is not limited to dispute resolution. The EPDB can, for example, also act if DPAs do not fulfil their duties of mutual assistance, and plays an important role in promoting the exchange of information. *See also*: Matos Brandao 2023.
1550. Data Protection Commissioner, Press Release of 22 May 2023, Data Protection Commission announces conclusion of inquiry into Meta Ireland https://www.dataprotection.ie/en/news-media/press-releases/Data-Protection-Commission-announces-conclusion-of-inquiry-into-Meta-Ireland accessed 24 March 2025.
1551. European Data Protection Board 12 May 2023 IN-20-8-1, Meta Platforms Ireland (previously known as Facebook Ireland Limited).
1552. European Data Protection Board 12 May 2023 IN-20-8-1, Meta Platforms Ireland (previously known as Facebook Ireland Limited), para. 272.
1553. Data Protection Commissioner, Press Release of 22 May 2023, Data Protection Commission announces conclusion of inquiry into Meta Ireland https://www.dataprotection.ie/en/news-media/press-releases/Data-Protection-Commission-announces-conclusion-of-inquiry-into-Meta-Ireland accessed 24 March 2025.
1554. Meta 2023.

in this case but also challenged the general legality of the consistency mechanisms before the GC.[1555] Consequently, the GC's decision in this case will be of the utmost importance for the GDPR's current institutional set-up. The case is currently still pending.

The *Meta v. EDPB* case clearly illustrates the relevance of institutional design and choices. The case demonstrates how the consistency mechanism can play an important role in countering the negative effects of the enforcement bottlenecks that may arise as a result of the decentralised and country-of-origin model of the GDPR. At the same time, this case once again shows the potential conflict that may arise between regulators. The Irish authority has appealed various EDPB decisions.[1556] This reveals a tension between the Irish DPA and the EDPB as well as their disagreement on the application and interpretation of the GDPR.[1557]

The shortcomings of the GDPR's cooperation mechanisms have been acknowledged in both literature and policy-making.[1558] Gentile and Lynskey, for example, highlight the fact that the cooperation mechanism is subject to minimal procedural rules and that there is a lack of clarity regarding key concepts. The EDPB also addressed the matter by publishing Guidelines on Article 60 GDPR in order to 'analyse and give guidance on the concrete application [of Article 60]'.[1559] With the Guidelines, the EPDB envisions that 'an ethos and obligation of sincere cooperation should permeate the interpretation and application of Article 60 GDPR'.[1560] Despite the EDPB's efforts, in a review of the GDPR, the Commission highlighted that 'further progress is needed to make the handling of cross-border cases more efficient and more harmonised'.[1561] To this end, the Commission has submitted a Proposal for a regulation laying down additional procedural rules for the enforcement of the GDPR. This proposed Regulation, *inter alia*, aims to reinforce existing cooperation mechanisms by addressing the 'disparities in the form and structure of relevant and reasoned objections submitted by DPAs concerned during the cross-border procedure'.[1562] Since the existing

1555. GC Case T-325/23, *Meta Platforms Ireland v. European Data Protection Board* (Case in Progress).
1556. GC 29 January 2025 Joined Cases T-70/23, T-84/23 and T-111/23, *Data Protection Commission v. European Data Protection Board.*
1557. Francis 2023, p. 169.
1558. Gentile and Lynskey 2022, p. 807; Gellert 2024.
1559. European Data Protection Board, Guidelines of 14 March 2022 on the application of Article 60 GDPR, 02/2022, para. 4.
1560. Gentile and Lynskey 2022.
1561. Communication from the Commission to the European Parliament and the Council of 24 June 2020, Data Protection as a pillar of citizens' empowerment and the EU's approach to the digital transition – two years of application of the General Data Protection Directive, COM(2020)264 final, p. 5.
1562. Proposal for a Regulation of the European Parliament and Council of 4 July 2023 on a Regulation laying down additional procedural rules relating to the enforcement of Regulation 2016/679, COM(2023)348 final, p. 3.

disparities may be detrimental to the 'efficient conclusion of the dispute resolution procedure', the proposed regulation lays down further details in this regard.[1563] The proposal, for example, lays down detailed requirements for the form and structure of relevant and reasoned opinions, specifies the information to be provided by the lead DPA, clarifies the role of all the actors involved and introduces procedural deadlines for the dispute resolution mechanism.[1564]

In sum, the GDPR provides a complex and extensive framework for the allocation of competences in cross-border cases. The starting position is a decentralised system based on the country of origin principle. At the same time, both the decentralisation and the country of origin principle are not absolute. In certain circumstances, the EDPB – a *European* body composed of different DPAs – can issue a binding opinion. In such cases, the system is thus not fully decentralised.

The current institutional system of the GDPR comes with significant challenges. The effective use of the consistency mechanism may partially resolve these challenges since an intervention by the EDPB can resolve a deadlock resulting from the lead supervisory authority's unwillingness to act. Currently, the consistency mechanism is subject to ongoing proceedings before the GC and to upcoming legislative changes. The upcoming developments will be relevant for the competition and data protection law interplay because they will determine with *which data protection authority* a competition authority should cooperate.

9.5.2 Agency Mandates and Portfolios

The issue of agency mandates and portfolios of competition authorities has been a topic of ongoing debate. Although data protection authorities tended to have less complicated portfolios, current trends show that the portfolios of data protection authorities are also broadening and, hence, becoming more complex. In The Netherlands, the Dutch DPA, for example, acts as the coordinating supervisor in the field of algorithms and AI.[1565]

In the context of the expansion of DPA's agency mandates, the question arises of whether the enforcement of competition and data protection law should become the responsibility of a single integrated authority. Reyna

1563. Proposal for a Regulation of the European Parliament and Council of 4 July 2023 on a Regulation laying down additional procedural rules relating to the enforcement of Regulation 2016/679, COM(2023)348 final, p. 3.
1564. Proposal for a Regulation of the European Parliament and Council of 4 July 2023 on a Regulation laying down additional procedural rules relating to the enforcement of Regulation 2016/679, COM(2023)348 final, p. 5.
1565. *See:* Autoriteit Persoonsgegeves Directie Coördinatie Algoritmes, 'Werkagenda coördinered algoritmetoezicht in 2024' (2024) https://www.autoriteitpersoonsgegevens.nl/documenten/werkagenda-coordinerend-algoritmetoezicht-2024 accessed 24 March 2025.

discusses the possibility of the merging data protection authorities with other national bodies.[1566] This institutional proposal is reminiscent of the Dutch debates on the integration of the ACM (*see* cf. section 8.3.2). In my view, merging DPAs and NCAs is neither feasible nor desirable. By merging data protection and competition authorities, the policy coherence of the integrated authority cannot be ensured. Despite the fact that there is a clear link between data protection and competition law, the respective legal branches have distinct characteristics and diverge on various points. DPAs are not merely market supervisors, but have an important task related to the protection of the fundamental right to data protection and privacy as well. This function is not sufficiently related to the tasks of NCAs to justify a merger of the authorities. On top of this, an integrated authority is arguably hard to reconcile with the GDPR's strict independence requirement. Article 52 GDPR requires the *complete independence* of DPAs. In this context, the Article 29 Working Party – the predecessor of the EDPB – opposed granting an excessively large role to the Commission within the EDPB. [1567] In a similar vein, merging DPAs and NCAs could constrain this complete independence. In my view, the EU (data protection) framework puts up an insurmountable obstacle.

9.6 THE GDPR AND COMPETITION LAW: COOPERATION

This Section studies the cooperation mechanisms governing the interaction between competition authorities (i.e., the Commission and NCAs) and DPAs. As explained above, unlike the field of competition law, the GDPR is largely enforced in accordance with the country of origin principle. Due to this divergence in the allocation of competences, the relevant NCA and DPA are not necessarily based in one and the same Member State. This means that cooperation can be either mono- or multi-jurisdictional.[1568] Both dimensions will be addressed in turn.

9.6.1 Mono-Jurisdictional Cooperation

The Section analyses mono-jurisdictional cooperation between data protection and competition authorities. In line with the scope of the research, I examine The Netherlands, Germany and the EU in turn.

1566. Reyna 2024, p. 17.
1567. Article 29 Working Party 23 March 2012, Opinion 01/2012 on the data protection reform proposals, 00530/12/EN WP 191, p. 17.
1568. *See* Synthesis I: Part II.

9.6.1.1 The Netherlands

In *The Netherlands,* the cooperation between the Dutch DPA and NCA is governed by the *Samenwerkingsprotocol tussen Autoriteit Consument en Markt en Autoriteit Persoonsgegevens* (Cooperation Protocol ACM and AP) (henceforth: Cooperation Protocol).[1569] Additionally, both the ACM and AP are part of some polycentric initiatives, including the *Markttoezichthoudersberaad* (Market Supervisory Council) (henceforth: MTB) and the *Samenwerkingsplatform Digitale Toezichthouders* (Cooperation Platform Digital Supervisors) (henceforth: SDT). This Section focuses on the Cooperation Protocol. The MTB and SDT are, given their polycentric and cross-disciplinary nature, discussed in section 9.8.1.

The main purpose of the Cooperation Protocol is: (i) to set out general principles for cooperation and to establish arrangements on the exchange of information between the AP and the ACM; and (ii) to establish general principles for handing matters where the tasks assigned to the respective authorities are related or overlapping.[1570] Cooperation under the Cooperation Protocol covers multiple topics, including the issues of 'payment' with personal data and the relevance of data for competition in markets.[1571] Furthermore, the Cooperation Protocol ensures that arrangements do not have to be made on an ad hoc basis, while its public availability enhances transparency regarding the cooperation between the ACM and the AP.[1572]

The exchange of information and communication between authorities is a key element of the cooperative relationship.[1573] Article 8 of the Cooperation Protocol emphasises that the authorities can inform each other about relevant developments related to their respective tasks as well as about upcoming press releases and publications. When the AP and ACM participate in fora for international cooperation, they may share relevant information, insofar as this is not prevented by the confidentiality principle. Additionally, the ACM and AP can alert each other to potential violations within the exclusive area of competence of the other authority. Beyond general information-sharing mechanisms, Article 7 Cooperation Protocol establishes specific rules for the exchange of data and information. In order to exchange

1569. Samenwerkingsprotocol tussen Autoriteit Consument en Markt en Autoriteit Persoonsgegevens, 18 June 2020, Staatscourant 2020, 36741 (henceforth: Cooperation Protocol).
1570. Article 2 Cooperation Protocol.
1571. ACM Besluit 21 maart 2023, ACM/UIT/594498 https://www.acm.nl/system/files/documents/woo-besluit-over-samenwerkinsprotocol-acm-en-ap.pdf accessed 24 March 2025.
1572. Preamble Cooperation Protocol.
1573. Article 3 Cooperation Protocol stresses that the authorities shall realise an *efficient and careful exchange of information* (*een een efficiënte en zorgvuldige uitwisseling van informatie*).

(sensitive) information, authorities need a legal basis.[1574] The Cooperation Protocol's provisions on the exchange of information are established in formal law. Article 19(2) GDPR Implementation Act and Article 7(2)(a) Establishment Act ACM provide a legal basis for the respective authorities. The Cooperation Protocol further elaborates on the exchange of information, stating in Article 7(3) that information cannot be used for a purpose other than that for which it was provided.[1575] Lastly, arguably the Cooperation Protocol does not merely establish a possibility to cooperate and exchange information, but arguably also a duty. In some circumstances, the sharing of information is mandatory when requested.[1576]

Apart from the provisions relating to the exchange of information, the Cooperation Protocol also defines practical aspects of the interaction between the ACM and the AP. For instance, Article 4 Cooperation Protocol stipulates that both organisations must designate a first point of contact for the other supervisor. Furthermore, according to Article 5 Cooperation Protocol, the authorities consult at least once a year, but more frequently if needed. Consultation can take place at either the managerial or at staff level.

The ACM has published some interesting insights on its cooperation with the AP, highlighting the potential of the bilateral agreement and the structural cooperation between the two authorities.[1577] It emphasised that the Dutch arrangement and degree of cooperation can serve as an example for other Member States. Yet, in practice, the experiences with cooperation have been mixed. Challenges arose, for example, because the Dutch DPA was reluctant to provide advice due to a lack of capacity. Additionally, notwithstanding the existing legal basis, the ACM has appeared hesitant to share information and data. Despite these difficulties, cooperation has always proved negotiable and solvable at the working level.[1578] Overall, the trend in cooperation has been positive. However, the ACM highlights that cooperation could further be improved by structurally embedding 'linking pins' in both organisations. Moreover, fostering structural contacts, investing in each other's work and in personal relationships and organising joint events could further enhance cooperation. In this context, the ACM highlights that

1574. Zwenne, Steenbruggen and Reker 2016; Sickinghe 2011, p. 204; Kuipers and Gaasbeek 2013. *See also*: Court of First Instance Rotterdam 24 December 2024 Case ROT 21/4781 and 21/4782, *Apple v. ACM*, para. 10.3. In this case, the District Court Rotterdam ruled that the exchange of information between two Dutch supervisory authorities met this requirement, since there was a Cooperation Protocol based on a legal basis in Dutch formal law.

1575. According to Article 7(3) Cooperation Protocol, the requesting authority shall explicitly state the purpose for which the information is requested.

1576. Kroes and Kreijger 2025.

1577. ACM Besluit 21 maart 2023, ACM/UIT/594498 https://www.acm.nl/system/files/documents/woo-besluit-over-samenwerkinsprotocol-acm-en-ap.pdf accessed 24 March 2025.

1578. ACM, Verslag 13 February 2020 https://www.acm.nl/system/files/documents/vergaderverslag-13-2-2020_0.pdf accessed 24 March 2025.

effective cooperation is becoming increasingly important, particularly in light of developments in online markets. In order to keep realising this cooperation, the ACM aims to prolong the structural cooperation between both authorities.[1579]

9.6.1.2 Germany

The GWB does not contain general provisions on cooperation between the *Bundeskartellamt* and DPAs. However, Section 50f GWB contains a specific provision on the exchange of information. According to Section 50f GWB, the *Bundeskartellamt*, the Federal Commissioner for Data Protection and the *Land* commissioners for data protection are permitted to exchange information, including personal data and business secrets, irrespective of the type of procedure and as long as this is necessary for the purpose of fulfilling their respective duties. The authorities can use the information exchanged in their proceedings.[1580]

Despite the exchange of information being the only type of cooperation set out in German law, broader cooperation between the authorities occurs in practice.[1581] In the *Meta Bundeskartellamt* case, the *Bundeskartellamt*, for example, consulted the Federal Commissioner for Data Protection, the regional data protection authority of Hamburg to inform them of the action it had taken. Furthermore, the *Bundeskartellamt* obtained confirmation that the above-mentioned DPAs were not conducting parallel investigations and that the case did not raise the DPA's objections. By engaging in this consultation, the *Bundeskartellamt* fulfilled its obligations of sincere cooperation.[1582] Additionally, the *Bundeskartellamt* has reported cooperation in various other cases. In a Section 19a GWB case concerning several Google services, the *Bundeskartellamt*, for example, exchanged views with German data protection authorities. Similarly, it consulted with the German data protection authorities on a case concerning self-preferencing and/or the impeding of other companies from using Apple devices by Apple's rules on the use of its App Tracking Transparency Framework.[1583]

Consequently, although the German framework does not impose obligations of cooperation and is limited to provisions that facilitate the

1579. ACM, Verslag 13 February 2020 https://www.acm.nl/system/files/documents/vergaderverslag-13-2-2020_0.pdf accessed 24 March 2025.
1580. However, according to Section 50f GWB prohibitions on the use of evidence shall remain unaffected.
1581. Jackwerth 2022, para. 47.
1582. CJEU 4 July 2023 Case C-252/21 *Meta Bundeskartellamt*, paras 60-61; paras 555-556; *Bundeskartellamt* 6 February 2019, *Facebook*, B6-22/16. The *Bundeskartallamt* also cooperated with the Irish DPA. *See also* section 9.6.2.1.
1583. OECD 2024, para. 14; Bundeskartellamt 14 June 2022, 'Bundeskartellamt reviews Apple's tracking rules for third-party apps' (2022) https://www.bundeskartellamt.de/SharedDocs/Meldung/EN/Pressemitteilungen/2022/14_06_2022_Apple.html accessed 12 March 2025.

exchange of information between authorities, DPAs and the German NCA engage in voluntary cooperation at the national level.

9.6.1.3 The EU

The GDPR introduces various provisions addressing the cooperation between the Commission and the EDPB. While these provisions are not specifically designed to address the intersection of competition law and the GDPR, they may facilitate dialogue between the Commission and the EDPB.

As explained in section 9.5.1, the European Data Protection Board plays a crucial role in the cross-border application of the GDPR. Under Article 68(5) GDPR, the Commission has the right to participate in the EDPB's activities and meetings. In the initial GDPR Proposal, the Commission envisioned a much stronger role for itself. According to Article 58(4) GDPR Proposal, the Commission could, for example, request that a matter be handled through the GDPR's consistency mechanism.[1584] Furthermore, the proposed Article 59 GDPR would have allowed the Commission to adopt an opinion on decisions made through the consistency mechanism or by the EDPB. The EDPB would be required to 'take the utmost account of the Commission's opinion'.[1585] Throughout the legislative process, the role of the Commission in GDPR enforcement has been toned down. The independence of data protection authorities was a key objection to a strong involvement of the Commission. The Article 29 Working Party – stressed that '[n]othwithstanding the role of the Commission as guardian of the Treaties, the Working Party has strong reservations to the role foreseen for the Commission in individual cases which have been dealt with under the consistency mechanism, as it encroaches upon the independent position of DPAs'.[1586]

Hijmans notes that the adjustments to the mechanism also affect the relationship between competition law and the GDPR. He argues that 'the synergies between enforcement of EU data protection law and EU competition law would be easier to deal with if the Commission in its role as enforcer of EU competition law had a strong interlocutor in the domain of data protection, at EU level'.[1587] It is hard to deny that a mechanism facilitating dialogue between the Commission and the EDPB could be beneficial for a more holistic and integral application of EU data protection and competition law. However, the objections concerning independence

1584. Commission Staff Working Document Impact Assessment Report Accompanying the document Proposal for a Regulation of the European Parliament and of the Council on contestable and fair markets in the digital sector (Digital Markets Act), SWD(2020) 363 final (DMA Proposal); *See* section 9.5.1.

1585. Article 59(2) GDPR Proposal.

1586. Article 29 Working Party 23 March 2012, Opinion 01/2012 on the data protection reform proposals, 00530/12/EN WP 191, (2012)WP 191, 17.

1587. Hijmans 2019, p. 372.

cannot be overlooked. In this light, the debate on the scope and reach of the consistency mechanisms of the GDPR exposes one of the main challenges of cross-disciplinary cooperation between authorities. While greater integration may be beneficial from a coherence perspective, such an approach also carries risks regarding the principle of independence. These concerns are particularly relevant in the field of data protection law, where the principle of independence is interpreted broadly.[1588]

Apart from its observational role in the EDPB, the Commission may ask the EDPB for advice. According to Article 70(1)(b) GDPR, the EDPB may 'advise the Commission on any issues relating to the protection of personal data in the Union, including the proposed amendment of [the GDPR]'. Apart from this general provision on the advisory function of the EDPB, Article 70 also provides that the EDPB may advise the Commission in very specific situations.[1589]

While the main objective of Article 70 GDPR is the *consistent application of the GDPR,* the EDPB's role is not limited to the intra-disciplinary data protection context. Instead, the EDPB has expressed the commitment to 'intensify engagement and cooperation with other regulators (e.g. competition authorities)'.[1590] The EDPB fulfilled this aspiration in the context of the *Google Fitbit* merger by highlighting 'the implications that this merger may have for the protection of personal data'.[1591] It also stressed its willingness to advise the Commission on the proposed merger if so requested by the Commission. In 2020, the Commission appeared rather unwilling to engage in cooperation with the EDPB. In an interview with Bloomberg, Vestager highlighted that 'cooperation with privacy regulators would not discuss specific cases because we would invite people who may not be privy to' confidential reviews of a merger.[1592] According to Docksey, the *Google Fitbit* case was a 'lost opportunity for effective cooperation between EU data protection and competition regulators'.[1593] The example mentioned above

1588. Article 52 GDPR.
1589. According to Article 70(1)(d) the EDPB may, for example, advise the Commission on the format and procedure for exchange of information between controllers, processors and supervisory authorities for binding corporate rules; Article 70(1)(q) provides that the EDPB may provide the Commission with an opinion on certification requirements. *See also*: Article 70(1)(r) and (s) for further possibilities to advice or provide opinions.
1590. European Data Protection Board 15 December 2020 'EDPB Strategy 2021-2023' https://www.edpb.europa.eu/sites/default/files/files/file1/edpb_strategy2021-2023_en.pdf accessed 24 March 2025, para. 7; European Data Protection Board 16 January 2025 'Position paper on Interplay between data protection and competition law' https://www.edpb.europa.eu/system/files/2025-01/edpb_position-paper_20250116_interplay-between-data-protection-and-competition-law_en.pdf accessed 24 March 2025.
1591. European Data Protection Board 19 February 2020 'Statement on the implications of mergers' https://www.edpb.europa.eu/sites/default/files/files/file1/edpb_statement_2020_privacyimplicationsofmergers_en.pdf accessed 24 March 2025.
1592. White and Ali 2020.
1593. Docksey 2020, p. 242.

concerns a merger case. As explained in section 1.3.3, mergers do not fall within the scope of the analysis. However, the statement put forward by Vestager clearly exemplifies the issues that may arise in the context of cooperation between the Commission and the EDPB. Importantly, the attitude of the Commission has changed since 2020 and that it could be more receptive to cooperation with the EDPB nowadays.[1594] However, since there are no explicit provisions on the exchange of information and evidence, the concerns expressed by former Commissioner Vestager remain valid.

9.6.1.4 Mono-Jurisdictional Cooperation: Final Thoughts

The examples of Germany, The Netherlands and the EU show that the different frameworks provide mechanisms for mono-jurisdictional cooperation. At the national level, both The Netherlands and Germany have clear mechanisms in place. These mechanisms facilitate (voluntary) cooperation. Importantly, the frameworks also provide a legal basis to exchange information between authorities. At the EU level, the bilateral cooperation mechanisms between the Commission and the EDPB are less well developed. The absence of an explicit legal basis for the exchange of presents a particular challenges.

9.6.2 Multi-Jurisdictional Cooperation

Beyond cooperation *within* one legal order, the intersection between the GDPR and competition law can require *multi-jurisdictional* cooperation. This situation arises in particular when the Commission or an NCA of Member State A takes action against an undertaking established in Member State B. In such cases, the DPA of Member State B would qualify as the lead supervisory authority.[1595] In this light, cooperation would be necessary between the Commission or the NCA of Member State A and the DPA of Member State B.

9.6.2.1 *Meta Bundeskartellamt*

The above-mentioned scenario is not merely hypothetical; it occurred in the *Meta Bundeskartellamt* case. This case is not only interesting because of the substantive issues at stake – which have received ample academic attention

1594. In June 2020, the Commission, for example, committed to the encouragement of cooperation between regulators, including competition regulators. *See:* Communication from the Commission to the European Parliament and the Council of 24 June 2020, Data Protection as a pillar of citizens' empowerment and the EU's approach to the digital transition – two years of application of the General Data Protection Directive, COM(2020)264 final, p. 16.

1595. *See* section 9.5.1.

– but also due to its strong institutional implications. In the case, the *German Bundeskartellamt* applied German competition law to Meta while incorporating considerations of data protection law. Given that Meta's main establishment is in Ireland, the Irish DPA would be the leading supervisory authority.

The CJEU acknowledged that, when assessing an abuse of a dominant position, it may be necessary for the NCA concerned to assess whether or not the undertaking's conduct complies with the rules on the protection of personal data laid down in the GDPR.[1596] If a competition law authority can take into account data protection considerations, this raises the question of how such an analysis impacts the position of DPAs and how the competences of competition and data protection authorities interact. The answer to this question has multiple dimensions.

First, the CJEU clarifies that the GDPR's one-stop-shop mechanism does not preclude NCAs from addressing data protection considerations, as 'the rules on cooperation laid down in the GDPR are not addressed to the national competition authorities but govern cooperation between the national supervisory authorities concerned and the lead supervisory authority as well as, where appropriate, cooperation between those authorities and the European Data Protection Board and the Commission'.[1597]

Second, the CJEU highlights that 'by merely noting the non-compliance of a data processing operation with the GDPR for the sole purpose of establishing an abuse of dominance and by imposing measures […] [the NCA] does not carry out any of the tasks set out in Article 57 [GDPR], nor does it make use of the powers reserved to the [DPA] under Article 58 [GDPR]'.[1598]

Third, the CJEU emphasises that the NCA and competent (leading) DPA 'must cooperate with each other in order to ensure the consistency of application of [the GDPR]'.[1599] Despite this obligation, the EU framework lacks mechanisms for the realisation of such cooperation.[1600] Regardless of the absence of such mechanisms in EU law, the various national authorities involved 'are all bound by the duty of sincere cooperation enshrined in Article 4(3) TEU'.[1601] The CJEU continues by stressing that this duty of sincere cooperation requires NCAs to 'consult and cooperate sincerely' with national or leading DPAs. The CJEU also acknowledges the risk of divergent

1596. CJEU 4 July 2023 Case C-252/21 *Meta Bundeskartellamt*, para. 48.
1597. CJEU 4 July 2023 Case C-252/21 *Meta Bundeskartellamt*, para. 48.
1598. Data Protection Commission 4 January 2023, 'Data Protection Commission announces conclusion of two inquiries into Meta Ireland' https://www.dataprotection.ie/en/news-media/data-protection-commission-announces-conclusion-two-inquiries-meta-ireland accessed 24 March 2025.
1599. CJEU 4 July 2023 Case C-252/21 *Meta Bundeskartellamt*, para. 52.
1600. CJEU 4 July 2023 Case C-252/21 *Meta Bundeskartellamt*, para. 43.
1601. CJEU 4 July 2023 Case C-252/21 *Meta Bundeskartellamt*, para. 53; *See* section 3.4.2.

interpretations of the GDPR by DPAs and NCAs and derives more concrete obligations to cooperate from the principle of sincere cooperation.[1602]

Building on the principle of sincere cooperation, the CJEU sets out some specific obligations for NCAs. The extent of the obligations is context-dependent. If a DPA or the CJEU already has decided on 'conduct or a similar conduct', NCAs cannot depart from this decision, although they can draw their own conclusions from the perspective of the application of competition law.[1603] Furthermore, the CJEU outlines specific obligations requiring NCAs to consult with DPAs. As explained in section 7.6.2, these cooperative obligations also have a pre-emptive dimension.

Concerning the duty to consult with the DPA, the CJEU sets out multiple scenarios in which the NCA must (attempt to) consult the competent DPA. Such consultation is necessary where: (i) the NCA has doubts about the scope of the assessment carried out by the competent DPA; (ii) the conduct is under examination of DPAs, but no decision has yet been adopted; or (iii) the NCA concludes that there is a violation of the provisions of the GDPR in the absence of an investigation by a DPA. In such cases, the NCA must seek cooperation in order to 'dispel its doubts or to determine whether it must wait for the supervisory authority concerned to take a decision before starting its own assessment'.[1604] When consulted, the relevant DPA 'must respond to such request for information or cooperation *within a reasonable period of time*'.[1605] In the absence of a timely reply, the NCA may continue with its own investigation. Similarly, the NCA may continue its investigation if the leading DPA has no objection to the investigation being continued without having to wait for the DPA's decision.[1606]

9.6.2.2 *Meta Bundeskartellamt*: Open Questions

In the *Meta Bundeskartellamt* case, the CJEU paved the way for multi-jurisdictional cross-disciplinary cooperation between competition and data protection authorities based on the principle of sincere cooperation. This first step towards stronger cooperation is praiseworthy and inevitable given the ever-closer relationship between data protection and competition law. Yet, certain concerns and open questions remain.

The question whether an NCA can rule that conduct is *compliant* with the GDPR remains unanswered. In the context of the duty of sincere cooperation, the CJEU only addresses the scenario of non-compliance with the GDPR. This raises the question of whether an NCA can determine that certain behaviour does *not* violate the GDPR without the involvement of a

1602. CJEU 4 July 2023 Case C-252/21 *Meta Bundeskartellamt*, paras 54-55.
1603. CJEU 4 July 2023 Case C-252/21 *Meta Bundeskartellamt*, p. 56.
1604. CJEU 4 July 2023 Case C-252/21 *Meta Bundeskartellamt*, para. 57.
1605. CJEU 4 July 2023 Case C-252/21 *Meta Bundeskartellamt*, p. 58.
1606. CJEU 4 July 2023 Case C-252/21, *Meta Bundeskartellamt*, p. 59.

DPA.[1607] Given the tasks and competences of the respective authorities, it is highly unlikely that a DPA would be bound by an NCA's conclusion of compliance with the GDPR. It became apparent from the *Meta Bundeskartellamt* judgment that NCAs can draw GDPR conclusions for 'the sole purpose of establishing an abuse of a dominant position'.[1608] Yet, a conclusion of compliance would lead to an awkward situation and could be detrimental to the consistent interpretation of the GDPR if a DPA were later to rule that the same conduct violates the GDPR. In this context, explicitly clarifying that NCAs are not entitled to determine GDPR compliance would be a good choice. In my view, this limitation for NCAs can be inferred from Article 4(3) TEU and, therefore, already applies in practice. However, for legal certainty, it would be desirable to explicitly establish this limitation. This approach would mirror Article 10 of Regulation 1/2003 and the *Tele2Polska* case, which provided that NCAs cannot decide that EU competition law is inapplicable.[1609]

Furthermore, the current institutional framework is not appropriate for the facilitation of cooperative enforcement. Consequently, it remains unclear how such cooperation should be structured in practice.[1610] In the *Meta Bundeskartellamt* case, the German NCA fulfilled its obligations to cooperate, also vis-à-vis the Irish DPA.[1611] However, the precise threshold for cooperation remains unclear. In other words, the CJEU provided a general rule on cooperation, but the (procedural) details still need to be worked out.[1612] At this point, there are no fora for cooperation between NCAs and DPAs from different jurisdictions. Despite the fact that such cooperation mechanisms are in place in a mono-jurisdictional context, no suitable institutional mechanisms are available in the multi-jurisdictional context. The mono-jurisdictional example of The Netherlands demonstrates that cooperation between enforcers of different legal branches is challenging, even when mechanisms are in place.[1613] The absence of a proper forum may therefore be detrimental to effective cooperation between NCAs and DPAs. Moreover, the CJEU leaves multiple important practical questions unaddressed. For example, it remains unclear at which level the exchange of information and cooperation should occur. Is it sufficient that case handlers communicate with each other or is consistency to be ensured at the managerial level? A duty to cooperate without the necessary practical arrangements in place will inevitably lead to cooperation on an informal basis. Such informal cooperation carries a risk and may compromise the

1607. Majcher 2024.
1608. CJEU 4 July 2023 Case C-252/21, *Meta Bundeskartellamt*, para. 49.
1609. CJEU 3 May 2011 Case C-375/09, *Tele2Polska*. *See also* section 8.4.2.
1610. Abate, Bianco and Casalini 2024, p. 26.
1611. CJEU 4 July 2023 Case C-252/21, *Meta Bundeskartellamt*, paras 60-61.
1612. Hriscu 2023, p. 374.
1613. *See* section 9.6.1.1.

procedural rights of the parties involved. For instance, confidential information and evidence can and should not be exchanged without a proper legal basis. Furthermore, informal cooperation occurs behind closed doors making it inherently opaque and intransparent. This begs the question of whether procedural rights, such as the right to access to the file and effective legal redress, are adequately protected.[1614] Against this background, it is imperative that the EU and national legislators take action to establish a multi-jurisdictional and cross-disciplinary cooperation framework for competition and data protection law.

9.7 SUB-CONCLUSION GDPR

Given the increasing overlap and interaction between competition law and the GDPR, the relevance of cooperation mechanisms facilitating collaboration between enforcers of the respective legal branches also becomes greater. The previous sections examined the existing mechanisms that can realise such cooperation. It became apparent that clear differences emerge between *mono-* and *multi-jurisdictional* cooperation.

In the *mono-jurisdictional* context, various mechanisms facilitate cooperation between data protection and competition authorities. In The Netherlands, the respective enforcers cooperate under a Cooperation Protocol which is based on national formal law. In Germany formal laws primarily govern the exchange of information rather than establishing general mechanisms for cooperation. Nevertheless, multiple instances of cooperation between data protection and competition authorities exist. At the EU level, the GDPR allows for a degree of cooperation between the Commission and the EDPB. However, these mechanisms primarily concern the coherent application of the GDPR rather than cross-disciplinary cooperation.

In the *multi-jurisdictional* context, cooperation is more complex. The EU framework does not provide a framework in this regard. As a result, the CJEU has invoked the general principle of sincere cooperation in order to establish certain duties of cooperation. NCAs incorporating data protection considerations into their competition law analysis must consult and cooperate with DPAs, at least in specific circumstances. In the *Meta Bundeskartellamt* case, the CJEU ruled that certain obligations of cross-disciplinary cooperation can be derived from the duty of sincere cooperation. The endorsement of the need for and relevance of cross-disciplinary cooperation is a welcome development. However, the current frameworks and obligations as set out by the CJEU remain too vague. Experiences in the *intra-disciplinary* context of the GDPR and competition law demonstrate that a detailed framework is essential in order to build such cooperative relationships. Ongoing initiatives for a procedural GDPR framework highlight the

1614. Picht 2023, p. 3.

relevance of such rules. Currently, the mechanisms that are in place to streamline the cooperation between DPAs and NCAs are underdeveloped, leaving many fundamental questions unaddressed. Such uncertainties hinder the development of a cooperation framework. The relationship between the Commission and DPAs also not clearly defined. This may result in serious tensions if the approach of *Meta Bundeskartellamt* were to be extended to EU competition law.

9.8 POLYCENTRIC COOPERATION AND 'SUPER' REGULATORS

So far, the analysis has focused on the interaction between regulators of *two* legal branches, i.e.: (i) competition law and the DMA; or (ii) competition law and the GDPR. However, both at the national and EU level, a trend towards broader cooperation can be observed. In academic literature and in the regulatory landscape, various initiatives promoting *polycentric* cooperation have emerged. This form of cooperation transcends the interaction between enforcers of two legal fields, facilitating instead collaboration among enforcers of *more than two* legal fields. This section studies existing fora for polycentric cooperation. Subsequently, I contend that the introduction of a cross-disciplinary polycentric 'super' regulator would not be a desirable solution.

9.8.1 Existing Mechanisms of Polycentric Cooperation

In the current frameworks for competition law, DMA and GDPR enforcement, various examples of fora for polycentric cooperation can be identified. This Section studies the different polycentric fora in turn.

9.8.1.1 The Digital Clearing House

The *Digital Clearing House* constitutes one of the early initiatives of multilateral polycentric cooperation. In 2016, the EDPA called for greater cooperation between different regulators in the digital sector.[1615] In 2017, the European Parliament endorsed the need for cross-disciplinary cooperation in a resolution, after which the 'Digital Clearing House' was established.[1616]

1615. European Data Protection Supervisor March 2014, 'Privacy and competitive in the age of big data: The interplay between data protection, competition law and consumer protection in the Digital Economy' https://www.edps.europa.eu/sites/default/files/publication/14-03-26_competitition_law_big_data_en.pdf accessed 24 March 2025.

1616. European Parliament resolution of 14 March 2017 on fundamental rights implications of big data: privacy, data protection, non-discrimination, security and law-enforcement (2016/2225(INI)).

This Digital Clearing House consists of an *informal* network of authorities aimed at strengthening synergies between various legal branches. The Digital Clearing House has hosted several meetings in the past. However, the latest meeting seems to have taken place in 2020, and it is not clear whether the initiative is still active.[1617]

The EDPS advocates the establishment of a 'Digital Clearinghouse 2.0' which would provide a forum for regulators 'to identify emerging areas and practices of cross-regulatory concerns, facilitate coordination and exchange of knowledge, experiences and resources'. The initiative should enable the interaction between 'a number and diversity of relevant authorities' by adopting a 'variable geometry'.[1618]

9.8.1.2 The High-Level Group of Regulators

Despite the fact that the Digital Clearinghouse seems to have been inactive in the last few years, polycentric cooperation is still a relevant topic in the context of the EU. At the EU level, the High-Level Group of Regulators, introduced in Article 40 DMA, is particularly relevant. The High-Level Group is an example of *a polycentric cross-disciplinary* network: it facilitates cooperation between enforcers of multiple legal branches, including data protection law, competition law and the DMA.[1619] The High-Level Group, chaired by the Commission, comprises of: (i) the body of the European Regulators for Electronic Communications; (ii) the European Data Protection Supervisor and European Data Protection Board; (iii) the European Competition Network; (iv) the Consumer Protection and Cooperation Network; and (v) the European Regulatory Group of Audiovisual Media Regulators.[1620] Meetings are held at the request of the Commission, at the

1617. *See:* https://www.edps.europa.eu/data-protection/our-work/subjects/digital-clearinghouse-20_en accessed 24 March 2025.
1618. European Data Protection Supervisor 15 January 2025 'Towards a Digital Clearinghouse 2.0 – Concept Note' https://www.edps.europa.eu/data-protection/our-work/publications/other-documents/2025-01-15-towards-digital-clearinghouse-20_en accessed 20 March 2025, para. 17, paras 40-50.
1619. Witt 2023, p. 659; Maher 2024, p. 275.
1620. The composition of the High-Level Group should ensure a 'high level of expertise and a geographical balance'. The mentioned bodies and networks shall have an equal number of representatives and the maximum number of members may not exceed 30. According to the Commission's decision on setting up a High-Level Group, the European Bodies referred to in Article 40(2) DMA can nominate six representatives, the European Data Protection Supervisor shall nominate one representative and the European Data Protection Board shall nominate five representatives. Representatives are appointed for a term of two years, which is renewable once. Each member of the High-Level Group can define its own rules and internal procedures on representation. Absent or indisposed representatives may be replaced by an alternate representative. *See:* Article 3 Commission decision of 23 March 2023 on setting up the High-Level

request of a majority of the Members or at least once a year.[1621] The High-Level Group decides, as far as possible, by consensus.[1622] Despite the non-binding nature of decisions of the High-Level Group, its recommendations create a form of 'soft accountability' among peers and may be leveraged politically.[1623]

EU bodies and networks can nominate 'the heads of national authorities of Member States or equivalent' as representatives to the High-Level Group. Participants are not remunerated for the activities in the group but can be reimbursed by the Commission for travel and subsistence expenses.[1624] The lack of reimbursement highlights one of the potential challenges of cooperation in polycentric networks. The involvement in the network adds to the tasks of national authorities. Given that these authorities often operate with limited financial and human resources, they may not always have the capacity to actively participate in these initiatives.[1625]

The High-Level Group can provide the Commission with advice and expertise in areas that fall within the competences of its members and are relevant to any general matter related to the implementation of the DMA or the promotion of a consistent regulatory approach across regulatory instruments.[1626] The High-Level Group is not involved in individual DMA investigations or proceedings and focuses on broader policy issues.[1627] The High-Level Group *in particular* identifies and assesses current and potential interactions between the DMA and *sector-specific rules.*[1628] This suggests that the High-Level Group primarily serves as a forum for discussing the interaction between the DMA and regulatory and sector-specific regulation.[1629] Against this backdrop, the ECN is a more suitable forum for discussions on the interaction between the DMA and competition law without broader regulatory implications.

The institutional structure of the High-Level Group reveals the intricate interplay between national and EU authorities and bodies. While it provides a *horizontal* forum, enabling interaction between the Commission and various EU bodies, it has a *vertical* dimension as well. Some of the bodies

---

Group for the Digital Markets Act, C(2023)1833 final (henceforth: Decision on the High-Level Group); Article 40(2)(3) and (4) DMA; Maher 2024, p. 275. Preamble DMA, para. 93.

1621. Article 40(4) DMA. The Commission can convene additional ad hoc meetings, also when urgent advice is required. *See:* Article 5(2) Decision on the High-Level Group.
1622. If a vote is necessary, the outcome is decided by simple majority. Members who abstained or voted against an opinion, recommendation or report can annex a document summarising their position. *See:* Article 40(8) Decision on the High-Level Group.
1623. Maher 2024.
1624. Article 11 Decision on the High-Level Group.
1625. Yakovleva, Geursen and Arnbak 2020, p. 1480.
1626. Article 40(5) and (6) DMA.
1627. Article 2(2) Decision on the High-Level Group; Annual Report DMA 2023, para. 47.
1628. Article 40(6) DMA.
1629. Preamble Decision on the High-Level Group, recital 3.

and networks, including the EPDB and the ECN, consist of representatives of national authorities. In practice, representatives of the High-Level Group will often be affiliated to a national authority and will also report back to national authorities.[1630] Consequently, the High-Level Group serves as an interesting example of a combination of horizontal and vertical networks. National authorities join forces in *multi-jurisdictional intra-disciplinary* networks. These networks, in turn, engage in *cross-disciplinary* cooperation at the EU level.

The establishment of the High-Level Group should be applauded. It demonstrates that the EU legislator recognises the relevance of *polycentric* cooperation. The High-Level Group presents an opportunity to reinforce cross-disciplinary cooperation throughout the EU.[1631] To fully exploit its potential, it is crucial that the High-Level Group does not merely exist on paper but engages in actual discussions. In this light, it is encouraging that the High-Level Group has already taken several initiatives by arranging several meetings and by establishing sub-groups. [1632] Consequently, the Group appears to be genuinely engaging with issues at the intersection between different areas of law and will be able to actively work on resolving potential tensions arising from overlapping regulatory frameworks.[1633]

9.8.1.3 The Digital Markets Advisory Committee

The High-Level Group is not the only cooperation mechanism introduced by the DMA. In addition, Article 50 DMA states that the Commission shall be assisted by a *Digital Markets Advisory Committee* (henceforth: DMAC). This DMAC, chaired by the Commission, is a comitology committee within the meaning of Regulation 182/2011.[1634] The DMAC is composed of representatives of the Member States and aims to 'integrate national expertise in the platform economy' in decision-making in the context of the DMA.[1635] The procedural rules governing the DMAC are laid down in the Rules for Procedure for the Digital Markets Advisory Committee.[1636]

1630. This is not always the case, since the European Data Protection Supervisor also joins the High-Level Group.
1631. De Streel et al. 2023, p. 186.
1632. Annual Report DMA 2023, para. 47; High-Level Group for the Digital Markets Act Public Statement of 22 May 2024 on Artificial Intelligence https://digital-markets-act.ec.europa.eu/high-level-group-digital-markets-act-public-statement-artificial-intelligence-2024-05-22_en accessed 20 March 2025.
1633. De Streel et al. 2023, p. 186.
1634. The Commission does not have a voting right. Article 3(2) Regulation 182/2011.
1635. European Commission, Explanatory Memorandum to Proposal of 15 December 2020 for a Regulation of the European Parliament and of the Council on contestable and fair markets in the digital sector (Digital Markets Act), COM(2020)842 final, 2020/0374(COD), p. 9.
1636. Digital Markets Advisory Committee, Rules of Procedure for the Digital Markets Advisory Committee of 13 January 2023, (2023)2699502.

Member States have discretion to determine the composition of their delegation. Recital 101 of the DMA's Preamble stresses that delegations 'can include, *inter alia,* experts from competent authorities within the Member States'. This means that a Member State can be represented by independent authorities, such as an NCAs or DPAs. However, experience with other comitology committees shows that such bodies are in practice often comprised of officials from ministries. These officials, who are not independent, likely have less (regulatory) expertise.[1637] Regarding the intersection between competition law and DMA, this means that although NCAs can be appointed as DMAC representatives, their inclusion is not guaranteed. During the legislative procedure of the DMA, NCAs plead for a more systemic role in the DMAC.[1638] Since NCAs are not structurally embedded in the DMAC, and the High-Level Group only operates at the policy level, it is important that NCAs and the Commission can engage in cooperation in the context of competition law and the DMA in another forum. The ECN is an example of such forum.[1639]

In accordance with Regulation 182/2011, the DMAC can act in two capacities.[1640] In an *advisory procedure,* the DMAC delivers an opinion of which the Commission shall take the 'utmost account'.[1641] Furthermore, the DMAC can adopt either a positive or a negative opinion in an *examination procedure* relating to an implementing act. In the case of a positive decision, the Commission shall adopt the implementing act, while the Commission shall refrain from adoption in the case of a negative opinion.[1642] The advisory procedure is most relevant in the context of the DMA, and applies, for example, to decisions relating to the suspension of an obligation,[1643] an exemption on grounds of public health and public security,[1644] market investigations for designating gatekeepers,[1645] market investigations into systemic non-compliance,[1646] interim measures,[1647] commitments,[1648] non-compliance,[1649] periodic penalty payments and[1650] certain implementing acts.[1651] The DMA relies on the examination procedure only in one instance,

1637. De Streel and Monti 2022, p. 61; Chirico 2021, p. 498.
1638. European Competition Network 2021, p. 9.
1639. Reyna 2024, p. 18.
1640. De Streel et al. 2023, p. 186; Larouche and De Streel 2021, p. 26.
1641. Article 50(2) DMA and Article 4 Regulation 182/2011.
1642. Article 5 Regulation 182/2011.
1643. Article 9 DMA.
1644. Article 10 DMA.
1645. Article 17 DMA.
1646. Article 18 DMA.
1647. Article 24 DMA.
1648. Article 25 DMA.
1649. Article 26 DMA.
1650. Article 31 DMA.
1651. Article 46 DMA.

i.e., implementing acts laying down detailed arrangements for the cooperation between the Commission and national authorities provided for in Articles 37 and 38 DMA.[1652]

In sum, the DMAC serves as a forum for Member States to influence the Commission's decision-making. So far, the DMAC has held several meetings and published multiple opinions.[1653] The Annual Review of the DMA indicates that the Commission has implemented (at least some) of the DMAC's advice. Based on the results of the consultation of the DMAC, the Commission, for example, simplified the procedures for access to the file laid down in the Implementing Regulation.[1654] Despite these successes, the DMAC's actual influence has been questioned in legal literature. According to Monti, the DMAC enters into the procedure relatively late, which could result in a 'marginal role in the day-to-day supervision of gatekeepers'.[1655]

9.8.1.4 National Initiatives for Polycentric Cooperation

Initiatives for polycentric cooperation are not limited to the EU level. Several noteworthy initiatives also exist at the Member State level. In The Netherlands, initiatives include the Digital Regulation Cooperation Platform, the SDT, and the *Markttoezichthoudersberaad,* the MTB. In Germany, the Digital Cluster Bonn facilitates the interaction between multiple authorities. The national polycentric fora are addressed in turn.

First, in 2021, various Dutch regulators with competences in the field of digital services established the *SDT*. This initiative involves cooperation between the Dutch ACM, the AP, and the financial and media supervisor. The SDT aims to address the risks and opportunities associated with digital markets. In order to protect the broad range of public interests and objectives protected by the respective supervisors, the SDT serves as a forum to invest in and share knowledge and skills. The SDT aims to identify new (European) rules in the field of Big Tech, data and the platform economy in order to effectively and efficiently enforce these regulations.[1656] To achieve this, the SDT will establish various chambers, including a chamber of general consultation, a chamber for DSA supervision and a chamber for AI and algorithms.[1657] To date, the SDT has published two documents in which specific principles are stressed. The first document relates to effective

1652. Article 46(1) sub 1 and 46(2) DMA.
1653. *See:* https://ec.europa.eu/transparency/comitology-register/screen/committees/C114400/consult?lang=en accessed 25 March 2025; *See also*: Maher 2024, p. 275.
1654. Annual Report DMA 2023, para. 6.
1655. Monti 2021a, p. 6.
1656. *See:* https://www.autoriteitpersoonsgegevens.nl/over-de-autoriteit-persoonsgegevens/samenwerking accessed 25 March 2025.
1657. SDT 2023a.

information provision online and the second document to online marketing for children.[1658]

The introduction of a cross-disciplinary platform with a digital focus is a positive development. The SDT may contribute to the synergies between the respective legal branches by fostering knowledge-sharing and by developing a more holistic view. This can help to align the views of the different regulators and can contribute to better-informed enforcement. However, and despite the potential of such cross-disciplinary cooperative fora, it is difficult to assess how successful the initiative has been so far. The websites of the respective authorities provide limited details about the functioning of the SDT. It is not clear how the interaction is shaped in practice and how far-reaching cooperation between authorities will be. So far, cooperation largely has taken place behind closed doors, making the actual functioning of the network rather opaque.[1659]

Second, the MTB promotes cross-disciplinary cooperation in The Netherlands. This forum, established in 2009 and predating the SDT – does not specifically target digital markets. Instead, the initiative casts a wider net by covering a broader range of topics. This wide scope is reflected in the diverse range of supervisors involved. Apart from the ACM, AP and financial and media supervisor – which also participate in the SDT – the MTB includes the Dutch Central Bank, the Financial Supervision Office, The Netherlands Gambling Authority, the Dutch Healthcare Authority and the Copyright Supervision Board.

The MTB seeks to create a forum in which the respective supervisors can join forces and work collectively on overarching themes and questions. According to the AP's website, a joint approach may lead to more efficient and effective supervision.[1660] By facilitating a structural forum for interaction, the MTB could contribute to an ongoing dialogue between supervisors. It is important to note that the cooperation within the MTB is limited to more general issues rather than the specific challenges associated with digital markets. In 2014, the MTB, for example, published its vision on 'Criteria for good supervision'. In this document, the authorities highlight several parameters of proper supervision, relating to professionalism, efficiency and effectiveness.[1661]

1658. SDT 2023b; SDT 2023c.
1659. Kager and Van der Geest 2021.
1660. *See:* https://www.autoriteitpersoonsgegevens.nl/over-de-autoriteit-persoonsgegevens/samenwerking accessed 25 March 2025.
1661. MTB 2014.

Third, in Germany, cross-disciplinary cooperation between authorities can be realised in the *Digital Cluster Bonn.*[1662] The Digital Cluster Bonn was established in 2024 and comprises the German financial supervisor, the Federal Office of Justice, the Federal Office for Information Security, the Federal Commissioner for Data Protection, the *Bundeskartellamt* and the *Bundesnetzagentur*. The Digital Cluster Bonn aims to provide a structural forum to build a continuous cooperative relationship based on trust. The EU regulations in the realm of digital markets are one of the focus points of the Digital Cluster Bonn. The authorities represented aim to share know-how and best practices in order to develop a common position. The regulators involved have shared a Memorandum of Understanding.[1663] Since the Digital Cluster Bonn is relatively new, its added value will be proven in the future.

9.8.2 One Step Further: Towards a 'Super' Regulator?

As explained above, an increased emphasis on cross-disciplinary initiatives is apparent. Despite the potential and current development of these initiatives, some scholars have advocated further integration of supervisors, for example, by the creation of a single platform regulator at the EU level. Such a 'super' platform regulator would guarantee the oversight of digital markets. Interestingly, the suggestion for a highly-integrated supervisor is not a novelty, but was already proposed in the context of the rise of the 'IT supervisor'.[1664]

The suggestions relating to the establishment of a 'super' regulator diverge in their reach and scope. The tasks of a digital authority could be to safeguard the application of secondary EU legislation, thereby complementing the competences of antitrust authorities.[1665] In this case, the enforcement of novel instruments such as the DMA and the DSA would become the responsibility of a newly created agency at the EU level. In a more far-reaching scenario, the new EU agency would also take over competences of existing national authorities and of the Commission by combining supervision of EU regulatory, data protection and competition law. In this scenario, one entity would act as a 'single EU-wide regulator for the biggest digital platforms'.[1666] In my view, the creation of such a 'super regulator' is neither feasible, nor desirable at this point in time.

1662. For more information, *see:* https://www.digitalclusterbonn.de accessed 25 March 2025.
1663. Digital Cluster Bonn Press Release 15 January 2024, ' Sechs Bundesbehörden arbeiten bei der Digitalisierung enger zusammen' https://www.bundeskartellamt.de/SharedDocs/Meldung/DE/Pressemitteilungen/2024/15_01_2024_Digital_Cluster.html accessed 25 March 2025.
1664. Garcia-Murillo and MacInnes 2003, p. 63; Yesilkagit 2014, p. 4.
1665. Lancieri and Morita Sokwski 2021, p. 165.
1666. De Streel and Monti 2022, p. 27.

Although such a 'super' regulator would arguably be well-placed to consider the overarching EU-wide interest and may help to avoid differentiated enforcement, it is unlikely that this avenue will be taken in the near future. First and foremost, it is unlikely that there will be political willingness at the Member State level to transfer such far-reaching powers to the Commission. The legislative procedure of the DMA, for example, shows that Member States envision a role for NCAs in the supervision of personal data markets.[1667] At the same time, the institutional framework required is difficult to realise constitutionally. The EU has limited competences to delegate enforcement to agencies.[1668] Furthermore, the most far-reaching scenario would require a separation between competition law applicable to digital markets and competition law applicable to non-digital markets. In order to achieve this, the Treaty would arguably have to be amended. Another problematic issue regarding a 'super regulator' would be the concentration of power within this authority.

Apart from these political and constitutional objectives, it is questionable whether the establishment of a super regulator would be desirable from an institutional design perspective. As explained in section 8.2.1, the element of *policy coherence* is one of the key evaluative criteria to assess institutional design. Given the fundamental differences between the selected legal branches (*see*, for example, sections 5.4.3 and 6.4.3), it is unlikely that the functions within this agency would be sufficiently related.[1669] Furthermore, the example of the integrated model of the ACM demonstrated that efficiency and budgetary reasons often play a role in the design of agencies.[1670] The establishment of a 'super' regulator at the EU level would require significant investments in the new authority. These hefty investments may constitute yet another political hurdle for the introduction of a 'super' regulator.[1671]

9.9 CONCLUSION

The aim of this chapter was to provide a cross-disciplinary analysis of cooperation mechanisms in the field of: (i) competition law and the DMA;

1667. Ministers of France, Germany and The Netherlands 27 May 2021, Friends of an effective Digital Markets Act – Strengthening the Digital Markets Act and Its Enforcement https://www.netherlandsandyou.nl/web/pr-eu-brussels/about-us/our-ideas-for-europe/digital-policy accessed 21 March 2025.
1668. De Streel and Monti 2022, p. 27.
1669. Kovacic and Hyman 2013, p 11.
1670. *See* section 8.3.2.
1671. De Streel and Monti 2022, p. 27.

and (ii) competition law and the GDPR. In order to map the cooperation mechanisms that are in place in the context of the selected legal branches, the scheme below structures the existing cooperation mechanisms according to the typology proposed in the previous chapter.

Table 9.1 Typology Institutional Design and Cooperation Competition Law and DMA

Typology Institutional Design and Cooperation Competition Law and DMA		
(1) Institutional design: DMA	*1a level of centralisation*	Limited centralisation approach
	1b agency mandate or portfolio	Mandate of the DMA enforcer is broader than just the DMA, often combined with competition law
(2) Cooperation	*2a dimension(s)*	Cross-disciplinary multi-jurisdictional; multi- and bilateral
	2b legal basis	DMA; national law
	2c forum	European Competition Network; Digital Markets Advisory Committee; High-Level Group of Regulators
	2d intensity	Consultation; cooperation in individual cases
	2e stage	Allocation of cases; investigative stage; decision-making stage

Table 9.2 Typology Institutional Design and Cooperation Competition Law and GDPR

Typology Institutional Design and Cooperation Competition Law and GDPR		
(1) Institutional design: GDPR	*1a level of centralisation*	Decentralised; country of origin model; dispute resolution by EDPB
	1b agency mandate or portfolio	Traditionally narrower mandates, but expanding

(2) Cooperation	*2a dimension(s)*	Cross-disciplinary multi-and mono-jurisdictional; multi- and bilateral
	2b legal basis	National laws; GDPR and the principle of sincere cooperation
	2c forum	European Data Protection Board, but only to a very limited extent
	2d intensity	Consultation; cooperation in individual cases
	2e stage	Investigative stage

The chapter and the tables above show that the frameworks of competition law, the DMA and the GDPR address the issue of cross-disciplinary cooperation to a varying extent. The DMA establishes extensive frameworks for cooperation between the Commission in its capacity as DMA enforcer and NCAs by providing fora and procedures for cooperation. Furthermore, the structural role of DG COMP in both competition law and DMA enforcement may add to the coherent application of the respective fields. Overall, the mechanisms for cooperation embedded in the DMA have the potential to guarantee a certain degree of coherence.

However, some specific issues may give rise to coherence problems. Despite the potential of the newly established mechanisms, there are some uncertainties as to how the cooperation will play out in practice. The consequences of a violation of Article 38(2) and (3) DMA have not yet been crystallised. Moreover, the practical relevance of the DMAC, for example, remains to be proven. Furthermore, despite the vast experience with cooperation within the ECN, the Network Notice – which is currently focused on cooperation between enforcers of competition law – will need updating in order to accommodate cooperation with the Commission in its capacity as DMA enforcer. In this light, it is hard to judge to what extent the established mechanisms are capable de facto of safeguarding coherence. The annual review of the DMA showed that cooperation between the Commission in its capacity as DMA enforcer and NCAs is not merely something that exists on paper. The respective authorities have engaged in cooperation in several cases. This cooperation is inevitable for the coherent application of competition law and the DMA and should be sustained in the future.

The cooperation between DPAs and competition authorities is more challenging. In the mono-jurisdictional context, there are several mechanisms in place to streamline the interaction between competition and data protection authorities. In The Netherlands, this framework is rather formalised, and authorities appear to be cooperating in the German context too. In both jurisdictions, the exchange of information is regulated in national laws. The Commission could engage with the EDPB, given its (limited) role in this body. However, these mechanisms are far less elaborate than the national frameworks for cooperation. In this context, a legal basis for the exchange of information is, for instance, absent.

Multi-jurisdictional cooperation between DPAs, NCAs and the Commission appears to be the largest gap in the current legal framework. The CJEU has addressed this gap by deriving certain duties to cooperate from the principle of sincere cooperation. The fact that cooperation between authorities builds on the principle of sincere cooperation is not a novelty in itself and is also not problematic per se.[1672] However, given the complexity of cooperation between enforcers with overlapping jurisdictions, general principles are not sufficient to shape the relationships between institutions.

Apart from cooperation between authorities enforcing: (i) competition law and the DMA; and (ii) competition law and the GDPR, this chapter identified multiple polycentric initiatives. The High-Level Group of Regulators, the Dutch SDT and MTB and the German Digital Cluster Bonn are the clearest examples in this regard. Polycentric fora offer a clear opportunity for cooperation between different authorities of overlapping competences, transcending the interplay between two legal fields. This can facilitate a more holistic approach. However, at the same time, the plethora of fora available can further complicate the regulatory landscape. It may be unclear how the different cooperation mechanisms relate to each other. On top of this, authorities need resources in order to effectively participate in cooperation mechanisms.[1673] If too many cooperation fora are established, without taking into consideration the question whether authorities have sufficient resources to participate in these bodies or networks, the initiatives run the risk of becoming a dead letter.

In sum, there are multiple mechanisms in place that facilitate cooperation between enforcers of competition law, the GDPR and the DMA. Given the overlap between the legal branches, these cooperation frameworks are desirable, and even inevitable. It is praiseworthy that the cross-disciplinary dimension of cooperation has been receiving increasing attention, also at the legislative level of the EU. At this point, the cooperation mechanisms that are in place to streamline cooperation between enforcers of the DMA and competition law are, despite the fact that there are some open questions, rather promising and can contribute to the coherent application of the respective fields. On top of this, the polycentric and broader initiatives offer opportunities beyond the intersection of two overlapping legal branches. These initiatives thus offer opportunities for a more holistic approach towards the supervision of personal data markets. As explained above, the cooperation mechanisms between competition and data protection authorities are, at this point, underdeveloped, particularly in the multi-jurisdictional

---

1672. The consistency mechanism in the GDPR is, for example, also grounded in the principle of sincere cooperation (*see:* CJEU 15 June 2021 Case C-645/19, *Facebook v. Belgian DPA*, paras 53, 60 and 63).
1673. Yakovleva, Geursen and Arnbak 2020, p. 1480.

context. The absence of well-developed cooperation mechanisms may be detrimental to the coherent application of both legal branches.

This chapter mapped cooperation mechanisms that are relevant for the complementary application of the GDPR, DMA and competition law. The gaps identified will further be analysed in light of the coherence principle in Synthesis II and in the Conclusion.

Synthesis II: Part III

Part II identified that, in the context of personal data markets, the competences of enforcers of competition law, the DMA and the GDPR overlap to a certain extent. Part III aimed to map which mechanisms are in place to facilitate cooperation between the enforcers of these overlapping legal branches in order to identify potential gaps in the legal framework.

In order to conduct the mapping exercise in a structured way, Part III took a two-step approach. *First,* Chapter 7 studied the mechanisms of pre-emption and hierarchy of norms. If norms overlap, but one provision clearly takes precedence over another, the risk of incoherence is minimal because the methods for identifying and resolving conflicts are well articulated. However, in the context of personal data markets, overlapping norms do not merely clash, but are also complementary in nature. Furthermore, the fact that authorities integrate norms of other legal fields into their assessments leads to a further norm overlap.[1674] In the context of such complementary norms, the rules of pre-emption and hierarchy of norms do not provide useful tools to guarantee coherence. Therefore, complementary norms call for mechanisms of cooperation, rather than for mechanisms to determine which rule should take precedence. Therefore, *second,* Chapters 8 and 9 addressed the mechanisms that can facilitate cooperation between authorities.

This synthesis builds on Chapters 7-9 by identifying potential gaps in the rules and frameworks governing the interplay between competition law, the DMA and the GDPR. The analysis serves as a stepping stone for the Conclusion and pursues the analysis through the lens of coherence.[1675]

Part II identified various dimensions of overlapping competences. The analysis is structured along the lines of those dimensions. Accordingly, the

---

1674. Yakovleva, Geursen and Arnbak 2020, p. 1465.
1675. *See* section 1.4.

analysis starts with an assessment of intra-disciplinary overlaps in the field of competition law. Next, the cross-disciplinary overlaps between: (i) competition law and the DMA; and (ii) competition law and the GDPR are addressed in turn. The cross-disciplinary overlaps are analysed from both a mono- and multi-jurisdictional perspective.

The Intra-disciplinary Dimension: Competition Law

The debate on intra-disciplinary overlaps in competition law can be approached from different angles. On the one hand, norms of EU and national competition law overlap to a certain degree. On the other hand, the multi-level enforcement framework of EU competition law can result in overlapping competences of the Commission and NCAs.

The competition law framework provides an elaborate and formalised system governing the interplay between EU and national competition law. As a starting point, EU competition law is hierarchically superior to national competition law. Therefore, national competition law provisions cannot prejudice the application of EU competition law. In cases of *conflict*, it is obvious that EU competition law prevails. Consequently, the consistency between EU and national competition law is well-articulated through the clear principle of norm hierarchy.

However, the question of to what extent EU competition law pre-empts national competition law is much more complicated. The principle of pre-emption concerns the question of whether a conflict between laws arises, rather than which framework should take precedence in the case of a conflict. In the context of competition law, it is not always clear whether or to what extent the EU framework leaves room for national provisions.

The classificatory system of Article 3(2) Regulation 1/2003 is incredibly complex and relies on various ill-defined concepts.[1676] It is, for example, unclear what is meant by 'rules with a predominantly different objective' or by 'stricter rules'. Due to the lack of clear definitions and interpretations, it is hard to establish into which category a national (competition) rule would fit. As a result, it is not always evident whether or not the EU framework leaves room for such rules. Thus, from this perspective, the relationship between national and EU law is not well-articulated. This causes a potential threat to the coherence of the system because the framework does not provide a clear answer to the question of whether certain national rules can or cannot co-exist alongside Article 102 TFEU. This coherence problem is particularly problematic in the context of personal data markets. Various national legislators have established or are contemplating the introduction of novel competition rules, *inter alia,* to govern the position of Big Tech.[1677] In Germany, the legislator has already provided such a framework with the adoption of Section 19a GWB. In my view, the EU framework leaves room

1676. Brook and Eben 2023a.
1677. Snoep 2023c; Arnoudo 2024.

for this particular rule. However, it is unclear under which precise conditions national legislators can adopt (competition) rules governing the position of large platforms.

The relationship between different enforcers of competition law, i.e., the Commission and NCAs, is governed by an elaborate cooperation framework. Cooperation takes place in several fora, and essential elements of cooperation – including the exchange of information – are formalised. These cooperation mechanisms are based on the principle of sincere cooperation and provide a detailed elaboration of the general duty to cooperate.[1678] Despite the fact that the system of cooperation in competition law generally works well, there are certain issues that can be detrimental to the coherence of the system. The *first* risk relates to the uncertainties as to the legal consequences of violations of key obligations, in particular the duty of parallel application (Article 3(1) Regulation 1/2003) and the duty to inform the Commission about investigative measures or decisions on infringements of Article 102 TFEU (Article 11(2) and (3) Regulation 1/2003). Compliance with these obligations is a prerequisite for the cooperative enforcement of EU competition law since the application of Article 102 TFEU triggers the cooperative obligations and the Commission needs to be informed in order to exercise its managerial tasks within the ECN. Against this backdrop, the uncertainties regarding the legal consequences of a violation could be detrimental to the overall functioning of the system. The different building blocks do not align with each other because the legal consequences of non-compliance with provisions that trigger the functioning of the cooperation mechanisms are unclear and subject to debate. In the *Meta Bundeskartellamt* case, for instance, the fact that the *Bundeskartellamt* refrained from applying Article 102 TFEU deprived other competition authorities of the opportunity to engage in discussions and influence the decision.[1679]

A *second* risk relates to the lack of a clear system for the allocation of cases which may result in parallel procedures by different authorities. The competition law framework does not provide a binding mechanism for case allocation, apart from the 'drastic' Article 11(6) Regulation 1/2003. Yet, this issue does not need addressing in the near future. At this point, there seems to be sufficient goodwill and mutual trust among competition authorities. On top of this, even if a significant problem of parallel procedures were to arise, the Commission already has the possibility to invoke Article 11(6) Regulation 1/2003.

A *third* coherence issue may arise in situations where the Commission and NCAs engage in parallel proceedings covering different relevant markets. In such a situation, neither Article 11(6) Regulation 1/2003 which establishes that NCAs are relieved of their competence to apply Article 102 TFEU if the Commission initiates proceedings, nor the principle of *ne bis in*

1678. Cseres 2024, p. 7.
1679. Brook and Eben 2023b, pp. 28-29.

idem limits the possibility of parallel proceedings. This is not problematic per se, especially if there are good reasons for carving out certain parts of the relevant market. However, this approach should not be used as a mechanism to circumvent the drastic consequences of the application of Article 11(6) Regulation 1/2003. In other words, it is not desirable for the Commission to leave certain parts of the (geographic) market untouched, solely because an NCA had already started an investigation on its national territory. Yet, this seems to happen in practice, for example, in the *Amazon Buy Box* case. By circumventing the application of Article 11(6) Regulation 1/2003, the Commission jeopardises the functioning of the cooperation mechanisms provided for in Regulation 1/2003. Admittedly, even in cases of such parallel proceedings related to different markets, the relevant NCA and the Commission can – and do – cooperate. This mitigates the risk of an incoherent application or interpretation of EU competition law. Yet, the current framework does not provide rules on the circumstances under which this situation is desirable or which (procedural) guarantees must be observed. In this light, artificially creating a separation between relevant markets affects the interconnection of the building blocks of the EU competition law framework. This poses a risk to the coherent application of EU competition law.

In sum, despite the fact that the competition law framework is overall rather coherent and well-structured, my research identified certain gaps relating to the application of the framework that may pose threats to the functioning of the cooperation mechanisms. The upcoming revision of Regulation 1/2003 presents a good opportunity to address these uncertainties and shortcomings. Suggestions for improvements will be provided in the final conclusion (*see* cf. section 10.4).

The Cross-Disciplinary Dimension I: Competition Law and the DMA

The DMA establishes a framework that is closely related to but is not part of EU competition law. In line with the regulatory tradition of the EU, the DMA and competition law are partially overlapping and complementary instruments.[1680]

The relationship between the DMA and competition law is governed by the principles of hierarchy of norms and pre-emption. When considering the hierarchy of norms, it is important to distinguish between EU and national competition law. Article 102 TFEU – an instrument of primary EU law – is hierarchically superior to the DMA, which is an instrument of secondary EU law. Conversely, as an EU law instrument, and in line with the principle of primacy of EU law, the DMA takes precedence over national competition law. These principles of hierarchy of norms ensure that conflict between norms can be resolved by establishing a hierarchical relationship. Consequently, in the event of conflicting norms, the EU law framework establishes

1680. Larouche and De Streel 2021.

a mechanism to resolve the clash. This safeguards the consistency of the framework.

The question of *whether* a conflict of norms arises is more problematic, particularly in the context of national competition law. At first glance, the DMA seems straightforward with regard to its relationship with EU competition law. Reflecting the superior nature of EU primary law, Article 1(6) DMA stresses that the DMA is to be applied *without prejudice* to EU competition law. The DMA can – for the reasons described above – not pre-empt the application of EU competition law. However, Article 1(7) DMA complicates the relationship between EU competition law and the DMA by stressing that national competition law authorities cannot take decisions that run counter to decision of the Commission under the DMA. The fact that Article 1(7) DMA implies a certain degree of executive pre-emption as it limits NCAs from interpreting EU competition law in a manner that runs counter to a DMA decision of the Commission is difficult to reconcile with Article 1(6) DMA.[1681] As a result, Article 1(6) and 1(7) DMA do not neatly align. Those building blocks do not fit seamlessly together, creating a coherence problem.

The relationship with national competition law is even more complicated. Article 1(6) DMA provides a classificatory system determining which instruments of national competition law are pre-empted by the DMA. Article 1(6) DMA follows a similar logic to Article 3(2) Regulation 1/2003 and also relies on various vague concepts. The interpretation of the concepts of national competition rules, rules applicable to undertakings other than gatekeepers and further obligations are, for example, unclear. As a result, the application of Article 1(6) DMA presents problems similar to those concerning the application of Article 3(2) Regulation 1/2003. Due to the lack of a clear classificatory system, it remains unclear to what extent the DMA leaves room for national (competition) laws governing personal data markets, such as Section 19a GWB.[1682] The fact that the DMA does not provide clear guidance on the extent to which different frameworks can co-exist means that the relationship between the instruments is not sufficiently well articulated. This creates a coherence risk.

Apart from the principles of pre-emption and hierarchy of norms, the relationship between competition law and the DMA is shaped by mechanisms of cooperation. This reflects the complementary relationship between the instruments: parallel or consecutive application of competition law and the DMA requires cooperation between the authorities concerned. In the DMA, the EU legislator – unlike the Commission in its initial proposal – explicitly addresses the issue of cooperation. The inclusion of cross-disciplinary cooperation mechanisms in the DMA will have a positive effect on the coherent application of the respective instruments. Despite the fact

---

1681. Beems, Van de Gronden and Rusu 2021, p. 69.
1682. *See* section 7.5.2.3.

that the adoption of cross-disciplinary cooperation mechanisms is a welcome development and can serve as a foundation for a collaborative relationship between the Commission and NCAs in the context of DMA enforcement, certain coherence-related risks remain. Cooperation between authorities is realised in the ECN. Since the Network Notice establishes that the ECN focuses on the 'effective and consistent application of the [EU] competition rules' and the DMA does not fall within the competition law framework, the Network Notice needs updating.[1683] Furthermore, the consequences of decisions adopted in violation of Article 38(2) and (3) DMA, which requires NCAs to inform the Commission of their intention to launch an investigation or impose obligations on gatekeepers based on the national laws referred to in Article 1(6) DMA, are unclear.[1684] As explained in the intra-disciplinary context of competition law, such obligations to notify are of key importance for the functioning of the framework for cooperation. Consequently, the fact that the consequences of violating these obligations remain unclear poses a risk for the functioning of the system and can, therefore, affect the coherence of the framework.

The Cross-Disciplinary Dimension II: Competition Law and the GDPR

In their application to personal data markets, competition and data protection law overlap, particularly because the assessment of abuse of dominance in a competition law context can incorporate data protection considerations. This overlap renders cooperation between competition authorities and data protection supervisors extra important. In the current institutional framework, there are important differences between *mono-* and *multi-jurisdictional* cooperation mechanisms.

Regarding *mono-jurisdictional* cooperation at the national level, the inquiry considered The Netherlands and Germany. In both countries, there are clear mechanisms in place to facilitate interaction between the respective national DPA and NCA. These national mechanisms facilitate the exchange of information between authorities thereby reinforcing the coherence between the two legal branches in the Dutch and German context. At the EU level, the Commission can engage in cooperation with DPAs in the context of the EDPB, albeit only to a limited extent.

Cooperation at the *multi-jurisdictional* level is more problematic. The EU framework does not provide a framework for cooperation between DPAs and NCAs from different Member States. This amounts to a clear gap in the legal framework, as the *Meta Bundeskartellamt* case clearly illustrated the need for this type of cooperation.[1685]

1683. Network Notice, para. 3.
1684. In the context of unilateral conduct, Article 1(6) DMA refers to the following national laws: national competition rules prohibiting abuses of dominant positions and national competition rules prohibiting other forms of unilateral conduct.
1685. CJEU 4 July 2023 Case C-252/21, *Meta Bundeskartellamt*.

The CJEU resolves the lack of a cooperation framework by relying on the general principle of sincere cooperation. Although this provides a partial solution, open questions remain. It is, for example, unclear which forum should facilitate cooperation or which legal basis should permit the exchange of information between authorities. Furthermore, many uncertainties remain as to the practical details of cooperation. This amounts to a gap in the institutional framework governing the interaction between NCAs and DPAs and hypothetically also the interaction between the Commission and DPAs. Given these gaps, the institutional framework is not comprehensive nor complete and, in turn, not coherent.

The gaps in the framework governing multi-jurisdictional cooperation in data protection and competition law may also cause problems in the broader EU law context. As explained in section 3.4.3, in order to justify a violation of the principle of *ne bis in idem,* duplicated proceedings must be conducted in a sufficiently coordinated manner. Furthermore, the coordination between the competent authorities must be predictable.[1686] Hence, due to the absence of cooperation mechanisms governing the multi-jurisdictional interaction between competition and data protection authorities, it will be difficult to justify the sanctioning of a legal person for a GDPR violation if this same person has already been fined for a competition law violation for the same facts. The CJEU makes it unequivocally clear that an NCA, by integrating data protection considerations in a competition law assessment, does not *replace* the leading DPA, nor monitors or enforces the GDPR.[1687] Yet, in the absence of cooperation mechanisms between authorities, the *ne bis in idem* principle could impose limitations on the DPA's competence to apply the GDPR to the legal person that has been sanctioned for an infringement of Article 102 TFEU for the same facts. In order to justify a *ne bis in idem* violation, the proportionality requirement demands coordination between authorities. Consequently, the absence of mechanisms facilitating the interaction between DPAs and competition authorities can amount to an obstacle in successfully justifying a *ne bis in idem* violation. This problem can only be resolved by introducing well-defined mechanisms for multi-jurisdictional cooperation. In designing such mechanisms, the strict independence requirements for DPAs cannot be overlooked.[1688]

Polycentric Cooperation

The interplay between competition law, the DMA and GDPR can also be addressed in fora for polycentric cooperation. The scope of these fora extends beyond the interaction between two fields of law and encompasses the interaction between enforcers of a plethora of legal areas. Such initiatives can play an important role in facilitating a consistent cross-disciplinary

1686. CJEU 22 March 2022 Case C-117/20, *bpost*, para. 58.
1687. CJEU 4 July 2023 Case C-252/21, *Meta Bundeskartellamt*, para. 49.
1688. Article 52 GDPR requires 'complete independence' of DPAs.

approach.[1689] They have the potential to significantly contribute to overarching coherence between: (i) different instruments; and (ii) different jurisdictions. Currently, mechanisms for polycentric cooperation are becoming increasingly relevant. Such cooperation is no longer confined to informal initiatives like the Digital Clearing House, but is actively endorsed at both the EU and the national level. Notable examples include the establishment of the High-Level Group, the SDT and the Digital Cluster Bonn, all of which are commendable developments.

Nevertheless, it is important to note that the initiatives primarily support high-level cooperation.[1690] The fora can contribute to the realisation of common goals or shared priorities, but are not the most effective avenue for facilitating cooperation relating to individual cases. Authorities do not tend to meet very frequently and in meetings multiple perspectives and mandates have to be reconciled. On top of this, in polycentric fora for cooperation a legal basis to share information concerning individual cases is often absent. In sum, while these broad initiatives can complement bilateral cooperation, they cannot replace well-functioning frameworks that govern the particular interaction between the enforcers of two legal branches.

Conclusion

This synthesis assessed the institutional frameworks and cooperation mechanisms of competition law, the GDPR and the DMA in light of the principle of coherence. The analysis identified various risks and potential coherence problems, both of a minor and more significant nature. The next chapter – the final conclusion – further elaborates on the gaps identified in light of the requirement of coherence and aims to provide recommendations.

1689. Which is, for example, one of the explicit objectives of the High-Level Group of Regulators. *See:* Article 3(2) Commission Decision of 23 March 2023 on setting up a High-Level Group for the Digital Markets Act, C(2023) 1833 final.

1690. The Digital Markets Advisory Committee is an exception in this regard. Decision-making in this forum can relate to individual cases.

Chapter 10
Conclusion

10.1 INTRODUCTION

Over the past few decades, rising digital and personal data markets have presented opportunities for the economy and society, but at the same time have posed significant challenges. The *powerful position* of large platforms is a matter of serious concern. In the regulatory context of the EU, several frameworks potentially curb this position of power. These different frameworks, as well as the competences of institutions supervising personal data markets increasingly collide. Overlapping competences are not problematic per se but come with the risk of divergent approaches, scattered enforcement and undue spending of enforcer's resources. Cooperation mechanisms can streamline the application of overlapping competences and can thereby mitigate the risks associated with norm overlaps.[1691] These institutional dynamics are at the heart of the analysis. Ultimately, the objective of inquiry assessed to what extent the institutional frameworks and cooperation mechanisms of national and EU competition law, the DMA and the GDPR can guarantee the coherent application of these instruments to personal data markets. By adopting a unidirectional approach, I placed competition law as the focal point of the analysis. The research considered the EU, German and Dutch context.

This Conclusion aims to answer the main research question of to what extent the institutional frameworks and cooperation mechanisms of national and EU competition law, the DMA and the GDPR can guarantee the coherent

1691. Yakovleva, Geursen and Arnbak 2020, pp. 1467 and 1479.

application of these instruments to personal data markets. To this end, section 10.2 presents an overview of the key findings. Subsequently, section 10.3 provides a coherence analysis. Next, section 10.4 offers recommendations for improving the coherence between the institutional frameworks of competition law, the DMA and the GDPR. Section 10.5 proposes potential avenues for further research. Lastly, section 10.6 puts forward my final remarks.

10.2 KEY FINDINGS

In order to answer the main research question, this inquiry adopted a three-step approach. *Part I* set the scene by providing the context of enforcement in the multi-level legal order of the EU and provided an overview of the functioning of personal data markets. *Part II* examined regulatory responses to conduct on personal data markets, focusing on the interplay between competition law, the DMA and the GDPR. *Part III* analysed the cooperation mechanisms that can facilitate the interaction between the enforcers of these legal branches.

Part I established the relevant context for the research by introducing the concepts of personal data markets, institutions and institutional design, and by outlining the regulatory context of the EU. On personal data markets, which constitute a subset of digital markets, undertakings operate business models that rely on the collection, exchange and/or monetisation of personal data.[1692] Due to their characteristics, such as the presence of multi-sided platforms, network effects, economies of scale and scope and the monetisation of personal data, such markets can be prone to tipping. Accordingly, one undertaking can 'win' the market and get to benefit from a positive feedback loop. This results in high barriers to entry, reinforcing the position of the dominant platform, which can be further cemented by the creation of a so-called platform ecosystem. The powerful position of large platforms gives rise to multiple concerns. Within the regulatory framework of EU law, multiple legal branches – including competition law, the DMA and the GDPR – enable public enforcers to address the powerful position of Big Tech. These legal branches are enforced within the multi-level legal order of the EU. While national rules are enforced by national authorities, EU law is enforced at both the national and the EU level, resulting in a complex interplay between national and EU institutions. As set out in sections 3.3 and 3.4, several important principles govern this complicated regulatory interplay. The principles of institutional and procedural autonomy, sincere cooperation, and *ne bis in idem* are particularly relevant in this regard. This project has focused on institutional frameworks and cooperation between enforcers. Institutions are defined as 'formal and informal bodies that are charged by a society with making, administrating, enforcing or adjudicating

1692. For a more extensive taxonomy of personal data markets *see:* S. Schneider et al. 2023.

its laws or policies' and institutional design covers the institution's mandates and organisational design, which includes the structures and processes that have a bearing on enforcement and the application of the law.[1693]

Part II built upon Part I and analysed the application of competition law, the DMA and the GDPR to personal data markets. The analysis focused particularly on the interplay between these legal branches. I concluded that the characteristics of personal data markets are a catalyst for an increasing overlap between competition law, the DMA and the GDPR. This overlap largely results from two main developments, as highlighted in Synthesis I. *First*, due to their characteristics, personal data markets are prone to 'tipping' and tend to be highly concentrated.[1694] The competition law framework can partially resolve issues relating to market power but is not equipped to deal with all the challenges associated with such markets. The EU legislator aimed to resolve these shortcomings by introducing a novel instrument: the DMA. Despite the fact that the DMA was adopted against the background of the shortcomings of competition law, it is not a competition law instrument.[1695] This results in an overlap between this novel (regulatory) instrument and traditional competition law. *Second,* due to the monetisation of personal data, the level of data protection has become a competitive parameter.[1696] As a result – in certain circumstances – data protection considerations must be taken into account in assessing an abuse of a dominant position.[1697] This leads to an integration of GDPR considerations in competition law assessments.

Overlapping competences between enforcers can manifest themselves in different ways. On the one hand, multiple authorities can have the competence to start parallel or consecutive procedures by applying their 'own' regulatory framework. This situation occurs in particular in relation to EU competition law, national competition law and the DMA. On the other hand, authorities can rely on concepts from one area of law to interpret rules of another framework. The German *Bundeskartellamt*, for example, borrowed rules of data protection law in order to interpret German competition law, thereby 'internalising' or integrating GDPR considerations. This manifestation of norm overlap creates clear ties between legal fields.

The overlapping competences identified in Part II result in a need for cooperation between authorities to mitigate the risks associated with these

1693. Balogh and Cseres 2013, p. 345.
1694. *See* Chapter 2.
1695. Commission Staff Working Document Impact Assessment Report Accompanying the document Proposal for a Regulation of the European Parliament and of the Council on contestable and fair markets in the digital sector (Digital Markets Act), SWD(2020) 363 final, p. 10.
1696. CJEU 4 July 2023 Case C-252/21, *Meta Bundeskartellamt*, para. 51; Commission Notice of 22 February 2024 on the definition of the relevant market for the purpose of Union competition law, C/2024/1645, para. 15.
1697. CJEU 4 July 2023 Case C-252/21 *Meta Bundeskartellamt*, para. 48.

overlaps. *Part III* studied the mechanisms that are in place to facilitate cooperation and started with an analysis of mechanisms of pre-emption and hierarchy of norms. If there are clear mechanisms that resolve conflicts between norms, it will be clear which set of rules takes precedence and the risks of incoherencies are minimal. The principles of pre-emption and norm hierarchies are useful in order to guarantee the coherent application of norms, but are not sufficient as such. As identified in Part II, in relation to competition law, the DMA and the GDPR, norms are often applied complementarily, meaning that the joint application of norms results in synergies.[1698] This scenario necessitates the application of both sets of overlapping norms and requires cooperation mechanisms in order to guarantee the coherent application of norms. Synthesis II built on Part III and provided the groundwork for the coherence analysis below. The synthesis mapped the main gaps in the cooperation frameworks. In this Conclusion, in line with the main research question, I build on the syntheses and further theorise the assessment by providing an analysis through the lens of coherence.

10.3 COHERENCE ANALYSIS

Section 1.4 defined and operationalised the criterion of *coherence.* In the context of this inquiry, coherence consists of two components, i.e., consistency and cohesion. *First*, consistency demands the absence of contradictions. *Second*, the criterion of cohesion requires that frameworks form a unified and systemic whole serving overarching objectives and/or principles. To further exemplify this criterion, I rely on the operationalisation criteria of *comprehensiveness, completeness* and *articulateness.*[1699] Comprehensiveness and completeness require that there are no gaps or irresolvable issues in the system. The principle of articulateness calls for explicit methods for determining whether a conflict arises (i.e., principles of pre-emption) and how a conflict can be solved (i.e., principles of hierarchy of norms) are available.

As concluded in Synthesis I and II, the interplay between: (i) EU and national competition law; (ii) competition law and the DMA; and (iii) competition law and the GDPR is not identical. Moreover, the available cooperation mechanisms are context-dependent. Against this background, as the respective overlaps diverge to a significant extent, general conclusions do not tell the whole story. For this reason, before drawing overarching

---

1698. *See* Synthesis I: Part II.

1699. Kress also lists the criteria of monism, unity and justification. These criteria are well-suited to analyse the coherence of a theory, but are less suitable to analyse the degree of coherence of the institutional framework of competition law, the DMA and the GDPR. Kress 2010. *See* section 1.4.

conclusions, the specificities of the different legal branches are addressed in turn.

10.3.1 Coherence: EU and National Competition Law

In the context of EU and national competition law, the framework for cooperation is elaborate and largely formalised. There are multiple fora for cooperation and the interaction between authorities is streamlined within the ECN. Within the cooperation framework for competition law, no clear contradictions were identified. Therefore, the framework is *consistent*.

Since no major gaps were identified, I contend that the framework governing the interaction between national and EU competition law is largely *complete* and *comprehensive* on paper. Yet, some (practical) issues may jeopardise the comprehensiveness of the framework. These issues do not relate to the rules of the framework itself, but rather to: (i) its practical application; or (ii) the lack of clarity regarding the consequences of violations of important obligations.

First, in its application of EU competition law, the Commission can circumvent the applicability of certain cooperation mechanisms. By artificially carving out parts of the relevant market, the application of Article 11(6) Regulation 1/2003 can, for example, be avoided. As a result, NCAs are not relieved of their competence to apply EU competition law, leading to (potential) parallel proceedings. Moreover, undertakings are not protected by the *ne bis in idem* principle, as the parallel procedures do not cover the same relevant markets.[1700] Consequently, in this scenario, a gap arises in the institutional framework. This gap results from the way in which the EU competition law framework is applied, rather than from the institutional framework itself. *Second,* the consequences of a violation of the duty of parallel application or NCA's obligation to notify the Commission of investigations or intended decisions are not crystalised.[1701] Article 3(1) Regulation 1/2003 requires the parallel application of EU competition law and national competition law in cases with an effect on trade between Member States, thereby triggering the applicability of the cooperation mechanisms. Moreover, notification to the Commission is of the utmost importance for the system's functioning. Consequently, in order to avoid undermining the competition law framework's comprehensiveness, the Commission and NCAs should observe the obligations of the framework.

Considered through the lens of the operationalisation criterion of articulateness, the relationship between EU and national competition law is more problematic. The relationship between EU and national law is set out

---

1700. CJEU 25 February 2021 Case C-857/19, *Slovak Telekom*, para. 30; CJEU 20 April 2023 Case C-815/21P, *Amazon v. Commission*, paras 27 and 31.
1701. Article 11(3) and (4) Regulation 1/2003.

in Article 3(2) Regulation 1/2003. However, since this provision is incredibly complex, and relies on multiple ill-defined concepts, such as 'national competition law', 'stricter', and a 'predominantly different objective', doubts arise as to the pre-emptive effect of EU competition law. Consequently, there are uncertainties regarding the extent to which the competition law framework allows for national (competition) laws. This means that it is not clear whether a conflict between EU and national competition law arises in a particular case. The framework is thus not well articulated which amounts to a coherence problem. The issue is particularly pertinent in relation to digital markets, as various Member States have established new (competition) frameworks in order to address the position of Big Tech, and it is not precisely clear to what extent EU law leaves room for such frameworks.

10.3.2 Coherence: Competition Law and the DMA

The DMA provides a framework for cooperation between the Commission and NCAs in the context of competition law. Section 7.5.1 identified a potential contradiction within this framework. While Article 1(6) DMA establishes that the application of the DMA is 'without prejudice' to the application of national and EU competition law, Article 1(7) DMA provides that NCAs cannot take decisions that 'run counter' to a Commission's DMA decision. It is, therefore, unclear how the DMA cannot prejudice the application of national and EU competition law by an NCA, while simultaneously imposing a certain degree of executive pre-emption.[1702] Since these provisions appear contradictory, the framework is not entirely *consistent.*

Considering the *completeness* and *comprehensiveness*, no major gaps were identified in relation to the cooperation framework between NCAs and the Commission in the context of the DMA. Relying on experience with Regulation 1/2003, the DMA contains a solid framework governing the interaction between authorities, including a forum for cooperation and a legal basis for the exchange of information.[1703] Overall, the framework can be considered complete and comprehensive. Nevertheless, some issues, and open questions relating to violations of cooperation obligations remain. The Network Notice, for example, needs to be updated in order to extend the scope of the ECN to cooperation in the field of the DMA. Furthermore, the consequences of violations of Article 38(2) and (3) DMA, which establish that NCAs should inform the Commission of national (competition) law investigations or the imposition of obligations on gatekeepers, are not clear. This does not amount to a coherence problem of the framework as such, but can nevertheless jeopardise the functioning of the framework.

1702. *See* section 7.5.1.
1703. Article 38 DMA.

Like the competition law discussion set out in section 10.3.1, the *articulateness* of the relationship between the DMA and competition law is problematic. Considering the relation between *national* competition law and the DMA, Article 1(5) and (6) DMA apply a logic similar to that of Article 3(2) Regulation 1/2003. Unfortunately, the DMA also relies on vague and ill-defined concepts, such as 'national competition rules', 'further obligations' and 'applicable to undertakings other than gatekeepers'. This means that the classificatory system of this provision – to a certain extent – triggers problems similar to the issues identified in the context of competition law. This is unsurprising given the fact that the enforcement and institutional frameworks are partially modelled on Regulation 1/2003.[1704] As a consequence of the unclarities relating to Article 1(5) and (6) DMA, the framework does not clearly establish the relationship between national competition law and the DMA. Consequently, it is not well articulated to what extent the DMA leaves room for national competition laws.

10.3.3 Coherence: Competition Law and the GDPR

Regarding competition law and the GDPR, the degree to which cooperation frameworks in the field of competition law and the GDPR are coherent is context-dependent: mono-jurisdictional mechanisms are far more developed than multi-jurisdictional frameworks. Before addressing the cohesion of both dimensions in more detail, it should be stressed that no clear *inconsistencies* have been identified in the institutional frameworks.

Considering the cohesion of the frameworks in a *mono-jurisdictional* context, frameworks for cooperation have been well developed in the national context. In both Germany and The Netherlands, elaborate frameworks enable the interaction between authorities, also providing a legal basis for the exchange of information. Consequently, the frameworks are sufficiently *complete* and *comprehensive*. At the EU level, the Commission can interact with the EDPB. While this can facilitate a certain degree of coherence, certain uncertainties remain. In the past, Vestager pointed out that cooperation on individual cases is complicated, particularly because there is no legal basis for the exchange of information.[1705] Given the lack of a legal basis, the frameworks are *not* fully *comprehensive* and *complete*.

The *multi-jurisdictional* framework is even less coherent and more under-developed. In the cross-disciplinary and multi-jurisdictional context of competition law and the GDPR, no explicit mechanisms for cooperation are in place. In order to fill this gap, the CJEU derives certain obligations from the principle of sincere cooperation.[1706] Despite the fact that this approach

1704. *See* section 5.3.3.
1705. White and Ali 2020.
1706. CJEU 4 July 2023 Case C-252/21, *Meta Bundeskartellamt*, paras 53-54.

provides some guidance, it does not provide a resilient solution. Important prerequisites for cooperation, such as a legal basis for the exchange of information and a forum for cooperation, remain non-existent. This represents a clear gap in the institutional framework. Consequently, the framework is not sufficiently *comprehensive* and *complete* and, therefore, not coherent.

With respect to the criterion of *articulateness* and considering the relationship between competition law and the GDPR, there are mechanisms in place to resolve potential conflicts. The GDPR does not limit the national legislator's freedom to adopt competition laws, because this instrument does, unlike the DMA, not have a pre-emptive effect on national competition law. Yet, in the case of conflicting norms, the GDPR takes precedence over national laws according to the primacy of EU law. This can be particularly relevant in relation to the German competition law provisions on data sharing. While the application of the doctrines of essential facilities and refusal to supply in the context of personal data is still rather controversial in the context of EU competition law, the German competition law framework explicitly establishes a potential obligation for the sharing of data.[1707] If the requested data sets contain personal data, sharing may violate the GDPR. This potentially amounts to a conflict between German competition law and the GDPR. Yet, no genuine problem of coherence arises in this scenario because it is clear that EU law takes precedence over national law. Hence, German competition law cannot limit the application of the GDPR and the relationship between the rules is well *articulated.* Considering this notion of articulateness, the relationship between the GDPR and Article 102 TFEU is more complicated. The GDPR, an instrument of secondary law, cannot limit the application of Article 102, i.e., an instrument of primary law. However, despite the fact that the CFR as such does not fall within the scope of the analysis, it should be acknowledged that the right to data protection is not merely enshrined in the GDPR, but also in the CFR and in Article 16 TFEU. Article 102 TFEU is not hierarchically superior to Article 16 TFEU or to the CFR. Therefore, if a situation falls within the scope of the CFR, a more nuanced approach is required. When confronted with this scenario, the CJEU would have to carry out a weighing exercise by balancing the interests of data protection and competition law.

10.3.4 Overarching Conclusions

The analysis above shows that, in light of the coherence analysis, important differences are present between the different areas of the law. Consequently, the answer to the main research question is complicated and demands a nuanced approach. Coherence is a matter of degree: none of the frameworks

1707. *See* section 4.4.2.2.

is fully coherent, but the frameworks of competition law and the DMA are clearly 'more' coherent than the framework governing the interaction between the GDPR and competition law. The different operationalisation criteria of the principle of coherence served as a useful normative tool to uncover these differences. While the coherence problems in the areas of competition law and the DMA largely relate to the articulateness of the different rules, the framework governing the relationship between the GDPR and competition law is incomprehensive and incomplete.

Moreover, the bilateral interactions between the different frameworks cannot be considered in isolation, but should be considered in the broader regulatory context of the EU. This means that – despite the differences between the frameworks – some important principles are of overarching relevance. These overarching conclusions aim to complement the context-dependent conclusions provided in the previous section.

The principle of *sincere cooperation* constitutes the backbone for multi-jurisdictional cooperation between authorities in the EU. This principle is the foundation for cooperation mechanisms established in Regulation 1/2003 and in the DMA. In the context of transdisciplinary multi-jurisdictional cooperation between data protection and competition authorities, the CJEU falls back on the principle of sincere cooperation in the absence of any specific cooperation frameworks.[1708] Although the principle provides tools for filling potential gaps in the legislative framework, it is not sufficiently clear and cannot substitute a well-functioning cooperation framework.[1709]

Considering the complementary application of different legal branches, the principle of *ne bis in idem* cannot be overlooked. It provides an important limitation by prohibiting double jeopardy and plays a vital role in safeguarding the (procedural) rights of undertakings. The importance of cooperation between authorities in cases of the parallel or consecutive application of legal branches is reflected in the CJEU's interpretation of the *ne bis in idem* principle. Violations of this principle can only be justified if there are rules which predict that there will be coordination between competent authorities and if the proceedings are conducted in a sufficiently coordinated manner.[1710] In the case of the imposition of sanctions imposed on one and the same (legal) person for the same facts, coordination between authorities is, thus, a prerequisite under EU law. This means that well-functioning cooperation mechanisms must be in place. I contend that such mechanisms are absent in the context of the multi-jurisdictional cooperation between competition and data protection authorities. Moreover, the protective function of the *ne bis in idem* principle can be put in jeopardy if the Commission carves out certain national markets in order not to relieve NCAs of their competence to apply

1708. CJEU 4 July 2023 Case C-252/21, *Meta Bundeskartellamt*, para. 53.
1709. Csatlós 2018, p. 67.
1710. CJEU 22 March 2022 Case C-117/20, *bpost*, para. 58.

EU competition law. If the Commission makes such carve outs without viable economic reasons, the application of the *ne bis in idem* principle is circumvented. Consequently, the principle does not provide protection against parallel or consecutive proceedings. Despite the fact that the principle of *ne bis in idem* is not applicable in this scenario and is, therefore, not violated, the undertaking concerned faces parallel proceedings. The absence of proper protection against double jeopardy in this scenario is problematic.

Consequently, while the principle of sincere cooperation can resolve certain coherence-related problems, it cannot fully resolve the issues identified in the previous Section. The principle of *ne bis in idem* clearly illustrates and further reinforces the need for well-functioning cooperation mechanisms, since a violation of this principle cannot be justified in the absence of coordination between authorities.

10.4 RECOMMENDATIONS

This inquiry has identified various gaps and shortcomings in the institutional frameworks and mechanisms for cooperation in the areas of competition law, the GDPR and the DMA. Resolving these issues will be a challenging exercise: cooperation takes place in the multi-level legal order of the EU. Due to the complexity of this legal order, the interplay between EU and national law and the differences between the legal branches, it is impossible to provide a one-size-fits-all solution. The suggestion to establish a 'super' platform regulator, for example, does not take stock of political reality nor of the nuances of the division of competences between the EU and the Member States, of the limitations of the Treaties and of general EU principles, including the principle of institutional autonomy. Moreover, the solution does not acknowledge the difference between the different legal branches. This issue is particularly relevant for the interplay between competition law and the GDPR. Despite their partially overlapping objectives, these branches also pursue different goals. In this light, competition problems and data protection problems are not always identical. Moreover, the requirement of independence is particularly strict in the context of DPAs. The proposal for a 'super' regulator does not sufficiently take these nuances into consideration. In my view, it is, hence, clear that the coherence problems cannot be resolved by the mere introduction of a single legal instrument or new institution.

Despite the fact that it is impossible to provide an all-encompassing solution to the coherence problems, several measures for the improvement of cooperation between authorities, thereby contributing to the coherent application of competition law, the GDPR and the DMA, should be implemented.

First, the institutional dimension and interactions between frameworks should be addressed at an early stage of any legislative procedure in order to enable discussions on the optimal institutional solution. The failure to address the role of NCAs in the initial DMA proposal, for example, represents a significant missed opportunity.[1711] Institutions and enforcement are of the utmost importance for the effective application of the law. The fact that the EU is currently working on a myriad of initiatives relating to data, platforms and digital markets makes the need to address the interaction between these instruments even more prominent. In order to streamline overlapping rules and competences, the relationships between overlapping norms must be mapped properly throughout the legislative procedure. In this mapping exercise, the relevance of institutional design and cooperation should not be overlooked.

Second, considering the pre-emptive effect of both EU competition law and the DMA, it is essential to clarify certain concepts. At this point, the fact that the classificatory provision of Article 3(2) Regulation 1/2003 and Article 1(5) and (6) DMA rely on ill-defined concepts, such as 'national competition law', 'stricter' and a 'predominantly different objective' makes it unclear to what extent the EU framework leaves room for additional national (competition) laws. This results in blurred lines between permissible experimentation by Member States and harmonised areas.[1712] Further interpretative guidance on the concepts relied on in Article 3(2) Regulation 1/2003 and 1(6) DMA is imperative to clarify the pre-emptive effect of competition law and the DMA. Providing further clarity on the notion *of national competition* rules is of particular importance. If it were more evident which national laws amount to competition law, it would become clearer which national laws can be adopted and which initiatives are not allowed in light of the pre-emptive effect of EU competition law. Therefore, the notion of national competition law should be defined as an *autonomous* concept of EU law. If the national qualification of a law were determinative, Member States could circumvent the pre-emptive effect of EU law by labelling economic regulation as competition laws.[1713]

Although it is clear that the concept of national competition rules should be established at the EU level, defining this concept is not a straightforward exercise, particularly in light of regulatory developments. Various instruments, such as the DMA and Section 19a GWB, do not neatly fit within the 'traditional' categories of competition law and economic regulation. Instead, these novel instruments are regulatory and competition law 'chimeras'.[1714] Consequently, in the current regulatory reality, the boundaries between economic regulation and competition law are not crystal clear. Yet, in order to establish the pre-emptive effect of EU competition law and the DMA, the

1711. Commission Staff Working Document Impact Assessment Report Accompanying the document Proposal for a Regulation of the European Parliament and of the Council on contestable and fair markets in the digital sector (Digital Markets Act), SWD(2020) 363 final (DMA Proposal).
1712. Wagner-von Papp 2024, p. 344.
1713. Drexl et al. 2023, p. 865.
1714. Zilsdorf 2023.

dichotomy between competition law and economic regulation is a determinative factor. Consequently, although the distinction between competition law and economic regulation is blurry in practice, the notion of national competition law should be defined clearly.

By focusing on the objectives of the national laws, Regulation 1/2003 invokes an 'unworkable test' that must be abolished.1681[1715] The DMA's definition of competition offers a better alternative, although uncertainties remain. Recital 10 of the DMA's Preamble stresses that national competition rules regarding unilateral conduct should be based on an individualised assessment and should allow for efficiency and objective justification arguments. Safeguarding the coherence of the EU legal framework requires that Regulation 1/2003 adopts the definition provided in the DMA. Next, it is essential that the CJEU further clarifies the boundaries of 'national competition rules' if it would be confronted with a case on Article 3(2) Regulation 1/2003 or Article 1(5) and (6) DMA.[1716] In order not to excessively reduce the relevance of national initiatives and benefit from experimentation at the national level, the notion of competition law should not be defined too narrowly.[1717] Accordingly, per se rules cannot be considered national competition law, while more flexible rules or rules allowing for efficiency or objective justification defences should be qualified as such. More concretely, in my view, Section 19a GWB leaves sufficient room for an individualised assessment and should be classified as national competition law.

The notion of national competition laws is not the only concept that requires clarification. Other determinative concepts, such as 'further obligations' and 'stricter obligations' are also insufficiently clear. Given the fact that Article 1(5) and (6) DMA to a certain extent replicate the test of Article 3 Regulation 1/2003, clarifications on one provision can provide useful guidance that can be transposed to its counterpart. Admittedly, not all notions set out in the respective provisions are not identical. Where the DMA refers to *further* provisions, competition law relies on the concept of *stricter* provisions. At this point, it remains uncertain whether the notions of further and stricter obligations have an identical meaning. In the context of competition law, 'stricter rules' can take various shapes, including rules with a broader personal scope, material scope or stricter sanctions. The concept of 'further obligations' seems also to cover rules with a broader personal or material scope, but stricter sanctions do not neatly fit within this category. Consequently, the concept of further obligations may be narrower than the concept of stricter rule. The CJEU should provide more clarity in this regard.

Third, considering cooperation between the Commission and NCAs in the context of DMA enforcement, the cooperation framework clearly

1715. Brook and Eben 2022.
1716. Van den Boom 2022, pp. 65-68; Graef 2024, p. 165.
1717. Drexl et al. 2023, p. 14; Graef 2024, p. 174; Käseberg and Gappa 2024a, p. 24.

resembles existing competition law mechanisms. This is promising because – as mentioned above – the framework for cooperation between NCAs and the Commission is rather well-functioning. Yet, in order to accommodate cross-disciplinary cooperation between NCAs and the Commission in its capacity as DMA enforcers, further adjustments and clarifications must be implemented. First, the scope of the Network Notice needs to be extended in order to allow cooperation in the context of the DMA.[1718] Second, at this point, the relationship between Article 1(6) and 1(7) DMA is not sufficiently clear. In this light, the CJEU should interpret the phrase 'run counter' within the meaning of Article 1(7) DMA and provide guidance on its precise meaning. In other words, clarification is needed as to the degree to which Article 1(7) DMA can impose limitations on NCAs in their application of EU competition law.

Fourth, another point potentially resulting in coherency issues is the unclarity on the legal consequences of violations of important provisions, such as the duty of parallel application, i.e., Article 3(1) Regulation 1/2003, as well as Article 11(3) and (4) Regulation 1/2003, which establish that NCAs shall notify the Commission about EU competition law investigations or decisions. If Article 11(4) Regulation 1/2003 is violated in a systemic way, this will jeopardise the overall functioning of competition law's cooperation mechanisms. Similarly, uncertainties exist in the context of the DMA. The consequences of violations of Article 38(2) and 38(3) DMA, which require NCAs to notify the Commission about certain investigations under national competition law or about the imposition of obligations on gatekeepers, are not clear. In my view, decisions adopted in violation of these provisions are not necessarily invalid and unenforceable. Yet, systematic violations of these obligations would jeopardise the functioning of the cooperation mechanisms established in the DMA. Since compliance with these obligations to cooperate is a prerequisite for the overall functioning of the cooperation mechanisms in the DMA and in competition law, the Commission should continuously monitor whether these obligations are complied with. If certain Member States would violate Articles 3(1), 11(3), 11(4) Regulation 1/2003 or Article 38(2) or 38(3) DMA, Commission should launch an infringement procedure.[1719] However, since infringement procedures tend to be long, this avenue should only be taken in exceptional cases of systemic violations.[1720]

Fifth, while the frameworks of competition law and the DMA mostly require smaller tweaks and clarifications, the institutional framework governing the interplay between NCAs and DPAs demands more substantial

1718. Currently, para. 3 of the Network Notice refers to 'the effective and consistent application of [EU] competition rules'.
1719. Article 258 TFEU.
1720. The European Court of Auditors concluded that infringement procedures take too long. *See:* European Court of Auditors 17 December 2024, 'Infringement procedures: Enforcing EU law takes too long' https://www.eca.europa.eu/en/news/NEWS-SR-2024-28 accessed 25 March 2025.

reforms. At this point, the interaction between NCAs and DPAs in a multi-jurisdictional context is merely governed by the principle of sincere cooperation. This principle provides a proper basis for cooperation, but is not sufficiently concrete to serve as a foundation for building relationships between authorities. Additionally, the exchange of information lacks any legal basis. Given the multi-jurisdictional and cross-border nature of this issue, the EU legislator is best placed to take action. The EU legislator should introduce secondary EU legislation harmonising cooperation between NCAs and DPAs in a cross-border context. The *Meta Bundeskartellamt* case clearly signals the need for such harmonisation. This form of cooperation cannot be realised by bilateral cooperation agreements at the national level. Under the consistency mechanisms of the GDPR, every national DPA can potentially qualify as lead supervisor. Moreover, both the Commission and NCAs of the different Member States can apply EU competition law. In order to facilitate cooperation between every potential authority involved, 27 DPAs would have to negotiate bilateral agreements with (at least) 27 NCAs. An extensive collection of bilateral agreements is not a suitable instrument for the introduction of a well-functioning cooperation mechanism. In order to make sure that further clarity is provided as to the level of cooperation and the division of tasks between authorities, top-down action of the EU is required.[1721] The new EU instrument should provide a harmonised procedure to facilitate cross-border cooperation between NCAs and DPAs. To achieve this, the EU legislator should adopt a directive. The new instrument could be based on Article 103 TFEU, Articles 16 and 114 TFEU. The EU legislator does not have to reinvent the wheel. Rather, it can draw inspiration from existing frameworks. EU legislation on cooperation between national authorities, such as the DMA, Regulation 1/2003 and the ECN+ Directive will provide useful insights. Article 38 DMA can serve as inspiration to draw a framework for the exchange of information. This provision establishes a basis to exchange information in a cross-disciplinary setting and, consequently, provides a useful template. More concretely, provisions mirroring Article 38(1) and (5) DMA should be transposed to the cross-disciplinary context of competition law and the GDPR. According to this provision, authorities shall have the power to provide each other with any information regarding any matter of fact or of law, including confidential information, for the purpose of coordination of enforcement. Beyond providing a legal basis for the sharing of information, the harmonised framework should introduce single points of contact in data protection and competition authorities.[1722] Establishing dedicated teams responsible for cross-disciplinary cooperation would facilitate an easier interaction between authorities. The dedicated

1721. Yakovleva, Geursen and Arnbak 2020, p. 1492.

1722. Such a single point of contact would not be a novelty. In the context of cooperation between the Dutch DPA and NCA, Article 4 Cooperation Protocol sets out that both authorities should establish a first point of contact.

teams could also receive additional training on the relevant legal landscape and cross-disciplinary developments.[1723] In addition to the harmonised framework, (informal) high-level cross-disciplinary interactions between authorities can enhance cooperation. Such interactions allow authorities to identify potential synergies while also minimising obstacles to cooperation. Regular meetings between different authorities, working groups or joint events can help to create a spirit of cooperation. Consequently, the importance of polycentric initiatives, such as the High-Level Group, the Dutch SDT and the German Digital Cluster Bonn should be endorsed and actively supported at the EU and national level.

10.5 AVENUES FOR FURTHER RESEARCH

This inquiry assessed the interplay between competition law, the DMA and the GDPR from an institutional perspective. Beyond the conclusions outlined above, several avenues for further research merit consideration.

First, the scope of this project is limited to a unidirectional analysis focusing on competition law. Yet, other dimensions of the overlap are also interesting and deserve further attention. The interplay between the DMA and the GDPR is, for example, very relevant.[1724] At this point, there are few examples of research on substantive overlaps between these areas of law. Hence, the institutional dimension of the DMA and GDPR intersection is still underexplored. This presents an interesting avenue for further research.

Second, this project relied on a legal doctrinal methodology. It mapped and assessed the institutional frameworks of competition law, the DMA and the GDPR. However, a broader and multi-disciplinary approach could provide further insights into the law in practice. In order to analyse the effectiveness of cooperation mechanisms, it could be interesting to conduct an empirical study based on: (i) a (quantitative) analysis of documents on the cooperation between authorities, including annual reports of authorities and documents that can be obtained via open government acts; and/or (ii) a qualitative analysis of interviews conducted with (former) officials of the respective authorities.

Third, the analysis focused on the application of the principle of coherence. However, overlapping competences of different authorities in the EU have a broad range of implications. For instance, decision-making in

1723. European Data Protection Board 16 January 2025 'Position paper on Interplay between data protection and competition law' https://www.edpb.europa.eu/system/files/2025-01/edpb_position-paper_20250116_interplay-between-data-protection-and-competition-law_en.pdf accessed 24 March 2025, para. 24.
1724. European Data Protection Board 16 January 2025 'Position paper on Interplay between data protection and competition law' https://www.edpb.europa.eu/system/files/2025-01/edpb_position-paper_20250116_interplay-between-data-protection-and-competition-law_en.pdf accessed 24 March 2025.

joint bodies and networks can result in accountability and transparency issues. These principles would provide suitable normative tools in order to further unravel the implications of norm overlaps in the regulatory landscape of the EU.

Fourth, while this inquiry has focused on the interaction between public enforcers, private enforcement represents another enforcement pillar to achieve the objectives of competition law, the DMA and the GDPR, which can ultimately help to address issues associated with personal data markets.[1725] Consequently, the increasing interaction between these legal domains is not only relevant from a public enforcement perspective but can also have implications for private enforcement. A cross-disciplinary analysis of private enforcement across the areas of competition law, the DMA and the GDPR presents a compelling and timely avenue for further research.

Lastly, the interplay between the primary law instruments of competition and data protection deserves further academic attention. While the principle of primacy provides a norm hierarchy in the context of competition law and the GDPR, the relationship between Article 102 TFEU on the one hand, and Article 16 TFEU and Articles 7 and 8 CFR on the other hand, is more complicated. These provisions all constitute primary EU law, and Article 6 TEU stresses that the CFR and the Treaties have 'the same legal value'. Consequently, there is no norm hierarchy in place. In the case of a conflict, the CJEU would have to weigh and balance data protection and competition law concerns. The weighing and balancing of these primary norms in the context of data protection and competition law is currently underexplored in the literature.

10.6 FINAL REMARKS

The rise of personal data markets presents numerous challenges that also impact the institutional frameworks of the EU and the Member States. In order to effectively regulate personal data markets, a proper understanding of the interplay between different frameworks is of vital importance. At this point, the interrelation between different branches of the law is not always addressed sufficiently. Both the EU and various Member States have introduced multiple instruments in order to address the challenges associated with Big Tech. Given the magnitude of the risks related to large platforms, these efforts are praiseworthy. However, as a result, the regulatory landscape has become ever more crowded and complex. In order to effectively apply the different instruments, the relationship and interactions between the different tools and levels should not be overlooked. This complexity further reinforces the need for cross-disciplinary cooperation and research. Research should not only focus on the substantive dimension but also take into account

1725. Podszun 2022d, p. 254.

the implications for different enforcers at the national and EU level. The institutional dimension deserves more attention, especially since cooperation between authorities has become increasingly complex. This inquiry showed that different domains of the law – i.e., competition law, the GDPR and the DMA – should not be considered in isolation. The various legal branches are not silos, but are interconnected, necessitating interaction between authorities as well. At this point, the mechanisms in place do not suffice to facilitate the coherent application of the different rules. Considering the institutional dimension of this discussion, it is not always clear who should do what.[1726] Yet, in light of overlapping competences, well-functioning mechanisms of cooperation are a prerequisite for the effective oversight of personal data markets. Therefore, institutional frameworks need updating and clarification. Only if authorities do not operate in isolation but cooperate sufficiently, can many hands make light work indeed.

1726. Hyman and Kovacic 2014.

Bibliography

Literature

Abate, Bianco and Casalini 2024

C. Abate, G. Bianco and F. Casalini, 'The Intersection Between Competition and Data Privacy', OECD Roundtables on Competition Policy Papers No. 310 (2024) https://www.oecd.org/en/publications/the-intersection-between-competition-and-data-privacy_0dd065a3-en.html accessed 24 March 2025.

Acquisti 2004

A. Acquisti, 'Privacy in Electronic Commerce and the Economics of Immediate Gratification' (2004) https://dl.acm.org/doi/10.1145/988772.988777 accessed 4 March 2025.

Acquisti and Grossklags 2005

A. Acquisti and J. Grossklags, 'Privacy and Rationality in Individual Decision Making' (2005) 3 IEEE Security & Privacy 26 https://doi.org/10.1109/msp.2005.22 accessed 29 August 2025.

Acquisti, John and Loewenstein 2013

A. Acquisti, L. John and G. Loewenstein, 'What Is Privacy Worth?' (2013) 42 The Journal of Legal Studies 249 https://doi.org/10.1086/671754 accessed 29 August 2025.

Acquisti 2014

A. Acquisti, 'The Economics and Behavioral Economics of Privacy' in J. Lane, V. Stodden and S. Bender (eds), *Privacy, Big Data, and the Public Good: Frameworks for Engagement* (Cambridge University Press 2014).

Acquisti, Taylor and Wagman 2016

A. Acquisti, C. Taylor and L. Wagman, 'The Economics of Privacy' (2016) 54 Journal of Economic Literature 442 https://doi.org/10.1257/jel.54.2.442 accessed 29 August 2025.

Actis Perinetto and Marquis 2017

P. Actis Perinetto and M. Marquis, 'Abuse of Dominance in Regulated Sectors in Italy: Recent Enforcement Trends' in P. Parcu, G. Monti and M. Botta (eds), *Abuse of Dominance in EU Competition Law* (Elgar Online 2017).

Akman 2019

P. Akman, 'An Agenda for Competition Law and Policy in the Digital Economy' (2019) 10 Journal of European Competition Law & Practice 589 https://doi.org/10.1093/jeclap/lpz055 accessed 29 August 2025.

Akman 2022

P. Akman, 'Regulating Competition in Digital Platform Markets: A Critical Assessment of the Framework and Approach of the EU Digital Markets Act' (2022) 47 European Law Review 1, 85.

Akman 2024

P. Akman, 'A Critical Inquiry into "Abuse" in EU Competition Law' (2024) 44 Oxford Journal of Legal Studies 405 https://doi.org/10.1093/ojls/gqae008 accessed 29 August 2025.

Akman, Fumagalli and Motta 2024

P. Akman, C. Fumagalli and M. Motta, 'The European Commission's Draft Guidelines on Exclusionary Abuses: A Law and Economics Critique and Recommendations' (2024) https://papers.ssrn.com/sol3/papers.cfm?abstract_id=5027376 accessed 5 February 2025.

Alexiadis and De Streel 2020

P. Alexiadis and A. De Streel, 'Designing an EU Intervention Standard for Digital Platforms' (2020) https://cadmus.eui.eu/handle/1814/66307 accessed 11 March 2025.

Allen and Flores 2013

J. Allen and N. Flores, 'Report for the Dutch Ministry of Economic Affairs: The Role of Government in the Internet' (2013) https://www.analysysmason.com/globalassets/x_migrated-media/media/analysys-mason-report-for-ministry-of-economic-affairs-230413.pdf accessed 10 June 2023.

Alexy and Peczenik 1990

R. Alexy and A. Peczenik, 'The Concept of Coherence and Its Significance for Discursive Rationality' (1990) 3 Ratio Juris 130 https://doi.org/10.1111/j.1467-9337.1990.tb00076.x accessed 29 August 2025.

Allen et al. 2020

D. Allen et al., 'Some Economic Consequences of the GDPR' https://papers.ssrn.com/sol3/papers.cfm?abstract_id=3160404 accessed 14 March 2025.

Andriychuk 2022

O. Andriychuk, 'Do DMA Obligations for Gatekeepers Create Entitlements for Business Users?' (2023) 11 Journal of Antitrust Enforcement 1, 123 https://doi.org/10.1093/jaenfo/jnac034 accessed 29 August 2025.

Appeldoorn and Vedder 2010

J. Appeldoorn and H. Vedder, *Mededingingsrecht. Beginselen van Europees en Nederlands Mededingingsrecht* (Europa Law Publishing 2010).

Arena 2011

A. Arena, 'The Doctrine of Union Preemption in the E.U. Internal Market: Between Sein and Sollen' (2011) 17 Columbia Journal of European Law 477.

Arena 2018

A. Arena, 'The Twin Doctrine of Primacy and Pre-emption' in R. Schütze and T. Tridimas (eds), *Oxford Principles of European Union Law* (Oxford University Press 2018).

Arnoudo 2024

L. Arnoudo, 'New Competition Regulatory Tools: Towards a Structure-Behavior-Performance Framework' (2024) 3 Concurrences 119735, 58.

Arsenidou et al. 2020

E. Arsenidou et al., 'Cooperation Within the ECN and Strengthening of National Competition Authorities' in E. Rousseva (ed.), *EU Antitrust Procedure* (Oxford University Press 2020).

Autorité de la Concurrence and Bundeskartellamt 2016

Autorité de la Concurrence and Bundeskartellamt, 'Competition Law and Data' (2016) https://www.bundeskartellamt.de/SharedDocs/Publikation/DE/Berichte/Big%20Data%20Papier.pdf?__blob=publicationFile&v=2 accessed 15 May 2024.

Avbelj 2011

M. Avbelj, 'Supremacy or Primacy of EU Law: (Why) Does It Matter?' (2011) 17 European Law Journal 725 https://doi.org/10.1111/j.1468-0386.2011.00560.x accessed 29 August 2025.

Ayata 2021

Z. Ayata, 'A Comparative Analysis of the Control of Excessive Pricing by Competition Authorities' (2020) 35 Turlane European and Civil Law Forum 101.

Azoulai 2015

L. Azoulai, 'The Complex Weave of Harmonization' in D. Chalmers and A. Arnull (eds), *The Oxford Handbook of European Union Law* (Oxford University Press 2015).

Bach 2020

A. Bach, '§ 32b GWB' in U. Immega et al. (eds), *Wettbewerbsrecht* (C.H. Beck 2020).

Balasingham and D'Amico 2024

B. Balasingham and A. D'Amico, 'Beyond Exclusion: Revisiting Exploitative Abuses in Digital Platform Markets' (2024) Journal of Antitrust Enforcement https://doi.org/10.1093/jaenfo/jnae050 accessed 29 August 2025.

Baker 2021

J. Baker, 'Protecting and Fostering Online Platform Competition: The Role of Antitrust Law' (2021) 17 Journal of Competition Law & Economics 2, 493 https://doi.org/10.1093/joclec/nhaa032 accessed 29 August 2025.

Baldwin, Cave and Lodge 2012

R. Baldwin, M. Cave and M. Lodge, *Understanding Regulation: Theory, Strategy, and Practice* (Oxford University Press 2012).

Balogh and Cseres 2013

V. Balogh and K. Cseres, 'Institutional Design in Hungary: A Case Study of the Unfair Commercial Practices Directive' (2013) 36 Journal of Consumer Policy 343 https://doi.org/10.1007/s10603-013-9236-y accessed 29 August 2025.

Bamberger et al. 2020

K. Bamberger et al., 'Can You Pay for Privacy? Consumer Expectations and the Behavior of Free and Paid Apps' (2020) 35 Berkeley Technology Law Journal 327.

Barkhuysen 2021

T. Barkhuysen, 'Handhaving van de AVG: de AP kan het niet alleen' (2021) 96 Nederlands Juristenblad 585.

Bauermeister 2022

T. Bauermeister, 'Section 19a GWB as the German "Lex GAFA": Lighthouse Project or Superfluous National Solo Run' (2022) 26 Yearbook of Antitrust & Regulatory Studies 75 https://doi.org/10.7172/1689-9024.yars.2022.15.26.4 accessed 29 August 2025.

Bechtold and Bosch 2021

S. Bechtold and W. Bosch, '§ 19a GWB' in S. Bechtold and W. Bosch (eds), *GWB: Gesetz Gegen Wettbewerbsbeschränkungen* (C.H. Beck 2021).

Beems, Van de Gronden and Rusu 2021

B. Beems, J. van de Gronden and C. Rusu, 'Gatekeepers and EU Competition Law: Exploring New Enforcement Avenues' in P. Wolters et al. (eds), *Digitalisering en conflictoplossing* (Wolters Kluwer 2021).

Beems 2023

B. Beems, 'The DMA in the Broader Regulatory Landscape of the EU: An Institutional Perspective' (2023) 19 European Competition Journal 1, 1 https://doi.org/10.1080/17441056.2022.2129766 accessed 29 August 2025.

Beems, Van de Gronden and Rusu 2023

B. Beems, J. Van de Gronden and C. Rusu, 'The Added Value of the DMA's Enforcement Framework' (2023) 15 The Competition Law Review 51.

Beems and Rusu 2024

B. Beems and C. Rusu, 'Marktafbakening anno 2024. De nieuwe Bekendmaking en digitale markten' (2024) 72 SEW, 10, 399.

Behrens 2014

P. Behrens, 'The "Consumer Choice" Paradigm in German Ordoliberalism and its Impact on EU Competition Law' (2014) https://papers.ssrn.com/sol3/papers.cfm?abstract_id=2568304 accessed 10 March 2025.

Bergqvist 2020

C. Bergqvist, 'What to Make of Google Android?' (2020) https://papers.ssrn.com/sol3/papers.cfm?abstract_id=3630974 accessed 10 March 2025.

Berkley Law Borderlines 2022

Berkley Law Borderlines, 'Digital Markets Act' (21 April 2022) https://www.law.berkeley.edu/podcast-episode/digital-markets-act/ accessed 10 March 2025.

Bieber and Solomé 1996

R. Bieber and I. Solomé, 'Hierarchy of Norms in EU Law' (1996) 33 Common Market Law Review 907 https://doi.org/10.54648/119846 accessed 29 August 2025.

Biondi and Gentile 2019

A. Biondi and G. Gentile, 'National Procedural Autonomy' in H. Ruiz Fabri (ed.), *Max Planck Encyclopedia of International Procedural Law* (Oxford University Press 2019).

Blume 2010

P. Blume, 'Data Protection and Privacy: Basic Concepts in a Changing World' (2010) 56 Scandinavian Studies in Law 152.

Bobek 2011

M. Bobek, 'Why There Is No Principle of "Procedural Autonomy" of the Member States' in B. De Witte and H. Micklitz (eds), *The European Court of Justice and the Autonomy of the Member States* (Intersentia 2011).

Boerman, Kruikemeier and Zuiderveen Borgesius 2017

S. Boerman, S. Kruikemeier and F. Zuiderveen Borgesius, 'Online Behavioural Advertising: A Literature Review and Research Agenda' (2017) 46 Journal of Advertising 363 https://doi.org/10.1080/00913367.2017.1339368 accessed 29 August 2025.

Böhm, Eucken and Großmann-Dörth 1936/2008

F. Böhm, W. Eucken and H. Großmann-Dörth, 'Unsere Aufgabe' in N. Goldschmidt and Wohlgemuth M (eds), *Grundtexte zur Freiburger Tradition der Ordnungsökonomik* (Mohr Siebeck 1936/2008).

Bois and Van Cleynenbreugel 2021

J. Bois and P. Van Cleynenbreugel, 'National Institutional Autonomy and EU Law: Time to Reframe the Stakes of Interdisciplinary Scholarship?' (2021) https://www.academia.edu/73303360/National_Institutional_Autonomy_and_EU_law_time_to_reframe_the_stakes_of_interdisciplinary_scholarship_EUDAMONIA_Working_Paper_2021_1 accessed 13 June 2023.

Bok-Wicherts et al. 2020

J. Bok-Wicherts et al., 'Evaluatie van de Autoriteit Consument en Markt' (2020) https://zoek.officielebekendmakingen.nl/blg-969588.pdf accessed 11 March 2025.

Bostoen 2017

F. Bostoen, 'Most Favoured Nation Clauses: Towards an Assessment Framework under EU Competition Law' [2017] European Competition and Regulatory Law Review 222.

Bostoen 2018

F. Bostoen, 'Online Platforms and Vertical Integration: The Return of Margin Squeeze?' (2018) 6 Journal of Antitrust Enforcement 3, 355 https://doi.org/10.1093/jaenfo/jny006 accessed 29 August 2025.

Bostoen 2019

F. Bostoen 'Online Platforms and Pricing: Adapting Abuse of Dominance Assessments to the Economic Reality of Free Products' (2019) 35 Computer Law Security Review 263 https://doi.org/10.1016/j.clsr.2019.02.004 accessed 29 August 2025.

Bostoen and Mândrescu 2020

F. Bostoen and D. Mândrescu, 'Assessing Abuse of Dominance in the Platform Economy: A Case Study of App Stores' (2020) 16 European Competition Journal 431 https://doi.org/10.1080/17441056.2020.1805698 accessed 29 August 2025.

Bostoen 2022a

F. Bostoen, 'The General Court's Google Shopping Judgment Finetuning the Legal Qualifications and Tests for Platform Abuse' (2022) 13 Journal of European Competition Law & Practice 2 https://doi.org/10.1093/jeclap/lpac010 accessed 29 August 2025.

Bostoen 2022b

F. Bostoen, 'The ACM's Apple Decision: To Boldly Go Where No Enforcer Has Gone Before' (2022) 10 Journal of Antitrust Enforcement 583 https://doi.org/10.1093/jaenfo/jnac024 accessed 29 August 2025.

Bostoen 2023a

F. Bostoen, *Abuse of Platform Power: Leveraging Conduct in Digital Markets under EU Competition Law and Beyond* (Concurrences 2023).

Bostoen 2023b

F. Bostoen, 'Understanding the Digital Markets Act' (2023) 68 Antitrust Bulletin 2, 263 https://doi.org/10.1177/0003603x231162998 accessed 29 August 2025.

Bostoen 2025

F. Bostoen, 'Artificial Intelligence and Competition Law' in N. Smuha (ed.), *The Cambridge Handbook on the Law, Ethics and Policy of Artificial Intelligence* (Cambridge University Press 2025).

Botta 2013

M. Botta, 'Testing the Decentralization of Competition Law Enforcement: Comment on Toshiba' (2013) 381 European Law Review 107.

Botta 2019

M. Botta, 'Exploitative Conduct in Digital Markets: Time for a Discussion after the Facebook Decision' (2019) 10 Journal of European Competition Law & Practice 465 https://doi.org/10.1093/jeclap/lpz064 accessed 29 August 2025.

Botta and Wiedemann 2019

M. Botta and K. Wiedemann, 'The Interaction of EU Competition, Consumer, and Data Protection Law in the Digital Economy: The Regulatory Dilemma in the Facebook Odyssey' (2019) 64 The Antitrust Bulletin 428 https://doi.org/10.1177/0003603x19863590 accessed 29 August 2025.

Botta 2021

M. Botta, 'Sector Regulation of Digital Platforms in Europe: Uno, Nessuno e Centomila' (2021) 12 Journal of European Competition Law & Practice 500 https://doi.org/10.1093/jeclap/lpab046 accessed 29 August 2025.

Bougette, Budzinski and Marty 2022

P. Bougette, O. Budzinski and F. Marty, 'Self-Preferencing and Competitive Damages: A Focus on Exploitative Abuses' (2022) https://papers.ssrn.com/sol3/papers.cfm?abstract_id=4028770 accessed 11 March 2025.

Brammer 2005

S. Brammer, 'Concurrent Jurisdiction under Regulation 1/2003 and The Issue of Case Allocation' (2005) 42 Common Market Law Review 1383 https://doi.org/10.54648/cola2005041 accessed 29 August 2025.

Brauneck 2023

J. Brauneck, 'Der Digital Markets Act (DMA): das neue, bessere digitale EU-Wettbewerbsrecht?' (2023) 27 Recht Digital 28.

Bredenoord-Spoek and De Jong 2020

M. Bredenoord-Spoek and S. De Jong, 'De renaissance van de voorlopige maatregelen in het mededingingsrecht' (2020) 3 Markt & Mededinging 89 https://doi.org/10.5553/menm/138762362020023003002 accessed 29 Au gust 2025.

Breton 2022

T. Breton, 'Statement Commissioner Breton: Sneak Peek – How the Commission Will Enforce the DSA & DMA: Blog of Commissioner Thierry Breton' (Brussels, 5 July 2022) https://ec.europa.eu/commission/presscorner/detail/en/STATEMENT_22_4327 accessed 12 March 2025.

Brook and Eben 2022

O. Brook and M. Eben, 'Who Should Guard the Gatekeepers: Does the DMA Replicate the Unworkable Test of Regulation 1/2003 to Settle Conflicts between EU and National Laws?' (2022) https://papers.ssrn.com/sol3/pa pers.cfm?abstract_id=4305810 accessed 29 August 2025.

Brook and Eben 2023a

O. Brook and M. Eben, 'Article 3 of Regulation 1/2003: A Historical and Emperical Account of an Unworkable Compromise' (2023) 12 Journal of Antitrust Enforcement 1, 45 https://doi.org/10.1093/jaenfo/jnad037 acce ssed 29 August 2025.

Brook and Eben 2023b

O. Brook and M. Eben, 'Another Missed Opportunity? Case C-252/21 Meta Platforms v Bundeskartellamt and the Relationship Between EU Competition Law and National Laws' (2024) 15 Journal of European Competition Law & Practice 1, 25 https://doi.org/10.1093/jeclap/lpad047 accessed 29 August 2025.

Brüggemann and Parmentier 2022

N. Brüggemann and H. Parmentier, 'Article 14: Advisory Committee' in K. Dekeyser et al. (eds), *Regulation 1/2003 and EU Antitrust Enforcement: A Systemic Guide* (Kluwer Law International 2022).

Budzinski 2007

O. Budzinski, 'Wettbewerbsfreiheit und More Economic Approach: wohin steuert die Europäische Wettbewerbspolitik?' [2007] Marburger Volkswirtschaftliche Beiträge.

Budzinski, Gaenssle and Stöhr 2016

O. Budzinski, S. Gaenssle and A. Stöhr, 'Der Entwurf zur 10. GWB Novelle: Interventionismus oder Laissez-faire?' (2016) https://papers.ssrn.com/sol3/papers.cfm?abstract_id=3619034 accessed 11 March 2025.

Budzinski and Polk 2021

O. Budzinski and A. Polk, 'Die 10. GWB-Novelle: Neue Wettbewerbsregeln für die Digitalökonomie' (2021) https://www.econstor.eu/bitstream/10419/246744/1/1777252415.pdf accessed 10 March 2025.

Budzinski and Mendelsohn 2021

O. Budzinski and J. Mendelsohn, 'Regulating Big Tech: From Competition Policy to Sector Regulation?' (2021) https://papers.ssrn.com/sol3/papers.cfm?abstract_id=3938167 accessed 12 March 2025.

Budzinski 2023

O. Budzinski, 'Die 11. GWB-Novelle: Vom Schutz des Wettbewerbsprozesses zur Verbesserung von Wettbewerbstrukturen?' in A. Kirk, P. Offergeld and T. Rohner (eds), *Kartellrecht in der Zeitwende – Auf dem Weg zur 11 und 12 GWB Novelle* (Nomos 2023).

Bueren and Crowder 2024

E. Bueren and J. Crowder, 'Sustainability and Competition Law in Germany' in P. Këllezi, P. Kobel and B. Kilpatrick (eds), *Sustainability Objectives in Competition and Intellectual Property Law* (Springer 2024).

Buiten 2018

M. Buiten, 'Regulating Data Giants: Between Competition Law and Data Protection Law' in K. Mathis and T. Avishalom (eds), *New Developments in Competition Law and Economics* (Springer 2018).

Buiten 2021

M. Buiten, 'Exploitative Abuses in Digital Markets: Between Competition Law and Data Protection Law' (2021) 9 Journal of Antitrust Enforcement 270 https://doi.org/10.1093/jaenfo/jnaa041 accessed 29 August 2025.

Burchardt 2019

D. Burchardt, 'The Relationship Between the Law of the European Union and the Law of Its Member States: A Norm – Based Conceptual Framework' (2019) 15 European Constitutional Law Review 73 https://doi.org/10.1017/s1574019618000512 accessed 29 August 2025.

Butorac Malnar and Kunda 2024

V. Butorac Malnar and I. Kunda, 'Designating Gatekeepers and Very Large Online Platforms under the EU Digital Acquis' (2022) 6 Journal of European Consumer and Market Law 242.

Bygrave 2002

L. Bygrave, *Data Protection Law, Approaching Its Rationale, Logic and Limits* (Kluwer Law International 2002).

Bygrave 2014

L. Bygrave, *Data Privacy Law: An International Perspective* (Oxford University Press 2014).

Caminade, Chapsal and Penglase 2021

J. Caminade, A. Chapsal and J. Penglase, 'Interim Measures in Antitrust Investigations: An Economic Discussion' (2021) 17 Journal of Competition Law & Economics 2, 437 https://doi.org/10.1093/joclec/nhaa027 accessed 29 August 2025.

Canto 2014

C. Canto, 'Van Consistentie Naar Coherentie: De Betekenis En Bevordering Van Rechtseenheid in Rechtsfilosofisch Perspectief' in T. Gerverdinck et al. (eds), *Wetenschappelijke Bijdragen* (Boom Juridische Uitgevers 2014).

Cappai and Colangelo 2021

M. Cappai and G. Colangelo, 'A Unified Test for the European Ne Bis in Idem Principle: The Case Study of Digital Markets Regulation' (2021) https://papers.ssrn.com/sol3/papers.cfm?abstract_id=3951088 accessed 5 March 2025.

Carey 2020

P. Carey, *Data Protection: A Practical Guide to UK Law* (Oxford University Press 2020).

Carugati 2023

C. Carugati, 'The Antitrust Privacy Dilemma' (2023) 19 European Competition Journal 2, 167 https://doi.org/10.1080/17441056.2023.2169310 acc essed 29 August 2025.

Cengiz 2009

F. Cengiz, 'The European Competition Network: Structure, Management and Initial Experiences of Policy Enforcement' (2009) https://cadmus.eui.eu/handle/1814/11067 accessed 20 March 2025.

Cengiz 2010

F. Cengiz, 'Multi-Level Governance in Competition Policy' (2010) 35 European Law Review 660.

Chalmers 2024

D. Chalmers, *European Union Law* (Cambridge University Press 2024).

Chiriţoiu 2017

B. Chiriţoiu, 'Convergence Within the European Competition Network: Legislative Harmonization and Enforcement Priorities' in A. Almăşan and P. Whelan (eds), *The Consistent Application of EU Competition Law* (Springer 2017).

Chirico 2021

F. Chirico, 'Digital Markets Act: A Regulatory Perspective' (2021) 12 Journal of European Competition Law & Practice 7, 493 https://doi.org/10.1093/jeclap/lpab058 accessed 29 August 2025.

Cioffi 2021

J. Cioffi, 'Beyond Competition: The Regulatory Turn & the Emerging Era of Intervention in Platform Firms & Markets' [2021] Policy Brief in Research Project Governing Work in the Digital Age, https://www.denkfabrik-bmas.de/fileadmin/Downloads/Publikationen/Brief-2_Cioffi_final_FINAL-ua.pdf accessed 3 March 2025.

Claassen and Gerbrandy 2016

R. Claassen and A. Gerbrandy, 'Rethinking European Competition Law: From a Consumer Welfare to a Capability Approach' (2016) 12 Utrecht Law Review https://doi.org/10.18352/ulr.321 accessed 29 August 2025.

Claes 2015

M. Claes, 'The Primacy of EU Law in European and National Law' in D. Chalmers and A. Arnull (eds), *The Oxford Handbook of European Union Law* (Oxford University Press 2015).

Clifford and Ausloos 2018

D. Clifford and J. Ausloos, 'Data Protection and the Role of Fairness' (2018) 37 Yearbook of European Law 130 https://doi.org/10.1093/yel/yey004 accessed 29 August 2025.

Colangelo and Maggiolino 2019

G. Colangelo and M. Maggiolino, 'Antitrust Über Alles. Whither Competition Law after Facebook?' (2019) 42 World Competition 355 https://doi.org/10.54648/woco2019020 accessed 29 August 2025.

Colangelo 2025a

G. Colangelo, 'The EU Essential Facilities Doctrine after Android Auto: A Wild Card Without Limiting Principles?' (2025) https://papers.ssrn.com/sol3/papers.cfm?abstract_id=5176785 accessed 31 March 2025.

Colangelo 2025b

G. Colangelo, 'The Privacy/Antitrust Curse: Insights from GDPR Application in Competition Law Proceedings' (2025) 70 The Antitrust Bulletin, 1, 113.

Colaps 2017

A. Colaps, 'Big Data: Is EU Competition Law Ripe Enough to Meet the Challenge?' in R. Mastroianni and A. Arena A (eds), *60 Years of EU Competition Law Stocktaking and Future Prospects* (ES 2017).

Costa-Cabral and Lynskey 2015

F. Costa-Cabral and O. Lynskey, 'The Internal and External Constraint of Data Protection on Competition Law in the EU' https://eprints.lse.ac.uk/64887/1/Lynskey_Internal%20and%20External%20Constraints%20of%20Data%20Protection%20_Author_2015.pdf accessed 14 March 2025.

Costa-Cabral and Lynskey 2018

F. Costa-Cabral and O. Lynskey, 'Family Ties: The Intersection Between Data Protection and Competition Law in the EU' (2018) 54 Common Market Law Review 11 https://doi.org/10.54648/cola2017002 accessed 29 August 2025.

Craig and De Búrca 2015

P. Craig and G. De Búrca, *EU Law: Text, Cases, and Materials* (Oxford University Press 2015).

Crane 2011

D. Crane, *The Institutional Structure of Antitrust Enforc*ement (Oxford Scholarship Online 2011).

Crémer, De Montjoye and Schweitzer 2019

J. Crémer, Y. De Montjoye and H. Schweitzer, 'Competition Policy for the Digital Era' (2019) https://op.europa.eu/en/publication-detail/-/publication/21dc175c-7b76-11e9-9f05-01aa75ed71a1/language-en accessed 3 March 2025.

Crémer et al. 2023a

J. Crémer et al., 'Enforcing the Digital Markets Act: Institutional Choices, Compliance, and Antitrust' (2023) 11 Journal of Antitrust Enforcement 315 https://doi.org/10.1093/jaenfo/jnad004 accessed 29 August 2025.

Crémer et al. 2023b

J. Crémer et al., 'Fairness and Contestability in the Digital Markets Act' (2023) 40 Yale Journal on Regulation 101.

Cremona 2008

M. Cremona, 'Defending the Community Interest: The Duties of Cooperation and Compliance' in M. Cremona and B. De Witte (eds), *EU Foreign Relations Law: Constitutional Fundamentals* (Hart Publishing 2008).

Csatlós 2018

E. Csatlós, 'The European Competition Network in the European Administrative System: Theoretical Concerns' (2018) 17 Yearbook of Antitrust & Regulatory Studies 53 https://doi.org/10.7172/1689-9024.yars.2018.11.17.3 accessed 29 August 2025.

Cseres 2006

K. Cseres, 'The Controversies of the Consumer Welfare Standard' (2006) 3 The Competition Law Review 121.

Cseres 2013

K. Cseres, 'Integrate or Separate: Institutional Design for the Enforcement of Competition Law and Consumer Law' [2013] Amsterdam Centre for European Law and Governance Working Paper Series https://papers.ssrn.com/sol3/papers.cfm?abstract_id=2200908 accessed 5 March 2025.

Cseres 2017

K. Cseres, 'Rule of Law Values in the Decentralized Public Enforcement of EU Competition Law' in A. Jakab and D. Kochenov (eds), *The Enforcement of EU law and Values* (Oxford University Press 2017).

Cseres 2024

K. Cseres, 'Defending the Rule of Law Through EU Competition Law: The Case of Hungary' (2024) https://papers.ssrn.com/sol3/papers.cfm?abstract_id=4878282 accessed 25 March 2025.

Curtin and Manucharyan 2015

D. Curtin and T. Manucharyan, 'Legal Acts and Hierarchy of Norms in EU Law' in A. Arnull and D. Chalmers (eds), *The Oxford Handbook of European Union Law* (Oxford University Press 2015).

De Baere and Roes 2015

G. De Baere and T. Roes, 'EU Loyalty as Good Faith' (2015) 64 International & Comparative Law Quarterly 829 https://doi.org/10.1017/s0020589315 000421 accessed 29 August 2025.

De Bree 2012

R. De Bree, 'ACM: evolutie uit zuinigheid?' (2012) 4 Markt & Mededinging 144.

De Groes and Raats 2021

K. De Groes and T. Raats, 'Implementation of the ECN+ Directive in the Netherlands: Strengthening Cooperation with National Competition Authorities' (2021) 5 European Competition and Regulatory Law Review 294 https://doi.org/10.21552/core/2021/3/23 accessed 29 August 2025.

Dekker, Gerbrandy and Niels 2019

C. Dekker, A. Gerbrandy and G. Niels, 'Wij staan op het punt om uit het peloton te demarreren naar de koplopers, Interview met Martijn Snoep door Redactie M&M 18 april 2019' [2019] Markt & Mededinging 87.

De Moor-van Vught 2010

A. De Moor-van Vught, 'Handhaving en toezicht in een Europese context' in S. Pront-van Bommel (ed), *De consument en de andere kant van de elektriciteitsmarkt: inleidingen op het openingscongres van het Centrum voor Energievraagstukken van de Universiteit van Amsterdam op 27 januari 2010* (Universiteit van Amsterdam, Centrum voor Energievraagstukken 2010).

Derlén and Lindholm 2015

M. Derlén and J. Lindholm, 'Characteristics of Precedent: The Case Law of the European Court of Justice in Three Dimensions' (2015) 16 German Law Journal 5, 1073 https://doi.org/10.1017/s2071832200021040 acce ssed 29 August 2025.

Deringer 1963

A. Deringer, 'The Distribution of Powers in the Enforcement of the Rules of Competition under the Rome Treaty' (1963) 1 Common Market Law Review 30 https://doi.org/10.54648/cola1963005 29 August 2025.

De Smijter and Sinclair 2014

E. De Smijter and A. Sinclair, 'The Enforcement System Under Regulation 1/2003' in J. Faull and A. Nikpay (eds), *The EU Law of Competition* (Oxford University Press 2014).

De Streel 2008

A. De Streel, 'The Relationship Between Competition Law and Sector Specific Regulation: The Case of Electronic Communications' [2008] Reflets et Perspectives de la Vie Économique 53.

De Streel and Larouche 2016

A. De Streel and P. Larouche, 'An Integrated Regulatory Framework for Digital Networks and Services: CERRE Policy Report' (2016) https://cerre.eu/wp-content/uploads/2020/07/160127_CERRE_IntegratedRegulatoryFramework_FinalReport.pdf accessed 17 March 2025.

De Streel et al. 2020

A. De Streel et al., 'Digital Markets Act: Making Economic Regulation of Platform Fit for the Digital' (2020) https://cerre.eu/publications/digital-markets-act-economic-regulation-platforms-digital-age/ accessed 12 March 2025.

De Streel and Monti 2022

A. De Streel and G. Monti, 'Improving EU Institutional Design to Better Supervise Digital Platforms', CERRE Report (2022) https://cerre.eu/publications/improving-eu-institutional-design/ accessed 20 March 2025.

De Streel and Alexiadis 2023

A. De Streel and P. Alexiadis, 'The European Way to Regulate Big Tech: The EU's Digital Markets Act' in D. Moura Vincente, S. de Vasconcelos and C. Chen (eds), *The Legal Challenges of the Fourth Industrial Revolution* (Springer 2023).

De Streel et al. 2023

A. De Streel, 'Effective and Proportionate Implementation of the DMA' (2023) https://cerre.eu/wp-content/uploads/2023/01/DMA_Book-1.pdf accessed 21 March 2025.

Deutscher 2021

E. Deutscher, 'Google Shopping and the Quest for a Legal Test for Self-preferencing under Article 102 TFEU' (2021) 6 European Papers 1345.

Deutscher and Makris 2016

E. Deutscher and S. Makris, 'Exploring the Ordoliberal Paradigm: The Competition-Democracy Nexus' (2016) 11 The Competition Law Review 181.

Devroe 2009

W. Devroe, 'Limits of Differentiation in European Economic Law: *Ne bis in idem* and Minimum Versus Maximum Harmonisation' (2009) 16 Maastricht Journal of European and Comparative Law 141 https://doi.org/10.1177/1023263x0901600201 accessed 29 August 2025.

De Witte 2021

B. De Witte, 'Direct Effect, Primacy and the Nature of the Legal Order' in P. Craig and G. De Búrca (eds), *The Evolution of EU Law* (Oxford University Press 2021).

Docksey 2020

C. Docksey, 'Article 70 Tasks of the Board' in C. Kuner, L. Bygrave and C. Docksey (eds), *The EU General Data Protection Regulation (GDPR): A Commentary* (Oxford University Press 2020).

Dougan 2019

M. Dougan, 'Primacy and the Remedy of Disapplication' (2019) 56 Common Market Law Review 1459 https://doi.org/10.54648/cola2019123 accessed 29 August 2025.

Dougan 2000

M. Dougan, 'Minimum Harmonization and the Internal Market' (2000) 37 Common Market Law Review 853.

Douglas 2021

E. Douglas, 'Digital Crossroads: The Intersection of Competition aw and Data Privacy' (2021) Report to the Global Privacy Assembly Digital Citizen and Consumer Working Group https://globalprivacyassembly.org/wp-content/uploads/2021/10/1.3h-version-4.0-Digital-Citizen-and-Consumer-Working-Group-adopted.pdf accessed 3 March 2025.

Drexl 2017

J. Drexl, 'Designing Competitive Markets for Industrial Data. Between Propertisation and Access' (2017) 8 Journal of Intellectual Property, Information Technology and Electronic Commerce Law 257.

Drexl et al. 2023

J. Drexl et al., 'Position Statement of the Max Planck Institute for Innovation and Competition of 2 May 2023 on the Implementation of the Digital Markets Act (DMA)' (2023) 72 GRUR International 9, 864 https://doi.org/10.1093/grurint/ikad067 accessed 29 August 2025.

Dunne 2015

N. Dunne, *Competition Law and Economic Regulation* (Cambridge University Press 2015).

Dunne 2020

N. Dunne, 'Fairness and the Challenge of Making Markets Work Better' (2020) 84(2) Modern Law Review 230 https://doi.org/10.1111/1468-2230.12579 accessed 29 August 2025.

Dunne 2021

N. Dunne, 'Fairness and the Challenge of Making Markets Work Better' (2021) 84 Modern Law Review 230 https://doi.org/10.1111/1468-2230.12579 accessed 29 August 2025.

Dworkin 1986

R. Dworkin, *Law's Empire* (Fontana 1986).

Dzino and Rusu 2019

N. Dzino and C. Rusu, 'Public Enforcement of EU Antitrust Law: A Circle of Trust' (2019) 12 Review of European Administrative Law 127 https://doi.org/10.7590/187479819x15656877527214 accessed 29 August 2025.

Dzino, Van de Gronden and Rusu 2019

N. Dzino, J. Van de Gronden and C. Rusu C, 'ECN+ Richtlijn: toegevoegde waarde en betekenis voor het publieke handhavingssysteem in Nederland' (2019) 12 SEW 530.

Eben and Robertson 2021

M. Eben and V. Robertson, 'The Relevant Market Concept in Competition Law and Its Application to Digital Markets: A Comparative Analysis of the EU, US, and Brazil' (2021) 18 Journal of European Competition Law and Economics 417.

Eben 2024

M. Eben, 'The Draft Revised Market Definition Notice: The European Commission Brings the Relevant Market Further into the 21st century' (Kluwer Competition Law Blog, 26 January 2023) accessed 10 March 2025.

Economides and Lianos 2021

N. Economides and I. Lianos, 'Restrictions on Privacy and Exploitation in the Digital Economy: A Market Failure Perspective' (2021) 17 Journal of

Competition Law & Economics 4, 765 https://doi.org/10.1093/joclec/nhab007 accessed 29 August 2025.

European Competition Network 2021

European Competition Network, 'Joint Paper of the Heads of the National Competition Authorities of the European Union: How National Competition Agencies Can Strengthen the DMA' (2021) https://www.bundeskartellamt.de/SharedDocs/Publikation/EN/Others/DMA_ECN_Paper.pdf?__blob=publicationFile&v=2 accessed 12 March 2025.

European Union Agency for Fundamental Rights 2018

European Union Agency for Fundamental Rights, *Handbook on European Data Protection Law* (Publications Office of the European Union 2018).

Evans 2020

D. Evans, 'The Economics of Attention Markets' (2027) https://papers.ssrn.com/sol3/papers.cfm?abstract_id=3044858 accessed 17 March 2025.

Ezrachi 2018

A. Ezrachi, 'EU Competition Law Goals and the Digital Economy' [2018] Oxford Legal Studies Research Paper.

Ezrachi and Stucke 2016

A. Ezrachi and M. Stucke, *Virtual Competition: The Promise and Perils of the Algorithm-Driven Economy* (Harvard University Press 2016).

Ezrachi and Stucke 2018

A. Ezrachi and M. Stucke, 'The Fight Over Antitrust's Soul' (2018) 9 Journal of European Competition Law & Practice 1 https://doi.org/10.1093/jeclap/lpx070 accessed 29 August 2025.

Farinhas 2025

C. Farinhas, 'Interim Measures in Digital Markets: Interaction between the DMA and Regulation 1/2003' (2025) 2 Utrecht Law Review 21 https://doi.org/10.36633/ulr.1118 accessed 29 August 2025.

Feintuck 2010

M. Feintuck, 'Regulatory Rationales Beyond the Economic: In Search of the Public Interest' in R. Baldwin, M. Cave and M. Lodge (eds), *The Oxford Handbook of Regulation* (Oxford University Press 2010).

Feteira 2015

L. Feteira, *The Interplay Between European and National Competition Law after Regulation 1/2003: 'United should we stan'?* (Kluwer Law International 2015).

Filistrucchi et al. 2014

L. Filistrucchi et al., 'Market Definition in Two-Sided Markets: Theory and Practice' (2014) 10 Journal of Competition Law & Economics 293 https://doi.org/10.1093/joclec/nhu007 accessed 29 August 2025.

Fox 1987

E. Fox, 'The Battle for the Soul of Antitrust' (1987) 75 California Law Review 917 https://doi.org/10.2307/3480656 accessed 29 August 2025.

Fox 2010

E. Fox, 'Antitrust and Institutions: Design and Change' (2010) 41(3) Loyola University Chicago Law Journal 473.

Fox 2019

E. Fox, 'Platforms, Power and the Antitrust Challenge: A Modest Proposal to Narrow the U.S. – Europe Divide' (2019) 19 Public Law & Legal Theory Research Paper Series 101.

Francis 2023

J. Francis, 'The Battle for the Soul of the GDPR: Clashing Decisions of Supervisory Authorities Highlights Potential Limits of Procedural Data Protection' [2023] Minnesota Law Review 167.

Franck and Peitz 2021

J. Franck and M. Peitz, 'Digital Platforms and the New 19a Tool in the German Competition Act' (2021) 12 Journal of European Competition Law & Practice 513.

Frank and Emma 2024

M. Frank and L. Emma, 'The European Commission's Challenge to Consent or Pay: Demystifying the Digital Markets Act?' (2024) 4 World Competition 427 https://doi.org/10.54648/woco2024026 accessed 29 August 2025.

Freeman and Rossi 2012

J. Freeman and J. Rossi, 'Agency Coordination in Shared Regulatory Space' (2012) 125 Harvard Law Review 1134.

Fuchs 2019

A. Fuchs, 'GWB § 18' in U. Immenga et al. (eds), *Wettbewerbsrecht* (C.H. Beck 2019).

Furman et al. 2019

J. Furman et al., 'Unlocking Digital Competition. Report of the Digital Competition Expert Panel' (2019) https://assets.publishing.service.gov.uk/media/5c88150ee5274a230219c35f/unlocking_digital_competition_furman_review_web.pdf accessed 20 March 2025.

Gal and Aviv 2020

M. Gal and O. Aviv, 'The Competitive Effects of the GDPR' (2020) 16 Journal of Competition Law & Economics 349 https://doi.org/10.1093/joclec/nhaa012 accessed 29 August 2025.

Gal and Petit 2021

M. Gal and N. Petit, 'Radical Restorative Remedies for Digital Markets' (2021) 37 Berkeley Technology Law Journal.

Galetta and De Hert 2015

A. Galetta and P. De Hert, 'The Proceduralisation of Data Protection Remedies under EU Data Protection Law: Towards a More Effective and Data-Subject-Oriented Remedial System' (2015) 8 Review of European Administrative Law 125 https://doi.org/10.7590/187479815x14313382198412 accessed 29 August 2025.

Gambaro 2018

M. Gambaro, 'Big Data Competition and Market Power' (2018) 11 Market and Competition Law Review 99 https://doi.org/10.7559/mclawreview.2018.326 accessed 29 August 2025.

Gappa and Käseberg 2024

S. Gappa and T. Käseberg, 'Article 38' in R. Podszun (ed.), *Digital Markets Act: Article-by-Article Commentary* (Bloomsburry 2024).

Garcia-Murillo and MacInnes 2003

M. Garcia-Murillo and I. MacInnes, 'The Impact of Technological Convergence on the Regulation of ICT Industries' (2003) 5 International Journal on Media Management 57 https://doi.org/10.1080/14241270309390019 accessed 29 August 2025.

Gebicka and Heinemann 2014

A. Gebicka and A. Heinemann, 'Social Media & Competition Law' (2014) 37 World Competition 149 https://doi.org/10.54648/woco2014017 accessed 29 August 2025.

Gellert 2020

R. Gellert, *The Risk-Based Approach to Data Protection* (Oxford University Press 2020).

Gellert 2024

R. Gellert, 'Publieke handhaving van de AVG: twee structurele spanningen die ten grondslag liggen aan nationale en grensoverschrijdende handhaving' (2024) 4 Tijdschrift voor Consumentenrecht en handelspraktijken 219.

Gentile and Lynskey 2022

G. Gentile and O. Lynskey, 'Deficient by Design? The Transnational Enforcement of the GDPR' (2022) 71 International & Comparative Law Quarterly 799 https://doi.org/10.1017/s0020589322000355 accessed 29 August 2025.

Georgieva and Schmidl 2020

L. Georgieva and M. Schmidl, 'Powers' in C. Kuner et al. (eds), *The EU General Data Protection Regulation (GDPR): A Commentary* (Oxford University Press 2020).

Geradin 2002

D. Geradin, 'Competition Between Rules and Rules of Competition: A Legal and Economic Analysis of the Proposed Modernization of the Enforcement of EC Competition Law' (2002) 9 Columbia Journal of European Law.

Geradin 2015

D. Geradin, 'Loyalty Rebates after Intel: Time for the European Court of Justice to Overrule Hoffman-La Roche' (2015) 11 Journal of Competition Law & Economics 579 https://doi.org/10.1093/joclec/nhv023 accessed 29 August 2025.

Geradin 2016

D. Geradin, 'The Power of Arbitral Tribunals to Raise Public Policy Rules Ex Officio: The Case of EU Competition Law' [2016] TILEC Discussion Paper 2016-027.

Geradin 2021

D. Geradin, 'What Is a Digital Gatekeeper? Which Platforms Should Be Captured by the EC Proposal for a Digital Market Act?' (2021) https://papers.ssrn.com/sol3/papers.cfm?abstract_id=3788152 accessed 12 March 2025.

Geradin and Katsifis 2021

D. Geradin and D. Katsifis, 'The Antitrust Case Against the Apple App Store' (2021) 17 Journal of Competition Law & Economics 503 https://doi.org/10.1093/joclec/nhab003 accessed 29 August 2025.

Geradin, Karanikioti and Katsifis 2021

D. Geradin, T. Karanikioti and D. Katsifis, 'GDPR Myopia: How a Well-Intended Regulation Ended Up Favouring Large Online Platforms: The Case of Ad Tech' (2021) 17 European Competition Journal 47 https://doi.org/10.1080/17441056.2020.1848059 accessed 29 August 2025.

Geradin, Katsifis and Karanikioti 2021

D. Gerardin, D. Katsifis and T. Karanikioti, 'Google as a *De Facto* Privacy Regulator: Analysing the Privacy Sandbox from an Antitrust Perspective' (2021) 17 European Competition Journal 3, 617 https://doi.org/10.1080/17441056.2021.1930450 accessed 29 August 2025.

Geradin 2022

D. Geradin, 'Apple's Constructive Refusal to Comply with the Law: A Harbinger of Things to Come?' (The Platform Law Blog, 19 March 2022) https://theplatformlaw.wpcomstaging.com/2022/03/18/apples-constructive-refusal-to-comply-with-the-law-a-harbinger-of-things-to-come/ accessed 10 July 2025.

Gerard 2010

D. Gerard, 'Regulation 1/2003 (and Beyond): Balancing Effective Enforcement and Due Process in Cross-Border Antitrust Investigations' (2010) https://papers.ssrn.com/sol3/papers.cfm?abstract_id=1359310 accessed 18 March 2025.

Gerber 1994

D. Gerber, 'Constitutionalizing the Economy: German Neo-liberalism, Competition Law and the "New" Europe' (1994) 42 The American Journal of Comparative Law 25 https://doi.org/10.2307/840727 accessed 29 August 2025.

Gerber and Cassinis 2006

D. Gerber and P. Cassinis, 'The "Modernisation" of European Community Competition Law: Achieving Consistency in Enforcement – Part 1' (2006) 27 European Competition Law Review 10.

Gerbrandy 2009

A. Gerbrandy, *Convergentie in het mededingingsrecht* (Boom Juridische Uitgevers 2009).

Gerbrandy 2017

A. Gerbrandy, 'Solving a Sustainability-Deficit in European Competition Law' (2017) 40 World Competition 4 https://doi.org/10.54648/woco2017035 accessed 29 August 2025.

Gerbrandy 2019

A. Gerbrandy, 'Rethinking Competition Law within the European Economic Constitution' (2019) 57 Journal of Common Market Studies 127 https://doi.org/10.1111/jcms.12814 accessed 29 August 2025.

Gerbrandy et al. 2020

A. Gerbrandy et al., 'Country-report for Fide 2020: Competition Law in the Digital Economy' https://www.uu.nl/sites/default/files/rebo-Gerbrandy-Fide%20report%202020.pdf accessed 11 March 2025.

Gerbrandy and Phoa 2022

A. Gerbrandy and P. Phoa, 'The Power of Big Tech Corporations as Modern Bigness and a Vocabulary for Shaping Competition Law as Counter-Power' in M. Bennett, H. Brouwer and R. Claassen (eds), *Wealth and Power* (Roudledge 2022).

Gil González and De Hert 2019

E. Gil González and P. De Hert, 'Understanding the Legal Provisions That Allow Processing and Profiling of Personal Data: An Analysis of GDPR Provisions and Principles' (2019) 19 ERA Forum 597 https://doi.org/10.1007/s12027-018-0546-z accessed 29 August 2025.

Giurgiu and Larsen 2016

A. Giurgiu and T. Larsen, 'Roles and Powers of National Data Protection Authorities' (2016) 2 European Data Protection Law Review 342 https://doi.org/10.21552/edpl/2016/3/9 accessed 29 August 2025.

Gorecka 2020

A. Gorecka, 'Is "Privacy" a Means to Protect the Competition or Advance Objectives of Innovation and Consumer Welfare?' in M. Tzanou (ed.), *Personal Data Protection* (IGI Global Publishing 2020).

Gorecka 2024

A. Gorecka, *The Interface Between Competition Law and Data Privacy Law* (Springer 2024).

Graef 2014

I. Graef, 'How Can Software Interoperability Be Achieved under European Competition Law and Related Regimes?' (2024) 5 Journal of European Competition Law & Practice 1, 6 https://doi.org/10.1093/jeclap/lpt069 accessed 29 August 2025.

Graef 2016

I. Graef, 'Blurring Boundaries of Consumer Welfare: How to Create Synergies Between Competition, Consumer and Data Protection Law in Digital Market' (2016) https://papers.ssrn.com/sol3/papers.cfm?abstract_id=2881969 accessed 10 March 2025.

Graef 2018

I. Graef, 'Algorithms and Fairness: What Role for Competition Law in Targeting Price Discrimination Towards Ends Consumers?' (2018) 24 Columbia Journal of European Law 3, 541.

Graef, Clifford and Valcke 2018

I. Graef I, D. Clifford and P. Valcke, 'Fairness and Enforcement: Bridging Competition, Data Protection, and Consumer Law' (2018) 8 International Data Privacy Law 200 https://doi.org/10.1093/idpl/ipy013 accessed 29 August 2025.

Graef 2015

I. Graef, 'Market Definition and Market Power in Data: The Case of Online Platforms' (2015) 38(4) World Competition 473 https://doi.org/10.54648/woco2015040 accessed 29 August 2025.

Graef 2021

I. Graef, 'Consumer Sovereignty and Competition Law: From Personalization to Diversity' (2021) 58 Common Market Law Review 2, 471 https://doi.org/10.54648/cola2021026 accessed 29 August 2025.

Graef 2022

I. Graef, 'What the Dutch Apple Case Can Teach us about Future Challenges for Competition Enforcement' (2022) 10 Journal of Antitrust Enforcement 570 https://doi.org/10.1093/jaenfo/jnac023 accessed 29 August 2025.

Graef 2023

I. Graef, 'Meta Platforms: How the CJEU Leaves Competition and Data Protection Authorities with an Assignment' (2023) 30 Maastricht Journal of European and Comparative Law 325 https://doi.org/10.1177/1023263x231205836 accessed 29 August 2025.

Graef 2024

I. Graef, 'Regulating Digital Platforms: Streamlining the Interaction Between the Digital Markets Act and National Competition Regimes' in I. Graef and B. van der Sloot (eds), *The Legal Consistency of Technology Regulation in Europe* (Hart Publishing 2024).

Granger and Irion 2018

M. Granger and K. Irion, 'The Right to Protection of Personal Data: The New Posterchild of European Union Citizenship?' in S. De Vries, H. De Waele and M. Granger (eds), *Civil Rights and EU Citizenship* (Edward Elgar 2018).

Grünwald et al. 2023

A. Grünwald et al., 'Germany Adopts Competition Enforcement Act' (Kluwer Competition Law Blog, 12 July 2023) accessed 10 October 2023.

Guastaferro 2015

B. Guastaferro, 'Sincere Cooperation and Respect for National Identities: The Unitary and the Pluralist Twists of the European integration process' [2015] Neo-Federalism Working Paper Series https://www.federalism.eu/assets/2017/07/wp_2_15.pdf accessed 20 March 2025.

Guastaferro 2018

B. Guastaferro, 'Sincere Cooperation and Respect for National Identities' in R. Schütze and T. Tridimas (eds), *Oxford Principles of European Union Law: The European Union Legal Order Volume I* (Oxford University Press 2018).

Guerra 2018

G. Guerra, 'An Interdisciplinary Approach for Comparative Lawyers: Insights from the Fast-Moving Field of Law and Technology' (2018) 19 German Law Journal 579 https://doi.org/10.1017/s2071832200022793 accessed 29 August 2025.

Guest 1992

S. Guest, *Ronald Dworkin* (Edinburgh University Press 1992).

Haket 2020

S. Haket, 'Popławski II: A Half-Hearted Embrace of Hierarchical Supremacy' (2020) 13 Review of European Administrative Law 1, 155 https://doi.org/10.7590/187479820x15881424928435 accessed 29 August 2025.

Hancox 2021

E. Hancox, 'Judicial Approaches to Norm Overlaps in EU Law: A Case Study on the Free Movement of Workers' (2021) 58 Common Market Law Review 1057 https://doi.org/10.54648/cola2021067 accessed 29 August 2025.

Harrison, Zdzieborska and Wise 2022

P. Harrison, M. Zdzieborska and B. Wise, 'Navigating ne bis in idem: Bpost, Nordzucker and the Digital Markets Act' (2022) 21 Competition Law Journal 2 https://doi.org/10.4337/clj.2022.02.01 accessed 29 August 2025.

Haucap and Heimeshoff 2013

J. Haucap and U. Heimeshoff, 'Google, Facebook, Amazon, eBay: Is the Internet Driving Competition or Market Monopolization?' [2013] International Economics and Economic Policy 49 https://doi.org/10.1007/s10368-013-0247-6 accessed 29 August 2025.

Haucap 2019a

J. Haucap, 'Competition and Competition Policy in a Data-Driven Economy' (2019) 4 Intereconomics 201 https://doi.org/10.1007/s10272-019-0825-0 accessed 29 August 2025.

Haucap 2019b

J. Haucap, 'Data Protection and Antitrust: New Types of Abuse Cases? An Economist's View in Light of the German *Facebook* Decision' [2019] CPI Antitrust Chronicle.

Heath and Reingold 2021

R. Heath and O. Reingold, 'Europe's Top "Tech Cop" Is Ready to Take on Big Tech with America' (Politico, 13 October 2021).

Heideman 2025

T. Heideman, 'Corrigerende Structurele Maatregel: Commentaar op art. 58a Mw' in D. Kuipers and R. Wesseling (eds), *Tekst & Commentaar Mededingingsrecht* (Wolters Kluwer 2025).

Heinz 2019

S. Heinz, 'Bundeskartellamt Ends Abuse Probe after Amazon Agrees to Changing Business Terms for Dealers' (Kluwer Competition Law Blog, 30 July 2019) https://legalblogs.wolterskluwer.com/competition-blog/bundeskartellamt-ends-abuse-probe-after-amazon-agrees-to-changing-business-terms-for-dealers/ accessed 17 October 2023.

Helberger, Kleinen-von Königslöw and Van der Noll 2015

N. Helberger, K. Kleinen-von Königslöw and R. Van der Noll, 'Regulating the New Information Intermediaries as Gatekeepers of Information Diversity' (2015) 17 Info 50 https://doi.org/10.1108/info-05-2015-0034 accessed 29 August 2025.

Helberger, Zuiderveen Borgesius and Reyna 2017

N. Helberger, F. Zuiderveen Borgesius and A. Reyna, 'A Perfect Match? A Closer Look at the Relationship Between EU Consumer Law and Data Protection Law' (2017) 54 Common Market Law Review 1427 https://doi.org/10.54648/cola2017118 accessed 29 August 2025.

Hellwig 2006

M. Hellwig, 'Effizienz oder Wettbewerbsfreiheit?: zur normativen Grundlegung der Wettbewerbspolitik' (2006) https://www.econstor.eu/bitstream/10419/26904/1/521158753.PDF accessed 11 March 2025.

Henten, Smarajiva and Melody 2003

A. Henten, R. Samarajiva and W. Melody, 'Designing Next Generation Telecom Regulation: ICT Convergence or Multisector Utility?' (2003) https://regulationbodyofknowledge.org/wp-content/uploads/2013/03/Henten_Designing_Next_Generation.pdf accessed 19 March 2025.

Herweijer 2003

M. Herweijer, 'Juridisch onderzoek' in J. Broeksteeg and E. Stamhuis (eds.), *Rechtswetenschappelijk onderzoek: over object en methode* (Boom Juridische Uitgevers 2003).

Hijmans 2016

H. Hijmans, 'The European Union as a Constitutional Guardian of Internet Privacy and Data Protection' (2016) https://dare.uva.nl/search?identifier=c9db9f1d-3759-44b0-8501-fb2e69fc1dd6 accessed 19 March 2025 accessed 29 August 2025.

Hijmans 2019

H. Hijmans, 'The DPAs and Their Cooperation: How Far Are We in Making Enforcement of Data Protection Law More European' (2019) 2 European Data Protection Law Review 362 https://doi.org/10.21552/edpl/2016/3/11 accessed 29 August 2025.

Hilpold 2021

P. Hilpold, 'So Long Solange? The PSPP Judgement of the Constitutional Court and the Conflict Between the German and the European "Popular

Spirit"' (2021) 23 Cambridge Yearbook of European Legal Studies 159 https://doi.org/10.1017/cel.2021.3 accessed 29 August 2025.

Hoffman, Herrmann and Kestler 2024

J. Hoffmann, L. Herrmann, L. Kestler, 'Gatekeeper's Potential Privilege: The Need to Limit DMA Centralization' (2024) Journal of Antitrust Enforcement 12, 126 https://doi.org/10.1093/jaenfo/jnad040 accessed 29 August 2025.

Holland 2010

H. Holland, 'Privacy Paradox 2.0' (2010) 19 Widener Law Journal 893.

Holzwarth and Woolfson 2022

J. Holzwarth and T. Woolfson, 'Article 3: Relationship Between Articles [101 and 102 TFEU] and National Competition Laws: Commentary' in L. Prete et al. (eds), *Regulation 1/2003 and EU Antitrust Enforcement: A Systematic Guide* (Kluwer 2022).

Hondius 1980

F. Hondius, 'Data Law in Europe' (1980) 16 Stanford Journal of International Law 87.

Honnefelder and Kolassa 2016

S. Honnefelder and D. Kolassa, 'An Academic View on the Role and Powers of National Competition Authorities. Background to the ECN Plus Project' (2016) https://www.europarl.europa.eu/RegData/etudes/STUD/2016/578971/IPOL_STU(2016)578971_EN.pdf accessed 19 March 2025.

Hoofnagle, Van der Sloot and Zuiderveen Borgesius 2019

C. Hoofnagle, B. Van der Sloot and F. Zuiderveen Borgesius, 'The European Union General Data Protection Regulation: What It Is and What It Means' (2019) 28 Information & Communications Technology Law 65 https://doi.org/10.1080/13600834.2019.1573501 accessed 29 August 2025.

Hoppner 2020

T. Hoppner, 'Digital Upgrade of German Antitrust Law: Blueprint for Regulating Systemic Platforms in Europe and Beyond?' (2020) https://papers.ssrn.com/sol3/papers.cfm?abstract_id=3575629 accessed 11 March 2025.

Hornung 2023

P. Hornung, 'The Ecosystem Concept, the DMA, and Section 19a GWB' (2023) 12 Journal of Antitrust Enforcement 3, 396 https://doi.org/10.1093/jaenfo/jnad049 accessed 29 August 2025.

Hriscu 2023

A. Hriscu, 'C-252/21 Meta v Bundeskartellamt' (2023) 9 European Data Protection Law Review 371.

Humpe et al. 2024

C. Humpe et al., 'Unpacking the Digital Markets Act: A Milestone Ruling Against ByteDance and Its Implications for Potential Gatekeepers' (2024) 23 Competition Law Journal 2, 104 https://doi.org/10.4337/clj.2024.02.03 accessed 29 August 2025.

Hutchinson 2012

T. Hutchinson, 'Defining and Describing What We Do: Doctrinal Legal Research' (2012) 17 Deakin Law Review 1 https://doi.org/10.21153/dlr2012vol17no1art70 accessed 29 August 2025.

Hyman and Kovacic 2014

D. Hyman and W. Kovacic, 'Why Who Does What Matters: Governmental Design and Agency Performance' (2014) 82 George Washington law Review 1446.

Ibáñez Colomo 2013

P. Ibáñez Colomo, 'Three shifts in EU competition policy: towards standards, decentralization, settlements' (2013) 20 Maastricht Journal of European and Comparative Law 363 https://doi.org/10.1177/1023263x1302000303 accessed 29 August 2025.

Ibáñez Colomo 2018

P. Ibáñez Colomo, *The Shaping of EU Competition Law* (Cambridge University Press 2018).

Ibáñez Colomo 2021

P. Ibáñez Colomo, 'The Draft Digital Markets Act: A Legal and Institutional Analysis' (2021) 12 Journal of European Competition Law & Practice 561 https://doi.org/10.1093/jeclap/lpab065 accessed 29 August 2025.

Ibáñez Colomo 2023

P. Ibáñez Colomo, *The New EU Competition Law* (Hart Publishing 2023).

ICN 2024

ICN, 'Competition Law Enforcement at the Intersection Between Competition and Privacy: Agency Considerations' (2024) https://www.internationalcompetitionnetwork.org/wp-content/uploads/2024/12/Intersection-project-agency-considerations.pdf accessed 19 March 2025.

Immenga 2006

U. Immenga, 'Ökonomie und Recht in der europäischen Wettbewerbspolitik' [2006] Zeitschrift für Wettbewerbsrecht 346.

Intven, Oliver and Sepúlveda 2000

H. Intven, J. Oliver and E. Sepúlveda, *Telecommunications Regulation Handbook* (The World Bank 2000).

Jackwerth 2022

K. Jackwerth, 'Great Expectations: The Facebook Case and Subsequent Legislative Approaches to Regulate Large Online Platforms and Digital Markets' (2022) 3 Journal of Intellectual Property, Information Technology and Electronic Commerce Law 200.

Jacobides and Lianos 2021

M. Jacobides and I. Lianos, 'Ecosystems and Competition Law in Theory and Practice' (2021) 30 Industrial Corporate Change 1199 https://doi.org/10.1093/icc/dtab061 accessed 29 August 2025.

Jans et al. 2007

J. Jans et al., *Europeanisation of Public Law* (Europa Law Publishing 2007).

Jansen 2013

O. Jansen, 'De zelfstandige last en de bindende aanwijzing' in D. Doorenbos, M. Somsen and G. Naber (eds), *Onderneming en sanctierecht* (Kluwer 2013).

Joncheray 2022

N. Joncheray, 'Article 16: Uniform Application of Community Competition Law – Commentary' in K. Dekeyser et al. (eds), *Regulation 1/2003 and EU Antitrust Enforcement: A Systemic Guide* (Kluwer Law International 2022).

Jones, Sufrin and Dunne 2019

A. Jones, B. Sufrin and N. Dunne, *Jones & Sufrin's EU Competition Law: Text, Cases and Materials* (7 edn, Oxford University Press 2019).

Jorens et al. 2017

Y. Jorens et al., 'Analytical Report for the European Commission on Mutual Assistance and Sincere Cooperation: An Inquiry Into the Cooperation to Enforce the Coordination Regulation to Combat Fraud and Error' (2017) https://ec.europa.eu/social/BlobServlet?docId=19403&langId=en accessed 5 March 2025.

Kager and Van der Geest 2021

P. Kager and R. Van der Geest, 'Opinie: Samen st(r)a(f) je sterker' (2021) 6 Tijdschrift voor Internetrecht.

Kalimo and Majcher 2017

H. Kalimo and K. Majcher, 'The Concept of Fairness: Linking EU Competition and Data Protection Law in the Digital Marketplace' (2017) 42 European Law Review 210.

Käseberg and Gappa 2024a

T. Käseberg and S. Gappa, 'Article 1' in R. Podszun (ed.), *Digital Markets Act: Article-by-Article Commentary* (Bloomsburry 2024).

Käseberg and Gappa 2024b

T. Käseberg and S. Gappa, 'Article 3' in R. Podszun (ed.), *Digital Markets Act: Article-by-Article Commentary* (Bloomsburry 2024).

Katz and Sharpio 1985

L. Katz and C. Sharpio, 'Network Externalities, Competition, and Compatibility' (1985) 75 American Economic Association 424.

Kerber 2007

W. Kerber, 'Should Competition Promote Efficiency? Some Reflections of an Economist on the Normative Foundations of Competition Law' [2007] 9 Marburger Volkswirtschaftliche Beiträge.

Kerber 2016

W. Kerber, 'Digital Markets, Data, and Privacy: Competition Law, Consumer Law and Data Protection' (2016) 11 Journal of Intellectual Property Law 856 https://doi.org/10.1093/jiplp/jpw150 accessed 29 August 2025.

Kerber and Specht-Riemenschneider 2021

W. Kerber and L. Specht-Riemenschneider, 'Synergies Between Data Protection and Competition Law' (2021) https://papers.ssrn.com/sol3/papers.cfm?abstract_id=3977039 accessed 14 March 2025.

Kerber and Zolna 2022

W. Kerber and K. Zolna, 'The German Facebook Case: The Law and Economics of the Relationship Between Competition and Data Protection Law' (2022) 54 European Journal of Law and Economics, 217 https://doi.org/10.1007/s10657-022-09727-8 accessed 29 August 2025.

Kessedjian 2007

C. Kessedjian, 'Public Order in European Law' (2007) 1 Erasmus Law Review 25 https://doi.org/10.5553/elr221026712007001001003 accessed 29 August 2025.

Kestemont 2018

L. Kestemont, *Handbook on Legal Methodology* (Intersentia 2018).

Khan 2017

L. Khan, 'Amazon's Antitrust Paradox' (2017) 126 Yale Law Journal 710.

Kjolbe 2020

L. Kjolbe, 'Consistent Application of EU Competition Law, The Case for Revisiting the Consistency Toolbox in Regulation 1/2003' (2020) 11 Journal of European Competition Law & Practice 456 https://doi.org/10.1093/jeclap/lpaa056 accessed 29 August 2025.

Klamert 2014

M. Klamert, *The Principle of Loyalty in EU Law* (Oxford University Press 2014).

Klamert 2015

M. Klamert, 'What We Talk About When We Talk About Harmonisation?' (2015) 17 Cambridge Yearbook of European Legal Studies 360 https://doi.org/10.1017/cel.2015.12 accessed 29 August 2025.

Klamert 2019

M. Klamert, 'Article 4 TEU' in M. Kellerbauer, M. Klamert and J. Tomkin (eds), *The EU Treaties and the Charter of Fundamental Rights: A Commentary* (Oxford University Press 2019).

Klamert 2022

M. Klamert, 'Supremacy, the Uniformity of EU Law, and the Principle of Equality' [2022] Austrian Law Journal 82.

Knapstad 2024

T. Knapstad, 'Digital Dominance: Assessing Market Definition and Market Power for Online Platforms under Article 102 TFEU' (2024) 20 European Competition Journal 293 https://doi.org/10.1080/17441056.2023.2280334 accessed 29 August 2025.

Koenig and Bremenkamp 2022

C. Koenig and F. Bremenkamp, 'Competition Law Sanctions in Germany' in T. Tóth (ed.), *The Cambridge Handbook of Competition Law Sanctions* (Cambridge University Press 2022).

Kokolakis 2017

S. Kokolakis, 'Privacy Attitudes and Privacy Behaviour: A Review of Current Research on the Privacy Paradox Phenomenon' (2017) 64 Computers & Security 122 https://doi.org/10.1016/j.cose.2015.07.002 accessed 29 August 2025.

Komninos 2022

A. Komninos, 'The Digital Markets Act: How Does It Compare with Competition Law?' SSRN https://papers.ssrn.com/sol3/papers.cfm?abstract_id=4136146 accessed 29 August 2029.

Koops 2014

B. Koops, 'The Trouble with European Data Protection Law' (2014) 4 International Data Privacy Law 250 https://doi.org/10.1093/idpl/ipu023 accessed 29 August 2025.

Körber 2016

T. Körber, 'Ist Wissen Marktmacht? "Überlegungen zum Verhältnis von Datenschutz" "Datenmacht" und Kartellrecht: Teil 2' (2016) 8 NZKart 348.

Körber 2019

T. Körber, 'Die 10. GWB-Novelle als "GWB-Digitalisierungs-Regulierungs-Gesetz"' [2019] NZKart 633.

Körber 2020

T. Körber, 'Art. 2 FKVO' in U. Immega et al. (eds), *Wettbewerbsrecht* (C.H. Beck 2020).

Körber 2023

T. Körber, 'Die 11. GWB Novelle: zwichen freiem und verwatelm Wettbewerb' [2023] Zeitschrift für Rechtspolitik.

Kovacic 2012

W. Kovacic, 'The Institutions of Antitrust Law: How Structure Shapes Substance' [2012] Michigan Law Review 6.

Kovacic and Hyman 2013

D. Hyman and W. Kovacic, 'Competition Agencies with Complex Policy Portfolios: Divide or Conquer' [2013] GWU Legal Studies Research Paper.

Kozak 2020a

M. Kozak, 'Mutual Trust as a Backbone of EU Antitrust Law' (2020) 4 Market and Competition Law Review 127.

Kozak 2020b

M. Kozak, 'ECN+ Directive: A Missed Opportunity of Strengthening the Rights of Parties' in C. Rusu et al. (eds), *New Directions in Competition Law Enforcement* (Wolf Legal Publishing 2020).

Kress 2010

K. Kress, 'Coherence' in D. Patterson (ed.), *A Companion to Philosophy of Law and Legal Theory* (Wiley-Blackwell 2010).

Kroes and Kreijger 2025

Q. Kroes and P. Kreijger, 'Commentaar op art. 14 UAVG' in H. Kranenborg and G. Zwenne (eds), *Tekst & Commentaar Privacy- en Gegevensbeschermingsrecht* (Wolters Kluwer 2025).

Kuipers and Gaasbeek 2013

P. Kuipers and P. Gaasbeek, 'ACM en informatieverstrekking: een weerbarstige materie' (2013) 5/6 Sanctierecht & Complinace 210.

Kuschewsky and Geradin 2014

M. Kuschewsky and D. Geradin, 'Data Protection in the Context of Competition Law Investigations: An Overview of the Challenges' (2014) 37 World Competition 69 https://doi.org/10.54648/woco2014005 accessed 29 August 2025.

Lamadrid de Pablo and Bayón Fernández 2021

A. Lamadrid de Pablo and N. Bayón Fernández, 'Why the Proposed DMA Might Be Illegal under Article 114 TFEU, and How to Fix It' (2021) 21 Journal of European Competition Law & Practice 576 https://doi.org/10.1093/jeclap/lpab059 accessed 29 August 2025.

Lancieri and Pereira Neto 2020

F. Lancieri and C. Pereira Neto, 'Designing Remedies for Digital Markets: The Interplay Between Antitrust and Regulation' [2020] FGV Dereito DP Research Paper Series.

Lancieri and Morita Sokwski 2021

F. Lancieri and P. Morita Sokwski, 'Competition in Digital Markets: A Review of Expert Reports' (2021) 26 Stanford Journal of Law, Business & Finance 65.

Langer and Sauter 2017

J. Langer and W. Sauter, 'The Consistency Requirement in EU Law' (2017) 24 Columbia Journal of European Law 39.

Larouche and De Streel 2021

P. Larouche and A. De Streel, 'The European Digital Market: A Revolution Grounded on Traditions' (2021) 12 Journal of European Competition Law & Practice 542 https://doi.org/10.1093/jeclap/lpab066 accessed 29 August 2025.

Lavrijssen and Ottow 2012

S. Lavrijssen and A. Ottow, 'Independent Supervisory Authorities: A Fragile Concept' (2012) 39 Legal Issues of Economic Integration 419 https://doi.org/10.54648/leie2012025 accessed 29 August 2025.

Lenaerts, Van Nuffel and Corhaut 2021

K. Lenaerts, P. Van Nuffel and T. Corhaut, *EU Constitutional Law* (Oxford University Press 2021).

Levi-Faur 2011

D. Levi-Faur, 'Regulatory Networks and Regulatory Agencification: Towards a Single European Regulatory Space' (2011) 18 Journal of European Public Policy 810 https://doi.org/10.1080/13501763.2011.593309 accessed 29 August 2025.

Lianos 2013a

I. Lianos, 'Some Reflections on the Question of the Goals of EU Competition Law' (2013) 3 CLES Working Paper Series.

Lianos 2013b

I. Lianos, 'Competition Law Remedies in Europe? Which Limits for Remedial Discretion?' [2013] CLES Research Paper Series.

Lianos 2018

I. Lianos, 'Polycentric Competition Law' (2018) 17 Current Legal Problems, 1, 161 https://doi.org/10.1093/clp/cuy008 accessed 29 August 2025.

Liebowitz and Margolis 1994

S. Liebowitz and E. Margolis, 'Network Externality: An Uncommon Tragedy' (1994) 8 Journal of Economic Perspective 133 https://doi.org/10.1257/jep.8.2.133 accessed 29 August 2025.

Lilico and Sinclair 2017

A. Lilico and M. Sinclair, 'Dynamic Competition in Online Platforms' https://assets.publishing.service.gov.uk/media/5a8212bc40f0b6230269ab13/Digital_Platforms_report_new_BEIS.pdf accessed 4 March 2025.

Lindeboom 2022

J. Lindeboom, 'Rules, Discretion, and Reasoning According to Law: A Dynamic-Positivist Perspective on *Google Shopping*' (2022) 13 Journal of European Competition Law & Practice 2, 63 https://doi.org/10.1093/jeclap/lpac008 accessed 29 August 2025.

Lintvedt 2022

M. Lintvedt, 'Putting a Price on Data Protection Infringement' (2022) 12 International Data Privacy Law 1 https://doi.org/10.1093/idpl/ipab024 accessed 29 August 2025.

Lynskey 2015

O. Lynskey, *The Foundations of EU Data Protection Law* (Oxford University Press 2015).

Lynskey 2017

O. Lynskey, 'Aligning Data Protection Rights with Competition Law Remedies? The GDPR Right to Data Portability' (2017) 42 European Law Review 793.

MacCormick 1978

N. MacCormick, *Legal Reasoning and Legal Theory* (Clarendon 1978).

Maher and Ştefan 2010

I. Maher and O. Ştefan, 'Competition Law in Europe: The Challenge of a Network Constitution' in D. Oliver, T. Prosser and R. Rawlings (eds), *The Regulatory State: Constitutional Implications* (Oxford University Press 2010).

Maher 2024

I. Maher, 'Regulatory Design in the EU Digital Markets Act: No Solo Run for the European Commission' (2024) 12 Journal of Antitrust Enforcement 273 https://doi.org/10.1093/jaenfo/jnae029 accessed 29 August 2025.

Maier-Rigaud 2012

F. Maier-Rigaud, 'On the Normative Foundations of Competition Law: Efficiency, Political Freedom and the Freedom to Compete' in D. Zimmer (ed.), *The Goals of Competition Law* (Edward Elgar 2012).

Majcher 2023

K. Majcher, *Coherence Between Data Protection and Competition Law in Digital Markets* (Oxford University Press 2023).

Majcher and Robertson 2024

K. Majcher and V. Robertson, 'The Twin Transition to a Green and Digital Economy: The Role for EU Competition Law' in J. Nowag (ed.), *Research Handbook on Sustainability and Competition Law* (Edward Elgar 2024).

Majcher 2024

K. Majcher, 'Interaction Between EU Competition Law and Data Protection in Digital Markets: Striving for Coherence' in P. Parcu, J. Rossi and M. Botta (eds), *Research Handbook on Competition and Technology* (Edward Elgar Publishing 2024).

Malinauskaite 2022

J. Malinauskaite, 'Competition Law and Sustainability: EU and National Perspectives' (2022) 13 Journal of European Competition Law and Practice 5 https://doi.org/10.1093/jeclap/lpac003 accessed 29 August 2025.

Mândrescu 2018

D. Mândrescu, 'The SSNIP Test and Zero-Pricing Strategies: Considerations for Online Platforms' (2018) 4 European Competition and Regulatory Law Review 244 https://doi.org/10.21552/core/2018/4/4 accessed 29 August 2025.

Mândrescu 2024a

D. Mândrescu, 'The Apple App Store: A New Kind of Hallmark Case' (Kluwer Competition Law Blog, 18 March 2024) https://legalblogs.woltserskluwer.com/competition-blog/the-apple-app-store-a-new-kind-of-hallmark-case/ accessed 25 July 2024.

Mândrescu 2024b

D. Mândrescu, 'Applying Article 102 TFEU to Multisided Online Platforms: Discrimination, Leveraging and Undefined Abuses of Dominance' (2024) https://papers.ssrn.com/sol3/papers.cfm?abstract_id=4814850 accessed 11 March 2025.

Mantzari 2020

D. Mantzari, 'Interim Measures in EU Competition Cases: Origins, Evolution and Implications for Digital Markets' (2020) https://papers.ssrn.com/sol3/papers.cfm?abstract_id=3544877 accessed 11 March 2025.

Markert 2019

K. Markert, 'GWB § 20' in U. Immenga et al. (eds), *Wettbewerbsrecht* (C.H. Beck 2019).

Marsden and Podszun 2020

P. Marsden and R. Podszun, Restoring Balance to Digital Competition: Sensible Rules, Effective Enforcement (2019) https://www.kas.de/documents/252038/7995358/Restoring+Balance+to+Digital+Competition+%E2%80%93+Sensible+Rules%2C+Effective+Enforcement.pdf/7cb5ab1a-a5c2-54f0-3dcd-db6ef7fd9c78?version=1.0&t=1601365173489 accessed 11 March 2025.

Martens et al. 2020

Martens et al., 'Business-to-Business Data Sharing: An Economic and Legal Analysis' https://papers.ssrn.com/sol3/papers.cfm?abstract_id=3658100 accessed 14 March 2025.

Massa 2020

C. Massa, 'Sincere Cooperation and Antitrust Enforcement: Insights from the Damages and ECN+ Directive' (2020) 16 European Competition Journal 126 https://doi.org/10.1080/17441056.2019.1705631 accessed 29 August 2025.

Masquelier 2021

R. Masquelier, 'After 19 Years of Complete Oblivion, Are Interim Measures the European Commission's New Panacea to Enforce Article 102 TFEU in the Digital Age?' (2021) 5 European Competition and Regulatory Law Review 24 https://doi.org/10.21552/core/2021/1/6 accessed 29 August 2025.

Mathisen 2010

G. Mathisen, 'Consistency and Coherence as Conditions for Justification of Member State Measures Restricting Free Movement' (2010) 47 Common Market Law Review 1021 https://doi.org/10.54648/cola2010045 accessed 29 August 2025.

Matos Brandao 2023

D. Matos Brandao, 'The One-Stop-Shop and the European Data Protection Board's Role in Combatting Data Supervision Forum Shopping' (2023) 13

International Data Privacy Law 313 https://doi.org/10.1093/idpl/ipad014 accessed 29 August 2025.

Mayr 2022

M. Mayr, 'Redefining the Ne Bis in Idem Principle in EU Competition Law: Bpost and Nordzucker' (2022) 13 Journal of European Competition Law & Practice 553 https://doi.org/10.1093/jeclap/lpac053 accessed 29 August 2025.

McIntyre 2023

R. McIntyre, 'Decentralisation and Recentralisation: An Institutional Analysis of EU Competition Law and the Digital Markets Act' (2023) 8 LSE Law Review 227 https://doi.org/10.61315/lselr.516 accessed 29 August 2025.

Menard and Shirley 2005

C. Menard and M. Shirley, *Handbook of New Institutional Economics* (Springer 2005).

Mestmäcker 2005

E. Mestmäcker, 'Die Interdependenz von Recht und Ökonomie in der Wettbewerbspolitik' in Monopolkommission (ed.), *Zukunftperspectiven der Wettbewerbspolitik* (2005).

Meta 2023

Meta, 'Our Response to the Decision on Facebook's EU-US Data Transfers' (22 November 2023) https://about.fb.com/news/2023/05/our-response-to-the-decision-on-facebooks-eu-us-data-transfers/ accessed 24 March 2025.

Meta 2024

Meta, 'Our Response to the European Commission's Decision on Facebook Marketplace' (14 November 2024) https://about.fb.com/news/2024/11/our-response-to-the-european-commissions-decision-on-facebook-marketplace/ accessed 10 March 2025.

Miasik and Szwarc 2021

D. Miasik and M. Szwarc, 'Primacy and Direct Effect: Still Together – Popławski II' (2021) 58 Common Market Law Review 571 https://doi.org/10.54648/cola2021030 accessed 29 August 2025.

Micheletti and Parry 2025

F. Micheletti and J. Parry, 'Time Was Right for US Big Tech Penalties, EU Competition Chief Says' (Politico, 23 April 2025).

Midri 2023

M. Midri, 'The Amazon Case in Light of Cooperation Between the EU Commission and the Italian Competition Authority' (2023) https://papers.ssrn.com/sol3/papers.cfm?abstract_id=4544271 accessed 21 March 2025.

Miller 1971

A. Miller, *The Assault on Privacy: Computers, Data Banks, and Dossiers* (The University of Michigan Press 1971).

Mohr 2023

J. Mohr, 'Digital Markets Act und § 19a GWB als zentrale Bestandteile des Wettbewerbsrechts im 21. Jahrhundert' in M. Ruffert (ed), *Die Regulierung digitaler Platformen* (Nomos 2023).

Molinari 2021

C. Molinari, 'Sincere Cooperation Between EU and Member States in the Field of Readmission: The More the Merrier?' (2021) 23 Cambridge Yearbook of European Legal Studies 269 https://doi.org/10.1017/cel.2021.10 accessed 29 August 2025.

Monteleone 2015

S. Monteleone, 'Addressing the Failure of Informed Consent in Online Data Protection: Learning the Lessons from Behaviour-Aware Regulation' (2015) 43 Syracuse Journal of International Law and Commerce 69.

Monti 2014

G. Monti, 'Independence, Interdependence and Legitimacy: The EU Commission, National Competition Authorities, and the European Competition Network' (2014) https://cadmus.eui.eu/handle/1814/29218 accessed 11 March 2025.

Monti and Mulder 2017

G. Monti and J. Mulder, 'Escaping the Clutches of EU Competition Law: Pathways to Assess Private Sustainability Initiatives' (2017) 42 European Law Review 635.

Monti 2021a

G. Monti, 'The Digital Markets Act: Institutional Design and Suggestions for Improvement' (2021) https://research.tilburguniversity.edu/en/publications/the-digital-markets-act-improving-its-institutional-design accessed 5 March 2025.

Monti 2021b

G. Monti, 'The Operation of the More Economic Approach after *Intel* and *Generics*' in P. Parcu, G. Monti and M. Botta (eds), *Economic Analysis in EU Competition Policy* (Elgar Online 2021).

Monti 2022

G. Monti, 'Taming Digital Monopolies: A Comparative Account of the Evolution of Antitrust and Regulation in the European Union and the United States' [2022] Antitrust Bulletin 1, 40 https://doi.org/10.1177/0003603x211066978 accessed 29 August 2025.

Morozovaite 2022

V. Morozovaite, 'Hypernudging in the Changing European Regulatory Landscape for Digital Markets' (2022) 15 Policy & Internet 1, 78 https://doi.org/10.1002/poi3.329 accessed 29 August 2025.

Mota Delgado and Petit 2023

M. Mota Delgado and N. Petit, 'Article 3 of Regulation 1/2003 and the Doctrine of Pre-Emption' in A. Claici, A. Kominos and D. Wealbroeck (eds), *The Transformation of EU Competition Law – Next Generation Issues* (Wolters Kluwer 2023).

Motta and Peitz 2020

M. Motta and M. Peitz, 'Intervention Triggers and Underlying Theories of Harm. Expert Advice for the Impact Assessment of a New Competition Tool' (2020) https://competition-policy.ec.europa.eu/system/files/2021-03/kd0420575enn.pdf accessed 3 March 2025.

MTB 2014

Markttoezichthoudersberaad, 'Criteria voor goed toezicht' (2014) https://www.acm.nl/sites/default/files/old_publication/publicaties/12609_criteria-voor-goed-toezicht-2014-02-11.pdf accessed 25 March 2024.

Mundt 2023

A. Mundt, 'Paradigmenwechsel in der 11. GWB Novelle?: Die Sicht der Praxis' [2023] NZKart.

Musielak 2021

M. Musielak, 'The Evolution of Classical Evaluation Standards in Competition Law: The Legal Assessment of Tying in View of Challenges Raised by Digital Markets' (2021) 35 Studia Prawa Publicznego 113 https://doi.org/10.14746/spp.2021.3.35.4 accessed 29 August 2025.

Neframi 2010

E. Neframi, 'The Duty of Loyal Cooperation: Rethinking Its Scope Through Its Application in the Field of EU External Relations' (2010) 47 Common Market Law Review 323 https://doi.org/10.54648/cola2010017 accessed 29 August 2025.

Newman 2002

P. Newman, 'Network Effects and Externalities' in P. Newman (ed.), *The New Palgrave Dictionary of Economics and the Law* (Palgrave Macmillan 2002).

Newman 2015

J. Newman, 'Antitrust in Zero-Price Markets: Foundations' (2015) 164 University of Pennsylvania Law Review 149.

North 2012

D. North, *Institutions, Institutional Change and Economic Performance* (Cambridge University Press 2012).

Nowag 2024

J. Nowag (ed.), *Research Handbook on Sustainability* (Edward Elgar Publishing 2024).

O'Callaghan 2018

L. O'Callaghan, 'The Intersection Between Data Protection and Competition Law: How to Incorporate Data Protection, as a Non-Economic Objective, into EU Competition Analysis' (2018) 21 Trinity College Law Review 109.

OECD 2013

OECD, Hearings The Digital Economy (2019) DAF/COMP(2012)22.

OECD 2020

OECD, Consumer Data Rights and Competition: Background note DAF/COMP(2020).

OECD 2024

OECD, The Intersection Between Competition and Data Privacy: Note by Germany DAF/COMP/WD(2024)42.

Ogus 1994

A. Ogus, *The Context of Regulation: The Market and Private Law* (Hart Publishing 1994).

Oppermann and Chmeis 2017

B. Oppermann and A. Chmeis, 'The Uniform Application of Articles 101 and 102 TFEU in German Competition Law' in A. Almăşan and P. Whelan (eds), *The Consistent Application of EU Competition Law* (Springer 2017).

Otto 2020

J. Otto, '§ 32b GWB' in U. Loewenheim et al. (eds), *Kartellrecht* (C.H. Beck 2020).

Ottow 2012

A. Ottow, 'Europeanization of the Supervision of Competitive Markets' (2012) 18 European Public Law 191 https://doi.org/10.54648/euro2012009 accessed 29 August 2025.

Ottow 2014

A. Ottow, 'Erosion or Innovation? The Institutional Design of Competition Agencies: A Dutch Case Study' (2014) 2 Journal of Antitrust Enforcement 25.

Parker and Van Alstyne 2005

G. Parker and M. Van Alstyne, 'Two-Sided Network Effects: A Theory of Information Product Design' (2005) 51(10) Management Science 1494 https://doi.org/10.1287/mnsc.1050.0400.

Pauer 2023

N. Pauer, 'The 11th Amendment of the German Act Against Restraints of Competition: A "New Competition Tool," Facilitated Disgorgement and the DMA's Enforcement' (2023) 14 Journal of European Competition Law & Practice 6, 354 https://doi.org/10.1093/jeclap/lpad033 accessed 29 August 2025.

Petit 2015

N. Petit, 'Intel, Leveraging Rebates and the Goals of Article 102 TFEU' (2015) 11 European Competition Journal 26 https://doi.org/10.1080/17441056.2015.1033215 accessed 29 August 2025.

Petit 2020

N. Petit, *Big Tech and the Digital Economy: The Moligopoly Scenario* (Oxford University Press 2020).

Petit 2021

N. Petit, 'A Theory of Antitrust Limits' (2021) 28 George Mason Law Review 1399.

Petterson 2022

D. Petterson, 'Sector-Specific Ex Ante Regulation in Digital Markets: A Complement or Substitute to Antitrust Enforcement' (2022) 4 Europarättslig tidskrift.

Picht 2022

P. Picht, 'Relative Marktmacht, Geoblocking and Digitalisierung' (2022) 4 Schweizerische Zeitschrift für Wirtschafts- und Finanzmarktrecht 315.

Picht 2023

P. Picht, 'CJEU on Facebook: Gdpr Processing Justifications and Application Competence' (2023) https://papers.ssrn.com/sol3/papers.cfm?abstract_id=4521320 accessed 19 March 2025.

Podszun 2020

R. Podszun, 'Der Verbraucher als Marktakteur: Kartellrecht und Datenschutz in der "Facebook"-Entscheidung des BGH' [2020] Gewerblicher Rechtsschutz und Uhreberrecht 1268.

Podszun 2022a

R. Podszun, 'Competition in the Digital Economy: What Next after the Digital Markets Act? – Statement for the Economic Committee of the German Bundestag' (2022) https://papers.ssrn.com/sol3/papers.cfm?abstract_id=4096357 accessed 5 March 2025.

Podszun 2022b

R. Podszun, 'A Learning Experience: Is the EU's Administrative Model Fit for Purpose?' in K. Dekeyser et al. (eds), *Regulation 1/2003 and EU Antitrust Enforcement: A Systemic Guide* (Kluwer Law International 2022).

Podszun 2022c

R. Podszun, 'Should Gatekeepers Be Allowed to Combine Data? Ideas for the Draft Digital Markets Act' (2022) 71 GRUR International 3, 197 https://doi.org/10.1093/grurint/ikab131 accessed 29 August 2025.

Podszun 2022d

R. Podszun, 'Private Enforcement and Gatekeeper Regulation: Strengthening the Rights of Private Parties in the Digital Markets Act' (2022) 13 Journal of European Competition Law & Practice 4, 254 https://doi.org/10.1093/jeclap/lpab076 accessed 29 August 2025.

European Competition Journal 1 https://doi.org/10.1080/17441056.2022.2156729 accessed 29 August 2025.

Riesenkampff 2011

A. Riesenkampff, 'Vom Wettbewerbsschutz zum Verbraucherschutz?' in S. Bechtold, J. Jickeli and M. Rohe (eds), *Recht, Ordnung und Wettbewerb Festschrift zum 70 Geburtstag von Wernard Möschel* (Nomos 2011).

Riley 2003

A. Riley, 'EC Antitrust Modernisation: The Commission Does Very Nicely: Thank you!' (2003) 11 European Competition Law Review 604.

Robertson 2020

V. Robertson, 'Excessive Data Collection: Privacy Considerations and Abuse of Dominance in the Era of Big Data' (2020) 57 Common Market Law Review 161 https://doi.org/10.54648/cola2020006 accessed 29 August 2025.

Robertson 2021

V. Robertson, 'Antitrust and Digital Markets: A Guide to the European Competition Experience in the Digital Economy' in H. Kurz et al. (eds), *The Routledge Handbook of Smart Technologies: An Economic and Social Perspective* (Routledge 2021).

Robertson and Majcher 2022

V. Robertson and K. Majcher, 'Protecting Personal Data and the Environment: Doctrinal Challenges for EU Competition Law in Our Day and Age' [2022] European Law Review 622.

Robertson 2024

V. Robertson, 'The Complementary Nature of the Digital Markets Act and EU Antitrust Rules' (2024) 12 Journal of Antitrust Enforcement 325 https://doi.org/10.1093/jaenfo/jnae013 accessed 29 August 2025.

Rodrigo, Allio and Andres-Amo 2009

D. Rodrigo, L. Allio and P. Andres-Amo, *Multi-Level Regulatory Governance: Policies, Institutions and Tools for Regulatory Quality and Policy Coherence* (OECD Working Papers on Public Governance No. 13, 2009).

Roosendaal, Van Lieshout and Van Veenstra 2014

A. Roosendaal, M. Van Lieshout and A. Van Veenstra, 'TNO Report: Personal Data Markets' (2014) https://publications.tno.nl/publication/34612412/riZsP9/TNO-2014-R11390.pdf accessed 3 March 2025.

Ruiz Feases 2020a

A. Ruiz Feases, 'Consistency and Modernisation of EU Competition Law: A View from the Concept of Appreciability' (European University Institute 2020).

Ruiz Feases 2020b

A. Ruiz Feases, 'Sharping the European Commission's Tools: Interim Measures' (2020) 16 European Competition Journal 404 https://doi.org/10.1080/17441056.2020.1805697 accessed 29 August 2025.

Rusu, Looijestijn-Clearie and Veenbrink 2018

C. Rusu, A. Looijestijn-Clearie and M. Veenbrink, 'State of the Art and Prospective Directions in Digitalisation of Economic Law' in M. Veenbrink, A. Looijestijn-Clearie and C. Rusu (eds), *Digital Markets in the EU* (Wolf Legal Publisher 2018).

Rusu and Van de Gronden 2024

C. Rusu and J. Van de Gronden, 'The Interaction Between the Digital Markets Act and Merger Control Instruments' (2024) 24 Mededingingsrecht in de Praktijk 3, 20.

Sauter 2016

W. Sauter, *Coherence in EU Competition Law* (Oxford University Press 2016).

Sauter and Mulder 2023

W. Sauter and J. Mulder, ' Hoe ver gaat rechtstreekse werking? Artikel 102 VWEU als toetsingsgrond van niet-meldingsplichtige concentraties door nationale mededingingsautoriteiten: HvJ EU 16 maart 2023, C-449/21,ECLI:EU:C:2023:207 (Towercast/Autorité de la concurrence)' (2023) 26 Markt & Mededinging 136 https://doi.org/10.5553/menm/138762362023026004005 accessed 29 August 2025.

Schäfers and Houdijk 2012

T. Schäfers and J. Houdijk, 'The Netherlands' New Authority for Consumer and Markets: Towards a Problem-Based Approach' (2012) 35 World Competition 659 https://doi.org/10.54648/woco2012049 accessed 29 August 2025.

Schiavello 2001

A. Schiavello, 'On "Coherence" and "Law": An Analysis of Different Models' (2001) 14 Ratio Juris 233 https://doi.org/10.1111/1467-9337.00179 accessed 29 August 2025.

Schinkel 2011

M. Schinkel, 'Het Marktwerkingspaleis' (2011) 4 Markt & Mededinging 138.

Schmidt 2019

H. Schmidt, 'Taming the Shrew: Is There a Need for a New Market Power Definition for the Digital Economy' in B. Lundqvist (ed.), *Competition Law for the Digital Economy* (Edward Elgar 2019).

Schneider 2018

J. Schneider, 'Testing Art. 102 TFEU in the Digital Marketplace: Insights from the Bundeskartellambt's Investigation Against Facebook' (2018) 9 Journal of European Competition Law 213 https://doi.org/10.1093/jeclap/lpy016 accessed 29 August 2025.

Schneider et al. 2023

S. Schneider et al., 'Exploring Design Elements of Personal Data Markets' (2023) 33 Electronic Markets https://doi.org/10.1007/s12525-023-00646-3 accessed 29 August 2025.

Scholten and Ottow 2014

M. Scholten and A. Ottow, 'Institutional Design of Enforcement in the EU: The Case of Financial Markets' (2014) 10 Utrecht Law Review, 5, 80 https://doi.org/10.18352/ulr.302 accessed 29 August 2025.

Scholten 2021

M. Scholten, 'EU (Shared) Law Enforcement: Who Does What and How?' in S. Montaldo, F. Costamanga and A. Miglio (eds), *EU Law Enforcement: The Evolution of Sanctioning Powers* (Routledge 2021).

Schroeter and Hoyng 2021

B. Schroeter and A. Hoyng, 'De Digital Markets Act als instrument voor het mededingingsbeleid in perspectief' [2021] Markt & Mededinging 1.

Schütze 2006

R. Schütze, 'Supremacy Without Pre-emption? The Very Slowly Emergent Doctrine of Community Pre-emption' (2006) 43 Common Market Law Review 1023 https://doi.org/10.54648/cola2006051 accessed 29 August 2025.

Schütze 2010

R. Schütze, 'From Rome to Lisbon: "Executive Federalism" in the (New) European Union' (2010) 47 Common Market Law Review 1385 https://doi.org/10.54648/cola2010059 accessed 29 August 2025.

Schwartz 2000

P. Schwartz, 'Internet Privacy and the State' (2000) 32 Connecticut Law Review 815.

Schweitzer 2021

H. Schweitzer, 'The Art to Make Gatekeeper Positions Contestable and the Challenge to Know What is Fair: A Discussion of the Digital Markets Act Proposal' (2021) https://papers.ssrn.com/sol3/papers.cfm?abstract_id=3837341 accessed 1 March 2024.

Schweitzer et al. 2022

H. Schweitzer et al., 'Data Access and Sharing in Germany and in the EU: Towards a Coherent Legal Framework for the Emerging Data Economy' (2022) https://www.rewi.hu-berlin.de/de/lf/ls/mzg/pub/final-report-08-07-2022-fin-01.pdf/@@download/file/Final%20Report-08-07-2022(FIN-01).pdf accessed 11 March 2025.

Schweitzer and Metzger 2023

H. Schweitzer and A. Metzger, 'Data Access under the Draft Data Act, Competition Law and the DMA: Opening the Treasures for Competition and Innovation?' (2023) 72 GRUR International 337 https://doi.org/10.1093/grurint/ikad012 accessed 29 August 2025.

Schwintowski 2023

H. Schwintowski, 'Die Beseitigung von Störungen des Wettbewerbs: Auswirkungen der 11. I.GWB-Novelle auf die Praxis' [2023] Energie- und Wettbewerbsrecht in der Kummunalen Wirtschaft.

Scott 2019

M. Scott, 'Margrethe Vestager's Vast New Powers' (Politico, 10 September 2019).

SDT 2023a

Samenwerkingsplatform Digitale Toezichthouders, 'Effectief digitaal toezicht cruciaal voor verantwoorde digitalisering' (2023) https://www.autoriteitpersoonsgegevens.nl/uploads/2023-10/SDT%20-%20Effectief%20digitaal%20toezicht%20cruciaal%20voor%20verantwoorde%20digitalisering_0.pdf accessed 25 March 2025.

SDT 2023b

Samenwerkingsplatform Digitale Toezichthouders, 'Uitgangspunten voor effectieve transparantie' (2023) https://www.acm.nl/system/files/documents/uitgangspunten-effectieve-transparantie.pdf accessed 25 March 2025.

SDT 2023c

Samenwerkingsplatform Digitale Toezichthouders, 'Uitgangspunten voor reclame en marketing gericht op kinderen online' (2023) https://www.autoriteitpersoonsgegevens.nl/documenten/sdt-uitgangspunten-voor-reclame-en-marketing-gericht-op-kinderen-online accessed 25 March 2025.

Senden 2004

L. Senden, *Soft Law in European Community Law* (Hart Publishing 2004).

Shelanski 2013

H. Shelanski, 'Information, Innovation, and Competition Policy for the Internet' (2013) 161 University of Pennsylvania Law Review 1663.

Sickinghe 2011

F. Sickinghe, 'Fusie NMa, OPTA en Consumentenautoriteit. Kwaliteitsoffer voor kostenbesparingen?' (2011) 7/8 Mediaforum 203.

Sinclair 2017

A. Sinclair, 'Proposal for a Directive to Empower National Competition Authorities to be More Effective Enforcers (ECN+)' (2017) 8 Journal of European Competition Law & Practice 625 https://doi.org/10.1093/jeclap/lpx084 accessed 29 August 2025.

Snoep 2021

M. Snoep, 'De rol van nationale toezichthouders bij handhaving van de Digital Markets Act' [2021] Markt & Mededinging, 4/5, 203.

Snoep 2023a

M. Snoep, 'De toezichtsrevolutie voor onlineplatforms: ook een nieuwe wereld voor toezichthouders' (2023) https://www.acm.nl/nl/publicaties/blog-martijn-snoep-de-toezichtsrevolutie-voor-onlineplatforms-ook-een-nieuwe-wereld-voor-toezichthouders accessed 31 October 2024.

Snoep 2023b

M. Snoep, '"Plugging Gaps" in Antitrust Enforcement' (Speech at the Conference for Antitrust, Regulation & the Political Economy, Brussels, 2 March 2023) https://www.acm.nl/en/publications/speech-martijn-snoep-plugging-gaps-antitrust-enforcement accessed 11 March 2025.

Snoep 2023c

M. Snoep, 'Kleine Overnames, Grote Problemen' (2023) https://www.acm.nl/nl/publicaties/blog-martijn-snoep-kleine-overnames-grote-problemen accessed 25 March 2025.

Snoep 2024

M. Snoep, 'Updating Competition Enforcement' (2024) https://www.acm.nl/en/publications/blog-martijn-snoep-updating-competition-enforcement accessed 11 March 2025.

Sousa Ferro 2020

M. Sousa Ferro, 'The System for EU Antitrust Enforcement is Misguided and Unfair: Let's Change It' (2020) 11 Journal of European Competition Law & Practice 8, 413 https://doi.org/10.1093/jeclap/lpaa063 accessed 29 August 2025.

Stefan et al. 2019

O. Stefan et al., 'EU Soft Law in the EU Legal Order: A Literature Review' (2019) https://papers.ssrn.com/sol3/papers.cfm?abstract_id=3346629 accessed 18 March 2025.

Steppe 2017

R. Steppe, 'Online Price Discrimination and Personal Data: A General Data Protection Regulation Perspective' (2017) 33 Computer Law & Security Review 6, 768 https://doi.org/10.1016/j.clsr.2017.05.008 accessed 29 August 2025.

Steppe, Devroe and Deblander 2024

R. Steppe, W. Devroe and G. Deblander, 'Final Report: Support Study for the Evaluation of Regulations 1/2003 and 773/2004' (2024) https://competition-policy.ec.europa.eu/system/files/2024-09/20240324_DG%20COMP_Evaluation%20Reg%201%20-%20WEB-PDF.pdf accessed 11 March 2025.

Stöhr and Mendelsohn 2024

A. Stöhr and J. Mendelsohn, 'Durchsetzung des § 19a GWB: Erste Erfahrungen und Verhältnis zum Digital Markets Act' (2024) https://papers.ssrn.com/sol3/papers.cfm?abstract_id=4707355 accessed 19 March 2025.

Streinz 2021

T. Streinz, 'The Evolution of European Data Law' in P. Craig and G. De Búrca (eds), *The Evolution of EU Law* (Oxford University Press 2021).

Stucke and Grunes 2016

M. Stucke and A. Grunes A, *Big Data and Competition Policy* (Oxford University Press 2016).

Subiotto, Lepetska and Nobbs 2022

R. Subiotto, R. Lepetska and K. Nobbs, 'The Application of Article 102 TFEU by the European Commission and European Courts' (2022) 13 Journal of Competition Law & Practice 51 https://doi.org/10.1093/jeclap/lpac002 accessed 29 August 2025.

Sunstein 2000

C. Sunstein, 'Introduction' in C. Sunstein (ed.), *Behavioral Law and Economics* (Cambridge University Press 2000).

Svantesson 2018

D. Svantesson, 'Enter the Quagmire: The Complicated Relationship Between Data Protection and Competition Law' (2018) 34 Computer Law & Security Review 25 https://doi.org/10.1016/j.clsr.2017.08.003 accessed 29 August 2025.

Svetlicinii 2023

A. Svetlicinii, 'The Elephant in the Room Turns Twenty: The Effect on Trade and the Enforcement of the EU Competition Law by the National Competition Authorities' (2023) 14 Journal of European Competition Law & Practice, 8, 483 https://doi.org/10.1093/jeclap/lpad060 accessed 29 August 2025.

Szydlo 2010

M. Szydlo, 'Leeway of Member States in Shaping the Notion of an "Undertaking" in Competition Law' (2010) 33 World Competition 549 https://doi.org/10.54648/woco2010048 accessed 29 August 2025.

Tavares 2018

M. Tavares, *A Constitutional Analysis of Multijurisdictional Conflicts in the EU Legal Order Confirms That Diversity Is Possible in EU Competition Law* (King's Research Portal 2018).

Thaler and Sunstein 2009

R. Thaler and C. Sunstein, *Nudge* (Penguin Putnam Inc 2009).

Thépot 2025

F. Thépot, 'Market Power and Gatekeepers: Complements or Substitutes?' (2025) 4 Market and Competition Law Review 1, 41.

Tombal 2021

T. Tombal, 'Data Protection and Competition Law: Friends or Foes regarding Data Sharing?' (2021) https://papers.ssrn.com/sol3/papers.cfm?abstract_id=3826325 accessed 14 March 2025.

Tountopoulos 2012

V. Tountopoulos, 'Failure of NCAs to Comply with Article 11(4) of Regulation 1/2003 and Legal Consequences' [2012] Zeitschrift für Wettbewerbsrecht 474 https://doi.org/10.15375/zwer-2012-0404 accessed 29 August 2025.

Townley, Morrison and Yeung 2017

C. Townley, E. Morrison and K. Yeung, 'Big Data and Personalized Price Discrimination in EU Competition Law' (2017) 36 Yearbook of European Law 683 https://doi.org/10.1093/yel/yex015 accessed 29 August 2025.

Townley and Türk 2019

C. Townley and A. Türk, 'The Constitutional Limits of EU Competition Law: United in Diversity' (2019) 64 The Antitrust Bulletin 235 https://doi.org/10.1177/0003603x19844626 accessed 29 August 2025.

Trebilcock and Iacobucci 2010

M. Trebilcock and E. Iacobucci, 'Designing Competition Law Institutions: Values, Structure, and Mandate' (2010) 41 Loyola University Chicago Law Journal 455 https://doi.org/10.54648/5095415 accessed 29 August 2025.

Tucker and Wellford 2014

D. Tucker and H. Wellford, 'Big Mistakes Regarding Big Data' [2014] The Antitrust Source 1.

Tuominen 2020

T. Tuominen, 'Reconceptualizing the Primacy–Supremacy Debate in EU Law' (2020) 47 Legal Issues of Economic Integration 245 https://doi.org/10.54648/leie2020015 accessed 29 August 2025.

Tzanaki and Nowag 2023

A. Tzanaki and J. Nowag, 'The Institutional Framework of the DMA: From Hybrid to Mature?' (2023) https://papers.ssrn.com/sol3/papers.cfm?abstract_id=4574518 accessed 26 June 2025.

Tzanou 2013

M. Tzanou, 'Data Protection as A Fundamental Right Next to Privacy? "Reconstructing" a Not so New Right' (2013) 3 International Data Privacy Law 88 https://doi.org/10.1093/idpl/ipt004 accessed 29 August 2025.

Van Alsenoy 2019

B. Van Alsenoy, *Data Protection Law in the EU: Roles, Responsibilities and Liability* (Larcier Intersentia 2019).

Vanberg 2009

V. Vanberg, 'Consumer Welfare, Total Welfare and Economic Freedom: On the Normative Foundations of Competition Policy' (2009) 9 Freiburger Diskussionspapiere zur Ordnungsökonomik.

Vanberg and Ünver 2017

A. Vanberg and M. Ünver, 'The Right to Data Potability in the GDPR and EU Competition Law: Odd Couple or Dynamic Duo?' (2017) 8 European Journal of Law and Technology 1.

Van Cleynenbreugel 2012

P. Van Cleynenbreugel, 'Institutional Assimilation in the Wake of EU Competition Law Decentralisation' (2012) 8 The Competition Law Review 285.

Van Cleynenbreugel 2020

P. Van Cleynenbreugel, 'Case (Re-)Allocation Against the Backdrop of Procedural Convergence: Time for a Regulation "2" Upgrade' (2020) 11 Journal of European Competition Law 8, 418 https://doi.org/10.1093/jeclap/lpaa054 accessed 29 August 2025.

Van Cleynenbreugel 2022

P. Van Cleynenbreugel, 'BPost and Nordzucker: Searching for the Essence of Ne Bis in Idem in European Union Law' (2022) 18 European Constitutional Law Review 357 https://doi.org/10.1017/s1574019622000190 accessed 29 August 2025.

Van de Gronden and De Vries 2006

J. Van de Gronden and S. De Vries, 'Independent Competition Authorities in the EU' (2006) 2 Utrecht Law Review 32 https://doi.org/10.18352/ulr.16 accessed 29 August 2025.

Van de Gronden and Rusu 2021

J. Van de Gronden and C. Rusu, *Competition Law in the EU. Principles, Substance, Enforcement* (Edward Elgar 2021).

Van de Gronden 2022

J. Van de Gronden, *Mededingingsrecht in de EU en Nederland* (Uitgeverij Paris 2022).

Van de Gronden and Rusu 2024

J. van de Gronden and C. Rusu, *Competition Law in the EU. Principles, Substance, Enforcement* (Edward Elgar 2021).

Van de Waerdt 2020

P. Van de Waerdt, 'Information Asymmetries: Recognizing the Limits of the GDPR on Data-Driven Markets' (2020) 38 Computer Law & Security Review https://doi.org/10.18352/ulr.16 accessed 29 August 2025.

Van de Waerdt 2023

P. Van de Waerdt, 'Meta v Bundeskartellamt. Something Old, Something New' (2023) 8 European Papers 1077.

Van den Bergh and Weber 2021

R. Van den Bergh and F. Weber, 'The German Facebook Saga: Abuse of Dominance or Abuse of Competition Law?' (2021) 44 World Competition 29 https://doi.org/10.54648/woco2021003 accessed 29 August 2025.

Van den Boom 2022

J. van den Boom, 'What Does the Digital Markets Act Harmonize?: Exploring Interactions Between the DMA and National Competition Laws' (2022) 19 European Competition Journal, 1, 57 https://doi.org/10.1080/17441056.2022.2156728 accessed 29 August 2025.

Van den Boom, Bostoen and Monti 2024

J. van den Boom, F. Bostoen and G. Monti, 'The Netherlands: DMA Enforcement Paradise?' (2024) https://papers.ssrn.com/sol3/papers.cfm?abstract_id=4869454 accessed 10 June 2025.

Van den Boom and Hinck 2024

J. van den Boom and S. Hinck, 'ByteDance v. Commission: The EU Has Set First Bars for Gatekeeper Designation Decisions under the Digital Markets Act' (Verfassungsblog, 30 July 2024) https://verfassungsblog.de/bytedance-v-commission-dma-gatekeeper-designation/ accessed 20 December 2024.

Van den Boom and Podszun 2025

J. van den Boom and R. Podszun, 'Procedures in the DMA: Non-compliance Navigation: Exploring the European Commission's Space for Discretion and Informality in Procedure and Decision-Making in the Digital Markets Act' (2025) European Competition Journal, 1 https://doi.org/10.1080/17441056.2025.2464959 accessed 29 August 2025.

Van Dijck, Nieborg and Poell 2019

J. Van Dijck, D. Nieborg and T. Poell, 'Reframing Platform Power' (2019) 8 Internet Policy Review https://doi.org/10.14763/2019.2.1414 accessed 29 August 2025.

Van Gestel, Micklitz and Maduro 2012

R. Van Gestel, H. Micklitz and M. Maduro, 'Methodology in the New Legal World' [2012] EUI Working Papers https://cadmus.eui.eu/handle/1814/22016 accessed 1 February 2024.

Van Gorp and Batura 2015

N. Van Gorp and O. Batura, 'Study for the ECON Committee: Challenges for Competition Policy in a Digitalised Economy' (2015) https://www.europarl.europa.eu/RegData/etudes/STUD/2015/542235/IPOL_STU(2015)542235_EN.pdf accessed 3 March 2025.

Varnali 2021

K. Varnali, 'Online Behavioural Advertising: An Integrative Review' (2021) 27 Journal of Marketing and Communications 93 https://doi.org/10.1080/13527266.2019.1630664 accessed 29 August 2025.

Vedder 2004

H. Vedder, 'Spontaneous Harmonization of National Competition Laws in the Wake of the Modernization of EC Competition Law' (2004) 1 Competition Law Review 1, 5.

Veenbrink 2019

M. Veenbrink, 'Bringing Back Unity: Modernizing the Application of the Non Bis in Idem Principle' (2019) 42 World Competition 67 https://doi.org/10.54648/woco2019005 accessed 29 August 2025.

Veenbrink, Van de Gronden and Aronstein 2022

M. Veenbrink, J. Van de Gronden and I. Aronstein, 'The Enforcement of Competition Law in the Netherlands' in T. Tóth (ed.), *The Cambridge Handbook of Competition Law Sanctions* (Cambridge University Press 2022).

Verhoeven 2010

M. Verhoeven, 'The Costanzo Obligation and the Principle of National Institutional Autonomy: Supervision as a Bridge to Close the Gap' (2010) 23 Review of European Administrative Law 23 https://doi.org/10.7590/real_2010_01_03 accessed 29 August 2025.

Vestager 2019b

M. Vestager, 'Statement by Commissioner Vestager on Commission Decision to Fine Google € 1.49 Billion for Abusive Practices in Online Advertising' (Brussels, 20 March 2019) https://ec.europa.eu/commission/presscorner/detail/en/STATEMENT_19_1774 accessed 10 March 2025.

Vestager 2021

M. Vestager, 'Competition in a Digital Age' (Speech at the European Internet Forum, 17 March 2021) https://ec.europa.eu/newsroom/comp/items/705929 accessed 12 March 2025.

Vestager 2022

M. Vestager, 'Shared Objectives for Framing the Tech Economy' (Speech at the Riesenfeld Award Ceremony, 22 February 2022) https://lawcat.berkeley.edu/record/1266833/files/Vestager%20Formatted%20%28No%20Spaces%29DOI.pdf accessed 11 March 2025.

Vezzoso 2021

S. Vezzoso, 'The Proposed Digital Markets Act: What Kind of (Regulatory) Animal Is It?' (WavesBlog, 31 March 2021) https://competitionwave.blogspot.com/2021/05/the-proposed-dma-what-kind-of.html accessed 20 March 2025.

Vinocur 2019

N. Vinocur, 'How One Country Blocks the World on Data Privacy' (Politco, 24 April 2021).

Vogiatzoglou and Valcke 2022

P. Vogiatzoglou and P. Valcke, 'Two Decades of Article 8 CFR: A Critical Exploration of the Fundamental Right to Personal Data Protection in EU Law' in E. Kosta, R. Leenes and I. Kamara (eds), *Research Handbook on EU Data Protection Law* (Elgar Online 2022).

Voigt and Von dem Bussche 2017

P. Voigt and A. Von dem Bussche, *The EU General Data Protection Regulation (GDPR)* (Springer International Publishing 2017).

Von Bogdandy and Schill 2011

A. Von Bogdandy and S. Schill, 'Overcoming Absolute Primacy: Respect for National Identity under the Lisbon Treaty' (2011) 48 Common Market Law Review 1417 https://doi.org/10.54648/cola2011057 accessed 29 August 2025.

Von Grafenstein 2018

M. Von Grafenstein, *The Principle of Purpose Limitation in Data Protection Laws. A Risk-based Approach, Principles, and Private Standards as Elements for Regulating Innovation* (Nomos 2018).

Vranken 2006

J. Vranken, *Exploring the Jurist's Frame of Mind. Constraints and Preconceptions in Civil Law Argumentation* (Kluwer Law International 2006).

Wagner-von Papp 2022

F. Wagner-von Papp, 'Die 11. GWB-Novelle: Geht es Oligopolen an den Kragen?' [2022] NZKart 605.

Wagner-von Papp 2023a

F. Wagner-von Papp, 'Sektoruntersuchung und Störung des Wettbewerbs: "Paradigmenwechsel" zum "Marktdesign"?' in A. Kirk, P. Offergeld and T. Rohner (eds), *Kartellrecht in der Zeitenwende* (Nomos 2023).

Wagner-von Papp 2023b

F. Wagner-von Papp, 'Who Should Mind or Mend the Gap Between Articles 101 and 102 TFEU?: National Experiments and Twenty Years of Article 3 Regulation (EC) 1/2003' (2023) https://papers.ssrn.com/sol3/papers.cfm?abstract_id=4599326 accessed 19 March 2025.

Wagner-von Papp 2024

F. Wagner-von Papp, 'Digital Antitrust and the DMA: In Praise of Institutional Diversity' (2024) 12 Journal of Antitrust Enforcement 338 https://doi.org/10.1093/jaenfo/jnae034 accessed 29 August 2025.

Weatherill 1995

S. Weatherill, *Law and Integration in the European Union* (Clarendon Press 1995).

Weatherill 2012

S. Weatherill, 'Maximum Versus Minimum Harmonization: Choosing between Unity and Diversity in the Search for the Soul of the Internal Market' in N. Shuibhne and L. Gormley (eds), *From Single Market to Economic Union : Essays in Memory of John A Usher* (Oxford University Press 2012).

Weinstock Netanel 2000

N. Weinstock Netanel, 'Cyberspace Self-Governance: A Skeptical View from Liberal Democratic Theory' (2000) 88 California Law Review https://doi.org/10.2307/3481227 accessed 29 August 2025.

Werden 2021

G. Werden, 'Exploitative Abuse of a Dominant Position: A Bad Idea that Now Should be Abandoned' (2021) 17 European Competition Journal 682 https://doi.org/10.1080/17441056.2021.1930451 accessed 29 August 2025.

Whish 2015

R. Whish, 'Intel v Commission: Keep Calm and Carry On!' (2015) 6 Journal of European Competition Law & Practice 1 https://doi.org/10.1093/jeclap/lpu108 accessed 29 August 2025.

Whish and Bailey 2018

R. Whish and D. Bailey, *Competition Law* (9 edn, Oxford University Press 2018).

Whish and Bailey 2021

R. Whish and D. Bailey, *Competition Law* (10 edn, Oxford University Press 2021).

Whish and Bailey 2024

R. Whish and D. Bailey *Competition Law* (Oxford University Press 2024).

White and Ali 2020

A. White and H. Ali, 'Google-Fitbit Probe Isn't for Data Watchdogs, Vestager Says' (Bloomberg 25 February 2020).

Widdershoven 2019

R. Widdershoven, 'National Procedural Autonomy and General EU Law Limits' (2019) 12 Review of European Administrative Law 5 https://doi.org/10.7590/187479819x15840066091222 accessed 29 August 2025.

Wiedemann 2021

K. Wiedemann, 'Data Protection and Competition Law: Why a Coherent and Consistent Approach is Necessary' (2021) 52 International Review of Intellectual Property and Competition Law 915 https://doi.org/10.1007/s40319-021-01090-6 accessed 29 August 2025.

Wiggers, Struijlaart and Dibbits 2019

M. Wiggers, R. Struijlaart and J. Dibbits, *Digital Competition Law in Europe* (Wolters Kluwer 2019).

Wils 2013

W. Wils, 'Ten Years of Regulation 1/2003: A Retrospective' (2013) 4 Journal of European Competition Law & Practice 293 https://doi.org/10.1093/jeclap/lpt038 accessed 29 August 2025.

Wils 2019

W. Wils, 'The Obligation for the Competition Authorities of the EU Member States to Apply EU Antitrust Law and the Facebook Decision of the Bundeskartellamt' https://papers.ssrn.com/sol3/papers.cfm?abstract_id=3424592 accessed 14 March 2025.

Wils 2024

W. Wils, *EU Antitrust Enforcement. Law, Economics, History, Policy & Practice* (Concurrence 2024).

Wintgens 1993

L. Wintgens, 'Coherence of the Law' (1993) 79 Archiv für Rechts- und Sozialphilosophie 483.

Wirtz 2006

M. Wirtz, 'Collisie tussen CAO's en mededingingsrecht' (PhD, Universiteit Utrecht 2006).

Witt 2019

A. Witt, *The More Economic Approach to EU Antitrust Law* (Hart Publishing 2019).

Witt 2022

A. Witt, 'Platform Regulation in Europe: *Per se* Rules to the Rescue?' (2022) 18 Journal of Competition Law & Economics 670 https://doi.org/10.1093/joclec/nhac001 accessed 29 August 2025.

Witt 2023

A. Witt, 'The Digital Markets Act: Regulating the Wild West' (2023) 60 Common Market Law Review 625 https://doi.org/10.54648/cola2023047 accessed 29 August 2025.

Yakovleva, Geursen and Arnbak 2020

S. Yakovleva, W. Geursen and A. Arnbak, 'Kaleidoscopic Data-Related Enforcement in the Digital Age' (2020) 57 Common Market Law Review 1461 https://doi.org/10.54648/cola2020744 accessed 29 August 2025.

Yesilkagit 2014

K. Yesilkagit, 'To Merge or Not to Merge: The Institutional Re-design of Telecommunications Regulation in the Netherlands' in D. Aubin and K. Verhuist (eds), *Multi-Level Regulation in the Telecommunications Sector* (Palgrave Macmillan 2014).

Yeung 2017a

K. Yeung, '"Hypernudge": Big Data as a Mode of Regulation by Design' (2017) 20 Information, Communication & Society 118 https://doi.org/10.1080/1369118x.2016.1186713 accessed 29 August 2025.

Yeung 2017b

K. Yeung, 'Making Sense of the European Data Protection Law Tradition' in L. Andrews et al. (eds), *Algorithmic Regulation* (London School of Economics and Political Science 2017).

Yeung and Bygrave 2022

K. Yeung and L. Bygrave, 'Demystifying the Modernized European Data Protection Regime: Cross-Disciplinary Insights from Legal and Regulatory Governance Scholarship' (2022) 16 Regulation & Governance 137 https://doi.org/10.1111/rego.12401 accessed 29 August 2025.

Yun 2020

J. Yun, 'Does Antitrust Have Digital Blind Spots?' (2020) 20 George Mason University Law & Economics Research Paper.

Ziller 2014

J. Ziller, 'Hierarchy of Norms: Hierarchy of Sources and General Principles In European Union Law' (2014) https://papers.ssrn.com/sol3/papers.cfm?abstract_id=2467982 accessed 18 March 2025.

Zilsdorf 2023

D. Zilsdorf, 'Markiert der Digital Markets Act die Endstation von § 19a GWB?' (2023) 5 Kommunikation & Recht 305.

Zingales 2017

N. Zingales, 'Between a Rock and Two Hard Places: WhatsApp at the Crossroad of Competition, Data Protection and Consumer Law' (2017) 33 Computer Law & Security Review 553 https://doi.org/10.1016/j.clsr.2017.05.018 accessed 29 August 2025.

Zingales et al. 2019

L. Zingales et al., 'Stigler Committee on Digital Platforms: Final Report' (2019) https://www.chicagobooth.edu/-/media/research/stigler/pdfs/digital-platforms---committee-report---stigler-center.pdf accessed 25 March 2025.

Zippro 2008

E. Zippro, *Privaatrechtelijke handhaving van mededingingsrecht* (Kluwer 2008).

Zuiderveen Borgesius 2015

F. Zuiderveen Borgesius, 'Behavioural Sciences and the Regulation of Privacy on the Internet' in A. Alemanno and A. Sibony (eds), *Nudge and the Law A European Perspective* (Hart Publishing 2015).

Zwenne, Steenbruggen and Reker 2016

G. Zwenne, W. Steenbruggen and M. Reker, 'Rechtsbescherming bij het gebruik van big data door toezichthouders: een verkenning' (2016) 7 Tijdschrift voor Toezicht 29.

Table of Cases

EU

National

Table of Opinions

EU

European Commission Guidelines of 1 September 2006 on the method of setting fines imposed pursuant to Article 23(2)(a) of Regulation No. 1/2003, C 210/8, 85, 170
Directive 2006/123/EC of the European Parliament and of the Council of 12 December 2006 on services in the internal market, OJ L376/36; Regulation (EU) 2022/2065 of the European Parliament and of the Council of 19 October 2022 on a Single Market For Digital Services and amending Directive 2000/31/EC (Digital Services Act), OJ L277/1, 121, 131, 166, 302, 304
European Commission Report of 29 April 2009 on the functioning of Regulation 1/2003, COM(2009) 206 final, paragraph 21, 207, 252
Commission Staff Working Paper of 29 April 2009 accompanying the Communication from the Commission to the European Parliament and Council, Report on the functioning of Regulation 1/2003, SEC(2009)574 final, 16
Communication from the Commission – Guidance on the Commission's enforcement priorities in applying Article 82 of the EC Treaty to abusive exclusionary conduct by dominant undertakings [2009] OJ C45/02, 65, 67, 68, 71, 72
Article 29 Data Protection Working Party and Working Party on Policy and Justice 1 December 2009, Joint contribution to the Consultation of the European Commission on the legal framework for the fundamental right to protection of personal data, 02356/09/EN, 162
Regulation 182/2011 of the European Parliament and of the Council of 16 February 2011 laying down the rules and general principles concerning mechanisms for control by the Member States of the Commission's exercise of implementing powers, [2011] OJ L55/13, 250, 300, 301
Consolidated version of the Treaty on European Union [2012] OJ C326/13, 56
Proposal of 25 January 2012 for a Regulation of the European Parliament and of the Council on the protection of individuals with regard to the processing of personal data and on the free movement of such data (General Data Protection Regulation), COM(2012)11 final, 281
Article 29 Working Party 23 March 2012, Opinion 01/2012 on the data protection reform proposals, 00530/12/EN WP 191, 286, 290
Charter of Fundamental Rights of the European Union of 26 October 2012, OJ C326/391
European Data Protection Supervisor March 2014, 'Privacy and competitive in the age of big data: The interplay between data protection, competition law and consumer protection in the Digital Economy' https://www.edps.europa.eu/sites/default/files/publication/14-03-26_competitition_law_big_data_en.pdf accessed 24 March 2025, 23, 24, 56, 297
Communication from the Commission to the European Parliament and the Council of 9 July 2014, Ten Years of Antitrust Enforcement under

of application of the General Data Protection Directive, COM(2020)264 final, 154, 155, 157, 164, 284, 292

European Commission, Press Release 10 November 2020 'Antitrust: Commission sends Statement of Objections to Amazon for the use of non-public independent seller data and opens second investigation into its e-commerce business practices', IP/20/2077, 264

European Commission, Proposal of 15 December 2020 for a Regulation of the European Parliament and of the Council on contestable and fair markets in the digital sector (Digital Markets Act), COM(2020)842 final, 25, 29, 300

European Data Protection Board 15 December 2020 'EDPB Strategy 2021-2023' https://www.edpb.europa.eu/sites/default/files/files/file1/edpb_strategy2021-2023_en.pdf accessed 24 March 2025, 291

European Commission, Explanatory Memorandum to Proposal of 15 December 2020 for a Regulation of the European Parliament and of the Council on contestable and fair markets in the digital sector (Digital Markets Act), COM(2020)842 final, 2020/0374(COD), 300

Commission Staff Working Document Impact Assessment Report Accompanying the document Proposal of 15 December 2020 for a Regulation of the European Parliament and of the Council on contestable and fair markets in the digital sector (Digital Markets Act), SWD(2020)363 final, 270

European Commission, Press Release 15 December 2020, Europe fit for the Digital Age: Commission proposes new rules for digital platforms, IP/20/2347, 54, 121

Regulation (EU) 2021/1232 of the European Parliament and of the Council of 14 June 2021 on artificial intelligence [2021] OJ L 231/1 (AI Act), 10

EDPB Binding decision 1/2021 of 28 July 2021 on the dispute arisen on the draft decision of the Irish Supervisory Authority regarding WhatsApp Ireland under Article 65(1)(a) GDPR https://www.edpb.europa.eu/system/files/2021-09/edpb_bindingdecision_202101_ie_sa_whatsapp_redacted_en.pdf accessed 14 March 2024, 163

EPDB and EDPS 13 September 2021, Lack of resources puts enforcement of individuals' data protection rights at risk https://www.edps.europa.eu/press-publications/press-news/press-releases/2022/edpb-edps-lack-resources-puts-enforcement-individuals-data-protection-rights-risk_en accessed 14 March 2025, 164

Regulation (EU) 2022/1925 of the European Parliament and of the Council of 14 September 2022 on contestable and fair markets in the digital sector and amending Directives (EU) 2019/1937 and (EU) 2020/1828 (Digital Markets Act) OJ L 265/1, 272

Amendments adopted by the European Parliament on 15 December 2021 on the proposal for a regulation of the European Parliament and of the Council on contestable and fair markets in the digital sector (Digital Markets Act) (COM(2020)0842 – C9-0419/2020), 137

European Data Protection Board, Guidelines of 14 March 2022 on the application of Article 60 GDPR, 02/2022, 282, 284
Communication from the Commission to the European Parliament, the European Council, the European Economic and Social Committee and the Committee of the Regions of 2 March 2022, Towards a green, digital and resilient economy: our European Growth Model, COM(2022)83 final, 55
European Data Protection Board, Guidelines of 12 May 2022 on the calculation of administrative fines under the GDPR, 04/2022, 163
Regulation (EU) 2022/868 of the European Parliament and of the Council of 30 May 2022 on European data governance and amending Regulation (EU) 2018/1724, OJ L 152/1 (Data Governance Act), 10
EDPB and EPDS 12 September 2022, OUT2022 – 0068 https://www.edpb.europa.eu/system/files/2022-09/letteronbudget_out2022-0068.pdf accessed 14 March 2025, 164
European Commission, Call for Evidence for An Initiative – Guidelines on Exclusionary Abuse by Dominant Undertakings, Ref. Ares (2023)2189183, 27/3/2023, 68
Data Protection Commission 4 January 2023, 'Data Protection Commission announces conclusion of two inquiries into Meta Ireland' https://www.dataprotection.ie/en/news-media/data-protection-commission-announces-conclusion-two-inquiries-meta-ireland accessed 24 March 2025, 293
Digital Markets Advisory Committee, Rules of Procedure for the Digital Markets Advisory Committee of 13 January 2023, (2023)2699502, 300
Commission Decision of 23 March 2023 on setting up a High-Level Group for the Digital Markets Act, C(2023)1833 final, 130, 298–299, 318
Proposal for a Regulation of the European Parliament and Council of 4 July 2023 on a Regulation laying down additional procedural rules relating to the enforcement of Regulation 2016/679, COM(2023)348 final, 164, 165, 171, 172, 284, 285
Regulation (EU) 2023/2854 of the European Parliament and of the Council of 13 December 2023 on harmonised rules on fair access to and use of data and amending Regulation (EU) 2017/2394 and Directive (EU) 2020/1828, L 2023/2854 (Data Act), 10
Commission, DRAFT Guidelines on the application of Article 102 of the Treaty on the Functioning of the European Union to abusive exclusionary conduct by dominant undertakings, [...](2024)xxx draft, 32, 57, 61, 67
Annual report on Regulation (EU) 2022/1925 of the European Parliament and of the Council on contestable and fair markets in the digital sector and amending Directives (EU) 2019/1937 and (EU) 2020/1828 (Digital Markets Act), COM/2024/106, 131
Commission Notice of 22 February 2024 on the definition of the relevant market for the purpose of Union competition law, C/2024/1645, 8, 28, 56, 118, 321
High-Level Group for the Digital Markets Act Public Statement of 22 May 2024 on Artificial Intelligence https://digital-markets-act.ec.europa.eu/hig

h-level-group-digital-markets-act-public-statement-artificial-intelligence-2024-05-22_en accessed 20 March 2025, 300

Regulation (EU) 2024/1689 of the European Parliament and of the Council of 13 June 2024 laying down harmonised rules on artificial intelligence and amending Regulations (EC) No. 300/2008, (EU) No. 167/2013, (EU) No. 168/2013, (EU) 2018/858, (EU) 2018/1139 and (EU) 2019/2144 and Directives 2014/90/EU, (EU) 2016/797 and (EU) 2020/1828 (Artificial Intelligence Act), OJ L 12.7.2024, 10

European Commission 25 June 2024, Commission sends Statement of Objections to Microsoft over possibly abusive tying practices regarding Teams, IP/24/3446, 71, 140

European Commission 1 July 2024, Commission sends preliminary findings to Meta over its 'Pay or Consent' model for breach of the Digital Markets Act, IP/24/3582, 140

Commission Staff Working Document of 5 September 2024, Evaluation of Regulation 1/2003 and 773/2004, SWD(2024)216 final, 83, 206, 249, 256, 259, 261

European Commission 19 September 2024, Commission starts first proceedings to specify Apple's interoperability obligations under the Digital Markets Act, IP/24/4761, 140

Commission Staff Working Document 3 October 2024, Fitness Check of EU consumer law on digital fairness, SWD (2024)230 final, p. 58, 16

Letter EDPB of 7 October 2024, EDPB on the interplay between EU data protection and competition law, COM A4/MK, 15

European Commission 11 November 2024, 'Commission fines Meta €797.72 million over abusive practices benefitting Facebook Marketplace', IP/24/5801, 71, 77, 80, 141

European Court of Auditors 17 December 2024, 'Infringement procedures: Enforcing EU law takes too long' https://www.eca.europa.eu/en/news/NEWS-SR-2024-28 accessed 25 March 2025, 331

European Data Protection Supervisor 15 January 2025 'Towards a Digital Clearinghouse 2.0 – Concept Note' https://www.edps.europa.eu/system/files/2025-01/towards_a_digital_clearinghouse_2_0_january_2025_en_0.pdf accessed 20 March 2025, paragraph 17, 256, 298

European Data Protection Board 16 January 2025 'Position paper on Interplay between data protection and competition law' https://www.edpb.europa.eu/system/files/2025-01/edpb_position-paper_20250116_interplay-between-data-protection-and-competition-law_en.pdf accessed 24 March 2025, 291, 333

Questionnaire to the Commissioner-Designate Teresa Ribera, Executive Vice-President for the Clean, Just and Competitive Transition, available at: https://hearings.elections.europa.eu/documents/ribera/ribera_writtenquestionsandanswers_en.pdf accessed 29 August 2025, 54

National

E65D948.1_cid362?__blob=publicationFile&v=5 accessed 31 March 2025, 253
ACM 11 April 2028, 'ACM Signaal 2018' https://www.acm.nl/nl/publicaties/acm-signaal-2018 accessed 31 March 2025, 89
Uitvoeringswet Algemene verordening gegevensbescherming of 5 May 2018, Stb. 2018, 212 (GDPR Implementing Act), 272, 301, 302
Hamburgisches Datenschutzgesetz of 18 May 2018, HmbGVBI. 2018, 67, 161
Ministry of Economic Affairs and Climate Policy, Letter to The Speaker of the House of Representatives, 17 May 2019, Future-proofing of competition policy in regard to online platforms, CE-MC/1912902f8, 24, 29, 88, 95
Kamerstukken Tweede Kamer der Staten Generaal, Wijziging van de Mededingingswet en de Instellingswet Autoriteit Consument en Markt in verband met de implementatie van richtlijn (EU) 2019/1, 2019/2020 35 467, 93, 94
Benelux Memorandum of the Belgian, Dutch and Luxembourg competition authorities on challenges faced by competition authorities in a digital world, 2 October 2019, https://www.acm.nl/sites/default/files/documents/2019-10/benelux-memorandum-over-toezicht-mededinging-in-digitale-economie.pdf accessed 20 March 2025, 88, 95
ACM, Verslag 13 February 2020 https://www.acm.nl/system/files/documents/vergaderverslag-13-2-2020_0.pdf accessed 24 March 2025, 288, 289
Samenwerkingsprotocol tussen Autoriteit Consument en Markt en Autoriteit Persoonsgegevens, 18 June 2020, Staatscourant 2020, 36741, 287
Entwurf eines Gesetzes zur Änderung des Gesetzes gegen Wettbewerbsbeschränkungen für ein fokussiertes, proaktives und digitales Wettbewerbsrecht 4.0 und anderer wettbewerbsrechtlicher Bestimmungen (GWB-Digitalisierungsgesetz), 19 October 2020, 19/23492, 105
ACM, 'ACM Annual Report' (2021) https://www.acm.nl/sites/default/files/documents/2021-acm-annual-report_0.pdf accessed 11 March 2025, 89
Gesetz zur Änderung des Gesetzes gegen Wettbewerbsbeschränkungen für ein fokussiertes, proaktives und digitales Wettbewerbsrecht 4.0 und anderer Bestimmungen (GWB-Digitalisierungsgesetz), 18 January 2021, Bundesgesetzblatt Jahrgang 2021, 1, 101
Ministers of France, Germany and The Netherlands 27 May 2021, Friends of an effective Digital Markets Act – Strengthening the Digital Markets Act and Its Enforcement https://www.netherlandsandyou.nl/web/pr-eu-brussels/about-us/our-ideas-for-europe/digital-policy accessed 21 March 2025, 271, 305
Referentenentwurf des Bundesministeriums für Wirtschaft und Klimaschutz 15 September 2022, Entwurf eines Gesetzes zur Verbesserung der Wettbewerbsstrukturen und zur Abschöpfung von Vorteilen aus Wettbewerbsverstößen (Wettbewerbsdurchsetzungsgesetz), 115

Bundeskartellamt, Guidelines for the Setting of Fines in Cartel Administrative Offence Proceedings 7 October 2021 https://www.bundeskartellamt.de/SharedDocs/Publikation/EN/Leitlinien/Guidelines_setting_fines_Oct_2021.pdf?__blob=publicationFile&v=5 accessed 12 March 2025, 114

ACM, 'Focus Werkzaamheden ACM 2022' (2022) https://www.acm.nl/sites/default/files/documents/focus-2022.pdf accessed 11 March 2025, 92

Deutscher Bundestag 7 January 2022 'Die Anwendbarkeit von § 19a GWB im Lichte des europäischen Gesetzgebungsverfahrens zum Digital Markets Act' WD 7 – 3000 – 114/21; PE 6 – 3000 – 067/21, 226

Bundeskartellamt 14 June 2022, 'Bundeskartellamt reviews Apple's tracking rules for third-party apps' (2022) https://www.bundeskartellamt.de/SharedDocs/Meldung/EN/Pressemitteilungen/2022/14_06_2022_Apple.html accessed 12 March 2025, 109, 289

Memorie van Toelichting Voorstel Uitvoeringswet Verordening (EU) 2022/1925 van het Europees Parlement en de Raad van 14 september 2022 over betwistbare en eerlijke markten in de digitale sector, en tot wijziging van Richtlijnen (EU) 2019/1937 en (EU) 2020/1828, 2023-2024, 36 495, 3 (Uitvoeringswet digitalemarktenverordening)(Explanatory Memorandum Dutch Draft Implementing Act DMA), 272

Voorstel Uitvoeringswet Verordening (EU) 2022/1925 van het Europees Parlement en de Raad van 14 september 2022 over betwistbare en eerlijke markten in de digitale sector, en tot wijziging van Richtlijnen (EU) 2019/1937 en (EU) 2020/1828, 2023-2024, 36 495, 2 (Uitvoeringswet digitalemarktenverordening)(Dutch Draft Implementing Act DMA), 272

Bundeskartellamt 14 November 2022, 'Extension of ongoing proceedings against Amazon to also include an examination pursuant to Section 19a of the German Competition Act (GWB)' (2022) https://www.bundeskartellamt.de/SharedDocs/Meldung/EN/Pressemitteilungen/2022/14_11_2022_Amazon_19a.html accessed 12 March 2025, 109

Bundeskartellamt 23 November 2022, 'Meta (Facebook) responds to the Bundeskartellamt's concerns – VR headsets can now be used without a Facebook account' (2022) https://www.bundeskartellamt.de/SharedDocs/Meldung/EN/Pressemitteilungen/2022/23_11_2022_Facebook_VR_Brillen.html accessed 12 March 2025, 109

Letter Ministerie van Binnenlandse Zaken en Koninkrijksrelaties aan de Voorzitter van de Tweede Kamer der Staten-Generaal 22 December 2022, 2022-0000689652, 161

ACM Besluit 21 maart 2023, ACM/UIT/594498 https://www.acm.nl/system/files/documents/woo-besluit-over-samenwerkinsprotocol-acm-en-ap.pdf accessed 24 March 2025, 287, 288

ACM, Uitvoerings- en handhavingstoets Digital Markets Act (DMA), 29 March 2023, ACM/INT/468084, 131

Entwurf eines Gesetzes zur Änderung des Gesetzes gegen Wettbewerbsbeschränkungen under anderer Gesetze, 16 May 2023, BT-Drs. 20/6824, 132

Data Protection Commission 22 May 2023, 'Data Protection Commission announces conclusion of inquiry into Meta Ireland' https://www.dataprotection.ie/en/news-media/press-releases/Data-Protection-Commission-announces-conclusion-of-inquiry-into-Meta-Ireland accessed 24 March 2025, 283

Autoriteit Persoonsgegeves Directie Coördinatie Algoritmes, 'Werkagenda coördinered algoritmetoezicht in 2024' (2024) https://www.autoriteitpersoonsgegevens.nl/documenten/werkagenda-coordinerend-algoritmetoezicht-2024 accessed 24 March 2025, 285

Digital Cluster Bonn Press Release 15 January 2024, 'Sechs Bundesbehörden arbeiten bei der Digitalisierung enger zusammen' https://www.bundeskartellamt.de/SharedDocs/Meldung/DE/Pressemitteilungen/2024/15_01_2024_Digital_Cluster.html accessed 25 March 2025, 304

Bundeskartellamt 13 February 2025, 'Bundeskartellamt has concerns about the current form of Apple's App Tracking Transparency Framework (ATTF)' (2025) https://www.bundeskartellamt.de/SharedDocs/Meldung/EN/Pressemitteilungen/2025/02_13_2025_ATTF.html?nn=49120 accessed 29 August 2025, 180

Autorité de la concurrence, Press Release 31 March 2025, Targeted advertising: the Autorité de la concurrence imposes a fine of EUR 150,000,000 on Apple for the implementation of the App Tracking Transparency ('ATT') framework https://www.autoritedelaconcurrence.fr/en/press-release/targeted-advertising-autorite-de-la-concurrence-imposes-fine-eu150000000-apple accessed 29 August 2025, 180

Index

INFORMATION LAW SERIES

1. Egbert J. Dommering & P. Bernt Hugenholtz, *Protecting Works of Fact: Copyright, Freedom of Expression and Information Law,* 1991 (ISBN 90-654-4567-6).
2. Willem F. Korthals Altes, Egbert J. Dommering, P. Bernt Hugenholtz & Jan J.C. Kabel, *Information Law Towards the 21st Century,* 1992 (ISBN 90-654-4627-3).
3. Jacqueline M.B. Seignette, *Challenges to the Creator Doctrine: Authorship, Copyright Ownership and the Exploitation of Creative Works in the Netherlands, Germany and The United States,* 1994 (ISBN 90-654-4876-4).
4. P. Bernt Hugenholtz, *The Future of Copyright in a Digital Environment, Proceedings of the Royal Academy Colloquium,* 1996 (ISBN 90-411-0267-1).
5. Julius C.S. Pinckaers, *From Privacy Toward a New Intellectual Property Right in Persona,* 1996 (ISBN 90-411-0355-4).
6. Jan J.C. Kabel & Gerard J.H.M. Mom, *Intellectual Property and Information Law: Essays in Honour of Herman Cohen Jehoram,* 1998 (ISBN 90-411-9702-8).
7. Ysolde Gendreau, Axel Nordemann & Rainer Oesch, *Copyright and Photographs: An International Survey,* 1999 (ISBN 90-411-9722-2).
8. P. Bernt Hugenholtz, *Copyright and Electronic Commerce: Legal Aspects of Electronic Copyright Management,* 2000 (ISBN 90-411-9785-0).
9. Lucie M.C.R. Guibault, *Copyright Limitations and Contracts: An Analysis of the Contractual Overridability of Limitations on Copyright,* 2002 (ISBN 90-411-9867-9).
10. Lee A. Bygrave, *Data Protection Law: Approaching its Rationale, Logic and Limits,* 2002 (ISBN 90-411-9870-9).
11. Niva Elkin-Koren & Neil Weinstock Netanel, *The Commodification of Information,* 2002 (ISBN 90-411-9876-8).
12. Mireille M.M. van Eechoud, *Choice of Law in Copyright and Related Rights: Alternatives to the Lex Protectionis,* 2003 (ISBN 90-411-2071-8).
13. Martin Senftleben, *Copyright, Limitations and the Three-Step Test: An Analysis of the Three-Step Test in International and EC Copyright Law,* 2004 (ISBN 90-411-2267-2).
14. Paul L.C. Torremans, *Copyright and Human Rights: Freedom of Expression – Intellectual Property – Privacy,* 2004 (ISBN 90-411-2278-8).
15. Natali Helberger, *Controlling Access to Content: Regulating Conditional Access in Digital Broadcasting,* 2005 (ISBN 90-411-2345-8).
16. Lucie M.C.R. Guibault & P. Bernt Hugenholtz, *The Future of the Public Domain: Identifying the Commons in Information Law,* 2006 (ISBN 978-90-411-2435-7).

17. Irini Katsirea, *Public Broadcasting and European Law: A Comparative Examination of Public Service Obligations in Six Member States,* 2008 (ISBN 978-90-411-2500-2).
18. Paul L.C. Torremans, *Intellectual Property and Human Rights: Enhanced Edition of Copyright and Human Rights,* 2008 (ISBN 978-90-411-2653-5).
19. Mireille van Eechoud, P. Bernt Hugenholtz, Stef van Gompel, Lucie Guibault & Natali Helberger, *Harmonizing European Copyright Law: The Challenges of Better Lawmaking,* 2009 (ISBN 978-90-411-3130-0).
20. Ashwin van Rooijen, *The Software Interface between Copyright and Competition Law: A Legal Analysis of Interoperability in Computer Programs,* 2010 (ISBN 978-90-411-3193-5).
21. Irini A. Stamatoudi, *Copyright Enforcement and the Internet,* 2010 (ISBN 978-90-411-3346-5).
22. Wolfgang Sakulin, *Trademark Protection and Freedom of Expression: An Inquiry into the Conflict between Trademark Rights and Freedom of Expression under European Law,* 2011 (ISBN 978-90-411-3415-8).
23. Stef van Gompel, *Formalities in Copyright Law: An Analysis of their History, Rationales and Possible Future,* 2011 (ISBN 978-90-411-3418-9).
24. Nadezhda Purtova, *Property Rights in Personal Data: A European Perspective,* 2012 (ISBN 978-90-411-3802-6).
25. Brad Sherman & Leanne Wiseman, *Copyright and the Challenge of the New,* 2012 (ISBN 978-90-411-3669-5).
26. Ewa Komorek, *Media Pluralism and European Law*, 2012 (ISBN 978-90-411-3894-1).
27. Joris van Hoboken, *Search Engine Freedom: On the Implications of the Right to Freedom of Expression for the Legal Governance of Web Search Engines,* 2012 (ISBN 978-90-411-4128-6).
28. Natali Helberger, Lucie Guibault, Marco Loos, Chantal Mak, Lodewijk Pessers & Bart van der Sloot, *Digital Consumers and the Law: Towards a Cohesive European Framework*, 2012 (ISBN 978-90-411-4049-4).
29. Tatiana-Eleni Synodinou, *Codification of European Copyright Law: Challenges and Perspectives,* 2012 (ISBN 978-90-411-4145-3).
30. Heather Ann Forrest, *Protection of Geographic Names in International Law and Domain Name System Policy*, Second Edition, 2017 (ISBN 978-90-411-8839-7).
31. Sari Depreeuw, *The Variable Scope of the Exclusive Economic Rights in Copyright*, 2014 (ISBN 978-90-411-4915-2).
32. Vikrant Narayan Vasudeva, *Open Source Software and Intellectual Property Rights*, 2014 (ISBN 978-90-411-5228-2).
33. Frederik J. Zuiderveen Borgesius, *Improving Privacy Protection in the Area of Behavioural Targeting*, 2015 (ISBN 978-90-411-5990-8).
34. Paul L.C. Torremans, *Intellectual Property Law and Human Rights*, Fourth Edition, 2020 (ISBN 978-94-035-1304-1).

35. Irini A. Stamatoudi, *New Developments in EU and International Copyright Law*, 2016 (ISBN 978-90-411-5991-5).
36. Lodewijk W.P. Pessers, *The Inventiveness Requirement in Patent Law: An Exploration of Its Foundations and Functioning*, 2016 (ISBN 978-90-411-6731-6).
37. Susy Frankel & Daniel Gervais, *The Internet and the Emerging Importance of New Forms of Intellectual Property*, 2016 (ISBN 978-90-411-6789-7).
38. Axel M. Arnbak, *Securing Private Communications: Protecting Private Communications Security in EU Law – Fundamental Rights, Functional Value Chains, and Market Incentives*, 2016 (ISBN 978-90-411-6737-8).
39. Christina Angelopoulos, *European Intermediary Liability in Copyright: A Tort-Based Analysis*, 2017 (ISBN 978-90-411-6835-1).
40. João Pedro Quintais, *Copyright in the Age of Online Access: Alternative Compensation Systems in EU Law*, 2017 (ISBN 978-90-411-8667-6).
41. P. Bernt Hugenholtz, *Copyright Reconstructed: Rethinking Copyright's Economic Rights in a Time of Highly Dynamic Technological and Economic Change*, 2018 (ISBN 978-90-411-9103-8).
42. Manon Oostveen, *Protecting Individuals Against the Negative Impact of Big Data: Potential and Limitations of the Privacy and Data Protection Law Approach*, 2018 (ISBN 978-94-035-0131-4).
43. Tatiana Eleni Synodinou (ed.), *Pluralism or Universalism in International Copyright Law*, Second Edition, 2025 (ISBN 978-94-035-2688-1).
44. Martin Senftleben, *The Copyright/Trademark Interface: How the Expansion of Trademark Protection Is Stifling Cultural Creativity*, 2021 (ISBN 978-94-035-2370-5).
45. Tito Rendas, *Exceptions in EU Copyright Law: In Search of a Balance Between Flexibility and Legal Certainty*, 2021 (ISBN 978-94-035-2395-8).
46. Martin Senftleben, Joost Poort, Mireille van Eechoud, Stef van Gompel & Natalie Helberger (eds), *Intellectual Property and Sports: Essays in Honour of P. Bernt Hugenholtz*, 2021 (ISBN 978-94-035-3733-7).
47. Marijn Sax, *Between Empowerment and Manipulation: The Ethics and Regulation of For-Profit Health Apps*, 2021 (ISBN 978-94-035-3791-7).
48. Thomas Tombal, *Imposing Data Sharing among Private Actors: A Tale of Evolving Balances*, 2022 (ISBN 978-94-035-4160-0).
49. Belle Beems, *The Interaction between Enforcers of Competition Law, the DMA, and the GDPR: An Inquiry into the Coherence of Enforcement across Legal Domains*, 2026 (ISBN 978-94-035-4259-1).

www.ingramcontent.com/pod-product-compliance
Ingram Content Group UK Ltd.
Pitfield, Milton Keynes, MK11 3LW, UK
UKHW020228290926
15470UKWH00001B/422

9 789403 542591